D1026696

LITERARY
OUTLAW

Avon Books are available at special quantity discounts for bulk purchases for sales promotions, premiums, fund raising or educational use. Special books, or book excerpts, can also be created to fit specific needs.

For details write or telephone the office of the Director of Special Markets, Avon Books, Dept. FP, 1350 Avenue of the Americas, New York, New York 10019, 1-800-238-0658.

LITERARY OUTLAW

THE LIFE AND TIMES OF
WILLIAM S. BURROUGHS

TED MORGAN

AVON BOOKS ◆ NEW YORK

If you purchased this book without a cover, you should be aware that this book is stolen property. It was reported as "unsold and destroyed" to the publisher, and neither the author nor the publisher has received any payment for this "stripped book."

AVON BOOKS
A division of
The Hearst Corporation
1350 Avenue of the Americas
New York, New York 10019

Copyright © 1988 by Ted Morgan
Front cover photograph by Wolfgang Wesener
Published by arrangement with Henry Holt and Company, Inc.
Library of Congress Catalog Card Number: 88-9290
ISBN: 0-380-70882-5

All rights reserved, which includes the right to reproduce this book or portions thereof in any form whatsoever except as provided by the U.S. Copyright Law. For information address Henry Holt and Company, Inc., 115 West 18th Street, New York, New York 10011.

First Avon Books Trade Printing: April 1990

AVON TRADEMARK REG. U.S. PAT. OFF. AND IN OTHER COUNTRIES, MARCA REGISTRADA, HECHO EN U.S.A.

Printed in the U.S.A.

OPM   10 9 8 7 6 5 4 3 2

*This book is dedicated
to the memory of Brion Gysin*

Contents

Note on Method

In the course of this book, the author uses techniques such as inner monologues and stream of consciousness. The reader may well ask how the author got inside his subject's head. The answer is that the author interviewed the subject exhaustively, over a period of four years, for more than 100 hours, and that the subject has an unusually retentive memory. He remembers, for instance, entire passages of Shakespeare which he learned in Mr. Kittredge's course at Harvard, and he also remembers his state of mind at a given moment in the past. In this way, the author is able to reconstruct what the subject was thinking, in the sometimes rambling and associative style that reproduces the process of thought. The subject has been given the opportunity to go over such passages to check their accuracy. In other instances, when the author quotes from the subject's work without identifying it, those passages are rendered in italics. Finally, when a name has been changed to protect someone's identity, the reader will be notified when the character is introduced.

LITERARY
OUTLAW

THE INDUCTION
1983

S ome of the faces could be recognized from their likeness on the dust jackets or reviews of their books, or, in some cases, on the cover of *Time*. There was Erskine Caldwell, who many thought was dead; there were the elongated granitic features of John Kenneth Galbraith; there was Malcolm Cowley, his face crumpled by age, who had known Hart Crane; there were the husband-and-wife teams, seated apart, as at a dinner party: Eleanor Clark and Robert Penn Warren, Shirley Hazzard and Francis Steegmuller. Some notable faces were missing, either because they lived too far away, or were ailing, or were busy elsewhere, or couldn't be bothered: Mary McCarthy, Saul Bellow, John Updike, Norman Mailer, Philip Roth, Arthur Miller, James Baldwin, James Dickey, Paul Bowles, Kurt Vonnegut, William Styron, Allen Ginsberg.

The occasion was the annual Ceremonial of the American Academy and Institute of Arts and Letters, which was being held this Wednesday afternoon, May 18, 1983, in the auditorium at 632 West 156th Street, in New York City. Seated on the stage in six rising tiers divided by an aisle were 128 of the 250 members, in the three disciplines of art, literature, and music.

The members gathered at noon for cocktails, and as they basked in the warm glow of springtime and inclusion, a few of them made the first mistake of the day by overimbibing, perhaps from conviviality or anxiety (if they were scheduled to speak), or a mixture of both. Drinks were downed as waiters passed trays of smoked salmon canapés and *escargots en croûte*. At one, the refreshed members repaired to the Great Terrace for lunch at round tables under a vast yellow-and-white-striped tent, the lunch being complemented by a Meursault and a Beaujolais picked by the eminent composer and Francophile Virgil Thomson. What an august assembly, to have Virgil Thomson as its *sommelier*! At three, the Ceremonial proper would begin, to induct new members and hand out cash prizes. The afternoon's highlight would be the awarding of the Gold Medal for fiction to Bernard Malamud, by Ralph Ellison.

Malcolm Cowley could remember when William Faulkner had given the Gold Medal to John Dos Passos. Faulkner got more and more restless as the afternoon and the speeches wore on, and started crossing out lines from his talk, until, when his turn came, he got up and said, "Here it is, Dos, take it," handing him the medal. Faulkner would be hard to beat for the shortest speech on record.

Cowley had been a member for thirty-five years, nearly half the life of the Institute, which went back to 1898. It was followed six years later by the Academy, an inner sanctum of fifty, so that even when a writer or painter or composer thought he had arrived by being elected to the Institute, there was still a pecking order.

What Cowley had not seen firsthand in those thirty-five years he had found out for himself. How Robert Underwood Johnson, a magazine editor and third-rate rhetorical poet, who was secretary of the Institute, was so protocol-conscious that when he was named permanent secretary of the Academy, he wrote himself an "I-have-the-honor-to-inform-you" letter, which he answered with an "I-am-happy-to-accept" letter. Johnson found a benefactor for the Academy in the person of Archer M. Huntington, who combined great wealth inherited from his railroad-magnate stepfather with an interest in Spanish literature. Huntington gave the Academy a plot of land between Upper Broadway and the Hudson River, a stately Venetian Renaissance building, and an endowment.

From the start, there were quarrels between ancients (known as stalwarts) and moderns (known as "locofocos"). Theodore Roosevelt and Woodrow Wilson were the stalwarts' idea of acceptable members, as Presidents who also wrote books, while avant-garde poets like Stephen Vincent Benet and Carl Sandburg were not. As leader of the stalwarts, Robert Underwood Johnson lobbied hard to keep "eccentrics" out. He thought *John Brown's Body* was crude, and at an institute dinner in 1933, he read aloud a poem by Sandburg (whom he called Sandbag), on shaving in a Pullman car, as a shocking example of his vulgarity. When H. L. Mencken was proposed, Johnson wrote forty letters to keep him out, which he was unable to do, any more than he could keep out Benet and Sandburg. The level of his indignation may have affected his health, and he died in 1933, at the age of eighty-three.

Cowley remembered most of the little tempests that had shaken the Academy. He remembered John O'Hara, who felt that many lesser writers had been admitted ahead of him, breaking down and weeping on the stage when he was awarded the Gold Medal; and the fracas when Lewis Mumford, who had lost a son in World War II, resigned from the Academy when the Gold Medal was awarded to the isolationist historian Charles Beard. He remembered the only member ever to have been expelled, the painter of German descent Hunt Diedrich, who had mailed his antiwar appeals on Academy letterheads. Ezra Pound, although charged with treason, was not expelled.

More recently, Graham Greene had resigned as an honorary member because the Institute would not speak up against the Vietnam War, and Mumford, who had been readmitted, had again walked out in 1966 over Vietnam. There was quite a lot of dissension in the ranks over that one, but Cowley did not think the Institute should take a stand—it was not, after all, a political club, and taking a stand would only stir up trouble and lead to the loss of valuable members.

With the passage of the years, he had seen former "locofocos" turn stalwart, and campaign against Abstract Expressionists and free-verse poets. He had seen major writers wait fifteen years before being elevated from the Institute to the Academy. Ralph Ellison's election had been held up because he had published only one novel, *Invisible Man*. Cowley had once asked him, "Ralph, when are you going to finish your next book?" Another strange case was that of Glenway Wescott, who had not brought out a book in nearly forty years but was working on his memoirs. He did not want them published in his lifetime because they included a frank account of his homosexuality, a subject on which he had old-fashioned qualms, but he did read an excerpt at an Institute dinner.

Then there was the question of women, for in the old days of stalwart supremacy, there had been long years with not a single woman member, but those days were over, and now there were women of every description, from outstanding fiction writers like Eudora Welty and Shirley Hazzard to Susan Sontag, the well-known panelist. Cowley remembered Caroline Gordon blaming her ex-husband Allen Tate for keeping her out, while in fact he was working hard to get her in, but she simply wasn't known enough as a writer. As far as Cowley was concerned, the decisive question of literary merit was not "Does it menstruate?" Once Arthur Miller had brought his wife Marilyn Monroe to the Ceremonial, and Cowley, watching her in the audience from his chair on the stage, found himself absorbed by the depth of her décolleté, which seemed to descend from her neck right into the orchestra pit. After the Ceremonial, the poet Phyllis McGinley said, "No one noticed my new hat."

The Institute cast a pretty fine net, but some of the biggest fish got away. Sinclair Lewis had refused membership in 1925, not wanting to "become safe, polite, obedient, and sterile," and attacked the Institute in his Nobel Prize speech in Stockholm, but in 1935 he had second thoughts and joined. Hemingway turned it down, not wanting to be just another fish in the aquarium. Edmund Wilson and James Thurber did not think it was a writer's business to join the establishment. Cowley felt that refusing to join was a mistake. The Academy could do some good—there was an Artists and Writers Revolving Fund, which gave cash to down-and-out practitioners of the arts—and if you were a member you could help direct the flow. The dinners were companionable, some of your colleagues became your friends, and once you were in the Academy, your hotel bills were paid if you were in town on Academy business.

In recent years there had been three other famous Refuseniks—J. D. Salinger, who had sent a wire saying I DO NOT FEEL FREE; Gore Vidal, who had said something snippy to the effect that he was not quite ready for the geriatric ward; and Vladimir Nabokov, who wrote, in his persona of permanent exile: "Socially, I am a cripple. Therefore all my thinking life I have decided not to 'belong.' "

But over the years, Cowley thought, the Institute had done a pretty good job of collecting the best talent from the different schools of American writing. They had kept up with the avant-garde, bringing in banned writers like Henry Miller, "difficult" writers like John Barth, William Gass, and John Hawkes, relatively young poets like John Ashbery and Galway Kinnell, and counterculture figures like Allen Ginsberg, who had spent his entire adult life railing at the Establishment. Cowley liked Ginsberg, whom he had first met in San Francisco in the fifties, when he and his friends wore jeans and drank beer out of cans. Perhaps the Institute had a civilizing influence, for now he was drinking tea out of bone china and wearing vested suits. The trouble with Ginsberg was that he was always pushing to get his friends in—at one point he had tried to get his boyfriend Peter Orlovsky in, which Cowley found appalling.

Cowley usually supported the election of controversial figures—he was after all an Old Bohemian who had championed new writers from Hart Crane to Jack Kerouac. But among the five writers being inducted into the Institute that afternoon, there was one whom he had opposed, and that was William S. Burroughs, author of *Naked Lunch* and many other works of an "advanced" or experimental nature. Cowley did not often feel that someone ought to be kept out, but he was lukewarm or even cool to the merit of Burroughs' work. Replete with homosexual sex scenes, hanging-ejaculation scenes, and scatology, much of it was frankly disgusting. At the November meeting, when new members were discussed, the Burroughs case had been pretty stormy, with some members speaking out quite violently against him. The members had a very high boiling point—oddly enough, there had not been much trouble over Henry Miller—but with Burroughs it was reached. Cowley was reminded of the storm over the composer John Cage in earlier years.

There were allusions to Burroughs' personal life. He came from a Socially Registered St. Louis family, and his grandfather had invented a model of adding machine widely adopted by American business. But after graduating from Harvard he had rebelled against the values of his family and class, and had professed and written about his homosexuality and addiction to heroin and other drugs. He had engaged in various criminal activities, being arrested on several occasions. Despite his homosexuality, he had married and had a son, but in Mexico City he had (in what was supposedly an accident) shot and killed his wife. His work had been declared obscene and had been banned by U.S. Customs. Was this the sort of person one wanted in the Institute? Cowley did not think that a man's personal life should be a determining factor in membership, but in Burroughs' case, he could not see any literary value to the work.

The election of Burroughs once again drew the line between the stalwarts and the "locofocos," and took six years: he was first nominated in 1977, and did not get in until 1983. The chief "locofoco" this time was Allen Ginsberg, who lobbied for Burroughs as tirelessly as Robert Underwood Johnson had lobbied against Mencken, writing letters, buttonholing sympathetic members, finding seconders, drafting citations, and going through the paperwork year after year.

Ginsberg had been elected in 1974, in belated acknowledgment of the changes of the sixties, so that there might be some kind of balance in the Institute between the combed poets and the shaggy poets. But aside from himself, there was still a Harvard East Coast axis heavily weighted toward the conservatives. Among the poets there was Howard Nemerov, an Establishment type, and Howard Moss, who as poetry editor of *The New Yorker* passed on his own work, which he published with predictable regularity, and William Jay Smith, who was basically a government type, thought Ginsberg, sent abroad by the U.S.I.A. They had their little network and got their friends in.

Well, Ginsberg would push to get *his* friends in, too. He would promote the kind of writer who wasn't normally asked into the Academy. What was the point of joining unless he could shake things up? His first success came in 1975, when he managed to obtain for Burroughs a $3,000 award in recognition of his creative work. The citation, written by Ginsberg, read: "To William Burroughs, invisible man, explorer of souls and cities, whose literary exploration of dense worlds of international consciousness, amounts to homemade, individualistic, self-invented Yankee Tantra."

But when it came to getting Burroughs elected, there seemed to be nothing but hurdles. One hurdle was the method of election. The number of vacancies depended on the number of deaths that year in the literature department. Then Ginsberg had to find a nominator and at least two seconders. Then there was a departmental ballot that weeded out the nominees from twenty-five or so to a few more than the number of vacancies. Then there was a ballot for all three branches, who voted for as many candidates as there were vacancies. One problem was that the people in the other branches often didn't know who the writers were— they only knew the people in their own fields, so they had to trust the nominator and see the name reappear a few times until they became familiar with it.

Now Burroughs had a number of admirers in the Institute, among them Mary McCarthy and Christopher Isherwood, whom Ginsberg recruited as seconders in 1977, the year of his first attempt. He was so discouraged when Burroughs was turned down that he sent the Institute an angry letter: "By some mischance the bulk of poets and prose writers nominated for election this year are men of talent but not men of genius . . . something has gone completely wrong with the Academy and Institute by my lights, and I want that opinion registered forthrightly—we have a mediocrity scandal." The writers elected that year were Hortense Calisher, Elizabeth Hardwick, Joseph Heller, and Ada Louise Huxtable.

"What am I doing here?" the disappointed Ginsberg asked himself. "Why should I lend my name to this club of fakes?" The only advantage he could see was that from time to time he pried some money loose from the fund for his needy friends. Other than that, he wouldn't even have stayed in. When the poet Gregory Corso was so severely beaten in January 1983 by the San Francisco police that he had to be hospitalized, the fund sent him $1,500 to pay his hospital bill.

But the Burroughs election seemed stalled, and one day in a meeting Ginsberg lost his temper and said, "There's nothing but a bunch of *New Yorker* writers here." Howard Moss got up and said he objected to that, and Ginsberg mumbled a sort of apology: "No, it's not just that, it's true, but on the other hand . . . " Then it got to the point where they were nominating John Hollander and Richard Howard, who to Ginsberg were just kids who had never contributed anything real to the advancement of poetry, so at another meeting, speaking out of long frustration, Ginsberg said, "I'm not sure I belong here." And the venerable Glenway Wescott, who had been there forever and was the chairman of a major committee, said, "Perhaps you don't." Ginsberg shuddered when he heard those words, because Wescott had spent years in Paris and known Gertrude Stein, and you would think he would have a soft spot for modernism, but in his dotage he seemed possessed by the stalwart spirit of Robert Underwood Johnson. Ginsberg had been saying that the Academy should bring in what was alive and valuable rather than collect fossils, and Wescott had countered that an Academy was an Academy and not a school for creative writers, which Ginsberg thought was bullshit.

Wescott's attitude was part of another snag in the Burroughs election, which Ginsberg called the "snooty gays" versus the "scruffy gays." He had hoped to count on the gay vote, but even here there were divisions, for the "snooty gays" detested Burroughs. It was as though they felt he had given homosexuality a bad name. Glenway Wescott referred to him as "that awful man," Ned Rorem as "that dreadful fellow," and Virgil Thomson said his work was "pornography for queers." Ginsberg felt very much alone. In 1981, however, an unexpected ally joined the Burroughs camp. This was Leon Edel, known among some of his colleagues as "Leon Idol" for his worshipful and overprotective biography of Henry James. Ginsberg had sat next to him at meetings and found him congenial, and on August 24, 1981, Edel wrote Ginsberg from his home in Honolulu, agreeing to second Burroughs: "I am not sufficiently familiar with the writings of Burroughs to write a new citation, but have made a few suggestions on yours. . . . One doesn't need to push too hard. I doubt whether Burroughs has been passed over for any other reason than that there are few vacancies at any time and it is always a slow process. I am willing to second him—I don't think I should be the nominator when I simply have not read him except in small bits and pieces. One just has to persist."

Ginsberg was beginning to understand the log-rolling that went on in the Institute. Edel was willing to second a writer whose work he knew only "in small bits and pieces" as a favor to Ginsberg, which would presumably be returned when Edel nominated someone. At last Ginsberg was making headway. He enlisted fresh supporters, among them Norman Mailer, Peter Matthiessen (with whom he had a connection through their both being Buddhists), John Ashbery, Galway Kinnell, and the novelist Hortense Calisher, who overlooked Burroughs' reputation as a woman-hater, seeing herself as an ally of offbeat people. As for John Ashbery, he thought *Naked Lunch* was an important work and wanted to help out in a difficult election, while Galway Kinnell, another admirer of *Naked Lunch*, agreed with Ginsberg that Burroughs was the kind of writer who *should* be a member.

Ginsberg also saw the importance of making deals with members in other branches. He traded off with the sculptor Marisol—she would vote for his nomination in literature and he would vote for hers in art. He realized that he had to tone down the wording of his citation. He had been writing extravagant paragraphs—"Mr. Burroughs has influenced the world from Buenos Aires to Helsinki"—but that didn't work. You had to be laconic and write, "It is time the Academy recognized Mr. Burroughs' merit," or, "It would be to the Academy's advantage to have Mr. Burroughs as a member."

So Ginsberg wrote a citation which was, by his standards, laconic: "Burroughs is original genius, prose-poet with extraordinary ear for assonance and speech styles; naked eye for hypnotic detail; penetrating mind, innovator of forms, ideas, moods, and cultural symbols; master-influence on several generations of poets and theater-music performers. He improves with age, as do his books. . . . " Nominated by Ginsberg in 1982, and seconded by Hortense Calisher, Leon Edel, Christopher Isherwood, Galway Kinnell, and Peter Matthiessen, Burroughs was at last elected in 1983. Ginsberg, a believer in the old Jewish message, "Today the world is created in you," had done it. The renegade, the pariah, the outsider, the literary outlaw was brought into the fold of his more conventional peers.

The first inkling the Institute had that Burroughs was "different" was when he was asked to send some material for an exhibit of manuscripts by new members. Rather than a manuscript, he offered to send a work of art entitled *Gun Door*. Burroughs is a gun nut and there is nothing he likes better than to go out into a field and fire away at targets. At that time he was experimenting with bags of paint attached to plywood panels. He would fire a shotgun blast at this assemblage, which would pockmark the plywood and splatter paint all over it, creating a unique artistic effect. The startled librarian, Casindania P. Eaton, replied that although *Gun Door* sounded like "a most interesting object," Burroughs had been elected to the Department of Literature, not to the Department of Art, so that "we shall not be able to use it at this time." Burroughs sent a few manuscript pages instead.

Burroughs was pleased to accept membership in the Institute. He did not at all feel that, having drawn a bead on the Establishment in his writing, a major theme of which was the denunciation of all control systems, he was now, at the age of sixty-nine, being coopted by that very Establishment. After all, Henry Miller had been a member, and Norman Mailer, who was a member, had once knifed his wife and been placed under psychiatric observation. Had they been coopted? Had Ginsberg? As a known drug user who had sometimes been held up by interminable searches at borders, his attitude was "Listen, I want all the medals on my chest I can get . . . gets you respect from customs agents." There was in fact a purple-and-gold Institute rosette worn on the suit lapel, but no one knew what it was, and people jocularly inquired of Burroughs when he wore it, "Does that thing mean your forefathers came over on the *Mayflower*?"

So, as the members took their seats on the afternoon of May 18, 1983, there was Burroughs on the same stage as such eminent figures of the literary-academic-political complex as John Hersey, George Kennan, John Kenneth Galbraith, and Arthur Schlesinger, Jr., who, as president of the Academy and Institute, opened the Ceremonial with brief remarks about the future of art in the nuclear age. The distinguished historian of the ages of Jackson and the second Roosevelt had not voted for Burroughs (who had been two years ahead of him at Harvard), not because of his lifestyle but because he felt the work was too disconnected and random and self-promoting and lacking literary merit. But the Burroughs thing was good for the Institute, Schlesinger thought, in the sense that no one could say it was a citadel of reaction.

And then came the induction of new members, and Hortense Calisher read the brief citation for Burroughs: "William Burroughs' *Naked Lunch* marked him as an innovator in the form and content of the novel, and as a cultural symbol. He is a prose-poet with an ear for assonance and speech style and an eye for hypnotic detail. . . ." Burroughs stood up and took a little bow . . . thank God he didn't have to give a speech, he thought . . . it was all quite painless. He was sorry Allen Ginsberg couldn't be there, because of a poetry reading commitment. He didn't see it as a consecration of his work but just as something that happens if you live long enough.

The applause was scattered. Some of the stalwarts, including Schlesinger and Barbara Tuchman, who were seated side by side, front row center, quite obviously sat on their hands. Although, thought Hortense Calisher, you couldn't read too much into the lack of applause. Some of the members were old and deaf, the acoustics were bad, and it was an exhausting day, with drinks and lunch and the race to the toilet, and all the speeches—you had to gear yourself just to get through it.

In the audience, James Grauerholz, who had been Burroughs' secretary for ten years, was overjoyed to see him on stage, because in terms of his critical standing it was a tremendous boost. It was something the critics couldn't argue with. It wasn't just that Burroughs was an outcast in the sociological sense, as an addict and a homosexual; it was that he stood for a whole counterculture movement that the critics hated with vehemence. It reminded Grauerholz of the line in the movie *Terms of Endearment*, where Jack Nicholson offers Shirley MacLaine a drink, and she asks why she should accept, and he says, "To kill the bug that is up your ass."

And then, after the awards had been handed out, came the high point of the day, the Gold Medal for fiction to Bernard Malamud, which was to provide yet another small tempest in the history of the Institute, a tempest that was quite illuminating in terms of Burroughs' induction. For in the Institute were many writers who had known each other for years, who had taught at the same universities, shared houses and meals, gone to the same parties, and dedicated books to one another. Hemingway had once described this hothouse phenomenon as "angleworms in a jar." It was a literary cronyism from which Burroughs was excluded. His only close friend in the Institute was Allen Ginsberg. So that in what was about to happen Burroughs was like an observer of some curious tribal rite to which he was totally foreign, and only half-comprehending, underlining once again that even though he was now a member of the Institute, he was still, and always would be, an outsider.

Ralph Ellison, who was presenting the Gold Medal, had made his reputation as an outsider, but had long been part of the inside coterie. He came from Oklahoma City, where as a boy he shined shoes and picked cotton. Oklahoma, the forty-sixth state, had no tradition of slavery. Ellison grew up in a white neighborhood, where his mother was the custodian for some apartments. He felt the stigma of race somewhat differently from a young black growing up in the twenties in the South, but perhaps for that reason he felt it all the more deeply, and with all the more clarity, for being less oppressed.

In 1945 he began writing *Invisible Man*, published in 1952 and immediately recognized as one of the important American novels of the twentieth century. A word often used to describe it was "seminal." It was in any case a hard act to follow. For the next thirty years, Ellison taught and lectured and received honors and gave readings on his work-in-progress.

But the long-promised novel, *And Hickman Comes*, was still unfinished.

Along the way, Ellison had made friends with Malamud, who taught at Bennington, where Ellison sometimes came to read or visit. But in 1971, there was a crack in the friendship when Malamud published his novel *The Tenant*, the story of a Jewish novelist named Harry Lesser, who refuses to leave a building that is due for demolition. A black squatter, Willie Spearmint, also a writer, moves into an abandoned apartment and starts showing his work to Lesser. Willie says things like "I'm gon win the fuckn Noble Prize. They gon gimme a million bucks of cash." Willie has a white girlfriend whom Harry takes away from him. In revenge, Willie steals the manuscript Harry has been working on for years and destroys it.

When the book came out, friends of Ellison's told him that the jive-talking, paranoid, violence-prone Willie Spearmint was based on him. His friend Bern had exploited him, as Jews were forever exploiting blacks, by modeling this despicable character on him. For years, although he said nothing to Malamud, he had chafed under the suspicion that Willie Spearmint was an injurious caricature of Ralph Ellison.

In spite of all this, they had remained friends. A few days before the Ceremonial, they had seen each other, and Malamud, alluding to the Gold Medal, had said, "Ralph, you'll be getting one, too—you're next." And Ellison, who had for decades been struggling with a second novel that he could not part with, had replied, "No, Bern, I'm finished."

And now, in front of 127 of his peers onstage and 700 guests in the audience, Ellison was about to make public his rancor over *The Tenant*, even as he awarded his old friend one of the highest honors in American literature.

In an evident state of animation after the cocktails and the wine at lunch, Ellison said, reading from a typed text, that the presentation was "in a certain way my pleasure, although an agony." He then went on at some length about Malamud's emergence from anonymity and his Jewish tradition, and the shared experience of novelists of minority background. It was clear that he was wound up, and that it would take some time for him to unwind, and as he rambled on, the audience, weary from hours of speeches, became restive.

Sitting next to Grauerholz was Terry Southern, the irreverent author of *Candy*, who scribbled coarsely humorous notes as Ellison resolutely swam against the tide: "He certainly isn't invisible now . . . " And ten minutes later: "A mind destroyed by syph . . . " And later yet: "Give them an inch . . . "

Onstage, Barbara Tuchman turned to Arthur Schlesinger and whispered, "You've got to stop this." Schlesinger knew that Ellison's talk was going on too long, but did not feel that he could do him (and his wife, Fanny, who was in the audience) the discourtesy of cutting him short. So Mrs. Tuchman took matters into her own hands and began to applaud, and the audience picked it up and applauded, too, which prompted another Terry Southern comment: "This really *is* the *March to Folly*."

"I hope you're not telling me to shut up," Ellison said. "Come on, come on, the best is yet to come." A few minutes later, there was more applause, and again Ellison said, "I told you, the best is yet to come." "And now," he announced, "the biographical aspect. Twelve years ago, when *The Tenant*, Malamud's sixth novel, was published, I felt trapped. People insisted that I was the model for the Negro writer who appeared in that work under the name of Willie Spearmint." Ellison said he had a conversation with a friend who was sure he was Willie. "Do you think," Ellison replied, "that I once lived in a tenement and became so vicious that I destroyed one of Malamud's manuscripts?" "Why are you being so literal?" the friend asked. "I wouldn't want you to think I was capable of destroying another writer's work," Ellison said.

As Malamud in astonishment listened to Ellison pour out his long-buried resentment, he grimaced inwardly and reflected on the dilemma between life and art. He thought of himself as an inventive novelist, able to give form to a character through the power of imagination. And now he was being accused of having simply copied from life. It was something he talked to his students about—which was more real, what was true or what was imagined? The imaginative novelist could outguess you; he was one step ahead of you, having made up what you might mistake as real.

Impatient for the proceedings to be over, since he had foregone cocktails and wine at lunch and wanted his late-afternoon drink, Burroughs was bored to death by Ellison's speech. Ellison seemed quite deliberately determined to be annoying. It was remarkable how someone could talk for half an hour and say absolutely nothing.

Like Burroughs, most of the audience was unaware of the psychodrama taking place onstage. There was ever louder applause, to which Ellison responded defiantly with "You just won the right to listen to the rest of it." Finally, however, he came to the task at hand: "Contrasting my lingering annoyance at being elected the model for Willie Spearmint with my pleasure at this moment," he said, "I will get on with my assignment [ear-splitting applause]—Bern, will you approach me?"

Everyone was grateful for the brevity of Malamud's acceptance speech, and soon members and their guests were threading their way through congested exits from the auditorium to the reception on the terrace. There was considerable head-shaking and tongue-wagging over Ellison's remarks, which some saw as washing dirty laundry in public, while others said that such incidents were bound to take place in the climate of cronyism that so many Institute writers shared. In twenty years of attending Ceremonials, Richard Hayes, an editor and collaborator of Jerzy Kosinski, had never seen anything like it. Rolling his eyes heavenward, he intoned, "I have heard the chimes at midnight."

After a festive dinner with friends, Burroughs got back to the apartment on the Bowery he stays in when he is in New York, which, being windowless, is known as the Bunker. Stewart Meyer, an old friend, was waiting up for him. "William, did you make a speech?" Meyer asked. "Yes," said Burroughs, "I said thank you for your paltry ribbons." "You didn't really say that, did you?" Meyer asked. "No, Stew," Burroughs said, "I just said thanks. These people, twenty years ago, they were saying I belonged in jail. Now they're saying I belong in their club. I didn't listen to them then, and I don't listen to them now."

· ONE ·

ST. LOUIS

1914–1931

Pershing Avenue, an elm-lined residential thoroughfare of plain-fronted brick houses in St. Louis, owes its name to World War I, having been rechristened from Berlin Avenue not long after the outbreak of hostilities. On Pershing Avenue—named after the American commander in the war—you can tell the seasons by the ways of tidying up: in the summer, the freshly mowed lawns; in the autumn, the bags in driveways filled with dead leaves. The avenue, in the middle of Middle America, is a monument to hard work, conventional behavior, proper values, shared assumptions, and sedentary, rooted, community-minded lives. Its houses, not immoderate or ostentatious, indicate a satisfactory level of affluence.

The three-story house at 4664 Pershing Avenue had a slate roof, a fifty-foot front lawn, and a large backyard with a garden and a fish pond, separated from the neighbors by high wooden fences overgrown with morning glories and rose vines. The windows were leaded, a fire burned in the living room on chilly evenings, the dining room and study were commodious, and cheerful bedrooms occupied the other two floors.

It was in one of those bedrooms, on February 5, 1914, that William Seward Burroughs II was born. His heritage combined two familiar American types: the Yankee inventor and the Southern preacher. The inventor was his paternal grandfather, William Seward Burroughs, born in 1857 in Rochester, New York, then known as "the flour city" because of its mills. The "Seward," after Lincoln's far-sighted secretary of state, who bought Alaska from the Russians, was an expression of hope that the boy would make something of himself.

William Seward's father, Edmund Burroughs, was a mechanic and an inventor in his own right—he took out patents on a railroad jack and on sliding knives to cut paper, but never made any money and was in fact often unemployed. As a result, he discouraged his son from following in his footsteps, wanting him to take a steady, white-collar job. When William graduated from high school at the age of eighteen, he found employment as a clerk in the Cayuga County National Bank, in nearby Auburn.

A bank clerk in those days spent his time writing columns of figures in black and red ink in cloth-bound ledgers and tallying them by hand. If the columns didn't balance he was in trouble. Every morning, he came into the office, removed his detachable cuffs, adjusted his green eyeshade, perched on a high stool next to the other clerks, and put in eight hours or more of unimaginable drudgery, until the numbers blurred his vision, until the battalions of dollars and cents melted and liquefied in his brain pan in a puddle of tedium.

William Seward Burroughs stayed at the bank for seven years. He married when he was twenty-one. During those years of scratchy nib pens, endless rows of figures, and the anxiety of error, the sensible idea occurred to him that there must be a better way. And the better way was a machine that would replace all the burned-out bank clerks across the nation. Born of his own seven years of frustration in the salt mines of clerking, the idea of a machine that could add and tally and spit out the error-free results on a strip of paper became an obsession.

The work had ruined his health. He was in the early stages of tuberculosis, and doctors recommended a warmer climate. His father had moved to St. Louis, and William Seward decided to follow there. His life from then on becomes a parable of entrepreneurial capitalism in the land of limitless opportunity, where anything was possible, where a poor young man, hard-working and inventive, could, in a decade, make a fortune and found a great corporation.

In an inventive age, examples abounded—the typewriter in 1868, the telephone in 1876, the cash register in 1879, the fountain pen in 1884, and the Kodak camera in 1888. It was easy—all you needed was the streak of genius to make something that had never been thought of before, plenty of cash to develop your invention, self-confidence bordering on megalomania, and a nod from the patent office.

Of course there had been calculating machines since the abacus, but no one had come up with a machine that could, with one stroke of the handle, add a column of figures and print the operation on paper at the same time. Burroughs later added a wide carriage so bookkeeping journals could be printed, and the now-familiar cash-register tape became the tally of the day's transactions.

In 1882, at the age of twenty-five, William Seward Burroughs arrived in St. Louis, a city of foundries, with an ample supply of toolmakers, still largely German in its ethnic stock. It was his good fortune soon after he got there to meet a kindred spirit, a young Canadian named Joseph Boyer, who was like him an inventor, and who like him had migrated to St. Louis in search of opportunity. Boyer, who ran a little machine shop at 244 Dickson Street, making mostly bottle molds for dairies and breweries, had patented a pneumatic hammer, and was working on a device to record the speed of trains.

Burroughs rented bench space from Boyer, along with equipment and an assistant. Having been around inventors, Boyer knew that most of them were big-talking dreamers whose schemes never hatched, and it was with a healthy dose of skepticism that he listened to Burroughs boast that "someday there will be one of my machines in every city bank in the land, and that means over 8,000 machines."

And yet, Boyer had to admit, Burroughs approached his task with the fervor of a religious fanatic. He would be at his bench making drawings when Boyer left the shop in the evening, and he would be there still when he returned the next morning. When the St. Louis damp stretched his drawing paper, he switched to polished copper plates, striking a center or drawing a line under a magnifying glass.

Burroughs found a couple of backers who put up $700 in exchange for fourteen shares of stock in a nonexistent company. Boyer was impressed and invested some of his own money. There was no doubt Burroughs had a knack. Boyer had seen him once, in a couple of hours, design a collapsible chicken coop that folded up when it was not being used.

Burroughs called his machine the Arithmometer, and in 1886, the American Arithmometer Company was incorporated under a Missouri charter with a capital stock of $100,000 divided into 1,000 shares, among Burroughs and three investors. The company was founded mainly on hope, for he did not yet have a patent and had not yet produced any machines. By this time he had a growing family, Mortimer, born in 1885, and Horace, born a year later, who would be followed by two daughters, Jenny and Helen.

Two years later, however, the great day came: Burroughs was granted the first patent for a key-operated recording and adding machine. The stockholders voted to increase the capital stock to $200,000. By this time, in St. Louis investment circles, the "mad mechanic's" adding machine had become something of a joke. It was customary to say, instead of "He has money to burn," "He has money to buy adding machine stock."

Under pressure from stockholders to come up with the goods, Burroughs produced fifty machines in 1889. There was only one problem—they didn't work. Depending on how hard you pulled the handle, the machines came up with different sums. Operating the handle correctly required a magic touch. Complaints poured in from the banks where the machines had been sent, and they had to be recalled. Banks lost interest, stockholders were discouraged, the company faced failure.

Burroughs hated failure, which in puritanical Darwinian fashion he equated with evil. If you failed, IT WAS YOUR FAULT, it was because of some moral taint. One day, in an alcoholic pique, he paid a stealthy visit to his workroom, where the fifty recalled machines were stored. He sat there for a long time staring at them—a vision of failure, of hopes delayed, of having his judgment and ability doubted. The chorus of complaints rang in his ears: "I tried to list four figures and your machine came up with a row of zeros." Suddenly he rose, picked up one of the machines, and threw it out the window . . . and then another and another. The machines were evil and had to be destroyed. Then he called Boyer over and, pointing to the pile of mangled metal on the pavement, said: "There, I have ended the last of my troubles."

PLUCK HIS ONLY ASSET, an obituary subhead would later read. The little drama of persistence was played out in a matter of days, with Burroughs experiencing the "Eureka!" moment, when lightning strikes. The solution to variations in the handle-pulling force was a "dash-pot," an oil-filled metal cylinder drilled from solid bar steel, about two inches in diameter and five inches long, with a piston punctured by two small holes to regulate the flow of oil. This gave a uniform motion to the shaft mechanism whatever the force applied to the handle. The "dash-pot," a device also used to keep heavy doors from slamming, buffered the variations.

The new machines went out in 1891, and they worked. In fact, they were the answer to every bookkeeper's dream. The banks snapped them up at $425 apiece. At last they had attained the dignity of a marketable commodity. As Burroughs noted in his demonstrations, "Let me say that there is no halfway point in the mechanical world. A machine of this nature is either a complete success or a complete failure."

The product was launched in the midst of that glowing late-nineteenth-century era of business optimism and the "we-can-do-it" spirit:

"How long will a Burroughs last? Frankly we don't know. We have never seen one wear out."

"Satisfied customers are saying, 'The Burroughs pays for itself many times over.' "

Salesmen imbued with absolute faith that their product was a humanitarian blessing fanned across the nation, stalking the P.B.—the Prospective Buyer. William H. Mason traveled 1,200 miles, including several hundred miles seated next to a stagecoach driver, to sell a single machine to a bank in Sonora, Texas, for a ten-dollar commission. Another salesman summed up, in his own way, the ethics of free-enterprise capitalism:

> Each time I find a new P.B.,
> I add to my prosperity . . .
> So conscience-free, I give true worth.
> I sell the best machine on earth.
> I'll show you, as well as I can,
> Just why I am a Burroughs Man.

Burroughs kept improving his brainchild, with duplicate copies on the paper strip, and a ribbon reverse that later became standard on typewriters. Rival machines like the Comtograph were developed, but quickly went out of business.

As his fortune improved, his tuberculosis grew worse. For years, he had worked until exhaustion under the handicap of TB, and was a heavy user of alcohol to keep him going. Single-minded and obsessive, it was up to his wife, Helen, to remind him to eat and wear clean clothes—she sometimes said that she had five children, two boys, two girls, and a husband. Not that Burroughs was much of a family man. He had that "don't-let-the-children-come-near-me-when-I'm-working" look.

In 1896 Burroughs moved to Citronelle, Alabama, with his family. Citronelle was situated in a pine forest, 320 feet above sea level, near the Gulf of Mexico, and was highly recommended for tuberculars. When his wife died, he married his nurse, Mrs. White, who helped him raise the children. They were good children—Jenny and Helen and Horace and Mortimer. Mortimer was a sociable lad if a bit ineffectual. One day he was eating a candy bar in the living room, which he hid under the couch when he saw his father approach. Burroughs, who could not stand anything sticky to the touch, reached under the couch and withdrew his fingers smudged with chocolate, which made him so irate that he spanked his son.

In Citronelle, Burroughs worked about four hours a day on his experiments and spent the rest of the day walking in the woods. His appetite returned and he felt that he was improving. In 1897 he resigned from the company, feeling too far removed to keep up with its operations. He kept tinkering, helping out a neighbor who sold firewood in bundles with a device that did the bundling automatically. In fact, however, he was getting worse, and he died on September 14, 1898, at the age of forty-one. At that same age, his grandson and namesake was just getting started on his writing career, having published his first book at the age of thirty-nine.

Burroughs was buried in St. Louis, and a stained-glass window dedicated to his memory was installed in the Presbyterian church in Citronelle, bearing the inscription: "As the hare panteth after the water brooks, so panteth my soul for Thee, O God."

It was not long after his death that Burroughs' dream of selling 8,000 machines was realized. So many machines were sold that in 1904 Boyer moved the entire company and its 465 employees aboard the Clover Leaf Limited to a new and spacious factory in Detroit. He had never liked the hot St. Louis summers anyway. A year later, Boyer, by now president of the American Arithmometer Company, renamed it the Burroughs Adding Machine Company. That year, 7,800 machines were sold, as many as Burroughs had predicted the entire U.S. market could absorb.

Burroughs was the father of the adding machine, but Joe Boyer was the father of the Burroughs company. He ran it after Burroughs resigned, and remained its president for nineteen years. He lived exactly twice as long as Burroughs, until the age of eighty-two. He saw the company grow from assets of $5 million in 1905 to assets of $430 million in 1920, and profited far more than did the Burroughs family, for Burroughs was as indifferent to money as to food and clothing. When he moved to Citronelle he sold quite a bit of his stock and put the rest in trust for his children with the Mississippi Valley Trust Company in St. Louis. So that when he died his children held in trust 485 shares, compared to the 16,380 shares that Boyer held. Over the years, there were stock splits, which made the Burroughs family holdings worth quite a bit, but it was still only a fraction of what Boyer was worth. The company was founded by Burroughs and bore his name, but the "Burroughs millions" were a fable. Burroughs put his energy into inventing the adding machine, and his partners put their energy into capital formation. Other entrepreneurs of the period, such as the Fords and the Rockefellers, amassed enormous wealth and founded dynasties. But Burroughs was a shooting star, who left his children little more than a bright afterglow.

In contrast and complement to the strain of Yankee ingenuity handed down by one grandfather, William Seward Burroughs II had on his mother's side the strain of the Bible-thumping, fire-and-brimstone Southern clergyman. His other grandfather, James Wideman Lee, born in 1849 in Rockbridge, Georgia, was a Methodist circuit-riding minister, a God-fearing moralizer who spread the gospel through the Georgia backwoods. Lee is, of course, one of the most common family names in the South, and thousands of the clan claim kinship to Robert E. Lee. But there was nothing very grand about these particular Lees, who traced their origins back to dispossessed eighteenth-century tenant farmers, a jump ahead of being sharecroppers. In 1875, when he was twenty-six, James Wideman Lee married thirteen-year-old Eufala Ledbetter. Two years later, she gave birth to the first of twelve children, of whom only six survived to adulthood, including Laura Lee, the mother of William S. Burroughs II, and Ivy Lee, his uncle.

It was through Eufala's firstborn, Ivy Ledbetter Lee, that her husband's ministerial message, "If you want to win the game of life and honor the God who made you, work hard and save," found its application in the business world. For Ivy used the nimbleness with words inherited from his father to realize his ambition of corporate success. William Seward Burroughs did it with an invention, and Ivy Ledbetter Lee did it with language. One was the Father of the Adding Machine and the other was the Father of Public Relations. Ivy Lee made the robber barons look like nice guys, and lied so often on their behalf that he became known as "Poison Ivy."

He graduated from Princeton in 1898, and the possibility that modesty was not his outstanding trait can be inferred from the class prophecy in the *Nassau Herald*: "Under his arm he carried a book entitled *Great Men Who Have Met Me*. . . . He hummed to himself a little tune of his own composition, entitled, 'Only Me, Ivy Lee.' "

After a few years spent working for New York City newspapers, he found his true calling, as a press agent for big business. At a time when corporations were seen as greedy and arrogant and indifferent to the public good, Ivy Lee pushed the notion of "The public be informed" rather than "The public be damned!" It was better to tell the truth, even if the truth was damaging, than to have your enemy catch you concealing it. If the Pennsylvania Railroad, one of his clients, had a train wreck, he put out the facts on the accident, even if the railroad was to blame. If the railroad wanted to lobby Congress for a rate increase, it could make a better case if it had clubhouses for workers, college scholarships for their children, and a pension plan. You conveyed an image of candor and public service, while in fact you continued to cover up when you could.

Around 1913, when Ivy Lee's name was on the rise, it happened that the Rockefeller name was at a low. In Colorado, 9,000 miners had walked off the job at coal mines where the Rockefellers were the principal owners. The workmen lived in company houses and shopped in company stores and voted for company candidates. The United Mine Workers came in to organize them and moved them out of the company houses and into a tent city. On October 17, 1913, deputy sheriffs shot up the tent city with a machine gun, and the state militia was called out. In April 1914 there was another battle, which became known as the Ludlow Massacre, in which two women and eleven children were killed. President Wilson sent in federal troops. The Rockefellers were branded as killers in newspapers across the country.

In May 1914, Ivy Lee was invited to the office of John D. Rockefeller, Jr., who said: "I feel that my father and I are much misunderstood by the press and the people of this country. I should like to know what your advice would be about how to make our position clear."

Here was the new Machiavelli being consulted by the twentieth-century Prince. Ivy Lee advised that management should give plausible accounts of the strike, to make it acceptable to public opinion. He advised an end to ivory-tower seclusion—personal contact between employer and employee was desirable. John D. Rockefeller, Jr., was dispatched to Colorado to visit the mines. He chatted with the workers, heard their grievances, and danced with their wives at a social. It did more good than a dozen speeches, and the strike was settled that December. But it later came out that Ivy Lee's candid press handouts had been based on cooked data from the coal operators, which he hadn't bothered to check. It wasn't so much the truth that Ivy Lee was selling, but a shell game. And where was the pea? Under Ivy Lee's hat.

His services were appreciated, and in 1915 he resigned from his other accounts to devote himself full-time to the Rockefellers. His next assignment was to transform John D. Rockefeller, Sr., who had always shunned the press, from monster into humanoid. He soon had old John D. skipping through his P.R. hoops—distributing shiny dimes to newsboys, cutting his ninetieth-birthday cake in public, playing golf with a reporter, gnarled and weasel-faced, in knickers. After all these years typecast as the villain, old John D. became a media darling. Instead of "Rockefeller, Man or Demon," it was "Rockefeller Gives Another Million to Unemployment Fund," philanthropy being the cornerstone of a better image. Ivy Lee, who called himself "an adjustor of relationships," refused to take credit for the change. "I just raised the curtain and let the people look in," he said.

Like the "Burroughs Man," who added to his prosperity by finding a new P.B., Ivy Lee did all right for himself. He had a town house at 4 East Sixty-sixth Street in New York, a list of clubs as long as your arm, and friends in high places. He was in the Social Register, and his daughter Alice was presented at the Court of St. James's. A song of the period had the line, "Even Rumania has Ivy Lee-mania, gosh how the money rolls in." A six-footer with a round, fleshy face, he conveyed a sense of prosperity and well-being, and his half-smile was that of a man who knows more than he lets on.

But after rising to a position of eminence in the American business community, Ivy Lee self-destructed because of blind faith in his own procedures. He really did believe that every problem was an "image" problem that would go away with a little P.R. If he could sell Rockefeller to the American public, why not sell Hitler?

When the Nazis came to power in 1933, he was paid a $33,000-a-year retainer by I. G. Farben to make the new German government and its leaders popular in the United States. Visiting Germany that year, he met Hitler and Goebbels and returned full of admiration. These were the men who would restore German confidence, he said, and was not a confident and healthy Germany essential for Europe?

Ivy Lee saw international affairs and the rise of fascist ideologies as matters that could be handled like corporate strategy. His advice to Nazi leaders was essentially what he had told Rockefeller. People had to be reassured so they didn't think you were a monster. Foreign Minister Von Ribbentrop should say that Germany did not want to rearm. Vice Chancellor Von Papen should say that Germany did not want the Saar basin. Hitler should say that the storm troopers were organized for the sole purpose of preventing a return to Communism. When William E. Dodd, the American ambassador to Germany, met Ivy Lee on his second trip to Berlin in January 1934, he wrote in his diary that "Ivy Lee has shown himself at once a capitalist and an advocate of fascism."

Ivy Lee realized too late that the Third Reich was not the clone of Standard Oil. You could have Hitler hand out dimes until the Rhine froze over and the Nazis still wouldn't be nice guys. Ivy Lee now had his own image problem. He was seen as Hitler's press agent, and his reputation hit bottom. In the Senate, Robert La Follette called his work "a monument of shame." In the House, the Un-American Activities Committee asked him in May 1934 to testify, and it came out that he was being paid to present Hitler in a favorable light.

The turmoil affected his health, and a cerebral hemorrhage felled him that October, at the age of fifty-seven. Billy Burroughs, then twenty, saw him in New York shortly before his death. He spoke of his many talks with Hitler. "The last time I saw him," he said, "Hitler told me, 'I have nothing against the Jews. This is all exaggerated.' " He had just bought a new car, and there was something wrong with it, and he said: "I didn't dream it would fall apart like this," which seemed to Billy an unconscious reference to his own situation. He had demonstrated the power, but also the limitations, of public relations. He had helped Rockefeller and other business leaders to find acceptance. But in so doing he had believed that acceptance depended on image rather than substance. As Robert Benchley put it, "Mr. Lee . . . has devoted his energies to proving, by insidious leaflets and gentle epistles, that the present capitalist system is really a branch of the Quaker Church, carrying on the work begun by St. Francis of Assisi."

Through his inventor grandfather, and through his preacher grand-father, by way of his uncle Ivy, William Seward Burroughs II was offered two examples of laissez-faire capitalism in its purest form. The inventor made something that could be said to advance progress, in that a machine took over dull clerical work, and got rich in the bargain. The press agent borrowed the style and sermonizing of the preacher to get his message across—what was good for the Rockefellers was good for the country.

These examples had a bearing on Burroughs' vocation as a writer. He was like a son whose father has embezzled a fortune, and who promises to pay back every cent on the dollar. He had a sense of mission. His uncle had debased the language, turned it to purposes of trickery and deceit. He would, in his own writing, restore integrity to language. To use language honestly, or to expose the ways language was used dishon-estly, was a sacred trust, not to be taken lightly, which helps explain why it took Burroughs so long to get started. He knew early on that he was a writer, but did not start work on his first book until he was in his late thirties, as though paralyzed by the magnitude of his task.

At the same time his inventor grandfather had lost what should have been his—the corporation that bore his name. Burroughs the grandson was in the position of a disowned heir. He was like "El Desdichado" in Gerard de Nerval's sonnet, quoted by another St. Louis writer, T. S. Eliot, in *The Waste Land*: "*Le Prince D'Aquitaine à la tour abolie*"— the prince whose tower has been destroyed. *Desdichado* means brought down, overthrown, disinherited. Burroughs the writer had to reclaim the name appropriated by the company, and vindicate the inventor who had lost the family birthright, with the help of his children.

For when their father died, the children, still in their teens, inherited the stock held in trust for them, which the executors, in collusion with company management, persuaded them to sell. "Ahem, I must tell you for your own good, holding on to these shares is basically unsound"— Burroughs imagines the scene, adding, "My father could be talked into anything." They were bought out for $100,000 apiece, which in today's dollars would be about a million. A tidy sum, but nothing compared with what they would be worth today if they had hung on. Only Mortimer, Burroughs' father, held on to a small number of shares, which he sold in 1929, three months before the stock market crashed. Burroughs, then fifteen, remembers his father coming home with a check for $276,000, "the highest balance ever to appear on his bank statement. With a measly quarter million in the bank, we were not accepted by families with ten, twenty, fifty million. No one wanted those ratty Burroughses about." He estimates that his father's small share in the company, had he held on to it, would today be worth about $20 million, adding, "Twenty million reasons not to write." For it is his conviction that wealth stifles the creative impulse. So that his exclusion from the family fortune was a blessing in disguise, allowing him to carry out the goal of making a name for himself as a writer.

It was after James Wideman Lee moved to St. Louis to take over an affluent Methodist parish there, Methodism still being in those days a religion of bankers, that Laura Lee met Mortimer Burroughs. James Wideman Lee was a fine-looking old gentleman with a white mustache who knew everyone in the congregation by name, and wrote a book on how to win the game of life, entitled *The Geography of Genius*. His wife, Eufala, was active in the Women's Temperance Union and frequently said she would rather have a son of hers come home dead than drunk. After her husband died from the complications of a broken hip, she took to travel, and once brought home some shawls from India, living on to the age of eighty-nine.

Laura Lee was a beauty, with thick chestnut hair, a perfect oval face, the high Lee forehead, a lovely mouth, lovely skin, and a willowy hourglass figure. Mortimer Burroughs was handsome in a clean-cut preppy way. He had a good mind, went to M.I.T., and was the sensible member of the family. Mortimer invested his money, while Horace used his to make a splash, buying a coach-and-four. After an illness, Horace began using morphine and speedily went through his inheritance, committing suicide in 1915, at the age of twenty-nine, by breaking a window pane in a roominghouse in Detroit and cutting his arm on the jagged fragments. Mortimer's sister Jenny was a drunk, and he would sometimes get calls from the desk sergeant at the police precinct, asking him to come and get her or they would have to lock her up. Finally, in exasperation, Mortimer gave her a one-way train ticket to Seattle and she was not heard from again. As for his other sister, Helen, she married a man named Mercer and went to live in Colorado Springs.

Laura and Mortimer married in 1910, when she was twenty-two and he was twenty-five, and went to Detroit, where Mortimer worked briefly as a salesman for the Burroughs Company. It was there that their first son, also Mortimer, was born in 1911 (to distinguish them, the father was called Mote and the son was called Mort). Soon after, they returned to St. Louis and moved into the house on Berlin/Pershing Avenue. With the proceeds of his Burroughs shares, Mote started a plate glass company. He and Laura were in the Social Register but not in the St. Louis Country Club, an important distinction in the stratified society of that city. Their friends were the *haute bourgeoisie*, like the lawyer Eugene Angert, and O. K. Bovart, editor of the *St. Louis Post-Dispatch*. Their next-door neighbor, Rives Skinker Matthews, was a prosperous hardware dealer who always wore a black tie and a high starched collar, and went to his office in a Packard limousine. Skinker Boulevard, which traced the city limits when the city had limits, was named after his grandfather.

The marriage was apparently a happy one. Billy Burroughs never once heard his parents' voices raised in anger or argument, and they remained faithful to each other. His father was a decent man who performed small acts of kindness. When one of Billy's schoolmates broke the glass of a portrait hanging on the auditorium wall with a basketball, Mortimer Burroughs repaired it free of charge. And yet there was in Mortimer a remoteness that his son could never bridge. What was he *really* like? Billy never found out. There were all too few father-son conversations that he could remember. Mortimer was an atheist, and once told his son, "I know what happens to you when you die. There was a little dog, and his name was Rover, and when he was dead, he was dead all over." "Well now, Dad," Billy asked, "what about reincarnation and all that?" "If you can't remember, what difference does it make?" replied his father. "Maybe you can remember," Billy said. "Oh, I suppose *you* know," said his father in irritation. "Well, maybe I do, Dad," Billy said.

Billy and Mort had to go to Sunday school as long as their preacher grandfather was alive, but after his death they were let off. One day Mort was spanked for fighting on Sunday, which seemed to Billy sheer hypocrisy, coming from his father.

His mother wasn't religious either, but she was psychic. She had a feel about people, like an animal. His father would be about to get involved in some business deal and she would say, "No, no, he's a crook, I can tell," and she would be right. Once his brother was out late and his mother dreamed that he came to her with his face covered with blood and said, "Mother, we've had an accident." In fact that night his brother had been in a car accident and his face had been covered with blood, although his injuries were minor.

Billy felt that his mother had been crippled by her Bible Belt upbringing, which imposed, among other things, an abhorrence for bodily functions. She suffered from headaches and backaches, and there was something deeply sad about her, as though she expected doom to arrive at any moment. He also felt that his mother was never really accepted by St. Louis society. The rich St. Louis matrons said, "Let's get together," but rarely did.

To others, Laura seemed cold and unaffectionate. "She never kissed me on the cheek in her life," said her daughter-in-law Miggy, who married Mort. "She found it hard to like people. Also, she was an unconsciously tactless woman. She'd walk into a room and say, 'This is the ugliest room I've ever seen.' " Sometimes her behavior verged on the cruel. "She asked me to meet her once at Stix, Baer & Fuller to buy nightgowns," Miggy said. "I was hoping she would give me one, but no, that wasn't it. She wanted me to admit that my family had no money and that I could not afford one.

"With her it was always vanity first," Miggy continued. "When she was told her boys had to wear glasses, she said, 'Don't bother about glasses, just sit them in the front row.' But she was smart, with a good sense of humor," Miggy went on. "She was good at everything she did, although she was impractical. She was the sort who could cook a French sauce but couldn't bake a potato."

Her specialty was flower arranging, and her reputation spread to the point that the Coca-Cola Company commissioned her to write three books on the subject, along with helpful hints on interesting ways to serve refreshments. She appears on the cover of the first volume, sitting on a couch in a white silk dress, a pearl choker around her throat, surrounded by flowers, a bottle of Coke in her lap.

Billy grew up in a family where displays of affection were considered embarrassing, although he was clearly his mother's favorite. According to Miggy, "Laura was crazy about Billy and didn't love Mort. It was always 'Billy this and Billy that. He's just the funniest person I know.' " When he was older, his mother told him, "I worship the ground you walk on."

Billy shared a room with his brother as a boy, but they were too dissimilar for there to be much close communication between them. One of Billy's earliest memories is that he was holding a ten-pin to throw one day as he said, "Will you play with me, Mort?" and threw it the instant Mort said no, hitting him in the head. Alerted by the cries, his father came in and Billy got spanked.

Mort took after his father; he was sturdy and healthy-looking, whereas Billy was thin and long-boned like his mother, and there was no color in his cheeks. Mort became the good son and Billy became the prodigal son. Mort went to Princeton and then to Harvard to study architecture, but he graduated during the Depression, when there was not much demand for architects. So for a while he worked for his father, who by that time had sold his plate glass business and become a landscape gardener. Then when the war came he went to work for Emerson Electric, which was later absorbed by General Electric, as a draftsman, and stayed there until he retired. All his adult life he lived in St. Louis on a different Pershing Avenue, in University City, and was a loyal and dutiful son. And it was perhaps because the place of good son was occupied that Billy was free to go and work out his destiny, living in all sorts of places in all sorts of ways, absent and out of touch, in and out of trouble. And although he was a frequent embarrassment to his parents, they continued to support him for many years, with amazing patience and devotion, when it would have been so easy to write him off as a bad bet. And Mort, of course, deeply resented his brother's feckless existence, when he, Mort, had been strapped in the straitjacket of family responsibility that Billy had escaped, had been made to play the role of the loyal and upstanding son because of Billy's defection.

So the texture of the brotherly relationship was based on the different roads they had taken, and came out in small ways rather than in open hostility. In a dignified WASP St. Louis family, small ways were enough. It was just that Billy and Mort never agreed on any subject. Take the little argument they had about the atom bomb when Billy visited St. Louis in 1965, when both brothers were in their fifties.

Mort said: "We were perfectly justified to drop the bomb."

Billy said: "Don't you realize the Japs were completely beaten? Look, you got some people over there in a cabin, you got a posse here, they got pistols, you've got rifles. They can't possibly hit you. Are you going to storm that cabin? No, you wait 'em out. That's all we had to do was wait 'em out."

Mort said: "That's the most ridiculous thing I ever heard."

Billy said: "Well, I think the Hiroshima thing was ridiculous."

Billy Burroughs grew up in post–World War I St. Louis, a city on the west side of the Mississippi, ten miles below its juncture with the Missouri. At that time, the subdivisions beyond the city limits, like Clayton and Webster and Groves, were known as "the county."

On March 9, 1914, a little more than a month after his birth, thirty-nine persons died when the Missouri Athletic Club burned down. It was the worst fire in the city's history. But generally, St. Louis was known as a fun-loving place, a place of joiners and clubs like the Public Questions Club, the Great Books Club, the Toastmaster's Club, the Twentieth Century Club, the Wednesday Club, and the Upper Glenmore Rose Garden Society. There was also the St. Louis Country Club for the upper crust. Rogers Scudder, a childhood friend of Burroughs', remembers his mother saying with horror, "They finally let a German into the country club."

For there was a strong German strain in St. Louis. The Anheuser-Busch family had built a brewery there, and from its proceeds a great estate on Gravois Road. Joseph Pulitzer had founded the *St. Louis Post-Dispatch*, adopting as his own Goethe's maxim, *"Mut verloren, alles verloren"*—"Courage lost, all lost."

It was a city of odd traditions, such as the Veiled Prophet Ball. Each year, the Veiled Prophet, whose name was never disclosed, but who was supposed to be from the Mysterious East, was escorted by Bengal Lancers to his throne at the ball, a white-tie affair, and crowned the "Queen" who would reign over St. Louis society for the next twelve months.

Billy Burroughs' St. Louis was a mix of places appealing for one reason or another to a boy's interests. There was the Winter Garden where you went ice-skating, and Joe Garavelli's restaurant on De Baliviere, where you went on Thursday, the cook's day off. There was the 415, where you ordered catfish by the pound, and the Women's Exchange on the corner of Euclid and McPherson, where they sold the best fudge in town. There was the Fawk Fur Factory, which gave off a peculiar smell, supposedly from the processing of seals—the story was that the Fawks had adopted a French boy, but he showed up with his two brothers and they had to take all three.

The old money lived on Portland Place or Van Devanter, while on Lindell Avenue stood the mansions of the new rich, like the Sayman Soap man, who had started selling his soap in the street from a horse-drawn cart. When the horse died he had it stuffed and stood it in the front hall of his fine new house. In contrast there was Market Street, the skid row of Billy's adolescence, with its tattoo parlors and pawn shops—brass knuckles next to a beat-up guitar in a dusty window.

T. S. Eliot, recalling his St. Louis childhood, remembered mainly the moods and majesty of the Mississippi, the steamboats blowing in the New Year, the river in flood with its floating cargo of dead Negroes and chicken coops, the river tame and sluggish . . . "I feel that there is something in having passed one's childhood beside the big river which is incommunicable to those who have not," he wrote.

Burroughs recalled most vividly another river, the Rivière des Pères, an open sewer thirty feet across that meandered through the city and emptied into the Mississippi. It flowed through some of the better neighborhoods, effluence amid the affluence. With his inseparable companion and first cousin Pryne Hoxie, who lived around the corner from Pershing, on McPherson, Billy would stand on the grassy banks of the River of the Fathers as turds shot out into the polluted water from vents along the sides: "Hey looky . . . someone just did it . . . " "You smell like the Rivière des Pères" was a common St. Louis saying.

With Pryne Hoxie also he would sit on his back porch of a summer evening drinking a cold Whistle, an orange drink, and watching the misty blue sky darken as the smells of coal gas and the open sewer drifted over the city. Or they would jump off the ten-foot stone pillars linked by a chain at nearby Washington University, or go to Forest Park and catch frogs in the pond. He and Hoxie saw each other every day—they even had an identifying cry: *Woo-Woo-Woop*.

It is a recurring theme of Burroughs' life that those close to him died violently—this book has more corpses in it than *Hamlet*—and Pryne Hoxie was the first to go. He died at eighteen while at Princeton, in a car crash. His jugular was severed by a broken windshield. Mrs. Hoxie, whose husband, Bob, had also died at about that time, went to see a spirit medium in East St. Louis who put her in touch with her son and husband—it seems they were having playful wrestling bouts in the hereafter. When informed of his former playmate's fate, Burroughs was disturbed by the apparent intellectual deterioration that the deceased undergo.

The Burroughs family had a gardener, a maid, a nanny, and a cook, who prepared roasts and squab and quail and wild duck. For dessert they sometimes had block ice cream from Delmonico's, orange ice on the outside and another flavor on the inside. Christmas was the time for turkey and Virginia ham, and almond cookies from Germany shaped like stars and half-moons, called *Kuchen*.

In the summer, they went to Harbor Beach, a postcard town on Lake Huron, sloping up from the lake into low hills, a town of neat white frame houses and steep winding streets. The hills were bright green in the summer, surrounded by meadows and fields and streams with stone bridges, and further inland there were woods of oak and pine and birch. It was a seasonal outpost of an idyllic pastoral America. The summer people owned cottages and had the town to themselves. Most of them ate in a communal dining hall and were summoned to meals by a bell. Ringing the bell at the wrong time was a favorite prank of the summer kids, as was raiding the icebox for ginger ale and Whistle.

On the surface, it seems an idyllic childhood, but there was a dark side, with a suggestible child falling under the influence of servants who had their private undertakings, possibly improper, possibly corrupt. The old Irish cook, Burroughs later reflected, was like one of the witches in *Macbeth*. She taught him how to call the toads. He made a sort of hooting sound, and the toad that lived under a rock in the pond in his backyard would come out. She taught him the curse of the blinding worm, how to bring the blinding worm out of rotten bread. You took some moldy bread and ran a needle through it in a certain way, and you buried it under a fence post in a pigsty, and you said, "Needle in thread, needle in bread, eye in needle, needle in eye, bury the bread deep in a sty." And the worm would go into the eye of the person you were cursing and blind that person. To ward off the curse, you had to say, "Cut the bread and cut the thread, and send the needle back on red."

"It's a secret," the Irish cook said. "Don't tell anyone." Many years later, in the Empress Hotel in London, Burroughs dreamed that a white worm was crawling out of his eye and woke up screaming. The Irish cook awakened in the boy a deep and lingering interest in witchcraft and the occult. One day when he was in Forest Park with his brother in the late afternoon he looked into a grove of trees and saw a little green reindeer, very delicate, with pale thin legs. *Annihilating all that's made / To a green thought in a green shade.* The reindeer, he later reflected, was his totem animal, which is revealed to you in a vision, and which you must never kill. Another time, he woke up after having made a house of blocks and saw little men playing in the house, moving very fast.

His nanny, Mary Evans, was Welsh, and the Welsh are known to dabble in magic. She taught him another curse:

> Trip and stumble
> Slip and fall
> Down the stairs
> And hit the wall.

She had certain expressions that Burroughs still remembers. Whenever he asked her how they were going to get somewhere, she would say,

"By shank's pony." Once when he suggested they light the fire, she said, "It will light"—and it lit. It was evident to the boy that she had magic powers.

Billy formed a hysterical attachment to Mary Evans, to the point that when she went out on Thursday, her day off, he would throw a tantrum, screaming, "All I want is nursy." This indicates that she was using the old nanny trick of sexual stimulation to control the boy. Sometimes she took him along on her day off, when she went to see her boyfriend, who was a veterinarian. He called Billy in to watch once when he put a couple of dogs to sleep.

And then one day when he was four, the trusted and beloved nurse introduced evil into his life. The sense of something gross and improper done to a small helpless child is overpowering but to this day blocked out. A feeling of something very drastic, very unpleasant, but what? To this day he can't be sure. *I hear the dark mutterings of a servant underworld.*

He knows that it was one of the times he went with nursy on her day off. It turned on some ride, some expedition with the boyfriend. They were out of doors, perhaps in a wood. He sees the man's grinning face, and hears nursy saying, "Come on, Billy, it won't hurt you." He remembers his brother saying later, "Should we tell on nursy?" He remembers a dream where he is being threatened by nursy—"And your eyes will be put out if you tell . . ." And some months afterward his mother said, "Nursy is going away," and there was no tantrum, he took it very calmly.

Years later, his psychoanalyst, Dr. Federn, who had been a pupil of Freud, lost his patience: "What IS this that has affected you your whole life?"

"I just don't remember, doctor, I just don't know."

He wants to remember, and runs through various scenarios to find the one that fits. A phrase from one of his books springs to mind: "The White Defenders . . . " Mary Evans told him to do something bad . . . the boyfriend had his pants down . . . Mary pushed him forward and asked him to do it for her . . . at the last moment he rebelled and the boyfriend screamed in pain. Was it that? Perhaps . . . he can't be sure.

Although he did not tell his mother, he felt a loss of confidence in the family for not responding. They should have known that Mary Evans, despite all her impeccable references, was a bad person. "The feeling I get about your parents," a friend told him once, "is that they weren't there."

On the surface, life went on as usual, and Billy at age six started riding the Chocolate Bus (because it was brown) to the Community School, a progressive school with all sorts of interesting ideas. The children were encouraged to express themselves by playing at caveman and making stone axes. They modeled clay and beat out copper ashtrays, and learned the Pearlman style of writing where you moved your arm but not your hand, which was supposed to produce a beautiful slanting script, while in fact all it did was wear your elbow out.

Miggy, who later married Mort, remembers Billy at the Community School as withdrawn, unable to make friends, living in a dream world. He was known for taking books home, she said. Actually, Billy had been very slow to read. His parents thought there was something wrong. Then all at once he started. His father often read to him—*Treasure Island, Kidnapped, Moby Dick,* Victor Hugo's *Toilers of the Sea,* with its never-to-be-forgotten encounter with the octopus.

Already, Billy had formed a feeling of apartness. His father had a workshop in the basement and liked to make things out of wood, like tables and chairs and pirate chests. Mort was down there with him, learning and helping. One day Billy, who was three years younger than Mort, came in and picked up a hammer. "Look at the way he hammers," his father said, and then: "Don't touch the tools." Billy was excluded from the workshop, excluded from the closeness between father and oldest son that came from working together and making things. He grew up convinced that he was no good with tools and never would be.

It was made abundantly clear to Billy that he was not like the others. The father of a schoolmate said: "That boy looks like a sheep-killing dog." One day he went to the house of Sis Francis, another schoolmate. Her mother was home, sitting on the sofa and reading the *Atlantic Monthly.* She was a cold woman, who viewed her husband, a nice bumbling guy and a bit of a drunk, with contempt. Burroughs had a revelation about women—they were great wasters of time, content to spend all eternity reading magazines or playing bridge. Women were either evil, like Mary Evans, or useless, like Mrs. Francis.

It got back to him that Mrs. Francis's sister, Mrs. Senseny, had said, "That boy looks like a walking corpse." Years later, when she died, his first thought was, "It's not every corpse that can walk." Also years later, he finally understood what it was about him that had put people off. It was the writer's appraising eye, the eye that sees, and that, because it sees, seems ill-intentioned.

He also felt ill at ease because he was unsure of his family's position in St. Louis society. To bear the name of a famous company that you didn't own a part of didn't mean much. It was like a Potemkin village made out of cardboard.

Audrey was a thin pale boy, his face scarred by festering spiritual wounds. . . . Doormen stopped him when he visited his rich friends. Shopkeepers pushed his change back without a thank you. . . . Audrey was painfully aware of being unwholesome.

In 1926, his parents sold the Pershing Avenue house and built a handsome white frame house on a five-acre lot in the suburb of Ladue, at 700 South Price Road. Set back from the road, the house could dimly be seen through screens of branches. By that time Mortimer Burroughs was fed up with landscape gardening, because the millionaires who hired you would find some quibbling reason not to pay. He and Laura decided to open a gift and antique shop near their new home, at 10036 Conway Road. It was called Cobblestone Gardens, and they sold garden furniture and porcelain birds and snowflake paperweights and that sort of thing. Once a year they went to Chicago for the gift show.

There were in those days two private high schools in St. Louis where the right people sent their children: John Burroughs (named after the naturalist), which was co-ed, and Country Day, for boys only. The public schools were for riff-raff. Billy had started going to the Burroughs School in 1925, when they still lived on Pershing Avenue, taking the Clayton trolley every day, but now that they were on Price Road, the school was only a short walk away. His brother went to Country Day and said to Billy, "Call yours the sissy school and I'll know what you mean."

Billy attended the John Burroughs School from the seventh through the tenth grade. He was not a joiner or a team player. He didn't go in for sports and thought the whole idea of school spirit was pointless. He went to class and did his homework without enthusiasm. He hated Latin, and when Mrs. Grossman handed out the assignments, he would ask, "Do we have to do this?" He asked the question once too often, and was sent to see the principal, Wilford M. Aiken, who seemed to Billy "a great big fat fraud, like most school principals."

The other Latin teacher, Mr. Baker, taught him something he never forgot. This was the lesson of Hannibal's campaign against Caesar. Hannibal defeated the Roman army but stopped short of Rome. He didn't follow up, which Billy thought was the worst sin of all. "When you got things goin' for ya, follow up! There are only two rules of gambling, plunge when you're winning and quit when you're losing." Another Mr. Baker taught sociology and was a Communist. "They're doing a great experiment over there," he would say. An embittered, sardonic man, he would say, after having asked a question you couldn't answer, "Are you one of those strong, silent types?"

Ann Russe, who was in the eighth grade with Billy, remembers him sitting in the back of the class and aiming an Eversharp pencil at the other students as though it was a gun. Several times she felt her scalp prickle and turned to see the pencil aimed at her. Ann was invited in February 1927 to Billy's thirteenth birthday party. She was spending the night with Sis Francis, and after the party Mrs. Francis was late picking them up, so Mr. Burroughs produced a soccer ball for them to kick around the living room. Ann, showing off, bounced the ball off her head and broke a cut-glass sconce on the wall. Mr. Burroughs vanished, but Mrs. Burroughs appeared, and said in a low, strained voice, "I got it in Italy . . . I don't know how I can replace it." Ann Russe was ready to commit suicide. The Burroughs home was so exquisitely furnished. But Mrs. Burroughs, she felt, had no warmth. Mr. Burroughs, it was said, made Billy learn five new words a day and use them in sentences.

The year he turned thirteen was the year of the great tornado. Billy was at school, standing in the entrance to the boys' locker room, when he saw the sky turn black and green. Lightning struck a cornice of the main building and knocked off some bricks. When he went over there he found all the girls running down the halls, screaming hysterically. The tornado killed 300 people (though no one the Burroughses knew), and was included in a book about famous disasters. There were entire blocks where the fronts of houses had been sheared off, so that you could see the inside, as in dolls' houses. There were two things St. Louis children always heard their elders talk about: the 1903 World's Fair ("Meet me in St. Louis, Louie") and the 1927 tornado.

A year later, Billy had a small disaster of his own, almost losing his left hand. He was in the basement playing with his chemistry set in its wooden case, mixing red phosphorus and potassium chlorate, when it blew up in his hand. Luckily, his father was next door in his tool shed and drove Billy to the hospital in University City. The surgeon, Dr. Masters, gave him an adult dose of morphine and operated for two hours, getting the wood splinters out. This was before penicillin, and the fear of a secondary infection kept Billy in the hospital for six weeks.

The accident did not deter him from his interest in explosives. With black powder and a piece of iron, he made a bomb, which he threw through the window of the principal's house on the school grounds. The bomb did not explode, but the principal's wife, Mrs. Aiken, called Billy's mother to tell her what he had done, and he had to apologize.

The summer of 1929, when he was fifteen, his father having inflated his bank account by selling the last of his Burroughs shares, the family toured France with a car and driver—the château country, two weeks in

Cannes, the Pyrenees. Billy was sick of châteaus but found wonderful gun shops that carried trick canes. He had developed a fondness for guns and would sometimes go duck shooting with his father. In any case, that summer in France, he bought a sword cane and a shooting cane. His mother was amused when the chauffeur said *"L'essence n'arrive pas,"* which meant "We're out of gas," but sounded like "The essence does not arrive."

Billy felt that the other boys at John Burroughs saw him as "not quite right." "You're a character," said one, "but you're the wrong kind." Yet it was at school that he formed one of the lasting attachments of his life, with a handsome, brown-eyed, curly-haired boy named Kells Elvins, whose family had a town in the lead-mining region of Missouri named after them. The Elvinses lived down Price Road from the Burroughses. Kells' father, Politte Elvins, was a former congressman and a lawyer for the St. Joseph Lead Company.

Billy thought Politte was a nasty, crapulous old man. He was a fierce anti-Semite, who would say: "You know what I like about this place— the view over the Jewish cemetery. I like to see it fill up." Politte had syphilis, which affected his mind. The stories about him were endless, and later in life, Burroughs remembered him as an extravagant comic figure, a sort of demented W. C. Fields. He once ordered scrambled eggs and when they arrived he threw them at the waitress, shouting, "Where are my beans?" When a cyclist rode over his toe, he hooked out his cane and caught the cyclist by the neck, pulled him off his bike, and drubbed him with his cane. He was a terrible driver, and once, going ninety miles an hour, he cut off a woman in a limousine driven by a black chauffeur. The woman caught up alongside him and lowered the window to tell him off, but Politte shouted, "Nigger lover!" and gunned the engine.

Billy was strongly attracted to Kells. He already knew he was homosexual. Indeed, he was certain that he had been born that way, dismissing psychological explanations having to do with his parents or his nurse. Kells was his first love, but it was a love that could not be admitted or expressed, and was never sexual. He was, however, clearly smitten. His schoolmates saw it and said to Billy, "You're his slave." Billy would walk Kells home with his arm around Kells's shoulder. Kells was friendly but unresponsive, although occasionally there were ambiguously physical games, as when Kells would playfully take Billy on his lap and strum him like a banjo, which gave Billy a hard-on.

Kells was everything Billy wasn't. He was athletic and popular, and had great élan. He was a terrific womanizer, which young Burroughs much admired and still remembers: "Kells sure had a way with women . . . he always had three or four beauties on a string . . . from the time he was just a kid he was getting all the ass he wanted. The technique was simple. Most people want it too much, but as soon as you sit back as though you don't need it, they'll line up at your door. As Blake said, the lineaments of gratified desire, that's what's most attractive to a woman. If someone's gettin' it and gettin' it steady, he's gonna get it more and more . . . Kells had the trick."

As Burroughs tells it, Kells was the classic Don Juan, who needs to seduce one woman after the other while disliking them profoundly. "When he'd had about three drinks," Burroughs recalls, "he'd say, 'Show me a good woman in *anything*.' He would beat them down and reduce them to tears. They'd cry on my shoulder and I'd say, 'I'm sorry, but if you want to put up with it that's your concern.' "

Burroughs and Kells were lifelong friends, their lives intersecting over and over, at Harvard, in Texas, in Mexico, in Tangier, in Copenhagen. But "never in the whole time I knew him did it ever get physical."

At school, there was a class where the students composed plays by volunteering lines that were copied on the blackboard, as in:

First Woman: I hear there is a tiger roaming about the village.

Second Woman: One doesn't feel safe with that tiger about.

Third Woman: It's getting dark. I think we'd better go home.

They also wrote compositions that they read before the class. One of Billy's friends, Gene Angert, a gauntly handsome and fragile boy, like a young T. S. Eliot, read a story that ended with the line, "The boat went down and the captain tried to swim but the water was too deep, and he cried help, help, I'm drowning." Burroughs never forgot that line, which in retrospect seemed to sum up Gene's life, for while at Harvard he was institutionalized as a schizophrenic.

For Billy, writing was an alternative to the disappointing world around him. At the age of eight, inspired by Ernest Thompson Seton's *Biography of a Grizzly Bear*, he wrote *Autobiography of a Wolf*. In Seton's book, the old bear, saddened by the death of his mate, slinks off to die in the animal cemetery. In Billy's ten-page opus, the wolf, saddened by the death of his mate, killed by hunters, was attacked by a grizzly and killed. Billy's mother showed the book to her friends, who asked Billy, "You mean biography, don't you?" and Billy replied, "No, I was right there with the wolf." It was an autobiography because Billy identified with the wolf and *became* the wolf.

When Billy was thirteen, he came across a book that would have an enormous impact on the unfolding of his life and work. Written by someone calling himself Jack Black, *You Can't Win* was the memoirs of a professional thief and drug addict. Billy immersed himself in the world of "gopher men" who tunneled under banks, safecrackers, con men, and fences. It was a world with its own code of conduct, an exciting alternative to the humdrum St. Louis environment.

Jack Black left school at fourteen and went to work in a cigar store that was a front for poker and dice games, running errands for the old cons and relishing their colorful language: "If it was rainin' soup I couldn't buy myself a tin spoon," or "I've got a string of debts longer than a widow's clothesline."

Jack became a burglar, which is how he came across Salt Chunk Mary, the fence. Salt Chunk Mary bought or sold anything that was stolen, but "she was righter than a gold guinea." She always had a pot of beans and a chunk of salt pork on the stove, and the first thing you heard when you stepped into her house was "Did you eat yet?" Her hair was the color of sun-burned brick and her small blue eyes glinted like ice under a March sun. Salt Chunk Mary "Could say 'no' quicker than any woman I ever knew, and none of her 'nos' ever meant yes. . . . She named her price, and she didn't name another."

Salt Chunk Mary was a member of the Johnson family, a band of crooks with their own code of ethics. The Johnson family minded their own business. They were loyal and honest with one another, and helped those in trouble. Even though they were outlaws and thieves, they were square in their dealings, and their word was their bond. Billy saw in the Johnsons a model of moral behavior in marked contrast to the hypocrisy, busybodiness, and double-dealing of the right-thinking citizens of the St. Louis establishment. In St. Louis, you were nothing if you didn't own something. St. Louis hummed with tales of loss and chicanery, how so-and-so had been done out of what he had. People actually said: "I can buy and sell that person." He saw that there existed a society of outcasts and misfits, who were, in their own way, decent people, living by their own rules. And who were the real thieves anyway? Jack Black the safecracker, or the trustees of the Burroughs estate who had conned his father into selling his shares?

In the turn-of-the-century period of the book, morphine and opium were as cheap as tobacco—fifty cents' worth would last you all day. "No fiend is ever at a loss for a sound reason for taking a jolt of hop," wrote Jack Black. "If he is feeling bad he takes a jolt so he will feel good. If he is feeling good, he takes one to make him feel better, and if he is feeling neither very bad nor very good he takes a jolt just to get himself straightened around." Jack became an addict, hanging out with other addicts: "Their bony arms were gray, like pieces of petrified wood. The skin was pocked with marks, mottled and scarred from the repeated, hourly stabbing of the needle. Their shirtsleeves were encrusted with dried blood from the many punctures."

For Billy, who already saw himself as an outsider, *You Can't Win* was a revelation. He felt somehow that Jack Black and Salt Chunk Mary and Gold Tooth and Foot and a Half George and all the others were his kind of people. He was not alone. The Johnsons became a part of his personal mythology. The world was divided into "us" and "them." In later life, any stranger who did him an act of kindness in a tight situation was a Johnson, like the cop in the paddy wagon after his arrest in New Orleans who slipped him a joint, or the pharmacist in Mexico City who cheerfully filled his prescription for morphine after half a dozen others had snarlingly turned him down.

You Can't Win was the blueprint for Burroughs' first book, *Junky*. It had the same relation to *Junky* as *Biography of a Grizzly Bear* had to *Autobiography of a Wolf*. Just as eight-year-old Billy became the wolf and wrote about the wolf in the first person, the adult Burroughs became a small-time criminal and drug addict and wrote about that, following the example of Jack Black and his thief's memoirs. In *You Can't Win*, there is a set of values, from Salt Chunk Mary's sense of honor to Jack Black's hatred of cops ("I always say a copper is a copper until you cut his head off"), that Burroughs would make his own.

Increasingly, Billy took refuge in fiction. It had occurred to him that he belonged to another species. He was afraid of others, and felt the need to play it cool and conceal himself. He felt at the same time inferior to others and better than others—it was hopelessly confusing. He was a physical coward, terrified of any kind of fighting. He was slight, only realizing much later, when he saw the muscles of his jock schoolmates turn to fat, that a slight build is an advantage in the long run. He wasn't sickly, though his mother tried to make out that he was.

Finding himself inadequate, he imagined himself as a fictional character. He read a pirate book and saw himself as the coldest and nastiest of the pirates, assigning a lesser role to Gene Angert, who said: "I want to be cold and nasty, too." Billy's name was Brundage. He picked a little rat gambler off the floor by the scruff of the neck and ran a cutlass through his throat. The crew was chilled by the cold brutality of the act. They rushed him and he killed six of them before they finally killed him.

My God, the memory of that high school prose! The flavor returns like the flavor of chicken croquettes and canned peas in the school dining-room. Crime stories, inspired by *You Can't Win*. A murderer tortured by remorse who succumbs to brain fever. A sinister fortune-teller: "With an inarticulate cry the man leaped to his feet and whipped out an automatic, spitting death at the fortune-teller. Blood splattered her crystal ball, and on the table lay a severed human hand." Action-packed Westerns: "Tom was quick but Joe was quicker." Hanging scenes galore: "Hardened old sinner that he was he still experienced a shudder as he looked back at the three bodies twisting in the breeze, etched against the beautiful red sunset." The hanging scenes were inspired by pulp Westerns and by newspaper articles, since hanging was still the form of capital punishment in Missouri.

Then there was an English period—seven young gentlemen were planning an expedition to the Pole. "Why Reggie, you're as excited as a child," said Lord Cheshire. "I am and I glory in it. Let's forget we are gentlemen." "You seem to have done that already," said Lord Cheshire acidly.

Some of these stories Billy read in class, and others he thought of selling to magazines, such as this one for *True Confessions* about a decent young man, grieving the loss of a favorite dog, who fell into the hands of a sinister hypnotist who plied him with marijuana injections. The distressed young man walked up to a cop and said, "If you don't lock me up I shall kill you." The cop sapped him without a word but a wise old street detective took a liking to the boy and set him straight. So the young man opened an antique shop in St. Louis and became prosperous.

Billy entertained the idea of becoming a writer. Writers were rich and famous. They lounged around Singapore and Rangoon smoking opium in yellow pongee suits. They sniffed cocaine in Mayfair and penetrated forbidden swamps with a faithful native boy. They lived in the native quarter of some exotic city, languidly caressing a pet gazelle.

His first published prose, however, was not one of his blood-curdling stories but a sardonic one-page essay written at the age of fourteen and accepted by the school literary magazine, the *John Burroughs Review*, for its February 1929 issue. Entitled "Personal Magnetism," it is worth quoting in full as an example of the consistency of Burroughs' thinking:

"Are you bashful? Shy? Nervous? Embarrassed? If so, send me two dollars and I will show you how to control others at a glance; how to make your face appear twenty years younger; how to use certain Oriental secrets and dozens of other vital topics."

I am none of these things, but I would like to know how to control others at a glance (especially my Latin teacher). So I clipped the coupon, beginning to feel more magnetic every minute.

In a week, I received an impressive red volume with magnetic rays all over the cover. I opened the book and hopefully began to read. Alas! the book was a mass of scientific drivel cunningly designed to befuddle the reader, and keep him from realizing what a fake it was.

I learned that every time one yawns, a quart of magnetism escapes, that it takes four months to recuperate from a cigarette. And as for a cocktail! Words fail me. Another common exit of magnetism is light literature of any kind, movies, and such unmagnetic foods as cucumbers and eggs. I never realized that a cucumber was so potent. They always impressed me as watery and tasteless.

And how is magnetism acquired? So far as I can make out, one must sit perfectly still for hours reading the dictionary or something equally uninteresting, then, laden with magnetism, one should arise with tensed eye (whatever that is) and with slow, steady steps, bear down on one's quarry like a steam roller.

Did I find out how to control others at a glance? I certainly did, but never had the nerve to try it. Here is how it is done: I must look my victim squarely in the eye, say in a low, severe voice, "I am talking and you must listen," then, intensify my gaze and say, "You cannot escape me." My victim completely subdued, I was to say, "I am stronger than my enemies." Get thee behind me Satan. Imagine me trying that on Mr. Baker!

I think the book was right in saying that by following its instructions I could make myself the center of interest at every party. Interest is putting it mildly!

In this adolescent effort, Burroughs is concerned, as he is in much of his later work, with debunking control systems. He sends away for the little red book and finds that Personal Magnetism as a method of control is a scam, a humbug, a ripoff. Already, he had adopted the guise of psychic explorer, just as he would later explore psychoanalysis, Scientology, Wilhelm Reich's orgone energy, Count Alfred Korzybski's theory of General Semantics, and other, more arcane systems.

The year of his first appearance in print, 1929, was also his last at the John Burroughs School. His mother was worried about his sinus condition and wanted him to spend his last two years of high school in a dry, healthy climate. She enrolled him in the Ranch School at Los Alamos, New Mexico. He had already spent a summer at the school's summer camp, where his fellow campers nicknamed him "Bull" because he was an incessant talker and advancer of improbable theories. He wisely did not object, although disliking the nickname intensely, thinking, the more you ask them not to the more they'll do it.

At the end of the school term, Wilford M. Aiken wrote on Billy's report card: "Capable boy—needs to develop more group spirit—good student and will become better when he has made a place for himself in groups of boys."

When Billy's class at John Burroughs, which graduated in 1931, held its fiftieth reunion, Gene Angert was dead, and Sis Francis had lung cancer, but reported from Pinehurst, North Carolina, "I'm going to beat this goddamned thing." It was amazing, thought Bill Turner, who had broken the glass pane that Mortimer Burroughs fixed for free, how upon seeing classmates after half a century, they shed the slight web of unfamiliarity after only a moment and came right into focus, unchanged. Ann Russe was the same high-spirited extrovert. Charles De Pew, the head of a reunion committee, gave his report in the same clear and concise manner. Alice Frank, who always looked around at whoever was reciting in class with piercing eyes, was still at it.

Burroughs sent a telegram regretting that he was unable to attend, and when it was read the response was something between a loud murmur and a soft cheer. Billy had not been the most popular kid in the class, but as Ann Russe reminded the others, he was their only claim to fame. But Charlie De Pew gave her a regular Jerry Falwell speech about how disgusting Burroughs was. Florence Steinberg said Burroughs had struck her as being dumb, and again Ann Russe took his defense, saying that Mort had been the handsome one, but Billy had all the brains. Who else among them had made it into the *Encyclopaedia Britannica*? That might well be, said Bill Turner, a retired big-league baseball manager, but he would wait until he was a little older before reading *Naked Lunch*.

· TWO ·

LOS ALAMOS

1929–1932

Ashley Pond was a Detroit businessman with a love of the strenuous life. He joined Teddy Roosevelt's Rough Riders but never got to the war, having contracted an almost fatal case of typhoid at the training base in Florida. He went to New Mexico to recover his health in the early 1900s, and fell in love with the clean beauty of the place, the deep ravines and furrowed mesas, the reddish cliffs of tufa, the forests of ponderosa pine, the pasque flowers among the pine needles in April, the Indian paintbrush in June. With its dry air and sunshine, it was, he felt, a setting that could not be equaled anywhere on earth.

Ashley Pond conceived the idea of a school that would turn boys into men by stressing the outdoor life and rugged activities. He noted that the Pueblo Indians segregated the boys of the tribe until they reached manhood. In the same manner, pampered boys from the East would become men when they were separated from oversolicitous mothers and placed on the back of a horse, and taught to camp in the mountains, and to hunt and fish and trap animals. There was no point in boys spending their days with their noses in books. It was an anti-intellectual, survival-of-the-fittest approach to education, designed to prepare the boys for the rough strategies of our laissez-faire system.

In 1915, Ashley Pond bought a 900-acre ranch about forty miles north of Santa Fe. The ranch sat on top of a mesa called the Pajarito ("little bird") that rose 7,300 feet above the Rio Grande Valley. To the east stood the Sangre de Cristo mountains, which at sunset glowed with a ruddy light that had once inspired the Spanish padres to compare them to the Redeemer's blood; to the south, the stubbier crests of the Jemez range. The ranch was planted with pine and juniper and cottonwood, the latter tree providing Pond with a name for his school: Los Alamos.

In 1917, Ashley Pond went looking for a school director, someone he could trust with the day-to-day business of running things, and found a man who fit the bill right in his backyard. This was A. J. Connell, a red-haired, florid-faced, blue-eyed Irishman, thirty-five years of age, who was serving as a ranger in the Panchuela District of the Santa Fe National Forest, and was also active as scoutmaster of the Santa Fe Boy Scout troop. Thus he combined the qualities of outdoorsman and experience with boys that Pond was seeking, even though he had never been to college, which didn't matter much to Pond, who thought most college boys were sissies.

A. J. Connell was another of those extravagant characters who periodically entered Burroughs' life, along the lines of Politte Elvins. Originally from New York City, he had worked for Tiffany's in some decorating capacity, but had gone west for his phlebitis, New Mexico being known as "get well" country. As a forest ranger, he packed a Luger and was known to have gotten the best of some pretty tough hombres. Bossy and short-tempered, his normal manner of speech was to make pronouncements, such as: "Of course there's no such thing as a man-eating shark. As for crocodiles, maybe they take a few pickaninnies, say 20,000 a year."

Connell gave the impression of toughness and decisiveness, but at the same time he had an oddly feminine side. His room at the Ranch School had so much magenta damask in it that it looked like the madam's parlor in a bordello, and he burned incense and constantly played Ravel's "Bolero" on his Victrola. His motto was "I know what's best for boys." Usually he referred to the boys as "gibbons" or "tailless apes," and showed a keen interest in their adolescent sexuality. There were no locks on the doors of the rooms, and it was Connell's habit to burst in on the boys to catch them masturbating. "I've caught 'em at it," he could be heard muttering under his breath, "CAUGHT 'EM AT IT!"

"Did you ever play with it 'till it went off way down deep?" was another of Connell's pet phrases. Arthur Chase, a brawny Harvard man who taught English at the school, also had the duty of measuring the boys six times a year to keep track of their physical improvement. They would line up naked as Chase read the numbers out for their necks, chests, and thighs. On these occasions Connell would appear and start feeling the boys' muscles, turning them around and showing a great deal of interest, which the boys called "gibboning." "It used to bother me," Chase recalled. "I always preferred it when he wasn't there."

In any case, under Connell's energetic administration, the school began to flourish. Pond's first brochure declared that "studying from books is absolutely unnecessary," but that noble principle had to be amended. A headmaster was hired, a curriculum was instituted (including such courses as "Animals and Their Habits"), and Connell recruited as teachers graduating students of Yale and Harvard, but not of Princeton, whom for some reason he regarded as unreliable wimps.

Los Alamos became known as a health school, where the spindly sons of the rich could be transformed into manly specimens. Each spring Connell went on a six-week promotional tour, concentrating on the Midwest, to convince parents of the Ranch School's benefits. The idea, he would explain, was to take city boys and have them regain their American heritage of outdoor wisdom. They would go on cattle drives, and lead an active robust life on the range, which promoted deep breathing and a strong pulse.

In 1929 he came to the Burroughs home on Price Road. He was already on friendly terms with Mr. and Mrs. Burroughs, Billy and Mort having spent several summers at the Los Alamos camp, and was invited to spend the night. "Mother and Dad went out that evening," Burroughs recalls, "and I was left in Connell's rather dubious company." They were in the living room listening to Connell's Victrola records when he suddenly said to fifteen-year-old Billy, "I want to see this gibbon stripped." Awed by such a figure of authority, Billy obediently complied. "Are you playin' with it, gibbon?" Connell asked, and Billy shook his head. "Have you ever done it with other boys?" Connell persisted. Billy hadn't, but he had thought about it—boys seemed to him the most exciting thing—and he found himself physically responding to Connell's suggestion in an embarrassing manner, so he quickly put his clothes back on. Billy was put off by Connell's manner, but at the same time saw that his own desires had been aroused, so he never mentioned the incident to his parents, for he was in a sense an accomplice. Some of the parents, however, did know about Connell's inclinations, and a Texas oilman told his son, "If he ever messes with you, you smack him one."

In September 1929, Billy left for New Mexico aboard the Atchison, Topeka & Santa Fe, which in fact stopped at Lamy, twenty miles short of Santa Fe; he took a bus the rest of the way. On both sides of the yellow gravel road there were pasturelands and clusters of barns and outbuildings and workers' cottages, and two large log buildings. One of these was the Big House, where the boys had rooms for studying, but slept on an unheated screen porch, even in winter, in flannel sheets and army blankets. On nights when the snow whipped through the screens, they were given striped canvas bedcovers. The other was Fuller Lodge, with its big-beamed ceiling, where the boys took their meals at tables of six. "At Los Alamos," Connell said, "everybody eats his share of everything," and that applied to strange dishes like calves' brains, unfamiliar fish from the Rio Grande, and baked bananas. The buildings were done in the style of the Southwest, with Indian rugs, rustic furniture, and flagstone floors.

At $2,400 a year ($24,000 in today's dollars), Los Alamos was one of the most expensive schools in the country, and those whose families could afford it included the son of General Wood, chairman of Sears, Roebuck, and the Marsden boys, whose father owned Humble Oil in Texas. But the year that Billy arrived was the year of the crash, and some of the families were wiped out in midterm (like the head of Chicago's Board of Trade), and had to be given full scholarships.

Billy had arrived in a largely self-sustaining community of 200 in a clearing on the edge of a ponderosa pine forest, with about forty students, a staff of twenty, and the rest consisting of ranch employees and their families. The school had its own water, pumped from a stream in a canyon, and Connell ran a black flag up a pole when the water got scarce. It had its own cows and dairy, run by a Methodist dairyman who pieced out his income with a little preaching. It had 400 acres of crops planted, beans and corn for the boys, and oats and alfalfa for the sixty-five horses. Adolfo Montoya, the head gardener, grew magnificent vegetables in the volcanic soil, and kept chickens. A trading post, which also operated as a post office, sold the necessities of life, such as candy and cartridges. One of the teachers was a magistrate and once tried a case—it was someone who had shot a deer out of season, for Los Alamos was a game refuge, abounding in deer and wild turkey, and it was said that the ratio of skunks to boys was about three to one.

Upon arrival, each boy was weighed and measured and assigned according to size to one of four patrols, from the small piñon to juniper, fir, and the tall spruce. Billy didn't like the regimentation, and didn't like the silly uniforms: short pants (khaki or flannel, depending on the season), khaki shirts, bandannas, Dakota Stetsons, and leather chaps for riding. Riding was a must, and Billy hated his horse, a sullen strawberry roan.

To Billy, the whole place was like a prison . . . Big House indeed! he thought. My God, they timed you on the john. He was always cold, and the school song began to take on ominous overtones:

> Far away and high on the mesa's crest,
> Here's the life that all of us love the best—
> Los Alamos!

> Winter days as we skim o'er the ice and snow,
> Summer days when the balsam breezes blow—
> Los Alamos!

Balsam breezes, shit, thought Billy. You fuckin' froze!

The days were tightly organized, which he didn't like either. At 6:30 A.M. the bell on a pole outside the kitchen rang and each boy had to drink two glasses of cold water. Then they went out in all kinds of weather, even if there was snow on the ground, and did fifteen minutes of calisthenics—three push-ups and waddle like a duck, and then "draw yourself up to your full height." Breakfast was at seven, then room-cleaning and classes until one fifteen. In the afternoon they sometimes did community work, which he particularly disliked, considering it arbitrary and pointless. You had to roll the tennis court, or build a trail, or weed Connell's garden, while some crew leader drunk with power was hanging over you.

Los Alamos was pretty isolated. There were rare trips to Santa Fe, and that was it. The mail arrived on the Denver and Rio Grande Western, which, since it sometimes took two weeks, was known as the Dangerous and Rapidly Growing Worse. There was no way to escape Connell and his *Reader's Digest* homilies, which Billy viewed with skepticism, such as "What is the safest place in America? Where you are." In civics class, Billy had the audacity to say he did not believe in capital punishment and was told, "Why shouldn't the law take its course?" The civics teacher kept repeating that if a thing was worth doing it was worth doing well, whereas Billy believed that if a thing was worth doing it was worth doing badly—you didn't have to be a Grand Master to enjoy a game of chess, or Annie Oakley to go target shooting. The civics teacher did not appreciate Burroughs' independence of mind, and for the remainder of the year addressed him as "our esteemed woodsman and scout." Burroughs learned that when young people are told to think, it means "think like we do." If your thinking is different, you're in trouble. He gradually lost interest in doing well, and in the yearbook put down as his ambition "traveling and loafing."

Billy thought of Connell as a dictator, which in some ways he was, since he had a terror of anything going wrong, and would say, "Accidents don't happen, they're caused." Connell was a mass of opposites. He later became a New Deal Democrat, furious that the stand-pat Republican parents of the boys criticized F.D.R., and yet he much admired Mussolini. He was courtly and charming with the boys' mothers, and yet he was a confirmed misogynist who never married and was convinced that women were the destroyers of boys, by making them soft and sorry for themselves. He didn't want women around, although he did have his sad-eyed spinster sister there teaching the piano. If a boy used his fork in a certain way, Connell said, "Don't be an old lady." If a boy was in the infirmary, and one of his friends asked how he was, Connell would say: "What are you, an old woman? Around here, we don't ask whether we're getting well."

That was another of his peculiarities: He could not abide any reference to illness or death. You had to be positive at all times. When a boy's mother brought lilies, Connell came in and said: "Who brought those in? Throw 'em out, I can't stand lilies." And when a group of boys was singing "My Grandfather's Clock," he stormed in on the line "when the old man died" and told them to stop at once.

Much later, Burroughs had a dream about Connell in which someone said, "He was a very minor prison official." Disliking the school, Billy adopted a "contra" stance. He did only fair in his studies the first year, dropping algebra, failing his French exam, and failing his English exam after leaving early, "which indicates either neglect or carelessness," said his report card.

There was a great emphasis on achievement, and grades were put in every week, and the boys were also ranked in terms of leadership ability. "The faculty looked at who was able to take charge," Arthur Chase recalled, "who could lead a patrol back to civilization and not into the ravine, and you can imagine that Billy was never ranked very high, because we figured if he was leading a patrol he might lead them into some mining camp and we wouldn't see them again for a couple of months."

The rule was that you had to stay outdoors between two thirty and four thirty every afternoon, and Chase remembers one afternoon when it was raining hard, seeing Billy standing in a doorway, this frail, wet, unhappy boy, just standing there waiting for four thirty to come around so he could go indoors.

There were a few things Billy did like about Los Alamos. He liked the rifle range and became a good marksman, further developing his lifelong fascination with guns. He spent hours throwing knives into posts and trees. You could see him walking down the corral as if he were Pat Garrett, with his arms at his sides and his shoulders hunched up, and suddenly he'd spin on his heels and fling his knife into a tree. He got pretty good at it. One time he hit one of Adolfo Montoya's hens and killed it, which got him further demoted in rank.

There was no question, though, thought his English teacher Arthur Chase, that Billy was the most original boy in his class. Already at fifteen, he had a fine sense of irony. His themes were a little macabre, although that was not so unusual—there's not much happy writing in that age group. But he wondered about Billy's ability to sustain anything for very long. "Billy," he would say, "I asked for 150 words and you gave me seventy-five, and this little story about a child playing with his brothers and sisters and rolling their skulls around, it has great possibilities, but it has to be built up."

Rogers Scudder, a St. Louis friend who went to the Ranch School with Billy, also remembers him as wry and sardonic, with a macabre side. He and Billy used to go dig in an old Pueblo Indian ruin, which for Scudder was the start of his interest in archeology. Billy found an anthill in the ruin and poured gasoline over it and lit it and started dancing a sort of parody of an Indian war dance with maniacal whooping as ants by the thousands fled the pyre, and Scudder was glad they were alone and that no one else had seen him.

Then, in March 1930, when he had just turned sixteen, Billy got into serious trouble. His mother came to visit, and took him and Rogers Scudder into Santa Fe. Billy and Rogers were wandering about, and Billy said, "I want to go into the drugstore and get some chloral hydrate." Rogers asked why and Billy said, "I want to see what it's like," so they went into the Capitol Pharmacy and Billy asked for some, and the druggist asked why he wanted knockout drops, and Billy, in a sepulchral voice, said, "to commit suicide." Glowering, the druggist thrust the bottle into his hand.

A few days later, Rogers Scudder was doing calisthenics with the other boys in the early morning chill when he looked up and saw a tottering Billy being half carried across the field by the school nurse. He had taken an almost lethal dose of chloral hydrate. Connell got after Rogers Scudder, saying: "Goddamn it, you had no right not to tell me about this . . . you should have known he would do something mad. The trouble with that boy is that his mother's made him think he's a genius and he's just a gibbon."

Of course, Connell had to inform Billy's father, writing him on March 22, 1930:

"Bill did a foolish thing last Sunday night. One day when he was in town with his mother he went to a drugstore and bought some chloral hydrate. He took a dose of it Sunday night and was unable to navigate Monday morning, so that I kept him in the infirmary. He claims that he just wanted to see how it worked. I believe he realizes now that it was a fool thing to do and I doubt if he will try anything like it again. I feel that Bill's greatest drawback is that he is not willing to recognize his responsibilities to others. It is very difficult to convince him that an act like that is simply anything more than his own affair. My anxiety, the unnecessary extra work occasioned the staff, or the effect on the other boys in the school, he never takes into consideration. I hope that this is the last of his foolishness."

The chloral hydrate episode is worth pausing over for several reasons. It was the first example of Burroughs purchasing a substance that would alter his consciousness. It showed him once again, as in his essay "Personal Magnetism," in the role of psychic explorer—he wanted to see what chloral hydrate was like, at the risk of harming himself. It was the first time he did something that seriously embarrassed his parents, causing his father to receive a stern letter from the school director. Finally, Connell's words, "I doubt if he will ever try anything like it again" must rank as a classic in the "famous last words" department, for Burroughs would spend the rest of his life trying the same thing, with different substances, over and over.

Burroughs has always felt that he has the ability to arouse instant enmity in certain people. They meet him and hate him on sight. At Los Alamos, one of his teachers, Henry Bosworth, seemed to have it in for him. Bosworth, a stocky World War I veteran with penetrating brown eyes, taught mathematics and boxing. Billy was small and thin and didn't like to box, and Bosworth viewed him as a malingerer. Billy liked to go in his room and sit against the radiator and read the Blue Books put out by that curious figure in publishing, E. Haldeman Julius, free-thinker and benevolent agnostic. In cheap editions not much bigger than playing cards, he published "risqué" writers like Anatole France and Guy de Maupassant, whom Billy devoured. Connell came around periodically to confiscate them, since at Los Alamos being bookish was a sign of decadence.

Bosworth was known for playing favorites. Some boys he liked a great deal, others he couldn't stand, and Billy was among the latter. Once when Billy was in charge on the sleeping porch, there was a commotion, and Bosworth came in and said, "All of you shut up. As for you, Billy, you worthless little pup, you're going to get yours." Then another time they went on a hike, and coming down a hill they disturbed a nest of yellowjackets and Billy was bitten four times. He knew that Bosworth carried a first-aid kit with something for insect bites, but when he complained that it hurt, Bosworth just looked at him blankly and did not offer to help.

To Billy, that was a declaration of war, except that there wasn't much he could do to retaliate. One morning, however, when the boys came in to breakfast, hilarity and consternation spread through the ranks. Hanging over the fireplace was the two-foot-high plaster-of-Paris Boy Scout figure that usually stood in the foyer of Fuller Lodge, and on the figure's uniform was pinned a sign that said, "Bozzy-bitch, goddamn him."

The identity of the boy who had hanged Henry Bosworth in effigy did not long remain secret, and Billy was summoned to Connell's office. "If it had been another boy," Connell said, "this might have been cause for dismissal. But why did you have to make it so vulgar?" The reason Billy was not more severely punished was that Bosworth himself was under a cloud. He had made improper advances to one of the boys, who had reported it to Connell, and it had been arranged that he would finish out the year and then leave the school. Connell could not, of course, allow a teacher who picked favorites and then propositioned them to remain.

But Connell was also losing patience with Billy, who was in one scrape after another. That October he was placed on probation as the result of an incident that landed him in the Santa Fe jail. The boys were allowed occasionally to go in supervised groups to Santa Fe for the weekend, staying at the La Fonda Hotel, and in mid-October Billy was part of such a group. On Saturday night, he sneaked out of the hotel through a fire door to buy some liquor and bring it back to his room. This was during Prohibition, but firewater was available if you knew where to look for it. Billy didn't know, but got into a conversation with a Mexican woman who said she might be helpful. As he was walking down the street with the woman, a policeman, attracted by the oddity of the couple, stopped Billy and questioned him, finally arresting him for vagrancy. When he didn't return to the hotel, his roommate alerted the teacher in charge of the group, Tom Waring, who spent the rest of the night vainly searching for him. The next morning, Billy was able to convince the cops that he was a student at Los Alamos, and they notified Waring, who was sick at the thought of facing Connell with a boy missing.

This led, on October 21, to another letter from Connell to Mortimer Burroughs: "I hope that the measures that I have had to take [general probation for an indefinite period] will bring Billy a little more to his senses, and that there will be no more violations of our rules; of course he will not have the opportunity again for another of this nature."

Actually, in spite of his errant ways, Connell was fond of Billy, and occasionally picked him to drive into Santa Fe with him on his twice-a-week excursions, an honor that was highly prized. They stayed at the La Fonda, where all the rooms opened on a patio, and a band played at dinnertime. On one of these occasions, Billy went to his room and at once masturbated. Later they went down to dinner—the band was playing "El Chocolate"—and after dinner he went into the bathroom and masturbated again. Ashamed of having masturbated twice in the same day, he decided to start a novel, establishing a curious connection between the sexual and the creative urges, one being used to atone for the excesses of the other. The novel, of which a page or two were completed on hotel stationery, had to do with someone who contacts four assassins to have an enemy killed. One was a woman and one was an elderly British gentleman with a hawklike face. Some of the dialogue went like this:

"He told me you would take care of it for a price."

"Of course we have our regular rates."

What do you do when you're sixteen years old and you wake up every morning with a hard-on and it takes an event of major proportions, like a flood or a final exam, to get your mind off sex? Billy didn't know why it was boys instead of girls; boys just seemed to click somehow. In his second year at Los Alamos he became enamored of a boy named Danny Franklin (this name has been changed), and fell into his self-defeating subservient mode. He knew he was doing it and yet he could not help making himself adoring and submissive to the point that he became an object of contempt to the boy.

Every man has inside himself a parasitic being who is acting not at all to his advantage. Why do you spill things? Why do you drop something? You have the equipment there not to drop something. Why isn't that capacity being used? Something is preventing it. And you come down to some sort of basic dualism. There isn't one person out there, but two. Acting against each other.

A couple of times, Billy got Danny Franklin to jack off with him under the sheets with a flashlight, but then Danny told him it was all wrong, and said, "I think you're going to be the sort of person who will be revolted by a naked woman." The more Danny Franklin ignored him, the more Billy made himself abject. Danny Franklin was cruel as only teenage boys can be, mocking Billy in front of his friends, whispering something to another boy as he walked by, finding small ways to humiliate him. Billy was in torment. His only relief was to confide his feelings to a diary.

His letters home were so forlorn that on March 30, 1931, his alarmed mother sent a telegram to Connell: "Billy's last two letters have sounded very blue and depressed. Do you know if anything special is worrying him? . . . If he does not soon feel better we have considered withdrawing him at Easter vacation." She planned to come out and see for herself what was wrong.

Now it was Connell's turn to be alarmed, for Billy, then seventeen, was due to graduate in June, and it would be a grave mistake for him to leave two months short of finishing. He had a talk with Billy, but could not find out anything definite that was troubling him. It was just the fact that he allowed things to accumulate, thought Connell. On March 31, Connell wired back: "Billy is coming out of his blues. Had a satisfactory talk with him this morning. He has selected April ninth as best time for your visit. I would advise going slowly about withdrawing. Believe would be a great mistake. . . ."

To Billy it was clear. He could not stay at the school, where he had laid himself open to the taunts of his classmates and the rejection of the boy he had so guilelessly admitted caring for. When his mother arrived on April 9, he insisted on returning to St. Louis with her. When she pressed him for a reason, he was forced to admit the truth. Homosexuality was a shocking thing in those days, it was still the love that dares not speak its name, and his mother was terribly upset.

They left in such a hurry that Billy didn't even have a chance to pack his things, which would be forwarded to him. Once in St. Louis, it was conveniently discovered that Billy's feet were bothering him, and on April 27 his mother wired Connell: "Have just been to hospital and received final report on Billy's foot. Doctors wish to give him treatments three times a week so all chance of sending him back this year is gone. We are sorry for him not to finish his term. Both feet in bad condition but left much worse. Regards to all. Am sorry. . . ."

Billy never returned to Los Alamos, from which he was honorably dismissed. His final report said: "He has good understanding but not much sense. His interest is in things morbid and abnormal, affects his sense of proportion in his work, making spotty and uneven results. His brain power, if rightly used, seems sufficient to get him to college, but there is doubt about his ability to direct himself." His mother sent him to an elderly psychiatrist named Dr. Schwab, who talked to him a bit about the Greeks, and assured Laura Burroughs that it was a phase he would soon grow out of.

When his box arrived from school, he hunted for his diary, turning cold at the thought that his classmates had somehow got hold of it and had read it aloud to one another. He found that the sight of his written words made him physically ill. The diary was so maudlin, so trite, the emotions expressed seemed so false. He could not bear to look at it, and destroyed it. He hoped that with the burning pages would also disappear the other self that revealed his feelings and made him a victim. The act of writing became to Burroughs embarrassing, shameful, false. It was an act he was incapable of attempting again until 1938, when his friend Kells Elvins started him writing once more.

Billy left Los Alamos thinking that the only thing he had learned was a hatred of horses. "Horses are a dying artifact," he still likes to say. "They will never make a comeback." Stressing leadership qualities amid surroundings that recaptured frontier days, Los Alamos was designed to turn out captains of industry, which it did: Roy Chapin, president of American Motors; John S. Reed of the Atchison, Topeka & Santa Fe; Arthur Wood, general counsel of Sears, Roebuck. It also turned out a leader of the counterculture, William S. Burroughs. And it might be argued that the same qualities that brought the captains of industry to their paneled offices brought Burroughs to his underground eminence— those qualities being in the main ambition and Emersonian self-reliance. Except that in the case of Burroughs, who was anti-everything at Los Alamos, those qualities were used not to rise within the system but to rise in opposition to it.

Also, Connell's sour views on women reinforced Billy's distrust of them, and some of Connell's misogyny may have rubbed off on him. In Connell, Billy had the example of a repressed homosexual who was tough and macho rather than an effeminate dandy in the Oscar Wilde mold. Connell was a homosexual *and* a frontiersman, a combination that would later appear in Burroughs' fiction.

For Burroughs, however, the true significance of his stay at Los Alamos had to do with the school's destiny. For after Pearl Harbor, when President Roosevelt had approved work on the atom bomb, the Army Corps of Engineers began looking for an isolated site to build the secret laboratory where the bomb would be made. It happened that J. Robert Oppenheimer, head of the Manhattan Project, as it was called, had taken a pack trip to Los Alamos as a teenager in 1922, and had been struck by the beauty of the place, a beauty he was about to destroy. For he suggested Los Alamos to General Leslie R. Groves, military director of the project, and they visited the school on November 16, 1942, in an unmarked car. It was cold, and a light snow was falling, but the boys and masters were out on the playing field in shorts, and paid scant attention to the two men huddled over maps. Los Alamos had definite possibilities. It was in the middle of a national forest, sixty miles from the nearest train station, and yet it had its own water and electricity. There were enough buildings to house the team of scientists, who could work on the bomb without fear of snoopers.

Two weeks later, on December 1, Secretary of War Henry L. Stimson wrote Connell the letter that meant the end of the Los Alamos Ranch School: "You are advised that it has been determined necessary to the interests of the United States and the prosecution of the war that the property of Los Alamos Ranch School be acquired for military purposes. Therefore . . . a condemnation proceeding will be instituted . . . to acquire all the school lands and buildings, together with all personal property owned by the school and used in connection with the operation."

The school was closed in February 1943, even as bulldozers were tearing up the frozen ground between the Big House and the Trading Post, and the last diplomas went out that June. Connell, who had known something was up since October, when low-flying planes had surveyed the mesa, had no choice but to comply. There was no appealing a decision made under the War Powers Act. Also, as a patriotic American, he was glad to be of help in the prosecution of the war. Indeed, the prospect of tons of bombs being dropped on thousands of Japanese civilians was one he approved of, saying: "We always said on the frontier, it's better to kill one bitch wolf than ten male wolves."

And yet the school had been Connell's whole life. He did not have any friends or outside interests. His one all-encompassing interest was his "gibbons." He did not have the heart to rebuild the school somewhere else. It wouldn't be the same. The Ranch School didn't travel, it could only work in its Los Alamos location. Connell outlived the school by exactly one year, for in February 1944 he died of pneumonia, at the age of sixty-two.

Once the school was closed the gibbons were replaced by eggheads—in fact, as General Groves put it, "the greatest collection of eggheads ever," notably Enrico Fermi, who had been awarded the Nobel Prize in 1938 for his work with neutrons, and the German-Jewish scientists just off the boat, courtesy of Hitler. They worked on the mesa top in splendid isolation, with assumed names—Fermi was "Eugene Farmer"—and had the same complaints as the boys: The houses were underheated, there weren't enough bathrooms, they were overworked.

Through his attendance at the Los Alamos Ranch School, Burroughs felt personally connected to the dropping of the Bomb. Connell's eviction was a parable for the age. The idyllic Ranch School, an outpost of the pastoral dream, which trained boys in the values of capitalist leadership, was commandeered by a government agency for a team of foreign-born scientists who gave away their secrets of mass destruction to the generals and the politicians, wrecking the America the school had represented.

For Burroughs, the Bomb and not the birth of Christ was the dividing line of history. The Bomb stole the relevance from all that had preceded it, and from its ramifications Burroughs constructed a worldview. It had all begun in the year of his birth, 1914, when Berlin Avenue had been changed to Pershing, and it culminated with the explosion of the Bomb. Burroughs was a "litmus person," in whom the horrors and perplexities of the age found a personal expression. As the great movements of history unfolded, they were acted out, on a small and private scale, in his own life.

T. S. Eliot, another "litmus person," was a pre-Bomb writer, who shored up fragments of culture against an eventual catastrophe. *The Waste Land* reads like an inventory of mementos buried in a time capsule so that future generations might know us. As a post-Bomb writer, Burroughs saw that America had made a Faustian pact, selling its soul for power, and losing its innocence. For America Before the Bomb, he felt a crushing nostalgia. Before the Bomb, America had been a safe and protected place, going its own way, pursuing its own dream. The way America was then comes up regularly in Burroughs' writing and conversation. In a New York restaurant once, when asked what he wanted to order, he replied, "A bass fished in Lake Huron in 1920."

After the Bomb, Burroughs had a sense of everything going wrong. He had visions of world death and death-in-life. He saw the survivors envying the dead, which was in the culture, a sixties rock group having called itself the Grateful Dead. His post-Bomb humor also entered the culture, as in this bit of graffiti on a New York wall: "If the Bomb falls, go up on the roof and get the best suntan of your life." The themes of his work were the themes of the post-Bomb age: the individual's powerlessness against state control, the feeling of being manipulated by unknown forces, with tormented characters fearing unidentified dangers, the need to connect sex and violence, the sense of doom relieved by gallows humor, the shattering of conventional narrative—what you might call a nuclear style. His books transcribed the prevailing fear of the second half of the twentieth century, when no one really knew whether he would reach the year 2000, the balance of terror practiced by the superpowers having seeped into our daily lives.

It was no accident that I went to the Los Alamos Ranch School where they couldn't wait to make the atom bomb and drop it on the Yellow Peril.

· THREE ·
CAMBRIDGE
1932–1938

Having been rescued by his adoring mother from an unendurable situation, and having failed to graduate from Los Alamos, Billy was enrolled in the fall of 1931 in a small St. Louis tutoring school run by Edgar C. Taylor, at 222 North Central Avenue. Taylor, a Rhodes Scholar and professional Anglophile who took Anglican orders to give himself the proper tone, admitted ten students a year with the understanding that he would get them into good colleges. A gifted fellow in many ways, he was also a self-advertiser and a poseur. Rogers Scudder thought of him as "a kind of fascinating charlatan," and Ann Russe, Billy's classmate at John Burroughs, remembers him at a party in 1937, looking elegant in front of a fireplace, and reminiscing about his exploits during his "wenching days." Then the conversation turned to the situation in Europe, and Taylor said with great emphasis, as though it was the last word on the subject, "I want war *now*."

With his appraising eye, Billy saw through Taylor's posturing. But he got through the year without incident, largely thanks to a perceptive English teacher named Jellinek, who taught full-time at Washington University and part-time at the Taylor School. Jellinek made him appreciate the classics, and he steeped himself in Milton and Wordsworth and Shakespeare. It was Jellinek who told him once: "I know you despise Taylor. I can see it in your face. But don't despise him. He's got a wife and kids, he's hooked. He's gotta make a living, don't you understand?"

Taylor must have been doing something right, for Billy got into Harvard, arriving in Cambridge to start his freshman year in September 1932. It was an interesting time—the height of the Depression, with 25 million unemployed, and the nation in a downward spiral. Franklin D. Roosevelt would be elected that November and launch the New Deal programs to get the country back on its feet. But Harvard was a world of its own. "I didn't see any bond salesmen selling apples," Burroughs recalls. Most of the students were apolitical, though Communism was fashionable among the faculty. There were Communist bookstores and Communist discussion groups and a publication called *The Harvard Communist*. F. O. Matthiessen, a noted professor of English literature, was an avowed Communist. A philosophy professor named Praul was another. At his urging, Billy read the *Communist Manifesto*, but he didn't like the sound of it, and told Praul, "Everyone's gonna work, but who's gonna make 'em work?" Praul explained the concept of the dictatorship of the proletariat, but Billy said, "Sounds to me like a lot of old people with beards are gonna be running the country."

Billy wasn't rebellious at Harvard, he wasn't placed on probation, and his parents did not receive embarrassing letters from the dean of students. But he soon began to hate the place. There was an "in" crowd made up of boys from Eastern prep schools, and they never accepted him. Once again, he had the sense of not belonging and adopted an attitude of passive resistance. "If Harvard doesn't bother me, I won't bother Harvard," he decided. No club wanted him, and he joined nothing. After his name and address, his listing in the senior yearbook is blank. In his freshman year he went out for sculls because you had to take one sport. After that, he went to class, got decent grades, and even enjoyed some of his classes. He liked Whiting's Chaucer course, and George Lyman Kittredge's famous Shakespeare course, which he audited. "Kitty" was a great Harvard character, white-maned and white-bearded, who always wore a gray suit and a red tie. He didn't have a doctoral degree, and when asked about it would say, "Who could examine me?" Billy remembers his *bon mot* about sexual intercourse: "The pleasure is momentary, the pains are infinite, and the posture is ridiculous." His classes started on the dot, he did not tolerate sneezing or coughing, and he would finish his lecture by coming down from the platform, still talking, reaching the door, and walking out just as the bell rang. A real showman. Kittredge assigned hundreds of lines of Shakespeare to learn by heart, which Burroughs, with his photographic memory, can still recite.

T. S. Eliot gave the Charles Eliot Norton lectures that year, one of which Billy attended. It was on the Romantic poets, whose excesses Eliot found deplorable. Using the Romantics as an example, he questioned the idea that people should be taught to think for themselves, and quoted someone who had said, "For God's sake, teach them to think like everybody else." Although disagreeing with his thesis, Billy found Eliot's talk humorous and well presented. Eliot gave weekly teas which Billy passed up, having heard that they were awkward affairs, with no one knowing what to say, while Eliot was polite and donnish.

One course that had a permanent influence on him was on Coleridge and taught by John Livingston Lowes, the author of *The Road to Xanadu*, a study of the genesis of Coleridge's work, in which he established the connection between drugs and creativity. Most of Coleridge's poems, with the possible exception of the *Rime of the Ancient Mariner*, had been composed under the influence of opium, and were in fact opium visions. Lowes called Coleridge's work "an abnormal product of an abnormal nature in abnormal conditions." He found in Coleridge's notebooks the signs of a personality haunted by the strange and fantastic, with entries such as these: "A dunghill at a distance sometimes smells like musk, and a dead dog like elder-flowers," and "Sometimes to a gibbett, sometimes to a throne—always to Hell." Lowes quoted that other great addict-writer, Thomas De Quincey, on the effects of opium: "Opium gives and takes away. It defeats the steady habit of exertion; but it creates spasms of irregular exertion. It ruins the natural power of life. But it develops preternatural paroxysms of intermitting power."

All of this Billy absorbed, although in those days there were no drugs on campus to experiment with. More routinely, this being the tail end of the Great Experiment, he made bathtub gin, mixing over the tub his simples of grain alcohol and Red Lion flavor.

In sophomore year he moved into Adams House, whose master was James Phinney Baxter III (later president of Williams College), bald and stern of expression, with a toothbrush mustache not unlike the Führer's, and wire-rim spectacles. Adams House was near the Yard but had no river view. It was not social or athletic; indeed it was sometimes described as a "social desert." It did, however, in spite of Baxter, have a vaguely bohemian reputation. A chess tournament was held there in the winter, already a bad sign, and speakers came and held forth on "Sanctions Against Italy" and "The New Age of Despots" and that sort of thing.

Billy was known as mildly eccentric because he kept a ferret in his room. The ferret was called Sredni Vashtar, after a story by Saki in which a ten-year-old boy trains his pet ferret to kill his bossy governess. It was a story likely to appeal to Billy because of his own childhood troubles with his nurse. But some of his friends were afraid to come to his room because ferrets were known to bite. The women who cleaned the rooms, known as "biddies," complained about the creature popping up from under the sofa.

Another item Billy kept in his room, against house rules, was a .32

revolver, with almost tragic consequences. He had gravitated to a circle of friends from St. Louis like Gene Angert and Rogers Scudder, and one of these was Richard Stern, a student at the business school. One day in Billy's room he and Stern were horsing around, and he pointed the gun, which he was sure was empty, at Stern's stomach. Stern, who was a fencer, made a quick lunge to deflect the barrel, and when Billy pulled the trigger, he blew a hole in the wall. Only then did he remember that the year before in St. Louis he had loaded the gun, thinking he heard an intruder downstairs. *Good God, that was a close fuckin' thing. You must always take it for granted that every gun is loaded. Just remember that and never point a gun at anybody. Unless you mean to use it.*

Billy and Richard Stern would go to New York on weekends, stay at the Savoy Plaza, and hang out in the Harlem after-hours clubs. There was Jimmy Daniels, who sang "Miss Otis Regrets" with his elegant, low-key delivery, and Clinton Moore, who ran a club, and gave him a phrase that he liked because it fitted his sense of fatalism. Billy was there one night with a sponge, who let him pick up the tab, and Moore said, "Some people are shits, darling."

It was through Richard Stern that Billy met some of the more outlandish characters then at Harvard, among them Graham Eyres Monsell, an upper-class Englishman whose father was First Lord of the Admiralty and who was at the business school. Billy thought he was glamorous because he was a lord and knew all sorts of people, but at heart he disliked him, recalling: "Ears Monsell—sounds like a Brooklyn gangster. He hung out with the undergraduates because he was in the habit of being deferred to and did not want to be with his equals. 'Like Cato give his little Senate laws/And sits attentive to his own applause.' He was a cat-hater, said he'd trained a dog to kill cats. But he was the one who told me vitamin A in large doses kills colds, which I've used a number of times. He was a fascist-minded elitist, not nearly as intelligent as he thought he was. I'm an elitist myself, but I don't want to be in the same lifeboat with *him*."

Another character was James Le Baron Boyle, a silver-tongued Irishman who claimed to be related to royalty but was actually the son of a Boston laundress. The lifelong friend of Richard Stern, Boyle drank a lot and was the life of the party; he became a teacher in a boys' school in Pennsylvania.

Once a week Billy had dinner with his brother, Mort, who was attending the School of Architecture after graduating from Princeton. Mort was so morose that he was known to Billy's friends as "Glum Burroughs." But he and Billy talked about books they had read, and discussed the merits of Freud.

Kells Elvins was also around, living off-campus with his bride and infant son. He had wed a St. Louis girl named Brick Orwig in a shotgun marriage; she had gone to the Veiled Prophet ball as a pregnant debutante, and no one had noticed, and the marriage was kept secret from St. Louis society.

In junior year Billy left Adams House for rooms in Claverly Hall, once one of the Gold Coast residences, on Mount Auburn Street. He didn't like the food or the master at Adams, and enjoyed the freedom of eating where he wanted to, at Durgin Park, which had sawdust on the floor and long tables with paper coverings, or Loch Ober's, or Bow's Waffle Shop, where he often had lunch with Robert Miller, a shy, introverted young man whose father ran a corset factory near Rochester, New York.

In Claverly Hall, Billy began to entertain, holding Sunday afternoon open houses to which he invited all the oddballs he could round up. There was one fellow called William P. Frere von Blomberg, who had gotten himself adopted by two elderly German baronesses, the sisters of the general who had been Hitler's first minister of defense. Von Blomberg wrote a gossip column in the *Boston American* and ended up as a traveling evangelist. There was also a broken-down actor who had a young attractive kid on a string, and the usual trio of Richard Stern and James Le Baron Boyle and Graham Eyres Monsell.

As for Gene Angert, who was so talented and beautiful, he was wandering around the Boston waterfront asking each of the old sea salts if he was the living Christ. Once he gave a party in his room, but by the time the guests got there he had drunk all the punch and was lying under the table. When he rushed up to Rogers Scudder one day and said, "I regard you as my Dr. Johnson," Scudder knew he was crazy. Indeed, he had to be committed to McLain's sanitarium outside Boston, where Billy visited him a number of times and was dismayed at his bizarre personality changes, from compulsively giggly to morose. He gave off that terrible ozone smell that schizophrenics have. From McLain's, he went to the Menninger Clinic, and then to a place for the terminally ill. It was a lesson in the fragility of human existence and the power of unknown, threatening forces.

Billy reflected that he was better off than Gene Angert, but not much. He was terribly unhappy because he was so frustrated sexually. He was in a sexual desert in the years when the sap is rising. Just when you want it most you can't get it. He had such a built-in ineptitude, such a block.

He always said the wrong thing. It was as if a being inside him did not want it to happen.

He had never had sex with either a man or a woman, and was in fact amazingly ignorant about it. His father, who was very prissy, had never had a man-to-man talk with him, of the "it's-time-you-knew-that-men-are-different-from-women" sort. Billy knew nothing about sex and had for some reason convinced himself, and still believed it when he was at Harvard, that children are born through the navel. It was during an evening with James Le Baron Boyle, Richard Stern, and Graham Eyres Monsell that he expressed this theory, which he thought was perfectly sound. They all shouted "WHAT!" and enlightened him as to the facts of life. He knew about female genitals, he explained, but didn't know the baby came out there—he thought it came out through the navel. Half a century later, when he was writing his novel *Western Lands*, he invented a mutant species that is born through the navel; although biology had proved him wrong, he created a woman who corresponded to his early belief—the world according to Burroughs, making the female genitals redundant. Whenever Burroughs thought of his persisting naïveté, he thought also for some reason of Jack Kerouac telling him, "You gotta be careful . . . women have poison juices." Jack, too, had gone through a naïve period, telling him: "When I was thirteen years old I went to this priest and I told him I had committed sins of impurity, and he said 'By yourself, my son?' and I said, 'Yes . . . and with another boy as well . . .' 'And how big was the other boy's thing, my son?' the priest asked. And that's when I lost my faith."

Relief from Harvard came during the summer vacations. In 1934 he went abroad with a St. Louis friend, Rex Weisenberger, who was fat and jolly and hated his mother. Rex had set up an elaborate electric train in his basement, which she threatened to throw out. "If you do that, Mother," he said, "I will cut the legs off your Hepplewhite dining room table." Tit for tat. The ship they crossed on provided for Burroughs one of those small humiliations he never forgets. He asked the steward for a cup of bouillon and the steward said, "Oh, those are for the passengers." *What did he think we were, stowaways?* His powerful sense of not belonging made him oversensitive to slights.

The ship stopped in Malta in early July, and Billy picked up a German newspaper which had an article in it that fascinated him, as it dealt with Hitler's purge of the Storm Troopers, whose leader, Ernst Roehm, was a homosexual. Roehm was Hitler's closest friend—they went back to the Beer Hall *Putsch* of 1923. But on June 30, Hitler personally drove to the hotel near Munich where Roehm and his entourage were staying and arrested his comrade-in-arms. "And a shameful sight greeted the eyes of the Führer," the article said. "There was Roehm with his *Lustknabe*—his pleasure boy—and indeed in a disgusting position." Roehm and many of his followers were shot.

Visiting Algeria, they went to the pre-Saharan town of Biskra, where they found the heat even worse than in St. Louis. They drank enormous beers called *Formidables* and told the hotel concierge, "Send everything cold you have up to the room." During the night, a bat flew into their room and Rex wanted to close the window. Billy thought that was ridiculous. "Of course, Rex, a lion might jump in," he said. "It's not funny," Rex said. "If that bat got to me I could die of a heart attack." Billy couldn't understand irrational fears, when there were enough real fears.

The following summer, he got a job as a cub reporter on the *St. Louis Post-Dispatch*. His father knew the managing editor, and every summer the paper hired a few college kids. At Los Alamos he had daydreamed about being a reporter. It sounded like a glamorous, exciting profession. But he soon found that he was grotesquely miscast. You had to have a hide like an elephant. Several times, he was sent out to get a picture of a child who had died in a summer accident, from drowning or by drinking lye. He thought it was an abject and disgusting assignment. Why in hell should the parents give him a picture? Either they were like whipped dogs and just handed it over or they did not want to give it and he would have to persuade them. He knew that a so-called good reporter would go to any lengths, would say, "Listen, I'll lose my job if I don't come back with a picture." And he would get it, whereas the parents should have said, "I don't give a shit whether you lose your job or not." He just wasn't cut out for this business of going around and trying to bulldoze the poor people.

Sometimes he'd cover the courts and police stations. "Have you got anything?" Sometimes he'd have to find out about a disappearance. "Was it voluntary?" Nine out of ten times it was. "If you're not a shit already," he thought, "this job will make you one." In his search for viability, he had found one more thing he wasn't cut out for.

His sexual frustration was so great that he was driven to women, and began to patronize a St. Louis whorehouse. The madam was a tough, no-nonsense country woman from the Ozarks who reminded him of Salt Chunk Mary. While he waited for the girl he had asked for, always the same one, he was shunted into a little room so he wouldn't see the judge coming down the stairs closing his fly, or the bank president, or his uncle. The girl was big-breasted, motherly, gentle, and effective. She provided a sense of release and pleasure and Billy felt he had done a socially acceptable thing. He was like the man in prison who says boys are better than nothing. The girl was alive, she had a warm body, and she was better than nothing.

Back at Harvard it was more of the same—sexual blockage, a sense of isolation, classes. Billy in his senior year finally got up the courage to pick up a piece of trade and have the kind of sex he wanted, but he paid dearly for it. It took two years for the symptoms of syphilis to become apparent—aching bones, a fluctuating rash, a flulike malaise. This was before penicillin, and the arsenic cure took eighteen months. He was later treated in New York by a Dr. Milton Feltenstein, who lectured him on the virtues of Communism while giving him intravenous injections of Salvarsan 606, so-called because its discoverer had made 605 tests before finding it. Billy responded that André Gide had visited the Soviet Union and pronounced it "the God that failed." "That is a vile slander," said Dr. Feltenstein, jabbing the needle into his arm.

Billy graduated in June 1936, but didn't attend the commencement. *It didn't mean a fuckin' thing.* He had his degree, but felt he had flunked out as a member of the WASP elite. There was something wrong with him. He just didn't belong. Members of the Porcellian and the Fly and the other snotty clubs all but crossed the sidewalk when they saw him coming.

Billy's graduation present was a European tour with the shy, round-faced Bob Miller. From Paris, where they stayed in the Hotel Montana and spent most of their time in cafés, they went to Vienna, and were captivated by the splendors of that great baroque city—the cathedral, the opera, the beaches on the Danube, the famous bath called the Romanische Baden, which was swarming with beautiful young boys; but they only looked.

Nazis were everywhere in evidence. When they went to Salzburg they were caught in a parade of Brownshirts. Chancellor Dolfuss had been murdered in 1934, but the *Putsch* had been bungled, and now the anti-Nazi von Schuschnigg was in tenuous control. Billy met an anti-Nazi named Fritz-Max Cahen, who said he was "steeped in the old German humanism" and that he was working on a book called *Men Against Hitler*. Several years later he arrived in New York and asked Billy to introduce him to wealthy Jews so that he could ask them for contributions to finance his plan to overthrow Hitler. Rubbing his hands, he said, "We will sure take in some thousands of dollars." *I realized then that his whole anti-Nazi act was a cheap con.*

Then it was on to Budapest, where they had an introduction to Baron

Yanche Wolfner, the model for a character in Christopher Isherwood's
"Mr. Norris Changes Trains" who ruled over the homosexual segment
of Budapest society. Billy and Bob Miller stayed in a pension in Buda
and Wolfner took them to a bar with Gypsy music. "Do you see anybody
in here that you want?" the Baron asked. Billy pointed to a boy and the
Baron snapped his fingers and the boy came over. There was something
to be said for Old World methods. Budapest boasted a homosexual hotel
called the King of Hungary, Wolfner informed them. One of the guests
had brought back a transvestite, and the outraged concierge had said,
"I'm sorry, sir, but you cannot bring a woman into this hotel."

Someone had told Bob Miller that the Yugoslav city of Dubrovnik, on
the Adriatic, was worth seeing, with its medieval walls, its partly Moslem
population, and its uncrowded beaches, and he suggested they go there.
Billy was willing. That was what Bob liked about Billy: he was placid,
good-natured, even-tempered, and entertaining with his dry wit—in short,
an ideal traveling companion.

They had a letter of introduction to Ilse Klapper, the person everyone
looked up in Dubrovnik, and she took them around. Ilse was a small-
boned woman of about thirty-five, with a shrewd birdlike face and brown
eyes that glinted like agate. She was straightforward and slightly mannish
and wore a monocle, and Billy liked her at once, liked her humor and
her lack of pretense. She saw through every phony. Born Ilse Herzfeldt
to a Jewish merchant family in Hamburg, she had married a doctor named
Klapper, who, although he was as Aryan as you could get, was fiercely
anti-Nazi. They had fled Germany in 1934 when the playing of Men-
delssohn's music was banned—this was true madness—and had settled
in Dubrovnik, where they were amiably divorced. Klapper practiced medicine illegally on an island near the harbor.

Ilse was living precariously on English lessons and on playing hostess
to visiting foreigners. She amused Billy with the story of her affair with
a married white Russian taxi driver. She had a tiny room in a hotel, and
one day he referred to it as "our little room," and she thought at once,
"I must get rid of this man." She had a dream that he came to her in
women's clothes, and the next day she got a begging letter from his wife,
and she wrote her lover, "Can't you write your own begging letters instead
of hiding behind a woman's skirts?"

She took them around to the beaches and the Gypsy cafés, and introduced them to a man who had written a book about Mount Athos, where
no women were allowed, not even hens, which Billy thought was a fine
idea. One evening they were having dinner in a garden restaurant with

a couple of English friends of Ilse's, one of them a famous hatmaker, when who should drop in but King Edward VIII and Wally Simpson (this was the year before his abdication). The royal yacht was in the harbor. Everyone stood up, and the waiters bowed and said, *"Guten Abend, guten Abend."* The English hatmaker made one of his *terribly amusing* English jokes, saying to the other Brit, "You should have gotten up and said, very softly, 'Good evening, sire.' " *Made me sick, this royalty nonsense.*

After Dubrovnik, they were due to head back to the States, but Billy made a startling announcement. He was returning to Vienna to enroll in the medical school at the university. He had decided to be a doctor but could not get into an American school, not having taken the required pre-med courses, since he was hopeless at math. But in Vienna they didn't have all these prerequisites. Anyone could enroll, although the attrition rate was high.

His parents, upon his graduation, had decided to give him a monthly allowance of $200 out of their earnings from Cobblestone Gardens, a tidy sum in those days. It was enough to keep him going, and indeed it guaranteed his survival for the next twenty-five years, arriving with welcome regularity. The allowance was a ticket to freedom; it allowed him to live where he wanted to and to forgo employment. And when there was an emergency, his parents were always there. Like the song said, *Now some write home/ To the old folks for coin,/ And that's their Ace in the Hole.* It sure was the time he was fined $273 or six months in jail in Beeville, Texas, for drunken driving, and his mother wired the money. Or when he was stranded in Algiers during the war with the French, his bed alive with bedbugs, and his father wired the money. *My name'd be mud/Like a chump playing stud/If I lost that old Ace in the Hole.*

The fall of 1936 found Billy living in the Dianabad Hotel, a combination hotel and Turkish bath, which was also used for sexual assignations, but not by him, for the syphilis contracted at Harvard had declared itself, and he had to go once a week to the doctor's for his intravenous arsenic shot, which nauseated him. His six months in Vienna were spent in syphilis-induced depression. He felt unclean and afraid of passing on his contagion, and his old-fashioned doctor didn't seem to know what the risk was. In any case, he felt no desire, and his days were inactive and lonely. Sometimes he took his meals with Dr. Frankel, a middle-aged man at the hotel. Sometimes he went to the Prater, the big amusement park. Sometimes he went to his classes in anatomy and *materia medica.* He was able to follow, having boned up on his German by reading a book in English side by side with the German, a trick he had picked up in one of Somerset Maugham's short stories.

Austria in 1937 was one year away from the *Anschluss*, but you could see it coming. Nearly every day in Vienna there were bombings and demonstrations. The students Billy talked to were Nazis, and if anyone was anti-Hitler, they sure weren't speaking up about it. In the newspapers there was a rising note of anti-Semitic hysteria. In the *Volkisher Beobachter*, Billy saw the emergence of a fiendish archetype. He saw a drawing of a Jew's head on a spider's body. He saw a photograph of a Jew accused of a crime, with the caption, "From his horrible Jew eyes speaks the criminal world of the Talmud."

As a homosexual, he felt himself to be a member of another persecuted group. The manipulation of archetypes applied also to queers. There were also articles about "the criminal world of the international homosexual." As he could see on a daily basis, a collective madness could seize a society, aimed at any outsider group.

It was a bad situation, getting worse, and on top of everything, in the spring of 1937 Billy came down with acute appendicitis. "We can't wait a single day," the doctor said. After the operation, he decided to go back to Dubrovnik for a couple of weeks to recuperate, and saw Ilse again. She was in a state of panic because her Yugoslav visa was about to expire, and as a Jew she could not renew it. Where could she go? Time was running out. The Nazis were making war noises and were likely to invade the Balkans.

Ilse felt that her salvation lay in finding an American who was willing to marry her. With an American husband, she could escape to the United States. She kept bringing the subject up with Billy, an older and experienced woman exerting pressure on a suggestible twenty-three-year-old. He was fond of Ilse, and he saw the chance to follow William Blake's precept: "He who would do good to another must do it in minute particulars." She was pushed by a desperate need, and he was malleable and willing to help, and agreed to marry her.

But when he informed his family of his plans, there was great agitation. His mother saw a grasping European femme fatale pursuing her gullible son in the mistaken belief that he was a rich American. There were heated transatlantic phone calls, entreaties, telegrams. Let's see if we can get her into the country without your marrying her, his mother said. But Billy did not back down. He took Ilse to Athens, where he had an introduction to the American consul, Henry Beck, who put through the paperwork. Then he went looking for a Greek Orthodox priest to perform the ceremony. The first priest refused—this naïve, submissive boy with this mannish, monocled, worldly woman in her late thirties—it looked fishy. *To hell with his fuckin' scruples, we'll get another one. All we need is a priest with no scruples who'll take ten dollars to get us hitched.*

With Henry Beck as a witness, the ceremony was performed in July 1937. It had its farcical aspects. Billy didn't have a ring, and Ilse had to peel the ring from her first marriage off her finger and hand it to him, and he stuck it back on. They were now man and wife, but in name only, for Ilse went back to Dubrovnik, and Billy, in response to the pleas of his alarmed parents, went home.

The question was, what to do next. Staying in St. Louis was out of the question. Medical school was out of the question. He thought psychology might have some answers, and enrolled in the graduate school at Columbia, but the statistics courses stopped him cold. Then he heard that Kells was at Harvard in graduate school and decided to join him there and take courses in archeology.

Kells was separated from his wife, and for most of 1938, he and Billy shared a small frame house on a quiet street in Cambridge near the Commodore Hotel. A black manservant did the cooking and cleaning. Billy took courses in the Navajo language and in Mayan archeology, and he had an ethnology teacher who said, "I'm not interested in why people do things, I'm interested in what they do." That made sense to Billy, who began to think of a career as an ethnologist.

But the more he saw of academic life, the less he liked it. The intrigues, the faculty teas, doing all the right things. It was worth your job to be seen in a queer bar. There was always someone you had to be on good terms with if you were going to get anywhere in the department. It was a little closed circle feeding on itself, a little whirlpool going round and round. He realized that he could never be an academic. The faculty life didn't suit his personality. If you had a negative attitude, it would be picked up immediately by the prickly egos in the department, and they would all say, "We'll fix him."

The year was not a total loss, however, for thanks to Kells, Burroughs broke the writing block that went back to his Los Alamos diaries. It was the act of collaboration that did it. Writing with another person released him from embarrassment. He and Kells were fooling around with a humorous routine about the captain of a sinking ship who dresses up like a woman to get into a lifeboat. It was based on the *Titanic* and the *Morro Castle*, which caught fire and burned off the Jersey coast in 1935, with a loss of 200 lives. The first mate was in the first lifeboat. On the *Titanic*, someone actually did get into women's clothes.

They acted things out, which Burroughs found to be a very good practice. *Lots of times what's wrong with a scene is that it couldn't possibly have happened. You've got people coming through the wall. Where was so and so when so and so came in? What door did he come in from?* Burroughs would write a paragraph and Kells would write a paragraph, or together they would work up the dialogue, splitting their sides with laughter.

Burroughs introduced a character he would use often, Dr. Benway, the irresponsible surgeon, who says, "Get me another scalpel, this one has no edge to it." As the jukebox plays a Fats Waller rendition of "The Star Spangled Banner," the passengers scramble for the lifeboats. Captain Kramer dons a kimono and wig and smears his face with cold cream. As drowning passengers grab for the gunwales, a lisping, knife-wielding paretic lops off their fingers.

The routine, called "Twilight's Last Gleaming," is the genesis for much of Burroughs' later work, with its combination of slapstick and surrealism, its cartoon characters and black humor. They sent it to *Esquire*, and got back a note saying, "Too screwy, and not effectively so for us." The discouragement of rejection put Burroughs off writing for another six years.

· FOUR ·
NEW YORK
1939–1941

In the spring of 1939, the Burroughs-Elvins household in Cambridge broke up. Kells, who was working on a master's in psychology, landed a job as a prison psychologist in Huntsville, Texas. There he could write his thesis on incest, based on interviews with convicts, one of whom had been sentenced to twenty years for knocking up his daughter, who had given birth to a girl. On the eve of his release, with six years off for good behavior, he went to see Kells and said: "Well, I guess the other one's about right now . . . Hell, I don't see nothin' wrong with raisin' your own tail."

Burroughs paid Kells a visit in Huntsville, where he was busy classifying convicts. One of them, a huge man, at least 300 pounds, complained that he could not adjust to prison life because he did not get enough to eat. Kells classified him as a "psychopathic eater," so that he was allowed to come to the dining room half an hour early and get a head start on meals. Kells studied the convicts' backgrounds. Most of the swindlers, he found, were the sons of ministers. "That's where they get their gift of gab," he told Burroughs.

From Huntsville, Burroughs went to New York, where there was a matter requiring his attention. His wife, Ilse Klapper Burroughs, was still trying to get out of Yugoslavia. As the wife of an American citizen, she had a right to a visa, and Burroughs testified at some sort of immigration hearing, before a distinguished white-haired gentleman with a flag on the wall behind him, who looked as though he was impersonating all the Presidents at once.

"Young man," he asked, "was this a perfectly sincere marriage, rather than a marriage of convenience?"

"Yes, it was," Burroughs replied less than candidly. "I love my wife and I want to have her in the United States with me."

He must have made a good impression, for three weeks later Ilse had her visa and arrived in New York. They lived apart, but saw each other regularly. "She never asked me for one cent," Burroughs recalls.

Ilse joined a growing Jewish refugee community in New York, and found a job as secretary to a fellow refugee, the German left-wing dramatist Ernst Toller, author of *Man and the Masses*. Toller, then forty-five, was a good example of a generation that could be described as defeated by history. Wanting to prove that he was a real German, he had volunteered for army service in World War I, and was thirteen months at the front before his health broke down and he was discharged as unfit. The meaningless slaughter he had witnessed, and the feeling that Germany had been betrayed by its leaders, made of him a Communist revolutionary, and he was a leader of the 1919 Bavarian Soviet Republic. Arrested and jailed, he was sentenced to death, but the firing squad refused the order to fire, and his sentence was commuted to five years, which he spent industriously turning out plays.

Toller went from defeat to defeat. In Germany, as an anti-Nazi. In Spain, as an anti-Franco loyalist. Having to flee to America only intensified his sense of uselessness, even though he went on lecture tours and published his memoirs. Through Ilse's reports, Burroughs was connected with the political diaspora of the thirties, when men who had fought on the losing side, whose beliefs and ideals had been stamped under foot, were evicted from their homeland. Ilse did not think much of Toller, who seemed a shell of a man, a windbag and a physical coward who was always talking about fighting fascism, she said, whereas "he'd shit himself if he heard a gunshot."

Toller sat around feeling sorry for himself. His young wife had left him, and he was no longer in demand as a lecturer. One day when she returned to his hotel suite from lunch, always on the dot of one, she found him trying to cut his wrists with a kitchen knife. She was sure he had timed the suicide attempt with her return.

On May 22, 1939, Burroughs took Ilse to lunch. As usual, the conversation was peppered with Ilse's caustic comments on Toller. "You can't imagine what he said this morning," she said. " 'Oh, for a great task!' " On her way back from lunch, she ran into someone who had just arrived from Europe, and stopped to chat—what happened to so and so—and got back about ten minutes late.

She sat down and started typing up some notes when a prickly sensation started up the back of her neck. She got up and pushed open the bathroom door. Toller was on the other side—he had hanged himself with his bathrobe cord. This time he has done it, Ilse thought. Even if she had gotten back on time it would not have helped, for his neck was broken.

Burroughs understood what had happened to Toller. He had died of bad news. He had read somewhere that there are two things a rat hates, to be thrown in the water and to have its whiskers cut. If it is thrown in the water it will manage to swim, but if in addition its whiskers are cut, it will drown. Toller had his whiskers cut and was thrown in the water—too much bad news.

At the funeral, he was eulogized. "He was as direct a martyr of the Nazi regime as if he had been murdered in a concentration camp," the rabbi conducting the ceremony said. The Austrian actor Kurt Kaznar, a friend and admirer of Toller's who had married a wealthy American woman, was at the funeral, and asked Ilse to be his secretary.

Once again, she reported on her employer to Burroughs, on his drunken wife and their disorderly household. "It is passing all the frontiers," she said, "it is not to believe." The Kaznars gave lavish parties, to which Ilse invited her husband. There Burroughs met John La Touche, who had written the lyrics for the musical *Cabin in the Sky*. "Touche" had a reputation as the funniest fellow around. He introduced everyone as the duke of so-and-so and the prince of so-and-so, and signed his letters "Loads of apples." He was famous for his skits, and did one on Burroughs: "I'm Bill Burroughs and I've got a gun. Don't come near me." Ilse reported that "Touche" was writing a musical based on the life of Byron, which he was tying in to the Greek Resistance. "He can write this shit by the yard," she said.

When the alcoholic Mrs. Kaznar expired from liver failure the maid accused her husband of having poisoned her. In the ensuing tumult, Ilse had to move on, and found a job in a travel agency. Burroughs continued to see her until 1945, when she returned to Europe.

In August 1939, Burroughs went to Chicago to attend five lectures by Count Alfred Korzybski, the author of a book he much admired, *Science and Sanity*. Korzybski was a Polish nobleman who had grown up on an estate near Warsaw but had come to the United States in 1915. A post–World War I Utopian, he hoped that the wreckage of Europe would be the dawn of a new age. He foresaw a government headed by a biologist, an engineer, a mathematician, and a sociologist, to develop human engineering. Human nature could be made to change, since man was the only creature with the capacity to improve. The beaver kept making the same dam over and over again, and the bee its honeycomb, but man could build on past achievement, man's mind was a storage house which could create a new ethics.

Burroughs was drawn to Korzybski's theory of General Semantics, which showed the errors of either/or Aristotelian thinking. Was an act instinctive or intellectual? Of course it was both. Was man the product of heredity or environment? It was simply mistaken to think this way. Either/or thinking created a gap between reality and the words used. In 1938, for instance, when Korzybski founded the Institute of General Semantics in Chicago, the words were "peace in our time" and "democratic appeasement," but the facts were war and dictatorship.

When Burroughs arrived in Chicago, he saw a heavy, bald, vigorous man of sixty with gleaming black eyes, who looked a little like Picasso. Korzybski's hopes for a new dawn were being scuttled by the dictators. Foreseeing the invasion of his beloved Poland, he was in a somber mood, telling his audience, "All you young men will be slaughtered—Hitler will invade Poland, but he will not call it a war, and then the conflict will spread." A month later it happened.

Korzybski still hoped to make reason prevail through his teachings. To demonstrate the gap between the word and the reality, he banged on a table and said, "Whatever this is, it is not a table." Emotions such as love, hate, and anger, he explained, occurred on a nonverbal level, so that what we called them had nothing to do with what they were.

"You think as much with your big toe as with your brain," Korzybski said, "and probably more effectively." Thought was not a tiny conscious area but the reaction of the whole organism to the whole environment. Words were inadequate to describe certain silent human processes, and Korzybski proposed the idea of thinking in pictures, which Burroughs adopted, as he did his ideas on language and either/or thinking. Korzybski helped him clarify his own views.

When the lectures were over, Burroughs went back to New York. He looked up a friend from Harvard, Bill Gilmore, who had literary ambitions but in the meantime was working as a fund-raiser for the Quakers. Gilmore knew W. H. Auden, who was living in Brooklyn, and took Burroughs over to meet him. Burroughs thought Auden was insufferable. He talked incessantly, and at dinner, disapproving of the conversation, he rapped on a glass and said, "It's time to change the subject." He would say, "As a Christian my opinion is . . . ," the point being that he was always talking "as" something, a tiresome way of buttressing his views. As for his poetry, Burroughs felt, it was almost profound. It went just so far and you waited for it to go further and it never did.

It was also thanks to Gilmore that Burroughs met Jack Anderson, who looked like the man in the Arrow shirt ad but had the mentality of a shopgirl. Gilmore, who had already made it with him, said, "He's very pretty and very willing." When they met at Tony's Bar on Fifty-second Street, Burroughs had that terrible sinking feeling of being smitten again, a feeling that distressed him because there was no way to control it. Jack's lack of education gave him a chip-on-the-shoulder attitude toward anything that was remotely intellectual. Whenever Burroughs ventured an idea, he would sneeringly ask, "Is that what Count Korzybski says?" Jack was completely oriented toward money. He had an office-boy job and hustled on the side, with both men and women.

Burroughs, who by this time was over his syphilis, had a room at the Taft Hotel on Seventh Avenue and brought Jack up there one night. He left the door unlocked and some hotel employee came through checking the rooms and saw them in bed together naked. Ten minutes later the house detective and the hotel manager barged in. "What's going on here?" Burroughs asked in the most convincing tone of offended propriety he could summon up under the circumstances.

"That's what we want to know," the hotel manager said.

"You're about the wisest prick I ever walked in on," the house dick said, which Burroughs thought was quite a compliment. "Didn't anyone ever kick the shit out of you?"

"You've got ten minutes to get your stuff packed," the manager said. "Then come downstairs, go over to the cashier's window, and we'll give you a refund."

Jack lived in a red-brick roominghouse on Jane Street in the village, and Burroughs went back there with him and took a room. He felt so little in control of his life and emotions that he decided to go into analysis with Dr. Herbert Wiggers, a tall, melancholy Freudian who had had rheumatic fever as a child. The Freudians insisted that the patient must provide all the information, and the analyst must not attempt any interpretation. *Vaster than empires, and more slow, this vegetable analysis may grow.* Over the years, he would try them all, the Freudians, the Jungians, the Adlerians, the Reichians, the Washington School, the Karen Horney School, the whole psychoanalytical panoply. He tried narcoanalysis, which used nitrous oxide to stimulate the subconscious—this was the stuff they gave during the war to shell-shocked amnesiac soldiers—and put you in a state between sleeping and waking. Burroughs began to talk in accents and take on different identities, a titled Englishman, an old Southern farmer. He came to know enough about analysis so that he thought of entering the profession, except that you needed a medical degree.

After ten years of it, he ended up thinking, "What is this nonsense?" He did not feel that much further advanced in any understanding of himself. Where it could lead it had led. Very few people really benefited from it, he felt. They mistook the dependence they built up on their analyst with the success of the treatment. The poor man tried to get away for a two-week vacation and his patients tracked him down . . . Oh, my God, Doctor, I have to see you, I HAVE TO SEE YOU! Sometimes there were odd, telepathic signals. Burroughs dreamed that another of his analysts, Dr. Federn, the pupil of Freud, was offering candy to little girls, and thought, this poor naïve European doesn't realize that people will think he's a dirty old man. Federn said it had actually happened, that he had offered candy to children and then worried what people would think. Over the years Federn had recorded 1,300 instances of telepathic contact with patients.

In any case, it was helpful on some level for Burroughs to discuss with Dr. Wiggers the problems he was having with Jack Anderson. By being too open about his attraction to Jack, Burroughs had once again fallen into the trap of making himself vulnerable to contempt. It was as if he deliberately picked hustlers like Anderson, who were sure to treat him shabbily.

He was next door, and at night he could hear Jack bring men or women back to his room, could hear the sound of laughter and glasses clinking, and then the voices getting lower and more intermittent and turning to sounds of lovemaking. Night after night he lived through it, hearing the muffled moans of pleasure and the cries of orgasm through the thin walls, and it was tearing him apart.

One day he was walking up Sixth Avenue from Forty-second Street, looking in pawnshop windows, when he came upon a cutlery store. In the window he saw knives and scissors and pocket microscopes and air pistols and toolkits that folded into small leather packets—he had as a child been given one for Christmas.

Saying to himself, "I must do it," he walked into the store and asked to see some poultry shears, the kind with one smooth and one sawtooth blade, the kind his father had used on the Thanksgiving turkey.

"That's stainless steel, sir. Never rusts or tarnishes."

"How much?"

"Two dollars and seventy-nine cents plus tax."

"Okay."

The clerk wrapped the shears in brown paper, and Burroughs paid with a five-dollar bill. Back in his room on Jane Street, he unwrapped the shears and put them down on the dresser in front of the oval mirror that turned on a pivot.

He looked at himself in the mirror and thought of Jack Anderson, who was so stupid and shallow that it was impossible to make any impression on him. He picked up the shears and placed the sawtooth lower blade against the end joint of his left little finger. Then he lowered the cutting blade until it rested against the flesh of his finger. Again he looked into the mirror, composing his face in an expression of impassiveness. He took a deep breath, and pressed the handle quick and hard. The tip of his finger fell on the dresser. He felt a deep sorrow for the severed finger joint, lying there alone and lifeless, a few drops of blood clinging to the white bone. Tears welled in his eyes.

When he turned his hand over to look at the stub, blood spurted up and splashed his face, which he cleaned with a towel. He bandaged his finger as best he could, and in a few minutes the bleeding stopped. He picked up the finger joint, wrapped it in Kleenex, put it in his vest pocket, and walked out of the hotel, saying to himself, "I've done it." He had performed his Van Gogh act, although Jack Anderson was a piss-poor Gauguin.

Waves of euphoria swept over him, and he stopped in a bar and knocked back a double brandy. Goodwill flowed out of him for the whole world. A lifetime of defensive hostility seemed to have dropped away.

The finger incident is in some ways like a replay of the childhood trauma with the nurse. In that still confused and dimly remembered event, with its ugly sexual context, he had been the victim, betrayed by a loved one. Now, once again, he was betrayed by Jack Anderson. Once again he was the victim, by turning his suffering and jealousy against himself. The cutting of the finger was a symbolic castration, an echo of the incident with the nurse and her boyfriend, when he had (perhaps, for he could never be sure) bitten the boyfriend's penis, his teeth the White Defenders. The sequence in both cases was confusion, betrayal, and pain.

And now he took the severed fingertip to his analyst Dr. Wiggers, as he had wanted but had been unable to take the story of the nurse to his father, for he might not have been believed. What was the credibility of a four-year-old? This time he had the evidence in his vest pocket.

Wiggers was horrified when the memento was displayed. He was sure Burroughs was going through a psychotic episode. In his own interest he should be placed under observation. He might do more harm to himself. Wiggers proposed to take him to Bellevue, but Burroughs shook his head.

"Really, Bill, you're doing yourself a great disservice. When you realize what you've done you'll need psychiatric care. Your ego will be overwhelmed."

"All I need is to have the finger sewed up. I've got a date tonight."

"Really, Bill, I don't see how I can continue as your psychiatrist if you don't follow my advice in this matter."

"Why don't you fix it yourself?"

"I haven't practiced since my internship, and I don't have the necessary materials in any case. This has to be sewed up right or it could get infected right on up the arm."

Fearing infection and weary of argument, Burroughs agreed to go to Bellevue for medical treatment only. While an intern sewed up his finger and put on a dressing, Wiggers urged him to commit himself overnight. Feeling overcome by a sudden faintness, Burroughs decided to place himself in the care of his psychiatrist, whom he trusted. "All right," he said, "I'll do what you say."

Wiggers went off to sign some papers and returned quite pleased with himself, saying, "I'm cutting red tape by the yard." The next thing he knew Wiggers was gone, and he was in a dressing gown in a ward with other men. My God, he thought, the lousy bastard shanghaied me into the nuthouse. On top of everything, his finger joint, which he had wanted to keep, had disappeared.

Once again, as in the case of the nurse, he was doubly betrayed. Just as his parents had neglected to take action against the evil nurse, his psychiatrist had tricked him into commitment to the psycho ward.

The following day, Burroughs was interviewed by a lady psychiatrist. "Do you hear voices?" she asked.

"When people talk to me, I can hear them talking, yes."

"No, I mean do you hear voices talking inside your head?"

"I suppose you could say I have a vivid imagination."

"Now, what about this self-mutilation?"

"Oh, that. Well, that's part of an initiation ceremony into the Crow Indian tribe."

Squinting, the lady psychiatrist asked, "Mr. Burroughs, why do you have mannerisms?"

"Well, I guess everyone has mannerisms."

"Not mannerisms like yours, Mr. Burroughs."

The lady psychiatrist diagnosed Burroughs as a schizophrenic, paranoid type. When Wiggers called to see how he was, Burroughs said: "What in hell have you done, you son of a bitch? Did you think I was going crazy or something?"

"I was afraid your ego would be overwhelmed," Wiggers said.

Burroughs called his father, who came at once to New York, saw the head psychiatrist at Bellevue, and arranged to have his son transferred to a private psychiatric hospital, Payne-Whitney. *My name'd be mud/Like a chump playing stud/If I lost that old Ace in the Hole.* Mortimer Burroughs was his usual taciturn self. He didn't even ask his son why he had cut off his finger. "Suffer in silence" was his motto.

After about a month, Burroughs was released from Payne-Whitney in the custody of his parents. He spent most of 1940 in St. Louis, living at home and working as a driver and delivery boy for Cobblestone Gardens. It was a low point in his life, like a return to childhood. He was bored and sullen, barely speaking to his parents. He hated the work, felt that he was doing penance. Once he had a delivery at the home of a wealthy Jewish couple. The wife answered the door and sent him around to the servants' entrance. Burroughs drove away clashing the gears and muttering, "Hitler is perfectly right." Since his sense of his own status was so fragile, any episode that linked him with the underclass was sure to make him seethe.

But even in St. Louis, under the supervision of his parents, he managed to get into trouble. Jack Anderson, with whom he had stayed in touch, and who had been apologetic after the finger episode, came to visit. One night Burroughs took his father's car and went out drinking with Jack in the red-light district in East St. Louis. Above the bar was a picture of Custer's Last Stand, distributed by Anheuser-Busch, which Burroughs was trying to convince the bartender was a rare and valuable object. "Yeah," the bartender said, "you already told me that ten times . . . anything else?" He walked to the other end of the bar and studied a *Racing Form*.

Jack picked up a dollar of Burroughs' money off the bar and said "I want to go into one of these houses." "All right," Burroughs said as he watched Jack leave through the swinging doors. "Enjoy yourself."

On the way home, Burroughs asked, "Want to try driving a bit? Only way to learn. Could you learn to play the piano by reading a book about it?" He took Jack's chin in his hand and kissed him lightly on the mouth. Jack laughed, showing sharp little eyeteeth.

"I always say, people have more fun than anybody," Jack said. Burroughs shuddered in the summer night. He really did have the mind of a chorus girl. "I suppose they do," he said.

Jack slid under the wheel, looking dubiously at the dashboard, for he had only driven twice in his life. With a grinding of gears the car lurched forward, bucked, almost stalled, then proceeded at a crawl.

"You'll never learn this way," Burroughs said. "Let's see a little speed."

It was three in the morning, with not a car on the road. "A little speed, Jackie . . . That thing under your foot . . . push it into the floor, Jackie." Equating speed with the sex that he wanted but was not getting from Anderson, Burroughs went on, in an odd, disembodied voice: "Push it all the way down, Jackie, all the way in . . . all the way, Jackie."

The car gathered speed, tires humming on the asphalt, the city spinning under them in the summer night. Burroughs felt that he was in a sealed capsule, beyond contact with the outside world. The light from the dashboard played on the two faces, one weak and handsome, the other thin and intense, a bookworm aspiring to be a man of action.

"You're learning fast, Jackie. Just keep your right foot on the floor." The speedometer had climbed to sixty. Jack swerved to avoid the metal mounds of a safety zone. The car hit a wet spot where the street had been watered and went into a long skid. There was the sickening crash of metal, and Burroughs flew out of the car door and slid across the asphalt. He picked himself up and ran his hands over his body. Nothing broken. Someone was holding his arm. A wrecker was towing away the car, its front wheels off the ground. He saw Jack between two cops, looking dazed, an ugly bruise on his forehead.

A police car took them to the hospital, where the doctor patched Jack's forehead and swabbed a cut on Burroughs' leg with Mercurochrome. Then they went to the police station, where Burroughs asked to call his father, who seemed to appear as he hung up the phone, conjured by an alcoholic trick of time, cool and distant as always.

It appeared that they had hit a parked car, whose owner had arrived. "So I met my wife at the train and took her to see the new car, and there wasn't any car. All four wheels knocked off."

"That will be all taken care of," Mortimer Burroughs told him.

"Well, I should think so! That car can't be fixed. There's nothing left of it."

"In that case you will get a new car."

"Well, I should think so! People driving like that should be in jail. Endangering people's lives!"

Mortimer Burroughs was huddled with the desk sergeant. They shook hands, and the sergeant accepted one of his cigars. No charges would be filed against Burroughs and Jack.

Jack was dropped off at his hotel, and Burroughs and his father drove in silence to the house on Price Road. Finally, Burroughs said, "I'm sorry, Dad . . . " "So am I," his father said.

"It's all right, Mother," Mortimer Burroughs called out upstairs as they entered the house. "Nobody hurt."

"Want some milk, Bill?" he asked, starting toward the pantry.

"No thanks, Dad," Burroughs said, and went upstairs to bed.

Burroughs had to get out of St. Louis and his parents' house, and began to see the war as the solution to his dilemma. He wanted to serve his country and do some fighting. America was bound to get into it soon. He could live out some of his childhood fantasies, becoming Mr. Brundage, the coldest and most brutal of the pirates. He liked the idea of danger, and saw himself volunteering for risky assignments, parachuted behind enemy lines.

He tried to enlist in the navy, but flunked the physical. The navy doctor said: "He is nearsighted and flat-footed. Put down that he is a poor physical specimen." Turning to Burroughs, he added, "You might get your commission if you can throw some weight around."

Then he tried the American Field Service, but a snotty young English public school type asked: "Oh, by the way, Burroughs, what were your clubs at Harvard? . . . No clubs?" Burroughs could feel the temperature drop. "And what was your House? Adams . . . I see. We'll consider your application."

Burroughs tried again, enrolling toward the end of 1940 in the Lewis School of Aviation in Lockport, Illinois, near Joliet, where the big prison was. He was hoping to get a pilot's license so that he could enlist in the Glider Corps. He knew that his eyesight was not good enough but figured that the demand for men would make them relax the standards.

The school was Catholic-run, and the first night he was there a priest came by and said, "It's kinda hard to swing right into it, isn't it?" Burroughs asked him what it was like to be a priest. "I do what I'm told," he said. Burroughs caught from those words the eerie feeling that the priest had the weight of great power behind him.

Flying was not much harder than driving. He did his 100 hours in Piper Cubs and got his license. The exam was easy, since the instructor knew the questions that were coming up. But when he tried to join the Glider Corps he was turned down because of his eyes. So the only thing he got out of the aviation school, since he didn't pilot again, was jaundice from the food.

He was back in St. Louis in June 1941, still looking for an outfit he could join. Through his father, he heard that a Colonel Donovan was setting up some sort of spy outfit in Washington. Donovan had recruited various eggheads for his Board of Analysts, which he called his College of Cardinals, and was looking for young Ivy Leaguers to serve as agents in the field. Armed with a letter of introduction from his well-connected uncle Wideman Lee, Ivy's brother, Burroughs went to the O.S.S. office

in Washington that July and had an interview with Donovan. They seemed
to get on fine, Burroughs thought. Then Donovan said, "Now I'd like
you to meet my director of research and analysis," who turned out to be
none other than his former Harvard housemaster, James Phinney Baxter,
who had disliked Burroughs from the days when he kept a ferret in his
room. As soon as Burroughs saw Baxter's purple-jowled face and officious
expression, he knew the jig was up.

He wanted to do his duty as a patriotic American, but everywhere he
turned, he was rejected. He was a misfit, a washout, a discard. There
was a functioning elite of officers' schools and intelligence outfits which
recruited among "his kind," but they vetoed him on sight.

Barring active service, Burroughs was looking for a way to migrate to
New York. His father, anticipating more trouble, also wanted him to find
something to do, and called up an old friend in New York who owed him
a favor, Colonel Massek. He had once loaned Massek $5,000 to start an
advertising agency, and now he told him on the phone: "My boy here
can't get a job. He's got such an awful personality, I don't know what
he's good for. He can't add a column of figures. He sounds terrible over
the phone."

"Okay," Massek said, "I'll hire him at thirty dollars a week."

The agency, Van Dolan, Givaurdon, and Massek, was a nickel-and-
dime, hole-in-the-wall outfit, staggering along with third-rate accounts.
Van Dolan was brash and overconfident. Givaurdon was a nasty little
shrimp who had apoplexy if you sat in his chair, but Burroughs liked
Massek, a sort of W. C. Fields type with an eccentric sense of humor and
a gamesman's view of life.

As the junior copywriter, Burroughs was given the accounts no one
else would touch. One was EndoCream, which contained female sex
hormones that made women look younger instantly, and had Egyptian
motifs on the box. Another was Cascade, a high colonic. The mixture
was added to water and placed in a bag with a nipple in the middle, that
was applied like an enema.

Burroughs reached new heights of lyricism in his ad copy for Cascade.
"It is no more like an enema than a kite is like an airplane," he wrote.
"Well done thou true and faithful servant—that is how many people feel
about their Cascade. Immeasurable relief sweeps over them. The waste
matter that has accumulated for years is often swept away without a trace.
You feel as if reborn."

Unfortunately, several overweight women who sat down on the bag a
little too vigorously reported colon inflammation and sued the company,

which at that point had a spot of trouble with the Interstate Commerce Commission.

All in all, this was a fairly happy time for Burroughs, who was living with Jack Anderson in an apartment on West Eleventh Street between Fifth and Sixth avenues. With Jack, life was at best a series of sexual compromises, but at least Burroughs wasn't cutting off any more fingers. In fact, whether due to analysis or a more stable relationship, he was able to vent his hostility against others rather than himself, which might be seen as a healthy development. Anderson had a wildly jealous girlfriend, who came around one evening to object that he was living with Burroughs. "I happen to love Jack," she drunkenly repeated. Since Burroughs wasn't responding, she took a swipe at him, knocking off his glasses. To his great surprise, since he hated quarrels, Burroughs found himself hauling off and whamming her one that sent her sprawling across the room and onto the couch. After that, the girl was more subdued. Jack as usual did nothing, and Burroughs was amazed that he had struck someone.

The war was everywhere, on the radio when you woke up, in the street when you went to work, at the office, on the newsreels. Middle-aged men came up to you at cocktail parties and wanted to demonstrate the stranglehold they had learned in their unarmed combat course.

The songs were a reminder of his own situation. He would never come in "On a Wing and a Prayer." Would he ever be the "Eager Beaver" with a two-day pass, givin' her that here it is Sunday shovin' off Monday line—look at that sad sack, wooin' her much too fast. She's sore, slammin' the door, and it's twenty-two miles to town! No matter, you had to "Accentuate the Positive."

Then came December 7, 1941, which upset everybody's plans. Upon hearing the news in Hollywood, where he was having lunch with John Barrymore, W. C. Fields at once went to the phone and ordered forty cases of gin. "Why only forty cases, W. C.?" queried Barrymore. "Because I think it's going to be a short war," Fields said. At the ad agency, Colonel Massek, a hero of World War I, tried to join up, but was turned down because of diabetes. Jack Anderson was drafted and sent to a base in Chicago for basic training. At the start of 1942, Burroughs was drafted and told to report to Jefferson Barracks outside St. Louis.

· FIVE ·

CHICAGO AND NEW YORK

1942–1944

I n Jefferson Barracks in the spring of 1942 there was one unhappy William Burroughs. He had volunteered his services in a number of quarters that he felt were commensurate with his intellect and abilities and had been rejected by them all. And now all of a sudden he was classified 1-A in the infantry. Brimming over with resentment, Burroughs thought, if I'm going into this thing, I'm going in as an officer, not as a fuckin' private. He liked the idea of danger and combat, but he wanted to be giving the orders, not taking them. He wanted to be wearing stripes and getting a lot of respect.

Once again, his mother came to the rescue. She knew David Rioch, a Washington neurologist involved in behavior modification studies for the government who had good connections with the military, and told him a little about Billy's psychiatric history. Rioch studied his Bellevue file and concluded, "I don't think that boy belongs in the military." He used his contacts to get Burroughs out on a civilian disability discharge—that is, he never should have been drafted in the first place because of mental instability.

Burroughs went to Chestnut Lodge, a psychiatric treatment center outside Washington, with which Rioch was connected, for a three-day evaluation. He knew that there was something wrong with him. He was aware of a deep psychic wound. There was a basic wrongness somewhere, and he thought at the time that it might be helped by analysis. He was impressed by the people at Chestnut Lodge, but he balked when he was told the treatment would probably take at least a year. As he thought of it later, it was the road not taken. Had he been treated, the wound might have healed, but who knows? Benefits are not always benefits . . . he might never have become a writer.

In the meantime, while waiting for Rioch's application to go through channels, which took four or five months, Burroughs sat around the barracks and read the complete works of Marcel Proust. Every evening at six his parents would drive out to bring him food packages. He was still the pampered younger brother.

In the barracks, Burroughs met a young man from Chicago named Ray Masterson, a short, thin, wiry, black-haired Irishman who was also awaiting discharge. Masterson told Burroughs that with so many men being drafted, jobs in Chicago were plentiful, and he decided to give it a try.

Discharged in September 1942, Burroughs left for Chicago and took a room on the North Side, across the hall from a drunken osteopath, a bear of a man who treated mostly athletes and had signed snapshots of big-league ball players. It was his custom to knock on Burroughs' door and say, "Bill, if you say one word I'll knock your block off."

Burroughs saw a lot of Ray Masterson, whose jealous wife was sure they were having an affair, which was not the case. "She's driving me crazy," Ray would say. "I wish she'd take the gas pipe." He'd stay at Burroughs' place to avoid scenes, and she would call up and say, "You're keeping him there living with you." "He's a grown man," Burroughs said. "He can walk out of here anytime he wants. If he stays over it's probably because he can't stand you." Then she insisted he put Ray on, and she screamed at Ray, "I hope he dies, I hope he gets torn to pieces . . . I'm coming over there with the cops."

The significance of the Chicago interlude in Burroughs' development is that it was his first deliberate attempt to live outside his class. Rejected by the WASP elite, he sought out lowlifes, characters like those in Jack Black's *You Can't Win*, and found acceptance among them. He lived in a poor neighborhood, where almost every kid on the block had a criminal record. They were Studs Lonigan types, unsuccessful burglars, penny-ante thieves, small-time gamblers and grifters. They weren't misfits, Burroughs decided, they just fitted into a different slot. That's what appealed to him: They formed a society of their own. He joined their Sunday afternoon crap games on the stoop. Invariably, this big fat cop would swoop down on them, and they would scatter and see the cop with his ass in the air grabbing all the change. Until one day somebody said, "Listen, the next time he runs up we'll just stand there, even if we spend the night in jail, why should we have this asshole grabbing our money?" They stood their ground, and there were no arrests.

Masterson was right about jobs in Chicago. Burroughs found work in a factory, but three days was all he could stand, taking bolts from here, and carrying them over there. Then he signed on with Merritt Inc., a detective agency that sent out teams to catch crooked store employees. This also palled, and Burroughs found a job with A. J. Cohen, Exterminators. He liked it because he could make his own hours, he drove around Chicago in his own Ford V-8 (in those days, they made Fords in any color you wanted, as long as it was black), and he got to meet all sorts of people. Chekhov said the reason he became a doctor was because of the house calls, which gave him access into the lives of families. Burroughs' new métier also involved house calls. He was assigned to apartment buildings which were required to have exterminator service, and rang doorbells: "Exterminator. You got any bugs, lady?"

He had to get ten signatures a day, which he could usually manage in two hours, so that he had the rest of the day free to bet on the horses and lose the money he earned. Then he'd go to the office at five o'clock and check in with his ten signatures. Some people didn't want the service, and they'd say, "Why should I sign if you haven't done anything?" "Well, I've come here and I've offered this service," Burroughs would reply.

He worked alone, carrying his kerosene spray for bedbugs, his pyrethrum powder and fluoride for roaches, his phosphorus paste for water bugs, his arsenic for rats, his bulbs and bellows. The fluoride did not work too well, for as a Southern defense worker told him, "They eat it and run around here fat as hawgs." Some customers complained that the city exterminators had been around and left some white powder that "draws roaches the way whiskey will draw a priest."

The pay wasn't bad, fifty dollars a week plus knockdowns. He'd go to a warehouse for a fumigation job and the manager would say, "We don't worry about the company, they make too much money, what will you take for the job?" And he'd go back on his day off and pick up ten, twenty dollars. Or a housewife would say, offering him a glass of sweet wine, "I am so bothered mit der bedbugs." "We're not allowed to spray beds, lady. Board of Health regulations." "Ach, so the wine is not enough?" She would disappear for a moment and return with a crumpled dollar bill.

Burroughs became an expert on bedbugs. He'd seen thousands of them. They weren't in the mattress, they were in the ticking. When you turned the mattress back you'd see great clusters of them. Another place you found them was in the springs, and if you had a wooden bedstead they went into the screwholes. He knew just where to find them—they might even be hiding in the wallpaper; you could see the little specks. Bedbugs were amazing survivors. They could live in an empty house for years in a state of suspended animation. Then, when the house was inhabited, they came out almost transparent, and the next thing you knew they were running around fat and red and gorged with blood. People thought it was smart to put the legs of their bed in cups of kerosene, but the bedbugs were smarter—they went up on the ceiling and dropped down.

Burroughs kept the job for eight months, longer than any other. *A distant cry echoes down cobblestone streets through all the gray basements up the outside stairs to a windy blue sky. "Exterminator!"*

That fall two of Burroughs' St. Louis friends, Lucien Carr and David Kammerer, arrived in Chicago. Carr, a handsome blond seventeen-year-old with slanting gray eyes and well-proportioned features, was a freshman at the University of Chicago. His mother, born Marion Gratz, was the daughter of a jute and hemp magnate. His father, Russell, left his wife when Lucien was an infant and went West, working as a sheepherder in Wyoming and a bank guard in Denver. He died in Denver when Lucien was a child. Lucien flew out for the funeral, looked down into his father's coffin, and said, "I don't know you, old man."

David Kammerer, who at thirty-one was three years older than Burroughs, came from a respected St. Louis family. His father was an engineer. Tall and thin with red hair, a big nose, and a high, squeaky voice, he was a *Punch* figure come to life. Burroughs liked him because he was a fellow outcast from St. Louis society, funny and unconventional. He had a friendly, open, and exuberant manner. When he dropped in on you, you were glad to see him.

When Lucien was in grade school, he joined a play group for boys run by Kammerer, who was then an instructor in English at Washington University. One afternoon a week, they drove out to St. Charles County in Dave's Model A and horsed around in the countryside. Once there was some rough and tumble in a hayloft, and Kammerer had to be taken to the doctor because he had broken a blood vessel in his penis. Boys aroused him sexually, and with one boy in particular—Lucien Carr—he became obsessed. Lucien Carr, the perfect example of the handsome upper-class boy that Kammerer could never be. Lucien Carr, presenting an image of idealized graceful blondness in contrast to Kammerer's clumsy manner and disorderly red hair.

Burroughs also liked Lucien, who made him think of Keats's line: "Two witches' eyes above a cherub's mouth." Once in St. Louis he was in an unheated house with Dave and Lucien, and he and Lucien curled up under a rug and Burroughs was sort of feeling Lucien up, and Dave was standing across the room and wringing his hands and saying, "What's this fruit stuff between you and Carr?"

Lucien was fond of Burroughs because he was funny and nonjudgmental. The story was that Burroughs had taken out this girl, Jane, who was supposed to be an easy lay, for a drive along the Missouri River, and that he had ripped open his shirt and started thumping his chest and saying, "Jane, there is a thunder in my chest." Thereafter, Lucien thought of him as "Thunder-in-my-chest Burroughs."

Another time, Lucien borrowed Burroughs' '36 Ford and went on a drunken spree in East St. Louis and blew the head off the engine. He waited four days and then called Burroughs: "You know, your car, it's over across the river and I don't think it's worth going over there to pick it up." "All right—fine," was all Burroughs said. Lucien did not offer an apology, and Burroughs did not ask for one. As someone who had been in his share of trouble, once involving a car, Burroughs was not in a position to lecture others. But Lucien appreciated his attitude, and that was the start of their friendship.

Kammerer made Lucien the focus of his existence. One summer, with Mrs. Carr's blessing, he took Lucien to Mexico, and reported to Burroughs that his advances had been rejected. But the more he was rejected the more obsessed he became. It was a contest of wills. Beyond the fact that Lucien was not homosexual, Kammerer wanted him with such intensity that he created in Lucien an equally intense resistance.

And yet Lucien was flattered by Kammerer's slavish and single-minded pursuit. When Mrs. Carr caught on, after finding letters from Kammerer, and sent Lucien to Andover, Kammerer followed him there, having been fired from Washington University for his part in a prank involving mock combat with fire extinguishers. And when Lucien later went to Bowdoin College in Maine, Kammerer tagged along and was still tagging along, now that Lucien had transferred to the University of Chicago. The story was that Lucien was trying to get away from Kammerer, but when you saw them together, they seemed to be the best of friends, drinking and horsing around. In Chicago, the high-spirited Carr-Kammerer team got Burroughs thrown out of Mrs. Murphy's roominghouse by tearing up a Gideon Bible and pissing out the window. Joe College stuff, 1910-style, Burroughs grumbled.

Burroughs at that time was cultivating his persona as a criminal in the making. He kept a gun in a sock in the back of his closet, and was dreaming up schemes to rob the world of its money. One plan was to blow up a Brink's truck as it went over a manhole. He had obtained street maps from City Hall showing manhole locations. The idea was to install a bomb under a manhole and detonate it as the armored truck drove over it. But the Brink's job never went beyond the planning stage. Then he decided to hold up a Turkish bath where he was a regular customer. He cased the joint and found out where the safe was, but on the appointed day he was drinking in a bar to get his courage up, and by the time he got to the baths the day's receipts had been collected.

Then there was some trouble between Carr and Kammerer. They went on a spree, and Carr wound up in the Cook County Hospital mental ward. Apparently, a distraught Lucien attempted suicide by putting his head in an oven, but failed to kill himself. Another version was that the whole thing was arranged to get Lucien a 4-F classification. In any event, Lucien's mother arrived and in the spring of 1943 Lucien moved to New York, transferring to Columbia as a second-term freshman. Soon after, Burroughs and Kammerer followed.

Burroughs found a place in the Village, at 69 Bedford Street. Kammerer lived around the corner, at 48 Morton Street, where he worked as a janitor in exchange for a room. Kammerer also found a job teaching in a high school, but he had grown a beard and was told to shave it. He did, but when he went to get his first paycheck they made him come back twice and he got fed up and quit, grew his beard back, and supported himself as a window-washer. His co-workers called him "the professor." On his first job, he lost his balance and dove through an open window into a ribbon-maker's office, and found himself lying on the floor, coiled in ribbons, like an Egyptian mummy.

Burroughs saw a lot of Kammerer. They went for dinner to Chumley's and the Minetta Tavern, and for drinks to the San Remo, where on occasion that village character Joe Gould would turn up. He was purportedly writing "The Oral History of the World," and smelled as though he hadn't taken a bath in twenty years. If you bought him a drink he'd do his seagull act, flapping his arms and making strange sounds.

Burroughs was friendly with a twenty-one-year-old Talk of the Town reporter for *The New Yorker* named Chandler Brossard, who lived in Kammerer's building and took them to a French restaurant, Au Bon Pinard, where the prix fixe dinner cost $1.50. Burroughs introduced him to eating calves' liver rare. Brossard, who was not homosexual, was fascinated by the elegant provincial style of the two St. Louis men. They were literate and charming and had interesting speech patterns. He told them about a strangely beautiful boy working as a checker at *The New Yorker* who seemed to have some literary talent. His name was Truman Capote, but Brossard said, "I can't introduce him to you vultures." When he did arrange a meeting, Burroughs didn't think he was beautiful at all—he had a squeaky voice and looked like a wizened, prematurely aged albino.

Lucien Carr came around often to see Kammerer, particularly when he needed a term paper in a hurry. Brossard thought he was a shallow little prick, and couldn't understand Kammerer's infatuation. "What's the matter with you anyway?" he asked Dave. "If he doesn't love me," Dave said, "why is he always around me?" On Jane Street, when Lucien jumped up to touch an overhanging branch, Dave said, "Isn't he wonderful?"

In Dave's room Carr and Kammerer were always wrestling on the floor, like the two men in D. H. Lawrence's *Women in Love*. It seemed to Brossard that men who spent so much time wrestling must like each other, even though Dave was kind of cuckoo, and Lucien was like some funny inauthentic soap opera ingenue. Burroughs also tried to reason with Kammerer, saying, "This is silly, Dave, what you're doing is selfish, you're not really interested in him, you're interested in yourself, and what you're trying to accomplish is not at all to his advantage."

Because naval cadets known as V-12s, who had to do ninety days of college to become officers, were occupying the student dorms at Columbia, Lucien had a room in Union Theological Seminary. One afternoon in December 1943, he was in his room playing records, and put on the Brahms Trio no. 1. There was a knock on the door, and a thin young man with horn-rimmed glasses and jug ears asked what the music was. The young man introduced himself—his name was Allen Ginsberg, he was seventeen years old, from Paterson, New Jersey, and was attending Columbia thanks to a stipend from the Y.M.H.A. there. As he rattled on, Ginsberg was struck by Lucien's blond good looks, and he was reminded of Rimbaud in the famous photograph with the tousled hair— Lucien had the same cat's eyes.

Allen's father Louis was a schoolteacher and old-fashioned poet whose rhymed and metered verse appeared occasionally on the editorial page of *The New York Times*. He loved jokes and word play and was known as the Paterson pundit or the Paterson punny man. "Is life worth living, it depends on the liver" was one of his expressions. "I've got no axiom to grind" was another.

His mother, Naomi, was a Communist who idolized Stalin and the party line. At the age of seven, Allen began accompanying her to party meetings off River Street in New York, where she sold little bags of garbanzos to raise money for worthy causes. Naomi was in and out of mental institutions. At one point, her doctor recommended a prefrontal lobotomy, which was performed. From the hospital, Naomi wrote Allen: "The wire is still on my head, and the sunshine is trying to help me. It has a wire department, but the wire that's outside my head, the sun doesn't touch."

Some of his mother's radicalism rubbed off on Allen, who at the age of fifteen began writing letters to the editor of *The New York Times*. The chief cause of World War II, he wrote on December 28, 1941, was that the United States had not joined the League of Nations, which he blamed on "the mental impotence and political infirmity on the part of a handful of U.S. Congressmen. . . . One can gather infinite consolation by speculation as to what will happen to those congressmen when they go to Hell . . . the devil has prepared a nice hot bath ready for many more senators."

Another letter protested the announced deportation of the West Coast labor leader Harry Bridges, for Allen was a student of labor history and his ambition was to become a labor lawyer. Indeed, one day on the ferry between Hoboken and New York, he had dropped to his knees and prayed that if he was admitted to Columbia he would devote his life to saving the working class in America.

Much taken with Lucien, Allen started hanging out with him at the West End. Lucien was very literary, and talked about such and such a scene in Dostoevsky and such and such a scene in Flaubert. There were all-night rap sessions about art and truth. Their literary mentors were renegades of culture like Rimbaud and Baudelaire. Lucien himself was Rimbaud-like, a combination of intellect and mischief, of heavy thoughts and unpredictable acts. When he had been drinking, which was often, he would chew broken glass or throw a plate of food on the floor. He was the master of the gratuitous act. "Know these words," Allen wrote in his journal, "and you speak the Carr language: fruit, phallus, prurience, clitoris, cacoethes [a bad habit or itch, as in "itch for writing"], feces, foetus, womb, Rimbaud."

One day, around Christmas 1943, Lucien asked Allen to come with him to see a friend who lived on Morton Street. On the subway downtown, they had an argument about art. The question was, if someone on the moon carved a walking stick, and no one saw it, was it art? In other words, did art have to be seen, or was it self-justifying?

Upon arriving, they found Kammerer at home with a thin, gray, cadaverous-looking man who introduced himself to Allen as William Burroughs. They were talking about a fight that had taken place in a lesbian bar, during which one woman had bitten another's ear, and Burroughs commented: "In the words of the immortal bard, ' 'tis too starved an argument for my sword.' " Allen was impressed. He had never heard Shakespeare quoted before in an ordinary conversation. Then, commenting on a young lesbian who lived in his building, Burroughs described her as "straightforward, manly, and reliable." Allen was struck by the originality of his mind, the sharpness of his comments, his sardonic humor.

To the seventeen-year-old college freshman, Burroughs seemed to be a fount of wisdom.

Going back to the discussion on the subway, Allen asked Burroughs what he thought art was. "Art is a three-letter word," Burroughs replied, trotting out Korzybski. Didn't they know anything about General Semantics? Didn't they know that a word was not the thing it represented? To Allen, he seemed to be cutting through the intellectual miasma so widespread at Columbia, the sophomoric attachment to concepts as if they had some ultimate meaning.

Burroughs, Allen thought, was remarkable. Here was this distinguished Harvard man and member of the University Club, always correctly dressed in a three-piece suit and snap-brim hat, who had theories on everything and rattled off page after page of Shakespeare. Allen began to jot down things he said, such as "I like disreputable characters. They amuse me." He noted that when Burroughs said, "I am glad to see you," he looked away, and that he washed his hands after receiving visitors.

Burroughs at that time was living a rather desultory life, collecting his monthly $200 allowance check at the University Club, which was sent on condition that he continue to see a psychiatrist, and working odd jobs. He was a bartender in Times Square for about two weeks, and he worked for the Shorten Detective Agency, mostly serving papers on people. He mentioned to Lucien Carr that he might try to join the merchant marine while the war was still on, but he didn't know how to go about getting papers. Carr said he had a friend named Jack Kerouac who had shipped out a couple of times and would give him advice.

Kerouac was a Canuck, raised in a Catholic blue-collar family in Lowell, Massachusetts. French was his first language. He didn't speak English until he was six, and had an accent well into his teens. His father, Leo, a fat and balding Archie Bunker type, was a linotypist. His mother, Gabrielle, played the piano and sang French-Canadian ditties when she wasn't quarreling with her husband. Jack won a football scholarship to the Horace Mann School, which brought him to New York and to the attention of Columbia coach Lou Little. He entered Columbia in the fall of 1940, playing halfback on the freshman team, but in his second game he cracked his right tibia and was out of action for the rest of the season. In sophomore year, there was a personality conflict with Little, who made fun of him and said he was too small to be a back. Kerouac quit school, and signed on the S.S. *Dorchester* to Murmansk in mid-1942. When he got back in October, Columbia still wanted him, but Lou Little benched him because he had lost weight at sea. So he enlisted in the navy, but found that he could not handle the discipline, and got himself discharged as "schizoid" in May 1943. A month later, he signed on the S.S. *George Weems*, which was carrying 500-pound bombs to Liverpool, as an ordinary seaman on the four-to-eight watch.

He was back in October, and moved into the apartment of his girlfriend, Edie Parker, at 421 West 118th Street. It was there that Lucien brought Burroughs in February 1944. "Not in the service?" Jack asked. "Oh, no," said Burroughs, "just 4-F, *phnunk*." *Phnunk* was the noise he made when he blew out his sinuses. To Kerouac, Burroughs appeared "inscrutable because ordinary looking . . . like a shy bank clerk with a patrician thin-lipped cold blue-lipped face, blue eyes saying nothing behind steel rims and glass, sandy hair, a little wispy, a little of the wistful German Nazi youth as his soft hair fluffles in the breeze."

Burroughs did not at that time pursue the merchant marine option, but the connection was made, with Kerouac on the one hand, and Ginsberg on the other, and this basic triangular friendship would be at the heart of a literary movement. Lucien Carr's role was as go-between, or in-troducer. There were visits back and forth. Burroughs gave parties on Bedford Street, emerging on one occasion from the kitchen with a plate of razor blades and light bulbs, and saying, "I've got something real nice in the way of delicacies my mother sent me this week, *hmf hmf hmf*." He gave Kerouac a two-volume edition of Spengler's *Decline of the West*, saying, "Edify your mind, my boy, with the grand actuality of fact."

Burroughs thought Jack should make the most of his merchant marine experience, and told him one day on a park bench on Broadway, "Why don't you wear a merchant seaman uniform like you said you wore in London for your visit there, and get a lot of soft entries into things, it's wartime isn't it, and here you go around in T-shirt and chino pants, and nobody knows you're a serviceman proud, should we say?"

"It's a finkish thing to do," Jack said.

"It's a finkish world," Burroughs replied.

Edie Parker, Jack's girl, came from a wealthy family in the Detroit suburb of Grosse Pointe. Her father was a playboy who had a yacht on Lake St. Clair and sold Packards, and her mother operated a chain of shoe stores. In the fall of 1941, Edie arrived in New York to take evening classes at Columbia. She lived with her grandparents, who had an apart-ment on West 116th Street. Edie was a lovely high-spirited girl who looked like the young Barbara Stanwyck. She was interested in boys, not books, and practically had her private platoon of V-12s.

Edie's grandfather wanted her in by ten-thirty, but fortunately he was a sound sleeper, and her grandmother was deaf, so she would go to bed with her clothes on and wait until she heard snoring, and then she'd stay out until all hours. She was dating a big, good-looking guy called Henry Cru, who was in the merchant marine, and that October, Henry introduced her to his pal Kerouac. Jack was shorter than Henry, but so handsome, with warm brown eyes and hair that fell into his eyes, and a shy manner. When he wrote her a love letter and called her his "little lost sparrow," she was hooked.

Then came December 7, and they all felt as if they had stuck their finger in an electric socket. One of Edie's cousins had a Cadillac delivered on December 8. It was the last car to come off the assembly line with five tires. The order had come down to "hold the spare." Henry Cru shipped out and left Edie in Jack's care, which was like having an ice cream cone put into your hand and being told not to eat it. Jack had quit Columbia and was working the switchboard at the Hotel Bates on 115th Street, where he had a room. She spent many happy hours in that room.

Neither of them used anything, and Edie soon found herself pregnant, but she didn't know whether it was by Jack or by Henry Cru. Terrified, she told her grandmother, who took her to see a doctor in the Bronx, on the Grand Concourse. By this time she was in her fifth month, and the doctor force-labored her, and the child came out stillborn but fully formed, a boy, which the doctor dropped in a bucket. In the summer of 1942, Jack shipped out for Murmansk.

Then Henry Cru came back and presented Edie with a three-carat diamond engagement ring, but she told him about the baby and said, "I don't know if it was yours, I slept with Jack more than you." In October, Jack was back from his Murmansk trip, and she and Henry Cru met him at the popular Columbia hangout, the West End Bar, at Broadway and 114th. "I have some very bad news," Cru said. "When you and I were gone, Edith had an abortion . . . and she thinks it was your child." Jack downed his drink in silence, slammed his fist on the table, got up, and walked out. At two in the morning he knocked on Edie's door and told her he loved her and that they would live together.

By this time, Edie was sharing an apartment with an eighteen-year-old Barnard girl she had met at the West End, Joan Vollmer Adams. Joan was from Loudonville, a suburb of Albany, where her father, David W. Vollmer, managed a plant belonging to the German filmmaker Gevaert, which was seized by the Alien Property Custodian in 1942, so that Vollmer operated the plant for the government.

Joan was five foot six, with a heart-shaped face, a small, turned-up nose, soft brown eyes that were set wide apart, and shoulder-length light brown hair with short bangs. She had a lovely complexion and a nice figure, with legs a little on the heavy side. When she walked her calves wiggled. Joan's beauty was more than the sum of its parts. She was soft and feminine, and wore silky clinging clothes and small bandannas tied close to her head. In her reserve, in her achievement of a personal style, she reminded Edie of Garbo.

"You should always cook eggs slowly," was Joan's advice in the kitchen on 118th Street. Joan did everything slowly, Edie reflected; she spoke, walked, dressed and read slowly, as if savoring every moment. She read everything, every newspaper and magazine. In *The New Yorker*, she liked the cartoons of William Steig, particularly the one of the dejected fellow saying, "My mother loved me but she died." Joan didn't get along with her mother, and felt that she had nothing in common with her parents' country-club existence. She had rebelled against her background by living the New York bohemian life.

Edie thought Joan was the most intelligent girl she had ever met. She had an independent mind, always questioning what anyone said, including her teachers at Barnard. In one of her marginal notes in her copy of Marx's *Capital and Other Writings*, there are echoes of Burroughs' thinking: "Maybe Marxism is dynamic and optimistic, and Freudianism is not. Is one more serviceable than the other? Why does it always have to be either/or?"

Joan's idea of a good time was to go to Child's at 110th Street and Broadway and sip *kümmel* and have deep conversations about Plato and Kant while listening to classical music. Or she would spend the entire morning in the bathtub, with bubble-bath up to her chin, reading Proust. If you wanted to talk to her you had to do it in the bathroom.

At that time she was married to a tall, curly-haired law student named Paul Adams, who had been drafted in the infantry and was stationed in Tennessee. But like Edie, Joan had an eye for the boys. She was the first girl Edie knew who had a diaphragm. Joan made sexual appraisals of men, of the sort men usually make about women, evaluating them as "cocksmen." When Kerouac returned from Liverpool in October 1943 and went straight to Edie's, he said, "The first thing I'm going to do . . ." and Joan said, "Oh, ho, Edie's going to get screwed tonight . . ." And that was the first night Edie gave him a blow job, because Joan had advised, "*Blow* Jack." "That old seadog Joan," Jack reflected, "had already been instructing her all summer, while I was at sea, how to please me at love."

In 1942, Joan had an affair with a Columbia student, and became pregnant. She decided to convince her husband that the baby was his, but to do that she had to get him to New York on leave in a hurry. Wondering with Edie what to do, she decided that she would pull an

Ophelia act and get sent to Bellevue. Edie took her down to Times Square one rainy evening, and Joan walked in the rain with one foot in the gutter and the other on the sidewalk, and then sat in front of the Horn and Hardon (as they called the Horn & Hardart cafeteria), acting goofy, talking to herself and playing with strands of wet hair.

In those innocent times, that was enough to get you committed. An ambulance arrived and took her to Bellevue, as Edie watched from across the street. Paul was summoned from his army base and got Joan out of the hospital and took her home. She told him she had flipped out because she missed him so much. Seven months later, in early 1943, Joan gave birth to a daughter, Julie.

Edie and Joan found a four-bedroom, sixth-floor apartment at 420 West 119th Street at forty-three dollars a month, in the rear, with a big, well-lit living room. There was plenty of room for guests, and at the start of 1944 a precocious, sixteen-year-old Columbia freshman named John Kingsland moved in. He was another of Joan's lovers, who had been thrown out of his dorm for bringing Joan up there.

Kingsland still had baby fat on his face, but wore three-piece Brooks Brothers suits and acted like a cross between Oscar Wilde and Noël Coward. He liked to tell stories of how he had put the employees of the department stores he patronized in their place. He looked like a juvenile version of the English actor Alan Mowbray, and one of his idols was Tallulah Bankhead, whose languid delivery he emulated, with the emphasis on certain words, saying things like "We've just come from the most *strikingly putrid* picture I've ever had the misfortune to see."

Joan and John Kingsland were updating the situation described in Raymond Radiguet's World War I novel, *Le Diable au Corps*: A married woman, with her husband away in the army, takes a boy as a lover. The real-life situation was just as dramatic as the novel, for Kingsland's parents, who lived in Brooklyn, got wind of the affair. One day the outraged parents appeared on Joan's doorstep and told her they were going to have her arrested for corrupting the morals of a minor. Kingsland held them off by promising to look for another room.

In the meantime, Joan was his tutor in matters of love. She also helped him with his term papers, writing one for his course on Dryden and the eighteenth century in the manner of a Dryden poem, which the professor, Joseph Wood Krutch, liked well enough to give him an "A." His papers were in fact so brilliant that Kingsland worried that his teachers would get suspicious.

Joan had a healthy appetite for sex, and the problem was that she would take her diaphragm out at night, and forget to reinsert it in the morning, and as a result she had to have two abortions. The abortions were a strain on her finances, and she found a job in a nursery school. Kingsland arranged to take all his classes in the afternoon, and spent the mornings in the apartment minding Julie. Then when Joan came home he went to class and to his evening job in the library. Joan asked her husband for a divorce, but he refused, which was just as well, because she continued to get his allotment.

Since they needed the money and had the space, they took in a boarder, Hal Chase, a graduate student from Denver studying anthropology. Hal was blond and handsome in an angular way and had that Colorado "white Indian" look. He thought of life on 119th Street as a psychodrama. No one went to class. People came and went like actors in a play, delivering soliloquies. When Jack was around, he wrote, talked, drank beer, and fucked Edie. When he shipped out, Edie was always flanked by at least two V-12s, flicking her cigarettes *à la* Barbara Stanwyck. The V-12s, or ninety-day wonders, had taken over Columbia, marching in groups up Broadway and Amsterdam Avenue—the streets and classrooms were filled with white-hatted blue uniforms.

Lucien Carr came around with his beautiful long-haired blond girl friend, Celine Young. Celine was a flirt, and one evening when Lucien was in the bathroom, she began to neck with Kingsland. This got back to Lucien via the talkative Allen Ginsberg, who wondered whether she had done it as a gesture of defiance or because she was cooling toward Lucien.

"As a matter of fact," Lucien said, "that night we copulated for the first time."

"*Bon Dieu!*" said Allen, who had secret hankerings for Lucien. "At last! Well!"

Then Celine was pregnant, and took female hormones to force a miscarriage, and miscarried in the bathtub on 119th Street, with Joan mopping up the blood. Another frequent visitor was the bushy-haired David Kammerer, who was jealous of Celine and always looking for Lucien: "I must find Lucien, I have a message for him." Edie didn't like Dave, because he dominated the conversation, and all he could talk about was Lucien. She and Joan had to clean up the mess these guys made. When Hal Chase heard Joan sweeping the floor with a whisk broom, he sometimes felt that she was trying to whisk him out. Joan was in fact annoyed with Hal, who raided the icebox daily, not even sparing Julie's milk, so that she finally had to bolt and lock it.

From time to time Burroughs would show up. He was older and more worldly, and would take them to a Chinese restaurant and teach them to use chopsticks, or to the Russian Tea Room for borscht. One night at the West End they were sitting with a fellow who started bragging that he had flown for Loyalist Spain, and went into graphic descriptions of dogfights over Madrid and Barcelona. Burroughs called his bluff, saying, "Well, I flew for Franco," and asking the fellow whether he had flown a Spad or a Heinkel, and discussing the merits of various planes, and recalling details of battles, deflating the fellow completely and pushing the gag to the point where he said that on such and such a day they had fought in a dogfight on opposite sides, but could shake hands now that the war was over.

All in all it was a carefree time, a time of free-form discussion groups, and watching the dawn come up after a night of listening to jazz, and evenings drinking in the West End, with the heavy oak booths that could seat six comfortably, or eight squeezing, and the sawdust on the floor, and Johnny the bartender in his white apron. Life had an almost stately pace. There were streetcars in the middle of Broadway then.

They were an extended family, a pre-sixties commune, with Joan and Edie as den mothers. It seemed to Hal Chase that in all the books he later wrote, Kerouac had tried to duplicate the marathon discussions they had on 119th Street. Hal's only complaint was that with all the talking and carousing, he didn't have time for normal activities. These people didn't want to learn, they wanted to emote, to soak up the world.

As in all families, there were little crises. One weekend when John Kingsland had to attend a family function in Brooklyn, Joan was so annoyed at being left alone that she slept with Jack Kerouac. When Kingsland got back, she announced what she had done, which did not overjoy him, or Edie for that matter. But they all stayed friends in spite of it.

A quarter of a century later, on October 24, 1969, at the funeral service for Jack in Lowell's St. Jean Baptiste Church, Edie reflected that those days on 119th Street had been the best of times. Looking around, she saw that Lucien was not there—the news had so upset him that he had bitten his tongue, so badly that he had to be hospitalized. Burroughs was out of the country, as usual. Allen was there, saying that Jack looked like a painted Buddha doll.

Jack had on a black-and-white-plaid sports jacket, white shirt, and bow tie. Edie was reminded of the time she and Lucien had taken him to Brooks Brothers and bought his first black-and-white sports jacket, after convincing him that the natural tailoring and understated shoulders would be to his advantage. When she saw the position of Jack's coffin, she thought of a little secret she and Jack had shared. He had lost his virginity about three feet to the left from where he was now lying, having brought a girl into the church one afternoon and fucked her in a confessional.

· SIX ·

"AND THE HIPPOS
WERE BOILED
IN THEIR TANKS"
1944

I n the summer of 1944, victory in Europe seemed within the grasp
of the Allies as thousands of troops successfully landed on defended
beaches in Normandy, and after weeks of fighting, began to enlarge
the pocket. On the home front, the commune had moved to 421 West
118th Street and was going full blast. There was an interminable discussion
about Wolfeans versus non-Wolfeans, with Kerouac arguing the merits
of Thomas Wolfe's confessional discursiveness, and Burroughs putting it
down as hogwash.

With Hal Chase, Burroughs and Kerouac acted out scenes from André
Gide's novel *The Counterfeiters*, the story of a motiveless murder. With
Ginsberg, they improvised comic skits. In one of these, Kerouac, wearing
a straw hat, played the innocent American, while Ginsberg was the oily
Hungarian who had escaped from the Nazis with his family heirlooms,
and Burroughs was the unscrupulous contessa who was leading the innocent American into the arms of the oily Hungarian. To make his performance more convincing, Burroughs wore a bonnet and spoke in a
squeaky accented voice. The charade in retrospect might be seen as a
timely parable on the loss of American innocence through involvement
in world affairs. Or, as Kerouac was later to write: "Shure did love
America AS America in those days."

Another topic of conversation was the Carr-Kammerer dilemma. As
Burroughs put it, "When they get together, something happens, and they
form a combination that gets on everybody's nerves." Now that Lucien

had a steady girlfriend, Kammerer was frantic. He explained at length to Burroughs that making it with Lucien was not what he was after, he wanted affection, a permanent attachment. Kammerer constantly rehashed the Lucien question—what had Lucien meant when he said this, and when he said that? Was Lucien really in love with Celine? Was Celine good for him? He didn't look well; she seemed to be sucking the life out of him, like a vampire.

Burroughs was fed up with Kammerer, and was also getting fed up with Lucien and his philosophizing. Lucien went on about the New Vision, which he had lifted from Yeats, and which had to do with a society of artist-citizens. "Rimbaud thought he was God," Lucien said. "Maybe that's the primary requisite. In Cabala man stands on the threshold of vegetable life and between him and God remains only a misty shroud. But suppose you actually projected yourself as God, as the sun, then what would you see and know?" As far as Burroughs was concerned, it was all in the "I-don't-want-to-hear-about-it" department.

Kammerer was so fixated that on one occasion he climbed up the fire escape of Lucien's dormitory, Warren Hall, in the middle of the night, went in the open window, and sat there for hours, just watching Lucien as he slept. "My Gawd," said Burroughs when Dave told him, "suppose you'd-a found the wrong room and hovered over a perfect stranger?"

Then he would go to the other extreme, after seeing Lucien neck with Celine on 118th Street, and vow that he would never see him again. One such time, he was with a friend on Morton Street when Lucien arrived and he barred the door and said, "Stay out of here. I told you never to come here again." Lucien barged in and Kammerer slugged him and Lucien fell on the floor, and said in amazement, "You never hit me before." Kammerer threw him out and locked the door, and then said to the friend: "You're welcome to stay. And come any time you want. But don't ever bring that little bastard here, I don't want him around." Then he added with a laugh, "I suppose he wants me to write a term paper for him."

For a variety of reasons, Lucien felt he needed to get away: away from Dave, away from Celine, away from school. One night at the West End, he said to Jack: "Let's you and me ship out. Don't tell a soul about this. Let's try to get a ship to France. . . . We'll walk to Paris. I'll be a deaf mute and you speak country French and we'll pretend we're peasants. When we get to Paris it will probably be on the verge of being liberated. . . . I feel like I'm in a pond that's drying up and I'm about to suffocate."

"Paris," Jack said. "All we have is a strip of the Normandy peninsula." But he thought, why not, he wouldn't mind getting out of the city for a while, and he needed the money, because Edie was bugging him about getting married. Jack had shipped out a couple of times already, he loved the sea, and had written something called *The Sea Is My Brother*. With Lucien along, he wouldn't be so much of a loner, which had caused problems on his previous voyages.

In a larger sense, both men felt the need to involve themselves in an epic situation, an adventure that would bring them to Europe at a historic time. Force-fed with literature, they saw themselves as akin to the heroes in novels. There were precedents in the books they had read for going away to sea and leaving friends and loved ones behind, which somehow validated their action.

Jack, who already had his papers, explained that Lucien would need a Coast Guard pass, a War Shipping Administration waiver, and membership in the National Maritime Union. When Lucien was set, they went down to the NMU hall on West Seventeenth Street, one day in late July. The long, low hiring hall was crowded with seamen sitting in folding chairs, or playing Ping-Pong, or thumbing through magazines at racks stocked with *The Pilot* (the union weekly), the *Daily Worker*, and *P.M.* A dispatcher called the jobs over the mike, most of them for Liberty ships carrying war matériel to Europe: "Barber Line Liberty on line eight. We need two A.B.'s, two ordinaries, a fireman water-tender, three wipers, and two messmen. This ship is going far, far away on a long cold trip . . . you better bring your long underwear."

Jack and Lucien put in their cards. The idea was to get on the same ship, but Lucien had no seniority and his card was sent back—so was Jack's for that matter, for he was in arrears on his dues. So they went down day after day, having great trouble finding a ship, but finally they signed on the S.S. *Robert Hayes*, Kerouac as an able-bodied and Lucien as an ordinary. "Report tomorrow at eight o'clock," the dispatcher said, "and bring all your gear."

When Jack got home and told Edie he was shipping out, she was furious. "You know why Lucien wants to ship out with you, don't you?" she said. "No, why?" Jack asked, throwing his pants on the chair.

"Because he's a queer and wants to make you."

"What?" Jack said.

"Don't what me. Some night at sea when he jumps on you you'll know what I'm talking about."

"You're nuts," Jack said.

"You've been living with me for a whole year, you've been promising to marry me, I've been giving you money, now you start hanging around with a bunch of queers and don't come home at night."

"Oh, for Christ's sake," Jack said.

Then he felt Edie's knee ramming his balls, and her knuckles punching his head. So he slapped her in the face and she went down, capsizing a bedside table that had talcum powder and an ashtray heaped with cigarette butts on it, and she lay there spitting out ashes, with talcum all over her face and her dress up over her knees, screaming: "You bastard! You're trying to mar my beauty!" But a few minutes later she was fine, and joined Jack on the bed, and said, "When you get back from this trip we'll get a new apartment."

That night, Burroughs gave a party, and Kammerer and Jack and Lucien were there, and Lucien said: "Well, we're shipping out tomorrow. We've been assigned to a ship and report at the pier tomorrow morning."

"Can I count on that?" Burroughs asked. "I'm getting sick of these abortive departures."

Burroughs had on an old seersucker jacket with a hole in the elbow no bigger than a dime, and suddenly Lucien stuck a finger in the elbow and ripped the sleeve. Kammerer joined the fun and ripped the back, and soon the jacket was hanging on him in shreds. Burroughs took the shreds and tied them together in a long rope, which he strung around the room like a festoon. Kammerer was in high spirits, not seeming to mind Lucien's departure.

The next morning, Jack and Lucien arrived at Pier 15 in Brooklyn, and Jack asked the guard, "Is the *Robert Hayes* here?" "She sure is, son," he replied. "She's all yours." They walked through a cool warehouse that smelled of coffee beans. Hundreds of longshoremen were loading ships on both sides of the wharf. Foremen yelled, winches creaked, a huge crane was lifting a 20mm antiaircraft gun to the flying bridge of a ship. A little truck trailing a string of wagons darted around a corner and almost ran them down.

To the right, they saw the great hull of the *Robert Hayes* streaked with oil and rust, water pouring from her scuppers. Several men carrying seabags came toward them, whom Jack recognized from the union hall. "I'm supposed to be goin' on as bosun," one of them said. "What about you?" "A.B. and ordinary," Jack said.

"Well, listen," the bosun said. "I shipped out with the mate on this one before and he is a bastard, let me tell you. The work's never good enough for him. None of us guys intend to sign on because the mate is a prick and we gotta see he acts right with us." They went aboard, and Jack led Lucien to an empty forecastle where they picked out two lower bunks. Then he took him up to the bow and had him lean over and look at the anchor and the anchor chain. Pointing out the jumbo block, he said, "This thing weighs over a hundred pounds, and it's just one of the little gadgets you work with on deck." He took Lucien topsides and showed him the wheelhouse, and belowdecks to the refrigerator storage.

The door was open, and they walked in and helped themselves to roast beef and cold milk from gallon cans. Then they went back to the forecastle, got some towels from the linen locker, and took showers. Jack stretched out on his bunk, turned on the bulkhead light over his pillow, and started to read a book, saying, "See? This is the way you do at sea, just lie down in your bunk and read." Lucien took a gas mask and a steel helmet from the top of his locker, put on the helmet, and said, "We're going to see action."

At this point, a six-foot-four, red-haired man wearing a dirty officer's cap and some old khakis stepped into the forecastle, yelling, "Did you sign on yet?"

"Are they signing on?" Jack asked innocently.

"Yeah, we're signing on."

"Well," Jack said, "the bosun . . . and the other guys . . . told us to wait until later."

"Yeah," said the red-haired giant, who Jack had realized was the bastard chief mate. "Get off the ship."

"Why?"

"Ask me once more and I'll throw you off myself."

"But . . ."

"Never mind buts. Who do you guys think you are anyway? You come on a ship, you sign on. If you don't want to sign, get off . . . and drop a couple of quarters in the kitty for using the shower."

Jack and Lucien were too stunned to move.

"Did you hear what I said?" the chief mate shouted. "Get off! I don't want anybody in my crew that won't cooperate."

"All right, don't get your water hot," Jack said. Turning to Lucien, he said, "Get your stuff. We're not staying on this damn ship." He picked up his bags, started for the gangplank, and hollered, "Fuck you all" down the alleyway.

In front of the gangplank, they saw the bosun who had told them not to sign on. "Listen," he said, "you guys want to sign on and they won't let you? Okay. That means you go down to the beef window at the union hall and collect a month's pay from the company, see? Union rules say a seaman can't be turned away once he's assigned to a ship. Do you follow me?"

Jack borrowed a quarter from the bosun so they could get home and said to the disconsolate-looking Lucien, who already saw himself marching on Paris with his steel helmet, "Don't worry, Monday we'll go to the beef window and get another ship."

Allen Ginsberg could not get over that this amazing group of people liked him and accepted him. He wasn't sure that he was likable. They liked him even though Jack and Lucien made fun of his ambition to be a labor lawyer, saying, "You don't know what the fuck you're talking about, you've never set foot in a factory." It was a topic of some hilarity. Uncertain about himself, about his sexual orientation, about what to do after college, Allen drew comfort from his new friends. Their world was certainly more real than the world of the university. What a group! Jack, with his unrestrained pursuit of experience, his appreciation of the beauty and ugliness of life, and his compassionate perception. Burroughs, with all his cynical humor and English lord mannerisms, had a melancholy strain. He saw that things would never be the same again. Partly it was the war, which gave one an apprehension of one's mortality. Partly it was something in the air, a feeling of transience. *We are such stuff as dreams are made of.* And Kammerer, who was so brilliant on Meredith and Hardy, and so obtuse on Lucien. Kammerer, who could sit cross-legged on the floor and go on for two hours on some arcane facet of Buddhism, was also a secret cripple, an intruder, lurking about unwanted. And yet one had to understand Kammerer, because Lucien was unstable, withdrawing the little he gave. Lucien was the intriguing bad boy, hard to resist—even Professor (Lionel) Trilling liked him.

Allen had a semihumorous sparring relationship with Lucien. Their talks were jousts, or fencing matches, in which the winner could claim *touché.* Allen jotted them down in his journal:

> Carr: "Really, Ginsberg, you bore me."
> Ginsberg: "Perhaps that shows a limitation on your part."
> Carr: "Now, Ginsberg, don't take refuge in insult."
> Ginsberg: "You're hypersensitive to insult."
> Carr: "Ah, first you tell me I'm limited, then you tell me I'm hypersensitive. Really, Ginsberg, you bore me."

In his journal, Allen wrote this assessment of Lucien:

> He said he could not write, he was a perfectionist. He compared himself not with those around him but with a high imagined self.

He feared that he was not creative, that he could not achieve his imagined potential. He rationalized his failures, but adopted the postures and attitudes of the intellectual for recognition. Carr and his scarred ego. He had to be a genius or nothing, and since he couldn't be creative he turned to bohemianism, eccentricity, social versatility, conquests.

After the Brooklyn fiasco, there had been no further attempt on the part of Lucien and Jack to ship out. The problem with Kammerer remained unsolved, and on August 13, 1944, Dave met Allen on a traffic island on Broadway to go over his predicament once again. He described his desperate affection. Should he give Lucien up or not? Allen saw a man with all defenses down, open and disarmed. He was like Verlaine in pursuit of Rimbaud, ungainly and ugly and obsessed. He needed advice, but Allen did not know what to tell him. Finally, Kammerer said he was shipping out, and suggested Allen do the same. "Oh, Ginsberg, heed the call of the artist," he said. "Reverend sybarite, forsake thy calling." "Art waits on humanity for the moment," Ginsberg said. "That's right," Kammerer replied. "Burroughs called you the bourgeois Rimbaud last night."

Later that day, Allen ran into Lucien, who said he had been to his room looking for him, and had found instead the journal entry Allen had written about him. With mock sorrow, Lucien said he had written a note in the margin: "Notice the tears in your most definitive work."

That night Allen went to the West End. Lucien arrived drunk after having had dinner with his mother, who had moved to New York, at her apartment on East Fifty-seventh Street. "I'll tell you about the fight I had with my mother," Lucien said. "I had a time with the old girl tonight. She's good in an argument. A good Phi Beta baby."

"What was it about?" Allen asked.

"My insanity record [from the mental hospital in Chicago]. She finally got me to burn it."

"No? Oh, what a misfortune. You've lost the only family heirloom. . . . How did she get you to?"

"She just asked me. So I argued. I told her to put a twenty-dollar bill in it and I'd do it. She said okay, but with my money. I offered to put ten in if she put ten, so she smiled and said no, either all your money or none at all. Then I offered to burn it free, only on the carpet. She said no, so I gave in, and we put a big ashtray on the table, lit the paper, and giggled while it burned. We even turned the lights out. . . . It's symbolic, I suppose."

"Yes, of her little Lucien's normalcy," Allen said. He asked Lucien where Celine was.

"Oh, up in Pelham," Lucien said. "She asked me up tonight. I don't know why I didn't go. I should have. There's nothing doing here."

Just then Kammerer walked in and came up to their booth, his long red face leering. "Well, well, fighting as usual," he said. Lucien rose and went to the bar with Dave, and Allen could see them knocking back drinks and arguing heatedly. Eventually they left, carrying a bottle.

At dawn the next morning, August 14, 1944, Burroughs was awakened by a knock on his door. He got up, put on his bathrobe, and answered. It was Lucien, wild-eyed and distraught. "I just killed the old man," he said.

"What?"

Lucien handed Burroughs a blood-stained pack of Lucky Strikes and said, "Have the last cigarette."

"So this is how Dave Kammerer ends," Burroughs said, half to himself.

"We were standing on the bank of the river and I stabbed him and threw him in the water."

"You'd better turn yourself in," Burroughs said. "You could plead some sort of self-defense."

"I'll get the hot seat," Lucien said.

"Don't be absurd. Get a good lawyer and do what he tells you to do. Say what he tells you to say. Make a case for self-defense. It's pretty preposterous but juries have swallowed bigger ones than that."

Lucien left, and Burroughs thought: So this is the way it ends. It had a sort of inevitability, going back to the early days in St. Louis. When he thought of Dave, he thought of what Toots Shor had said about Jimmy Walker at his coffin: Jimmy, Jimmy, when you walked in, you brightened up the joint. Burroughs tore the pack of Luckies into tiny pieces and flushed it down the toilet.

Not long after, around six that morning, Edie and Jack were asleep in their bedroom on 118th Street when Lucien barged in, threw Kammerer's glasses on the table, and said, "I just got rid of the old man."

"What'd you really do?" Jack asked.

"I stabbed him in the heart with my Boy Scout knife."

"What for?"

"He jumped me. He said I love you and all that stuff, and couldn't live without me, and was going to kill me, kill both of us." They had gone down to the Hudson with a bottle after leaving the West End and gotten into this drunken argument. Kammerer had threatened to do something to Celine.

"I stripped off his white shirt," Lucien went on, "tore it into strips, tied rocks with the strips and tied the strips to his arms and legs, then took all my clothes off and pushed him in. He wouldn't sink, that's why I had to take my clothes off, after, I had to wade in to my chin level and give him a push. Then he floated off somewhere. Upside down. Then my clothes were there on the grass, dry, it's hot as you know. I put them on, hailed a cab on Riverside Drive, and went to ask Burroughs what to do."

Jack got dressed and went to Morningside Park with Lucien to help him get rid of the evidence. As early as it was, it was already hot. He pretended to piss to draw attention as Lucien buried the glasses in the park. Then Lucien dropped the Boy Scout knife down a sewer grating, the knife he had owned since joining the Scouts at the age of twelve. Then Jack and Lucien went out drinking, and after that to the movies, to see *Four Feathers*.

It took Lucien two days to decide to go to the police. On the morning of August 16, he walked into the Manhattan district attorney's office with a lawyer, and told Jacob Grumet, the head of the Homicide Bureau, about the killing. Grumet was skeptical—there was no body. Was this kid some kind of nut? But Lucien was detained and spent his time reading poetry.

On August 17, the front-page banner in *The New York Times* said: INVADERS DRIVE EIGHT MILES INLAND ON RIVIERA. Amid the invasion news was a story headlined COLUMBIA STUDENT KILLS FRIEND AND SINKS BODY IN HUDSON RIVER.

"A fantastic story of a homicide," the story began, "first revealed to the authorities by the voluntary confession of a nineteen-year-old Columbia sophomore, was converted yesterday from a nightmarish fantasy into a horrible reality by the discovery of the bound and stabbed body of the victim in the murky waters of the Hudson River."

The Coast Guard had found Kammerer's body floating off 108th Street. Lucien had led police to the spot where he had buried Dave's glasses. In the *Daily News*, Lucien was shown pointing at the river, where he had dumped the body.

Lucien told the police that on Monday morning, August 14, between 3:00 and 4:00 A.M., while sitting on the grassy bank below Riverside Drive at the foot of 115th Street, Kammerer had made an indecent proposal, and a fight had ensued. Carr was five feet nine and 140 pounds, while Kammerer was six feet and 185 pounds. Carr was getting the worst of it and took out his Boy Scout knife and stabbed Kammerer.

When Chandler Brossard, who had been so fond of Kammerer, picked up the *Daily News* and saw Lucien on the front page, he thought, "This is the stuff of tragedy." He could see what had happened: They'd had a drunken fight, and Lucien had snapped and killed Dave. But these cries of total innocence were lousy. All you had to say was that a guy made a pass at you and everything was okay, including murder. There was more to it than that, as Brossard well knew from having watched Lucien in action.

When Allen Ginsberg saw the news, he thought of a song Lucien liked to sing:

> My friend was an honest cowpuncher
> Honest, straightforward and true.
> He still would be riding the ranges
> If it weren't for a girl named Lou.

For Lucien, it hadn't been a girl named Lou but Dave Kammerer. So this is where the experimentation had led, the thirst for experience, the New Vision, the long conversations, the inquiries on the nature of art, the attraction to the gratuitous act. Lucien had crossed the boundary from literary games to reality. He was like the precocious child who reads all the books, and whose mother says, "But if my little darling reads books like that at his age, what will he do when he grows up?" and who replies, "I shall act them out." If Lucien could kill, it had not been just talk. To what extent, Allen wondered, was Lucien's deed the logical outcome of their fondness for the doomed figures of literature? And of their smiling approval of his many extravagances? It was as though they had all done it together, as though they had *instructed* Lucien. He always said, "I'm going out to invoke Mephisto," and that night he found him.

At the same time, Allen knew that alcohol was to blame. Drink had made Lucien go berserk. Drink made people do things they didn't understand, it made unconscious motives surface. Allen wrote in his journal, "The libertine circle is destroyed with the death of Kammerer." He went back to the bench on the traffic island where they used to sit and thought, "I am quick, he is dead."

In the meantime, Burroughs and Kerouac had been arrested as material witnesses, for not reporting a homicide. So, Burroughs thought, he was supposed to rush to the nearest phone like a decent citizen, who is supposed to be a stool pigeon according to official ruling? The Kammerer killing was significant in that he and Jack were made to choose between their loyalty to a friend and their duty as citizens, and were punished for choosing their friend, which further alienated them from officialdom and its demands.

Burroughs was held in lieu of $2,500 bail, but his father arrived right on cue and posted the bond. When Burroughs went to the district attorney's office to give his deposition, Grumet was saying to Detective Sergeant O'Toole, a big Irishman with a shoulder holster, "That Carr is a very good-looking boy, wouldn't you say so?" "A sickly-lookin' bum," the detective replied. "Ha ha ha," laughed Grumet, "well, a comment from the police department."

Grumet asked Burroughs about the Carr-Kammerer relationship, and Burroughs said, "I don't think there was any sexual relationship."

"Did you know Kammerer was homosexual?"

"Yes, I frequently remonstrated with him but in vain."

"Did he ever make a pass at you?"

"Certainly not."

In contrast to Mortimer Burroughs, Leo Kerouac told Jack he had disgraced the family name and refused to bail out his son, who was invited to be a guest in the Bronx jail, known as the Bronx Opera House, where the stool pigeons sang arias. At his arraignment, he was told, "You came close to being an accessory." "I watched him get rid of the knife, I didn't help him get rid of the knife," Jack said. He was taken to the morgue in the basement of Bellevue to identify Kammerer's bloated blue body, red-bearded, his shirt torn, sandals on his feet. In Grumet's office, Detective O'Toole asked, "What would you do if a queer made a grab for your cock?" "Why, I'd k-norck him," Jack said.

O'Toole took Jack back to Grumet, saying, "He's okay, he's a swordsman."

"We've got the case here," Grumet told Jack, "of how the guy followed him around the country from one school to another getting him into trouble and getting him expelled." The case hinged on whether Carr was a homosexual, Grumet said. Jack said he wasn't.

The banner headline in the August 25 *New York Times* said: DE-GAULLE REPORTED LEADING SMASH INTO PARIS. Inside was the story that Lucien Carr had been indicted for second-degree murder and was being held without bail. The *Daily News* reported that the books Lucien was carrying as he entered the Tombs were Rimbaud's *A Season in Hell* and Yeats's *A Vision*.

Allen Ginsberg was struck by the divergence between the court system and the actual event. What did the lawyers, the regulations, and the paperwork have to do with reality? Lucien had come to the attention of the state, that was all. You could not attempt to convey an honest explanation of the situation, involving the reasons of the heart and the tragic overtones—that had nothing to do with what society had decided was standard procedure. The entire social apparatus that was brought into play was irrelevant to the main Dostoevskian theme.

Lucien was not taking it too badly. On September 30, he wrote Allen from the Tombs that although he missed their polemics and did not enjoy the inflexible discipline of prison life, one could learn much under duress—an amazingly strong animal, Man. Lucien was in a sanguine state of mind, reading Thomas Hardy's *Jude the Obscure*, and doing crossword puzzles, "at which I am a past master." If you knew what a wattled honey-eater was, or the Walloon name of a province in southern Belgium, or the name of the Anatolian goddess of fertility, you had it made. The presidential election was two months off, and among his upstanding fellow inmates there was many an admirer of the racket-busting former district attorney Thomas E. Dewey.

From Pelham, Celine Young wrote Kerouac that "had Lucien felt less pride in having Dave dog his footsteps, he might have gotten rid of Kammerer before this in a socially acceptable manner. . . . If he persists in the idea that he has done a messianic service by ridding the world of Dave, he is becoming too presumptuous a judge." Celine in a sense admired Dave's devotion to Lucien, risky and uncalculating as it was. Now that Lucien was in jail, Celine was breaking off with him. It was an ideal time. She had tried before and couldn't. Soon she would be dating Hal Chase, who bore a resemblance to Lucien.

Lucien's lawyer, Vincent J. Malone, could have asked for a jury trial, and might have gotten him off by pleading self-defense, because of the homosexual angle. But it was risky, because Detective O'Toole was unsympathetic, saying: "They traveled around—he says they didn't have sex—I don't believe it. I think this had something to do with jealousy." Malone also felt that it would be wrong for Lucien to get away with murder—he should do a little time. The second-degree murder charge against Lucien could fetch life. But because District Attorney Grumet was agreeable, Malone plea-bargained. Lucien would plead guilty to the reduced charge of first-degree manslaughter, and be sentenced at a hearing before a judge. It seemed fair, and it would save the taxpayers money.

At the hearing, Lucien's mother described Kammerer as a "veritable Iago," who had at every turn dissuaded him from the proper course, "purely for the love of evil." Lucien, wearing a clean and pressed brown suit, gave the judge his "honorable" look. District Attorney Grumet said:

"Your Honor, we're not pushing for a stiff sentence. Anything that could be done to rehabilitate this young man will be appreciated."

Lucien was sentenced to an indeterminate term of up to twenty years to be served in the Elmira Reformatory rather than Sing-Sing, in view of his age. There is nothing like a prison sentence to order one's thoughts, and he came out of Elmira after two years a changed man. It was as if by killing Kammerer he had sought to bring his life to a premature climax, so that the rest of it would be tranquil. Lucien stopped drinking and smoking and put on weight and grew a mustache and beard. When Burroughs saw him after his release, he thought, he has deliberately unbeautified himself. The arrogant *jeunesse dorée* element had vanished.

Lucien dropped out of the 118th Street group and found a job with a news agency. Allen grudgingly acknowledged that the social application had been right. It had been good for Lucien to go to jail for a short period. He had lost his "the world-owes-me-a-living" side. Now Lucien described himself as a "petit bourgeois," and did not want to be reminded of the past.

In 1956, he complained about being in the dedication of Allen's book *Howl*: "I value a certain anonymity in life and it always jars me when my friends, of all people, find it desirable to include mention of me in their works. I hope you bear that idiosyncrasy in mind in your next book—*Moan*." Again in 1962, he complained about the "dig-up-of-the-past, roll-in-your-own-shit" poetry. "Can't you word bandiers stick to your own ghosts and leave mine alone? . . . I'm being trapped annually into your broken record gyrations."

Burroughs felt that the whole thing had been mainly Kammerer's doing. Kammerer's obsession had brought matters to a head. There was something in Dave that had provoked Lucien to kill him. Dave saw death as the solution to his obsession, Mayerling-style. In death, he would live eternally with Lucien. Burroughs told Lucien, "You shouldn't blame yourself at all, because he asked for it, he demanded it." It was too complicated to explain to the police. They saw things in primary colors. Had Carr been homosexual? Had Kammerer made advances? It was like trying to explain that Othello had not murdered Desdemona because she was unfaithful but because she was Venetian.

The Columbia *Spectator* was close to the truth when it said in an editorial: "We only know that there is a complexity to the background of the case that will defy ordinary police and legal investigations. The search for motive will dig deep into the more hidden areas of the intellectual world."

One by-product of the Carr-Kammerer drama was that it started Burroughs writing again. As with Kells Elvins in 1938, he needed a collaborator to prod him into activity. Kerouac suggested that they write a novel about the killing. Each of them would write alternate chapters based on the part of the story he knew best. They would write it in a deadpan, Dashiell Hammett style, but it would be more than a detective story—it would be the first American existential novel.

The working title, "I Wish I Were You," indicating Kammerer's compulsion to transform himself into Lucien, was changed to the absurdist "And the Hippos Were Boiled in Their Tanks," a phrase Burroughs had heard a radio announcer use when in mellifluous tones he reported a fire in a traveling circus. Burroughs liked that kind of off-the-wall remark, which in this case was also literally true. Kerouac signed his chapters Mike Ryko and Burroughs used the name Will Dennison for his. The novel is a more or less factual account of the 118th Street circle and the events leading up to the murder, with Kerouac contributing some good descriptions of his attempts with Lucien to find a ship, and Burroughs walking away with the best lines, as in, "People in bars are always claiming to be boxers, hoping thereby to ward off attack, like a blacksnake will vibrate its tail in leaves and try to impersonate a rattlesnake."

"Hippos" is an intriguing example of the early work of two writers who would become famous, who at the time were subduing their individual voices to attain a uniformity of style. The literary agents Ingersoll and Brennan agreed to handle it, but it was turned down by every publisher it was sent to.

In 1952 Kerouac, who had by that time published his first novel, *The Town and the City*, was still trying to get "Hippos" published, and wrote Carl Solomon, an editor interested in his work, on April 7: "Burroughs and I wrote a sensational 200-page novel about Lucien's murder in 1945 that 'shocked' all publishers in town and also agents. . . . Allen remembers it . . . if you want it, go to my mother's house with Allen and find it in my maze of boxes and suitcases . . . Bill himself would approve of this move, we spent a year on it, Lucien was mad, wanted us to bury it under a floorboard."

For Burroughs, "Hippos" was another false start, tending to confirm that he had no future as a writer. He would have to find some other form of activity.

· SEVEN ·

JUNK

1945–1946

The libertine circle was not destroyed, as Allen had predicted, but for the moment it disbanded. Kammerer was dead, Lucien was in jail, Burroughs was visiting his parents in St. Louis, and Joan Vollmer took her daughter upstate to stay with her parents. Jack Kerouac arranged with Edie that if she put up the $100 in bail money they would get married, which they did on August 22, 1944, at City Hall. Celine Young was the maid of honor.

On September 1, Jack wrote Edie's mother that "the tragic events of the last few weeks catapulted us into a badly timed union." He and Edie were arriving in Grosse Pointe "under circumstances highly embarrassing to me." "At any rate," he went on, "in a world where death is rampant, as today, marriage is the least evil—that much is certain."

Edie agreed. She had what she wanted, which was Jack, who was so handsome and smelled so good, like the deep woods of Lowell. He had high body heat, and slept on his stomach with an arm above his head, so there wasn't much room for spreadoutski, as she put it. Edie's father found Jack a job as an inspector in the Fruehoff trailer factory, but Jack didn't take to Grosse Pointe, or to Edie's mother asking him, when she saw him writing in notebooks, "Will you ever be as good as Pearl Buck?" Edie felt that to please Jack she should be well-read, and she wrote Allen asking for a book list, in exchange for which she promised to keep their "secret"—which was that one night at 118th Street, Allen had jumped into her bed naked, in a state of arousal. But he was "a wet kisser" and she pushed him away.

Jack lasted about a month in Grosse Pointe, and the one thing he managed to accomplish there was to catch the mumps, which affected both of his testicles. They shriveled up to the size of filberts, so that he became convinced that he was sterile, though not impotent. Later, when his second wife gave birth to a daughter, he was sure the child was not his.

In October, he left for New York and shipped out as an able-bodied seaman, but jumped ship in Norfolk to escape the advances of a hulking bosun who called him "Pretty Boy" and "Baby Face." Back in New York, and thinking of himself as being like one of Balzac's provincials observing the big evil city, Jack got in touch with Allen, who was still at Columbia. Hearing that Burroughs was back, in an apartment on Riverside Drive, they decided to go see him. "We were like ambassadors to the Chinese emperor," Allen recalled, "making a delegation of ourselves to inquire into the nature of his soul. Quite literally and directly. Who is Burroughs? Why is he so intelligent? Will he be friendly or unfriendly?"

Burroughs was friendly, and loaned them books from his library: Kafka, Blake, Cocteau's *Opium*, the cyclical historians Vico and Pareto, Hart Crane's *Collected Works*. Allen had never heard of Hart Crane, and thought of Burroughs as an essential supplement to the education he was getting at Columbia. For his part, Burroughs was gratified to find two young disciples so eager to learn. He pointed out a passage in the preface of Spengler's *Decline of the West*, which said that with the culture declining, "therefore, young man, take to the slide rule rather than the pen, take to the microscope rather than the brush."

Soon Allen and Jack were making regular visits, and Burroughs suggested that since he was back in analysis, and was familiar with the methods, he might try analyzing them for an hour a day. Flattered that he would take the time, they agreed. This went on for some months, and Allen, trusting Burroughs, revealed himself, dropping his defenses completely. One day he broke down sobbing and repeating, "Nobody loves me, nobody loves me, nobody loves me." Burroughs felt that the outburst did not ring true, it was sheer histrionics. He wanted to say, but held his tongue, "Why should anyone love you?"

Jack talked about his father, who had developed cancer of the spleen, and his mother, who was overbearing and critical of his friends. During one of their sessions, in the spring of 1945, Burroughs said: "Trouble with you Jack is you're too hung up on your mother's apron strings. You're going around in circles. Are you man enough to break away?"

Jack was shaken. This was one of the first character critiques he had ever gotten, and it scared him a little. He went over to Hamilton Hall to tell Allen what Burroughs had said. Allen agreed with Burroughs, since Jack's mother didn't like him. They kept talking until 2:00 A.M., and Jack stayed the night in Allen's room, for Allen's roommate, Bill Lancaster, whose father was chairman of the National City Bank, was away.

Now it happened that on the previous day, to draw the attention of the Irish cleaning woman to the fact that his windows were dirty, Allen had scrawled in the grime "Butler has no balls" (referring to Nicholas Murray Butler, the formidably stuffy president of Columbia), over a cock and balls, and "Fuck the Jews," over a skull and crossbones. Instead of erasing the graffiti with a shrug, the cleaning woman had reported Allen to the dean's office.

The next morning, Allen was in his room with Jack when Dean Ralph Furey, the director of student-faculty relations, barged in and saw the offending messages on the windowpane. "Wipe that off," he ordered Allen in a cop voice. Then he spotted Jack, whom he already disliked for quitting the football team when Furey was an assistant coach. Jack had been banned from the Columbia campus and officially designated "an unwholesome influence on the students" as a result of being a material witness in the Carr case. But the only result of Jack's being there was that Allen was charged $2.63 for having an overnight guest.

Allen was sent in to see Dean Nicholas McKnight, known to the students as Woodrow Wilson, who said, "Mr. Ginsberg, I hope you realize the enormity of what you have done." He was told that he would have to take a leave of absence, and that he must not return until he could show a psychiatrist's letter stating that he was in a proper frame of mind to take on academic responsibilities.

The incident was a turning point for Ginsberg. He was a model student, with a busy curriculum, getting "A's," editing the humor magazine, *The Jester*, running the Philolexion (literary) Society, active on the debating team (he had lost to West Point on "Should armies and navies be permanently abandoned?"), and now he was suspended for what was basically a harmless undergraduate prank. That the university chose to make a big deal out of it only underlined the hidebound and narrow-minded nature of the academic community. The university was more and more an annex of government, with the V-12s and their special course in naval history, with the G.I. Bill, which amounted to open admissions and eroded standards, and with government grants ushering in an era of increasing interference—build us this, build us that, build us a nuclear reactor. Military funding was gobbling up university research. These so-called distinguished academics had done nothing to help Lucien when he was arrested, and now they were on Allen's case for some small thing. They were merely an arm of the establishment, enforcers of the status quo, part of the whole syndrome of shutdown. Even the best of them were conventional, thought Allen. Mark Van Doren was a fine teacher, but his verse was boring. He would write a line like "time's tooth devours," and never worry about a new way of expressing it, and he seemed not to have heard of Walt Whitman or Hart Crane. As for Lionel Trilling, he wanted to shape the best students for academic careers, to turn them into copies of himself.

In Allen's treatment by the powers at Columbia, in his friendship with two other troublemakers, Burroughs and Kerouac, there was the germ of an anti-Establishment, counterculture program. He was beginning to divide the world into "Us" and "Them." But for the moment, Allen went to Sheepshead Bay and enrolled in the Maritime Service Training Center to become a merchant seaman. From the center that July, he wrote Burroughs, to whom in the hours of analysis he had admitted his homosexuality, "I feel more guilty and inferior for reasons of faggishness than intellectualization will admit is proper." "Mountains of homosexuality, Matterhorns of cock, Grand Canyons of asshole" were "a weight on my melancholy head."

By that time, Burroughs was also trying to get into the merchant marine. He still wanted to take an active part in the war and thought that being a seaman would be glamorous and exciting. He wrote Jack on July 24, 1945, to congratulate him on returning to the sea, "maker and mother of men." He had to go to St. Louis to get his army medical survey from the Office of Demobilized Personnel, but by the time he got it the war was over.

On August 6, just before 8:00 A.M., the *Enola Gay* dropped "Little Boy" from 32,000 feet and turned Hiroshima into an earthwork. On August 9, the Flying Fortress *Bock's Car* dropped "Big Boy" over Nagasaki. On August 10, Japan sued for peace, and on August 14, President Truman proclaimed V-J Day. The Sheepshead Bay training center was closed down, and Burroughs never did get his papers.

Burroughs was back in New York on V-J Day, and he and Jack went out to celebrate what Jack called "surrender night." There was much drinking and madness. Thousands of servicemen roamed the streets, parlaying military victory into sexual conquest. Burroughs and Kerouac went to Times Square to pick up women but had no luck. It was Burroughs' appearance, Jack thought; he looked like Lucifer's emissary, *chargé d'affaires de l'Enfer*, and perhaps women caught a flash of red lining inside his coat.

What was certain was that after "Little Boy" and "Big Boy," nothing would ever be the same. It seemed to Burroughs that the end of classical culture, predicted by Spengler and Korzybski, had now come about, the end of culture and religion and the traditional values of society. After

Hiroshima, the human species existed in a world where everything was permitted. Where was that bearded and verifiable divinity who is filled with wrath at man's transgressions? He was not in strict attendance. Like the servicemen on V-J Day, He was off on a bat Himself.

That June, Joan was back in town with Julie and found a big apartment at 419 West 115th Street. Replying to a gloomy letter from Edie, whom Jack had abandoned in Grosse Pointe, Joan wrote on June 8: "You sound . . . almost as bad as me in Albany. Haven't you met any cocksmen out there yet? . . ." Joan had asked her husband for a divorce, and he had written back and "didn't seem too upset, and asked what I wanted to do. Don't know quite what to answer. He didn't suggest divorce but said we might separate and begin courting again. Poor little soul. But honestly, I think he might be just a little relieved."

The "libertine circle" began to reform in Joan's apartment. Allen, still suspended from Columbia, moved in, and so did Jack and Hal Chase, who to Allen represented "the hero of the snowy West." Hal had served in the ski troops and had trained in the Rockies and had reorganized the Indian artifacts in the Denver Museum. Allen admired his subtle, snaky-headed mind, and was strongly attracted, but Hal did not reciprocate.

Jack in the meantime was after Celine, whom he described as "ineffable, beautiful, self-corroding, doomed, a bit mad," but Celine said she loved him like a brother. Then Edie turned up and moved in with her long-absent husband. Edie got a job in the Zanzibar night club as a cigarette girl and would feed Jack and the others steak sandwiches from the kitchen when they came around. But eventually she was fired when she nestled a five-dollar tip a sailor had given her in the bra of her little red costume—the tips went to the house.

Joan was introduced by Jack to Benzedrine, which you could buy over the counter as inhalers at drugstores, removing the accordion-folded paper strips inside. One strip in a cup of coffee could send you spinning for the rest of the day. She and Jack were zonked out a lot of the time. Burroughs was a frequent visitor at 115th Street—at that time he had a small apartment near Columbus Circle—and it was easy to see that Joan liked him. She invited him to dinner and they talked about books. They liked the same stories, such as Conrad Aiken's "Silent Snow, Secret Snow." Jack and Allen thought Joan and Bill would make a great match, and Jack asked Burroughs, "Why don't you move in with that college widow?" On September 10, Joan wrote Edie, who was in Asbury Park with her grandparents, that "Jack and Burroughs came up. We had dinner, met Ginsberg, and spent the evening in fruity men's bars in the Village."

The group fell into its former ways, with endless verbalizing and "Dostoevskian confrontations." They were together constantly. It was like a marathon encounter session. As Hal Chase put it, "you could dip into the set at any point and stay with it for days on end."

It was only a matter of weeks after Joan had taken the apartment that her soldier husband Paul Adams showed up, fresh from the German front, and walked in to find a group of people high on bennies, piled on Joan's vast double bed in sybaritic disarray. Disgusted, he asked, "This is what I fought for?" "Why don't you get down from your character heights," mumbled Joan through her Benzedrine haze. Adams left and filed for divorce.

Jack's father, who had moved to Queens, was dying, and Burroughs went out to Ozone Park with him in November to visit. The frail old man was lying in bed, hardly able to speak, and Mrs. Kerouac was doing all the talking, sticking out her tongue and saying, "Pretty soon I'm going to be saying ya ya ya to you and you'll be six feet under ground." She struck Burroughs as a tough French peasant, mean and superstitious. She was always trying to separate Jack from his friends, and told him that Burroughs and Ginsberg were followed everywhere by the F.B.I. Jack's reaction was to drink another bottle of beer and refuse to face the situation. That was basic to his character—avoid the issue. He was uneasy in the presence of anything approaching an emotional scene.

Jack was writing and drinking and taking Benzedrine. He was a member of the 52–20 club—twenty dollars a week for fifty-two weeks for the unemployed. On Benzedrine, Jack could stay awake and talk continuously for thirty-five hours. But it caught up with him, and one day around Christmastime 1945 when he and Allen and Hal were coming back from a walk on the Brooklyn Bridge, and Allen was humming a Bach toccata, suddenly Jack's legs buckled, and the others had to carry him into a cab. He was hospitalized for thrombophlebitis, which was produced by a combination of Benzedrine and drinking.

A person is thrown into the water to sink or swim, so he learns something about the water. He learns that when you hit bottom, you are on the way up. Herbert Huncke was born in 1916 in Greenfield, Massachusetts, where his father worked for the Greenfield Tap and Die Company. His father was a German Jew who hated Jews and joined the Bund to establish his Aryan background. His mother was the daughter of a Wyoming cattleman who had a ranch in Laramie. The family moved to Chicago, where Herbert's parents separated. At the age of twelve, since his mother was unable to handle him, his father said, "Send him to me."

His mother gave him a dime to take the trolley, and he rode it to South Chicago, which became Gary, Indiana, and he hitchhiked all the way to Geneva, New York, where police picked him up and sent him home.

Having had his first taste of the road, Huncke vowed that he would never again be trapped by school and family. He hung around Rush Street and Chicago Avenue, picking up odd jobs and running errands for whores. At fifteen, he started smoking pot, and a year later he tried heroin. At first he was needle-shy—the idea of sticking a needle into his arm was terrifying. But over the years, after shooting up thousands of times, he viewed his veins with a friendly detachment, talking about them as if they were old familiars. "That one is a roller," he would say of a vein that slipped the needle. And of a small vein he couldn't hit, he would say, "I'll get you yet, you little bastard."

Huncke spent six years just floating around the country. A sparrow-like man with bright hazel eyes and sallow skin, there was something furtive and unthreatening about him. He seemed as harmless and ingratiating as a puppy, although his voice had a ring of false plausibility that would put an alert person on guard. He knew how to get by, staying here a week and there a week, alive to small opportunities. In Albuquerque, he helped out a fellow who was promoting a TB sanitarium for Greeks. In Miami he worked as a bellhop in a little hotel whose customers bet the horses. Everywhere he looked for junk. Everywhere he traveled alone, often carrying no more than a cigar-box toilet kit, often riding the freight trains, the soot ingrained in his skin.

Huncke hit New York around 1940, and started hanging around the Times Square area, where a community of hustlers gathered. Times Square in those days was picturesque without being sleazy. Instead of porn movie houses, it had art houses like the Apollo that showed French films such as *Pepe le Moko* and *Le Jour se Lève*. Horn & Hardart, where you could get a little pot of baked beans with a strip of bacon over it for a nickel, was open all night, and there were also Chase's and Bickford's and the Dixie Hotel with its arcade.

Huncke became a part of the community of homos, dips, paperhangers, and pimps. He didn't mind being known as a hustler, but he didn't want to be known as an open faggot, because faggots were everyone's property. Huncke presided at a table at Bickford's and was known as the Mayor. Occasionally he did a little breaking and entering, mainly into cars. When an opportunity arose, he took it. Once in Penn Station, a sailor asked him to watch his duffle while he took a shit, and Huncke walked off with it.

Arrested for breaking into a car, he did six months on Hart's Island,

and fought not to be pegged as a broad. He learned the cliques and classifications of prison life, the nuances of getting along with his fellow inmates. "I've jacked off other inmates under circumstances you wouldn't believe possible," he recalled, "like across two feet of concrete between cell doors."

A year after his first bust he was arrested again while filling a forged prescription, having used the same drugstore too many times. There was a custody battle between plainclothesmen and uniformed cops at the scene. Arguing about who should get the collar, they asked Huncke to arbitrate. "Look, who got here first?" asked a detective. "You guys did," Huncke said, trying to be fair. "Well, that's all there is to it," the detective said. The uniformed cop got mad and said, "You little bastard, I'll get you."

Huncke became a "chippy junky," turning on two or three days, then switching to liquor and Benzedrine, living from hand to mouth, hustling johns, breaking into cars. He met a young Italian named André, who was sharing an apartment on Henry Street with a big slob known as Bozo. Having tried and failed to make the grade in vaudeville, Bozo was now an attendant at the Creedmore sanitarium. André invited Huncke, who was always hard-pressed for a place to stay, to come to Henry Street, but Bozo didn't approve and moved out. Bozo was a sort of martyr type, the kind who wants to tell you that he never gets credit for the trouble he takes—he later O.D.'d on Nembutal, of which he had an ample supply through Creedmore. André then took up with a gorgeous Titian-haired hooker known as Vickie Russell, though her real name was Priscilla Arminger and she was the daughter of a judge in Detroit. Vickie was tall and willowy, with finesse and class—a real knockout. Then André walked out after a fight with Vickie, leaving Huncke alone in the apartment with her, until two other underworld characters turned up—Phil White and Bernie Barker (name changed).

Phil White, a tall and rawboned Tennessean, made Huncke think of a traveling preacher on a mule. He was a professional pickpocket and something of a thief. Beneath the con man smile he was cold-blooded, thought Huncke, and only interested in people to the extent that he could use them.

Phil had a habit. He also had a wife, an older woman named Kay, who worked as an editor at McGraw-Hill. A bitch on wheels, thought Huncke, bowing to the Almighty Dollar—which was his verdict on anyone who held a steady job. Kay was always trying to get Phil to quit drugs, and would say to Huncke: "You've got to do something about Phil. He's been taking this . . . junk, you know, and he can't do any good now, and a woman's got to have her tail."

Bernie Barker was a rather dashing fellow from Cleveland, not handsome, but slim and dapper and energetic. His brother Don was active in the N.M.U., but Bernie's ambition was to become a first-class gangster. In the meantime, he was working as a soda jerk up around Columbia—he could handle a busy soda fountain.

Huncke and Phil White both had seamen's papers through Barker's brother and decided to go to sea in September 1945. It would be a good way to kick their respective habits, and Kay White was all for it. They grabbed a tanker that was carrying high-octane gas to Honolulu and was short two messmen, but instead of kicking their habits they got worse habits. They made friends with the seaman in charge of the infirmary, who gave them all the morphine they wanted. So through the Panama Canal and on to Honolulu and back, Phil White and Huncke were in a morphine glow. Now Huncke really had a monkey, of whom he was fond because the monkey was even more irresponsible than he was, and he could lecture the monkey.

They were back on Henry Street and desperate for junk, when one day in January 1946 Bernie Barker dropped by and said, "Jesus, good to see you. Man, I've got a guy lined up, going to be down tonight, I want you to tell me what you think of him. He approached me the other day. He's been coming into the drugstore quite regularly, and he's been talking about capers of one sort and another. He just told me that he has a sawed-off tommy gun with an automatic pistol cartridge and some morphine Syrettes that he wants to get rid of." That sounded good to Phil and Herbert. Morphine Syrettes, the kind that are like little toothpaste tubes with a needle sticking out, were what they'd been using on the ship.

The guy with the sawed-off shotgun and the morphine Syrettes was William Burroughs. Increasingly, he felt like an exile in his own country, belonging nowhere. He once dreamed that he was being drafted into the English army. He could not find his passport to prove that he was American. They were checking through, saying, "No, sir, I don't see any passport here, sir." In his search for a viable identity, Burroughs deliberately sought out a criminal life. A community of outlaws, such as he had read about in Jack Black's *You Can't Win*, was perhaps the only place where a misfit such as he could belong.

The incongruity of his choice was what made Burroughs unique. He was the grandson of the inventor of the adding machine and belonged to a good St. Louis family. He had gone to Harvard and was a member of the University Club. He was a bourgeois bourgeoisphobe, retaining some of the attributes of his class. He wore conservative vested suits and snap-brim hats and looked like a junior executive in a brokerage house. His manner was courteous and reserved. His speech, despite its nasal Missouri twang, revealed him as a man of education and intellect. He seemed to have ingested all of Western thought and literature, which he regurgitated willingly. A more unlikely colleague of Huncke's dim-witted junky band would be hard to imagine.

Jack Anderson, the boyfriend who had crashed his car, with whom Burroughs had kept up, had a friend named Norman who worked in the Navy Yard. Norman stole a tommy gun, carrying it out piece by piece, and sixteen yellow boxes of morphine tartrate Syrettes. Burroughs bought them as a means of entrée into the criminal world. He had met Bernie Barker, who had done some serious stealing—he was part of a gang that had robbed a company in Delaware of a $180,000 payroll. Bernie was not modest about his exploits—in fact, he loved to talk about them, and about the gun he used: "Give me a .38 every time." About how he had cracked some guy's jaw with a roll of nickels in his fist: "No one can hang anything on you for carrying U.S. currency." Barker was the real thing, thought Burroughs, a professional criminal, a tough hombre. "Bernie doesn't mess around," he told Hal Chase. "He decides to do something and he does it. He goes to the West End and orders a drink at the bar and drinks it and turns on his heels and walks out—never a wasted moment." In imitation of Barder, Burroughs started wearing a trench coat, with his hat brim down low over his forehead, walking briskly forward the way Bernie walked.

Barker suggested that Burroughs meet him at the Henry Street apartment, where some friends of his might be interested in the Syrettes. Huncke in the meantime had done quite a decorating job on the railroad flat, the kind with a bathtub in the kitchen. He had painted the walls black, with yellow panels, and the ceiling red, with a wheel filled with different-colored little squares and triangles. Black-and-yellow floor-length drapes covered the windows, and the place looked like a cross between a Chinese opium den and Ali Baba's cave.

The evening that Burroughs showed up on Henry Street, Huncke saw a tall thin man in the doorway wearing a chesterfield coat and a gray snap-brim hat, gloves clutched in one hand. He thought Burroughs was the police. He asked Barker to step into the bedroom and said, "Who is this guy, he looks like trouble." Bernie vouched for him, and when they came back into the kitchen, Burroughs and Phil White were discussing the Syrettes. But Huncke was still suspicious and said, "I don't think I want to bother, really." Phil, however, was interested and said he would be in touch.

A few days later, Burroughs used one of the Syrettes and had his first experience with junk. He wanted to see what it was like, as he had done with the chloral hydrate at Los Alamos, in a spirit of general inquiry. Also, it seemed to be the thing to do as far as being a criminal was concerned. Using junk made him part of the group, it was a sort of rite of passage. Finally, there was in Burroughs the spirit of the self-mutilating scientist that the opium addict–writer Thomas De Quincey described in his *Confessions*: "I have conducted my experiments on this subject with a sort of galvanic battery and have, for the general benefit of the world, inoculated myself with the poison of 800 drops of laudanum a day (just for the same reason that a French surgeon inoculated himself lately with cancer, an English one twenty years ago with plague, and a third, I know not of what nation, with hydrophobia)." Burroughs would never say that he was taking junk for the general benefit of the world, but a spirit of scientific curiosity, with the risk of possible harm, was not absent from his experimentation.

Morphine was like nothing Burroughs had previously known. He had the feeling of moving off the ground at great speed. He seemed to be floating, as a wave of pleasure spread through his tissues. This was followed by a feeling of fear and the vision of a neon-lit cocktail lounge, and a waitress coming in with a skull on a tray. "I don't want your fuckin' skull," Burroughs found himself saying. "Take it back!"

A few days later, when Phil White came to buy, at four dollars a box, Burroughs laid out ten boxes of Syrettes and kept two, saying, "These are for me." Phil looked up, surprised: "You use it?" "Now and then," Burroughs said. "It's bad stuff," Phil said, shaking his head. "The worst thing that can happen to a man."

Soon, Burroughs was buying Syrettes from Phil, but at a higher price. Often, they would shoot up together. Phil would hit a vein in his leg and shoot the morphine in with an air bubble. "If air bubbles could kill you," he said, "there wouldn't be a junky alive."

Phil introduced Burroughs to a doctor on 102nd Street off Broadway, who would fill junk prescriptions. Burroughs also started hanging out at the Angler Bar on Eighth Avenue near Forty-second Street, where Huncke was often to be found. Overcoming his suspicion, Huncke permitted

Burroughs to buy him drinks and meals—he still had him pinned for a mark. Huncke took him back to Henry Street to meet Vickie, who explained her philosophy on how to treat johns. "Always build a john up," she said. "If he has any sort of body at all, say, 'Oh, don't ever hurt me.' You give him what he pays for. When you're with him you enjoy yourself and you want him to enjoy himself, too. If you really want to bring a man down, light a cigarette in the middle of intercourse."

One afternoon in Chase's, a girl carrying some books came over to Huncke's table and asked if she could sit down. "There's someone who wants to meet you," she said, "a Professor Kinsey. He's at Indiana University and he's doing research on sex. He's looking for people to tell about their sex lives, to be as honest about it as possible."

Huncke called Kinsey and asked what he was interested in. "All I want you to do is to tell me about your sex life, what experiences you've had, what your interest is, whether you've masturbated, how often, have you had any homosexual experiences, heterosexual. Just a complete record as far back as you can remember."

Huncke was willing, for a price. "I don't want to sound crude," he said, "but I think it's only fair to tell you, I do need money." Kinsey promised ten dollars, and Huncke went to his hotel and unburdened himself of a sexual history that must have stood out for its rich variety, from his first experience at the age of nine. Then Kinsey wanted to measure the size of his penis. He had a card with a phallus drawn on it and said he would mark the length when soft and when erect on the card. "Well, why not," Huncke thought.

As he left, Kinsey said, "Now, if there's anyone else that you know that you think might be interested in being interviewed by all means send them up. In fact, I'll tell you what. For every person you send me from Forty-second Street, I'll give you two dollars. I know you can use the money."

An enterprising recruiter, Huncke sent everyone he could think of up to see Kinsey, including Vickie and Burroughs, who may be the only writer of renown to have his sexual history on file, including his penis size soft and erect, at the Kinsey Institute for Research in Sex, Gender, and Reproduction, in Bloomington, Indiana. Unfortunately for the biographer, the file is closed.

Burroughs was the link between the uptown Columbia group and the Times Square Huncke group, between the students and the thieves, between the book-smart and the street-smart. He took Jack and Allen downtown to meet Huncke. To Allen, coming as he did from the campus, Times Square seemed like a heroic place. It was marvelous, with a dimension he'd never seen, a whole community, raunchy but not degrading. It was a world with its own charm and character, a more realistic society than Paterson or Lowell or St. Louis. In Paterson, "they didn't know nuttin' about nuttin'," thought Allen. His parents and their socialist friends were naïve and academic and newspaper-oriented. And here before him was a world that high school teachers didn't have a glimmer about. Allen wanted direct experience, he wanted to get away from the theoretical, like saying he planned to be a labor lawyer when he had never met a working man. Burroughs was offering the chance for a psychosocial exploration of a new world that seemed forbidden and strange. "I'm a seeker after cities and souls," Burroughs said.

Huncke was a crucial figure, a sort of Virgilian guide to the lower depths, taking them into a world that provided an alternative to the right-thinking banality of Columbia and its so-called teachers. Huncke was the first hipster, who had been on the street since age twelve, and who was basically the victim of police persecution, in and out of jail for drug possession. Huncke was an antihero pointing the way to an embryonic counterculture, which would arise from this Times Square world of hustlers and hat-check girls.

Allen skin-popped morphine Syrettes and felt he was a part of something intensely real. He also tried Benzedrine but it tangled up his brain—it was like a spider weaving a web that was very dense on one side but missing filaments on the other. Jack tried morphine, too, but said he was allergic to it, and threw up. He would stick to liquor.

At this point, in early 1946, Burroughs moved into Joan's apartment, and they became lovers. Although primarily homosexual and professing a caustic misogyny, Burroughs didn't mind having sex with women, and he must have been proficient at it, because Joan, a woman of wide experience at twenty-two, gave him high marks, saying, "You make love like a pimp." Primarily, however, their relationship was one between two remarkable intellects. Burroughs saw Joan as a woman of unusual insight. She was the smartest member of the group, he thought, certainly as smart as Allen, in many ways smarter, because there were limits to Allen's thinking, but none to Joan's. She started Burroughs thinking in new directions, got him interested in the Mayans, suggested that Mayan priests must have had some sort of telepathic control. She had an odd and original way of looking at things, and a great insight into character. For instance, she said about Jack that he had a natural inborn fear of authority and that if the cops ever questioned him his mouth would fall open and out would come the name they wanted.

Jack and Allen were delighted with their matchmaking. Burroughs would be lying on the couch in shirtsleeves, and Joan with her arms around him would exclaim, "Oh, Bill!" when he said something outrageous, while admiring the inventiveness of his mind. Joan was subdued and content when Burroughs was around, and waited on him hand and foot.

She was, however, taking more and more Benzedrine, and started hallucinating. She said she could hear this old couple downstairs who were calling her a whore and saying she ran a whorehouse. Then one day they got into a fight, she said, and it sounded like someone was being murdered, so Allen went down and knocked on the door but there was no one home.

Now that Burroughs was living with Joan, her juvenile lover, John Kingsland, abdicated the position while remaining a friend. He was intrigued by Burroughs, whom he saw shooting up in the bathroom and spending his days trying to score from writing doctors. On one occasion he accompanied Burroughs to the University Club, where Burroughs tried to kick his habit by swimming in the pool. Another time, they went to the Hotel Biltmore and sat in steam cabinets for hours. Burroughs also recruited Kingsland to score heroin for him, which got the eighteen-year-old into hot water. Burroughs sent him to 103rd Street with some money, but the people he was trying to buy from beat him up, thinking he was a rival pusher trying to muscle in. Then the campus police arrested him and took him down to Forty-second Street and sat him in the window of Bickford's to see if any users would come in and make a buy. Kingsland was suspended from Columbia, but a petition from his teachers got him reinstated on a parole basis, and he was able to graduate that June of 1946 (in three years), and said farewell to "the libertine circle."

Things began to go a little haywire on 115th Street. Huncke was breaking into cars and leaving the stuff he stole at the apartment. Once he was so stoned he stole the car as well and parked it outside. Burroughs was shooting in the main line and having trouble filling scrips. Every day he would meet Phil White to plan the day's junk program. He would have to go through these elaborate scenarios: "I'm just in from Detroit, doctor, and I've got a bad back . . ." Joan was on Benzedrine all the time and not making much sense.

Hal Chase, thinking the situation was out of control, moved out. He didn't see petty thievery and drug addiction as a valid form of rebellion in postwar America. Burroughs had a real talent for finding things to do that he wasn't suited for. Ginsberg and Kerouac wanted experiences they could write about, but Hal was an anthropologist, not a writer, and he wasn't comfortable with the idea of having experiences and then marketing them. Also, Hal was fed up with the Ginsberg game of "let's find your hidden homosexuality." Allen was a social homosexual, Hal thought. He had come out and said that he was becoming homosexual in order to succeed as a poet. Hal had the "post A-bomb feeling that so much of the world was dead and why weren't we dead," but what Burroughs and the others were doing did not seem like remedies, so he split.

Trouble was approaching, not as single spies but in battalions. Huncke was involved in various capers. He and Barker cracked a dress shop in Jamaica, and Phil White and Burroughs took one of the hot dresses to give to a doctor's wife in exchange for a scrip. Then Bernie was caught robbing a safe in a theater and was sent away. He had dropped a matchbook with an address on it that the police traced to the Henry Street apartment, and Huncke had to pack up and clear out in a hurry. At that time, Burroughs was keeping a one-room dump, also on Henry Street, which he let Huncke use. "Of course it never occurred to him to pay the rent," Burroughs said, which Huncke thought was a nasty crack, since he was down and out, whereas Burroughs had a stipend from his family. Huncke was coming uptown almost daily to deposit his stolen goods in Joan's apartment, even though he didn't feel comfortable around all these college people.

Then Huncke, fingered by someone he'd done drugs with, was arrested in Burroughs' Henry Street apartment, and Burroughs figured it wouldn't be long before they came after him. Phil White had talked him into forging the signature of a Dr. Greco on some blank prescriptions he had lifted from the doctor's office, and an inspector spotted the difference in the handwriting. He was easy to catch because he used his real name on the prescription.

A state inspector swore out a warrant charging Burroughs with violation of Public Health Law 334, for obtaining narcotics through the use of fraud, and one day in April 1946 two detectives came to the apartment on 115th Street to arrest him. He was taken to the Tombs and mugged and fingerprinted, and was locked up in his cell in a painful state of drug withdrawal, bathed in sweat, too weak to move, hearing voices drifting back and forth from cell to cell: "Forty years! Man, I can't do no forty years."

That night, Joan bailed him out and gave him some goofballs to tide him over. But she had to call his psychiatrist, Dr. Wolberg, to sign his surety bond, and Wolberg promptly notified Burroughs' parents, which led to a good deal of unpleasantness. It was the first they knew that he was taking drugs, and they were shocked. It seemed like only yesterday that Mortimer Burroughs had bailed his son out as a material witness in the Carr case, and now he had to pay for bail again.

While waiting for his case to come up, Burroughs had to finance his heroin habit. Three caps a day at three dollars each, bought from various connections, was more than he could afford, so he began "working the hole" with Phil White. They would ride the subways at night looking for drunks asleep in stations. Phil would spot a "flop" sleeping on a bench and they would get off and Burroughs would stand in front of the bench covering Phil with an open newspaper as Phil went through the drunk's pockets looking for his "poke." One time a lush woke up and started fighting, and Burroughs and Phil had to make a run for it. The experience was enough to convince Burroughs that working lushes was not his line.

In the meantime, Huncke was in Riker's Island for three months, in a dormitory with hundreds of beds and a pair of lockers between each bed. It was his first experience in the dorm, and he knew he had to watch himself because he was small and appealing. The first night he had to knock a guy over the head with a work shoe. He had learned never to accept anything. If a guy offered you a cigarette, "thanks anyway." Huncke was loaded down with blankets and sheets and a pillow and was looking for his bed, and here on the bed next to his was this tall, cadaverous-looking man with good features and a receding hairline, who introduced himself as Bill Garver—William Maynard Garver, of the Philadelphia Garvers.

Garver seemed like an interesting, unthreatening fellow, in his forties, too old to bother him sexually, and he and Huncke became friendly. He came from a good family—his father was a banker—and had been expelled from Annapolis for drunkenness. His skeletal though not undistinguished appearance came from being a junky, which he had been all his adult life. "Junk is the only thing in my life," he said. During the war he had worked as an orderly in a mental hospital, stealing the morphine and substituting milk sugar. Patients in pain were given milk sugar tablets. "After all, they're crazy anyway, they don't know the difference," Garver said. After getting away with it for two years, he was caught by one of the doctors, who said, "There's something wrong here, I think you know what I mean."

To finance his habit, Garver was now stealing overcoats, which he called "boosting bennies." He would walk into a place for a cup of coffee and walk out with someone's overcoat, which he would pawn for ten or twelve dollars. He had a record of ten arrests, all for petty larceny. Huncke told Garver to look up Burroughs when he got out, which he did. Still waiting for his case to come up, Burroughs went into pushing heroin with Garver, who introduced him to his contacts in the Village. Garver, thought Burroughs, didn't have the nerve to be a real thief so he stuck to overcoats. He knew the coatroom of every restaurant in New York, a rare if penny-ante field of expertise. "Fifteen apparitions have I seen / The worst a coat upon a coat-hanger," in the words of W. B. Yeats.

Every day, Burroughs had to sell enough caps to buy his next quarter ounce, and he was never more than a few dollars ahead, having to contend with unreliable and untrustworthy customers. "What a crowd," he thought. "Mooches, fags, four-flushers, stool pigeons, bums—unwilling to work, unable to steal, always short of money, always whining for credit." Burroughs was a conscientious pusher, punctual and honest. He delivered right to your door, and had a good roster of steady clients. One of these, Mel the waiter, always unshaved and dirty-looking, lived in a rooming-house on Jane Street. One time, Burroughs gave him a cap and he shot up as Burroughs looked out the window—he didn't like to watch junkies probing for veins—and when he turned around Mel had passed out; the dropper was hanging in his arm full of blood. His friend Ritchie pulled the dropper out and slapped his face with a wet towel. Mel came around partly and muttered something. He lay there on the unmade bed, his limp arm stretched out, a drop of blood forming at the elbow.

As they walked downstairs, Ritchie said that Mel had been after him for Burroughs' address. "Listen," Burroughs said, "if you give it to him, you can find yourself a new connection. One thing I don't need is somebody dying in my apartment."

With all the hassle, Burroughs was barely scraping by, what with short counts from wholesalers, the constant nibble of credit, customers coming up short, and his own habit, which he had to sustain daily. Garver said it was his own fault, he ought to cut the stuff more. "You're giving a better cap than anybody in New York City," he said. "Nobody sells sixteen percent stuff on the street. If your customers don't like it, they can take their business to Walgreen's."

Garver lived in a cheap roominghouse in the forties, where Burroughs would sometimes shoot up with him. Once he rummaged around in a bureau and brought out a worn manila envelope, which contained a discharge from Annapolis "for the good of the service," a faded letter from "my friend, the captain," and membership cards in the Masons and the Knights of Columbus. His claims to reality, Burroughs thought. "Every little bit helps," Garver said. He sat silent and reflective for a few minutes, then added, "Just a victim of circumstances." He handed Burroughs two overcoats and said: "I've about burned down all the pawnshops in New York. You don't mind pawning these coats for me, do you?"

By this time, Huncke was out of Riker's Island and was crashing at Phil White's place in Washington Heights. Phil's wife, Kay, had cracked down and refused to give him any more money to support his habit. Phil had borrowed a .32 from Burroughs and one morning he woke up junk-sick and took some goofballs. High as a kite, he told Huncke: "Come on, I'm going to take this fucking gun out. I won't use it but I'll stick somebody up."

"Oh, no," said Huncke, "I'm not going out with you with a gun, Phil."

"Then fuck you, I'm not going to share with you."

"Well, that's your business entirely," Huncke said.

Phil went out and came back at about one-thirty that afternoon, looking like he'd been dragged out from beneath a rock. "Oh, man, I shot a guy," he said, "a furrier, the son of a bitch didn't have any money and he started to scream, and I let him have it."

Huncke didn't know whether to believe him, but that evening in the late edition of the *Journal-American* there was a banner headline that said, MAD DOG NOONDAY KILLER. Well, thought Huncke, that wasn't Phil, that was Phil on goofballs.

Out of consideration for Burroughs, Huncke helped Phil get rid of the gun, taking it apart and wandering over the wilds of Brooklyn, throwing a piece here and a piece there.

In June 1946, Burroughs' case came up in Special Sessions. Since he was a first offender, the charge was a misdemeanor. Burroughs' father was there to provide backup, and the judge gave him a four-month suspended sentence, saying: "Young man, I am going to inflict a terrible punishment on you. I am going to send you home to St. Louis for the summer." The judge could not have known that having to go home and be in the custody of his parents like a misbehaving child *was* a terrible punishment for Burroughs.

He had a pleasant surprise when he arrived in St. Louis, however, for his old friend Kells Elvins was there, after having gone through some of the island battles in the Pacific as a captain in the marines. A Jap shell had exploded close enough to make him deaf in one ear, and he had also contracted malaria.

Burroughs and Kells dreamed up various moneymaking schemes, one of which was a home dry cleaning machine. Like the Alex Guinness character who invents a white suit that never gets dirty or wears out, therefore confounding the makers of deliberately inferior clothing, Burroughs now saw himself as a crusader for "white suit"–type products that would put the others out of business—concrete houses that would last forever, fluoride mouthwashes that would do away with cavities. He was reverting, in his imagination at least, to the ambitions of his paternal grandfather, and wrote Allen Ginsberg that he was planning to market "Death County Bill's Tooth and Gum Tablets, from the county without a toothache," but was being hassled by the Pure Food and Drug Department.

Kells' son, Peter, was assigned to type up the patent for the home dry cleaner, and Burroughs teased him on his slowness: "Well, Peter, you're supposed to have a little more skill at the typewriter." Noticing that the tip of one of Burroughs' fingers was missing, Peter asked him what had happened. "Oh, it's more beautiful that way," Burroughs said. Kells asked his mother if they could use her washing machine to try out their formula, but Mrs. Elvins wanted nothing to do with it, which frustrated the two inventors: what, this dull and unimaginative woman obstructing the brilliant experiments of two young Tom Edisons!

Kells, however, had a much better deal going than a dry cleaning machine. He had bought ten acres of citrus groves for $5,000 in the Rio Grande Valley, sixty miles of the richest farmland in America, in East Texas near the Mexican border, and grew Ruby Reds, Foster Pinks, blood oranges, lemons, and limes. He also had 100 acres of cotton. There was a support price for cotton, and if you had an allotment you couldn't lose. It all seemed like easy money, and Burroughs convinced his parents to advance the funds to buy fifty acres of Rio Grande cottonland. He had washed out as a criminal—he might as well try farming. In late June he went down to Pharr, Texas, with Kells and rented a house. Every day they drove out past the flimsy houses and the Bide-A-Wee tourist courts to look at their cotton, which was being picked by wetbacks in perfect weather—hot and dry. There was no particular reason for them to look, since neither of them knew the first thing about it. They just did it to pass the time until 5:00 P.M., when Kells would bang a tin pail in front of his house and yell, "Drinking time!" and the neighbors would come in and make martinis with homemade gin. Kells, who cultivated a macho, anti-intellectual manner, liked the farmers and the good ol' boys.

Burroughs soon learned that the economics of farming were not that simple. By the time your crop came in you were up to your ears in debt, because you'd borrowed money on your tractor, which cost thousands of dollars, and there wasn't much left over. If you hit a bad year—a hailstorm or a drought—you were wiped out. The big money was in vegetables, if you hit it right. Everybody read the bulletins the way you'd read a racing sheet, to find out what they were growing in the other winter vegetable areas, which were Louisiana, California, and Florida. Of course, a freeze in Florida was money in the bank in Texas. One year in the Rio Grande they hit it big on onions. The next year, you couldn't give onions away. One year Kells was going to clean up on peas, and another year on tomatoes, but something always went wrong. Everybody was always talking "should": "I should have hung on to that 100 acres on the lower lift; I should have took up them oil leases; I should have planted cotton instead of tomatoes." Burroughs wasn't into the vegetable gambit; he put all his land into cotton. He had an allotment, and the land was so good he made two bales an acre, whereas one bale an acre was considered a good yield, and the support price was $150 a bale.

Kells also made some oil investments. He was friends with Sid Murchison, who gave him tips. Murchison's favorite expression was "When are ya gonna get yourself cured?" Being cured meant being rich. "Hey, Clem, you've only got a couple of million, when are ya gonna get yourself cured?"

"Tell me about the man, Burroughs, tell me about Murchison's hands," Kells said. "The man's hands are twisted," Burroughs said, "from being in all that shale." "That's right," Kells said, "the man's got arthritis."

Kells was an advocate of the prolongation of life, and took Burroughs over the border into Mexico to take the Bogomoletz serum, which was illegal in the United States. The theory was that aging was caused by the deterioration of the connective tissue, which the serum could correct. You could tell how old your tissue was by pinching it and seeing if it snapped right back. They went to the Mexican doctor who had the franchise. In his office was a photograph of Bogomoletz at the age of eighty-six, with coal-black hair and a pretty girl on each arm. In his racket, thought Burroughs, you've got to be your own best advertisement. He took the serum and his arm swelled up alarmingly. Oh, well, he thought, a Mexican doctor will shoot anything into you if you pay him. The stuff was supposed to make you live to the age of 125, which Bogomoletz said was man's natural life span. Burroughs also took advantage of his visit to get a Mexican divorce from Ilse Klapper Burroughs.

Back in New York, in the summer of 1946, the "libertine circle" had once again disintegrated. Hal Chase was gone, Burroughs was gone, Ginsberg had shipped out, Edie Parker was in Grosse Pointe, and Kerouac had no fixed address. Without boarders, Joan had trouble raising the rent. She missed Burroughs, and relieved her unhappiness with Benzedrine.

Huncke, who had no place to stay, offered to move in with her, and helped out by robbing parked cars for luggage. Huncke was fond of Joan, but he knew he couldn't make her happy physically. She was much too strong and sexual, and nothing turned Huncke off faster than a woman who wanted to get fucked. Huncke thought of himself as Joan's protector in Burroughs' absence. When he took her down to Times Square, amid all these guys who were basically pimps at heart, he said she was his old lady. But that only annoyed Joan, who said: "Don't be telling people I'm your old lady. I'm perfectly capable of taking care of myself." Huncke inwardly laughed. He knew those guys; they'd have her turning tricks in no time.

Huncke brought around a fellow thief named Whitey, a good-looking blond, well-built, street-smart and virile, and he developed a crush on Joan, and soon they were having what she referred to as "a light affair." Whitey and Huncke brought their loot to 115th Street, and Joan complained that everything in the apartment was hot.

Huncke was egalitarian in his larceny, stealing from friends as well as strangers. He took Allen Ginsberg's phonograph and pawned it, and then wrote Allen a letter, apologizing for "overstepping the bounds of good fellowship." He advised Allen not to speak of his pilfering to others, "as it will place you in the role of being the proverbial sucker—if you forgive and continue allowing me parasitical advantages from my contact with you." Such was Huncke—advising his victims on the correct reaction to his stealing while hoping to remain on friendly terms with them.

He was in more trouble in August, when a valise disappeared from an after-hours joint in the Bronx where he was hanging out, and the consensus was that he was the culprit. One day two policemen showed up at Joan's apartment with the owner of the valise. Joan was terrified because of all the stolen goods on the premises. Huncke was arrested when it developed that he had upon his person the keys to a stolen car parked downstairs, and soon found himself in the Bronx jail at 153rd Street and River Avenue. On September 25 he wrote Allen pleading for a little cash: "Seriously, if you can—please, please bring over four or five dollars. I need it. Thus far—I am forced to bum fellow inmates for stationery—cigs—soap and other almost essentials. It becomes slightly rough on all concerned."

Joan owed for back rent and couldn't pay, so she and Whitey and Julie were evicted and bounced around from one hotel to another. Then Whitey, who was sweet but stupid, tried to crack a safe in a Howard Johnson's and was immediately arrested. That left Joan alone and broke. She left Julie with an aunt in Long Island and found a place to stay with a black friend of Huncke's called Spence, on West Forty-seventh Street.

Jack Kerouac went to see her and found her "out of her fuckin' mind on Benzedrine." When he came in, she immediately stripped. "Joan, what are you doing?" Jack asked. "Who are you, strange man?" she said. "Get out of this house." "I'm not a strange man, Joan, I'm Jack," he said. When she started shouting, "Jack is trying to rape me," he left.

Joan was in bad shape. John Kingsland, who saw her in October, wrote Edie Parker: "I saw Joan last weekend. She seemed to be losing her mind. It's a shame, don't you think?" One day, wandering around Times Square, she was picked up and taken to the Bellevue psycho ward. Four years earlier, she had faked a psychotic episode in order to bring her husband to New York. In retrospect, that was a dress rehearsal for the real thing. While she was in Bellevue, Whitey's trial came up, and she later learned that he had been sentenced to five to ten years in Sing-Sing. Her father, David Vollmer, came down from Loudonville to get Julie. It took Joan ten days to convince the doctors that she wasn't crazy. When she talked about junkies congregating on 103rd Street, they thought she was hallucinating. But she asked the doctors to call in the two detectives who had arrested Burroughs, who confirmed what she was saying.

When Burroughs heard, via Allen Ginsberg in October, that Joan was in Bellevue, he came to New York to get her. It was a rescue operation. It was not easy to be Burroughs' friend, but once he accepted you, he tried not to let you down. In his criminal persona, he liked the idea of having an "old lady," so he could talk to the others about "my old lady this" and "my old lady that." Also, he and Joan were companionable; they had the same interests, from drugs to the Mayan codices.

Joan agreed to go to Texas with him. They would find a little spread of their own and grow the best cash crop of all, marijuana. In November, they went to stay with Kells in the Rio Grande Valley while they looked for an isolated place. Finally, they found a broken-down, ninety-nine-acre farm about forty miles north of Houston. Burroughs kept his cotton land in the Rio Grande, which Kells would manage for him. They stayed in their new place the last week of November, starting repairs on the house, then drove to New York for a few days, where they saw Allen, who had been readmitted to Columbia and had a crush on a fellow student named Heaze. "Why you can't even get a Heazard-on," Burroughs joked. Giggling, Joan added, "It's his innate sense of delicacy." On December

8, they went to the Museum of Natural History to look at the Mayan codices, taking the recently sprung Huncke along. For six nights running, Allen took heroin with Burroughs, and felt no habit and no anxiety when he quit.

Burroughs went to St. Louis to spend Christmas with his parents, and Joan went to Londonville to get Julie. She and Julie took the train to Houston on January 2, 1947. Joan wrote Edie: "Although we're not married, Bill got a divorce, but I haven't yet. Let me have your news. Make it Mrs. W. S. Burroughs, New Waverly, Texas." When Joan and Julie got to Houston, Burroughs was there to greet them, and Joan announced that she was pregnant. Burroughs was not surprised. He knew exactly the night that the baby had been conceived, in a Times Square hotel room. *They say women always know . . . well, I know too . . . that was it . . . I just knew.* Joan asked him if he wanted her to get an abortion. Certainly not, Burroughs said, it was out of the question—abortion was a form of murder.

· EIGHT ·

TEXAS

1947–1948

New Waverly was a town five blocks long, forty miles north of Houston, with a gas station, a diner, and a post office. From the highway you took a pitted blacktop road for twelve miles, past weather-beaten cabins with elderly blacks sitting on front porches, and then an old logging road back into the pine woods, twisting down to the bayou, with an occasional old cedar dripping Spanish moss, until you came to a ramshackle clapboard house with a porch, in the middle of nowhere. There was a cistern, and a vine-covered old barn about ready to collapse. It was a setting out of Tobacco Road, for the house had no electricity, no hot water or bathtub, and the only heat came from a pot-bellied stove in the kitchen.

In this secluded spot, part of a depressed area called Pine Valley, where you could not see your neighbor's roof, Burroughs planned to grow marijuana, which according to Texas law was a felony with an automatic two-year sentence. But he would not be "like the poor cat i' the adage," in Shakespeare's words, who wanted fish but was afraid to wet its paws. His first priority was to obtain seeds, and he and Joan agreed that it would be a good idea to invite Huncke, recently released from the Bronx jail, to join them on their rural estate. He could bring some seeds, provide companionship, and score Benzedrine for Joan in Houston. On January 9, 1947, Joan wrote Allen Ginsberg:

"Bill really should write this but it would never be started if I left it to him. Julie and I made it down here all right and after some confusion managed to connect with Bill. This week we're staying at a tourist camp. . . . We have a Jeep, which while it bounces almost intolerably, is an incredible blessing as it actually navigates over our road, flooded as it is by five days of steady rain. So now we can carry loads in, things are looking up. Bill is enclosing fifty dollars. Would you, the goat as always, buy Huncke a train ticket as soon as possible. . . . It leaves N.Y. about 4:30 P.M. daily—train no. 11—*The Southerner*, Texas-Mexico section. . . . On top of all the rest, if you could spare the time to see Herbert safely on the train, it might be a sound idea. Not offensively, you understand. . . ."

Huncke thought it over. He was preparing to sail as second cook on a ship bound for Shanghai, but figured, they're probably surrounded by redneck Texans and will be glad to see a friendly face. He ended up taking the bus rather than the train, so out of his skull on various drugs that he forgot the mason jar of pot seeds he was supposed to bring. By the time they hit the Gulf of Mexico he was going through withdrawal, but fortunately Burroughs met him in Houston with some pantapon, a form of opium which Bill Garver had sent from New York.

Disappointed that he hadn't brought the seeds, Burroughs sent Huncke into Houston with some money to buy some. With a dowser's instinct on where to score, Huncke headed straight for the Brayos Hotel, an old-fashioned Southern-style place with wicker chairs and two-bladed ceiling fans. Around the corner was a stand with black shoeshine boys who made the shine rag snap. Huncke started rapping with one of them and said he was interested in buying some grass. "What I really want are some seeds," he said. "I'm visiting some friends here in Texas. We've got a big spot and we'd like to plant some grass. If I could get just a jar, it's worth twenty dollars to me."

"Well, man, I just might be able to do you some good," the shoeshine boy said. "Listen, I can't knock off here until a little later in the day, but if you want to we'll meet. I have a taxicab and we'll drive out to a couple of spots I know. I'll turn you on to a stick and you can decide if you want some or not. When they clean up, I'll tell them to save the seeds."

Mission accomplished, Huncke started back, but remembered that he had also promised to find Joan some inhalers. With the same unerring instinct, he hit on a drugstore that offered him as many as he wanted. He bought them by the dozen, and became such a good customer that the druggist gave him a discount. After that, Huncke did all the scoring for Burroughs, who didn't want to draw attention by patronizing the drugstore in the New Waverly area. Huncke also picked up liquor in Houston, because New Waverly was in a dry county.

Aside from scoring, Huncke was kept busy fixing the house. When he thought about it, he couldn't remember ever working so hard. He got yards of screening to enclose the old porch. He dug holes for fence posts. Since there was no well, he carried a water tank in a wheelbarrow down to the stream every day and filled it with a bucket. Now he realized why they'd invited him down: They needed a day laborer and water carrier.

Heeding Huncke's complaints, Burroughs brought in a dowser or water-witch to find a well—no one in that part of Texas would have dreamed of digging a well without one. This old fellow wearing baggy pants held up by one suspender and leading a one-eared mule came by and walked up and down with his wand until it dipped, and sure enough they found water there. Four-year-old Julie came up and said, "Hey, Bull, what's goin' on?" She couldn't pronounce "Bill," so she said "Bull." Burroughs would tell her stories about the gnomes that lived in the cistern—in fact, he had to keep a strainer on the cistern so the frogs didn't get in.

All in all, thought Huncke, it wasn't a bad life. He suspected that even Burroughs enjoyed it. With spring coming, the foliage was turning lushly verdant. The oak and persimmon trees were draped in Spanish moss, and everywhere there were armadillos and rosy-throated chameleons. There were also, in multitudes, scorpions, tarantulas, ticks, chiggers, and centipedes. Burroughs fixed a razor blade to the end of a stick to destroy scorpions, and sliced one in three pieces—each piece ran off in a different direction. "That's the ugliest thing I ever saw," Huncke said. Burroughs kept a scorpion count—his record was ten in one day. The house was overrun with rats as big as possums—one was so fat he got wedged in his hole, and Burroughs shot him. He had a .22 target pistol, and would set up cans and bottles to fire at.

Joan was pregnant and wore loose dresses. There were wild berry thickets near the house, and one afternoon Huncke saw Joan with a big crockery bowl in her arms, and Julie trotting along beside her, the two of them picking blackberries, and Joan was wearing a loose blouse that fell off her shoulders—she was really something to see.

One morning, Huncke heard some mewing under the house, and Julie called him and said, "Hunk Hunk Hunk, cat cat cat." Sure enough, there was a tiny white cat, which came out when Huncke put a saucer of milk out. It was covered with ticks, which he pulled off with tweezers, and it became Huncke's cat—the only creature he had ever found that would obey him. If Julie wandered away from the yard, the cat would meow up a storm.

There was always plenty to do around the house, aside from shopping trips to Houston. In the evening they smoked grass and listened to music on Burroughs' scratchy old phonograph. Huncke wanted to play Billie Holiday records, but Burroughs asked for Viennese waltzes. "Aw man," Huncke would say, "you don't want to hear that," and Burroughs would reply, "Oh, but I do." Huncke was reading *Tales of the South Pacific* by a new writer, James Michener, which made him laugh out loud. "You know, Bill," he said, "this book's on the bestseller list. You ought to write something like this, you old fart."

But Burroughs had no thought of writing. He was bent on bringing in his marijuana crop, which was speedily growing. One day his neighbor, a grizzled farmer named Arch Ellisor, dropped by and admired the tall cannabis plants. "That's a mighty fine stand, whatever it is," he said. "Oh," explained Joan, "it's some new kind of animal feed." Surrounding the cannabis was a cover crop of tomatoes. Ellisor told his wife: "They're growing 'maters over there. Don't they know you can't grow 'maters in that soil?"

Joan described Ellisor as the man with the Orphan Annie eyes, two little empty circles. He would arrive on horseback and say, "Well, how is everything today," waiting to be invited in for a whiskey. His grandmother was dying of cancer, and he provided graphic reports on her condition. "The old woman's about ready to go. Her breast is just literally eaten away," he said, making a scooping gesture in front of his chest. "There ain't nothin' left, poor old girl." A while later, he reported, "She's so bad she's crawlin' around on all fours." When she died, he invited Burroughs and Huncke and Joan to the funeral.

The other neighbor, Mr. Gilley, would come by just as often, through the piney woods where armadillos frolicked, pale blue eyes under a black Stetson. "Lawd, lawd, have you seen my brindle-faced cow?" he would ask. "Guess I'm takin' up too much of your time. Must be busy doin' somethin', feller says. Good stand you got, whatever it is. Maybe I'm asking too many questions. Talking too much. You wouldn't have a rope, would you? A hemp rope. Don't know how I'd hold that old brindle-faced cow without a rope if I did come on her." At one point, when Burroughs had a Jeep and a car, Gilley said, "Well, I see the rich man has got hisself another car—might give that Jeep to a poor man."

The strangest thing about the setup to Huncke was Burroughs' apparent indifference to Joan. He never expressed affection. They slept in separate rooms, and there seemed to be no physical contact between them. One night when he was trying to sleep he heard Joan knock on Burroughs' door. When the door opened, Huncke heard her say, "All I want is to lie in your arms a little while."

Huncke didn't think Burroughs was cruel or without feeling. But he found Burroughs' coldness toward Joan hard to take. Once they were walking in the woods and Joan was tiring from carrying Julie and Huncke said, "Why don't you fuckin' help her," and Burroughs responded that the Spartans knew how to deal with the excess baggage of female infants by throwing them off cliffs.

That kind of sardonic humor was Burroughs' way of coping with emotions, but Huncke never got used to it. You could never be completely sure whether he was kidding or not. Once, they came on a big hole in a clump of cedars and Burroughs dropped a rock down, saying, "Let's see how deep it is." They waited a long time until they heard it hit, and Burroughs said, "If only we had Kay White here we could shove her right down."

On the other hand, if anyone criticized Joan, Burroughs came to her defense. When Huncke said that she was a little extravagant in her shopping, Burroughs said, "Well, after all, she wants to see that we're fed properly." He never said anything about her Benzedrine habit, which was worse despite her pregnancy. Huncke kept right up with her, and they would spend evenings giggling and having strange conversations. Both of them, in their Benzedrine hallucination, began to see small white filaments coming out of their skin, living organisms, like tiny worms. This to Joan was connected to the post–atomic bomb fear of radiation, which was one of her main obsessions, so that the white filaments took on the relevance of a universal planetary disease, in the sense that atomic contamination was spreading everywhere. Fearing contamination, she took to examining her skin with a hand-held mirror, in the light of a kerosene lamp. Amphetamine, reflected Huncke, could lift you into some very strange states of mind. He had seen people dig things out of cracks in the floor, and imagine they were seeing microbes.

While Burroughs was working out his version of the American pastoral idyll, Jack Kerouac and Allen Ginsberg in New York found a fresh heroic figure to replace him in Neal Cassady. Here was the Western hipster, a child of the streets like Huncke, but with a manic drive and a genuine lyric dimension. He had grown up on Denver's skid row with a wino father, and began stealing cars at the age of fourteen. By the time he was eighteen, he'd already been arrested ten times. But he wasn't a victim like Huncke; he was more of an irrepressible natural force. A creature of Bunyanesque excess, Cassady claimed that he could throw a football seventy yards, run a hundred yards in under ten seconds, and broad-jump twenty-three feet.

As a child he had been a classroom show-off, skipping third grade by going up to his teacher and spouting facts at her. She was impressed by his fluency, and he found his true calling—the inspired rap. Largely self-taught, he had absorbed a vast number of unrelated facts, from the amount of coffee grown in Brazil to the weight of Trotsky's brain. He had grandiose visions where he saw himself confounding senators with his wisdom, and in the meantime used his big talk on the ladies. Basically, what he wanted was for everyone to say, "Neal is great."

Cassady was a friend of Hal Chase, who described him as "this unbelievable crazy quixotic man." Hal went to see Lionel Trilling and said that Cassady was a bright street kid who had done a lot of unconnected reading, a sort of valuable savage who should be given the chance to attend Columbia. Trilling agreed to set up a special admittance exam for him, but on the appointed day, Neal didn't show. Hal thought he had lost his nerve. For once Columbia was willing to try the unorthodox, but Neal copped out.

In any case, at the start of 1947, twenty-year-old Neal was in New York with his sixteen-year-old girlfriend LuAnne Sanderson, a sort of teenage Betty Grable, the daughter of a Denver cop. Jack and Allen took to Neal at once. He fit right into their cast of characters, as a creature of appetite and instinct who hungered after experience and was ready to try anything. Neal was a perpetual motion machine, investing every moment with his own brand of manic intensity. He explained to Allen that the reason for his manic side was that he was conditioned to dealing with people who had to be driven on by his assuming an urgent tone. Words like "crude" and "vulgar" didn't seem to apply to Neal, who could get away with describing "the heightened sensibility one experiences after a good bomber."

Allen could speak about literature as easily as Neal could speak about football. He admired Allen for that. Allen could put things so well that Neal found it hard to formulate. He could certainly profit from Allen's company. There was one slight hitch, which was that Allen was forcing himself on Neal physically, and even when Neal gave in, so as not to interrupt the flow of conviviality, he didn't enjoy it much.

Thus in February, in a letter to Burroughs, Allen disclosed his "liaison" with Neal, but soon after that Neal went back to Denver and wrote Allen that "I don't really know how much I can be satisfied to love you, I mean bodily, you know I, somehow, dislike pricks & men . . . I'm not sure whether with you . . . I was forcing a desire for you bodily as a compensation to you for all you were giving me."

Allen also informed Burroughs that he was seeing a psychiatrist but had no faith in the treatment. Burroughs, who had gone through half a dozen psychiatrists and was disappointed in all of them, replied that he was not surprised: "These jerks feel that anyone who is with it at all belongs in a nuthouse. What they want is some beat clerk who feels with some reason that other people don't like him. In short someone so scared and whipped down he would never venture to do anything that might disturb the analyst. I think you would do better with the Reichians who sound a good deal more hip."

In this letter was Burroughs' first use of the word that would later be used to qualify a generation—the word "beat," which he had picked up from Huncke, who used it to signify down and out or pathetic. It was used as well by Joan in a March twenty-third letter to Allen in which she said, "If you feel like seeing the beatest state in the union for a while during the summer, we'd all be awfully glad to see you."

The reference to Reich was an indication of the new field of psychic investigation that Burroughs was engaged in. He had been very impressed by Reich's book, *The Cancer Biopathy*, in which cancer was seen as the result of sexual repression in a sick society. The connection Reich made between individual illness and the social order was one that fitted Burroughs' own sense of alienation and sexual blockage. He was conditioned by his own experiences to accept the idea that a life-denying, repressive society could produce that alienation and blockage.

More specifically, Reich singled out drug addiction as a "biopathic phenomenon," writing that "addicts are always orgastically impotent . . . they attempt to get rid of their excitations artificially, but they are never completely successful. Usually, they are sadistic, mystical, vain, homosexual, and are tortured by consuming anxiety, which they attempt to work off by brutal behavior."

When Burroughs read Reich, he recognized his own predicament, and became a convert. But Wilhelm Reich was in fact a textbook case of the healer who cannot heal himself, of the reformer whose own life is a mess. He seemed to seek out conflict and difficulty, as though compulsively reenacting a scenario in which he, the holder of the flame, is banished by the established powers. He seemed to go around with a storm cloud over his head.

A student of Freud's in Vienna, Reich was repudiated by the master for seeing the cause of neurosis in blocked sexual energy. He developed a theory of sexual politics in which he saw the ills of society re-created in each individual, and joined the German Communist Party. But soon the party expelled him because he tended to substitute sexual blockage for the class struggle. He moved to Denmark and was expelled again, from the Danish Communist Party, and to Norway, where he was again the focus of controversy. In 1939 he came to the United States, in the hope that in a young, dynamic land, still in the midst of its own social experiment, his ideas might find, if not acceptance, at least tolerance.

Having dropped Communism, Reich developed the idea of a specific kind of energy he called orgone energy, which was present in all living matter. The blocking of this "good" orgone energy was a single-cause explanation for the devastations of human history and the emotional and physical ailments of individuals. Orgone energy was the life force, in contrast to such negative and destructive forms as nuclear energy.

Reich designed and built an Orgone Energy Accumulator, a box-shaped cubicle made of alternate layers of metallic and nonmetallic materials where a person could sit and absorb the healthful orgone energy. His proof that the device worked was that he measured different temperatures inside and outside the orgone box.

In 1941, Reich sent an orgone box to Einstein, who determined that the differences in temperature were caused by convection currents of air around the box, and wrote Reich off as a crackpot, thus making him the only man to have been rejected by the three great thinkers of his age— Marx (via the Communist parties), Freud, and Einstein.

The more he was dismissed, the more stridently Reich insisted on the correctness of his views. He claimed that the orgone box was an "indispensable weapon" in the treatment of cancer, which he connected with bad sex: "Cancer is living putrefaction of the tissues due to the pleasure starvation of the organism." He bought 280 acres near Rangeley, Maine, and set up a research institute called Orgonon, where he treated cancer patients.

The year that Burroughs took an interest in Reich, 1947, was also the year that Reich came to the attention of the Food and Drug Administration, which was mandated to protect the public against false medical claims. Reich was renting orgone boxes for ten dollars a month and putting out an Orgone Energy Bulletin that made various claims about its benefits.

There was a lengthy F.D.A. investigation, which was dropped and then resumed, and it was not until 1954 that the attorney general of the state of Maine filed an injunction at the request of the F.D.A. against the interstate shipment of orgone boxes. Reich went on trial in April 1956 for violating the injunction and was found guilty and sentenced to two years in jail, a victim less of government persecution than of his own willful mishandling of his case, never having been told that a man who acts as his own lawyer has a fool for a client. He died in prison that November, of heart failure, which he had always insisted was a biophysical manifestation of an emotionally heartbreaking experience.

During the time of his investigation and trial, Reich grew increasingly irrational. He refused to appear in court on the grounds that his appearance would lead to "possibly national disaster." He threatened to disrupt the weather on the Maine coast with orgone energy, to prove that it worked. He told his associates at Orgonon to carry firearms against the HIGs (Hoodlums in Government). He identified UFOs as spaceships powered by negative energy. At a hearing for the reduction of his sentence he argued that to imprison him would "lead to the downfall of the United States as a self-governing society at the hands of a few conniving masterminds," because only he knew the equations concerning space and negative gravity, which he carried in his head.

The moral of this dismal tale was that those whom the gods wish to destroy they first drive mad, except that in Reich's case it was not the gods but his own demons.

Burroughs in any case did not feel much sympathy for Reich at the time of his downfall. He thought Reich was "a goddamn fool" who could have stayed out of jail if he'd had any sense. He was, however, interested in some of Reich's ideas, while admitting that in the most charitable view they hovered in a twilight zone between cultist dogma and verifiable scientific truth.

But he thought there was something in the idea of pleasurable and unpleasurable orgasms, and of cancer as a disease of sexual decline. Someone with a satisfactory sex life, he thought, would be less likely to get cancer. He was sold on the orgone box, and over the years built them and used them in various places. He usually stayed in the box about twenty minutes, reporting an accumulation of energy as manifested in a tingling sensation on the skin. When he came out he felt invigorated, and on several occasions he achieved a spontaneous orgasm—"Look, no hands." Part of this may have been that what you got out of the box depended on your degree of receptivity. In any case, it could do no harm to go and sit in a metal-and-plywood box for twenty minutes, and come out feeling that it was keeping you healthy.

Beyond the orgone box, Burroughs saw that Reich's vision of society was not scientific but literary, and that he could adapt it to his own purposes. Reich's rejection of ideologies, his ambivalence toward authority, his view of politicians as parasites, were seeds falling on fertile ground. The notion of a stifling bureaucratic structure, of a life-denying social structure, of neurotic symptoms showing up on a national and global scale, would all show up in Burroughs' writing, and in this sense he was "Reichian." Indeed, in *Naked Lunch* there are a number of references to orgone energy, as though Burroughs was giving Reich a tip of the hat—"they wanta suck my orgones," "the invisible blue blowtorch of orgones," and the clientele of the Meet Café, including "sellers of orgone tanks."

For Huncke, life in New Waverly was a pleasant interlude, away from the dangers and temptations of New York. The situation, he wrote Allen on March 26, was "quite satisfactory. . . . As you know, some absorbing interest exists for Joan, Bill, and Julie. I like them. The house and its location: pine trees and moss-draped oaks and dead trees. Bayou and swamp and semitropical growth. Heavy heat and damp, chilling cold on and off during spring. Summer will be hot steadily, with terrific beating rain. . . . Bill is a good friend. He is exceedingly interested in guns. He has allowed me to shoot and I find them much less awe-inspiring. Bill is quite a guy. Joan is splendid. She is amazingly energetic and ingenious. Incidentally, I can do things, too, and Julie is growing rapidly and is beyond the average by far with self-reliance."

Spring warmed into summer, lush and green, and at two in the morning on July 21, Huncke was awakened by the sound of Joan knocking on Burroughs' door and saying, "Bill, I think it's time." "All right, just a few minutes," he said. As he got his clothes on, Joan turned to Huncke and said, "Well, I'm going to have my baby." They had made no arrangements, but there was a hospital in Conroe, about fifteen miles south of New Waverly, where Burroughs drove her. He returned the next morning, laconic as always, and said: "Joan's had her baby. It's a boy." The day after that, she was back, and the boy was named William Burroughs III. Huncke was surprised at how little fuss they made, treating the birth as an event like any other. Life went on as usual, with Bill seeming completely indifferent to Joan's comfort. Joan did not breastfeed the baby, because her system was loaded with amphetamines.

Soon after the baby's birth, Burroughs' parents came for a rare visit, to take a look at their new grandson and to check up on their son, who was supposed to be leading a healthy, drug-free life. Huncke thought Mortimer Burroughs looked very distinguished, and Laura was the gushing grandmother, hovering over the baby. She had bought boxes of clothing for Joan and the new arrival. Mr. and Mrs. Burroughs were steered away from the marijuana field in back, and Bill told them he wasn't using any drugs, which was their primary concern—not using any more than what he could get ahold of, thought Huncke, who had to wear a Stetson and pretend to be a local, to hide his New York drug scene origins.

Mr. and Mrs. Burroughs left New Waverly thinking that their son had made great progress, and was living a productive life on the farm as a model family man, with his wife and child and talkative little Texas friend. Their visit was followed by the arrival of Allen Ginsberg and Neal Cassady. Allen, still pursuing Neal, had gone to Denver, fantasizing about all the different things he would try with him sexually, but Neal wasn't interested, and Allen wrote in his diary, "I can't keep giving and not getting in return."

Allen wanted Neal to meet Burroughs, hoping he would see the quality in him, which was not readily apparent to everyone, and they hitchhiked to Texas, arriving in New Waverly on August 29. It was a bad time, because Burroughs was low on funds, waiting for his monthly check, and they were barely able to buy food. Joan and Huncke were scraping by on two tubes of Benzedrine a day. In addition, there was a great deal of sexual tension between Neal and Allen, with his "petitionary masochistic lust," as he called it. Huncke tried to play Cupid by turning over his room to the guests and proposing that they take some canvas from an old army cot and stretch it between the two sideboards of his bed to make a double bed, but the effort was a failure, and they ended up sleeping on the floor. With the collapse of the double-bed idea Allen's hopes also collapsed, and he resolved to stop making advances that were impossible to gratify, go to Houston, and find a freighter to ship out on.

On September 3, Allen went to the union hall and found a messman's job on a freighter leaving for France. September 5 was his last night before shipping out, and Neal promised to spend it with him in a Houston hotel, which Allen would pay for with money borrowed from Burroughs. They went in that afternoon with Huncke, who could get a suite for the price of a room in the hotel where he usually stayed, and that evening they hit some black music joints and got high on grass. Then Cassady drove them back to the hotel and took off in the Jeep, saying he would meet them later. He managed to pick up a girl and bring her back to the hotel, but when Allen saw her he protested that Neal had promised to spend the night with him. Neal told the girl to go into the next room while he took care of Allen. At this point, Huncke, who had been out making a connection, came in and saw Neal fucking Allen in the mouth with a kind of vehemence that seemed decidedly unpleasant—it was not for pleasure, he thought, but for humiliation. When he was finished, he went in and fucked the girl, after which he passed out. An infuriated Allen threw the girl out and struggled in vain with Neal's lifeless body. Huncke was annoyed. He had a good reputation at the hotel, they had a certain amount of respect for him as a paying customer, and now here was this wild-eyed maniac dragging in this piece of jailbait and having her wait her turn while he did it to Allen first—it was a bit too much.

The next morning when Neal woke up, Allen wanted to discuss matters, and kept postponing his departure, while Huncke warned him that if he didn't hurry up he would lose the job—which was exactly what happened: He lost the job and was in dutch with the union. Dejected, they went back to New Waverly and a highly displeased Burroughs. But the next day, Neal drove Allen into Houston for the last time, dropping him off at the union hall, and left him reading Henry James and musing on his fate. At least, thought Allen, it was an end to his state of sexual supplication.

"Incidentally," Cassady wrote Jack Kerouac in an account of his Texas visit, "the girl I'd had that night is now in the nuthouse, she was picked up babbling on the street the next morning. Too bad her beautiful body was matched by an idiotic mind."

Allen found a boat but Neal stayed on, much to Huncke's annoyance. As much of a hustler as he knew himself to be, he always considered the other person with some respect, and now here came Neal who didn't give a damn, who was a burden but unconscious of being one, who just sat on his ass reading Mezz Mezzrow's *Really the Blues*—Huncke could sense that Burroughs wanted him out, too, particularly when he said about Mezz Mezzrow, "Sure a nigger-lover, ain't he?" On top of everything, Huncke fumed, Neal was coming on to Joan, which he was sure Bill sensed—Neal couldn't help himself when there was a woman around. My God, he was even coming on to four-year-old Julie, and saying that she was already hep to many, many things, and that he would keep an eye on her and check her out when she was eight or nine to see how far she'd gone.

Neal, however, thought he was making himself useful. While Huncke went into Houston to get bennies for Joan and paregoric (tincture of opium) for Bill, who had a slight habit again, and who got up at ten thirty and started reading the paper and making comments—"Well, I see Peaches Browning got another divorce here"—he, Neal, was building a fence, laying a cement floor in the garage, and damming up the creek with cement. When he had some time to himself he went to Huntsville to a football game.

Then it dawned on Huncke why Burroughs was letting Neal freeload. Winter was coming, the pot had grown and been harvested, and he wanted to take it to New York and sell it, and needed Neal to help him drive the

Jeep. Joan also wanted out, she had a baby to take care of, and Billy wasn't a quiet baby, he squalled constantly. Huncke felt he could have done some of the driving, but he knew he made Bill nervous. Bill, trying not to hurt his feelings, said, "Well, Herbert, you know the car is not in the best of condition."

The Jeep, in fact, was too small to carry them all, so it was decided that Joan and the children would take the train and wait for them in Grand Central Station. There was some talk of making Huncke hitchhike, since he wasn't needed for driving and there wasn't enough money for his train ticket, but in the end, he squeezed into the backseat of the Jeep, surrounded by duffle bags filled with mason jars of pot.

They left on September 30 and covered the 1,860 miles to New York in three days, driving nonstop. Neal did most of the driving, because Burroughs' sight was poor, and at night, if another car was coming, he'd pull over to the side of the road—just like an old woman, thought Neal. They barely stopped for food—someone would run into a diner and pick up coffee and hamburgers. Once they pulled in off the road and Huncke looked up and saw a state trooper with his visored cap right in Bill's face. "All he wanted was a shot of whiskey," Burroughs said. Huncke couldn't help thinking that they had enough pot back there to land them in jail for a couple of years. Also, he was out of Benzedrine and going through withdrawal, but Bill wouldn't even stop at a drugstore—wait till we get to New York, he said.

When they checked Grand Central, Joan wasn't there. She had been waiting so long that the police had picked her up and taken her to Bellevue for observation. For some reason, they thought she was planning to abandon her children. Burroughs went to Bellevue and explained the situation, adding that he was a member of the University Club, and Joan was released.

The next item on the agenda was the marijuana, which turned out to be something of a problem, because it wasn't properly cured. All they had done was cut the plants and hang them upside down in the barn until they dried. They knew nothing about male and female plants, about separating the potent parts or about manicuring, so that when Huncke gave a sample to a hotel bellhop, he made a face and said, "Hey, man, that's awful, that's green tea . . . Jesus, it's terrible shit, it's not even cured."

Pushing the pot was a headache. It was so bulky, thought Burroughs, that if the cops came around it would be like being caught with a bale of alfalfa. Through Huncke's friend Vickie, who was back in town after a stint with a Philadelphia madam, Burroughs was introduced to a tough lesbian jazz pianist who agreed to keep the pot in her apartment until it was sold. But then Vickie told her she was crazy to take the risk, and the next time Burroughs and Huncke came around, she told them to take the stuff and get out, adding, "You're both mother-fuckers."

Burroughs tried baking it until it achieved the desirable greenish-brown look, but still there were no takers, even though he and Huncke roamed the metropolitan area from the Bronx to Newark. He had been talking about making thousands from his crop, but finally had to wholesale it to some Italians for $100, resolving never to push pot again.

By this time he was back on junk, thanks to the good offices of Bill Garver, the overcoat thief. One night in Yonkers he had too much and passed out, as he had seen his customers do when he was pushing: His eyes rolled back and showed the whites. Joan made coffee and walked him around the room to revive him. His parents, unaware that he was back on drugs, came to New York and set them up in a resort hotel in Atlantic Beach, where the off-season rates were reasonable. Joan stayed in her room with the children while Burroughs was out scoring with Garver.

Burroughs tried to kick with a reduction schedule, adding distilled water to the junk in increasing amounts, but that didn't work, so he decided in January 1948 to commit himself to the Federal Narcotics Farm in Lexington, Kentucky. The routine involved seven days of medication on dolophine, a synthetic morphine, and seven days of rest, after which they put you to work on the farm or in the cannery. The doctor who examined Burroughs assessed him this way: "Patient seems secure and states his reason for seeking cure is necessity of providing for his family."

By February, Burroughs was back in New Waverly with Joan and the children. Arch Ellisor, as a neighborly gesture, gave him two young pigs, saying, "You keep feedin' 'em and they'll be worth a heap of money." But Burroughs found that every time he fed them they squealed for more. He didn't have enough garbage so he had to start buying great bags of feed to shut them up. Finally he called Ellisor over and said, "Look, Arch, we've carried the fuckers as far as we can. Take 'em back!"

Fed up with farming, Burroughs put the New Waverly place up for sale. He still had his cotton land in Pharr, which he periodically visited. That May, while driving down to the Rio Grande Valley. he was drinking in the car with Joan when they got the itch, and decided to stop outside the town of Beeville and make love by the side of the road. Someone driving by reported this activity to the sheriff's office, and the next thing

Burroughs knew flashing lights were shining in his face and handcuffs were snapping on his wrists. He was placed under arrest for drunken driving and public indecency.

As it happened, Vail Eenis, the Beeville sheriff who had arrested Burroughs, was a famous Texas lawman in the tradition of Buckshot Frank Leslie and Whispering Tom Mayfield, one of those relics of the Old West around whom legends gather. Tall and thin, with cold gray-blue eyes, Eenis was storied in the state of Texas, and revered in Beeville County. Once he arrested two men for robbery, handcuffed them together, and went into a phone booth to call his office. One of the men drew a concealed .38 revolver and shot Eenis four times in the gut. Eenis drew his horn-handled, double-action, .44 Colt, put six bullets in one of the men, calmly reloaded, and put six bullets in the other. "With a look of faint disapproval on his face," commented Joan when she heard the tale.

Although he didn't mind shooting people in the line of duty, and was credited with killing at least nine, Eenis disapproved of drinking and fornicating in public. Actually, Eenis was quite cordial when he brought Burroughs before the judge. "He saw at once," Burroughs recalls, "that I was not a member of what Graham Greene calls the torturable classes." "You should be ashamed of yourself, pullin' a trick like that," he told Burroughs.

Eenis even managed a *bon mot* before the judge: "This here feller was disturbin' the peace while tryin' to get a piece." The district attorney asked Burroughs, "Do you do this sort of thing at home?" Burroughs said he did not, and the D.A. said: "So you come down here to do it, is that it?" Burroughs pleaded guilty, and the D.A. said, "If you are inclined to let this man off with a fine, your honor, I suggest that it be a substantial one."

Burroughs was fined $173 and had his license suspended for six months. He could not pay the fine, and spent the night in jail; Joan wired his parents for funds. When Eenis locked him up, he told Burroughs: "Listen, you did the smart thing. If you'd taken that in front of a jury, you'd be in here for six months." He also explained that they would have had to support his wife while he was in jail, so that they much preferred a guilty plea. Later that night, Eenis brought in a kid with blood all over his face, and explained that he was charged with robbery and assault. "If I hadn't a known his pappy I'd a killed this little fuck," he said. "Oh, I didn't do nuthin'," he mimed. "Well, it's no good takin' what somebody makes honest. So I drove him round the block three times and by the third time he was ready to pick out the money he took."

The next morning Burroughs' money order arrived and he paid his fine and was released. "How can I drive out of here with my license suspended?" he asked Eenis. "If anyone stops you, just refer them to me," Eenis said. He really was a little tin god, Burroughs reflected, and a mean son of a bitch to boot, but there was a certain fairness and integrity about him.

Having had enough of frontier justice and marijuana farming, Burroughs sold the New Waverly property and tried to think of the nearest place where there might be a drug scene and a gay scene. He decided on New Orleans, and moved his family there in June 1948. Off he went again, the Wandering WASP, at home nowhere, who somehow managed to get the law on his tail wherever he landed.

With the money from the sale, Burroughs bought a house at 509 Wagner Street in Algiers, a suburb across the Mississippi from New Orleans, reached by ferry. The house was dilapidated but there was a screened front porch and a big yard with several good-sized trees, where the children could play.

While Joan set up house once again and found druggists who would sell her inhalers, Burroughs was hoping to make a killing in winter vegetables. He had combined his holdings in Pharr with Kells Elvins. They had bought equipment together and hired a manager and planted peas, lettuce, and carrots, aside from cotton and Elvins' citrus grove. "If all my crops come in on schedule," he wrote Jack Kerouac, "I will be rolling in $ by cotton-picking time." At the same time, he was worried that "the government will put the snatch on a big hunk of what we sons of the soil wring out of the earth."

Burroughs' experience as a farmer in the Rio Grande Valley reinforced his conviction that conventional morality was a hoax, and that the line between the criminal and the law-abiding citizen was blurred. As a farmer, he violated the law every day, but his violations were condoned by a corrupt government. The Rio Grande Valley was only a few miles from the Mexican border, and the Border Patrol looked the other way when the illegal aliens arrived, providing cheap labor. The whole deal was handled by labor brokers who contracted to find the workers and get the crops picked. The broker simply backed a truck up to the river and rounded up the wetbacks who had waded or swum across. They worked a twelve-hour day for two dollars, and were sometimes kept on the job at the point of a gun. Some brokers went in for rough stuff, and shot workers who tried to leave the field. You might say that their civil rights had been violated, but no one did anything about it. Anyone wanting to sacrifice himself for a noble cause had only to try and organize farm labor in Texas. "In short," Burroughs wrote Allen Ginsberg, "my ethical position now that I am a respectable farmer is probably shakier than when I was pushing junk."

In a society where life was "nasty, brutish, and short," in the words of Thomas Hobbes, moral attitudes were pointless, and Burroughs determined to adopt a philosophy which he called "factualism." "All arguments, all nonsensical condemnations as to what people 'should do,' " he wrote, "are irrelevant. Ultimately, there is only fact on all levels, and the more one argues, verbalizes, moralizes, the less he will see and feel of fact." Or, as he put it to Kerouac, "The only possible ethic is to do what one wants to do."

Kerouac was in New York, trying to place his first novel with a publisher, and renewing his friendship with Lucien Carr, who had been released from the Elmira Reformatory and had a job with a news agency. One day in September, after staying up all night listening to Lennie Tristano records, they went for a walk down Sixth Avenue, and Jack reflected on intention—did we really understand what we were doing, or was all of life a mystery never to be resolved? They stopped in a bar and drank Pernod in iced glasses. There was the Cézanne-like light of day, thought Jack, and the light of Lucien's intelligence, and the Pernod brought in another light. Lucien ribbed Jack about being a "disreputable writer," and urged him to enter the economic system as he had done, and it seemed to Jack that they were communicating on the surface only, and that this lack of depth was in some manner similar to bad writing, and that if only people could feel love for each other without deviation, if only they could break through the shields and screens . . . the hours drifted by and soon the sun was sinking, and the sky was reddening, and they wandered into Washington Square, and saw a little girl fall down on her skates and scrape her knee, and stamp up and down because she was hurt, and Lucien said, "It's so wonderful the way children express their pain." He went over and patted the little girl on the head and told her she would be all right, and she pouted and blushed and turned away. Lucien was talking about his days at Elmira, and all the hopes he had nurtured there, and, tripping along on the edge of the fountain he said, "And you know, Jack, it gets more and more joyous all the time." And it occurred to Jack that Lucien was someone who by losing everything had been saved, and that Burroughs was the same way, he had thrown all his earthly possessions and pride away, and in a deeper sense, had been saved. Jack repeated the words inwardly: "It gets more and more joyous all the time . . . spoken in the reddening sun of Washington Square in the early fall of 1948." It all tied in with his writing, in which he was delving into the consciousness of his generation—there was a kind of furtiveness, as though they had an inner knowledge it was pointless to flaunt, a weariness with the conventions society had handed them. Later, they went back to Lucien's place on Twelfth Street, and his girlfriend Barbara was in bed and said, "What's the big idea of getting Lucien drunk the minute my back is turned?" "Be serious, Barbara," Jack said, as Lucien started dancing with a frying pan, and hitting himself with it softly, *bing-bong*, *bing-bong*.

· NINE ·

LOUISIANA

1948–1949

Embracer of marine commerce and purveyor of the lesser deadly sins, New Orleans was known for its tolerance. It was romantic and corrupt and tropical. Amid the smell of gardenias and the intricate ironwork of balconies, people lived in an atmosphere of mildew and lassitude. It was perfect for anyone who wanted to pledge himself, in the words of Lafcadio Hearn, "to the worship of the odd, the queer, the strange, the exotic, the monstrous." Crossing the Mississippi on the ferry from Algiers, you went down Morgan Street and hit downtown New Orleans, the Vieux Carré, Bourbon Street, Rampart Street, the Storyville red-light district.

In the French Quarter, Burroughs found a replica of the Times Square scene, with seedy bars and jazz joints crowded with servicemen, merchant seamen, gamblers, and drifters. By instinct, he sensed that the areas around Lee Circle and Exchange Place were junk neighborhoods. One night in Frank's Bar near Exchange Place, he caught the eye of a square-faced man, who looked like one of those terra-cotta heads you plant grass on, coarse-haired and vacant-eyed. The man's name was Pat Cole (name changed) and he was an old-time New Orleans junky.

After some preliminary conversation to establish their mutual interest in junk, Cole asked Burroughs if he wanted to score, and Burroughs gave him four dollars for two caps of heroin. One cap led to another, and a week later, Burroughs had a habit again. The problem with New Orleans was that the stuff was so easy to buy. The town was full of pushers underbidding each other for your business. You didn't have to look for it, it came looking for you. At the same time, the state laws were among the stiffest in the country. Possession was a felony, and there was a law making it a crime to be a drug addict, so that you could be arrested for having track marks on your arm.

Burroughs fell into a routine of scoring three caps a day, mainly through Pat Cole, and filling in the days by working around the house. Manual labor made the time pass. He also started pushing in a small way, to two or three regular customers like Seltzer Willy and Lonny the Pimp, and once again came up against the problem of being held up for credit: "You don't mind putting this one on the cuff, do you? You know I'm good for it."

Burroughs thought of kicking but couldn't as long as the stuff was available. He considered leaving New Orleans long enough to get the Chinaman off his back. Maybe on his next trip to Pharr, to see how his crops were doing . . .

On December 15, 1948, Jack Kerouac got a call from Neal Cassady, who was in San Francisco and had traded in his old Ford and all his savings for a maroon 1949 Hudson. Neal was now married, to a pretty blond Denver University coed named Carolyn Robinson, who had given birth to his daughter on September 6, and had recently left for Hollywood to work as a costume designer. Before joining his wife, Neal proposed to drive to New York, pick up Jack, and drive back out west.

"To save you the hitchhiking trip out to the coast, see, I will break in my new car, drive to New York, test it, see, and we will run back to Frisco as soon as possible and then run back to Arizona to work on the railroads. I have jobs for us, see. Do you hear me, man?"

"I hear you, I hear you."

"See, Al Hinkle is with me in the phone booth. Al is coming with me, he wants to go to New York. I will need him, see, to help me jack up the car in case I get a flat or in case I get stuck, see, a real helper and pal, see."

Al Hinkle was a friend from Denver who could have lifted the car single-handed and stood it on its end, being cast in the mold of a jolly giant, six feet six of muscle and brawn, with a cheerful, boyish manner. A brakeman on the Southern Pacific, he was at that time laid off and suggestible to Neal's schemes, one of which was to find money to finance their cross-country trip.

It happened that Hinkle was dating a pretty half-Greek, half-Portuguese San Francisco girl named Helen, who was about a foot and a half shorter than he was. Neal, sensing that Helen was well-heeled, urged Al to marry her and take her for a honeymoon on the trip, which he expected her largely to subsidize. Al did marry Helen on December 18, but Neal realized she would be hard to con when she vetoed the big jam session he had arranged for a wedding celebration. Now Neal told Al he was marrying a rotten bitch, and made disparaging remarks as he drove them to church.

Neal wanted to leave right after the wedding night, and Helen soon realized that the so-called honeymoon would be a nightmare. His idea of traveling was to drive without stopping. When she wanted to go to the bathroom, he said, "Piss out the window." When she suggested that newlyweds might want to stop for the night in a motel, he said, "Bang in the backseat. " In addition, he was constantly picking up people and asking them to pay for gas, and entertaining them with his nonstop rap, so that the car was crowded. By the end of the second day, when they arrived in Tucson, and Neal once again refused to stop for the night, Helen said she'd had enough. She was going on no farther. Was Al staying with her? Al was not, not wanting to lose face with his good friend Neal. He gave her his railroad pass and told her to take the train to New Orleans, where they would arrive shortly with Kerouac to visit Bill Burroughs. Armed with the pass, a little cash, and Burroughs' phone number (just in case), Helen Hinkle arrived in New Orleans and checked into a hotel. In the meantime, Neal and Al had detoured to Denver to pick up Neal's old girlfriend, the ripe and now eighteen-year-old LuAnne. Al was glad to have her along, because the Hudson had a radio but no heater. It was cold in Colorado in December, and he warmed his hands between her legs. By Christmas, they reached Rocky Mount, North Carolina, where Jack was vacationing with his mother, and a few days later they were in New York. Neal and the others put up at various places, including Allen Ginsberg's apartment, and were in no hurry to leave, as there was a round of parties, and it was Hinkle's first trip to the city.

At one party, Jack confided to Neal that he had told his novelist friend John Clellon Holmes that they were a Beat generation, a term he had borrowed from Huncke. But where Huncke meant "wiped out," Kerouac's usage had the connotation of upbeat and of beatific. There was hope for the Beat generation, as there was hope for anyone rowing against the current with optimism and ambition. One day Jack and Neal and LuAnne drove out to Woodmere, Long Island, to visit one of the unlikeliest members of the burgeoning counterculture group. Alan Ansen was a Harvard classics scholar, class of 1942, summa cum laude. He was an expert on almost everything, quoting Latin and Greek by the yard and singing entire operas by heart. He was also an obvious homosexual who had been denied a teaching post at Harvard because of trouble with the law over his proclivities, even though he did his best to be discreet, describing his double life in Long Island as *"New York Times*, wholesome walks in the suburbs, evening music, a perpetual ground bass of detective stories, and nights of quick closeting with complements."

A tall, burly man with close-cropped hair, Ansen had a slightly asymmetrical face, as if assembled by a police artist from the unreliable reports of witnesses. He was pedantic, but in an acceptably humorous way. When you asked him what his politics were, he said, "Whig." He lived with an elderly maiden aunt and a large collection of records and rare books in a fine house. When the aunt answered the bell and at first refused to let Neal and Jack in, Ansen screamed, "Get into that room, you stupid old bitch."

In no time at all they were loaded, and started acting out a Verdi opera, with Ansen singing in falsetto and LuAnne singing bass. Then, in a burst of drunken generosity, Ansen invited them to make long-distance phone calls. When LuAnne called a boyfriend in San Francisco, Neal got mad and knocked her down, losing his balance and falling on top of her, as Ansen shouted "Oh my God, mayhem, mayhem on my island, oh my God!"

In New Orleans, Helen Hinkle was about to be evicted from her hotel, because all the rooms were booked for the Sugar Bowl on New Year's Day. In desperation, she called Burroughs on December 28. From his voice, he sounded like a man in his sixties. He took her to lunch in a Chinese restaurant and expounded at some length on prefabricated housing that would last a thousand years and indestructible nylon stockings—he was still in his *Man in the White Suit* phase. Painfully thin, thought Helen, and there was something strained in his gait, so that he seemed much older than thirty-four. That day, he sent a telegram to Allen Ginsberg asking him to tell Neal and her husband that she was worried.

A couple of days later, when she had to vacate her room, a bellhop gave her the address of a rooming house. The first thing she noticed in her room was a jar of Vaseline on the mantel. Bells rang all night long and there were constant comings and goings in the halls. Realizing she was in a brothel, Helen called Burroughs, who offered to put her up. She was obviously furious with her wayward husband, he thought, and was, in the words of Robert Burns, "Gathering her brows like the gathering storm, nursing her wrath to keep it warm."

As she nursed her wrath, she also observed the Burroughs household, although she tried to absent herself as much as possible, leaving in the morning on the ferry and visiting antique shops and museums in New Orleans. Joan, you could see, had once been pretty, but now looked drab, mousy, unadorned, with straight and lifeless hair, chopped off short. She walked with a slight limp, the result of a mild case of polio contracted since their arrival in Algiers. One way that Helen was able to make herself useful was to buy inhalers for Joan. "You can have as many as you like," a druggist told her. "I'll sell you up to ten 'cause I know you won't misuse them." Misuse them? Helen didn't know what he was talking about. She bought one because it said on the label that it was good up to six months. Joan had to explain that she used them with greater frequency.

The household seemed to operate on the principle of total permissiveness. The children were allowed to go potty wherever they liked, whether it was on the dining room floor or in the Revere Ware in the kitchen. The little boy, not yet two, was beautiful, with fine blond hair, and the six-year-old girl was thin, with filthy, matted hair—apparently they washed when they felt like it. She had nightmares and had formed the habit of chewing her left arm, in the crook of which there was a large scar.

The state of the children was not negligence on Joan's part, Helen observed, but a deliberate attitude of leaving them largely to themselves. Far from being a sloppy housewife, Joan was forever cleaning the floors with Lysol and had discovered the first liquid detergent on the market, called Glim. She cooked two full meals a day, and was proud of the fact that Bill had found a butcher who sold chuck roast so tender you could broil it.

Joan was so pepped up by the amphetamines that on occasion, when she couldn't sleep, she did housework at night. There was a dead tree right outside the kitchen that was covered with small lizards, and one night Helen woke up and saw Joan raking the lizards off the tree. "You rake them off they'll only come back," she said. "I have all this energy, I have to do something," Joan replied. Once they took a walk to the river, and Joan told Helen she could see fire dancing on the water's surface.

Her relationship with Bill struck the newly married Helen as equally curious. They were obviously fond of and amused by each other, and their conversations on all sorts of subjects were witty and well-informed. It was only when they talked that Helen saw Joan really come to life. But they slept in separate rooms, and there was no physical contact between them that she could see.

As for Bill, he would read, shoot his air gun, and work around the house. He had found a termite-ridden log which he had sanded smooth, leaving the bark on the underside, and was building a table that he said would last a thousand years. Not realizing he was on heroin, Helen wondered why he spent so much time in the bathroom.

His way of relating to the kids was to tease and frighten them. Billy was Little Beast and he was Big Old Bear, and he would come after them like a lumbering bear and they would scream and run away. There were half a dozen cats around the house, and Bill had a habit of tying their paws with string and giving them baths. Helen would hear the cats screaming in the bathroom. It was so bizarre she didn't know how to react, although once she asked, "What is it with the cats?" and he mumbled an unintelligible reply. She wasn't sure whether it was some kind of experiment or whether Bill had an ornery streak. He taunted the cats terribly, saying to one, "I'll get you tonight." Later, when *Junky* was published, the following paragraph was deleted from the manuscript: "When I am on junk, I take pleasure in tormenting and terrorizing cats. I hold a cat out the window or provoke the unfortunate animal into biting or scratching, then slap it across the face with brutal force. I give the cats a bath and hold their bodies underwater."

Trying to be helpful, Helen offered to baby-sit, and one evening Bill and Joan went to the movies, but mostly they just stayed home, with Bill spending his days in New Orleans on various errands. As the days wore on and there was no sign of Al Hinkle, Burroughs lost patience. What kind of character was this Hinkle, to leave his wife without funds and not even let her know where he was? Did Hinkle expect him to billet his wife indefinitely? She was a perfect and conscientious guest, who paid her way as far as she was able, but why didn't he stop fucking around New York and get down there and retrieve her? She had been there two weeks.

Another pet peeve was "that bitch mother of Kerouac's," as Burroughs described her to Helen. She was an evil old woman, domineering, and making Jack feel guilty about everything he owed her. To all these guys, Helen reflected, maybe even to her own husband, a man she barely knew, after all, women were bloodsuckers. You used them but you didn't let them get any power over you. She was reminded of a catch phrase of the period: Mother, please, I'd rather do it myself. That was Neal, that was Jack, that was Burroughs, all fighting Momism.

Burroughs' irascibility was compounded by the heroin habit he was trying to kick and by developments in the Rio Grande Valley. His first crop of peas, from which he had been expecting $5,000, had frozen five days before harvest. All was not lost, however, for he and Kells had made $2,000 on eight acres of lettuce, which they would split, and still had thirty acres of carrots, which they hoped to cash in on at $200–$300 an acre. The California freeze was money in his pocket, and all they needed now was a hurricane in Florida and a hailstorm in Arizona.

On January 10, Burroughs sent another telegram and on the sixteenth he wrote Allen, "This Hinkle thing has assumed the proportions of a full-blown atrocity." Finally, Hinkle and the others left New York on January 19, and the trip to New Orleans went into *On the Road*, which Kerouac had begun, almost verbatim. The gobbling up of miles, Neal's manic need to criss-cross America, the importance of the car as a way to absorb the country, the driving day and night and coasting into gas stations and filling the tank while the attendant slept, the "warmest talk about the goodness and joy of life," the appreciation of the land's varied beauty and grandeur—schoolchildren waiting for a bus in the Florida panhandle, a black family in a wagon pulled by a mule in Biloxi, Mississippi—it all had an epic quality.

And then, as Jack would remember it, they were driving along the blue waters of the gulf, and listening to the "Chicken Jazz 'n' Gumbo" disk-jockey show, with the disk jockey saying, "Don't worry 'bout nothin'," and they inhaled the soft air of New Orleans, and the car bounced up on the Algiers ferry, and they crossed the Mississippi, the great brown father of waters rolling down from mid-America bearing Montana logs and Dakota mud and Iowa wheat, and they drove into old sleepy Algiers on a road that ran across a swampy field, and came to a dilapidated old house with sagging porches and weeping willows in the yard, the grass a yard high, a washtub on the back porch.

Helen happened to be home that afternoon, and Jack and Neal came in through the kitchen, wearing white mechanics' overalls, followed by her husband. "Who are you, buddy?" she felt like asking. Jack found a recipe for crepes suzette and at once wanted to make some. It seemed to Helen that all the banter and noise covered up a shyness with each other and a self-consciousness over the impression they made. It was a form of play-acting, which was not something she expected men to do. Neal the con man at once began to make excuses for the delay, and when she took Al into Joan's bedroom so they could have a quiet talk, LuAnne followed them in and asked, "Aren't you going to bang?"

That night, Burroughs took them into New Orleans to visit the French Quarter, and showed them the sword cane he carried for self-defense. Although genuinely glad to see Jack, and displaying all the bonhomie he could muster, Burroughs was not sympathetic to the little band's voyage. For sheer compulsive pointlessness, he thought, it compared favorably with the mass migrations of the Mayans. To cross the continent for the purpose of transporting Jack to San Francisco, where he planned to stay three days before heading back east, was an exercise in futility. Neal, of course, was the very soul of the journey, and exemplified pure, abstract, meaningless motion. Compulsive and dedicated, he was ready to sacrifice family, friends, even his very car itself to the necessity of careening from place to place. Wife and child might starve, friends existed only to be exploited for gas money, but Neal must move.

Burroughs' worst fears were confirmed the next day, when Neal put the bite on him for the continuation of their wretched trip. He said he was broke, which was true enough. Like most inveterate moochers, Neal seemed to feel that others were under some mysterious obligation to support him. Did he have any idea of how he appeared to others? Allen Ginsberg claimed that Neal had "charm" and a "graceful human nature," but Burroughs couldn't see it. In fact, when Neal saw that no money was forthcoming, he grew sullen, and acted as though Burroughs had lured him to New Orleans under false pretenses.

Jack, however, seemed much more sensible and self-assured than Burroughs remembered him, which may have had something to do with the fact that his novel was being considered for publication by the editor Robert Giroux at Harcourt Brace. He and Jack played at quick draw in the yard, and went to the races. Burroughs generally put down New Orleans, saying it was a very dull town, the bars were insufferably dreary, and it was against the law to go to the colored section. Joan read the want ads in the *Times Picayune*, saying it was the most interesting part of the paper. Her face, once plump and Germanic and pretty, had become stony and red and gaunt.

Burroughs tried to talk Jack out of continuing his trip with Neal. "Why don't you stay in New Orleans with me?" he asked. "If you go to California with this madman you'll never make it. We'll play the horses over to Graetna and relax in my yard. I've got a nice set of knives and I'm building a target. Some pretty juicy dolls downtown, too, if that's in your line these days." Then he would retire to the bathroom for his fix, clutching his necktie in his teeth for a tourniquet and jabbing the needle in his arm, hunting for a vein. In the afternoon they went to the bookie joint in Graetna, and Burroughs played the slot machine, missing the $100 jackpot by a hair. "Damn!" he said. "They got these things adjusted. You could see it right then. I had the jackpot and the mechanism clicked it back. Well, what you gonna do?" Back in the yard, Burroughs showed Jack how to disarm someone with a knife. Six-year-old Julie said, "Look at the silly men," and Neal Cassady said, "Wow! Wait till she grows up! Can you see her cuttin' down Canal Street with her cute eyes?

Neal announced that it was time to get moving. "I'm not going on any more trips with him," Helen Hinkle said. Neal's greatest pleasure, she knew, was to get lots of people into a car and start them fighting with one another—that was pure bliss. So Neal and Jack and LuAnne drove off into the sunset on January 29: "We wheeled through the sultry old light of Algiers, back on the ferry, back toward the mud-splashed, crabbed old ships, across the river, back on Canal, and out on a two-lane highway to Baton Rouge in purple darkness; swung west there, crossed the Mississippi at a place called Port Allen."

Reporting to Allen Ginsberg on the visit, Neal wrote that "Joan is brittle, blasé brittleness is her forte. With sharpened laughs and dainty oblique statements, she fashions the topic at hand. . . . Julie's hair is matted with dirt. . . . Normal disintegration of continued habit patterns (child-raising) has Joan laboring in a bastardized world wherein the supply of Benzedrine completely conditions her reaction to everyday life."

Al and Helen decided to stay in New Orleans for a while. Al landed a soft job answering the phone and taking orders for a tile company, and was paid in cash while collecting unemployment from the railroad. "Bring plenty to read," the boss told him. They found a place on Rampart Street, finally had a real honeymoon, and are married to this day. But to Burroughs, any job was a mistake. "A regular job drains one's very lifeblood," he wrote Allen Ginsberg. "It's supposed to. They want everything you've got."

It was not a particularly pleasant time for Burroughs, who had a showdown with his troublesome Italian neighbors ("that termite nest of dagos," as he called them), shortly after Neal's departure. They had wiseass kids who liked to throw rocks and who went around singing "Glory to the newborn Jew" at Christmastime. Now one of them threw a rock into his yard that hit little Billy in the head. Burroughs went over there with his gun in his shoulder holster, looking for the kids' father, who wasn't home, and got into a shouting match with the wife. "Listen, lady, keep your goddamn kids at home," he said, to which she replied, "Go back where you came from." "That's what you ought to do, go back to Italy," Burroughs said. "My husband will come over there and knock your glasses through your face, you four-eyed bastard," she said, and Burroughs answered, "If he does, he won't walk home." The conflict, however, did not go beyond the verbal level.

Once again, there was bad news on the agricultural front, when he heard in March that the bottom had fallen out of the carrot market. Instead of the thousands he was hoping for, he was lucky to get $500 for his share. Too bad. He had hoped to spend the carrot money on a ten-day cure in a private sanitarium. Maybe he would just take a train to some strange city with a pint of paregoric and plenty of goofballs (Nembutal tablets) and stay until he kicked.

Even more annoying than the carrot fiasco was the lecturing letter he received in March from Allen Ginsberg, who was back in New York after shipping out to Dakar; he had graduated from Columbia in February, 1949. Allen, who seemed to be in a moralizing, holier-than-thou frame of mind, accused him of living a lie for staying married to Joan while remaining a homosexual. What about Joan's sexual needs, Allen asked, was he thinking of her at all? With some indignation, Burroughs replied on March 19: "Now this business about Joan and myself is downright insane. I never made any pretensions of permanent heterosexual orientation. What lie are you talking about? Like I say, I never promised or even implied anything. How could I promise something that it is not in my power to give? I am not responsible for Joan's sexual life, never was, never pretended to be. Nor are we in any particular mess. There is, of course, as there was from the beginning, an impasse, and cross purposes that are, in all likelihood, not amenable to any solution."

Allen was writing poetry, and had gotten his first rejection slip from John Crowe Ransom at the *Kenyon Review*: "I like very much this slow, iterative, organized and reflective poem. At times it's like a sestina. . . . But still I think it's not for us exactly. I guess we need a more compacted thing." As luck would have it, Allen had some compacted things to send him. He was, however, disgusted with his work, which he saw as full of artificial passion, ventriloquism, and fake symbols. In addition, he was seeing an analyst to break away from homosexuality. Generally, he felt lost and unsure of himself.

Early in 1949, Herbert Huncke appeared at the door of his small apartment at 1401 York Avenue, having just been released from jail and needing a place to stay. Huncke had a way of taking over. He wore Allen's clothes, took over Allen's bed, and burned incense. Allen, who worked nights as a copy boy at the Associated Press, slept on the couch. Soon he began to think in terms of the Ionesco play in which a giant shoe appears in someone's living room, unbudgable and growing larger by the day. When he wrote Burroughs about his quandary, the reply was pitiless: "The more obligation Huncke is under to anyone, the more anyone has done to help him, the more certain he is to steal from or otherwise take advantage of his benefactor. It works out like an algebraic equation. Raise (x) benefits, you raise(y) resentment = everything of value seized and disposed of."

But Allen rationalized Huncke's parasitic side by seeing it as the repetition of an early family situation. Cast out by his father, Huncke had to keep testing those who befriended him. He was a wastrel and a criminal because he was rootless and had never owned anything. In addition, Allen admired his knowledge of the underground culture and saw him as a key figure in the formation of his own consciousness. Thus, Allen could not bring himself to throw Huncke out. He kept planning to give him an ultimatum, but Huncke developed a boil on his leg and stayed in bed for two weeks.

When he got better, Huncke brought around Vickie Russell and Little Jack Melody, a son of the Mafia. They were living together in Little Jack's family home in Maspeth, Long Island, where his mother had an altar in the basement with votive candles. Allen knew Vickie as a changeable shrew, worldly and irreverent, a naturally bitchy but gorgeous girl who went from overaffection to rejection of men, but always had a lover in tow. As for Little Jack, he didn't look like the gangster he was supposed to be (although Allen knew that he had done time for safecracking). Small and balding, Little Jack was elfin, almost doelike, and unfailingly eager to please. They started coming around every day, making his apartment their second home. Jack brought a Victrola and Billie Holiday records, and the marijuana flowed. Well, thought Allen, he had dreamed of having a pad with a friendly atmosphere, where his pals could come and drink and smoke pot and listen to music, and now he had it.

Since he didn't seem able to get rid of Huncke, and since Little Jack offered to sublet his place, Allen decided to go to New Orleans and see Bill, who he was worried had reached a stage of intellectual and spiritual failure, with his heroin habit and his marital dilemma—he seemed to be stagnating. Allen wanted to go down there and galvanize him into activity, get him to kick his habit and stop fiddling around with drugs and romanticized quasi-underworld activities. He thought of Bill and Joan almost as a substitute father and mother. But each time he started to leave, something came up.

At the end of March, 1949, it was the acceptance of Kerouac's *The Town and the City* by Harcourt Brace, with a $1,000 advance for Jack, and a round of celebrations. Allen thought it was a great book and was glad that Jack's efforts had been rewarded. In contrast to this good news were the activities of Huncke and his two friends, who had started pulling burglaries and bringing the loot back to Allen's apartment. One day he accompanied them when they were cruising for cars with suitcases and clothes in them to break into, but he insisted that he did not want to get involved, and Little Jack deferred to his wish "to keep his cherry," as he put it. Allen saw his apartment filling up with stolen goods—clothes, radios, a carved chest and two chairs removed from a Park Avenue lobby. One day, he came back from the dentist to find a cigarette machine standing in the kitchen. When he objected, they broke it up into parts and disposed of it.

Not knowing what to do, Allen sought out Lucien Carr for counsel. Lucien warned him that his involvement with Huncke and the others could get him into serious trouble. Then Huncke left the apartment in a fit of pique after Vickie called him "Little Jack's prat-boy." Huncke's method, Allen reflected, was to make people feel guilty about him. Allen finally told Little Jack and Vickie that he did not want his apartment to be used for burglary operations, but Little Jack said he had to pull a few more jobs because of the "desperacy" of his financial situation.

Then, on April 21, a fine spring day, Allen wanted to take some books over to his brother's on the West Side, and accepted a ride with Little Jack and Vickie, who had a carful of stolen clothes they were taking to a fence. But first they had to go to Maspeth to drop off a few dresses for Little Jack's mother. Coming back on Northern Boulevard shortly after noon, as Allen was recounting his trip to Dakar, Little Jack missed a turn, and made a U-turn over the center island, at which point a policeman flagged him down. Since Little Jack was driving a stolen car and had no driver's license, in addition to which he was out on parole, he stepped on the gas, with a patrol car in pursuit, saying, "We've got to outrun them." Vickie asked him where he was going, and he said, "Someplace where we can abandon the car."

Vickie observed that if they abandoned the car they would have to leave the clothes behind, and Little Jack said, "Fuck the clothes." Swerving to turn into a side street, he lost control of the car and crashed into a stone stanchion. The car turned over and Allen's glasses were knocked off. He managed to get out and walk away, and heard someone shout, "Turn off the ignition before the car explodes!" Little Jack and Vickie had run off, and Allen stumbled to a phone booth and called his apartment, finding Huncke there, and told him to "clean the place out." He knew that the police would have his address from the books and papers he had left in the car.

When he got back to York Avenue, he saw that Huncke had taken him literally—he was sweeping the floor. Then Vickie arrived, weeping, and saying, "Man, Jackie's been busted." Huncke had some portable radios there that were easy to hock, and said, "Well, look, let's get a few things together and get the fuck out of here." At that moment there was a knock on the door, and all three of them were arrested and taken to the Sixty-eighth Street precinct, where the cops slapped Allen around and asked him whether he liked men or women—they had evidently read some of the material he had left behind. He said he liked mostly men. To Huncke, the cops said, "We've got a streamer on you." Huncke could see the years in jail piling up. He and Allen were taken to the Long Island House of Detention, where Allen, behind bars, recited Jewish prayers, while Vickie went to the women's prison in Greenwich Village. The next day in *The New York Times*, the headlines read WRONG WAY TURN CLEARS UP ROBBERY, and COPY BOY JOINS GANG TO GET "REALISM" FOR STORY.

As it happened, of the four, only Huncke did time. He was sent away for five years, having no influence whatever. Vickie's magistrate father got her a suspended sentence. Little Jack's family arranged for him to be sent to Pilgrim State Hospital for observation, even though he had a record of eighteen previous arrests, and he was released a year later in the custody of his mother. As for Allen, out on bail, he sought advice from his supposedly wise professors at Columbia, who reacted in various ways. Meyer Schapiro talked about the universe for two and a half hours and told him about the time he had been jailed for vagrancy in Europe. Mark Van Doren sermonized: "What were you doing with common criminals, Ginsberg? . . . . A lot of us around here have been thinking maybe you'd better hear the clank of iron." A dismayed Lionel Trilling took him to see law professor Herbert Wechsler, who suggested he plead insanity, which he did, ending up in the Columbia Psychiatric Institute on 168th Street, and writing in his journal:

> All the doctors think I'm crazy.
> Truth is really that I'm lazy.
> I had visions to beguile 'em,
> Till they put me in asylum.

When Allen wrote Burroughs that the Wrath of God had descended upon him, he got back a testy reply: "Imagine being herded around by a lot of old women like Louis Ginsberg and Van Doren. Besides I don't see why Van Doren puts in his two cents' worth. Sniveling old liberal fruits. . . . All liberals are weaklings, and all weaklings are vindictive, mean, and petty. I don't see anything to gain from this Medical Center deal. A lot of New Deal Freudians. I wouldn't let them croakers up there treat my corn let alone my psyche."

In fact, Allen had a way of making every turn taken in his life seem to be the right one. He did find great gain at the Psychiatric Institute, for it was there that he met Carl Solomon, another key figure in his personal and artistic growth. Then twenty-one, Solomon was the son of a smoked fish salesman who had served in the American Expeditionary Force in World War I. Unlike Allen, sent by his mother to Communist camps as a boy, Solomon was raised in a patriotic, flag-waving family setting. He was a child prodigy of sorts, who could remember every baseball player and score since the beginning of the game. In 1943, he started City College at the age of fifteen, and two years later he joined the merchant marine, having seen movies that romanticized it, such as *Action on the North Atlantic*, with Humphrey Bogart. In May 1947, he took the liberty ship *Alexander Ramsey* to France and jumped ship in the port of La Palice. Then it was on to Paris, where he hired a French lady to teach him the language. One day in the rue Jacob, he came upon a gallery where a man with a thin face and shoulder-length hair was reciting a strange text. It was Antonin Artaud, the French poet and playwright, who had been confined for nine years in an insane asylum, and who proclaimed that "a lunatic is a man who prefers to become what is socially understood as mad rather than forfeit a certain superior idea of human honor." If you saw that the society around you was irrational, a retreat into what that society called madness would in fact be the only road to enlightenment. The text that Artaud read was on Van Gogh, who in his view was the perfect example of a man driven to madness and suicide by a loutish and philistine society. Deeply impressed, Carl Solomon nurtured a cult for Artaud. He tried to see life the way Artaud did, and to ask the questions that Artaud might have asked, such as: "Should I accept reality?" "Should I have a job?" "How can I justify this dissipated society? Can I justify it by Lautréamont's 'the marvelous is to be found in the banal'? . . . If so, I can find a job and get married." In 1949, while attending Brooklyn College, Solomon's attempt to go beyond the complacency of postwar campus life led him to commit an Artaud-like absurdist act. He stole a peanut-butter sandwich from the Brooklyn College cafeteria and showed it to the guard on duty. As a result, he was packed off to the Columbia Psychiatric Institute, where he met Allen. They became allies in a setting that each had entered by choice—Allen to escape a jail term, and Carl as an alternative to his stultifying existence at Brooklyn College. But the consequences for Carl were horrible, as if he were there to confirm Artaud's thesis that asylums are places where you go in sane and are driven mad. Carl was given insulin shock treatment, which has since been abandoned as too dangerous. The treatment put him into acute sugar withdrawal, or hypoglycemia, which in turn brought convulsions and amnesia. The doctors determined that his amnesia was the sign of some deeper psychosis and continued the insulin treatment. In the nine months that he was at the hospital, he went through fifty insulin comas, a parallel to Artaud's experiences in France with electroshock treatment. As Artaud had embraced "madness" as a heightened sense of artistic awareness, so did Carl Solomon, who explained to Allen that his insulin-packed body was a human pun, readable on several levels. He called Allen a "dopey daffodil," a foolish romantic like Wordsworth. He spouted Surrealist epigrams which Allen jotted down, and told him about some of the "gratuitous acts" he had committed, such as pretending he was W. H. Auden and signing autographs. He continued his antics in the hospital, once giving his doctor a handful of marbles "in the hope that you might kill yourself." "What do you mean, he might?" Allen asked. "I got my point across," Solomon said.

Carl was the most interesting person there, Allen thought. On the first day they had met, Allen told him about some of his mystical experiences, and Carl said: "Oh, well, you're new here. Just wait awhile and you'll meet some of the other repentant mystics." Carl amused Allen by telling the nurses that if he ever heard anyone say, "Mr. Solomon, you're raving," he would overturn the Ping-Pong table. He and Allen shared a hatred of the doctors, pale-lipped, four-eyed, ungainly psych majors, seersucker liberals, bloodless blue-eyed boys who went to proms and debated about socialism, vapid social scientists and rat experimenters: "What? Mr. Solomon won't eat today? Send him down to shock."

And so the hospital was the venue for a meeting with another kindred spirit, another character in Allen's cast, which already included Lucien Carr, Jack Kerouac, Burroughs, Huncke, and Neal Cassady, all rejecting the system and operating under their own impulses and beliefs. In this scheme, Solomon was the artist as outcast, misunderstood, branded a lunatic, punished by psychiatrists for his refusal to conform, an exile in his own country.

All these characters helped inspire the poem "Howl," but it was to Carl Solomon that the poem was dedicated, and it was of Carl Solomon (and Allen's mother) that Allen was thinking when he wrote the memorable first line, "I saw the best minds of my generation destroyed by madness." It was Carl Solomon he invoked and identified with: "Ah,

Carl, while you are not safe I am not safe. . . . I'm with you in Rockland, where we are great writers on the same dreadful typewriter. . . . Fifty more shocks will never return your soul to your body again from its pilgrimage to a cross in the void. . . ."

At about the same time that Allen was busted in New York, gathering material for a realistic story, as he told the police, Burroughs was busted in New Orleans. The chief of police had launched an antidrug drive, and the cops were stopping addicts on the street and examining their arms for needle marks. On April 6, he was driving near Lee Circle with his addict friend Pat Cole, who was well known to the police. They were driving very slowly, on the lookout for a connection, when a prowl car passed them; the cop at the wheel did a double take when he saw Pat. They were stopped and arrested, and in the glove compartment the police found an unregistered gun that Burroughs had brought in to pawn. Also in the car was a letter from Allen mentioning the sale and purchase of marijuana, which made the police think that Burroughs was a big-time pusher.

On the strength of the letter, they escorted Burroughs to his house and searched it, finding a jar of marijuana, a small amount of heroin, and half a dozen assorted firearms. Then they took him back to the lockup at the Second Precinct, where he was placed in a cell with four other men, three of them addicts.

Burroughs hoped that the case would be thrown out, because the police had searched his house without a warrant, or barring that, that he would be tried in federal court. If he was tried by the state, it meant a mandatory two-to-five-year sentence for possession, and a stay in Angola State Prison, which was known not to be a country club.

In the meantime, Joan found a clever, well-connected lawyer named Crile (name changed), who got bail set before Burroughs was arraigned, and came to the lockup to get him released. Crile looked at Burroughs quite awhile before introducing himself, then said: "I can see you don't feel much like talking now. We'll go into the details later on. Did you sign anything?"

Burroughs said he had signed a statement to a federal district attorney admitting possession of heroin, and taking the heroin home in his car.

"That was to get your car," Crile said. "You're charged in state. I talked to the federal D.A. an hour ago on the phone and asked if he was going to take the case. He said, 'Absolutely no. There's an illegal seizure involved, and under no circumstances will this office prosecute the case.'

I think I can get you over to the hospital for a shot. The man at the desk now is a good friend of mine. I'll go down and talk to him."

Within minutes, two cops escorted Burroughs to Charity Hospital in the wagon. The nurse at the receiving desk asked what was wrong with him. "Emergency case," one of the cops said. "He fell off a building."

Burroughs could hear two doctors nearby discussing his case. "After all, doctor," one of them said, "there is the moral question. This man should have thought of all this before he started using narcotics."

"Yes," the other one said, "there is the moral question, but there is also the physical question. This man is sick." He turned to a nurse and ordered half a grain of morphine, which Burroughs soon felt sweeping in pleasant waves through his body.

The next day, Crile made arrangements for Burroughs to take a cure in a private sanitarium, where he was driven in a police car with two detectives. As Burroughs got out of the car, Crile handed a wad of bills to one of the detectives and said, "Put this on that horse for me, will you?" "I'm not going to put any money on a horse," the detective replied indignantly, making no move to take the money. Crile laughed and tossed the money on the seat, saying, "Mack will." The bribe offer was a deliberate tactic, for when the detectives later asked him what in hell he was doing, right there in the police car in front of a witness, he said, "Why that boy was too sick to notice anything." Crile wanted witnesses to testify that his client was in bad shape at the time he signed his statement, and could call the two detectives to the stand.

While Burroughs was in the sanitarium, taking Demerol to kick his habit, and going through the "ants-crawling-under-the-skin" junk sickness for the first three days, Joan wrote Allen on April 13 to warn him that the cops had found his letter and might relay the information to New York City police. Hospitalizing Bill had been a good move, she said, as his father was about to swoop down from St. Louis to insist that he be hospitalized somewhere else for six months. The problem was, where would they go now: "New Orleans seems pretty much out of the question, as a second similar offense, by Louisiana law, would constitute a second felony and automatically draw seven years in the state pen. Texas is almost as bad, as a second drunken driving conviction there would add up to about the same deal. New York is almost certainly out—largely because of family objection. What else is there, really? Maybe Chicago—I don't know. It makes things rather difficult for Bill; as for me, I don't care where I live, so long as it's with him." This was Joan—loving, loyal, and unselfish, sticking by a man who was not a husband in the usual sense, who was unable to take care of her in the usual ways, whose life was a tangle of contradictions and failures, and who was incapable of helping her cure her own addiction to amphetamines.

The week-long cure was a success. Burroughs felt as good as new, and determined to avoid drugs while his case was pending. One stick of marijuana, one cap of heroin, could send him away for seven years as a second offender. He wanted to get out of New Orleans, where the police were still under orders to question known addicts "when and wherever encountered," making him subject to a search and a seventy-two-hour stay in a precinct lockup just for standing on a street corner.

He went to see Crile to ask him whether he could leave the state and visit his farm property in the Rio Grande Valley. "You're hot as a firecracker in this town," Crile said. "I have permission from the judge for you to leave the state. So you can go to Texas anytime you like."

"I might want to take a trip to Mexico," Burroughs said. "Would that be okay?"

"So long as you come back here when your case comes up," Crile said. "There are no restrictions on you. One client of mine went to Venezuela. So far as I know, he's still there. He didn't come back."

Burroughs wondered whether Crile was telling him to disappear. He was shrewd and farsighted, and seemed lucky. Criminal law was one of the few professions where the client bought someone else's luck, which usually was not transferable. But a good criminal lawyer could sell all his luck to a client, and the more luck he sold the more he had to sell.

In May, Burroughs moved his family to a rented house in Pharr, where he looked after his crops and built an orgone box with Kells Elvins, obtaining "unmistakable results." He was "immobilized in this valley of heat and boredom," the police having seized his car because heroin had been found in it. "This seizure of property," he wrote Jack Kerouac in June, "is a violation of the Constitution—if I had the money I'd take it to the Supreme Court."

Burroughs was fed up with America, seeing government interference everywhere. In Pharr, Border Patrol agents were deporting his field hands, and Department of Agriculture bureaucrats were telling him what, where, and when to plant. (In fact he was the beneficiary of New Deal programs in that he was paid a support price for his cotton.) In New Orleans, and all over the country, there were heavy punitive statutes against the use of marijuana, in spite of the 1944 La Guardia report on drug use describing marijuana as harmless. The report, of which he had a copy, stated that "marijuana is not a drug of addiction" and that "those who have been smoking marijuana for a period of years showed no mental or physical deterioration which may be attributed to the drug. . . . In most instances, the behavior of the smoker is of a friendly, sociable character." If that was the case, thought Burroughs, why were users sent to jail, any more than people who used alcohol? It didn't make sense.

He longed for a return to "our glorious frontier heritage of minding your own business." But the frontiersman had been transformed over the years into a wretched, interfering, liberal bureaucrat. He saw the country heading in the direction of a socialist police state, similar to England, and not too different from Russia. Harassed by the police and disappointed by the returns on his crops, Burroughs had the nativist reflex of his class and background, which had been drummed into him at the Los Alamos school. He had the same mentality as the businessmen who wanted an end to government regulations so that they could be left alone to work out their version of laissez-faire capitalism.

When Allen Ginsberg wrote that he was still thinking of becoming a labor lawyer, Burroughs was incensed. Allen must have been totally corrupted by those liberal psychiatrists, and was allying himself with a cancerous element that would stifle every vestige of free life in the United States. His opinion of labor leaders and unions, who wanted to put a stop to the cheap wetback labor in the valley, was close to the view expressed by Westbrook Pegler, the only columnist who in his eyes possessed a grain of integrity. The word "liberal," he believed, had come to stand for the most damnable tyranny, a smirking, mealy-mouthed tyranny of bureaucrats, social workers, psychiatrists, and union officials. The world of 1984 was not decades away, it was here and now.

Burroughs' own farm operation was a disaster, with acres of vegetables ploughed under, and he was selling out. By September, his cotton was picked. He had hoped to realize $15,000, but with high operating costs, and rising labor costs, and the $6,000 the government would snatch to pay the salaries of the "obscenity bureaucrats," he did not end up with much. His case in New Orleans was coming up on October 27, and there was every indication of an unfavorable outcome, in spite of the illegal seizure.

Burroughs decided to leave a country he had come to detest. Wherever he lived, he was hounded by the police. Busted in New York for forging a prescription, he had moved to Texas. Busted in Texas for drunken driving and public indecency, he had gone to New Orleans. Busted in New Orleans for possession, he was not about to stand trial, with the likelihood of spending a minimum of two years in Angola State Prison. He would go and live in Mexico, and wait for his case to be canceled when the statute of limitations ran out after five years. At the end of September 1949 he went to Mexico City to look for an apartment before moving his family down, beginning a period of exile that would, with the exception of short visits, last twenty-four years.

· TEN ·

MEXICO

1949–1952

When Burroughs moved his family to Mexico City in October 1949, it was a city of one million people with clean, sparkling air and the sky that special shade of blue that goes so well with circling vultures. A city of lottery ticket vendors crying the numbers, of peso-cab drivers signaling one more with their arm out the window, of newspaper boys chasing stray dogs, of yellow streetcars along Rosales, of women with their hair in knots and overweight men in green gabardine suits, of whores puckering their lips in the mirrors of *pulquerias*, of Indian families eating lemon-sprinkled slices of *jicama*, of weary *mariachis* eating *pozole* on the corner of Salto del Agua, of boys sleeping in the doorways of banks and churches, of smoky bars full of voices and guitars, of ever-honking cars dashing into the broad Reforma from Insurgentes, and of long lines in front of bus stops and hiring windows. Miguel Aleman was president, and the *mordida* was king—a pyramid of bribes reaching from the cop on the beat to El Presidente.

Burroughs took an apartment at 37 Cerrada de Medellin, a dead-end street in a quiet residential neighborhood. He felt that he had found a spirit of tolerance that was absent from life in the United States. Not only was Mexico incredibly cheap—you could buy a *garrofon* (gallon jug) of Glorias de Cuba, a local rum, for a dollar—but a man could walk the streets without being molested by cops. A Mexican cop had no status; he was on the level of a streetcar conductor.

Everything in Mexico City was to his liking. Drunks slept on the sidewalk and nobody bothered them. Everyone who felt like it carried a gun. Down here you didn't have to take nothin' off nobody. The most they could hand you for shooting someone was eight years. In Mexico, the frontier values he so admired were still in force. He had seen several cases in the papers where drunken cops, shooting an habitué in a bar, were themselves shot by armed civilians.

There was no holier-than-thou posturing, since all the officials were corruptible. The Mexicans really loved children, and it was unthinkable to be refused a room because of little ones. Billy and Julie played every day with the well-behaved neighbors' children, an agreeable contrast to the dago rock-throwing urchins in Algiers. The cost of medical treatment was reasonable because there were so many doctors; they advertised and cut prices. You could get the clap cured for two dollars, or buy penicillin and shoot it yourself. There was a general atmosphere of freedom from interference. Everyone seemed to have mastered the art of minding his own business, as in an Oriental culture. If a man wanted to carry a cane or wear a monocle, no one gave him a second glance. Boys and young men walked down the street arm in arm, drawing no attention. Burroughs chuckled over an article on the disgraceful conditions in Alameda Park, which said that "vicious people lie about on the grass drinking tequila, smoking marijuana, and shouting insulting remarks at passing police officers."

He signed up at Mexico City College on the G.I. Bill, which paid his books, tuition, and a seventy-five-dollar-a-month allowance. Despite his hatred of big government, he was not above benefiting from its programs. As he observed, "I always say, keep your snout in the public trough." He also had his family allowance of $200 a month, which went a long way south of the border. He took courses in Mayan and Mexican archeology, and thought of becoming a Mexican citizen and buying a ranch with the money from his Texas land. With hunting and fishing, he could realize his dream of self-sufficiency.

The one drawback to life in Mexico was that the Smith, Kline, and French Benzedrine inhalers that Joan was so fond of were unobtainable. She went through three weeks of suffering but pulled through thanks to faith and thyroid tablets. Now, however, as she wrote Allen Ginsberg, she was "somewhat drunk from 8:00 A.M. on. Evil spirits here sell tequila for forty cents a quart, and I tend to hit the lush rather hard." She had heard about Allen's hospitalization, and was not surprised, "as I've been claiming for three years [since her own commitment to Bellevue] that anyone who doesn't blow his top once is no damn good. . . . When I refer to it as a top-blowing, I'm sure you know what I mean. No percentage in talking about visions or super-reality or any such lay terms. Either you know now what I know (and don't ask me just what that is), or else I'm mistaken about you and off the beam somewhere—in which case you're just a dime-a-dollar neurotic and I'm nuts. . . . Bill is fine in himself, and so are we jointly. The boys are lovely, easy, and cheap (3 pesos = 40 cents) down here, but my patience is infinite."

Joan pretended not to mind when Burroughs went out at night to a gay bar called the Chimu. He knew just enough Spanish to pick up a boy, going up to one with the rather lame line *"Por que triste?"* ("Why are you sad?"), to which the boy responded that he wasn't sad at all, and then following up with a more direct approach: *"Vámonos a otro lugar"* ("Let's go somewhere else"). In the hotel room, "I ran one hand slowly over the boy's back, following with the other hand the curve of the chest down over the flat brown stomach. The boy smiled and lay down on the bed. Later we smoked a cigarette, our shoulders touching under the cover."

Having decided not to return for his court date in New Orleans on October 27, Burroughs was worried about being extradited and went looking for a good lawyer. One day in the lobby of the Reforma Hotel he was saying to someone, "I need an English-speaking criminal lawyer," when a man came up and said, "Pardon me, I couldn't help overhearing what you said . . . the man you need is Bernabé Jurado . . . what's your trouble, embezzlement?" "No, narcotics," Burroughs said. "Well, he's your man," said the passerby. Burroughs went to see Jurado, a tall handsome, flamboyant *hidalgo* who held court at the Opera Bar, near his office on the calle Madero. His sister was the actress Katy Jurado. One of his specialties was blocking extradition. In Mexico City there was an international community of fugitives who were being kept out of jail in their native lands thanks to the efforts of Bernabé Jurado—American numbers racketeers, Peruvian swindlers, Canadian embezzlers. Every time a foreign government tried to extradite one of his clients, Jurado would come up with a doctor's certificate saying that the client could not be moved, or he would pay off a judge, or he would send the client to a northern province whose governor was prepared to say, "There is no one here by that name."

In fact, there was no attempt to extradite Burroughs, but Crile, his lawyer in New Orleans, advised him on the phone to lay low for a while, saying, "I can't get the judge I want, and the judge I've got is very down on narcotics . . . you could go to jail." Laying low was fine with Burroughs, who had decided not to return to the United States under any circumstances.

It was also thanks to Bernabé Jurado that Burroughs met Dave Tercerero, a street peddler who sold crucifixes and bracelets that were supposedly silver but turned black within the day. Jurado had said, "Bring 'em around to my office," where Burroughs saw him, and, sensing something about him that he knew all too well, invited him to dinner. When

Burroughs said something about junk, Tercerero, who was known as "Old Dave" even though he was only fifty, because of his wizened and cadaverous appearance, turned back the lapel of his jacket to reveal a hypodermic needle pinned to the inside. "I've been on junk for twenty-eight years," he said. "Do you want to score?"

Was the Pope in Rome? Old Dave at that time was scoring from Lola La Chatta, the best-known local pusher, whose product Burroughs found inferior. "You can get better stuff buying codeine in drugstores," he told Old Dave. They decided to find doctors to write scrips, which was easy because there were so many doctors. The problem was finding druggists to fill them. When they showed their narcotics scrip, which was bright yellow, like a dishonorable discharge from the army, to a pharmacist, he read it aloud: "*Gotas para injectar*" ("Drops to inject") and snarled, "*No prestamos servicio a los viciosos!*" ("We do not serve addicts!"). From *farmacia* to *farmacia* they went, getting sicker with each step, for by now they both had a habit. Finally they entered a hole-in-the-wall *farmacia* miles from their regular rounds. Burroughs pulled out the *receta* (prescription), and the pharmacist looked at the scrip and said, "Two minutes, señor." They sat down to wait. There were geraniums in the window. A small boy brought Burroughs a glass of water, and a cat rubbed against his leg. The pharmacist returned with the morphine, and when they went outside, the neighborhood seemed enchanted—an open market with crates and stalls and a *pulquería* on the corner, kiosks selling fried grasshoppers and peppermint candy, boys in from the country in spotless white linen with rope sandals.

They had found a Johnson, but had waded through Shitville to find him. There had to be a better way, and there was. One of the writing croakers suggested to Old Dave that he apply for a government permit. He would get a certain amount of morphine per month at a low price. The doctor would put through his application for a hundred pesos. It seemed too good to be true, but Old Dave got on the program within ten days, allowing him to buy fifteen grams of morphine a month at two dollars a gram. The permit had to be signed each month by his doctor and the head doctor at the Board of Health. Then he could get it filled. The first time Burroughs saw the pharmacist bring out a boxful of morphine cubes, he felt like a kid who still believes in Santa Claus. He had never seen so much morphine all at once. He paid for the stuff, and they split it, with seven grams allowing him about three grains a day, more than he'd ever had in the States. He was in junky heaven, supplied with all he needed for thirty dollars a month.

Burroughs told Old Dave to give up the crucifixes. He didn't want him standing on street corners and getting arrested for vagrancy. He urged him not to get involved in anything illegal. Old Dave had been a thief on his visits to the United States, stealing suits in department stores with a false-bottomed suitcase, but in Mexico he did not steal, for repeat offenders could be sent to the Tres Marias penal colony without a trial. In Mexico, you were either a big operator with political and police connections, or you spent half your life in jail.

Old Dave lived modestly, and Burroughs kept him going. He had a beautiful girlfriend much younger than himself, named Esperanza, who was of course also on junk. They formed a little extended family of junkies, shooting up every day. At the end of the month when they ran short, Old Dave would go back to scoring *farmacias*. Sometimes he was able to score cocaine, and they shot speedballs, a mixture of morphine and cocaine. Dave was very good at hitting veins. He could have found a vein in a mummy, Burroughs said. Veins retreat and sometimes Burroughs couldn't hit, but Old Dave always could. Sometimes Burroughs would have to take off his shoe and find a vein in his foot.

When Burroughs was on junk, he wanted no sex or sociability, and spent all his time in the house. He was aware of the waste involved, and felt like one of those Tibetan Buddhists who push the "I've-got-it-all-inside" proposition to the extreme and wall themselves in a little cell with a slot where food is pushed in at them, and stay there till they die. He did not want to be that way, but could not help himself.

Joan, who had always been so tolerant, perhaps because her own Benzedrine habit facilitated tolerance, now lost her patience. Two days after connecting with Old Dave, Burroughs was cooking up a shot when Joan grabbed the spoon and threw the junk on the floor. Burroughs was usually a model of gentlemanly conduct with Joan, but this was the one thing he could not accept, and he slapped her twice across the face. Joan threw herself on the bed sobbing, then said: "Don't you want to do anything at all? Don't you want to visit some ruins? You know how bored you get when you have a habit. It's like all the lights went out. Oh, well, do what you want. I guess you have some stashed anyway."

Burroughs did have some stashed, but this was a signal that Joan was through with meekly accepting his addiction. As deep as their attachment was, she was having doubts about following down the road to self-destructiveness, and mentioned the possibility of a divorce, their common-law marriage being considered legal in Mexico. But the subject was held in abeyance when Lucien Carr and his girlfriend arrived that August of 1950.

Lucien felt that Joan and Bill had an understanding on some deep level that people rarely achieve, something on a psychic level that you could actually feel. Sitting in the living room of their small apartment, he watched them play their favorite game. They sat at opposite ends of the room, and each one took a sheet of paper and divided it into nine squares, and drew a picture in each of the squares, and when they had finished they compared the drawings, and there was an uncanny correlation—they had both drawn a scorpion, and they had both drawn a bottle, and they had both drawn a dog—about half the drawings were the same. To Lucien, this degree of telepathic communication was spooky, and it seemed to him that if either of the two was psychically stronger it was she, that if any signals were being sent, like saying I will draw a rat and you will also draw a rat, they were coming from her.

Lucien's visit was brief. He was trying to decide whether to smuggle some dope back to the States, and Burroughs told him what would happen if anything went wrong—his car would be seized, for one thing. At the same time it was not likely that anything would go wrong. Lucien decided not to take the risk.

After Lucien's departure, Joan went to Cuernavaca and filed for divorce. There was a small crisis when Old Dave was picked up for peddling without a license and sent to Carmen, the city prison, for fifteen days. Burroughs could well imagine the withdrawal sickness he was going through, and also knew that the *comandante* conducted thorough searches of visitors, confiscating the drugs he found. Burroughs brought Old Dave a basket of fruit. He had a piece of opium wrapped in cellophane hidden in his mouth. After being searched, he was let into the yard with Old Dave, who was gaunt and dehydrated, his eyes dulled by pain. Burroughs cut an orange in half, slipped the opium out of his mouth, and stuck it in the half he handed Dave. He could see the pain and sickness melt away when Old Dave bit into the orange. He picked up right away, and started complaining about his fellow inmates, who would steal the pants off you while you slept. "Such a lousy people they got in here," he said.

Once out of jail, Old Dave wanted to go on his annual pilgrimage to Our Lady of Chalma, outside Mexico City. Burroughs went along, and they walked the forty miles in two days. They took plenty of morphine—in fact, Old Dave took about twenty envelopes to sell at the shrine, knowing all the users would be there. The first night they stayed at a farmhouse and slept in a haystack, and in the morning the farmer's wife brought Burroughs what he remembers as one of the best breakfasts of his life—blue corn tortillas with two fried eggs and strong coffee.

The town was like a feudal village, with narrow cobblestoned streets and a warren of houses with open patios. The river ran right through it, forming pools where the locals washed their clothes. The story was that Our Lady of Chalma had pointed to the base of a tree outside town and a stream had started flowing beneath it. A dowser before her time, Burroughs thought. The tree was still there, with bits of paper attached to the branches, the prayers of the faithful.

The church itself was like Lourdes, filled with pictures of people who had been divinely saved, off boats, or falling from ladders, and piles of crutches that the faithful had left behind—they had limped in and walked out. Ostensibly, Our Lady of Chalma handled the crutch-and-wheelchair contingent, but sub rosa she was the patron saint for thieves and pushers, many of whom Old Dave recognized. It was like an alumni reunion. He was furious when he saw his chief rival in the crucifix game, a dark-skinned, sharp-featured Mayan whom he called the Black Bastard, and who was in the habit of following him around and badgering his croakers. Old Dave was full of contempt for the Black Bastard, who did the last two miles of the pilgrimage on his knees, which Dave thought was ostentatious. Old Dave did a little genuflecting in front of the Madonna, nothing showy, and went from pew to pew selling his glassine envelopes. To Old Dave, it was a very satisfying trip, combining religious observance and financial gain, but to Burroughs this worship of a plaster saint was sordid and depressing, and he was glad to get on the bus back to Mexico City.

The news upon his return was that Kells Elvins had arrived with his new and pregnant wife, Marianne. Disgusted with the uncertainties of farming in the Rio Grande Valley, Kells had sold his land and planned to take some courses at the college. He and his wife took an apartment in a new building overlooking a remodeled golf course on the highway to Guadalajara.

The first time that Burroughs and Joan came to visit, Marianne Elvins, a well-bred and attractive woman, was so distracted by their appearance that in retrospect she could not recall one word of the conversation. Joan was a large, shapeless woman, with a doughy face and the kind of eyes that used to be placed in antique dolls, made of blue glass and quite vacant, reflecting everything and seeing nothing. She seemed placid and shy, and reminded Mrs. Elvins of a well-meaning mental patient let out for the afternoon. At one point, her pocketbook dropped on the floor and fell open. Pills of every color and shape cascaded out and rolled across the rug. Clumsily, Joan got down on her hands and knees and picked them up by the handful, pushing them back into her purse, smiling and murmuring to herself. Neither Burroughs nor Kells paid the slightest attention to her.

Burroughs was cadaverous-looking—thin lips, bad teeth, yellow fingers, and eyes like death. Once in an Acapulco resort, Marianne Elvins saw a scorpion on the tile floor of their bungalow, and knew immediately that it was a malignant creature. She felt the same way about Burroughs. The prospect of spending much time in the company of these two freaks was intolerable, which Kells seemed to understand, since he did not press the matter. Once, they went to dinner at the Burroughses' apartment. Joan had cooked a roast beef, which she placed on the table, practically raw, for Burroughs to serve. He attacked it like a wild animal, tearing off hunks of meat which he threw at their plates, and then picked up a great slab of beef in both hands and gnawed at it voraciously like Charles Laughton playing Henry VIII.

Marianne Elvins was having enough problems with her husband, who had a Jekyll-Hyde personality. He was attractive, charismatic, and well read, and could hold everyone spellbound with his conversation. All in all, he was the most graceful man she had ever met. He was also alcoholic, volatile, and sadistic, and overly tolerant of the hangers-on who provided him with an audience. He required women, but did not like them, and had no close women friends.

When he was drunk he went at Marianne. One evening, when Kells' son, Peter, by his first marriage, was visiting, he started on a story Marianne did not want him to tell, and she said, "If you tell that story I'm going to throw this bottle of milk right at your head," so he continued telling the story and she threw the milk, and a look of such fury crossed his face that Peter was sure he was going to throw her off the balcony, but then he collected himself and said, "If you're going to do a job you might as well do it right," and poured the rest of the milk over his own head. In the end, when her daughter, Tao, was born, Marianne decided to clear out, seeing that Kells was not ready to stop drinking.

But one very important thing Kells was able to do for Burroughs, and that was to start him writing again, as he had done in 1938. Burroughs was unable to start on his own, completely lacking self-confidence. He needed someone to tell him that he had talent and could do it. Kells suggested that he simply set down, in a straightforward, reportorial manner, his adventures as a junky, which he proceeded to do.

He worked through the fall, despite his habit, writing the book like a diary, remembering with his photographic memory exactly what had been said, writing every day, taking the same amount of morphine every day, on an even keel, and by December he had a first draft.

One morning just before Christmas, 1950, he was awakened at eight by a knock on the door, which he answered in his pajamas. It was an immigration inspector, who said, "Get your clothes on, you're under arrest." Apparently the woman next door had turned in a long report on his drinking and drug taking, and there was something wrong with his papers. Burroughs knew the inspector would take a bribe, but since he was head of the Deportation Department, and had gone to the trouble of making a house call, he wouldn't go away for peanuts. After lengthy negotiations he had to cough up $200.

Now that he had been chiseled out of $200 and squealed on by a neighbor, his early impression of Mexico as an idyllic repository of frontier values was radically revised. He fumed that the typical Mexican family dinner usually ended up with everybody staggering around blind stupid drunk but still able to get in there with knives and machetes and broken bottles, and then some cop reeled in drunker than the rest and shot three or four before he realized he was in the wrong house and the people he shot were not the ones who beat his time with some bitch he used to lay who had actually been dead five years. Mexico was not simple or jolly or idyllic. It was an Oriental society that reflected two thousand years of disease and poverty and degradation and stupidity and slavery and brutality and psychic and physical terrorism. Mexico was sinister and gloomy and chaotic. Mexico City had the highest murder rate in the world. When a Mexican killed someone it was usually his best friend. Friends were less frightening than strangers.

Burroughs' plan to become a citizen and buy a ranch no longer seemed appealing. His papers, which he had spent a thousand dollars to obtain, were still hanging fire and now the immigration department had lost his entire file. And even if his papers came through, his land would always be liable to confiscation. If you wanted to make a living or start a business, the government put every obstacle in your way. His own Mexican lawyer said, "You cannot trust these bastards." So he had decided not to invest one nickel or buy one square foot of property, and not even to try for citizenship, but to stay on as a tourist.

With the New Year, 1951, Burroughs resolved to kick, for his behavior was increasingly erratic. One day he started petting the cat, and tightened his hold when it tried to escape. He brought his face down to touch his nose to the cat's, and the cat scratched his face. He held it at arm's length, slapping it back and forth across the face with his free hand. The cat screamed and clawed, and started spraying piss all over his pants. He went on hitting, his hand bloody from scratches, until the cat twisted loose and ran in the closet, where he could hear it whimpering with terror. "Now I'll finish the bastard off," he said, picking up a heavy painted cane. At this point Joan intervened. He put down the cane, and the cat scrambled out of the closet and ran downstairs. "Bill," Joan said, shaking her head, "aren't you ashamed of yourself? Sometimes I don't know. Sometimes I just don't know."

Burroughs kicked, but started drinking heavily, which carried its own set of problems. One night he was sitting drunk in a bar, staring at a moldy bull's head over the rows of bottles, when a cop came and sat next to him. They started talking, but in his mind it was the cop of his dreams, an irritating presence who came in unasked whenever he was about to take a shot or go to bed with a boy. As if in a dream, he found himself drawing his gun and pressing it into the cop's stomach. The bartender grabbed his arm, twisted it away, and took the gun. Examining it, he said, "*Está cargado*" ("It's loaded"). Of course, Burroughs thought, what good is an unloaded gun? The cop took him firmly by the arm and said, "*Vámonos, gringo*" ("Let's go"). But once they were outside, instead of arresting him, as Burroughs had expected, the cop gave him a little push and said, "*Andale, gringo*" ("Get going"), keeping the gun. Burroughs was quite satisfied, despite the loss of his gun, to have had a showdown with a Mexican policeman.

The next morning he woke up in a cheap hotel room, with his money, his fountain pen, and his pocketknife gone. Maybe he could hit Kells for a few pesos. It was a long walk to the golf course, but he found Kells in front of his apartment, walking his Norwegian elkhound, and looking dapper in whipcord slacks and a suede jacket. Burroughs told him about losing his gun and Kells said: "You're going to get your head blown off carrying that gun. What do you carry it for? You wouldn't know what you were shooting at. You bumped into trees twice yesterday on Insurgentes. You walked right in front of a car. I pulled you back and you threatened me. I left you there to find your own way home, and I don't know how you ever made it. Everyone is fed up with the way you've been acting lately. If there's one thing I don't want to be around, and I think no one else particularly wants to be around, it's a drunk with a gun."

"You're right, of course," Burroughs said.

"Well, I want to help you in any way I can. But the first thing you have to do is cut down on the sauce and build up your health. You look terrible. Then you'd better think about making some money. Speaking of money, I guess you're broke, as usual." Kells took out his wallet and handed Burroughs a fifty-peso note, saying, "That's the best I can do for you."

Burroughs took the fifty pesos and drank tequila for eight hours straight. The next morning he started vomiting at ten-minute intervals until all he brought up was green bile. Old Dave came around and held him up as he vomited dribbles of bile into the toilet. "You got to quit drinking, Bill," he said. "You're getting crazy." Burroughs went to bed and in the afternoon, he stopped vomiting and managed to drink some grape juice and a glass of milk.

"It stinks like piss in here," he said. "One of them cats must have pissed under the bed."

"No, nothing here," Old Dave said as he sniffed around the bed. He sniffed near the pillows and said, "Bill, it's you that smells like piss."

Burroughs smelled his hands and said, "Good Lord! I got uremic poisoning! Go out and get me a croaker."

"Okay, Bill, I'll get you one right away."

"And don't come back with one of them five-peso scrip-writing bums!"

Old Dave returned with a Chinese doctor—evidently one of his scrip-writers—who said there was no uremia since Burroughs could urinate and did not have a headache.

"How come I stink like this?" Burroughs asked.

"He says it's nothing serious," Old Dave said. "He says you have to stop drinking. He says better you go back to the other than drink like this." Old Dave took the doctor into the hall, where Burroughs could hear him ask for a morphine scrip.

Wanting a second opinion, he asked Old Dave to find Kells and have him bring around his doctor. "All right," Old Dave said, "but I think you're wasting your money. This doctor is pretty good."

"Yeah, he's got a good writing arm."

In an hour, Old Dave was back with Kells and another doctor, who sniffed and smiled and nodded at Kells. The doctor explained in Spanish that Burroughs had incipient uremia and would have to stop drinking for a month. Picking up an empty tequila bottle, he said, "One more of these and you were dead." He wrote out a prescription for an antacid preparation, shook hands, and left.

For a while, as he recovered from the uremia, Burroughs was off junk and off booze. He was back in touch with Allen Ginsberg, who had been released from the psychiatric hospital and was trying to live a conventional heterosexual life. Allen reported that he had lost his cherry to Helen Parker, an older woman with two children, one of whose attractions was her connection with great literary figures, having been engaged to Dos Passos and known Hemingway. Burroughs wrote him that it was not so simple to overcome queerness, and Allen replied, "You don't really want me to get over being queer." Burroughs wrote back that he would be glad to see anyone switch to women if they weren't putting a con on themselves. "I am acquainted with the drawbacks of being queer," he added. "Better acquainted than you. Like you say, 'It multiplies problems' . . . But the point is not how dissatisfied you are with being queer. The point is do you get everything you want in the way of sex from a woman?"

Burroughs regarded his homosexuality as a handicap and a drawback but also as a condition from which there was no escape. Yes, it created all sorts of problems, but those problems had to be faced, as the condition was not about to go away. Allen's attempts at sex with women seemed to him a form of wishful thinking. You had to accept what you were. He had read a book called *The Homosexual in America*, whose author recommended that queers learn to turn the other cheek. That was an attitude Burroughs found nauseating. He wasn't going to take any guff for what he was, and if people didn't like it, as the song said, " 'tis their misfortune and none of my own." Burroughs was disgusted with Allen's let's-take-our-place-in-a-normal-society routine. Maybe the nut croakers had fucked him up permanently. Did Allen actually think that laying a woman made someone a hetero? Burroughs had been laying women for fifteen years and hadn't heard any complaints from them. But what did that prove except that he was hard up at the time? Laying a woman or a thousand women merely emphasized the fact that a woman was not what he wanted. "Better than nothing, of course, like a tortilla is better than no food," he wrote Allen. "But no matter how many tortillas I eat I still want a steak."

This letter to Allen was annotated by Joan, who was not only fully aware of Burroughs' tastes and predilections, but was able to joke about them: "Around the 20th of the month, things get a bit tight and he lives on tortillas."

Burroughs sent Allen the draft of his book on junk, which seemed to Allen, in his present solid-citizen phase, to be a justification of addiction. Bridling at this interpretation, Burroughs wrote: "I don't justify nothin' to nobody. As a matter of fact the book is the only accurate account I ever read of the real horror of junk. I don't mean it as a justification or deterrent or anything but as an accurate account of what I experienced during the time I was on junk."

Over his uremia, Burroughs started hitting the bars again, and one day ran into his old friend from Columbia days, Hal Chase, in the Hollywood Steakhouse, known as the Hollywood Stinkhouse. Still studying anthropology, Hal had gone to Mexico on a grant to learn the Zapotecan language, and had been in the hinterland. Burroughs found him attractive, with his blond, angular good looks, and got drunk enough to suggest they spend the night together. Hal said he wasn't interested, and tried to brush the whole thing off lightly, but Burroughs was mortified, feeling that he had been rejected in front of a third party (the bartender) in a nasty, bitchy way designed to insult him. He had been put in the position of the detestedly insistent queer, who is too insensitive to realize that his attentions aren't wanted. He decided that Hal was just a bore, and a hypochondriac to boot, always talking about the ailments he might or might not have, tetanus or typhoid, going to the hospital for tests, wanting to show you his urine test. When Hal left for Salina Cruz, supposedly to build a boat, Burroughs thought, "The sooner he sails off into the sunset the better."

In June 1951, Burroughs and his family moved to an apartment at 210 Orizaba, in a two-story house near the Sears, Roebuck building. It was not far from the bar patronized by American students, the Bounty, at 122 Monterey, which Burroughs began to make his headquarters. The Bounty was run by two Americans, Marvin Apt from Miami and John Healey, a good-hearted Irishman from Minnesota, who had been a tail-gunner on a B-17 and was now enjoying the benefits of the G.I. Bill and cheap Mexican liquor. Healey had an apartment above the bar and occasionally slept with Juanita, the fat and fortyish Mexican woman who owned the building. The Mexican front man for the Bounty was Luis Carpio, who had spent his childhood in Gary, Indiana, and was known as a *pocho*, a term for a Mexican who hated other Mexicans.

The Bounty was the meeting place for the G.I. Bill students who would rather hang out and get drunk than study. Merrymaking of epic proportions went on there, sometimes exploding into fights and shootings. The drinks were cheap and anything went. Burroughs, who always carried a gun, was known as one of the more colorful regulars, having on one occasion shot a mouse that someone had caught and was holding up by the tail. The bullet had gone through the mouse and lodged in a wall, and the bullet hole was shown to visitors as part of the Bounty's decor.

Another regular was Arnold Copeland, who had the knack of regurgitating at will. On one of the rare occasions that he attended class, he threw up in front of one of the teachers, saying, "Doc French, your course makes me sick." When Copeland got drunk, he would do an impersonation of a dying Mexican. When a Mexican came into the Bounty, and many did, Copeland would stare at him until the man came over and asked him what he wanted. When Burroughs wondered out loud why he was always starting trouble, Copeland said, "Because they're so horrible." Then he shouted, "I tell you, we will all die like dogs."

Copeland took a dislike to Burroughs for remonstrating with him about the Mexicans. He carried a .25 automatic, and one day he went up to Burroughs and said, "You don't know shit—you don't even know what the fucking Boy Scout motto is." Burroughs pulled out a .45 automatic and put it down on the counter and said, "Yaaasss—Be Prepared."

Another time, John Healey threw a good-bye party for Marvin Apt, who was going back to Miami—a *despedida*. They had bought a kid goat in the country, which they were going to barbecue. They saw Burroughs walking down Insurgentes, wearing his usual long drab trench coat and slouch hat, and looking sinister, and Healey said, "Hey, Bill, we're going to have a party tomorrow night—why don't you drop up?" Marvin Apt added, "But no guns, Bill." "Not even a little one?" Burroughs asked. When he got there they fanned him down, as a joke. Healey was in the kitchen, handing out plates of goat through a little serving window, and could see Burroughs sitting there with his legs crossed, wearing his usual three-piece suit, and there was a small automatic stuck in his garter.

Two other Bounty regulars were Eugene Allerton (name changed) and Eddie Woods, who had been friends since childhood in Tampa, Florida. They had been wild kids, skipping school and going down to used-car lots and hot-wiring cars, and joyriding until they ran out of gas, which was scarce in wartime. In 1946, sixteen-year-old Allerton joined the army, and fifteen-year-old Woods joined the air force, one step ahead of reform school. Allerton was tall and Woods was husky, and they both looked older than their age. Allerton spent three years in Germany in the Counter-Intelligence Corps, operating a cryptograph machine and writing extracts from field agents' reports. He got out in early 1949, at the same time as Woods, and they went out on the town in Tampa and were arrested as juveniles for violating curfew, and had to pay a twenty-five-dollar fine—welcome home, soldier. Allerton decided to go to Mexico City College on the G.I. Bill, a far more attractive idea than working. His aim in life, he liked to say, was "Get rich, sleep till noon, and fuck 'em all." Woods joined him there in August 1951.

Allerton lived in a room upstairs from the Bounty and went to class from time to time. He shopped around for classes with long reading lists, so that he could sell the books, which were paid for by the G.I. Bill. You could get 50 percent of the face price. *Art Through the Ages* was his favorite course; it had lots of big books with color plates, and Allerton took it two years in a row. Most of his time, however, he spent in the Bounty, drinking rum and Coke.

It was there that Burroughs saw him, and was immediately attracted, although Allerton was not conventionally handsome, being tall and thin with a round face and jug ears. But he was clean-cut and boyish, and had a self-directed "I-don't-care-who-owns-the-place" manner. He had that very American look of false innocence, with something cold and calculating behind it. He wasn't strong or tough, but had learned a few things in the C.I.C. Once at the Bounty someone pushed him and said, "Get out of my way, skinny," and Allerton hooked a thumb in his belt, pushing down, and brought his other hand up under his jaw, decking him, and stepped on his face.

In the early summer of 1951, the thirty-seven-year-old Burroughs looked for occasions to connect with this twenty-one-year-old, slightly disdainful straight youth. He was afraid that his wanting showed through his clumsy efforts. It was hard for him not to give himself away. One night at the Bounty when Allerton had had a few they got into a conversation and Allerton recounted some of his C.I.C. experiences—one of their agents had conned them by inventing an entire spy network. As Burroughs listened to him laugh at his own story, he thought: He is without guile, like a child who has never been hurt.

To hold his attention, Burroughs invented comic routines, connecting with the oldest tradition of storytelling—it went back to cavemen sitting around a fire. It went back to Scheherazade holding the sultan's attention to stay alive. It was the frantic, attention-grabbing format that is probably at the source of all literature: "It is an ancient Mariner / And he stoppeth one of three . . ."

This was not material he planned to use for fiction, for he did not yet think of himself as a writer. The routines were comic extrapolations of his experience, such as the information he had picked up on oilmen in Texas. They were an uninhibited bunch, who would find investors to buy leases, and when the geologist's report was negative, they'd say, "That boy is disappointed, and so are we . . . That's the way it is, heh heh heh." Dry-hole Dutton had brought in twenty dry holes before he struck oil. Then he bought a yacht, and he'd go into Corpus Christi and pick up people in bars and sail around and wake up in the morning and say, "What are these people doing on my yacht? Throw 'em off and let 'em swim ashore." So Burroughs hardly had to exaggerate when he went into his oilman routine: "Well, that's the way it goes. Some holes got lubrication and some is dry as a whore's cunt on Sunday morning."

Allerton thought he was a good raconteur and began to appreciate his company. One night Burroughs got him drunk on brandy and took him to a hotel and went to bed with him. Allerton responded without hostility or disgust, but in his eyes Burroughs saw a curious detachment. He already knew that loving a straight guy was doomed to failure, because even if he was willing to have sex it would be grudgingly. But on some level Burroughs was after the unobtainable. He saw himself as disembodied, which was why he needed other male bodies, not only to make love to but to occupy. His purpose was to possess and inhabit the lover. He was, as he put it, "straining with a blind worm hunger to enter the other's body, to breathe with his lungs, learn the feel of his viscera and genitals." Perhaps, as Auden put it, homosexuality was a form of envy, a wanting of the other's maleness.

When Allerton avoided Burroughs, he tried to win him back with favors, buying him meals, and getting his camera out of hock for 400 pesos. When Allerton refused him, his body going rigid with annoyance, Burroughs found it difficult to control his hurt. It seemed to him not only that he was doomed to failure in any love relationship, but that he was setting up his failure by going after a straight man. On one of the rare occasions when Burroughs was able to get him into bed, Allerton said, *in medias res*, "This does seem to be rather superfluous."

Even though he realized that no reciprocal relationship would be possible, Burroughs could not let Allerton go, and invited him on a trip to South America. "It won't cost you a cent," he said. "Perhaps not in money," Allerton replied. "All I ask is be nice to Papa, say twice a week," Burroughs said. "That isn't excessive, is it?" Allerton finally agreed to go, saying, "It's always nice to see places you haven't seen before."

In all this, Joan was the passive and acquiescing observer. She either had to accept Burroughs as he was, which he made no attempt to conceal, or leave him, which she had thought of doing, but had decided against. Their destinies were intertwined. There was in spite of everything a rare form of communion between them. One evening shortly before his departure, Burroughs and Joan were playing the drawing game, and Joan drew a picture of herself with little puffs of smoke around her head, and the caption "troglodyte," or cave-dweller. Troglodyte was also a word commonly used in the Mexican press to describe heinous criminals, as in "Troglodyte so-and-so killed his mother and cut her up into small pieces."

On July 9, 1951, Joan wrote Allen Ginsberg: "Bill has taken off for Panama and possibly Ecuador, in company with a pretty boy from school. . . . He and the kid are going to look over prospects down there, and if they find anything that looks good the children and I will go on down. I think they're going to Panama City, and if that turns out to be too expensive, they'll go to Ecuador and maybe even Peru. We like Mexico, but Gobernación apparently doesn't like us—one damn fine after another, no prospects of getting any papers, no possibility of any job or investment."

In the meantime, Allerton and Burroughs had arrived by plane in Panama City, and repaired to a nightclub called the Blue Goose, which Burroughs had heard was an incomparable den of drugs and vice. But it did not live up to its billing, being just another drab cathouse bar. That was the trouble with Burroughs, Allerton thought, he was always picking things up in *Argosy* or some other magazine and giving them a little more credence than they deserved. He had this fixation about going to Ecuador and finding a hallucinatory drug the Indians used that he had read about somewhere, called yage.

From Panama City, they took a small plane to Quito, the capital of Ecuador, high in the Andes. It was cold and the air was thin and the town was full of ugly people and llamas. Tibet must be like this, Burroughs thought. A bitter wind from the Andes peaks blew rubbish through dirty streets.

They left for the coastal town of Manta, and stayed at the Hotel Continental. When Burroughs asked for sex once too often, Allerton said: "I want to register a complaint concerning breach of contract. You said twice a week." They spent a few days on the beach. The houses had bamboo walls, and vultures roosted on the roofs. They moved down the coast to the harbor city of Guayaquil, which was built on a river, with many parks, squares, and statues. Burroughs was getting sick of the inevitable statue of Bolívar, whom he called "the Liberating Fool." The one in Guayaquil had a sort of limp-wrist look, which Burroughs pointed out to Allerton saying, "What a flaming queen." That night, Allerton said he wanted to sleep alone, and Burroughs went into his possession routine, which could only distance Allerton all the more: "If I had my way we'd sleep every night all wrapped around each other like hibernating rattlesnakes. Wouldn't it be booful if we could juth run together into one gweat big blob?" Even if it was intended to be funny, Allerton thought, the baby talk was repulsive.

The river was the color of urine, so dirty you could not see half an inch below its surface. Allerton was quite happy sitting on the beach all day. They were thinking of buying a boat and sailing it back to Mexico, and picked out a modified lateen rig, and were wondering, should they go as the crow flies, or should they hug the shore, since neither of them knew anything about sailing, except that the sun set in the west. Allerton later reflected that had they bought the boat, modern American literature would have been deprived of one of its finer lights. But they were spared from being lost at sea by a border skirmish with Peru, so that Ecuador banned the sale of boats to foreigners.

Then they heard that near Ambato, deep in the jungle on the border with Peru, there was an American botanist who lived with the Indians and knew something about yage. The bus to Ambato was a jolting fourteen-hour ride. It wasn't even a bus, but a two-and-a-half-ton truck with benches close together in the back, made for small Indians. Allerton was in agony, his balls ached, and when he said he had to throw up, Burroughs gave him his hat—it was the only thing he could do, they were wedged in on the bench until the next stop. At the mountain pass, far above the tree line, they stopped at a hut for a snack of chick peas, and soon saw the snow-covered peak of Chimborazo. Then from Ambato to Puyo they drove along the edge of a thousand-foot gorge. It was the most miserable trip Allerton had ever made, but Burroughs took it rather well. He was calm in adversity. But then, reflected Allerton, he'd had plenty of practice.

Puyo was the end of the line. After that, it was jungle. Burroughs wanted to set out at once to find the botanist, Dr. Fuller, but Allerton asked if they could wait until the rains stopped. "They got like a saying down here," Burroughs said. " 'I'll pay you when it stops raining in Puyo.' " Allerton wondered how they would find Fuller, since "there aren't too many street signs in the jungle," but Burroughs said he had directions.

And so they set out on muddy trails, which were maintained by the Ecuadorian army so a donkey could get through, up steep slopes and across streams, watching for *quebradas*, deep crevices cut by streams, some of which were four feet wide and sixty feet deep. Every once in a while they would come up to an Indian and ask him how much farther Dr. Fuller was, and invariably the Indian would answer, "Three more hours." Allerton wanted to rest, but Burroughs said, "No, if you rest your legs get stiff."

Finally they reached the doctor's house, across a river from an Indian village. A thin, wiry man, Fuller lived there with his wife, a large red-headed ex-nurse. They reminded Burroughs of Jack Sprat and his wife. Fuller struck Allerton as a mad-doctor type, going on endlessly about how he was due the entire credit for the development of the medical uses of curare, but one of his assistants had stolen his research material and published first. (In fact, Fuller had nothing to do with the discovery of curare.) Curare, which was used as a muscle relaxant, was a poison the Indians put on their darts to shoot monkeys. Pretty soon the monkey was so relaxed it fell out of its tree. Used in proper doses, it worked well in surgery.

Burroughs and Allerton had brought a rather miserable present, a raunchy loin of pork, but Fuller seemed glad to have it, since their diet was skimpy. The Indians fished with dynamite obtained from a nearby Shell drilling operation, and were by now reduced to sprat-sized catches. They had exhausted all the game with shotguns bought with their wages from Shell, and were now chasing groundhogs with machetes. "As like fools as pilchards are to herring," thought Burroughs, in the words of the immortal bard. The only one left who still used curare was Dr. Fuller in his experiments.

Fuller at first was cordial, but when he heard that they were planning to stay awhile, he grew suspicious, asking a great many questions, as if they were emissaries from hostile interests come to steal more of his research. At the same time, he bragged about saving the daughter of an Indian chief, who had an "incurable" ailment, which gave him entrée into tribal rites. If that was the case, Burroughs said, perhaps Fuller could help them find some yage, which he was willing to try as a scientific experiment. Fuller was noncommittal on this point.

He grudgingly put up cots on the porch for them to stay overnight, but it was clear he would have preferred them to leave before sundown. During the night he heard a frog croak and rushed out to capture it so that he could inject it with curare. He too suffered from the absence of wildlife, for he had no experimental animals, but was too lazy to leave. The reason the frog was croaking was that it had been caught by some tree snakes, but Fuller wrestled it away from the snakes and triumphantly carried it to his laboratory.

That night, sleeping on the porch under a mosquito net to keep off the vampire bats, Burroughs dreamt that he was standing in front of the

Bounty, and heard someone crying. He saw his son, and knelt down, and took the child in his arms. The sound of crying came closer, and soon he was crying, too. He held little Billy close to his chest. A group of people were standing there in convict suits, and Burroughs wondered what they were doing and why he was crying. When he woke up, he stretched out a hand toward Allerton, then pulled it back, and turned around to face the wall.

Realizing that Fuller was not going to be helpful, and indeed resented their presence, Burroughs decided to head back. Allerton was just as glad to get out of one of the less desirable places he had ever been in. The whole trip had been a fiasco, and Burroughs projected a calm and detachment that he did not feel, realizing that he would have to return another time.

Lucien Carr had two weeks of vacation coming in August 1951 and wanted to drive down to Mexico in his battered Chevrolet. "I can't drive all that way alone," he told Allen Ginsberg. "Somebody's got to keep me awake." Allen agreed to join him. He had never been out of the country, except for his trip to Dakar, and, having read Jack's manuscript, he wanted to experience the road.

When they got to Mexico City, Burroughs was gone, but Joan was there taking care of the children. Julie, by then eight, had become very pretty, and Allen told Joan, "She'll be giving you competition soon." "Oh, I'm out of the running," Joan replied. Her face had changed, Allen noted. It was lined and swollen. She had lost that Botticelli delicacy. Her hair was limp, and she walked with a limp. Allen assumed it was the drinking, for there was a bottle of tequila on top of her dresser. They went to a little hole-in-the-wall *cantina* on the corner and had *huevos rancheros*, which Allen had never eaten and thought were delicious. Joan seemed to be taking Bill's absence in stride, with ironic detachment. "Oh, Bill," she said, "who knows when he'll be back?" She talked about him the way you would talk about the weather.

Joan and Lucien, who had never spent much time together, found that they hit it off. They both liked to drink and had the same kind of sense of humor. That evening they left Allen to baby-sit and went to the Bounty. Two Mexicans were playing Pedro Infante songs on the jukebox, and Joan said, "That one is called '*El Cobarde*,' which means 'The Coward'— I think they put it on to provoke you." "Well, that's interesting," Lucien said, as he tossed back shots of Oso Negro gin, with a little Coca-Cola to take the edge off. Another song came on and Joan said: "I think that because of your alcoholic consumption you have now been accepted. This one is called '*El Borracho*,' which means 'The Drunkard.' " "Well, that's something of an improvement," Lucien said.

What followed was a week-long marathon drinking binge, combined with a road trip through western Mexico that terrorized Allen and the children. It was one of the wildest, drunkenest trips Lucien had ever taken in his life. They left Mexico City in the direction of Guadalajara, the tires squealing as Lucien skidded around hairpin mountain turns, with Joan egging him on, saying, "How fast can this heap go?"

In back with the children, who were huddled on the floor with their hands over their eyes, Allen was furious at Lucien, and said, "I can't stand this, you're scaring the kids." But he didn't want to say it too often because he didn't want to scare the kids worse. He felt he had to stay under control so they wouldn't panic. Obviously, there was a desperate quality in Joan that Lucien was playing right into. Lucien was so drunk at one point that he couldn't hold the wheel, which he turned over to Joan as he lay on the floor working the pedals. That night they got to Lake Chapala and drove the car onto a concrete pier where they spent the night. The next morning, they saw that they were about two feet from having driven the car into the lake.

The next day they drove to the live volcano of Parícutin, which was in eruption when they arrived. You were not supposed to go in without a guide, but drunk again on Mexican gin, Lucien bumped over the fields of hardened lava, until the car got stuck in a crack and they decided to spend the night there. Molten lava from the volcano several miles away flew in the dark sky, and you could hear a roar like a subway under the street, a very palpable roaring of the powers of the earth, and Allen was overcome with a sense of the volcano's destructive force, which made him realize how the earth you were standing on could turn ugly.

The next day they stayed at a hotel on a river, a lovely place that reminded Allen of Blake's drawing of Eden. Lucien and Joan went swimming drunk, and Lucien came out alone, saying the current was quite swift. Allen was happy that his two friends were getting along so well, that they were connecting in their intoxicated ecstasy, but at the same time he was afraid they were playing some kind of desperate game of dare. Allen felt the resonance of the past, felt that Joan was in a situation with Bill where he didn't treat her properly, felt that in Lucien she had found someone her own age who was more appreciative. But now she had floated downstream, Ophelia-like, and as he and Lucien ran up and down the bank calling her name he remembered her phrase, "I'm out of the running," and thought it was a poignant remark coming from a woman of only twenty-seven, in reply to his casual sophomoric statement, which he had meant as a compliment, "Your daughter will give you competition." They finally found Joan sitting on the bank in silent contemplation of the dark waters, and took her back to the hotel, and who knows, it was possible that she and Lucien made love that night, Allen wasn't sure, but Lucien did let pass that if he hadn't been already committed to a girl in New York . . .

Time was running out, and they headed back to Mexico City, but Lucien, still drunk, insisted on seeing a lake that was on the map, and they drove over a dirt road with watermelon-sized rocks, skidding and tumbling and banging, and there turned out to be nothing there, the lake had dried up years ago, and there was nothing to eat and no place to sleep, and it was the middle of the night so they slept in the car.

The next day they reached Mexico City, and with Lucien pressed for time, they dropped Joan and the kids at a bus stop at one of the *glorietas* near Chapultepec Park, and their last sight of her was Joan standing there wistfully, holding four-year-old Billy with one hand and waving good-bye with the other. To Allen it was a poignant farewell, for he felt that she and Lucien loved each other, and Lucien said on the trip back that he had thought of taking her with him, but that she was the wife of a friend, with two children, and it just wasn't in the cards.

A couple of days later, Hal Chase, who was back in Mexico City, ran into Joan in the street. Her head made that proud little welcoming shake he remembered, and he put his arm around her shoulders because she looked so awful. There were open sores on her arms and she seemed to have lost some of her hair. She told Hal that she had an incurable blood disease and said, "I'm not going to make it." Hal was shocked. Joan had been a beauty, graceful and delicate. Now she limped away awkwardly, swinging one arm more than the other.

At the beginning of September, Burroughs and Allerton returned to Mexico City. The trip had been a failure in that they had not been able to find any yage, and yet there had been some incidental pleasures, including the pleasure, at least for Allerton, of leaving places you never wanted to see again. Joan was glad Bill was back, and told him he had just missed Allen and Lucien.

Burroughs was depressed. Something weighed down on him, which he could not identify. Perhaps it was coming back to the routine of family life after the freedom of travel. Perhaps it was the dilemma of being married to Joan, who did nothing but drink from morning to night, when he wanted to be with Allerton, who remained friendly but unaccommodating. No, it wasn't only that, it was something else, something deadening and oppressive, an inescapable sense of dread and foreboding, which Burroughs tried to drown in alcohol.

As usual, there were money problems, and Burroughs decided to sell his .380 automatic. He didn't like it much anyway. It was a cheap gun, which he had tried out with Marvin Apt, and it shot low. John Healey had a buyer, and he was due to bring the gun over to his apartment above the Bounty on the afternoon of Thursday, September 6, 1951.

In Quito, Burroughs had bought a Scout knife with a tarnished metal handle, like something from a turn-of-the-century junk shop, which he had spotted in a tray of old knives and rings. On September 6, at about three in the afternoon, he heard the knife-sharpener's whistle, and took the knife down to him. Walking down the street toward his cart, the sense of depression and loss that had been weighing on him intensified to the point that tears began to stream down his face. It was a feeling so strong that it seemed to fill his chest, making it difficult to breathe, and he wondered what on earth could be wrong. He gave the knife to the sharpener and went back to his apartment and started drinking. Then, around six, it was time to go to Healey's place, and they left the children with neighbors.

When he and Joan got there, the buyer had not arrived, but Healey was there with Gene Allerton and Eddie Woods. Evidently, a party had been going on for some time, for Healey's living room was strewn with empty Oso Negro bottles. By the time Healey left to tend bar downstairs, the four remaining guests were feeling no pain.

In what happened next, the versions sometimes differ and sometimes overlap, and as there is no reason to accept one at the expense of the others, it seems preferable to give all three.

The Burroughs version: "Let's see, Joan was sitting in a chair, I was sitting in another chair across the room about six feet away, there was a table, there was a sofa. The gun was in a suitcase and I took it out, and it was loaded, and I was aiming it. I said to Joan, 'I guess it's about time for our William Tell act.' She took her highball glass and balanced it on top of her head. Why I did it, I don't know, something took over. It was an utterly and completely insane thing to do. Suppose I had succeeded in shooting the glass off her head, there was a danger of glass splinters flying out and hitting the other people there. I fired one shot, aiming at the glass."

The Allerton version: "It was a convivial gathering, just the four of us. We were sitting around drinking, with Bill at a table, and Joan sitting across from him. The conversation was desultory. Bill had a gun. That was nothing unusual. Even I had one, a Belgian automatic I had picked up overseas, though it often wound up in the hock shop. When he said he was going to do his William Tell act, nobody said, 'Look, Bill, this is not a good idea.' There was nothing especially alarming about it. There had been some drinking, and Bill was known for his marksmanship. As for the reason Joan went along with it, you could ascribe it to her confidence in his marksmanship, or anything else you want to ascribe it to.

"At any rate, the gun fired low, and Joan was shot in the side of the head. We all sat there staring and not believing. But once I saw the red trickle, I was past disbelief. I knew what had happened. I had seen him pick up the gun and fire it. I think I was the first to move. The only thing I could think of doing was to get the hell out of there—I told you, I'm a natural coward. I knew that a Mexican medical student lived in one of the little cubicles on the roof, so I said I was going to get him. He wasn't there, so I came back down and from then on I don't recall any particulars. Someone else called the cops."

The Woods version: "On this particular day, Allerton came to me and said, 'Bill is a little short of cash and wants to meet this fellow who wants to buy some of his handguns. But he doesn't want to do it at his place, he doesn't want the guy to know where he lives, so he's going to meet this guy in Healey's place, and he wants you and me to be there as witnesses.' So we got there in the early afternoon, and Healey's living room was just a field of dead soldiers from the running party we always had the first of the month when the checks came in. Then Bill and Joan arrived, and Bill had an overnight bag, a little carry-all, I don't know how many handguns he had in there. Now I think you should take into account what my attitude toward Bill was at the time. I thought he was somewhat sinister, I thought he was a bad influence on my friend Gene. I didn't know what to make of him, and I was renting a room in Healey's apartment, and I didn't care for his holding his meeting there, but I was the new boy on the block and I couldn't object, and Allerton was involved, and we'd always been allies.

"So we were sitting around in this living room littered with bottles, and Joan was drinking gin with *limonada*, and Allerton and I were sitting on the sofa, and Burroughs was sitting in a chair within an arm's reach of me, so close that I could have reached over and grabbed his gun, and Joan was in a stuffed chair across from Gene and myself. I don't know how the conversation got around to it, but Burroughs said, 'Joanie, let me show the boys what a great shot old Bill is.' So she balanced her glass on her head and turned her head and said with a giggle, 'I can't watch this—you know I can't stand the sight of blood.' And then it dawned on me that he was actually going to pull the trigger, and I thought, 'My God, if he hits that glass there'll be shards flying all over the place, there'll be a hole in the wall, and how are we going to explain this to Juanita' . . . it just seemed ridiculous to me. So I started to reach for the gun, but then I thought, 'You better not, 'cause if it goes off and hits her . . . ' She was nine, ten feet away. And then bang, that was the first impression, the noise—we were temporarily deafened by the sound. The next thing I knew the glass was on the floor, and I noticed the glass was intact, it was rolling around in concentric circles, this six-ounce water glass. And then I looked at her and her head had fallen to one side. Well, I thought, she's kidding. Then I heard Allerton say, 'Bill, I think you hit her.' Then he cried 'No!' and started toward her, and then I saw the hole in her temple. Burroughs kept crying 'Joan, Joan, Joan!' He was out of it, in shock.

"Allerton went to get a doctor, and I went to Juanita's place, leaving Burroughs there, kneeling in tears at her side, saying, 'Talk to me, talk to me.' And as I left, I could hear her death rattle—*haaarrrhhh*. So I went to Juanita's and told her what had happened, and she called Burroughs' lawyer, and said she would call the police and an ambulance. She told me what Jurado, the lawyer, said—that Allerton and I were the only witnesses and we should lie low in a hotel someplace and call him that night and he'd tell us what to do."

An ambulance arrived and took Joan to the Red Cross Hospital. She was dead on arrival. Inspecting the apartment, the police noted a blood-splattered chair, three ashtrays on the floor, and, on a table, four empty bottles of Oso Negro gin, ten dirty glasses, and a Star .380 automatic.

Driving back with Lucien, Allen Ginsberg had the famous *turista* in the worst way, Montezuma's revenge, the Aztec two-step, but Lucien didn't want to stop, so he bought a big ceramic bowl. Then the Chevrolet broke down in Galveston, and Lucien flew to New York, leaving Allen behind in a five-dollar-a-night seashore motel while it was fixed. A couple of days later, Allen picked up a paper and saw that Joan had been killed. It hit him hard, because he had introduced Bill and Joan, and had what he thought of as a sacramental connection with them. Joan was the one woman he really respected and admired. She was smarter than Bill, he thought. Bill needed someone like her to overcome his general testiness and disdain of the flesh.

Remembering their frantic trip, and Joan's challenge to Lucien—"How fast can this heap go?"—Allen wondered to what extent Joan had challenged Bill to shoot the glass off her head. He had sensed a death wish on her part in Mexico, in her acceptance of Lucien's reckless driving, in her swimming off alone down the river, and he wondered whether, drunk as she probably was, she had somehow controlled the situation. On one hand it seemed to him that Joan wanted to die, and on the other he knew there was in Burroughs a sense of perverse irresponsibility, and that he might have been showing off for Allerton's benefit. Was Bill entirely to blame? It seemed to Allen that Joan in some way might have goaded him.

It was something unresolved that would not leave Allen's mind, and years later he dreamed that he went back to Mexico City and saw Joan leaning forward in a garden chair, her arms on her knees. She studied him with clear eyes and a downcast smile, her face restored to its delicate beauty. They talked and she asked, "What's Burroughs doing now?"

"Bill, he's in North Africa," Allen said.

"And Kerouac?"

"Jack still jumps with the same beat genius as before."

"I hope he makes it," Joan said. "Is Huncke still in the can?"

"No, last time I saw him he was on Times Square."

"And you?"

"New loves in the West."

And then Allen knew it was a dream, but nonetheless questioned her: "Joan, what kind of knowledge have the dead? Can you still love your mortal acquaintances? What do you remember of us?" She faded in front of him, and in the next instant he saw her rain-stained tombstone with an illegible epitaph under the gnarled branch of a small tree in the wild grass of an unvisited garden in Mexico.

After Joan's death, Burroughs knew that the rest of his life would be a form of atonement for that one inexplicable moment, not only for the wife he had killed but for the havoc he had brought to those closest to him, his son and his parents, and he was haunted by these lines of Edwin Arlington Robinson's:

> There are mistakes too monstrous for remorse
> To tamper or to dally with.

For the rest of his life, he would carry with him the dull, floating pain of his guilt. There would not be a single day that he would not be reminded in some way of what he had done. As a rational act, it could only be understood up to a point, and then you reached an opaque center. Perhaps there had been an element of provocation, he wasn't sure, and if there was, it was on a telepathic level, like that drawing of Joan's captioned "troglodyte." Perhaps the shooting was the drawing game carried to its terminal outcome. Even if that was the case, and she had somehow willed him to do it, he did not accept it as a cop-out. The glass on the head had been his idea. He was responsible. He had pulled the trigger and fired the bullet that had killed her.

You could say that it was an accident, but to Burroughs, there was no such thing as an accident. He believed that inimical forces caused accidents. In this case, he had been given foreknowledge that something awful was about to happen, that a smog of menace and evil was about to descend. He had broken out in tears, but he had not paid proper attention to the signals. If he had, he would have retrenched, cut his drinking, gone to bed.

The inimical force that had caused him to kill Joan, Burroughs believed quite literally, was an evil spirit that had possessed him. This was a concept more medieval than modern, although whether the evil spirit is seen as coming from within or from without, the result is the same. A divided personality with a capacity for wickedness can look for a psychological explanation, or can believe that he is possessed by malignant forces. Both explanations are metaphors for the nature of evil, which religion and the "ologies" do not satisfactorily define.

In any case, Burroughs believed that there were occasions when an outside being took possession of him. This was not on the level of a "save-me-from-myself" apology. Being occupied by an evil spirit was not an excuse for throwing oneself on the mercy of the court. Quite the contrary: Each time a battle was lost in his struggle with the invading entity, the price was high, the sentence heavy.

One might protest that the evil spirit was a post facto explanation, devised after Joan's death, and better than saying he had shot her deliberately. But the threat of an outside malevolent presence ready to invade him was something Burroughs had felt all his life, even as a young boy— the sense of dread that he could not name, the scene with the nurse and her boyfriend. However far fetched it may seem, it was real to him. He lived with it from day to day.

Joan was a self-designated victim. There was a quality of doom in her marriage to Burroughs. She was like an athlete who takes on an impossible feat of endurance, and breaks under the strain. In the name of living her own life, of defying convention, of finding an alternative to the smugness and hypocrisy of middle-class American life in the forties and fifties, she destroyed her physical and mental health, and finally lost her life. In the vanguard of the counterculture, she became one of its early casualties. As brief as her life was—she was twenty-seven when she died—it was baffling, impenetrable. One sees the cute Barnard girl, taking bubble baths, wearing angora sweaters, looking for "cocksmen" among the V-12s with Edie Parker. And then one sees a woman with a tired, lined face, limping down the street, watching horrified as tiny white worms crawl out of her skin, and one wonders how it can be the same person. The one thing she proved was that you could not take unlimited amounts of amphetamines with impunity.

In her choice of husbands, she was one of those women who take pride in marrying hard cases. She stayed with Burroughs even though he was a homosexual and a drug addict, even though he was often cold and remote, even though there was little of the usual physical affection between husband and wife. There was something brave in her resolve to keep on. But Burroughs, being an addict himself, was in no position to rehabilitate her. On principle, he could not bring himself to give advice. He could not tell Joan to stop taking Benzedrine when he was himself on junk.

The irony of Joan's death was that it unlocked Burroughs' literary vocation. Thanks to Joan, he was able to pursue a career as a writer. One form of atonement was a description of his demons, and one form of defense against them was the written word. With Joan's death, the strands of his life converged—his sense of disinheritance, his fears of alienation and possession, his need to articulate his disgust with the state of American society:

"I am forced to the appalling conclusion that I would never have become a writer but for Joan's death, and to a realization of the extent to which this event has motivated and formulated my writing. I live with the constant threat of possession, and a constant need to escape from possession, from Control. So the death of Joan brought me in contact with the invader, the Ugly Spirit, and maneuvered me into a lifelong struggle, in which I have had no choice except to write my way out."

Aside from Joan's death, there was one other factor that helped Burroughs to become a writer, and that was the example of a kindred spirit, the English writer Denton Welch. In 1933, at the age of eighteen, while an art student in London, Welch was riding a bicycle when he was struck from behind by a woman motorist. His spine was fractured, and he lived in constant pain, mostly bedridden, until his death at the age of thirty-one, writing three autobiographical books in the interval.

Burroughs identified with Denton Welch, thinking of him almost as an alter ego, and memorizing passages of his books. Both Burroughs and Welch had become writers as the result of a terrible accident. Like Burroughs, Welch had felt a sense of foreboding on the day that left him an invalid for the rest of his life. Bicycling to Surrey to visit his uncle's vicarage, he stopped to have coffee and biscuits in a beautiful little eighteenth-century house converted to a luncheonette, and noticed the brass handles on the paneled shutters of the huge sash windows, some of which were broken or missing, and was struck by a sense of universal damage and loss. If he had lingered a little longer over his coffee, or if he had left at once instead of daydreaming, he would have missed his appointment with the motorist. Describing the intersection points where a moment's difference would have meant so much, Welch was able to charge a visit to a church where two nuns prayed, or a billboard advertising Players cigarettes, with a sinister significance. His anticipated feeling of impending doom was exactly like Burroughs'.

Welch would not have started writing except for the accident, a reminder of the origins of Burroughs' own vocation. Like Burroughs, he saw all of his writing as autobiographical. Like Burroughs, he was a homosexual with unfulfilled erotic needs. Indeed, this passage from Welch's journal applies as well to Burroughs:

"When you long with all your heart for someone to love you, a madness grows there that shakes all sense from the trees and the water and the earth. And nothing lives for you, except the long deep bitter want. And this is what everyone feels from birth to death."

Finally, in his deep admiration for Denton Welch, Burroughs was identifying with the victim of the accident, as if he had been, as its instigator and survivor, the true victim of Joan's death.

Joan was buried in Mexico City and Burroughs was locked up in Lecumbere prison, known as the Black Palace. He was fortunate that he had not shot his wife in the United States, where, added to his previous offenses, the charge of homicide would probably have put him away for quite a while. The pillars of the Mexican criminal justice system, however, were bribery and perjury, and in Bernabé Jurado Burroughs had a master in the use of both. Jurado came to see him in jail on the night of the shooting and said, "Well, your wife is no longer in pain, she is dead. But don't worry, I, Bernabé Jurado, am going to defend you, and you will not stay in jail. In Mexico is no capital punishment."

Jurado saw at once that the William Tell version was not serviceable. You could not tell a judge and a jury that you had tried to shoot a glass off your wife's head and had shot her instead and get away with it. It was too grotesque to be convincing. He summoned Woods and Allerton to his townhouse to coach them in the version that he had devised. Which was that Burroughs was a collector of firearms who was demonstrating an automatic to a potential customer. During the demonstration, he pulled back the slide to see if the weapon was loaded, and it fired. Happy to help a friend, Woods and Allerton synchronized their stories. It would have been counterproductive to tell exactly what had happened. As they left Jurado's house, they noticed that they were under surveillance, one man behind them and two on the opposite sidewalk, whom they playfully took on a long walk through the city.

According to the Mexican system, a pretrial hearing was held on September 9 before a judge, who had an office in the prison. Jurado had known the judge, Eduardo Urzaiz Jimenez, since law school, and told Burroughs, "He's a bastard, but he's fair, and he cannot be bought." "That's all I want," Burroughs said, "a fair judge." The prosecutor, Rogello Barriga, was an old friend of Jurado's who occasionally did legal work for him, which didn't hurt.

Taken to the judge's office, Burroughs stood on one side of an iron mesh grid, with the others on the other side—the judge and his stenographer, the prosecutor, Jurado, Woods and Allerton, and two policemen. Burroughs made a statement, which Woods and Allerton corroborated. There had been a friendly party, and he had eight or ten drinks. He had bought the automatic six months ago, and did not know whether it was loaded, not having handled it for three months. When he pulled back the slide to find out, the gun went off.

Woods borrowed one of the cops' .45s to show how it could happen, while thinking: This would never stand up in an American court, because it would be impossible to fire a gun that way unless your finger was depressing the trigger the entire time.

But the prosecutor didn't ask any embarrassing questions, and the judge ruled that Burroughs would be charged with *imprudencia criminal*—criminal imprudence, which carried a maximum sentence of five years. Burroughs pleaded guilty to the charge, and was released on bail until his sentencing in a year's time.

There was some perfunctory questioning about his common-law marriage, during which it came out that he and Joan had filed for divorce in 1950 in Cuernavaca, but were later reconciled. "I am sure she loved me as I loved her," Burroughs said.

Burroughs was released from Lecumbere on September 21 after posting a bond of $2,312. He had spent a total of thirteen days in jail. During his brief sojourn in the slammer he had been greatly impressed by the kindness and decency of the Mexican people. At his first interrogation at the eighth precinct, the cops had coached him: "You must admit this, you must deny that." In the chilly prison cell, where he slept on a slab of tin, a man had given him one of his two blankets. One of the guards told him that prison "requires much calm and much resignation," adding, "It's too bad when a man goes to jail because of a woman."

When Kells Elvins asked Jurado if there was any chance that Burroughs would go back to jail, he said, shocked: "What! Mr. Burroughs go back to prison? Do you think I want to jeopardize my reputation as a lawyer?" Jurado had sprung him in record time. The average for a homicide before bail was arranged was two months. Jurado held Burroughs up as an example of his excellent work and showed him off to prospective clients: "There he is! Thirteen days! No one else in Mexico could have done it."

It annoyed Burroughs when people said that he had been taken. Jurado charged but he delivered. Burroughs had paid him a $2,000 fee, sent by his father, and the only extra was $300 to bribe the four ballistics experts appointed by the court—he could not have made much on that. In Lecumbere he had met people with money and influence and less difficult cases who had been in three and four months. One fellow had run through ten lawyers and $5,000 and was still in. No, he had to hand it to Jurado; he had worked magic.

In Mexico, bail was in effect probation. Every Monday, Burroughs had to report to the prison and sign in. If he didn't, his bail would be rescinded and he would go back to jail. Burroughs would get there early, pacing around the little square until seven, and join the line of sixty or seventy Mexicans, some of whom signed with their thumbprints. It was a weekly reminder of what his fate had almost been.

In the American papers, and particularly in St. Louis, the Burroughs shooting was played up with headlines such as SON OF SCION SLAYS WIFE, and STUNT-SHOOTING OF WIFE DENIED. Once again, Burroughs had brought shame upon his parents, who sent Mort to Mexico to make arrangements for the return of little Billy. When they met in Jurado's office, Mort struck Gene Allerton and Eddie Woods as a dutiful, straitlaced sort who was fed up with bailing his brother out of messy situations but who had a family obligation which he intended to carry out. Afterward, when they went out for a drink, Mort started whining about his youth, when he had to go to night school and support a family while Bill had a free ride thanks to the allowance from his parents.

Burroughs was released from jail while Mort was there, and went to see him at the Reforma Hotel. Burroughs would always remember the occasion, for it was the one and only time that Mort broke through his reserve and showed some emotion. They actually hugged, and Mort started to cry, and Burroughs felt a closeness that would never be repeated. Burroughs spent the night at the hotel, since his apartment was on the other side of town, and Mort talked about the importance of family ties. They slept in the same bed, and Mort, who was a little drunk, put his arms around him and said, "Blood is a hell of a lot thicker than water." This show of affection on the part of his normally undemonstrative brother gave Burroughs a sharp sense of the loss of childhood, when the family had offered some security, and of his own deliberate break, while Mort had stayed and shouldered the responsibility and paid the price, and suddenly he felt abject and began to weep, and Mort said, "Don't, Bill, don't."

They agreed that Billy should go to St. Louis and live with his father's family. Mort also picked out and paid for a burial plot for Joan in the American cemetery, which was good for seven years, after which she was disinterred, and her remains were thrown on the bone-heap. When he got back to St. Louis, Mort told his wife, Miggy, that he was convinced his brother was crazy.

Then Joan's parents, Mr. and Mrs. Vollmer, arrived to get Julie, and Burroughs saw them at the American Consulate, a meeting he would have done anything to avoid. They kept up appearances and shook hands, but Joan's mother sat there just vibrating hostility. Burroughs could imagine what they thought of him, but he didn't think much of them either. They had never contributed one cent to Joan's support, and had written her off completely. They were taking Julie, and wanted to take Billy as well, since he was Joan's child. But Burroughs made them promise to stop in St. Louis and discuss it with his parents, which they did, and Billy stayed in St. Louis.

In December, Burroughs heard from Allen Ginsberg that Phil White, with whom he had rolled drunks in the subway, had hanged himself in the Tombs. Phil, who used to say "I don't see how a pigeon can live with himself," had set up a pusher on the promise that the prosecution would drop one narcotics charge and two larceny charges against him. They double-crossed him and only dropped the narcotics charge, and he was due to follow the pusher to Riker's Island. Unable to face being identified by his fellow convicts as a pigeon, he hanged himself while awaiting transfer.

One way or another, Burroughs reflected, we were held responsible for our acts. He, for instance, had been told that after his case was settled he would be deported as a "pernicious foreigner." Well, that was all right with him since he had burned the place down. If he kept on like this he would end up in Tierra del Fuego. For the moment, he was living very quietly as a result of his legal situation and a case of jaundice contracted during the trip with Allerton. Any more trouble and his bail would be revoked. He even went out without a gun, like a petit bourgeois. He did have a slight habit, having had to cut out drinking completely because of the jaundice. He was wondering where to go next. It had to be someplace where he was a virgin on the police blotter, as he detested limitations of any kind. He certainly wasn't going back to the States, which would be like putting on a straitjacket.

Early in 1952, Allerton left to visit his grandmother in Oklahoma. Mexico was getting a little uncomfortable. He was still under surveillance as a witness in the Burroughs case. Once, after escaping surveillance, he tried to beat the tab in a restaurant. He was walking briskly down the street when he heard the click of an automatic. He stopped walking, turned around, and saw a Mexican policeman pointing a .45. He was arrested and released, but felt it was time to move on. He was also tired of Bill pursuing him, although he had to admit it, Bill was a character. He had all the attributes of a gentleman: loyalty, honesty, generosity. On the other hand he had about every known vice. He drank a great deal, and he was a drug addict, a criminal, and a homosexual, even though he hated faggots and queens, like the one who used to come by the Bounty kissing everybody in sight and proclaiming, "I may be old but I'm still desirable." In spite of his vices, Allerton sensed, Burroughs had great strength of character—where others were overcome, he would survive.

In April 1952, Burroughs received some news that almost made up for all the horrible things that had been happening. The publisher A. A. Wyn had paid $1,000 for his book *Junky*. It was Allen Ginsberg's doing. It had seemed to Allen that Burroughs' only route to redemption was to exercise his talent for writing. As Burroughs sent him chapter after chapter, Allen began to appreciate his eye for the precise sociological detail and his absence of self-pity and self-protectiveness. Acting as Burroughs' agent, Allen did the rounds of his contacts in the publishing world. There was his Columbia classmate Louis Simpson, an editor at Bobbs-Merrill. He, too, had been in a mental hospital and undergone shock treatment. Allen remembered the story of a mutual friend visiting Simpson at his twentieth-floor apartment on East Seventy-second Street. Simpson asked him if he had a watch, and took it, and dropped it out the window, saying, "We're in eternity, we don't need time." Simpson, Allen thought, might appreciate Burroughs' "lower depths" vision, but he didn't, and turned the book down.

He next took it to Jason Epstein, an editor at Doubleday, who said: "The prose is not very good. This could only work if it was written by someone important, like Winston Churchill." What about the line "the taxi drivers were orienting themselves with their horns, like bats," Allen asked, which came from some reservoir of zoological information that would only have occurred to Burroughs. "Well, that's a good line but it doesn't make a book," Epstein said. Allen later realized it was hopeless to show Epstein anything new or original. He was willing to publish only what had already been done. Years later, Allen sent him the work of a younger poet, entitled "Factory," and got back a rejection letter saying, "Our younger editors don't think this is very good poetry, but they also point out that it is an attack on the factory system, and after all, what would we do without factories?" Allen amused himself by composing imaginary rejection letters from Epstein clones: "Dear Mr. Marx, Your long diatribe against the capitalist system is not without interest, but without free trade how could publishing exist?" "Dear Mr. Dostoevsky, This gloomy novel of yours may be of interest to the psychiatric community, but we do not feel that it would appeal to a general audience."

Well, there was always his friend from the nuthouse, Carl Solomon, who was working as an editor for his publisher uncle, A. A. Wyn. Upon his release from the hospital, Solomon had followed Allen's suggestion that they should both try to lead normal lives. He had found a girl and got married, and he and his wife were doing freelance editing when he was hired by Wyn (the husband of his mother's sister), who had a small trade house with a paperback division called Ace Books.

Allen hoped that Solomon could convince his uncle to publish the daring new work of his friends, and put him on to Jack Kerouac, who had not yet found a publisher for *On the Road*. But when Kerouac brought in the huge scroll the book was typed on in one uninterrupted paragraph, Solomon was horrified. He wanted "a James Michener–type box," something ready to go to the printer.

Solomon had a novel approach toward writers, which was to insult them, and he wrote Kerouac that his pose was "that of a nasty, stupid, worthless, idiot-brat son of a royal house." The hero of *On the Road*, he wrote, reminded him of a zinc penny, "symbol of the forties, inflation, the loss of respect for authority, the second war, demonism, the atomization of the American petit-bourgeoisie, the frustration of the kid clutching the penny, loss of contact with this earth.

"So I proceed to the classic and absurdly American problem of the Brilliant Young Punk's second book," Solomon went on. They were arguing over the size of the advance and Jack was acting "like an undertipped head waiter when because of a misunderstanding I clearly explained to you what you (torn between Bennett Cerf and the turd in the toilet bowl) take as an insultingly low figure. . . . We are interested in getting from you neither a book nor a turd of the month. . . . My uncle and I are money-changers. . . . You canucks are always smart businessmen. The French and the Jews uphold the democratic tradition."

On the rebound from his own Dadaist, Artaud-like extravagances, Solomon distrusted Kerouac's vagabond romanticism and did not publish *On the Road*, but when Allen sent him *Junky* he liked it, and so did his uncle, who thought it had a positive side, in that Burroughs had tried to break away from drugs. However, it had to be handled carefully, because the portrayal of drug addiction in those days was out of bounds as the subject of a book. Addiction was seen as an absolute evil. Addicts were called "dope fiends," and what was worse than a fiend?

To cover himself, Wyn decided to publish *Junky* as an Ace paperback, coupled in the same volume with a book by a former agent of the Federal Bureau of Narcotics, Maurice Helbrant. This way, the law enforcer and the lawbreaker would have equal time. The book came out in 1953 as a thirty-five-cent "two books in one." On one cover was *Junky*, by William Lee (Burroughs' mother's maiden name), with the subtitle *Confessions of an Unredeemed Drug Addict*. On the other, upside down, was *Narcotics Agent*, by Maurice Helbrant, the reprint of a book first published in 1941, which was described as "more thrilling than any fiction story."

Shortly after accepting *Junky* in the spring of 1952, Carl Solomon had a nervous breakdown, left his wife, smeared the walls of his apartment with paint, attacked books with knives, stabbing them repeatedly, stopped traffic by throwing his shoes at cars, and ended up in Bellevue. "I wasn't sure which it was," he said, "this reality or the other one, and there are so many realities."

For Burroughs there was only one reality, and that was—after so many years of failed hopes, going back to the routine sent to *Esquire* in 1938—publication. "I owe it all to Al Ginsberg," he wrote Kerouac on April 8. "He is a real friend." The publishers expected a commercial success and were clamoring for his new book, which he had been working on ten hours a day to get into shape. This was an account of his pursuit of Allerton. The two books would be a tale of two afflictions, drug addiction and homosexuality, and there was some talk at the time of running them together in one volume.

It seemed to Burroughs that they had all hit the jackpot. He was being paid a $1,000 advance, Jack had done well with *The Town and the City*, and Allen had a $1,000 grant and the assurance of publication of a book of poems with a preface by William Carlos Williams. Allen echoed this optimism, writing Kerouac, "I can't believe that between us three already we have the nucleus of a totally new historically important American creation."

With *Junky* coming out, Burroughs could at last call himself a writer. The book validated him, gave him a profession and a purpose. Every man needs a métier, in the words of Gertrude Stein, and at last he had one. Writing Allen that some of the boys at Mexico City College had gone to Alaska for jobs, he added, "Thank God I am a man of letters and don't have to expose myself to the inclemencies of near-Arctic conditions."

When it was published in 1953, however, the book went completely unnoticed. There was not a single review of what appeared to be a lurid paperback exploiting the taboo subject of drug addiction. No one but his friends knew Burroughs had written it, since he used a pseudonym to keep his parents from finding out he was the author.

Thus, *Junky* is an example of an important book that was ignored at the time of its publication. A short, autobiographical account of Burroughs' addiction, it follows the tradition of such picaresque novels as Laurence Sterne's *Tristram Shandy* and Céline's *Voyage au Bout de la Nuit*. Like Céline's Ferdinand, Lee the narrator is a magnet for events, and a spokesman to express the author's horror of society. Written in a deadpan documentary style that owed something to the private eye novels of Raymond Chandler and Dashiell Hammett, and begun at the urging of Kells Elvins as a memory exercise, *Junky* reads like a report, but from the wrong side, as though an account of a death in the electric chair had been written from the point of view of the condemned man.

On the surface, *Junky* appears to be an objective slice-of-life document on the subculture of addicts. But in the context of Burroughs' alienation, the book is about finding a place to belong. It is a sequel to Burroughs' favorite childhood book, Jack Black's *You Can't Win*. By taking drugs, Burroughs gained admittance to an outlaw society which he found morally no worse than so-called normal society. The addicts were a sorry lot, with their thieving and their whining for credit and their apathy, but the citizens of straight society were no better—informers, corrupt cops, and hypocrite doctors, with a sprinkling of Johnsons, or decent folk, on both sides. The narcotics agent is "the focal point for a hostile intrusive force. You could feel him walk right into your psyche and look around to see if anything was there he could make use of."

In writing that he had first tried junk out of curiosity and ended up hooked, Burroughs was masking his real motive, which was his attraction to a society of outcasts, and the use of junk as a means of entrée. In those terms, junk had a social use, in that it helped him gain acceptance, just as bringing a remote-controlled model boat to the pond in Central Park will help you to be accepted by the model-boat enthusiasts who gather there daily. Like any social group, the addict underworld had its code of conduct—suspicion of newcomers, the appreciation of experience, the dos and don'ts of scoring and pushing. It was all highly regulated, very much like the world outside. It was also a widespread urban subculture, with a universal language and etiquette, so that Burroughs could pick it up wherever he went, in New Orleans or Mexico City.

Thanks to junk, Burroughs found the place in society which he had been denied repeatedly, when he washed out as a newspaper reporter, an O.S.S. candidate, and in all his other vain attempts to join the mainstream. In this first book, he was content mainly to describe usages, like a visitor to some jungle tribe bringing back the details of their odd customs: They eat human flesh, don't you know . . .

There are, however, indications of future themes in embryonic form, so that the book finally is like a black-and-white photograph of a seedy urban neighborhood in the 1940s, with period cars parked in the street, painted over here and there with the visions of a master of the fantastic such as Hieronymus Bosch.

His hatred of insects, going back to the invasion of scorpions and centipedes in East Texas, makes its appearance: "One afternoon I closed my eyes and saw New York in ruins. Huge centipedes and scorpions crawled in and out of empty bars and cafeterias and drugstores on Forty-second Street. Weeds were growing up through cracks and holes in the pavement. There was no one in sight."

A monstrous, insectlike figure appears, hanging around junk neighborhoods and secreting a substance to prolong life (Burroughs had gone to Mexico to take the Bogomoletz serum, which he thought of as a con, and also connected the figure to the servant underworld which had harmed him in childhood): "What is his [the insect figure's] lost trade? Definitely of a servant class and something to do with the dead, though he is not an embalmer. Perhaps he stores something in his body—a substance to prolong life—of which he is periodically milked by his masters. He is as specialized as an insect, for the performance of some inconceivably vile function."

The image of the hanged man who achieves sexual orgasm just as his neck snaps can also be traced to his youth. Hanging was the method of capital punishment in Missouri when Burroughs was growing up, and he often saw photographs of hanged men in the newspapers. The linking of death by hanging with sexual orgasm had to do with a puritanical instinct that pleasure is wrongful and must be punished. There was a further connection with addiction, which brought suffering and the danger of death through withdrawal and overdosing. The hanged man represented the addict, in that his condition was one of terminal pain, with junk providing relief from pain, a form of pleasure the puritan conscience could condone.

Also in embryo was the idea of the quest, which in later Burroughs books would entail leaving behind a decaying body and a polluted planet. In *Junky*, he moves from place to place, finding one as unsatisfactory as the next. Finally, finding "nationwide hysteria" in the United States, he leaves the country. At the end of the book, far from giving up drugs, he is planning another trip to look for yage, which may be "the final fix." Perhaps the kick of yage will help him escape from his body, the kick being "the momentary freedom from the claims of the aging, cautious, nagging, frightened flesh."

When Burroughs and Allerton planned to sail up the coast of South America, they thought it might be better to hug the shore, since they were not experienced sailors. In *Junky*, not being an experienced writer, and lacking self-confidence, Burroughs hugs the shore, keeping his own experience in sight and seldom straying off into stylistic depths. There is a spare, clear-eyed quality to the writing and a precise, unromanticized rendering of a previously unexamined social group. Junk, as he put it, was a way of life, deserving of notice, and *Junky* is a memorable book, good enough to make a short list of exceptional confessional novels. Jack Kerouac thought it was like Hemingway, but better than Hemingway, and wrote a blurb: "A learned, vicious, Goering-like sophisticate makes the first intelligent modern confession on drugs. . . . Stands classic and alone." Chandler Brossard also admired *Junky*, and taught it in his writing class as the first novel of its kind.

Within a year of publication, *Junky* had sold 113,170 copies, a more than respectable sale for a paperback in those days. Burroughs found that being a published author had its irksome side. When he was asked in April 1952 for a biographic note, he felt as if someone had put to him that most inane of questions: "Tell me about yourself." He felt like writing back a parody of the author as a man of multiple occupations: He had worked as a towel boy in a Kalamazoo whorehouse, lavatory attendant, male whore, and part-time stool pigeon. He was currently living in a remodeled pissoir with a hermaphrodite and a succession of cats, which he took pleasure in torturing, favoring kerosene over gasoline because it burned slower.

When Carl Solomon wanted to know whether he minded being identified as a homosexual, he replied that he was in the vein of T. E. Lawrence and all manner of right Joes, and that as long as Solomon maintained the distinction between the strong, manly, noble types and the leaping, jumping, window-dressing, cock-sucking fags, it would be all right.

In May 1952, Jack Kerouac arrived on a visit, feeling gloomy because *On the Road* was being rejected all over the place. Bob Giroux, who had taken *The Town and the City*, did not want it. When Jack had brought in his 120-foot roll of paper and said he would not change a single word, Giroux said it was his first experience with the "my-words-are-sacred" attitude. "Even Shakespeare," he told Jack, "who they say didn't blot many words, blotted some—and Jack, you ain't Shakespeare."

Then Scribner's, which had accepted John Clellon Holmes's novel *Go*, turned him down. A friend of Jack's and Allen's, Holmes had used them as characters in the book. Kerouac thought Holmes's novel was terrible, whereas *On the Road* was inspired in its entirety . . . it was, he felt sure, as good as James Joyce's *Ulysses*, and as path-breaking, and should be treated with the same gravity. Was this the fate of an idiot, he wondered, or the general fartsmell of New York? He knew that Ginsberg and Holmes would give their right arm to match the writing in *On the Road*. All these cheap little shits were the same, and he'd wasted fifteen years of his life among the cruds of New York, from the millionaire Jews of Horace Mann who'd kissed his ass for football and now would hesitate to introduce their wives to him, to the likes of Ginsberg, a small-sized variant of a poet. As for Holmes, everybody knew he had no talent, and his book stank, while *On the Road* was great and unpublished. Allen had even fucked him up with Giroux when he had brought Neal to his office, and Neal right away tried to steal one of his books. But none of that mattered, for one of these years he was going to knock off three masterpieces in one year, like Shakespeare in his *Hamlet-Lear-Caesar* year.

Once he had the dust of great Mexico on his shoes, Jack felt better. He arrived by bus on a Saturday, and the women were making tortillas, and the radios were playing Perez Prado. He felt close to Bill, who looked like a mad scholar, surrounded by the pages of his new novel, which Jack suggested should be called *Queer*. Bill missed Joan terribly. She lived on in him. His son was gone, and his boyfriend had left, it seemed for good. His life was empty of everything save kicks and art. But he was the same wise philosopher, and when Jack complained about Holmes, Bill said that "envy or resentment is only possible when you cannot see your own space-time location."

They went to the bullfights, and to Lola's bar, and to the Mexican ballet, and took some peyote together, which launched Burroughs into a monologue about being a prisoner: "Ah, I feel awful, I feel worse than if I was suddenly a prisoner on the high Andes." Jack connected with two women, one a big-breasted American, the other a splendid Mexican whore, and began writing his new novel, *Dr. Sax,* a character partly based on Burroughs.

Then a friend of Jack's arrived, Slim Simon, the bass player, known as the Scooper, with the goatee and the thick crepe soles and the great driving style, who used to play at the Club 229 in San Francisco. He wanted to open his own bop joint with some local boys, and came around every day. But he made a poor impression on Burroughs, who could tell a junky on the mooch when he saw one. "No, I don't want to buy any," Slim said, "I'm kicking. Just let me have half a fix." Here was a guy driving around in a new Chrysler and too cheap to buy his own junk. What am I, Burroughs asked himself, the junky's benevolent society for Chrissakes?

Jack was getting on his nerves for the same reason. During the brief time he had money, it was like pulling an impacted molar to get him to part with any. After the first week he was flat and did not put out centavo one. Burroughs was picking up the tab in toto. Also, he asked Jack to keep the bag of grass he was smoking (which Burroughs had bought) out of the apartment, since he was out on bail and would be in serious trouble in case of a shakedown, and what did Jack do but ask Old Dave to bring him the bag so he could hide it somewhere. Old Dave tipped Burroughs off. But that was only one example of Jack's selfish, inconsiderate, and

downright insufferable behavior. Jack was so paranoid he thought everyone else was plotting to take advantage of him, so he had to act first in
self-defense. Whenever Burroughs bought food, Jack ate it all. If there
were two rolls left, he ate both of them. Once he flew into a rage because
Burroughs had eaten his half of the remaining butter. To share on an
equal basis was something he considered unreasonable. When in July
Jack talked about leaving, Burroughs loaned him twenty dollars to speed
him on his way. Jack, in the meantime, had soured on Mexico, complaining about the food and the lack of sanitation, and thought that Bill,
with his alternating periods of nagging and sullenness, had joined the
sinister forces working against him. They had talked of traveling to South
America together, but that was something Burroughs now refused to
consider. As for Jack, he was terrified by Burroughs' stories of deadly
South American snakes. All in all, Jack's two months in Mexico were a
strain on their friendship.

No sooner had Jack left than Bill Garver, the Times Square overcoat
thief, turned up, having collected an inheritance that gave him enough
to satisfy his habit in Mexico City, and having left a trail of bad debts in
New York. Burroughs went to meet him at the airport, and saw his tall,
bent frame, and his thin face with the white hair combed back. He had
blood all over his pants from having used a safety pin on the plane to
shoot up. Garver said the situation for addicts in the U.S. was bad: eight
years in Washington, D.C., for possession of an eyedropper.

Burroughs found him a room with a hotplate, a dresser, a full-length
mirror on the inside of the door, pink drapes, and an easy chair. Garver
brightened it up with photographs of Orozco paintings he cut out of
Mexican magazines. His wants were few—a little Nescafé, an occasional
ham sandwich, his newspaper, and his junk. In some ways, Garver felt,
the addict was not unlike the artist, in that they both liked to be alone
and didn't go running around looking for things to do. They had it all
inside, and did not turn away from the study of good books. Garver had
read H. G. Wells's *Outline of History* a hundred times, and was an
authority on Alexander the Great, "the only general I know of," he
would say, "who rode in front of his cavalry swinging a sword."

One day not long after Garver's arrival, Burroughs went to the office
of Bernabé Jurado, who asked him whether he knew anyone who was
interested in buying an ounce of heroin for $500. Burroughs passed the
offer on to Garver, who was looking for a heroin connection and together
they went to see Jurado, who took the stuff out of a drawer and put it
on the desk, saying, "I don't know anything about this stuff. All I use is

cocaine." He used it before trials, and sniffed it with tequila, placing it on his hand in lieu of salt.

Burroughs poured some out on a piece of paper. It was grayish-black and didn't look right. He and Garver rolled their sleeves up and took shots, as people walked in and out of Jurado's office, paying no attention. "It's H," Burroughs said, "but there's something not exactly right about it." Garver, already loaded on goofballs, thought it was all right and bought it.

The next morning at eleven, on a bright summer day, Burroughs opened his eyes to find Garver standing by his bed, looking cadaverous in his midnight-blue overcoat, his eyes gleaming wildly. "You just going to lie there on your bed," Garver asked, "with all these shipments coming in?"

"Why not?" Burroughs said, annoyed at the intrusion. "This isn't any fuckin' farm . . . Shipments of what?"

"Pure, drugstore M," Garver said. Then he pulled back the sheet and blanket and climbed into bed with Burroughs, shoes, overcoat, and all.

"What's the matter with you," Burroughs asked. "You crazy?"

Garver went "Hee hee."

Looking into his bright vacant eyes, Burroughs saw that he was not himself, and carried him back to his room, confiscating what was left of the ounce of heroin.

Soon Old Dave arrived with some laudanum, and they poured a good belt down Garver's gullet, which had a sedative effect. He stopped raving about "shipments" and went to sleep.

"Maybe he die," Old Dave said, "and they blame it onto me."

"If he dies you clear out," Burroughs said. "Listen. He's got six hundred dollars cash in his wallet. Why leave it for some Mexican cop to steal?"

They searched his clothes and his room looking for his wallet, but couldn't find it. The next day when Burroughs came around, Garver looked fine. He couldn't remember anything, but said, "Good thing I stashed my wallet." He turned up the mattress and the wallet sprang open, thick with crisp bills.

But Garver depressed him because he was such a wreck, on the nod all the time, fumbling five minutes for a word. The only thing that had ever held him together was the necessity of stealing, and without it he was falling apart.

In September, Allerton turned up. Burroughs was hurt that he had been in Mexico City five days before coming to see him, and made a scene. Allerton asked why they couldn't just be friends, with no sex. Burroughs explained that it was too much of a strain—just having him in town was ruining his digestion, sleep, and nerves. He felt that with Allerton he had done everything he possibly could and failed completely. Allerton was with a con man called the Colonel, and they were headed for Panama and points south, where the Colonel sold advertising space in nonexistent publications. Well, thought Burroughs, if he preferred the company of such dull characters to his own, there was nothing to be done. Burroughs still had Angelo, a Mexican boy he saw twice a week, but commercial sex left him absolutely cold.

He showed Allerton the manuscript of *Queer*, which chronicled their meeting and travels together, and Burroughs' painful and unrequited effort to connect with another human being. Allerton read it and said, "Well, it's not a bad yarn, but don't get the idea you're anything in the way of a writer." That seemed to be the consensus, for the people at A. A. Wyn decided that publishing *Junky* was dangerous enough without teaming it with a book about homosexuality that might land them all in jail.

He badly wanted to leave Mexico City, but his case still had not come up. There were endless delays. If it wasn't a religious holiday, the court secretary had gone on vacation and taken his file along. Then in November, there seemed to descend one of those bad luck periods that affect everyone. He had a habit again, and his pocket was picked of $200. But that was nothing compared to what had happened to Jurado. A car driven by a seventeen-year-old boy had sideswiped his Cadillac and damaged the fishtail. Jurado pulled the boy out of his car, and in the ensuing argument, shot him in the leg. The boy died of tetanus in the hospital. Whether the boy had been killed by Jurado or the people at the hospital was an interesting legal point, but Jurado didn't wait to find out and fled to Brazil.

Not long after Jurado's departure, the other lawyers in his office told Burroughs they would need more money to keep him out on bail. Once the shakedown began, Burroughs thought, there would be no end to it. He decided to follow Jurado's example and skip, even though it would mean forfeiting the $2,000 bond. (He later learned that he had been sentenced in absentia to two years suspended.) He had a friend, Tex Palmer, known as Tex the Trotskyite, who was resourceful and had a car. Tex was in a spot of trouble himself over some forged cashier's checks, and was also ready to skip. He suggested to Burroughs that they pull a bank robbery first, "and we can hole up in Bolivia where I've got some Trotskyite connections." Burroughs talked him out of that plan, and in December 1952 they left Mexico City, heading north, and crossed the border without incident. Burroughs had been there three years, but there was no one he wanted to say good-bye to.

· ELEVEN ·

COLOMBIA

1953

When four-year-old Billy Burroughs came to St. Louis in October 1951, he stayed at first with his father's brother, Mort, and Mort's wife, Miggy. Mr. and Mrs. Vollmer had brought him on a chilly day, and he had nothing on but a light shirt. They were terribly bitter, and Mrs. Vollmer said, "I hope Bill Burroughs goes to hell and stays there." Billy spoke a little English and a little Spanish and sang "La Cucaracha." He said, "There were mens under the bed and the mens were fighting." Billy was unmanageable. He screamed at night, and once he bit Miggy, who finally said, "I cannot cope any longer," and sent him to live with his grandparents. Laura was sixty-three and Mote was sixty-six and had a heart condition. They continued to operate their gift shop, Cobblestone Gardens.

Billy knew that his mother was dead, but not the circumstances. He had not had time to store up many memories of her. He remembered being in a crib with a net over it, under a tree—that must have been in East Texas. He remembered a tiled floor in Mexico City, and walking behind his mother up the steps to their apartment, and thinking that her calves were sort of heart-shaped. He remembered a trip in a car, and his mother saying, "How fast can this old heap go?"

His father had played a game with him called Our House. He had drawn a picture of the house. It was in the jungle, up on stilts, because the jungle was full of dangerous tigers and jaguars. There was Our House, and even Our Monkey. It was a safe place. But now his mother was dead, and his father was away, and his sister was gone, and he was living with his grandparents.

Billy was afraid of the dark. He slept in his grandparents' bedroom, and Laura would hold his hand across the beds until he fell asleep. Billy felt it was dangerous to reach across the darkness for his grandmother's hand. He might be intercepted, or worse, find that the hand he touched was not the familiar hand he knew. One day, two of his grandparents' friends in the gift business, Tom and Clark, came for tea. Laura mentioned that Billy was afraid of the dark and Tom looked at him teasingly and said, "Are you afraid there's something under the bed?" and everyone laughed the kind of laugh that is meant for the soothing of children, but Billy saw Tom's eyes as the only living things in the room, and they were not laughing. Billy asked his grandmother why it was that he, Billy, always seemed to look just before something happened, and she said it was a great gift. He wondered how she could say that and not realize that when he said the dark was dangerous, it *was*.

One day Mote was reading Billy Dr. Seuss's *Horton Hatches the Egg*, in which Horton the elephant does a favor for Mazie the Lazy Bird while she goes on vacation to Palm Beach. When Laura came home, Mote said, "Guess what? Billy and I have decided to move to Palm Beach."

At first it was said as a joke, but it began to seem like a good idea. Laura and Mote were at an age where they wanted to get away from the St. Louis winters. They also, according to Miggy, felt that the actions of their son had distanced them from their friends. It did not help one's social and professional position in St. Louis to have a son who had been jailed for shooting his wife. On one particularly cold day in March 1952, Mote said, "I've put a snowsuit on that child for the last time."

In the spring, they sold the house on Price Road and moved to Palm Beach, an island that was a concentration of green, in terms of vegetation and money. They bought a two-bedroom ranch house at 202 Sanford Avenue, which was lined with royal palms. The Kennedy estate, sur-rounded by ivied walls, was half a mile away, and some of the other names on the mailboxes in the vicinity were Rockefeller, Kellogg, and Dodge. Palm Beach was a perfect setting to demonstrate the insularity of great wealth. "We have three bridges that lead to the United States" was a Palm Beach saying. West Palm Beach, on the mainland, had orig-inally been developed as a dormitory for servants. On Worth Avenue, the shops had an understated elegance designed for customers who were not alarmed by high prices. Mote and Laura reopened Cobblestone Gar-dens at 233 Phipps Plaza, but soon moved to Worth Avenue, joining Cartier, Elizabeth Arden, and Brooks Brothers. Cobblestone Gardens was the shop where a charming and well-bred couple in their sixties would greet you at the door and sell you porcelain birds, music boxes, and garden furniture.

In December, having skipped from Mexico, Burroughs arrived in Palm

Beach to spend Christmas with his parents and son. Laura and Mote were discreet as always, and asked no questions concerning recent events. It was as though Burroughs was a blackboard, whom they could periodically erase, starting over with a clean slate. Burroughs was kicking, and went to see a local doctor who put him on cortisone and told him he was in perfect health.

He spent a good deal of time with his son, making up for his absence, taking him to the beach, and fishing off the jetty at the end of town, and showing him how fast he had walked through the jungle, and taking pictures, and driving past the estates that had tunnels leading under the public road to their private beaches. Billy copied his European style of eating, with fork upside down. Burroughs loved his son, and was aware of his duties as a father, but for the moment it was better that the child remain with his parents. He was homeless, and had no idea where he would settle. His only plan at present was to go back to South America and look for yage: "Let determined things to destiny hold unbewailed their sway."

By mid-January 1953, he was in Panama City, and it was the same old Panama, inhabited by the crummiest people in the hemisphere, half of whom seemed to be pimps: "Want nice girl? See naked lady dance? Hey, meester, you fuck my seester?" Discovering a bad case of piles, he checked into the American hospital to have them operated on. After four days in the hospital he was in a foul mood. Coming upon a group of American women in the hall, probably officers' wives, he overheard one of them say, "I don't know, I just can't eat sweets," and commented as he passed, "You got diabetes, lady."

He would leave for Bogotá when he was in a condition to travel. He was in pain and junk-sick, and whenever he sat down a little pool of blood collected, as if he was menstruating, so that he had to buy maroon slacks. Bill Garver had passed through and gone, having heard it was easier to score there than in Mexico, and Burroughs was glad to see the last of him.

By January 25, 1953, Burroughs was in Bogotá, a gloomy city at 9,000 feet. He felt the dead weight of Spain, somber and oppressive. His hotel room had no window, and the bed was too short. The next day, he went to the university to get some information from the botany department. Around noon, he found himself in a large dusty room full of plant specimens when a tall, husky man came in, with a strong face and close-cropped hair, wearing steel-rimmed glasses and Ivy League tweeds, who was muttering, "What have they done with my cocoa specimens" in a tone of refined annoyance. Ah, a fellow American, thought Burroughs.

He was in luck, for the man was Richard Evans Schultes, a world authority on hallucinogenic plants. At Harvard, Schultes had taken a botany course and realized that the study of narcotic and psychoactive plants was a wide open field of research. He had switched his major from pre-med to botany and written his senior thesis on peyote. He had what you might call a vocation, being amazed that such powerful substances, substances that had changed civilizations, existed in ordinary-looking plants that grew wild. There were about half a million species of plants, and primitive man, being curious, put them in his mouth. Some were nourishing, some alleviated illness, some made him sick, and some killed him—end of experiment.

Their use went back to the dawn of man. The Ebers papyrus, written in Egypt in 1500 B.C., told of message runners who developed ulcers and plastered their legs with green mud from the soil. They were applying antibiotic-secreting fungi. Some plants—and in these Schultes specialized—took you to wonderland. After getting his Ph.D. in 1941, he had gone to Colombia to study arrow poison plants in the northwest Amazon, also scouting rubber sources for the government. He lived there with the Indians for twelve years, eating what they ate and sleeping where they slept, traveling by canoe, delving into folk usage, using Indian assistants, learning the language, catching malaria and beri-beri.

The region was rich in plant hallucinogens, and Schultes collected 24,000 specimens, identifying six new psychoactive plants in years of hard exploration. In a spirit of scientific inquiry, he had sampled a wide variety of drugs, sacred morning glories, sacred mushrooms, peyote, various types of yage—what he hadn't tried hadn't yet been found.

On that day in January 1953, Schultes was working in the herbarium during his two-hour lunch break, when no one was around to bother him, and he saw this gaunt fellow come in, obviously an American, and asked if he could help. It turned out that Burroughs was Harvard '36 and Schultes was Harvard '37, and this common background induced a certain amount of good fellowship. Burroughs said he was looking for yage specimens, and Schultes pulled some out and saw at once from the way Burroughs handled them that he wasn't a botanist.

The meeting between Schultes and Burroughs illustrated two approaches to knowledge, the scientific and the romantic. Schultes had spent most of his adult life studying hallucinogenic plants; he was a recognized expert with a patiently accumulated fund of knowledge. Burroughs knew almost nothing about yage, but had a tenacity of purpose born of a devout hope—the hope that yage would be the ultimate mind-bending drug that would somehow change him in crucial ways. In the tradition of the romantic quest, he had simply started out, without preparation or instruction, rather like a primitive man, and had stumbled onto the expert who knew more about hallucinogenic plants than any other.

Schultes was puzzled that someone would come all this way without knowledge or training to look for yage, but explained that the drug came from a vine known botanically as banipsteriosis, of which there were 100 species growing wild in the Amazon jungle. The bark from the stems of these jungle lianas, when pounded and boiled in water with or without other ingredients, made a vision-producing beverage widely used by the Indians. Depending on the region, the drink was called ahahuasca, caapi, or yage. The myth of creation among the Macuna Indians had it that they had come down from the Milky Way in a canoe driven by an anaconda snake, with a man and a woman and three plants—the cassaba or tapioca, the cocaine plant, and the yage. Now people might laugh at that, Schultes said, though they didn't laugh at the myth of Genesis, which had a snake chasing a woman with an apple in its mouth, so you had to ask yourself, which was more ridiculous?

In any case, the Indians included yage in their myth of origin, which indicated the importance it had in their society. It caused visual hallucinations, and the Indians used it to commune with the spirit world. The Ecuadorian Indians explained the altered state produced by yage by saying that during that time the soul left the body, and was wandering around in space with the ancestors, and when the soul came back the altered state was over.

Schultes told Burroughs he had tried yage. "I got colors but no visions," he said. Burroughs' best bet, he said, was to go down to the Putumayo River, which formed the border between Colombia and Ecuador and Peru, where he would find medicine men who made the stuff. He'd better take along a hammock, a rubber bag, and various medicines.

Traveling by bus and train, Burroughs headed toward the southwestern corner of Colombia, on the border with Ecuador, past Cali, a pleasant, semitropical town, and on to Popayan, a university town where U.S. residents told him: "They hate the sight of a foreigner down here. You know why? It's all this Point Four and Good Neighbor crap and financial aid . . . the more you give the bastards the nastier they get."

On January 30 he reached Pasto, which hit him in the gut with a punch of depression. High mountains all around, sod-roofed huts, a crummy-looking populace. The higher the altitude, it seemed, the uglier the people. Everyone had a harelip or one blind eye or one leg shorter than the other. Schultes had given Burroughs an introduction to a German who ran a winery. All the German did was complain about his health. His bad heart, his bad kidneys—"and I used to be tough as nails," he said. The German told him to go to Mocoa, about forty miles east of Pasto, where he would find yage.

Mocoa was one of those end-of-the-road towns, with muddy streets. After that, it was mule or canoe. He reached Puerto Limon by truck, where he found a *brujo* (medicine man) who agreed to prepare a cold water yage infusion in exchange for a quart of *aguardiente*. This was a far less potent preparation than boiling, but Burroughs had vivid dreams in color, and saw a composite city, part Lima, part Mexico City, and part New York. He continued down the Putumayo River, where the towns were called Puerto this and Puerto that, traveling by canoe with outboard motors.

In Puerto Assis, one of the members of the Policia Nacional asked to see his papers. There was at the time trouble with Peru, and Puerto Assis was right on the border. The cop noticed a mistake on his visa—the consul in Panama had dated it 1952 instead of 1953. Burroughs found himself under house arrest pending a decision from Mocoa. He was furious at being stuck in the dreary Putumayo town, with its dirt road along the river, its *cantina*, its few shops, and its mission of Capuchin fathers. The fathers, however, turned out to be good guys, who interceded for him and invited him to dinner, serving wine and liqueurs. They lived the life of Riley, Burroughs thought; when they snapped their fingers the natives jumped. But as the days wore on he felt that he was on his way to establishing himself in the capacity of village wastrel. Sepulchral telegrams arrived from Mocoa, saying, "We are studying the case of the foreigner from Ohio." By this time he had malaria and was running such a high fever that the doctor who came to his hotel exclaimed, "*Caramba!*" Finally it was decided that he would have to go back to Bogotá and get a new visa. It was like some lunatic board game, where if you landed on the wrong square you had to go back to your starting point.

The return to Bogotá in March, however, turned out to be a blessing in disguise, for Burroughs was able, thanks to Schultes, to attach himself to an official Cocoa Commission expedition, which included two English and two Colombian botanists. The Englishmen, Doctors Barclay and Halliday, from the Imperial Institute of Mycology, were specialists in broom rot, the disease of cocoa, and the Colombians went along to collect plant specimens, while Schultes was trying to convince the Indians to plant rubber trees, which they were reluctant to do, for it took fifteen years for a tree to produce rubber.

Back Burroughs went to Mocoa, where this time another German friend of Schultes, who owned a *finca* and did a little gold-panning, put him on to the real thing. Burroughs was taken to a thatch hut with a dirt floor, where a *brujo* of about seventy with a cherubic, unlined face sat in front of a bowl on a tripod. Behind the bowl there was a small wood shrine with a picture of the Virgin, a crucifix, a wood idol, a bunch of feathers, and a little package tied with ribbons. The *brujo* crooned over the bowl and shook a little broom over it, to whisk away evil spirits. After sampling it, he handed Burroughs an ounce of the black liquid in a plastic cup. It was oily in texture and bitter in taste. Burroughs' first thought was "That wasn't enough, I need more," which he recognized, based on precedent, as a dangerous reaction indicating that he had taken too much. Two minutes later his head began to spin. Blue flashes passed in front of his eyes. Rushing for the door as a wave of nausea hit him, he found that he could hardly walk. His feet were like blocks of wood. "All I want is out of here," he kept saying in uncontrolled hebephrenic repetition. Outside, he fell on all fours, retching and convulsed with spasms. The medicine man stood over him, saying something, which Burroughs understood as a request to return to the hut, and he shook his head. This *brujo*, he was sure, must specialize in poisoning *gringos*: "You've come to the right place—just drink this straight down."

He downed some Nembutals and felt a bit better, but was still delirious. He felt himself change into a Negress with convulsions of lust. Then he was a Negro fucking a Negress. Everything was writhing as in a Van Gogh painting. Complete bisexuality was attained. He was a man or a woman alternately or at will. Yage, he later reflected, really did what other drugs were supposed to do. It really bent your mind. It was the most complete negation possible of respectability. Imagine if every complacent, middle-class American took it. Imagine a small-town bank president turning into a Negress and rushing into nigger town in a frenzy to solicit sex from some buck Nigra. He would never recover the preposterous condition known as self-respect. Perhaps the preliminary sickness had been a motion sickness of transport to the yage state. H. G. Wells in *The Time Machine* had written of the vertigo of space-time travel.

In any case, the delirium lasted about four hours, after which Burroughs went back into the hut and lay down under a blanket. During the night he had chills like malaria but the next day he felt all right, and rejoined the Cocoa Commission expedition in Mocoa. The two Englishmen spent hours looking through microscopes for tiny spots on leaves, which led to some hilarity, while the two Colombians pressed specimens. Schultes complained about the buildup along the river, where there was now town after town—"You have to walk miles to get to the jungle." Burroughs noted that Schultes was in with the natives, and not above amorous dalliance with indigenous females. A coolness developed between the Colombians and the British, who thought they were deliberately procrastinating in the mornings to avoid an early start. "So long as they can collect any old weed they don't give a ruddy fuck," one of the English botanists told Burroughs.

Eventually they reached the naval base of Puerto Leguisomo, which was named for a hero of the last war with Peru, and were put up on a Colombian gunboat, the *Santa Marta*, where they were able to take showers. It was a great improvement over the jungle, thought Schultes, gleaming white and comfortable, with the sailors polishing the brass. But Burroughs in his disgruntled way complained that the Colombians ran a loose ship and said he wouldn't be surprised to see someone shit on the deck and wipe his ass with the flag.

Wanting to sample yage in other areas, Burroughs was eager to proceed with his trip, and found a plane back to Bogotá. When native hustlers approached him there, asking, "You speak English?" he replied, "Fluently." By May 5, he was in Lima, hanging around the bars near the Mercado Majorista. Lima was the promised land for boys, all available to the Yankee dollar. He had seen nothing like it since Vienna in 1936. But you had to keep an eye on the little bastards or they'd steal everything you had including your skivvies. He hid his money in his hatband.

Rather than stay in a hotel, he found a hole-in-the-wall near the public dump, a former shop with a pull-down shutter—it was cheap, and he could bring boys there. When he walked out on the sidewalk there were so many vultures he had to kick them aside. They came by the hundreds to the dump to eat the fish heads. He had never seen a city with more vultures than Lima; they were all over the public buildings in Bolivar Square. They were useful, however, in that they ate the garbage and kept the streets and beaches clean.

On May 15, he heard that *Junky* was out, and that Wyn had run an ad with blurbs from Kerouac and John Clellon Holmes. A week later he got $270 as part of his advance, and that night, a boy stole it. Peruvian boys, who had no inhibitions about showing affection, had none about stealing either. A few days later he was rolled again, losing his glasses and pocketknife. What a nation of kleptomaniacs! In all his experience as a homosexual, he had never seen such idiotic pilfering. The trouble was, he shared with the late Father Flanagan of Boys Town the deep conviction that there was no such thing as a bad boy.

He wondered about himself. Here he was thirty-nine years old, and it seemed that the older he got the less he knew, the less wisdom, maturity, and caution he had. Oh, well, if he had listened to his analyst he would have given up boys and become an assistant professor in some midwestern university, hatching a cancer of the prostate. Instead of which he was demonstrating judo to young boys in louche bistros—God keep me from ever being a wise old man praised of all, in the words of the immortal Yeats.

Peru was an improvement over Ecuador and Colombia in that the Peruvians didn't have the small country inferiority complex. In Peru they had *pochos*, Peruvians who did not like other Peruvians, which was a sure sign of a superior civilization. In Peruvian towns they had what you wanted, whereas in other South American towns they never did—in a river town they did not stock fish hooks, in a place infested with mosquitoes they had never heard of citronella. That was the way it was, a determination to be stupid and jerkwater. In mid-June, Burroughs left Lima for the high jungle, stopping in the farming center of Tingo Maria, which had a U.S. Point Four Agriculture station. It gave him the stasis horrors, the unendurable feeling of being just where he was and nowhere else, as if he would have to stay there forever. It reminded him of H. G. Wells's *The Country of the Blind*, where a man is stuck in a country where everyone has been blind for generations and they have lost all concept of sight. Pucallpa, another high jungle town, he liked better, although he fell in with some Peruvians at the hotel who drove him crazy with their stupid Spanish jokes. When they said that American literature did not exist, he lost his temper and told them Spanish literature belonged in the outhouse on a peg with the old Montgomery Ward catalogues.

On the waterfront he met a boy who said he had nothing to eat, and invited him for a sandwich at the hotel. When the boy arrived carrying a Bible with an inscription from "your friend the chief of police in Contamana," one of the Peruvians, a furniture salesman, put his hand to the back of his head and said, "And a very special friend, my dear, no?"

The hotel owner introduced him to a Protestant missionary, a member of an outfit called the Linguistic Institute, financed from some place in Oklahoma. They were all over Peru, teaching Indians the Bible. The missionary was going to take Burroughs upriver in his motorboat, but when he saw him take a drink he said, "Jesus will come to you." "That's all mythology," Burroughs said, ruining his chance for a ride. What a lousy Christer, thought Burroughs, and what a difference from the Capuchins, who didn't mind a drink and ate the local food, whereas this guy subsisted on Spam.

Burroughs had been about to make another yage connection, but the missionary said yage came from the devil. He finally made the connection, and this time he did not go into convulsions. When it got to be too much he took Nembutal. Taking yage five times, he built up a tolerance. It was without a doubt the most powerful drug he had ever experienced, producing a complete derangement of the senses. Yage was an insane, overwhelming rape of the senses.

Back in Lima in July, he was sick and discouraged. Lima was damp and depressing, and none of the Mercado boys were around. He felt the urge to leave right away, and took a bus to Talara, on the coastal desert in the north, and from there to Panama City, that mongrel town of pimps and whores and recessive genes. In Chico's Bar they were playing "It Wasn't God Made Honky-Tonk." The G.I.s all had that light-concussion Canal Zone look. A B-girl sat next to him, and when he declined to buy her a drink, she asked, "Why are you so mean?" "Look, if I run out of money who is going to buy my drinks?" he asked. "Will you?" The girl looked surprised and said, "Yes, you are right. Excuse me." He left Chico's and walked down the main drag, and a pimp seized his arm: "I gotta fourteen-year-old girl, Jack, Puerto Rican. How's about it?" "She's middle-aged already," Burroughs said. "I want a six-year-old virgin, and don't try palming your old bats off on me." The next day, coming back from the embassy on a bus after picking up his mail, with a newspaper resting on his knee, a *mestizo* sat next to him, snatched the paper, and started reading it. Burroughs snatched it back and said, "If you want to read my paper, ask for it. Where is your politeness?" "You are a Polish Jew?" the *mestizo* asked. "No, American," Burroughs said. "Lie. You Polish," said the *mestizo*. Burroughs was on the point of saying, "You ought to know an American when you see one, we run your jerkwater spic country," but told himself to watch his temper. It was time to leave. *Panama, how I hate your cheatin' guts.*

Passing through Mexico City, he ran across a couple of people from the Bounty days and asked if they had heard from Allerton, but no one knew where he was. Burroughs felt an ache of longing, remembering their trip. If he suddenly appeared, Burroughs would have a new routine for him, the Skip Tracer: "You meet all kinds on this job, kid. Every now and then some popcorn citizen walks in the office and tries to pay Friendly Finance with this shit. . . . Slowly he opens a thin brown hand, revealing a roll of yellow $1,000 bills. The hand turns over palm down and falls against the chair. . . . The bills lie there crumpled on the red tile floor. . . . Imperceptibly, the Skip Tracer straightened up: 'Keep that in case you're caught short, kid. You know how it is in these spic hotels. You gotta carry your own papers.' He walked to the door, polishing the nails of his left hand on the lapel of his worn glen-plaid suit. The suit gave off an odor of mold when he moved. He looked at his nails: 'Oh, about your account. I'll be around soon. That is within a few. . . . We'll come to some kind of an agreement.' The door opened and wind blew through the room. The door closed and the curtains settled back, one curtain trailing over a sofa as if someone had taken it and tossed it there."

By mid-August 1953, Burroughs was in Palm Beach for a brief visit with his family. His parents continued to support him with $200 a month, but it was clear they did not want him living where they lived. The trouble was, there were places where he might have liked to live but couldn't, because of legal problems—New Orleans, Mexico City, New York. In September, however, he went to New York for the first time in six years, to visit Allen Ginsberg.

It was a different city, a different country, a different planet, a different decade. There were no Roaring Fifties as there had been Roaring Twenties. The postwar equation did not lend itself to merry-making: two superpowers with the ability to destroy each other, the Russians having exploded their first atomic bomb in 1950. Then the Korean War started, the first example of the superpowers waging war by proxy in the Third World. The Pentagon replaced the W.P.A. as Big Spender. At home, Senator McCarthy exploited fears of Communism, federal employees went before loyalty boards, and "subversive" organizations were listed by the attorney general. Robert Oppenheimer, maker of the A-bomb, was charged with having Communist sympathies. Charlie Chaplin was refused entry into the United States on the ground of being a dangerous character—the Little Tramp, dangerous!

Life went on—Levittowns, *The Man in the Gray Flannel Suit*, "The $64,000 Question," Doctors Spock and Kinsey, *The Joy of Cooking*, "Are you now or have you ever been . . . ?," Jayne Mansfield, with her rayon hair and little-girl voice, and William F. Buckley, with his meretricious *God and Man at Yale*, were two examples of the moral hypocrisy of the fifties . . . the Eisenhower years . . . Eisenhower having been, in passing, president of the university from which Allen Ginsberg had been suspended and Jack Kerouac had been barred as an "unwholesome element."

Swept up in some degree by the mood of the fifties, Allen Ginsberg was trying to live a normal life as a regularly employed heterosexual. He lived at 204 East Seventh Street, right off Tompkins Square Park, he worked for the *World-Telegram*, making up the stock market quotations, and he had girlfriends. But in June, when the Rosenbergs were executed, he sent President Eisenhower a telegram: "You have the Rosenbergs' blood on your hands." When Fulton Lewis, Jr., said on the air that the Rosenbergs smelled bad, Allen thought, "An ugly image . . . the stinking Jew."

When Burroughs turned up in September, Allen invited him to stay at his apartment. They were making breakfast the morning after his arrival when a garrulous and disheveled young friend of Allen's appeared, wanting to sell a suitcase full of miniature liqueur bottles of various hues that he had stolen from a queer bar. The young man was Gregory Corso, who would become a leading figure of the Beat movement, and who had in common with the others that he was a misfit, self-invented, rebellious, and blessed by the Muse. If Ginsberg, Kerouac, and Burroughs were the Three Musketeers of the movement, Corso was their D'Artagnan, a sort of junior partner, accepted and appreciated, but with less than complete parity. He had not been in at the start, which was the alliance of the Columbia intellectuals with the Times Square hipsters. He was a recent adherent, although his credentials were impressive enough to gain him unrestricted admittance, and he added to the core group's ethnic diversity—a Canuck, a Jew, a WASP, and now, an Italian.

In one of his journals, Corso wrote: Gregorio Nunzio Corso, address Oblivion, school Death. It wasn't quite that bad, although his life did have a strong element of Dickensian pathos. His beautiful eighteen-year-old mother, Michelina, ran off with a lover back to Italy when he was six months old, in 1930. His father, Fortunato, placed him with foster parents, of which he had had three sets by the time he was ten. The agency that arranged the placements believed that it was not healthy for a boy to become attached to a foster mother. Never having known his real mother, Gregory loved his first foster mother as his own, and was grief-stricken when at the age of two he was separated from her. One day his first foster mother came to see him at his second foster home and gave him a quarter, which he lost. After that, he started wetting his bed.

In the third foster home, they gave him a rubber sheet and wouldn't let him drink water after 6:00 P.M.

When he was ten, his father, by now remarried, took him back, and he went to live on the Lower East Side. His father was an obstinate, uneducated Italian, who had never read a book or listened to classical music. When he got mad, which was often, he yelled, "I should have thrown you down the toilet bowl." His stepmother competed with his father on the decibel level, screaming, "He wets the bed, he wets the bed!"

In 1942, Gregory stole a radio from the lady downstairs and was sent to the Youth House for four months, which was heavily populated with older black youths belonging to gangs—the Comanches, the Lucky Gents, the Sabers. He was so regularly beaten that in despair he put both hands through a window and was sent to Bellevue for observation, and released. By this time his father was in the navy, and Gregory was sent to a Christian Brothers home, where he was made to stand on the main path from the cottage to the mess hall, holding his rubber sheet. He ran away and took to the streets.

Oh, yes, another thing—his obsession with watches, symbols of life's impermanence and pain—each hour wounds, the last one kills. When he stole a wristwatch from the dresser drawer of his third foster parents' bedroom, he was spanked. When he stole ten dollars from his father's pants and bought a Mickey Mouse watch, his father beat him with a razor strap. When he stole a watch with a gold case from a sleeping man, he wasn't caught, and hocked the watch.

Raised a Catholic, he had First Communion and Confirmation. He went to church every Sunday and said hundreds of Hail Marys for the poor. He kissed Cardinal Spellman's ring and a piece of the True Cross. He went to confession and made up venial sins to mask his true and mortal sin of masturbation, and when he admitted to masturbation he had to say 100 Our Fathers and 100 Hail Marys and he could not understand why, at thirteen, the only pure joy he knew was forbidden, and he broke from the church—he was through with the "Only-we-shall-see-the-face-of-God" routine.

His formal schooling ended at the sixth grade, but his street schooling continued, and when he was sixteen, he and two friends planned the holdup of a Household Finance office. Gregory was the master burglar who bought surplus World War II walkie-talkies from an army-navy store. The burglary was a success, netting $21,000, and Gregory took off for Florida. His two confederates, however, remained in New York, where their conspicuous spending led to their arrest. They gave away their partner, who was sentenced to three years in the state prison in Dannemora, New York. The judge said he was a threat to society because he had put crime on a scientific basis.

Small and jaunty, a sort of street-smart Italian combination of Tom Sawyer and the Artful Dodger, Gregory had to defend himself in prison from being a "freehole." If you allowed yourself to be fucked, you were finished. Black gangs tried to rape him, but he fought back fiercely, and the Mafia inmates did their bit to protect a fellow Italian. They gave him advice: "Don't you serve time, let time serve you." "When you're talking to six people, make sure you see seven"; in other words, self-esteem. Gregory started reading in prison, discovering the great printed acreage of literature, which anyone could make his own by the simple act of opening a book. He also discovered that for anyone who was small and puny, the best protection was to be a clown—if you could make people laugh, half the battle was won, and he worked at it with a frenzy, going the limit, falling on his face.

Just as Lucien Carr was transformed by his stay in prison (Lucien, who liked to say that Gregory's past was "institutional"), so was Gregory, but in a different way. What emerged from the sordid chapters of his life, the foster homes, the Youth House, Dannemora, was the love of beauty with a capital B, and the burgeoning of a poetic sensibility—the old flower-in-the-dunghill routine. As Jack Kerouac put it, Gregory had risen like an angel over the rooftops of the Lower East Side to become a poet.

Back to New York in 1950 came Gregory Corso, aspiring poet, who soon met Allen Ginsberg, aspiring poet. Ever the go-between and arranger, Allen took his discovery, the street-urchin-convict-poet, to see Mark Van Doren, who looked at his prison poems and pronounced, "Too much mother." He then showed Gregory's work to John Clellon Holmes, who said something about "green armpit poems."

A friendship formed, and one day Gregory asked Allen if he was queer. "Would it make any difference?" Allen asked. "It's all right," Gregory said, "but it wouldn't have been in prison." At that point, in 1951, Gregory was smitten with a sultry-eyed Latin American sculptress named Marisol Escobar, and was competing for her favors with a black man twice his size. One night in the Minetta Tavern, Miss Escobar's dusky suitor approached Gregory and said, "Don't go near Marisol again." Something snapped inside Gregory's head—suddenly he saw a gang of leering blacks holding him down and calling him a little wop and trying to tear his pants off—and he smashed his beer glass on the bar and pushed the broken glass into his rival's face.

Not knowing where to go, he went to Allen's, showing him his cut hands, and saying, "Look what I did—I could have blinded the man." Exhausted and distressed, he lay down on Allen's bed, but soon felt his belt being unbuckled. "Here I need some warmth from this guy and he's trying to put his little fat Jewish dick into me . . . at a time like that . . . come on!"

Their friendship survived this contretemps, however, and Gregory continued to show up at Allen's, as he did on the morning in September 1953 when Burroughs was there. Burroughs saw a young man with a lively, expressive face and a lot of wavy brown hair, who was rather like a hyperactive child, with a rap as manic as Neal Cassady's. He had a knack of saying things that other people might think but would not say. If there was a man with warts on his face, Gregory would observe, "They say you get warts from toads." Say your father was dying of cancer, he would ask, "Hey, did your old man kick the bucket yet?" There was in Gregory the need to defy, to be provocative, to be constantly testing every human relationship. That morning, when he saw that he had no takers for his liqueur bottles, he said he would make toast, and he burned the toast.

Gregory felt that Burroughs had taken an instant dislike to him. He sensed jealousy—here was this young Italian kid that Allen obviously liked. Gregory's intuition was correct, for in the odd way these things happen, Burroughs was now in love with Allen. Years before, in the Columbia days, Allen had said that he and Burroughs were destined to enter into some sort of extreme Lucien Carr–David Kammerer relationship, and when Burroughs heard about it he said, "Ridiculous, I'm not attracted to him."

But in the intervening years, Allen had become Burroughs' lifeline. When Joan died, he was not outraged or judgmental. He continued to offer sympathy and friendship. No matter what Burroughs had done, Allen got it across that his respect and fondness for him had not changed. Burroughs, who saw himself as monstrous in the eyes of others, was uplifted by Allen's loyalty. In addition, it was thanks to Allen that Burroughs had realized his ambition to be a published writer. Allen had believed in the book and had taken it around. Burroughs, with his perennial sense of isolation, had built up a tremendous dependence on Allen, as stalwart friend and able ally. Allen was his audience of one, to whom he wrote long letters while on his yage expedition, letters that were the initial form of a possible book.

Allen was flattered. Burroughs had been a mentor and elder statesman of their Columbia days. And now Burroughs needed him. His wish to be respected, his own fragile sense of worth, were gratified. And yet Allen was unprepared for the intensity of Burroughs' feelings. At the time he was seeing a black girl, Alene Lee, but she had been offended when he told her, "I've been in the bughouse and I've had enough trouble with my Jewish relatives and I can't bring home a colored girl." It wasn't prejudice on Allen's part but a kind of flippant social gaucherie, and a surrender to the mores of the fifties. In any case, he introduced her to Kerouac, who used her as the main character in *The Subterraneans*.

But when Burroughs showed an erotic interest, Allen was perplexed. He had never thought of Bill that way. His taste was for strong young guys, but Bill was thirty-nine to his twenty-seven. On the other hand, Allen thought, if he's really that involved, why not be generous? He knew what it was to have heartaches and be rejected, as he had been, innumerable times. And he felt, I am a remarkable person and he is a remarkable person, and we must surpass ourselves.

Allen accepted Burroughs' advances, not from desire but as an extension of friendship and an act of kindness. Sexually, it was too bizarre to be satisfying. For Burroughs in the act of sex underwent an amazing transformation. This reserved, sardonic, masculine man became a gushing, ecstatic, passionate woman. The change was so extreme and startling that Allen was alarmed.

What Burroughs wanted was to take the passive role. Allen was surprised to see that he could have an orgasm that way. There was nothing reciprocal in it. Having it done to him was enough. Allen did it a few times but got a bit squeamish about it, perhaps because Burroughs' reaction was so intense it scared him. He seemed to melt completely, to take on a different identity, as he had in narcoanalysis with Dr. Wolberg, to become some recognizable female type, a St. Louis dowager perhaps. His distinction and reticence gave way to a mushily romantic, vulnerably whimpering female persona, as if he was able to contain within himself the personalities of both sexes. To Burroughs, it was another instance of being possessed by beings over which he had no control, but to Allen it was unsettling. Also, Burroughs' thin, almost childlike body was not to Allen's taste, which ran more to the body-builder muscle man.

The other alarming factor was the depth of emotion that Burroughs demonstrated, which to Allen seemed inappropriate. Burroughs aspired to complete mutual possession. He wanted some kind of uncanny, primordial, protoplasmic union, some kind of complete symbiosis. He wanted to graft and absorb the other person. Allen later reflected that Burroughs' writing was shot through with images of this desire to possess. The character of Bradley the Buyer in *Naked Lunch*, going around and literally absorbing all the young junkies, was a parable of his own erotic fantasies.

In sex, Burroughs disclosed the secret of his multiple selves. Allen reflected that it left him in a dangerous position, for in dropping his guard he became a target for mockery. Allen wondered what he had gone through at the Los Alamos school, where, being unable to show his soft and feminine side for fear of being ridiculed, he had found acceptably oblique ways of presenting himself with parodies and routines.

Burroughs wanted to be made love to and possessed, but to Allen it was an unsatisfactory situation. The more evasive Allen became, the more Burroughs pressed for a total commitment. Allen's inability to respond made him feel guilty, and there were earnest discussions, in which Burroughs compared his relationships with Allerton and with Allen, and tried to come to terms with his extravagant demands—he was annoyed, for instance, that Allen continued to see girls. Burroughs felt more keenly than ever his inability to have a successful love relationship. It had not worked out with Allerton because he was straight, and now it was not working with Allen, even though Allen was homosexual. Allen was trying to think of a way to wind it all down without rejecting Burroughs. One day they went out for a walk and Burroughs was chiding him for his lack of response, and all the frustration that Allen had been storing over-flowed, and he turned to Burroughs and said, "I don't want your ugly old cock." Burroughs stood there, as if rooted in the pavement, and Allen saw his whole body shudder. It was the worst thing that Allen could have said, an intemperate answer born of defeat, a rejection of his body, a rejection of the deeper intimacy that Burroughs sought, the life commitment, in which Allen saw his entire life monopolized. Allen's outburst put an end to the erotic aspect, which in retrospect might come to be seen as a temporary aberration, a single scene in a long-enduring friendship.

His face had the look of a superimposed photo, reflecting a fractured spirit that could never love man or woman with complete wholeness. Yet he was driven by an intense need to make his love real, to change fact. Usually he selected someone who could not reciprocate, so that he was able—cautiously, like one who tests uncertain ice, though in this case the danger was not that the ice give way, but that it might hold his weight— to shift the burden of not loving, of being unable to love, onto the partner.

Burroughs fell back on his stance of sardonic diffidence, and Allen thought of a line of William Carlos Williams', "Unworldly love that has no hope of the world and that cannot change the world to its desire."

They remained friendly, and explored the new Village scene. It was very different from Columbia in the forties when the only hip people were the Times Square hustlers. Now there was a whole new generation, partly documented in Chandler Brossard's 1952 novel, *Who Walk in Darkness*, who knew what the word "hip" meant. They could be found at the San Remo bar and other Village hangouts, forming the nucleus of a counterculture.

Then there were those people whom it was impossible to classify, but who somehow found themselves in the Ginsberg-Kerouac-Burroughs orbit, like the classics scholar Alan Ansen, still sharing a house with his maiden aunt in Woodmere, Long Island. Ansen had in the meantime become secretary to W. H. Auden. In 1948 he went to hear Auden lecture at the New School on *The Merry Wives of Windsor*. "It's such a boring play," Auden told the audience, "but it did give us a great opera," and proceeded to play Verdi's *Falstaff* on the phonograph he had brought along. Instead of providing scintillating comment, he pretended to be absorbed in the libretto, which provoked the audience into restiveness. There were cries of "We came here to hear a lecture." Ansen, an Auden loyalist, responded with "Aw, shaddup!" and was rewarded with an introduction to the poet and an invitation to carry his record player home to Brooklyn. Then Ansen showed Auden a paper he had written on the "Sea and the Mirror" poems, and Auden complimented him by saying, "You've seen the figure in my carpet," and asked Ansen to be his secretary. Ansen's hope that the job would be a passport to the Muses was soon dashed, for all he did was pay bills and make travel arrangements. Auden discouraged all attempts at being Boswell to his Johnson. "It was not one of the great secretariats, like Beckett and Joyce," Ansen recalls.

By the time Burroughs was back in New York in the fall of 1953, Ansen's aunt had died, and he had rented the house to the novelist William Gaddis, which gave him a small income, enough to travel to Europe. Calling Allen Ginsberg one day, he was told that Burroughs was there. Burroughs was to him an intriguing but enigmatic figure, whom he had heard about from Allen but never met. "I very much want to meet him," he told Allen, and Burroughs got on the phone and said, "Come on in, man, take a cab, we'll pay at this end," which struck Ansen, who was something of a penny-pincher, as a lavish gesture.

Burroughs and Ansen hit it off so well they decided to travel to Europe together. They weren't sure where they wanted to go, but decided to start from Rome. "I'm going to steep myself in vice," Burroughs announced. But he had to steep himself in parental favor first to refurbish the old exchequer, and left for Florida, agreeing to meet Ansen in Rome at Christmastime. Once again, Burroughs was on the move, and this time he didn't know where.

Mid-December found him aboard the Greek liner *Nea Hellas*, complaining bitterly about the dirty staterooms, the terrible food, the hair in the jam, and the length of the trip—twelve days. He reached Rome before Ansen and felt miserable. It was cold, nothing was heated, and instead of bars, they had soda and ice cream joints with no place to sit down. You would be standing next to some citizen sucking on a banana split, and find a maraschino cherry in your dry martini. Then he had an argument with the hotel clerk, who had enough garlic on his breath to deter a covey of vampires, about visitors in his room.

Ansen arrived, and went around visiting churches, which to Burroughs were just piles of stone. Alan spoke enough Italian to negotiate several *affaires du coeur*. But after ten days, Burroughs hated Rome, and would rather have been anywhere else, even Quito. Ansen decided to go to Venice, where he would remain for years. Burroughs for some reason decided to head for Tangier. He had read Paul Bowles's novels, *The Sheltering Sky* and *Let It Come Down*, set in Fez and Tangier, which had a reputation for wickedness. It sounded like his kind of city—worth checking out.

· TWELVE ·

TANGIER

1954–1958

On February 5, 1954, Burroughs celebrated, if that is the right word, his fortieth birthday in Tangier. Forty, the halfway point of life, a time for taking stock, pausing, and asking hard questions: What have I accomplished? Have I met my goals? In what direction is my life going? For Burroughs, the answers were disappointing. At an age when most men are solidly established in their careers, he was still being supported by his parents, like an eternal adolescent. His one published book had made no ripple on the literary waters. His future as a writer was uncertain. He himself had no idea whether he would ever write another book.

His life since his graduation from Harvard could to some extent be summed up like a police rap sheet: forged prescriptions, drunk driving, possession of narcotics, and criminal imprudence, a south-of-the-border euphemism for homicide. He had succeeded in distancing himself from his class and family background, but his progress had been chaotic. He was a man tormented by his drug addiction and the memory of his wife, her head slumped, a trickle of blood running down her face. His life resembled one of his South American expeditions, in which he fell into every possible accident and error, losing his gear, being arrested for a misdated visa, shivering in the wind on a bare mountain slope above the tree line, chilled to the blood-making marrow with despair and loneliness.

Burroughs could not shake his feeling of apartness from the rest of the human race. *Enter the American tourist. He thinks of himself as a good guy but when he looks in the mirror to shave this good guy he had to admit that "Well, other people are different from me and I don't really like them." This makes him feel guilt toward other people.* Despite severe bouts of depression, he had the fortitutde to keep going. *I have crippling depressions. I wonder how I can feel this bad and live. Very few people are ever in contact with that area of human despair. I've survived by confronting it. I let it wash through me.*

It seems paradoxical to say this about a man who was indentured to narcotics, which might be seen as the worst form of self-indulgence, but Burroughs had considerable strength of character. He had deliberately set out to live a certain way, and would not be swayed from his purpose. He approached life with a sense of mission, as in his quest for yage. He had great personal courage, bordering on foolhardiness, as when he drank the potion prepared by the medicine man, knowing nothing about the proper dose, and it almost killed him. He had those very Emersonian qualities of self-reliance and a personal point of view, as if following Emerson's advice to the scholars at Dartmouth College: "Be content with a little light, so it be your own. Explore and explore. Be neither chided nor flattered out of your position of perpetual inquiry."

Although cast in the mold of the American original, as exemplified by Emerson and Thoreau, there was an added dimension to Burroughs, a dark side, which was his belief in a magical universe. This had been noted early on, in his Los Alamos report card, which mentioned his interest in the morbid and abnormal. *Yes, I had and have an insatiable appetite for the extreme and the sensational, for the morbid, slimy, and unwholesome. At Los Alamos I was reading Baudelaire,* The Flowers of Evil, *and burning incense. My nannies brought me up on black magic . . . trip and stumble, slip and fall . . . I would not have had such nurses had I not been receptive ground . . .*

As Wordsworth, in "Intimations of Immortality," trailed clouds of glory, Burroughs trailed clouds of witchcraft. As a five-year-old, looking down the hall of the house on Pershing Avenue, he had such a feeling of oppression and dread that he burst out crying. When his brother asked him what was wrong, he couldn't explain. It was a feeling of being hopelessly at a disadvantage, which he later identified as the visitation of an inimical spirit. In college, he read books on Tibetan magic, and the works of the French master of the occult Eliphas Levy, who gave him a key to success: *Vouloir sans désirer, voilà le secret du pouvoir.* (To want without desiring, there is the secret of power.) He studied the Golden Dawn, the psychic society that Yeats belonged to, and became a connoisseur of ghost stories.

To Burroughs, behind everyday reality there was a reality of the spirit world, of psychic visitations, of curses, of possession and phantom beings. This was the single most important element of his life, just as the single most important thing about Graham Greene is his vision as a lapsed Catholic.

At Los Alamos, Burroughs put a curse on a boy who had rejected him, and when the boy got sick, he felt that the curse had worked. In New York, he put a curse on a hoodlum friend of Jack Anderson's who had borrowed a gun which he did not return. A few days later, both his hands were blown off when a drum of gasoline he was handling exploded, and he died, another demonstration of the effectiveness of curses. *We assume that everything happens by accident. My attitude is that nothing happens by accident. Of course if you put a curse on someone it may boomerang, but you take the chance. It's like the Old West, if you shoot somebody, there are gonna be ten people looking for you. You may have to do it in self-defense. It's nothing to be undertaken lightly, but in many cases it has to be done. Another thing about curses, often they don't hit the person they're aimed at. As for me, I've won some and lost some.*

It was because the sense of dread persisted that Burroughs went into analysis. Through narcoanalysis he was able to identify several of the personalities that seemed to be competing for control of his being, but that did not alleviate the condition. Finally, he confronted what he felt to be his situation: External forces, some benign and some inimical, were trying to inhabit him, and he had to wage a daily battle to keep them in line. The world was divided between potential allies and potential enemies.

Burroughs was in the position of primitive man, who believes that the animal or human sacrifices he has offered to the gods have brought rain. There were forces out there that had to be appeased or guarded against. *In the magical universe there are no coincidences and there are no accidents. Nothing happens unless someone wills it to happen. The dogma of science is that the will cannot possibly affect external forces, and I think that's just ridiculous. It's as bad as the church. My viewpoint is the exact contrary of the scientific viewpoint. I believe that if you run into somebody in the street it's for a reason. Among primitive people they say if someone was bitten by a snake he was murdered. I believe that.*

A city built on low sand hills at the northwestern tip of the African continent, Tangier was unique for two reasons: Geographically, it was the only city overlooking both the Atlantic and the Mediterranean, thus straddling two worlds. Legally, it was an international zone. Whereas the rest of Morocco was under French rule, Tangier was governed by the consuls of eight European nations, and had three official languages—

French, Spanish, and Arabic—and two official currencies, the franc and the peseta. From this special position many benefits flowed.

Legend had it that the city's origin went back to the Greek hero, Hercules. Walking along the shores of the Mediterranean, en route to pick up some of the Golden Apples in the Gardens of the Hesperides (about sixty miles south of present-day Tangier), Hercules spied a lovely young woman dozing in the sun. It developed that she was married to a local giant named Antaeus, who was the son of Gaea, goddess of earth. As long as any portion of his anatomy touched the ground, he received powerful charges from mother earth that made him invincible. Antaeus challenged Hercules for ogling his wife, and they fought, but every time Hercules threw him, the giant bounced back. In one last, prodigious effort, Hercules lifted him off the ground and crushed him to death in his mighty arms. Then he buried him on the continent's northwest corner, where Tangier today stands. Antaeus was the god of losers, which made Tangier an appropriate haven for all the washed-up people who gravitated there, with stories of having been robbed of their wealth and their power and their strength.

The actual history of Tangier was one of foreign occupation, so that a certain kind of cosmopolitanism, at once wary and raffish, became inbred. The Berbers were followed by the Phoenicians and the Romans, the Portuguese in the fifteenth century, and the British in the seventeenth. A period of Moroccan monarchs ended in 1912, when the French and the Spanish partitioned Morocco, and Tangier was made a special zone.

Writers and artists passed through. Mark Twain came in 1867 and wrote that the houses of the native quarter were so jammed together it seemed like "a crowded city of snowy tombs." All the men seemed to be money-changers. At last he had found something uncompromisingly foreign. Matisse lived and painted there from 1911 to 1913.

Because of its special status, Tangier was a hub of unregulated free enterprise. Anyone with a valid passport could become a citizen of the city. It was a free port, with no import duties or income tax. Gold could be bought over the counter. Anyone with a letterhead and a storefront could open a bank, of which there were close to 100. Anyone with a fistful of cash could become a money-changer, of which there were more than 100. Post–World War II Tangier became a multinational boomtown, a capital of permissiveness. Smuggling was a respectable profession— drugs out and guns in. It was said that the CD license plates did not mean *Corps Diplomatique* but *Contrebandier Distingué* (distinguished smuggler).

Tangier being by definition a place where everything was freely bought and sold, it gained a reputation for wickedness. In his widely syndicated column, "As I Was Saying," Robert Ruark wrote in 1950 that "Sodom was a church picnic and Gomorrah a convention of Girl Scouts" compared to Tangier, which "contained more thieves, black marketeers, spies, thugs, phonies, beachcombers, expatriates, degenerates, characters, operators, bandits, bums, tramps, politicians, and charlatans" than any place he'd ever visited.

What Ruark did not catch was that although lenient, Tangier was also provincial. It was a small town, where you kept seeing the same people, and everyone knew everyone else. The Arabs, Spanish, French, and expatriate residents coexisted in polyglot harmony. In spite of languid law enforcement, there was little crime. The bulk of the population was made up of hardworking shopkeepers and merchants. There was also a glittering expatriate fringe of the wellborn and truly wealthy. Barbara Hutton wore a diadem and sat on a sort of throne when she received guests in her whitewashed, crenellated palace in the medina. On the Mountain, as an outlying hilly area was known, the inimitable David Herbert, younger brother of the Earl of Pembroke, maintained the traditions (and the cuisine) of English manor life.

When Burroughs arrived in January 1954, he caught at once the special character of the city, its quality of exemption. It was exempt from every interference. There was no pressure of any sort to curtail private behavior. Hard drugs were routinely sold over the counter. Kif and hashish were openly smoked in little clay pipes with wood stems. Boys were so plentiful you had to fight them off. Here at last was the sanctuary of complete noninterference he had sought in his wanderings. The cop stood there with his hands behind his back, a benign and unthreatening presence. In Morocco, no stigma was attached to homosexuality. According to the distinguished anthropologist Edward Westermarck, author of *Ritual and Belief in Morocco*, it was regarded with indifference by the Moroccans except in the case of boy whores or of men who practiced passive pederasty, who in the next world would be condemned to wash their faces forever with the urine of Jews.

Another attractive feature to Burroughs was the low place of women in the society. They were veiled and shrouded, so you hardly noticed them. From the country there arrived men on donkeys followed by women on foot, bent over almost double under their load of charcoal. There was no mistaking their subservient role. Tangier was also a place where magic was a part of daily life, where sorcerers mixed love potions and poisons, where members of secret brotherhoods went into trances and cast spells. In the souks the medicine men sold their wares—powders, bottled elixirs, bunches of herbs, bits of bark, dead lizards, colored stones—all arranged on anatomical charts spread on the ground.

Burroughs found a room in a house at 1 calle de los Arcos, near the Socco Chico (Little Market). The owner, Anthony Reithorst, a portly fellow known as Dutch Tony, made a living arranging assignations with boys in his quarters for visiting English and American gentlemen. Burroughs hung out at the Café Central in the Socco Chico, the meeting place and switchboard of Tangier, and as good a place as any to size up its inhabitants. He saw young Spaniards in gabardine trench coats talking about soccer, Arab guides smoking kif pipes, pimps and smugglers and money-changers, a parade of boys being appraised by expatriate queers, and above all, a parade of losers stuck in Tangier, where, in the words of Auden, "the lonely are battered like pebbles into fortuitous shapes."

Tangier was the world capital of the stranded. Here was a Danish boy waiting for a friend to arrive with his money and the rest of his luggage, who each day met the ferry from Gibraltar and the ferry from Algeciras. Here was a Spanish boy, waiting for a permit to enter the French zone where his uncle would give him a job. Here was an English boy waiting for a money order, having been robbed of his valuables by a girlfriend.

There was in Tangier a high concentration of people with vague and unlikely prospects, who sat around cursing their luck and hoping for deliverance. They would get a job on a yacht, or smuggle whiskey into Spain, or write a bestseller. At café tables they traded schemes, fantasies of diamond or gun-running, of starting nightclubs and bowling alleys and travel agencies, and Burroughs knew that in spite of their confident voices and decisive gestures, none of it would ever come to pass—the idea, the plan, the project would be allowed to disintegrate undisturbed. All their lives these people had taken wrong turns, they had drifted with an unlucky current, and they had ended up in Tangier.

Of course it was natural for Burroughs to fall in with the lowlifes. He was not invited to the castle to sit at Barbara Hutton's feet, or to the Mountain to have dinner with Lord David Herbert on the hibiscus-clad terrace. The friends Burroughs made were known as the Calamity Sisters. There was Eric Gifford, who worked for the English-language *Tangier Gazette* and took care of his elderly mother. Gifford had ability and intelligence, but nothing worked for him, he was either too late or too early. He had lost his money in a bee-raising venture in the Caribbean. It looked like a sure thing, but it turned out there was a local moth that infested the hives. The bee-raising venture was one brief chapter in a long saga of misfortune. "It's the sort of thing that could only happen to Eric," said his friends. Who but Eric could have been held for months in a detention camp as a Spanish Communist during the Franco years? Gifford had gone to good schools in England, he was willing to work and he spoke five languages, but he bore the indelible brand of bad luck and failure.

Then there was Bernie Butler (name changed), the shameless sponger, who looked like some aborted, early variant of homo sap, blackmailing the human race with his existence—"Remember me? I'm the boy you left behind with the lemurs and the baboons. I'm not equipped for survival like some people." His greedy blue eyes would search for a hint of uncertainty in yours, and he would make his pitch: "Nobody else will buy me a drink, will you?" If you bought him one, you would be rewarded with the story of his fall from wealth, of his betrayal by dishonest associates, of his promised inheritance: "Dear Aunt Harriet is dying, and I'm so afraid the nurse will get hold of her money." He had a regular route knowing that so-and-so was good for coffee, and so-and-so might be good for lunch.

Another character who passed through but didn't stay long was Porter Tuck, an American bullfighter who had been touring Spain as *El Rubio de Boston* (the Boston blond). He had taken a bad goring, a *cornada* in the lung, and there was a photograph of him in a Spanish magazine over the caption "Dead American." He thought of suing the magazine, but instead went to New York with all his bullfighting capes and got a job as a waiter in a Spanish restaurant. Over the years he went downhill and did some time for paperhanging. When Burroughs was in New York in 1965 he got a call in the middle of the night and it was Porter Tuck, whom he hadn't seen in years. "Can I come over and see you?" he asked. "For God's sake, Porter, it's three in the morning, come this afternoon." "That's a laugh," Porter Tuck said. The next day Burroughs turned on the radio and heard that he had shot himself on a bridge. I guess the magazine was right, he thought, he was dead and didn't know it. Some people died in installments, a bit here and a bit there. It was like the old joke about the razor: "Just try to shake your head ten years from now." Burroughs composed an epitaph for Porter Tuck.

> Nobody likes a walking stiff
> And they like him less with every whiff.
> So find yourself a plot of sod
> And lie down for the love of God.

Also in the "chequered career" category was Paul Lund, known as Paul of Birmingham. The son of a respectable import-export executive, Lund had turned to crime for fun and profit. In Birmingham, he stole the payroll of the Ladywood Hospital and held up the Grove Cinema. In Blackpool, he held up the Yellow-Way Coach Company. Over the years, he became an authority on English prisons. At the bottom of the list were the antediluvian "wheel prisons" like Dartmoor and Parkhurst and Winson Green, with a number of halls leading out like spokes from a central hub. The bedding was filthy, the food was inedible, and they still gave you "the cat" for certain offenses, which was known as "having your back scratched." Reading Gaol was the best nick in England, with only 150 inmates. The screws told him he had Oscar Wilde's old cell, B-23. Finally his father said, "If you must be a blackguard, Paul, go and be one somewhere else and not on my doorstep." Lund came to Tangier, and was soon involved in smuggling cigarettes from the Canary Islands. But he was caught at sea by the Italian coast guard and was imprisoned in Livorno, where he contracted tuberculosis. Back in Tangier, Lund wound down his criminal activities and opened a little bar, the Novara. In England he was facing what they call Pen Indef as an habitual criminal. Burroughs liked his stories of the English underworld and his picturesque lingo.

A good friend of Lund's was George Greaves, a big, fat, puffing Sydney Greenstreet character, whose adventures had taken him from his native Australia to Tangier, where he was the stringer for the London *Daily Express*. Greaves lived so obviously beyond his means that he was suspected of selling information to the Moroccan police and the various legations. Seen at all the parties, he was known for his lascivious and usually slanderous stories.

Greaves liked to invite his friends to breakfast, and once invited Burroughs and Paul Lund, to whom he said, "Listen, Paul, if you can get me a little information on arms shipments, I think a lot could be forgotten." "How could I look at meself in the mirror if I did something like that?" Lund asked. "Well, Paul," Greaves said, "you have to take a broad, general view of things." This seemed to Burroughs the highest expression of the justification of corruption that he had ever heard. He never tired of repeating it, mimicking George's slow and insinuating Down Under drawl. He was the most completely corrupt person Burroughs had ever met.

A cut above the Calamity Sisters was Don Cotton (name changed), a blond and blue-eyed man in his thirties from Ohio who had been a captain in the air force. Cotton wrote a social column in the weekly *Morocco*

Courier under the sobriquet Barnaby Bliss, and went around to parties collecting bits of gossip. He had an unsavory reputation as a police informer, dating to a crackdown on homosexuals after Moroccan independence in 1956, when Tangier lost its international status. "If they call me," Cotton told Burroughs, "I'm going to spill the beans on everybody. Think I'll leave Paul Bowles sitting up there in his ivory tower? I'll just blow the whistle." He was questioned by police and apparently gave some names. Paul Lund called him Grassy Gert, to "grass" meaning to squeal in British criminal argot.

A fellow boarder at Tony Dutch's, Cotton introduced Burroughs to the Tangier boys' scene. As an example of how inexpensive it was, he got two Arab boys to screw each other for sixty cents. "*Leche*, we want *leche* [milk]," Cotton said as boy number one lay down on his stomach on the bed and boy number two rubbed spit on his prick. The boy contracted, his breath whistling through his teeth, and he pushed himself off with both hands, showing the *leche* and asking for a towel. Then he lay down on his stomach and boy number one took over—he was more passionate and came almost at once. When Burroughs expressed surprise that they would perform so cheaply, Cotton said, "They are hungry." The whole episode made Burroughs feel sort of like a dirty old man.

It was thanks to the ubiquitous Cotton, however, that Burroughs met the one person in Tangier he most wanted to know, Paul Bowles. Bowles was an established writer with a growing reputation, who had published two novels and a collection of short stories that Burroughs admired. He was, in short, what Burroughs wanted to be. The two men had in common that, finding the United States inhospitable, they had chosen to live in the tolerant international climate of Tangier. They also shared a disgust with the life they saw around them, combined with a will to survive. Burroughs would have endorsed this passage from Bowles's short story "Pages from Cold Point": "Life is visually too hideous for one to make the attempt to preserve it. Let it go. Perhaps some day another form of life will come along. Either way, it is of no consequence. At the same time, I am still a part of life, and I am bound by this to protect myself to whatever extent I can."

Like Burroughs, Bowles had been unhappy as a child and had grown up with a feeling of apartness. Born in 1911 on Long Island, he was the only son of a failed concert violinist turned dentist. His grandmother told him that when he was six weeks old, his father had tried to kill him by throwing open the windows of his room during a midwinter snowstorm. Instead of a bond of trust between father and son, there was hostility and suspicion. In self-defense, Bowles became guarded and dissembling, retreating into a fantasy life. After briefly attending the University of Virginia "because Poe went there," he left for Paris when he was twenty and was taken up by Gertrude Stein and her group.

Like Burroughs, Paul married a woman he loved very much, even though he was a homosexual. In Jane Auer, he found the same slightly off-kilter quality that he had, the same way of looking at the world that others would find peculiar. They were allies in their strangeness. Paul was a composer, and Jane wrote a novel called *Two Serious Ladies*. It was through helping her with her novel that Paul first thought seriously about writing.

In 1947, leaving Jane in New York, he came to North Africa, wanting to get away from the atmosphere of literary coteries. "I want to take every poet and shove him down into the dungheap," he wrote a friend, "kick all his literary friends in the ass, and try to make him see that writing is not word-bandying . . . but an emotion seen through the mind."

Bowles traveled 3,000 miles by bus through Algeria, seeking out difficult places and uncomfortable situations. His logic was that if a place was unbearable, it was not surprising that he felt so ill at ease. It was useful to find places to live in that you could hold accountable for your anxieties. There were things that happened to Paul of which his friends said, "That's pure Paul," in the sense that they seemed to distill his off-center vision. In Algeria, for instance, a boy stole 400 francs from Paul, and when Paul uncharacteristically beat him up, the thief asked for an extra hundred to cover his hospital bills.

Paul went into isolation in the Sahara to write *The Sheltering Sky*, writing his parents that "living in the atmosphere of the novel has to become and stay more real than living in one's own life." His aim was, as he told a friend, to "look only, everywhere, all hours, for that new way of looking at the human thing, the heart."

In 1948, he moved to Tangier, where Jane joined him. They led separate sexual lives. Jane pursued a rough country girl named Cherifa, who sold grain in the market, while Paul had various Moroccan male friends. He didn't know why he stayed in Tangier, he said. It was out of inertia, or because it was cheap, or because it satisfied his capacity for being ill at ease. By the time Burroughs arrived in 1954, he had been there so long it was too much trouble to pull up stakes. The only way to live there, he said, was to remember constantly that the world outside was still more repulsive.

When Cotton brought Burroughs around that January, Bowles had paratyphoid and was not at his best. Burroughs saw a small blond man, finely made, like a Meissen porcelain figurine. He had a natural elegance of gesture and manner, and smoked kif in specially ordered filter-tip cigarettes, with a holder which he waved while talking. He spoke very deliberately, weighing every word, and always with a slight air of be- musement, as if the unspoken subtext of his conversation was Puck's "What fools these mortals be." Glad to be talking shop with a fellow writer, Burroughs told him he wanted to get out of his *Junky* contract, because his publisher was holding $350 of his royalties as a reserve against returns, but Bowles said that if he had signed the contract there was no way to change it, and advised him to get an agent. Burroughs did not seem to take to that idea, and Bowles wondered whether he thought agents were dishonest. At that point, Burroughs seemed rather gray and insubstantial to him, as though flickering in and out of focus. He looked furtive, like someone being questioned at a police station. Perhaps it was the drugs he was taking.

When Bowles made no effort to see him again, Burroughs felt snubbed, and wrote Allen Ginsberg that he was "a shameless faker." To Jack Kerouac, he wrote: "The one time I met Paul Bowles he evinced no cordiality. Since then he has made no effort to follow up the acquaint- ance—under the circumstances it is his place to make advances once he knows that I am here and who I am. He invites the dreariest queens in Tangier to tea but has never invited me, which, seeing how small the town is, amounts to a deliberate affront."

On thinking it over, however, he decided there had to be a reason for what he perceived as Bowles's coolness, which was that Bowles must be engaged in illegal currency operations and did not want anyone "tracking heat into his trap," particularly someone who might be suspected of dealing drugs. A currency dealer would shun like poison anyone to whose garments clung the leprous taint of narcotics.

Generally, Burroughs felt that he had for some reason, perhaps because of his addiction, been put in Coventry by the Tangier intelligentsia. The bar where writers and the international set gathered was Dean's, run by a dark gentleman named Joseph Dean, who was either an Egyptian of noble birth or a Jamaican of wealthy antecedents. (It was common in Tangier to hear several versions of a person's background—a certain doctor, for instance, was either a survivor of a concentration camp or a Nazi wanted for war crimes.) Just down the street from the Minzah Hotel, Dean was the barman of legend, a resident wit who offered free counseling with the free lunch. Dean's was a club, an information agency, one of the consolation prizes of life in Tangier. When Burroughs went there, however, he felt hostility. Dean did not want to serve him, as though he would bring the place bad luck. That was fine with Burroughs, who savored Dean's disapproval, rolling it on his tongue with a glass of good dry sherry.

The other fashionable gathering place was the 1001 Nights, a restaurant in a narrow wing of the Menehbi Palace on the Marshan, a plateau overlooking the straits where there were many large houses. The creation of the Swiss-Canadian painter Brion Gysin, the 1001 Nights marked perhaps the high point of expatriate life in Tangier, with its dazzling Moroccan food, its band of five musicians, and its dancing boys. It prospered only briefly, but there was nothing like it before or since. The decor was Moroccan—banquettes, wooden tables surfaced with tiles, and brass lanterns with colored glass panels. The menu was a wooden tablet into the surface of which the bill of fare had been artfully burned. Gysin's paintings, scenes of Morocco and the Sahara, hung on the walls.

Burroughs had been to an exhibition of Gysin's work in the Rembrandt Hotel soon after arriving in Tangier, and found the paintings undistinguished—he could draw, but had no real reason to do so. When he went to the restaurant, he found Gysin, a tall, broad-shouldered man with thick sandy hair and the ruddy, bony, narrow-eyed face of a Swiss mountaineer, cold and imperious. He was as niggardly in personal relations as he was in his paintings, thought Burroughs, who could make no contact with him. As a fashionable restaurateur, he had just the right sort of glacial geniality. "Last night the coatroom was stacked with mink," he told Burroughs. "There's a lot of money in Tangier." Gysin was crazy like a fox, Burroughs thought, and had a paranoid conceit. He was a man who never had one good word to say about anybody. As for the ferret-faced dancing boys, with their narrow shoulders and bad teeth, they reminded him of a bowling team from Newark.

As Burroughs settled into Tangier, he had his usual objections. Everybody had both feet in your business—some character he had never seen before had come up to him and said: "Your friend Ali is in the Socco Chico. Please give me one peseta." Their lousy weed tasted like it was cut with horseshit and had no more boot than corn silk. The Arabs were a gabby, simple-minded crew, who did nothing but smoke weed and drink mint tea and sit around playing card games. You couldn't put your garbage out in a container because the container would get stolen.

He was deeply hurt that he had not heard from Allen, who was traveling in Mexico, for four months. The withdrawal symptoms had been worse than with Allerton. He hadn't realized he was so hooked. He couldn't write or take an interest in anything. Nothing was worse than waiting day after day for a letter that didn't arrive. It seemed to Burroughs that he was always knocking himself out for his friends, who dismissed him as a vampire. But in spite of it all, he continued to love Allen, and nothing canceled love.

Perhaps he should attempt some account of Joan's death. His reluctance had nothing to do with bad taste, it had to do with fear. Not exactly the fear of discovering unconscious intent, but something more complex and horrible, the fear of realizing that her brain had drawn the bullet toward it. He remembered Kells Elvins' dream, the night of Joan's death, before he knew, of course. Burroughs was cooking something in a pot and Kells asked him what it was and Burroughs said, "Brains," and opened the pot to show him what looked like a lot of white worms. The idea of shooting a glass off her head had never entered his mind consciously, until out of the blue he had said: "It's about time for our William Tell act. Put a glass on your head, Joan." Why, instead of carrying it out, had he not given up the idea? Why indeed? He was afraid to go too deeply into the matter, although he knew that he had aimed from six feet for the very top of the glass.

In February things picked up when Burroughs met an eighteen-year-old Spanish boy named Kiki, whose anti-Franco father had been killed in the Civil War, and who lived with his mother and his brother. Kiki reminded him of Angelo in Mexico City, with the same slightly Oriental cast of face, the same very straight black hair, and the same brown eyes. It seemed to Burroughs that wherever he went he met a replica of the same boy. A good-natured, indolent youth, Kiki came to visit every day. The arrangement was satisfactory, for Burroughs did not like the bother of looking for boys. Rather than losing interest after a few times, as many homosexuals did, he liked to stay with the same person. He also preferred a simple relationship without emotional entanglement. He saw too many examples of Tangier queens making fools of themselves over Arab boys. Obviously there was a confusion of levels. The queens were thinking of love, while the boys thought in terms of practical advantage, of bettering themselves, of helping to feed their families. And why shouldn't they?

Kiki was a tranquil, healthy young male. Burroughs kept the sex on an adolescent level, and didn't ask him to do things he didn't want to do. Kiki's standard objection was, "*Tu me haces maricón*" ("You're turning me into a faggot"). It was so pleasant to loll around smoking pot and having sex. They would doze off in the delicious sleep of a hot afternoon in a cool darkened room, with the sweet, imperceptible drawing together in sleep, leg inching over leg, arm encompassing body, hips hitching closer, stiffened organ reaching out to touch warm flesh. Kiki was playful. He would blow smoke through his pubic hairs and say, "Abracadabra" as his cock rose out of the smoke.

At the same time, Kiki had his limitations, and Burroughs often felt lonely, for he had no one to talk to. If he went into one of his routines, Kiki gazed at him with pensive brown eyes like a puzzled deer, eyes that asked: "What is the American talking about? Should I laugh now? Is he good for an extra twenty-five pesetas today?"

With no companionship except for Kiki, Burroughs fell back on drugs. Over the counter he bought a German-made synthetic morphine called Eukodol, the best junk kick he had ever had. The manufacturer, having discovered that it had a side effect of euphoria, stopped making it, but there was still a supply in Tangier, which Burroughs proceeded to exhaust. At first, he shot Eukodol every four hours, then he narrowed it down to two. Between shots, he felt the gravity pull of junk in his cells. When he looked at himself in the mirror, he seemed almost transparent, his body pared down to bone and muscle. He looked down at his dirty trousers, which he had not changed in weeks. His life had but a single purpose: Eukodol.

The days slid by, strung on a syringe with a long thread of blood. He kept to his room, with the shutters closed. In April, there was trouble at the Farmacia. The police were cracking down because a German tourist had been found dead in a ditch of a drug overdose. "*Muy difícil ahora*" ("Very hard now"), the druggist said. Burroughs could sense the static, like a telephone off the hook. One day it took him hours to score for two boxes of Eukodol. In broken English, Tony Dutch complained that because of Burroughs there was now police surveillance of his house: "Ach, thirteen years and never before I haff such a thing in my house. And since two weeks are here in Tangier two good English gentlemens I know since long time, with them I could make gud business except my house is watched at by the Arabics."

Burroughs paced his room, repeating, "I have to quit." He offered Eric Gifford fifty dollars to help him take a reduction cure. The idea was that Gifford would keep his clothes so he couldn't go out, bring him food, and dole out decreasing amounts of drugs for ten days. But it was rough, and on the second day, May 10, Burroughs took the other boarder's clothes and sneaked out and bought a box of Eukodol ampules. Gifford discovered the unused ampules, which he confiscated, took Burroughs' money, and told the other boarder to lock his door. "By God," he said, "I'm being paid to do this and I'm going to do it right."

One reason Burroughs wanted to kick was that Kells Elvins had come to Tangier for a visit. He was now living in Rome with a new wife, a Danish beauty named Mimi Heinrich, and he was still trying to write. Kells was appalled at finding Burroughs in such a decrepit state. It was worse than Mexico. He had wanted to travel through southern Morocco with him, but he was damned if he was going anywhere with a junky who could get them both arrested. Kells did not like Tangier, which seemed to him a mixture of poor Arabs and snobbish Europeans. In the Parade Bar he got into a conversation with a man who answered in monosyllables and then let the conversation lapse. "You come here direct from the States?" Kells asked. "No, from Brazil." "And how did you come?" "By yacht, of course."

That was Tangier for you, thought Burroughs. No snotty uptown New York fags could compare with the ones they had here for utter pretentious, insincere, inhuman snobbishness. Anyone who came on straight and sincere was looked upon with contempt. As he reported to Allen Ginsberg, when in late June he took Kells to an Arab restaurant that was like a remodeled bus station, "Brion Gysin was there and wanted to cut me, but I am learning the practice of this dreary tribe. I never saw him, he never got the chance to cut me." Kells left for Madrid on July 3, and Burroughs wished he had left with him. Tangier was dragging him like a sea anchor.

Burroughs had cut junk almost to the vanishing point but was sick with a fever and swollen joints. He slept twenty hours a day and his weight was down to 125 pounds. Finally he called a doctor, who diagnosed rheumatic fever. There was a secondary ankle infection, and the doctor drew out a jigger full of pus. Kiki nursed him through his illness, fixing him soup and tea, stroking his head, and tucking him in. Burroughs felt a need for nonsexual intimacy, which Kiki provided. Kiki's mother, who at first had been upset at the arrangement, was now reconciled because Kiki contributed to household expenses.

Burroughs sometimes felt that he loved Kiki. Usually he was sweet and affectionate, although he could also be sulky and abusive. There were times when Burroughs felt faced with a hostile stranger, who shocked him with tirades of abuse that sometimes reduced him to tears. He had always felt the fear with those he loved that they really hated him and that he would suddenly be confronted with their hate. Kiki always said afterward that he was only joking, but once Burroughs got mad and slapped him. One night in August Kiki came in late and announced that he was going to have his arms and chest tattooed. Burroughs begged him not to ruin his beautiful copper-brown skin: "It's like you were going to put a plug in your lip, or a ring in your nose, or knock out your front teeth to put in gold teeth. It's a desecration." He gave Kiki ten dollars he could ill afford, his last sportcoat, and one of his two remaining pairs of pants on the promise that he would never get tattooed.

Although Burroughs was fond of him, Kiki was not his partner of choice. He still brooded about Allen and hoped that they might have a life together. In a dream, he was with Allen in the country, somewhere hot like Texas, red clay, roads and farms. He wanted to be with him, but Allen kept saying, "Today I am spending with Jack, tomorrow with so-and-so," and Burroughs asked, "What about me?" Feeling hurt and rejected, he packed his suitcase and started down the Amazon alone in a canoe.

Burroughs decided to go back to the United States and join Allen in California. "Seems I can't make it without him," he wrote Kerouac. "I learn that during last six months we separate." Allen had also had a dream about Burroughs while traveling in Mexico. He and Jack and Joan had gone to see a movie about Rome, in which there were scenes of Burroughs traveling by bus through Europe. "Can we ask the movie company to show us the unedited scenes?" Allen asked. "No," said Joan, "it's a bad idea. Leave them alone." A passing *paisano* said, "It's a sort of *mirácolo*, that by accident he was chosen and used in these scenes in the film." "No tamper with the *mirácolo*," Joan said. Bill was on a bus in Spain, looking solitary and grim. He had disguised himself with a brush mustache because he feared he was being pursued.

In June 1954, Allen was back from Mexico and went to visit Neal and Carolyn Cassady in San Jose, California. Allen resumed his pursuit of Neal, and one day Carolyn caught them in bed and there was a horrible scene. Neal ran off to his railroad job and Carolyn ordered Allen to leave, but he sat and faced her and actually watched her face turn green with anger and jealousy as she said, "You've always been in my way—ever since Denver—your letters have always been an insult—you're trying to come between us." Flashing across his mind as Carolyn upbraided him was the remembrance of a trip to Lakewood with his mother when he was fourteen. They had become separated and she had gone into a drug-store and had an attack of paranoia. He found her in the drugstore with a shoe in her hand, surrounded by cops. When he called out to her, she yelled at him that he was a spy.

Allen moved to San Francisco, got a job in market research, and started going out with Sheila Williams, who had been married at eighteen and had a four-year-old kid. When Burroughs heard that he was making it with a chick he was upset. U.S. chicks wanted it all. It would be the end, because at that point he couldn't stand being around Allen with no sex. There was a café scene in Frisco, Allen wrote Kerouac, and he had met the poet Robert Duncan, a friend of Ezra Pound's, "who runs a crappy tho' sincere Pound-type poetry circle." His poetry was no good because he was too hung up on his piddle-a-night sensibility, but he was a nice and curious person.

Upon hearing in September that Burroughs was on his way, Allen confided his feelings to Jack Kerouac: "The impossibilities of his demands are ultimately inescapable unless I let him carry me off forever to Asia or something to satisfy his concept of his despair and need— I do like him and would love to share a place with him if it could be done, which it will be—but he is going to be frantic and possessive you know—he was against his own will having tantrums of jealousy in NYC— even over Dusty [Dusty Moreland, a girl Allen was seeing] he was annoyed—the situation with Sheila will be a madhouse—I don't know how to manage it—Bill will enforce his idea so much he will make me reject it and take it as a hopeless horror—he has of course calmed down a lot since mid-summer but he still puts all his life in my hands—even I never went that far. . . . It's a real bitch, man . . . I can't be his one sole and only contact forever, I can only be his nearest and best—what a situation, surrounded by mad saints all clawing at each other and I the most weird."

In October 1954 Burroughs arrived in New York and ran into his editor on *Junky*, Carl Solomon, who was wearing the white uniform and peaked cap of a Good Humor man. My God, what was he doing selling ice cream, Burroughs wondered, when he should have been sending out his royalty statements? Burroughs felt he had been treated rudely and dishonestly by his publisher. Solomon explained that he had left his uncle's firm and was hiding out from his family, who were trying to kill him because he hadn't turned out well. He was, he proudly added, the top Good Humor salesman in his area. Burroughs wrote Allen that Solomon seemed quite mad, adding, "There was more foolery yet if I could but remember it."

Wanting to discuss the Allen situation, he went to see Jack Kerouac in Richmond Hills. Jack saw that he was distraught, and, hating to see a friend suffer, told him a white lie to make him feel better, saying:

"Allen really secretly wants to be with you as before. Otherwise, you see, Bill, he wouldn't write and discuss and rehash so much." Jack's true feelings were that maybe Allen didn't want Bill around because he had become so strange and frightening and secretive. Anyway, he really didn't want to get involved in the homosexual difficulties of Allen and Bill, and wished that they could all return to the Beat generation confessions and honesties of the 1947 period.

Allen was furious when Burroughs passed on Jack's hopeful assessment, and at once harshly replied that Burroughs' stringent requirements of love were exasperating and idiotic. Rather than join Allen in California, where he clearly was not wanted, Burroughs went to see his family in Palm Beach, where he met with a less than enthusiastic reception. There was no room in the house on Sanford Avenue, and he stayed in a hotel. "You probably won't *want* to stay more than two weeks," his mother said. The house was mortgaged, the shop was mortgaged, and they didn't know whether they could keep giving him $200 a month. But as Burroughs wrote Allen Ginsberg on October 15, "They have a bad conscience about me. Besides, they've been giving me money so long it's a habit. They don't have what it takes to kick the habit and me out on my ass, which is what I would do in their place."

Allen sent another negative letter, in which he said he had his needs, too, to which Burroughs replied, "I just wish your needs were more compatible with mine." He wondered what to do next. Here he was in Palm Beach, completely isolated, with censorious parents threatening to cut off his allowance. San Francisco was out of the question. He couldn't make it in the States, being virtually unemployable except in take-anything jobs. He was over forty, with no work record and no references. What could he say when a potential employer asked him, "What have you been doing for the last twenty years, Mr. Burroughs?" Since they didn't want him hanging around Palm Beach, he would blackmail his parents into sending him back to Tangier, where at least life was cheap and he had Kiki.

In San Francisco, Allen was relieved that Burroughs had not come out. He just knew that they would have gotten involved in some kind of absolute sad idiocy, and he would have to sit and listen to his routines, mercilessly applauding. He wasn't interested enough. Bill was like a vac-uum that constantly needed to be filled—you had to give him all your attention, and Allen's attention was turned in other directions. His ob-jection wasn't to queerness but to Bill's wild strong frightening uncanny chill thrill. Bill's letters were driving him to distraction, so how much worse would it be in person? Sometimes there were three letters a day. It was as if a letter specter was zipping around him. Finally he had to tell Bill, no, don't come. What a sad mess it was!

A couple of months later, as it turned out, Allen met his lifelong lover and companion, Peter Orlovsky, a handsome, blond, brawny nineteen-year-old, the son of a White Russian cavalry officer who had migrated to New York. Peter had a poetic though off-center sensibility. He was discharged from the army after saying, "An army is against love." He moved to San Francisco and went out every day with a bottle of Lysol to scrub the sidewalks, feeling that he had a mission to keep the city clean. He met the painter Robert La Vigne, who asked him to model, and through him he met Allen.

In the meantime, Burroughs had left Palm Beach and gone back to Tangier in November, 1954, feeling that if he stayed any longer it would unseat his reason. The place was a horror, with no slums, no dirt, no poverty. What a relief it was to get back to Tangier, with its smelly, dirty native quarter, its sunless streets and blind alleys, its disreputable Europeans and bogus fugitives. There was an end-of-the-world feeling about Tangier. When the druggist sold him his daily box of Eukodol ampules he smirked as if giving him the bait to a trap—perhaps the whole town was a trap and some day it would close.

Nothing much had changed, except that Paul Bowles had left for Ceylon. But that "paranoid bitch on wheels," Brion Gysin, was still there, as were the assorted losers and con men. Burroughs found a place in the Casbah, four rooms for twenty-three dollars a month, and Kiki often came to spend the night.

As his second year in Tangier began, Burroughs concentrated on trying to write, but it was horribly difficult. He was certain he had no talent, and sat for hours looking at a blank page. The paradox was that although he felt that he could accomplish nothing, writing appeared to him as an absolute necessity. And yet he had the impression that what he did write was only evasion, sidetracking, notes. He was walking around the shore of a lake, pretending to study the flora and the fauna, and afraid to jump in. What he did write he sent to Allen, who was still his receiver, and to whom he wrote, on January 12, 1955: "Allen, I need you so much your absence causes me, at times, acute pain. I don't mean sexually, I mean in connection with my writing." At the same time he was jealous that Allen had found Peter, and wrote: "Your setup with Peter sounds rather grim and beat. What do you *talk* about?" It was hard to come to terms with the reality that he and Allen would never have a life together. It was hard to come to terms with loss and suffering. The withdrawal pains were comparable to kicking junk. You could avoid the pain by avoiding emotional involvement, but that was not the answer, as Burroughs wrote to Kerouac: "I say we are here in human form to learn by the human hieroglyphs of love and suffering. There is no intensity of love or feeling that does not involve the risk of crippling hurt. It is a duty to take this risk, to love and feel without defense or reserve."

In 1955 Burroughs began to see that Tangier could serve as a model for the setting of his novel, which he called "Interzone." Tangier was as much an imaginative construct as a geographical location, a metaphor for limbo, for a dead-end place, a place where everyone could act out his most extreme fantasies. On one level, Tangier was a reconstruction of the world in a small place. He would attempt a novel-length work, even though he knew it would be unpublishable. He would write it in the style of his most outrageous routines, such as the talking asshole. He wasn't sure what he was writing about, but he began to see that it had to do with larval forms, transitions, emergent telepathic faculties, attempts to control and stifle new forms. He knew that the routine was his special form—it was unpredictable, with the author always trying to outdo himself, to go a little further, to commit some excess, since he was trying to hold the attention of a particular person. Before the book was written, he already had a title, courtesy of Jack Kerouac: *Naked Lunch.*

But to write steadily, Burroughs had to get out of the straitjacket of junk. All he did when he was on junk was wait for the next shot. While waiting, he could spend hours looking at his big toe. In May, he checked in to Dr. Aptel's clinic on the Marshan for a two-week sleep cure. He took barbiturates, chloral hydrate, and Thorazine, and lost thirty pounds. It struck him as a ridiculous cure because it upset the whole cycle of sleep and waking. But he saw it through, determined that he never wanted to see any more junk as long as he lived. He would rather sell lottery tickets like the dwarves and blind men in the Socco Chico than touch it again.

By July, he was hooked again. Two weeks had not been long enough to kick. He might have made it but for coming down with painful neuralgia in his back. That finished him, and he lapsed into Demerol, which was evil shit. It was heartbreaking to be hooked again after taking that awful cure. He was disgusted with his prevarications. Every day he found some excuse for buying the absolutely last box of ampules. What a dreary display of weakness. He might try having Kiki take his clothes away and measure out the pills, but oh God, he'd tried that so many times before. There was one bright spot, which was that Paul Bowles was back from

Ceylon and invited him to tea with Brion Gysin. "Oh, impossible, impossible," Brion said to Paul, "I know, I've seen him staggering around, he's just an old junky," but Brion came anyway, and the tea was quite a success. Bowles appreciated Burroughs' storytelling abilities and saw him for what he was—a genuine original. The best thing about him was that he always made sense and he was always funny. At any point of the night or day, the whole machine of his vitriolic humor was going full blast. In contrast to Bowles's diligent traveling and investigations of Moroccan life, Burroughs made no attempt to learn about the country or to speak the language. Bowles admired his "I-remain-myself-everywhere" stance, since he had, in the first years that he had lived abroad, fretted about becoming deracinated and adapting to an alien culture. But Burroughs made no effort to adapt, and the thought that he was an exile never crossed his mind, for wherever he might be, thought Bowles, he remained as American as the general store in a one-horse town.

Burroughs knew he had to kick to continue his work, but was reluctant to leave the safety of junk. A song from his youth rattled in his head, about an old black man who had sold his cabin and ⸳tch of ground to go north for better pay:

> But Dina she don't want to go,
> She says we're getting old.
> She's 'fraid that she will freeze to death,
> The country am so cold.
> That story 'bout the work and pay
> She don't believe it's true,
> She begs me not to do the thing
> That I am bound to do.

Dina was junk, which had all the claims on him that a wife of long standing might have. But in September, thanks to currency fluctuations that made the dollar worth more, Burroughs checked into a private room in the Jewish hospital. The cure was dolophine every four hours, which gave him bizarre ideas, "strange things I have in heart that will to hand." He was writing, but he had no control over what he wrote. "I am trying," he wrote Allen Ginsberg from the hospital on October 20, "to create something that will have a life of its own, that can put me in real danger, a danger which I willingly take on myself."

A few days later he left the hospital, off junk and feeling feisty. His attitude in his work, he wrote Allen, was "Let petty kings the names of parties know; where'er I come I kill both friend and foe." He was also feeling sexy, but was getting tired of monogamy with Kiki, which reminded him of Dryden's description of the Golden Age, "Ere one to one was cursedly confined." From his bedroom window, he watched the boys in the courtyard of the Italian school across the street with his eight-power field glasses—they wore shorts and he could see the goose pimples on their legs in the morning chill.

At this time there was a great deal of political agitation in Morocco. Demonstrators called for the return of King Mohammed V, exiled by the French. There were riots in the French zone, and in August the rioting spread to Tangier; its international status did not protect it from the nationalist surge. Burroughs saw store shutters slamming, women jerking their babies indoors, and people running through the streets giving the three-fingered salute (for Allah, the King, and Morocco). In September, the French promised to give Morocco independence, and in November the king made a triumphant return. One of his first pronouncements was that he would abolish Tangier's international status. It would become a Moroccan city like any other. This, of course, was like sounding the siren for Abandon Ship. Overnight, hundreds of homes and businesses posted FOR SALE signs. Forty tons of gold in Tangier vaults were transferred to Geneva. The Country Club lost membership so fast there were more caddies than golfers. Brion Gysin eventually had to close the 1001 Nights— the minks had fled.

In San Francisco, Allen Ginsberg was making the poetry scene and pushing his own work and the work of his friends. He showed Burroughs' and Kerouac's stuff to the ranking San Francisco poet, Kenneth Rexroth, who said that "*Dr. Sax* sounds like it was written on pot. The sentences are always diffuse, as if he were wandering, not driving forward to the point of the book. I know it's great writing, I just have the feeling he's gone astray somehow, on the wrong track. Now you take Burroughs, he'll never amount to anything, like Kerouac, but he knows how to write . . . he tells you straight off and you read through in a rush and he's going in one direction, tells you what happened, catches your attention and takes you fast." Rexroth read parts of Kerouac's *Vision of Cody* to Robert Duncan, who responded with: "As Katherine Mansfield said when she read *Ulysses*, 'This is obviously the wave of the future. I'm glad I'm dying of tuberculosis.' " Allen met the respected critic and friend of Faulkner and Hemingway, Malcolm Cowley, who told him, "Keep away from Burroughs, I understand he killed his wife."

Allen had quit his market research job and moved in with Peter Orlovsky, into a North Beach apartment at 1010 Montgomery Street. In August and September of 1955, he was putting down thoughts on scratch paper, and the thoughts had to do with madness. For Carl Solomon was straitjacketed in Pilgrim State Hospital, where he was given twenty-one electroshocks. Poor Carl, the disciple of Artaud, who had burned money to protest the evils of materialism.

In using Carl as his character, Allen could also write, without naming her, about his mother, Naomi. She was also in Pilgrim State, the largest mental hospital in the world, in Brentwood, Long Island, which houses 25,000. Allen could not write directly about his mother because he did not want to admit that it was he who had recently signed the commitment papers for her lobotomy. When Allen was seven, Naomi had become convinced that doctors had planted three big sticks down her back as antennae to receive radio broadcasts from the ceiling—the voices sent by President Roosevelt alternately praised her as a "great woman" and mocked her as a "radical" and a "bad girl." And this is where it had all led, with the son agreeing to his mother's lobotomy. Out of Allen's feelings of guilt, "Howl" was composed: "I saw the best minds of my generation destroyed by madness."

In October, Allen rounded up some of the young poets for a reading at Gallery Six, a remodeled auto repair shop with white walls. Invitational postcards were sent out, promising "all sharp new straightforward writing." On October 7, an audience of about 150 watched Kenneth Rexroth in a white turtleneck introduce the poets: Philip Lamantia, a twenty-eight-year-old former Surrealist; Philip Whalen, a Zen Buddhist from Oregon; Gary Snyder, another Buddhist and former lumberjack and seaman; Michael McClure, the youngest of the group; and Allen. In the audience, Jack Kerouac cheered them on with cries of "Go!" and "Yeah!" beating out the rhythms of the poetry on his wine jug as if he was at a jam session.

The evening belonged to Allen, a thin and rumpled twenty-nine-year-old who that night had a kind of incandescence, as though he'd been dipped in phosphorus. As someone in the audience later said, "When Allen read 'Howl,' it was like bringing two ends of an electric wire together." It was Allen's spiritual confession, and all his friends were in it, Burroughs, Kerouac, Neal Cassady, "who sweetened the snatches of a million girls trembling in the sunset . . ." It had an absolutely compelling incantatory quality, and seemed to be a manifesto for all the misfits of the fifties, the rejected, the deviants, the criminals, and the insane, who could unite under his banner.

Strong stuff, thought Lawrence Ferlinghetti, who had founded the City Lights bookstore and publishing company in North Beach in 1953. He had the sense that a barrier had been broken. It would be impossible to go back to the genteel drabness of academic poetry. As soon as he got home from the reading, he sent Ginsberg a telegram that was a paraphrase of the message Emerson had sent to Walt Whitman after reading *Leaves of Grass:* "I greet you at the start of a great career. When do I get the manuscript?"

" 'Howl' just blew things up completely," Rexroth said. "That night was the birth of the San Francisco renaissance." It led to divisiveness, however, for Rexroth had been challenged as king of the castle. Allen was brash when sober; when drunk he was insulting. At one of his Friday afternoon at-homes, Rexroth was approached by a boozy Allen, who said, "I'm a better poet than you."

Some months later, Rexroth's wife, Martha, ran off with the poet Robert Creeley, and for some reason Rexroth thought Allen had had a hand in her departure. At a party for the poet and anthologist Oscar Williams, Rexroth started cursing Allen as soon as he walked in the door. "There are no knives in heaven," Allen said, and Rexroth calmed down, taking Allen aside and asking him whether it was true that they had all held orgies with his wife in Allen's Berkeley cottage, and whether Allen had gone around giggling and ridiculing him because his wife had left him. Allen denied both charges, which he said were pure invention, and he and Rexroth resumed their increasingly uneasy friendship.

At the start of 1956, Burroughs took stock of his situation. The last two years had been a blur of drugs. His attempts to kick had failed, and once again he had a heavy habit. He was taking so much dope that he woke up in the middle of the night with someone squeezing his hand—it was his other hand. He heard about a doctor in London who treated addicts, and prevailed upon his parents to send him $500 to go there. When he went to the American Consulate to get his passport renewed, the consul said, "Well, Mr. Burroughs, you will of course satisfy the local people before you leave . . ." In other words, pay his bills, which he now had the money to do.

On the theory that drug addiction was a metabolic illness, Dr. John Yerbury Dent had developed a form of treatment that consisted in regulating the addict's metabolism with a morphine derivative called apomorphine, made by boiling morphine with hydrochloric acid. Dr. Dent had first tried apomorphine, an emetic used to treat cattle, on alcoholics, and found over the years that he could also use it with considerable success on heroin addicts. He took only two patients at a time, however, since he spent a great deal of time with each. He had been treating addicts for fifteen years when Burroughs came to his small clinic at 24 Addison Road. "Umm," said Dent, sizing up his gaunt new patient, "would you feel comfortable if you have a shot before we talk?" Once on the program, Burroughs was given one and a half grains of apomorphine, which produced vomiting in two minutes. The dose was then reduced to one-twentieth of a grain, which he received by injection every two hours, day and night, for six days. At the same time he continued to receive morphine injections in decreasing doses, first a quarter of a grain every six hours (one tenth of what he had been taking), and then an eighth of a grain. After six days, he was getting the apomorphine shots every four hours and the morphine shots every twelve hours. The entire treatment lasted fourteen days, and for the first four days and four nights, Burroughs couldn't sleep. No sedatives or sleeping pills of any kind were used. "You'll sleep when your body is ready to sleep," Dr. Dent said. It was pretty bad, but Dent came by to see Burroughs at 2:00 A.M., staying until five, and they had long talks about the Mayans. This time, Burroughs vowed, there would be no backsliding, not one shot of paregoric or codeine or Demerol. Dr. Dent gave him three tubes of apomorphine in case of emergency. It turned out to be the most successful cure he had ever taken, and he remained off drugs for several years.

Burroughs hated London, which seemed to him overregulated. He had seen a sign in a pub that said: "No liquor may be consumed after time is called. Drinking must stop at once, no time being allowed for consumption." So when time was called, Burroughs supposed, you had to spit your drink out on the bar.

As soon as he could, he left London for Venice to visit Alan Ansen, who had an apartment there on the top floor of a palazzo in the via delle Carrozze. Alan was in love with Venice, its lagoons and hidden riches. This was the last golden era, when people still had liveried servants and private gondolas, and the old families like the Volpis and the Cicognas held court in their *piani nobiles*. Burroughs, however, thought it was basically one big tourist postcard. Half the population seemed to be made up of real estate agents. A distinguished old fellow, the Count de Ville, who wore ribbons of various colors in the buttonhole of his lapel, invited them for an *aperitivo*. He was retired from the diplomatic service, and said, "I do not know whether they will give me another assignation." It turned out he wanted to rent them an apartment.

Burroughs took up rowing Venetian-style, that is rowing forward, in the direction you are looking, and went to dinner with Ansen in an eighteenth-century palazzo. In July they were invited to a cocktail party for the British consul at Peggy Guggenheim's palazzo Venier dei Leoni, opposite the Prefettura (city hall). Peggy's gondoliers were all in white with a turquoise sash. Since 1951, her palazzo had been open as a museum. Great paintings hung in the bathrooms, alongside her stockings, and the Calder mobile in the entrance, positioned too low, struck inattentive guests in the eye. Brancusi's "Two Birds" was in the sculpture garden, and on the white marble terrace overlooking the Grand Canal there was a six-foot-high bronze by Marino Marini of a horse and rider, who greeted passing gondolas with his head thrown back and outstretched arms and a penis in full erection. So as not to offend the nuns who came on holy days to be blessed by the patriarch in the Prefettura, Peggy asked Marini to cast the penis separately, so it could be unscrewed. But when it was stolen during a party, the new one was soldered on.

Burroughs, who drank heavily when he was not on junk, arrived at the party tanked, and when Ansen advised him that it was customary to kiss Peggy Guggenheim's hand, he said, "I will be glad to kiss her cunt if that is the custom," a remark that was overheard by one of her courtiers and promptly repeated, so that for the rest of his stay he was persona non grata. It was unreasonable of Peggy Guggenheim, Burroughs observed, to move in admittedly bohemian circles while demanding conventional behavior. She was strictly a Queen Bee.

He showed Ansen the six episodes of *Naked Lunch* that he had completed, and Alan advised him not to make it reportorial like *Junky* but to dramatize it and heighten it to an incessant state of experience, to "promise nothing which is not performed." It seemed to him that it needed a lot of work.

Ansen was under surveillance by the Venetian authorities, who, although tolerant of eccentric behavior, did draw a line, which he had crossed. One night, some sailors he had taken to his apartment attacked him, and he ran into the street naked and into a bar on the corner, where he seized a chair to defend himself. After that, there were intimations that his residence permit would not be renewed, and he began to worry that the drunken parties with Burroughs might further endanger his status. "The neighbors are spying on me," he said. Burroughs pointed out that to see into his apartment they would have to stand on chairs. "On chairs they would stand," Ansen said. In August, when his *soggiorno* wasn't renewed, he had to go to Austria and come back, so Burroughs decided it was time to head back to Tangier.

He returned via Tripoli and Algiers, two more names he could add to his planetary list of god-awful holes. In Tripoli there was a state of emergency due to the threat of war with Egypt, and at the American Embassy the staff were walking around with pistols in their belts. Algiers was a battlefield where the French and the *fellaghas* were fighting it out. Every day bombs went off and people were shot in the street. He went to see a movie—*Blackboard Jungle* dubbed in French—and wondered why he was the only one there, not realizing that grenades lobbed into movie theaters were commonplace. He ate lunch at the Milk Bar, where a bomb would explode soon after his departure, killing twelve people. There did not seem to be one safe place you could go to in the entire city of Algiers, but he was stuck there because planes were booked solid for weeks. He stayed in the decrepit Hotel Variétés, because he was running out of money. His bed was infested with bedbugs, he had never seen anything like it, his sheets were black with them. Finally he had to wire his parents for funds, and took a train back to Tangier. Oddly enough, he had not minded the sense of danger. Danger taught alertness. The Buddhists said that hell worlds were less dangerous than heaven worlds. What was that line of Edwin Arlington Robinson's? "Security, the friendly mask of change/At which we smile, not seeing what lies behind."

Burroughs was glad to be back in Tangier that September of 1956. It was the only place he could think of where he didn't want to be someplace else. The beauty of the town consisted of its changing combinations. There was always something that would surprise you, such as his growing friendship with Paul Bowles. The great event of the moment, said Paul, was Barbara Hutton's party for 200 guests on the roof of her casbah castle, to which Burroughs was not invited. It was the biggest party since the war, and invitations were sold on the black market for 20,000 francs. But at the door, a special squad checked names, and those with invitations bought from scalpers were turned away. One woman, the wife of a banker, went into hysterics and had to be dragged off. Others, who had arrived in evening dress, had to leave on foot through the dirty streets of the casbah, lined with Moslems observing the strange goings on. Paul, who went with Jane, was startled to see how strongly people felt about such things. After all, a party was only a party.

But what a party! In a drawing room stood a throne from India insured for a million dollars and encrusted with thousands of pearls, rubies, sapphires, and emeralds, upon which the hostess received her guests, who sat at her feet upon cushions embroidered with real gems, big ones. A little hard on the rear end, perhaps, although no one complained. There was a jazz orchestra on the top terrace, a group of Gypsies dancing in a patio, a Moroccan orchestra with dancing boys in another room, and a concert pianist on an inner balcony. Each guest had been insured against accident or loss. The flat roofs of adjacent houses were crowded with the curious. The party went on until nine the next morning.

Oblivious to the party of the decade, Burroughs took a room in the Hotel Muniria, at 1 calle Magallanes, with a private entrance that opened on a garden. He was off junk for the first time in three years, and he was on a health kick. In the morning he did the Hornibrook abdominal exercises he had learned in London, which guaranteed a flat stomach. Then he went rowing in the bay. So many simple things gave him pleasure now that he was off junk—the contracting and relaxing of muscles, sitting in a café, walking around town.

Tangier had independence jitters. In October there was a general strike, with thousands of Arabs marching down the boulevard and yelling, "Down with the French!" The Istiqlal, or Nationalist Party, was promising to protect foreign residents, and the king had been severe in punishing some of the worst rioters, in the city of Meknes. Tangier was comparatively safe, but you never knew, and Burroughs practiced exercises to help make himself invisible in the street. The first one was to see everyone before they saw you . . . if you could do that, they didn't see you. The other was not to give anyone a reason to look at you. Foreigners in Morocco had a tendency to stick out, but Burroughs was indistinct and anonymous-looking, and found that he could walk through town without being noticed. The real test was getting through a whole line of guides without being accosted, which he succeeded in doing. He became so good at it that the locals in his neighborhood dubbed him *el hombre invisibile,* which was self-defeating, for now he was noticed *because* he was invisible.

Off junk, he was writing daily. After his exercises and his rowing, he would get started around noon and work until evening, with no central plan, just writing along. He felt the power coming in. In Tangier the other dimension was always breaking through. Compared to this, what he had written so far was just kid stuff. Don Cotton, who had the room next door, said he could hear Burroughs' wild laughter along with the typing. Every other day he took some *majoun* (hashish candy), and the rest of the time he smoked a lot of weed, which stimulated the associative process and the flow of images. The book began to take shape. When Paul Bowles visited his room in the Muniria, the floor was covered with hundreds of yellow foolscap pages. Many of them had been stepped on;

you could see sole and heel marks on them. They were covered with rat droppings and bits of cheese sandwiches. Obviously, Burroughs ate at the same table where he typed. "What is all this?" asked Bowles, who, being meticulously neat, was put off by clutter. "That's what I'm working on," Burroughs replied. "Do you make copies before you throw it on the floor?" "Nope." "Then how are you going to read it?" "Oh, I figure it'll be legible." It was unbelievable, Paul thought. He spent half his time making those things, carefully, and the other half ruining them. Burroughs, however, although admittedly untidy, swept his room out daily and did not habitually leave papers on the floor.

Burroughs had built an orgone box in the garden of the Muniria, and he tried to sell Paul on it, but the whole argument did not sound compatible with anything Paul knew about science. "Just sit in it and you'll feel different when you come out," Burroughs said. The box reminded Paul of a dog kennel, but he sat in it to be agreeable, and it was a cold night, and he did feel different when he came out—he was shivering.

Paul told Burroughs that Tangier had been given five years to adjust to its loss of free-zone status. You could still use pesetas and francs. You could still get a bottle of Gordon's gin for under two dollars. For drugs like opium, you now needed a prescription, which Bowles's French doctor, Madame Roux, was always willing to provide, saying, "*C'est le roi des médicaments, monsieur.*" ("It is the king of medicines.") And yet a lot of people had sold out and left, and a lot of others who had stayed were going around with long faces, saying, "How much longer have we got?"

But none of that mattered to Burroughs, who was feeling better than he had felt in years. What he liked about Tangier was the feeling of being outside any social context. He felt that he could be completely himself, and disregard all social forms. He had a drink with some stuffy English people who mentioned that their yacht was tied to a buoy, and he said, "Tied to a boy—lucky chap," and laughed his low cackle of a laugh, but no one else thought it was funny. One evening, Paul was entertaining a rich American woman, and Burroughs started talking about yage, and the woman asked, "How long does it take to rot you?" and Burroughs replied, "Lady, you should live so long." He and Paul were getting along splendidly, their minds were alike, and the telepathy was flowing.

He heard from Jack Kerouac, who had been in Mexico, that Old Dave, his partner in addiction, to whom he had brought the opium in jail, hidden in an orange, and with whom he had gone to see the patron saint of pushers, had died. Poor Old Dave, he had just sat down on a curb one day and died. Jack reported that Allen Ginsberg was famous, on the basis of his one poem, "Howl." He was giving readings coast to coast. In New York, Jack was introduced as "that guy that 'Howl' is dedicated to." Jack thought Allen's success was due to the fact that no one since Henry Miller had had the guts to say cock and cunt in public. But Jack was not far behind, for he'd signed his contract for *On the Road* with Viking that January of 1957, and it would be out in October.

Jack was coming to see Burroughs in Tangier, he wrote, and in fact left New York on a Yugoslavian freighter on February 15, 1957. One morning he awoke to see Africa outlined on the blue sea, and the ship passed through the straits of Gibraltar, "where rough rocks groaning vegetate," in the words of Blake. Burroughs was waiting for him at the dock, healthy and tanned and vigorous, wearing chino pants and a pocketed shirt and a fisherman's hat, this scion of a great industrial family who had only been a-scioned $200 a month, Jack joked.

Burroughs got him a room at the Muniria for twenty dollars a month and said, "Tomorrow first thing after I've had my simple breakfast of tea and bread, we'll go rowing in the bay." Burroughs walked so fast he reminded Jack of an insane German philologist in exile. "Come on, step on it," he said. "Young man like you can't even keep up with old man like me."

"You walk too fast."

"Lard-assed hipsters, ain't good for nothin'."

As they walked, Burroughs showed Jack his switchblade, and said, "Yessir, without it I'd be dead now. Bunch of Ay-rabs surrounded me in an alley one night. I just let this old thing click out and said, 'Come on ya buncha bastards,' and they cut out."

"How do you like the Arabs?" Jack asked.

"Just push 'em aside like little pricks," he said, and suiting action to words, he walked through a knot of Arabs on the sidewalk, making them split on both sides, muttering and swinging his arms with a vigorous unnatural pumping motion.

As they rowed in the bay, Burroughs recounted his trip to Venice. It was full of rich old American bitches, he said, with Truman Capote blowing gondoliers in the middle of the Grand Canal. When Jack saw the mess in Burroughs' room, he volunteered to help with the typing. But the material he typed gave him nightmares. "Why are all these young boys being hanged in limestone caves?" he asked.

"Don't ask me," Burroughs said. "I get these messages from other planets. I'm apparently some kind of agent from another planet but I haven't got my orders clearly decoded yet. I'm shitting out my educated Middlewest background once and for all. It's a matter of catharsis, where I say the most horrible things I can think of. Realize that—the most horrible dirty slimy awful niggardliest posture possible . . . These great existential anarchists and terrorists, so-called, never even their own drippy fly/mentioneth." Writing the book seemed to be transforming Bill, Jack thought. He was so deeply into it that it was scary. Now his conversation was in routines, he was assuming different roles and identities. It all kept pouring out of him in mad monologues. He kept saying he was going to erupt in some unspeakable atrocity, such as waving his ding-dong at an embassy party, or slaughtering an Arab boy to see what his insides looked like. On paper, he was unleashing his word hoard, and his message was all scatological, homosexual, superviolent madness. Burroughs, Jack thought, was a quiet flowery sage who stood alone in a sea of facts. He might be put down for a hundred years, but he was the scientist who had found out the secret of how to control dictators by telepathy. He was also a great sad George Sanders in the movie of our minds, the great ultimate Sanders-of-the-river.

Burroughs introduced Jack to some of the local characters, including Paul Lund, who struck Jack as a dashing dog with a limey accent. He had a picturesque way of speaking. In the midst of a story about a lady he had met in Rome, he said, "There she is jugglin' me sweetbreads with her tongue."

Allen Ginsberg and Peter Orlovsky were due to follow Jack to Tangier, and one night in Burroughs' room, after dinner at the Paname, Burroughs began to cry. He told Jack that he had been in love with Allen for years. Once Allen had drawn two hearts pierced by Cupid's arrow, but by mistake the arrow's shaft only went through one heart. "That's what I mean," he told Jack. "This autocratic person can only fall in love with the image of himself." Burroughs admitted that when he had come to Jack's house in Richmond Hill in October 1954, it was because "the only connection I had at that agonized time was through you. You'd been getting long letters from him about what he was doing in Frisco. Laborsome human prose but I had to have some connection with him . . . and I had to see you as second best to nothing."

After about a month in Tangier, Jack got restless. He complained about the food, the Arabs, the sanitation. That was the trouble with Jack, thought Burroughs, he didn't like anything outside America. The clincher was that an old black guy who was always hanging around the Socco Chico sold him some bad hash. It was metallic-looking, and when Jack smoked it he came down with violent diarrhea. It was as if his bowels were telling him it was time to go, and on April 5 he took the boat for Marseilles. He left convinced that Burroughs was writing a great and haunting book and would one day be a really big writer.

The day before Jack left, Allen Ginsberg and Peter Orlovsky arrived. It was quite amazing that just at the moment when Burroughs needed help organizing and editing his material, his friends responded to his psychic call, and traveled thousands of miles to assist him. Low on money, Allen had been wondering how to finance the trip when $200 came in from the National Academy of Arts and Sciences, thanks to William Carlos Williams. Also, Peter had gotten his army disability pay as a nut case raised from $17.50 to $50 a month, after going in to see the psychiatrists and telling them that people were shadows. They took a freighter, and Allen was struck upon arrival in Tangier by the brilliant porcelain sky and the bright green water. You could see twenty miles across the straits to the ancient parapets of Europe, the south coast of Spain, and Gibraltar. Bill found them rooms in the Muniria, and they settled down to a daily schedule of typing and editing, working six hours a day and more, in relays. Alan Ansen arrived from Venice to join this writer's equivalent of a quilting bee, and was a great asset, having done the same sort of work for Auden. He read through all the typed pages and notebooks and made an index of all the material, the sentences, letters, routines, all indexed chronologically. He worked, said Allen, like a great professional pedantic scholar with an unruly library full of dignified ancient manuscripts. Over a period of two months, working steadily, they integrated and edited and typed the material, which was an incredible mosaic of Bill's fantasies over the past three years, until they had about 200 pages of finished manuscript typed in duplicate.

It was the first time Burroughs had seen Allen since their breakup in 1953, and there was some strain. Burroughs did not take to Peter, who had replaced him in Allen's affections. He thought Peter was nutty and embarrassing. He was always talking to people in the street, which was the wrong thing to do in Tangier. He would spot a group of mature Moroccan men wearing their traditional *djellabahs* and say, "Look at those hip young kids," and go up and talk to them, thereby confirming their views as to the craziness of Nazarenes. Burroughs tried to explain to him that you didn't do that, but could not get it through his head that from years of living in Tangier he knew something about the dos and don'ts. Burroughs got so he couldn't stand the sight of Peter. He just didn't want him around, and froze him out by not talking to him and not inviting him to meals. Once, when he was high on *majoun,* he started waving his machete at Peter and Allen in a menacing way. There was hostility in the air.

Allen tried to mediate and told Burroughs, "I think it would be good for both of you if you got along better," but to no avail. One night, high on *majoun,* Burroughs began to mock him for putting up with Peter's inanity, and Allen exploded and grabbed Bill's knife and cut open his khaki shirt. The situation did not improve. It wasn't jealousy, Burroughs explained to Allen, it was just that Peter got on his nerves. Alan Ansen didn't like him either, and called him "a freeloading bitch posing as an assistant mahatma."

In the evening they would sit on the hotel porch and drink sherry and watch the sunset, and then they would cook huge meals. There was plenty of weed and plenty of boys, and Allen was reading the Koran, and dug Surah 55, with the refrain "Which of the lord's treasures would you reject?" With the exception of the trouble with Peter, it was a hard-working and yet carefree time.

Allen wanted to meet Paul Bowles, who was traveling, but he telephoned Jane, introducing himself as "Allen Ginsberg, the bop poet." Jane, who was not at all well, having that April suffered a stroke that impaired her vision, did not know what to make of Allen, never having heard the word "bop."

Then Allen started playing "do you know." "Do you know Philip Lamantia?" he asked.

"No," Jane said.

"He's this very hip poet, been writing since he was thirteen, and he just had a vision in Mexico on peyote."

"Oy veg," Jane said.

"Honest, it was a real vision, and now he's a Catholic."

"Oy veg," Jane said.

"Do you know Charles Henri Ford?"

"Yes, because he's old," Jane said.

"Well, don't you take *majoun* day and night?"

"I hate all that, and I'm sure you shouldn't see me."

"Well, what about Zen?"

Jane thought to herself: This must be the Zen Buddhist-Bebop-Jesus Christ-Peyote group.

Allen asked her if she believed in God, and Jane said, "I'm certainly not going to discuss it on the telephone."

The standoffishness was a pose, however, for Allen did see Jane, whom he found cool and shy and intelligent, and who reminded him of Joan Burroughs.

Paul returned in May, back from Ceylon, and invited them all over, playing Indian music and rolling huge bombers. Allen sized him up as a little mechanical and remote—he was small, with close-cropped blond hair, and had a nervous stomach and wore nylon suits. With Jane, Allen came on in his usual bull-in-a-china-shop way. Jane was terrified of losing her sight, and Allen talked about William Carlos Williams, who also had eye trouble, and said, "Of course he was able to get a good seeing-eye dog."

Through Paul, Allen and Burroughs met the English painter Francis Bacon, who was forty-seven but looked thirty-five, with a spoiled tragic face. He said his reputation was a lot of chic shit and that his real love was gambling—he had once won $4,000 at Monte Carlo. He told Allen that he had also once been offered a gambling stake for allowing himself to be whipped, with a bonus for every stroke that drew blood. Bacon's painting technique was what he called psychic representation, the face formed as if by accident in a whirl of feathery brush strokes. Bacon said DeKooning was the great man in the United States, for bursting through the abstract and planting an image on the canvas.

Allen thought that Bacon painted the way Burroughs wrote. It was a sort of dangerous bullfight of the mind, where he placed himself in acute psychic danger of uncovering some secret that would destroy him. Burroughs had these unpublishable mad routines about talking assholes, with the recurring image of the spurting hard-on as the hanged man's neck snaps, and vast paranoiac theories of agents and psychic senders taking over the world in bureaucratic conspiracies. But Burroughs, although fond of Bacon, denied that there was any connection, and said: "Bacon and I are at opposite ends of the spectrum. He likes middle-aged truck drivers and I like young boys. He sneers at immortality and I think it's the one thing of importance. Of course we're associated because of our morbid subject matter."

In early June, Allen and Peter and Alan Ansen left for Spain and Burroughs was alone again. He had an invitation from Kells Elvins to visit Copenhagen, where Kells had moved with his Danish actress wife Mimi, after living in Rome a few years. Mimi was trying to break into Italian movies, and Kells took her to auditions at Cinecitta. Mimi did not get the parts, but on one occasion a director asked Kells to play a drunken American in a party scene, a part for which he was well suited, for the booze had done a job on him, and he was now puffy-faced and overweight.

He lived the dilettantish, expatriate, fringe Roman life with other would-be artists and writers. Kells had to his credit one story about an Athens bartender named Hercules, published in *Esquire*. He wrote letters home to his mother telling her what a disciplined writer he had become. To Burroughs he wrote about the beautiful people, film festivals, skindiving weekends, and drinking *grappa* and *sambuca* with his new friends. "Such a thing as too much fun, Elvins," Burroughs replied. Eventually, however, since there was movie work for Mimi in Denmark, where she was a star, they moved to the Charlottenlund section of Copenhagen.

Burroughs left for Copenhagen in July 1957, not only to see Kells, but on an intuition that it would be important for his book. He had four main zones, or sets, where the book takes place—the United States, South America, Interzone (which was Tangier), and Freeland—and in Scandinavia he found the real model for his imagined Freeland, a place of the living dead. He had already described it as a series of bars along a canal, which was what he found in Copenhagen. What he saw exceeded the most ghastly product of his imagination. All these people with their cradle-to-grave welfare state and their ordered socialist limbo were so unhappy compared to the Spanish and Moroccans in Tangier, who had nothing. Suicide was almost unknown in Morocco, but in Scandinavia it was endemic. The dead-level sanity and bone dullness of the Danes appalled him. It was a police state without police, populated by robots completely conditioned by the state. The only antisocial element was the juvenile delinquents, known locally as "Leather Jackets." It was all horribly depressing, the sandwich bars, the workmen in overalls listening to classical music on the radio, the lack of conversation, the general inanity and squareness of people. In a bar, he had a few drinks with a handsome young Dane, and said something about going back to his hotel. "You mean both of us go back there?" the young Dane asked. "That's the general idea," Burroughs said. "No, I can't . . ." long pause . . . "I have a wife." Why had he pinned it down like that, Burroughs wondered, then refused, and then lied? He thought of a scene for his book where this type of creature would be sent to a reconditioning center. "Calling Dr. Benway. You are wanted in reconditioning."

Kells was thriving, and Mimi was the first of his wives who seemed to like him, but Burroughs was ready to cross out Scandinavia. In some way, however, Scandinavia catalyzed the novel, which was now taking shape faster than he could write it down in his hotel room. Every time he reached an impasse, something happened to show him the way, so he stayed in Copenhagen through August and worked. The main theme, it was now clear to him, was the desecration of the human image by control addicts. As Lola La Chata, the Mexico City pusher, used to say, "Pushing is more of a habit than using."

When he got back to Tangier in September, bad news awaited him, news concerning the deaths of two friends. The first was Kiki, his Spanish boy, who, despairing that Burroughs would overcome his addiction, and alert to new opportunities, had left for Spain in 1956 with a Cuban band-leader. The Cuban was a jealous, violent type. In Madrid, when he found Kiki in bed with a girl, he stabbed him with a kitchen knife and killed him. Poor, gentle Kiki, thought Burroughs, it was so out of character for him to die a violent death.

The second death, reported by Jack Kerouac, was Bill Garver's in Mexico City. The overcoat thief, the oldtime *schmecker,* the dilapidated patrician, with all his sad mementos of onetime respectability, had finally packed it in, and was buried in the American cemetery with Joan.

As for Jack, with the publication of *On the Road* that September, he was experiencing the devouring quality of overnight notoriety. His prophecy in *The Town and the City* was coming true: "He was going to become famous, he was going to be the dark swift figure with twinkling feet that is seen in the Pathé Newsreels galloping across chalk-stripes in the terrific, mob-swarmed, autumn-dark stadiums of America as jubilance strides across the land."

Despite the mixed reviews, there was a consciousness of the book's importance as well as popular success, for *On the Road* hit the bestseller list for five weeks. Jack found himself in a swirl of publicity. At the Viking party, he was surrounded by interviewers as the original "100-mile man-uscript," as Jack called it, was unrolled on the carpet. There were articles everywhere, and Charles Olson and Nelson Algren and Norman Mailer praised him. Forty million viewers saw him on John Wingate's "Night-beat," as the big camera zeroed in, along with the dumb questions. "Do you ever smoke dope?" "What do you think of suicide?" "What are you seeking?" "I am waiting for God to show his face," Jack replied. Wingate's girl interviewer asked him if he thought sex was messy, and he said, "No, it's a gateway to paradise," and she said, "Oh, I don't think so," to which Jack replied, "Close the door and let's do it."

The West End Bar was full of young kids reading *Road.* Each day, Jack picked through piles of fan letters, from grandmothers to sixteen-year-old girls. He was living with Joyce Glassman, and they left the phone off the hook; it rang every five minutes. *Life* had taken 150 shots of him in the Village, and Brooklyn College asked him to lecture. Marlon Brando wanted to make a movie of *Road*. Kerouac had written an article, "Explaining the Beat Generation," for *Pageant* magazine. He said it was the second religiousness of Western civilization as prophesied by Spengler, and gave as an example Lucien Carr's attempt to gain asylum in a church after killing Dave Kammerer, the most Gothic mad event of all. The *American College Dictionary* sent him their definition of "Beat Generation" to revise: "Certain members of the generation that came of age after World War II who affect detachment from moral and social forms and responsibilities, supposedly due to disillusionment. Coined by Jack Kerouac." Jack sent this amendment: "Beat generation, members of the generation that came of age after World War II–Korean War, who join in a relaxation of social and sexual tensions and espouse antiregimentation, mystic-disaffiliation and material-simplicity values, supposedly as a result of Cold War disillusionment. Coined by Jack Kerouac." Over and over in interviews, Jack explained that "Beat generation" didn't mean angry at the world but weeping at the world. Everywhere he went, he was recognized. One evening when he walked into a bar, someone said, "Well, Kerouac came off the road in high gear . . . I hope he has a good set of snow tires."

Back in Tangier that September of 1957, Burroughs found that his own novel seemed to be taking a form of its own. All he had to do was transcribe. It came in great hunks, faster than he could get it down. With intensive work, he might finish by Christmas. It was developing into a saga of lost innocence, the fall, with some kind of redemption through knowledge of basic life processes. If anyone found the form confusing it was because they were accustomed to the conventional novel form, which was always a chronology of events that had already happened. Whereas this novel was concerned with events that were still happening at the writing, or had not yet happened. "The only way I can write narrative," Burroughs wrote Allen, "is to get right outside my body and experience it. . . . This can be exhausting and at times dangerous . . . one cannot be sure of redemption."

One curious by-product of this period of intensive work was the feeling that through his writing he had solved the dilemma of his queerness, which had been, all along, "a horrible sickness." In a dream, he saw his nonqueer self, an adolescent who stared at him angrily and said, "I hate you." No wonder, thought Burroughs, who had submerged and smothered that side of his being for years. But now it was coming out, as a direct result of his writing, and he was hoping to arrange a merger with the other side.

"Have reached point where I don't seem to want boys any more," he wrote Allen. "Can't make it. Must have some cunt. I was never supposed to be queer at all. The whole original trauma is out now. Such horror in bringing it out I was afraid my heart would stop."

Thus through writing he was hoping for the resolution to his divided self. The conflicting parts of his personality seemed capable of cohesion. In his work, Burroughs had finally faced his central conflict, making it one of the keys to the book—characters are repeatedly transformed through absorption and mutation: One character eats his son's sugar skull, another is turned into an insect, and a third into a crab; death itself turns into a maize seed.

The total immersion of the writer in his work created a parallel between the violence in the book and the day-to-day life of its author, who began to see himself as surrounded by dangers. A virus was spreading through Tangier, he believed, and had already struck a number of his friends. In escape there was safety. But even escape was perilous, for the Tangier-Madrid plane had crashed with no survivors. The plane may have carried a letter to Allen with a section of his manuscript, and he wrote Allen twice asking whether he had received it. Or were his worst fears true that the manuscript had gone down with the plane?

Burroughs was sick of Tangier and everyone in it, especially Don Cotton, who was now bringing around eight-year-old Arab boys—it was really disgusting to see these prepubescent gooks prowling around the Muniria looking for something to steal. And Cotton said gaily, "Oh, it's just that I feel inadequate with older people." The stupid bastard was in the middle of a particularly undesirable section of hell and didn't even know it.

He had to get out, and in mid-January 1958 he ended his three-year stay in the model for Interzone and left for Paris to join Allen Ginsberg. It was the first time in many years that he was leaving a place voluntarily, without the threat of police or legal action to spur him to flight.

· THIRTEEN ·

PARIS

1958–1960

When Allen Ginsberg and Peter Orlovsky left Tangier in June 1957, they went to Madrid to explore the Prado. By this time, after the publication of *Howl* and *On the Road,* the Beat phenomenon was getting some ink, and *Time* magazine offered Allen a plane ticket to come to Rome and be interviewed. Allen was constantly having to explain his position: The Beats were not rebels but questers, who had divorced themselves from a society devoted to making money. Walt Whitman had already warned that unless there was a spiritual infusion, America would wind up among the "fabled damned." Or, as Jack Kerouac put it, "It's beat, it's the beat to keep, it's the beat of the heart, it's being beat and down in the world and like oldtime lowdown and like in ancient civilization the slave boatmen rowing galleys to a beat and servants spinning pottery to a beat."

From Rome, Allen proceeded to Ischia, the island off Naples, to see Auden, who spent his summers there. Allen got so upset over Auden's disdainful attitude that he drank too much at dinner. When Allen announced that it was time for a revolution in American poetry, Auden said, "I wonder what *les jeunes* think they're doing now." That struck Allen as patronizing to the point of obtuseness. After all, William Carlos Williams, who had started the revolution, wasn't *les jeunes,* and Robert Creeley, who had been in correspondence with Ezra Pound for eight years, wasn't *les jeunes.* Here was Allen, a young poet full of enthusiasm for and acquaintance with the poetry of his time, coming to Auden for encouragement, and Auden was dismissing him like a classic reactionary. It was more than Allen could bear. Inflamed by drink, he said, "You've got a nerve, you old fool, you ought to be ashamed of yourself," and stumbled into the night, his hopes of a sophisticated weekend with a great poet completely dashed.

From Ischia, he joined Peter in Venice, where they stayed with Alan

Ansen, who was back from Austria, cooking huge meals in his apartment while Alan was in the other room making it with Italian boys. Like Burroughs the previous year, Allen and Peter made a poor impression on Peggy Guggenheim, who came for a drink and was caught in the middle of a towel-throwing rumpus between them, both bare-chested and glistening with sweat in the summer heat. Then it was on to Vienna in September, where they ate many different kinds of frankfurters with weird-colored mustard, and were thrown out of the opera because they didn't have ties on. They went back in with handkerchiefs around their necks and were thrown out again.

In the meantime, the self-described shit-stirrer Gregory Corso was in Paris, doing his thing. He too was getting some recognition, for City Lights was publishing his second book of poems. Gregory likened poetry to semen. It was fertile inside you, but once it spilled it died. There had to be a womb for poetry, not just an ear. Thus, he wrote with his "poetical cock" to produce the muse-baptized semen. Everyone was picking up on him with questions about the Beats, and he saw how poor Jack felt, taking the full blast of the media ovens back in the States. And yet Gregory knew he incited it with his funny mouth that said all he thought.

Gregory met Jean Genet, author of *The Thief's Journal,* then the most talked about writer in France, who arranged for him to stay in a friend's apartment, but got mad at him for painting on the walls. That Genet was offended by Gregory's vandalism was not without its humorous side, since he was a thief and a jailbird who had been released from prison thanks to a petition signed by some of France's most prestigious men of letters. But to every Frenchman, including Genet, property was sacred.

Genet kept saying, "I don't like Americans, why don't you speak French?" to which Gregory replied, "You French are decadent, why the fuck don't you wake up?" Truly, he thought, the French were the cheapest bastards on earth. That September, he cashed some bad checks, and left for Amsterdam to avoid arrest. He was acting as he had as a child when he wet his bed—since he had dreamed he was going to the toilet, it couldn't be him. So much of what he did today was still like that, screwing up with bad checks and then insisting he was not to blame.

From Amsterdam, he went to Venice to stay with Alan Ansen. The first night in Venice he was kicked out of Harry's Bar because some fellow Americans objected to his long, disorderly hair and sneakers. What a human garbage can that Alan Ansen was, Gregory thought, all he wanted to do was eat, but at the same time what an educated man, a walking book, you could talk to him about anything.

Ansen introduced him to Peggy Guggenheim. Gregory had a way with rich women, he knew how to make them laugh, the lure of money honed his wit. He was invited to the palazzo, and Peggy insisted on cutting his hair. They spoke of sex, but Gregory wasn't sure how to respond, for she was fifty-nine and no beauty. She tried to get him into bed, but for once he resisted. That was his first mistake. Then she asked Gregory to accompany her as she carried out a little ceremony in her garden. Her favorite pet dachshund was buried there. Into the sculpture garden she walked, carrying a pitcher of water and trailed by Gregory, past the Brancusis and the Giacomettis, to the small flowered plot of ground that was a canine grave, and reverently poured out the contents of the pitcher. "Gee, what a nice backyard you got," Gregory said. That was his second mistake. He was nonetheless invited to Peggy's next party, during which some prankster removed the penis from the Marino Marini naked rider. Naturally, suspicion fell on Gregory. "All right, Gregory, where is it?" Miss Guggenheim asked. "I can tell you where to look for it," Gregory said. "It was that German artist, Hundertwasser, that fucker took it." But Gregory's reputation weighed against him, and he was blamed for the disappearance of the bronze organ. That was his third mistake. Like the other Beats before him, he had struck out with Peggy Guggenheim.

In Venice, Allen had met a tall blond Dutch painter named Guy Harloff, who gave him the address of a cheap Paris hotel inhabited mainly by expatriate artists. Arriving in Paris in October 1957, Allen and Peter took a room in the hotel, which was located at 9 rue Git-le-Coeur, a Left Bank street that gave on the river Seine and was around the corner from the place Saint-Michel, one of the hubs of the Latin Quarter. It was directly across the river from the Paris police headquarters. The name Git-le-Coeur, which means "lies the heart," was said to go back to King Henry IV, who had a mistress on the street and said as he passed by one day, *Ici git mon coeur"* ("Here lies my heart").

There were thirteen categories of hotels in Paris, and the hotel at 9 rue Git-le-Coeur was at the bottom of the list. It did not even have a name, although it soon became known as "the Beat Hotel." It was a dingy place, with peeling walls that had once been painted gray, and cracked, dirty windows, and sparsely furnished rooms, without carpets or telephones, lit by a single forty-watt bulb. On each landing there was a toilet consisting of a hole flanked by two corrugated porcelain shoes, with shredded newspapers as toilet paper. On the ground floor there was a bathroom, and guests had to give advance notice if they wanted a bath, so that the water could be heated. Brion Gysin, who moved in at some point in 1958, and who paid the *supplément* for baths, maintained that if you put your head under the water you could hear the gurgling of an underground tributary of the Seine, the Bievre.

Time called it "the fleabag shrine where passersby move out of the way for rats," but with the rooms averaging thirty dollars a month, no one was complaining. It was not, however, merely the hotel's cheapness that drew a counterculture clientele, but its style, which was set by the legendary Madame Rachou, who ran the place. Madame Rachou was a short woman, "as high as three apples," in the French phrase, so short that when she was behind the zinc-topped bar she stood on an overturned wine case. She had curly white hair and a rather stern, bulldog-type face, but in fact she was the soul of tolerance and understanding. She had seen the world go by and did not judge. If you wanted to smoke dope in your room or invite an Algerian hustler to spend the night, that was all right with her. A dilapidated refuge of live and let live, the Beat Hotel resembled that legendary establishment described by Ludwig Bemelmans, which had a sign in the lobby that said, "No opium smoking in the elevators." In addition, Madame Rachou was arbitrary about whom she allowed to occupy her rooms. "She has her orders," Burroughs would say. Her first impression was final, she either liked you or she didn't. It was preferable to be introduced by someone in good standing, so that the hotel clientele grew into a sort of extended family.

Allen Ginsberg had a first draft of *Naked Lunch,* which he took around in November to show to Maurice Girodias, the founder of Olympia Press. In addition to its regular line of pornographic books, Olympia had begun to publish works of literary quality that mainstream publishers would not touch, such as Vladimir Nabokov's *Lolita* and J. P. Donleavy's *The Ginger Man.*

Maurice Girodias was the son of Jack Kahane, a wealthy Jewish gentleman from Manchester who married a French girl, Marcelle Girodias, and settled in Paris. In the thirties, Kahane founded Obelisk Press, and became the first publisher of Henry Miller, who used to drop around the office to borrow a few francs when young Maurice was filling in. His father died in 1939, and during World War II Maurice adopted his mother's name—it was that or the Yellow Star.

In 1953, Girodias launched Olympia Press, with its line of what he called d.b.s—dirty books, in the green-jacketed Traveler's Companion series. These were books written in English and sold in bookstores in France, mainly in Paris and a few other cities where tourists gathered. It was a seasonal operation. He would starve through a bleak touristless winter, but as soon as the first buds were on the trees, he would print (on credit) a catalogue announcing the new crop of d.b.s, as yet unwritten. The catalogue was crucial, for it was sent to 2,000 regular customers, most of them in England, and it was only when their orders came in that Girodias was able to commission authors and pay the printer. Here is where Girodias's inventiveness came into play, for each year he had to dream up provocative titles to lure potential customers—*With Open Mouth,* by Carmencita de las Lunas; *I've Got a Whip in My Suitcase,* by Beauregard de Farniente; *White Thighs*, by Count Palmiro Vicarion. With each new title, there was a short summary of the contents, and soon the checks started arriving in envelopes marked URGENT—PLEASE EXPEDITE AT ONCE, and the books weren't even written.

Fortunately, there were a lot of young American would-be writers and would-be poets hanging about Paris at the time, who were only too happy to accept a $500 fee to write a d.b. under the pseudonym that Girodias assigned. Patrick Bowles, a resident of the Beat Hotel, wrote *Roman Orgy* as Marcus van Heller. Iris Owens, who later wrote novels under her own name, wrote *The Woman Thing* as Harriet Daimler, and Girodias always maintained that she did her best work for him, that the pseudonym had somehow freed her creative powers. He also recruited from the *Merlin* group, young Americans and Brits who were putting out the literary quarterly *Merlin*. The poet Christopher Logue was Count Palmiro Vicarion, the novelist Alexander Trocchi was Carmencita de las Lunas, and Richard Seaver, long before his rise in publishing, translated Apollinaire's *Memoirs of a Young Rakehell*. Not everyone could write a d.b. George Plimpton, later founder of the *Paris Review,* sent a few trial pages which Girodias found so silly and vulgar that he had a hard time finding neutral words to express rejection.

Girodias produced about twenty d.b.s a year, in editions of 5,000. He saw himself as invading the priggish Anglo-Saxon world with his erotic armada. Aside from his mailing list of 2,000, he could count on about a dozen Paris bookstores, and half a dozen in Nice and Cannes, where American sailors bought armfuls of d.b.s. They took them back to the States and resold them. Without the Sixth Fleet, Girodias would have gone bankrupt. Brentano's in Paris was his single biggest outlet. There was a hidden shelf stocking Olympia Press books. Tourists in the know headed straight for it, and spent no time leafing through the d.b.s; they just bought them and left. Girodias was convinced that there were British visitors who came to Paris especially to buy his books, and maybe take in the Folies Bergères while they were at it.

As he fortified his mailing list and composed his annual catalogue and hurriedly got the books printed in time for the summer influx, Girodias had a nice little business going, except that he found himself embroiled in an ongoing struggle with the forces of censorship. Mild and soft-spoken, with the fretful manner of someone who thinks he is being followed, Girodias was an unlikely crusader. But he was forced into it, having a stubborn streak that made him unwilling to capitulate to harassment which he felt smacked of the police state.

It was, he felt sure, the example of four years of German occupation that had changed France. Censorship under the Germans was a way of life that people got used to, as they did to police surveillance and the use of informers. With time, most people began to accept strict political authority as God-given and normal—they became stooges. After the war, the socialist government in power reasoned that since the French were now accustomed to censorship, why not maintain it? The vice squad, or *Brigade Mondaine* (Worldly Brigade), which traditionally was responsible for gambling and prostitution, saw its responsibilities extended to obscene books. It amused Girodias that the postwar French governments seemed to be placing publishers on the same level as whores and pimps. In fact, as he soon realized, the inspectors of the Mondaine had found another way to collect bribes, the purpose of any vice squad being to generate new, income-producing vices. His vice was pornography, unknown in France, a country famous for its freedom of expression, until it was prosecuted by the *Mondaine*.

Every week, the Ministry of Interior published lists of banned books in the *Journal .Officiel*, and then the *Mondaine* would come around to the bookstores with the list and seize the books. All Olympia Press books were automatically banned, but fortunately there was a bureaucratic gap of about six months between the publication of a new Olympia title and its banning as obscene, and it was within this gap that Girodias managed to sell most of his books.

Nonetheless, he was brought to court and found guilty of *outrage aux bonnes moeurs par la voie du livre* (outrage to good morals by way of books). While appealing that charge, he was charged again, so that between 1953 and 1958 he accumulated six years in jail sentences, which he never served because he was always in appeal. In addition, he was banned from all publishing activities for ninety years and three months, an odd time frame emblematic of the arbitrariness of the proceedings. When de Gaulle came to power in 1958, in the middle of the Algerian war, the censorship laws were strengthened and Girodias virtually had to give up publishing. It was exhausting and expensive to be constantly fighting the entire government apparatus, with no hope of winning.

It was not, however, censorship that finished Girodias, but love of literature. His real trouble began when he deviated from the uncomplicated prurience of d.b.s to publish books with a high literary quality. In 1954, he brought out Samuel Beckett's *Watt,* ten years after it had been rejected by every other publisher, and he also published three other important Beckett novels in English: *Molloy, Malone Dies,* and *The Unnameable.* In 1955, an agent sent him *Lolita,* which had been turned down by a number of American publishers. Girodias loved it, for it seemed to him an apparently effortless transposition of the rich Russian literary tradition into modern American fiction. He wasn't worried about possible obscenity—the book would simply be banned as all his books were. Nabokov, however, *was* worried about what he called Lolitigation, and didn't want to be identified as a professor at Cornell, which he then was.

When *Lolita* appeared in September 1955, nothing much happened, except that Girodias was inundated with angry letters from his loyal clientele, who having bought the book on the basis of a blurb, accused him of betraying his sacred trust. What were these nonarousing and incomprehensible books by Beckett and Nabokov? "Why are you publishing junk like that?" irate aficionados of porn wanted to know. "Stick to the tried and the true." "You're giving yourself a bad name." "Trash like this is a sheer waste of time." "Any more like the last one and you can strike my name from your list." Many such complaints did Girodias receive.

Then, around December, Graham Greene said in the *Times Literary Supplement* that *Lolita* was one of the three best books of the year. When other London newspapers accused him of promoting pornography, the book became a *succès de scandale.* As it happened, there was a clause in his contract with Nabokov that gave Girodias 17.5 percent on all American sales, even though he was pretty sure that there would be no American sales, since he expected the book to be stopped at customs. The Customs Service was then the most active agent of federal censorship in America, deciding by fiat which books would be allowed into the country and which would be seized. If they were seized, which Olympia Press books usually were, they were denied the chance of obtaining an American copyright. But this time, Girodias knew not why, when he sent a copy of *Lolita* through the U.S. Customs, and wrote to ask what had happened, he received a reply that the book had been examined and found acceptable for American readers. What a bonanza, and what a fluke! A minor customs official had written a two-line letter that went against all the rules of his department and that enabled Girodias to secure the American copyright and to sell *Lolita* to an American publisher, Putnam's, who brought it out in 1958. The book's enormous success—it quickly rose to the top of the bestseller list, unseating *Dr. Zhivago*—made Girodias richer by $300,000. In another instance, however, that of *Candy* by Terry Southern and Mason Hoffenberg, Girodias was unable to obtain copyright, and when that book, too, was published by Putnam's, there immediately appeared a number of pirate editions in various parts of the country. (If you want to see an authentic Pavlovian reaction, just say the word "Girodias" to Terry Southern and watch the frothing at the mouth.)

For reasons buried in his psyche, Girodias was cavalier about money. When he didn't have it, he would employ almost any ruse to get it, but when he had it, it burned a hole in his pocket. At the age of fourteen, as soon as he had a few thousand francs, he would go and buy a shirt at Charvet, the most expensive men's store in Paris. Now, with his *Lolita* money, he had more grandiose plans. He bought a building on the rue Saint-Séverin, a few blocks away from the Beat Hotel, which he turned into a conglomerate of nightclubs and restaurants, called the Grande Séverine. In the cellar, the sixteenth-century vaults of which had been restored at great expense, there was a restaurant with a Brazilian samba band; on the ground floor a French restaurant; above that the Blues Bar, which served Soul Food and had Hazel Scott at the piano; and on the top floor a Russian nightclub called Chez Vodka, with a balalaika ensemble. The decor was eclectic. At one point, Girodias had unsupervised birds flying around the patio and crapping on the customers.

No surer scheme for losing unlimited amounts of money could Girodias have devised. It wasn't the censorship laws in France or the copyright laws in America that did him in, it wasn't the loss of his reputation among the porno patrons for publishing "literature," it was his obstinate delusion that he could operate nightclubs and restaurants at a profit. On top of that, in 1964 he opened a theater, and his first offering was an adaptation of the Marquis de Sade's *Bedroom Philosophers,* with the result that he was raided by the police and had to close down shop completely.

Girodias had no choice but to declare bankruptcy, as he was being sued by several authors for reasons that had to do with the nonarrival of money they felt was owed them—notably Nabokov and J. P. Donleavy, author of *The Ginger Man.* The most persistent was Donleavy, who kept up the litigation for more than fifteen years.

In 1972, Girodias saw the chance to outwit Donleavy and buy back his bankrupt company for next to nothing. A public auction of the assets was arranged by the bankruptcy receiver, which was to take place at the *Tribunal de Commerce*. Girodias had the fix in, so that the auction was not announced or publicized in any way. He figured that by maintaining complete secrecy, he would be the only bidder, and could win the prize for a few hundred dollars. When he arrived at the courtroom on the appointed day, however, he was surprised to see other people there. They looked like tourists, and he imagined that they must have gone astray, that perhaps they were looking for the *Sainte-Chapelle* and had somehow wandered into the commerce tribunal. But *sapristi!* when he started bidding, they bid against him, going up a thousand francs at a time, and the bidding soon reached nine thousand dollars, an amount that Girodias could not raise, and he had to drop out. He later learned that the other bidder was Donleavy's wife, who also had the fix in. Donleavy became the owner of Olympia Press, and Girodias reminded himself that after all, it was a mythical entity, with more liabilities than assets, such as Donleavy's suit, which was canceled now that he owned the company. And so, at an unheralded auction in a little-known tribunal, ended the short but notorious heyday of Olympia Press. A lot of the authors that Girodias had published were mad at him, but he could say in his own defense that if he had not published their work first, they would never have found a mainstream publisher. He had stepped in at a time when brilliant unpublished work was available, and he had helped to slay the beast of censorship. It was thanks to Girodias that you no longer had writers sitting in front of their typewriters and saying, "There's no point in my writing this sentence because I couldn't get it published." The trouble with Girodias, though, was that he constantly shot himself in the foot. For Nabokov, Donleavy, Terry Southern, and a number of others, however, Olympia had been a halfway house on the path to literary fame.

It was with the thought that only Girodias could publish a book as outrageous as *Naked Lunch* that Allen Ginsberg came to see him in November 1957 with Burroughs' manuscript under his arm. "I have this manuscript that I've brought back from Tangier," Allen said, "and it's by Bill Burroughs and it's the masterpiece of the century." Girodias wished he had a thousand francs for every time he'd heard that phrase, "masterpiece of the century." He probably heard it every day, there were so many people coming through promoting unpublishable writing. It was a phrase he had come to distrust, and when he saw the condition of the manuscript that Ginsberg handed him, he distrusted it even more. The manuscript seemed to have been nibbled at by the rats in the Paris sewers. It was completely dilapidated and unreadable, with pasted-over paper patches, and all sorts of loose bits and pieces. With his innate French sense of order, Girodias was offended by this . . . palimpsest. He was convinced that an untidy manuscript was a sign of perverse instability in the author. A manuscript like that smelled trouble, and there would be more trouble if he got involved. So he told Ginsberg that whatever it was, it wasn't a book, and that if he could get Burroughs to put it into shape he would be glad to take another look at it. Allen figured Girodias didn't want the book because it didn't fit his d.b. formula—it was emetic rather than erotic. Girodias was thinking in terms of books that he could peddle to 3,000 horny sailors off a Sixth Fleet carrier in Nice on a twenty-four-hour pass who wanted something to jack off to on the long voyage home. Allen was crestfallen because Girodias was his only hope, and it seemed to Girodias that he left with a mournful expression on his face.

Burroughs arrived in Paris in mid-January 1958, and Allen found him a room in the Beat Hotel, which he liked. The room smelled of dust and Gauloise cigarettes, and you could do pretty much what you wanted, nobody bothered you. Nobody came bursting in *pour faire la chambre,* they didn't care whether they made the chamber or not. You could paint on the walls and bring your own furniture in, and in the bar, a glass of wine was cheaper than a cup of coffee.

Allen had been apprehensive about seeing Burroughs again. Would Bill try to claim him, and start the sex *schlupp* lover routine? Who would save him, now that Peter Orlovsky had left for New York, from sordid sorrows with Satanic Bill? On January 19, they sat down and faced each other, and Allen confessed all his doubt and misery. But then Burroughs said that in the last few months he had gone through changes, and that his trip to Paris was not to claim Allen but to clear up his remaining blocks with the help of an analyst. He had fallen into such despair in Tangier that he had finally prayed to God and been answered, and seen his benevolent soul emerge. In his own way he had found what Allen already had, a vision of a large and peaceful central force. He had developed a method of meditation which consisted in letting his worst fantasies emerge rather than shutting them up or rejecting them as unwholesome. He had terrible fantasies, horrible homicidal fantasies such as killing Allen and killing Peter, and he had to come to terms with them and realized that they were a part of him. Allen agreed. All fantasies, such as Peter's of being drowned by Allen, or of suffering a lonely death, were parts of us which were TRUE. They had to be let out in full force, rather than suppressed, no matter how painful. Only when they were accepted as true did they lose their horror and their force, which came from trying to deny them, and then you could look at these vile parts of yourself unafraid. By consciously running through your fantasies, you could end up with a great feeling of liberation, attaining the level of the impersonal watcher, benevolent and clear.

Burroughs said he had gone far in this process, but that there was something underneath it all so horrible that he could not get at it— something to do with his nurse. He would begin to get near it, and then he would have such a feeling of fright that prickles would go up his neck and he couldn't continue. It was the memory of something so awful that he had suppressed it all his life, as if he had as a child murdered someone and blanked it out. To show Allen how he went into meditation and cleared his mind, Burroughs suggested that they try it together. He stood by the bed in silence, looking blank-eyed and strange, with a face like a mask, and Allen got scared, thinking he might turn into a monster and kill him. But Burroughs, sensing Allen's fear, came back to normal and they both relaxed.

Bill really had changed, Allen thought. He wasn't interested in sex, and he talked about trying women. He was affable with all the young hip pot-smoking cats that hung around the Beat Hotel, and became their favorite, talking to them endlessly about junk or growing tomatoes in Texas, and becoming this great monument of endless benevolent objective talk and practical judgments about everything from cancer to tea.

In the Beat Hotel, Burroughs found a congenial atmosphere that was not unlike Tangier, with a population of down-and-out young poets and artists, hustlers, dope dealers, and various other maladjusted types. He felt quite at home, surrounded by this ongoing Lower Depths, Left-Bank-Paris-in-the-Late-Fifties spectacle. Guy Harloff, the movie-Aryan Dutch painter who had led the Beats to the hotel, amused him by coming on with all this working-class Communist stuff, whereas Burroughs knew that his family was wealthy and gave him a generous allowance. That was why Madame Rachou extended credit and drinks on the cuff. His was the well-upholstered proletariat. Harloff was a bad drunk who would start breaking the furniture. Once when a little Jap was arguing with him he said: "What you talk? I beat you down to a pulp."

Then there was Sinclair Beiles, a scrawny young South African Jewish poet who had been in and out of institutions. He became a great admirer of Burroughs' work, since he, like Burroughs, tended to see society as a network of control mechanisms. "Once it gets out that Ego is CON-

TROL'S blind," he wrote Burroughs, "which prevents people from realizing they are entirely voice-sent into their straitjacket roles or careers or cells, then the whole pack of civilized bullshit collapses." Beiles would have lonely tantrums in his room, and the only one who could shut him up was the fat Swiss cleaning woman, who would bang on his door and say, "Be quiet, you dirty beast." He had an original and interesting but scattered mind, and was unpredictable in his behavior. Once he and Gregory Corso and Burroughs were walking along the Seine and stopped to look at a group of tourists boarding a *Bateau Mouche*. Sinclair Beiles suddenly dropped his pants in front of them and stuck his finger up his ass. "This is deplorable behavior," Burroughs said. Not to be outdone, Corso accused Beiles of being a social climber.

Another congenial and Tangier-like figure was the Arab pusher with very good heroin called the Hadj, which meant that he had made the pilgrimage to Mecca. The Beat Hotel was on his daily rounds, and among his regular customers were several authors of d.b.s, who, as they turned out their daily quota of fantasy sex, had no interest whatever in the real thing, being knocked out on junk: "Hey, how about an orgy in a Boy Scout camp?" "Naaahhh, it's been done and done." Girodias would give them advances to buy a typewriter, and they'd hock the typewriter to buy junk.

One of the worst offenders in that respect was Mason Hoffenberg, who had been in France since 1948 and was married to the daughter of the distinguished art historian Élie Faure. Despite his drug intake, Hoffenberg was a prolific author of d.b.s, not only as the coauthor of *Candy*, originally written under the pseudonym Maxwell Kenton, but as Hamilton Drake, author of *Sin for Breakfast*, and Faustino Perez, author of *Until She Screams*. In the opinion of Burroughs, Hoffenberg was a kicking junky, that is someone who gets on junk because what he really likes is the pain of withdrawal, and he was also one of those people who somehow bring death to those around them. "Why don't you get on or get off?" Burroughs asked him one day, telling him about Dr. Dent. Hoffenberg went to London in 1961 and was waiting in the entrance of Dent's clinic when he heard someone say, "I think he's gone." A few minutes later a nurse told Hoffenberg, "He can't see you." Dr. Dent had just died of a heart attack. Years later, back in New York, when he was on the methadone program, Hoffenberg was in the 55 Club on Christopher Street with a couple of junkies. He took off his coat, in a pocket of which he had two bottles of methadone, and went to the men's room, and when he came back his two friends were gone and so was the methadone. The dosage was too strong, or they didn't know how much to take, or something else went wrong—in any case, they both died. Hoffenberg was an early fan of *Naked Lunch,* which as a member of the Olympia stable he promoted to Girodias. "Maurice is a fool for not publishing it," he told Burroughs. He died in 1986.

Also reminiscent of Tangier was the fellow who went from one fruitless scheme to the other. One young fellow called Graham, who had been selling encyclopedias on army bases, arrived at the Beat Hotel. The trick was to wangle a way into the base, where salesmen weren't allowed. Then you'd go up to a soldier and ask, "Are you a vulture for culture?" Graham gave that up for Hong Kong suits—an Oriental tailor would take your measurements but you'd never see the suit. When last seen, he was headed for Puerto Rico, to raise woolly monkeys for zoos.

Mack Thomas, a saxophone-playing young Texan, was one of the young men who liked to drop in on Burroughs and talk. It seemed to Mack Thomas that Burroughs spent most of his time in his room, with his pants folded at the end of his bed, scribbling, going through notes, and complaining about the hotel's electric circuitry. Mack Thomas, who would go on to write two autobiographical books that displayed considerable talent, was perceptive in his appraisal of Burroughs. He saw a man who had never belonged and who never would and who would blame himself all his life. He wanted to belong on some prestigious level that he'd been cheated out of, and this was the form his ambition took. Others thought Burroughs was strange, but never did Mack Thomas think he was anything but stark raving sane.

And yet Burroughs was a man separate from the rest of humanity. Mack Thomas saw him on an almost daily basis, but never felt that he got close to him. You got to the point where he said, "No, you don't understand, don't come any closer." And so he went deeper into isolation, into the far end of solitude. "The night is my diocese and silence is my ministry," in the words of Thomas Merton. Burroughs seemed to have no identity concept other than man's basic depravity, no standard other than guilt and innocence. He was such an accumulation of irregularities that in a sense it was embarrassing to acknowledge his existence. And yet he had to be acknowledged, if only for his refusal to be homogenized.

Perhaps it had something to do with the genetic roulette. All the swallows that left for Capistrano did not get there. So that the only thing left for Burroughs was to cultivate his sense of indignation and defiance. Mack Thomas saw his writing as an application for permission to exist. He was always a man with a plan, and there was something relentless in his pursuit of it. Nothing stopped him. He was in an endurance contest with himself. And he was also doing penance, and his writing was also a documentary record of that penance. Mack Thomas sensed that Burroughs was one of those outcasts who would achieve distinction. After years of rejection, after orgies of rejection, he was still using indignation as energy and saying, "I'll show you, I'll give you creative imagination."

There was a random, happenstance flavor to life in Paris, with the direction of the day determined by who you happened to bump into. "The first dreamy warm day of spring," Allen wrote Peter Orlovsky on April 6, "we all left our coats home, me and Bill out for walk, found Gregory talking with young French girl with big purse, and in front Iris, one pornography writer girl [Iris Owens, who wrote for Girodias], and Al the Shades Levett, drummer, with a spade named Money, and another tall blond nervous type with a mustache, so we all drifted along toward Luxembourg Gardens, and on the way met a banjo artist, Jack Elliott, and his wife, and wandered in the park until who should we meet but Mason [Hoffenberg], also out for a junk cure constitutional walk, we all stopped and ate ice cream and talked about man-eating piranha fish and sharks."

One day Allen and Gregory ran into the director John Huston, who had just finished making a movie with Errol Flynn about white hunters in Africa, *The Roots of Heaven.* Gregory went up to him, and, by way of introduction, said, "Why do you always have guns in your movies, man?" "Don't you call me 'man,' " Huston replied, but accepted their invitation to have coffee in the Bonaparte, where they proceeded to tell him what a great movie *Naked Lunch* would make. Huston begged off, but invited them to a cast party he was giving on a houseboat in the Seine, thinking perhaps to introduce an antic element.

They showed up with Burroughs and a young, large, wild-eyed would-be actor by the name of B. J. Carroll, who, under the influence of abundantly flowing champagne, started baiting Errol Flynn, saying, "Hey man, I hear when you were flying an airplane someone popped a popper under your nose." "Go away, sonny," Flynn said, at which B. J. Carroll poured his glass of champagne over the star's head. A couple of bodyguards then grabbed B. J. Carroll and tossed him into the Seine. Allen was dismayed. The Beat generation was living up to the billing of all its attackers, creating public scandals in the houses of the mighty. It was really a shame, because up until then, Huston had been taking them quite seriously as young poet-intellectuals, and had invited them aboard the boat, and now they had egg on their faces.

Later in April, Ginsberg and Corso left for London, two agents pro-
vocateurs in stodgy old England. At a student gathering in Oxford, Corso
read his new H-bomb poem: "I love you H-Bomb, I see ermine round
your neck, you're so lonely, everybody wants to die by cancer electric
chair old age but not by glorious you . . ." An infuriated anti-Bomb
radical threw a shoe at Gregory and denounced him as a fascist. "Do
you know what it's like to die by an H-bomb?" the students shouted.
Here were the goddamned Americans, who had invented the bloody
thing, and who were now coming over to recite commercials for it—it
was too bloody much! Gregory called them limey creeps and there was
a big riot, and Allen and Gregory were saved from the English equivalent
of lynching by some friendly female students.

In London, they had lunch with Edith Sitwell and tea with Auden, who
had forgiven Allen for his agitated state in Ischia. Gregory, who liked to
make provocative remarks, asked Auden, "Are birds spies?" With sound
English common sense, Auden replied, "No, I don't think so, who would
they report to?" "The trees," said Allen.

Behind the foolery, there was in Allen a serious literary purpose. Everything he did in England, for instance, had some literary association. When
he made a pilgrimage to Burnt Norton, it was in homage to T. S. Eliot.
When he visited Stonehenge, it reminded him of Burke's idea that the
sublime always involves terror, and when he went to Salisbury Cathedral,
he thought of Henry James calling it "the blond among cathedrals." On
the path to a farm, he met a muscular gamekeeper who seemed to have
stepped from the pages of *Lady Chatterley*. He could not spend a day
without conjuring up all sorts of connections, because he was steeped in
British literary tradition.

Rather than thinking of himself as a rebel, Allen saw himself and his
friends as the true heirs of the modernist tradition. If they were rebels,
it was in what they thought of as the Whitmanesque sense of "Unscrew
the locks from the doors! Unscrew the doors themselves from their jambs!"
For the modernist tradition had to be rescued from the tenured philistines
who had falsely appropriated it, the Van Dorens and the Trillings and
the Tates and the Blackmurs, and all the other pusillanimous time-servers
who claimed to be at the center of American literature, which was controlled invisibly from the universities, by the teacher-writers. Allen wanted
to break their stranglehold, to get away from their faculty tea prose, from
their bloodless, gutless, overintellectual approach.

The direct link between the Beats and the modernist tradition, as he
saw it, was through the *Black Mountain Review,* a quarterly produced by

that border post of the counterculture, Black Mountain College, near Asheville, North Carolina. Charles Olson, the six-foot-seven, 250-pound poet who presided over both the high point and the demise of the college as well as the review, had been Ezra Pound's secretary after the war, before Pound was committed to St. Elizabeth's. The editor of the review was Robert Creeley, the poet with the eyepatch who had absconded with Rexroth's wife. On Olson's advice, Creeley wrote Pound asking how to put out a literary magazine, and Pound told him to push three or four writers in every issue and surround them with interesting transitory material, so that each issue didn't look like a grab bag. William Carlos Williams was another Grand Old Man of poetry that Creeley consulted.

Through these consultants, the *Black Mountain Review* was directly linked with two heirs of the modernist movement, Pound and Williams. In its final issue, number seven, in the fall of 1957, the review published work by Allen Ginsberg and Jack Kerouac, and a section of *Naked Lunch* by Burroughs, who was still using the pseudonym William Lee. Thus the lineage was established between modernism and the Beats. But in New York, the literary sachems didn't pick up on what was happening. The *Partisan Review* continued to conduct symposiums on such subjects as "Religion and the Intellectuals." Louis Simpson parodied "Howl" as "Squeal." Kerouac's books after *On the Road* were generally dismissed by important critics. Burroughs, due to the obscene nature of his material, couldn't get published through the front door the way Kerouac had. He couldn't even get published through the back door, for Ferlinghetti at City Lights turned down *Naked Lunch,* saying it was disgusting. Allen had no better luck when he sent a section of the book to Stephen Spender at *Encounter* magazine. Spender replied that he had no interest in "wading through yards and yards of entrails." So that for Burroughs, publication in the *Black Mountain Review* was a crucial break in the pattern of rejection.

Being published together in the *Black Mountain Review* underlined the fact that the Beats were now a bona fide movement. In fact they constituted one of the few American literary movements, for American writers are more often loners, competing with each other like Hertz and Avis to be Number One. In the view of their detractors, who called them Beatniks (a term born of the fear engendered by Sputnik), they were drugged eccentrics whose work was worthless, imaginary rebels advertising their private helplessness, who had created a "conformity of alienation." The liberal establishment scorned the Beats for standing outside the political arena. The Eisenhower Republicans saw them as a threat to American middle-class values and morality. They were repudiated by both the left and the right.

In fact, unlike their wild and crazy media image, the Beats were rather like the English between-the-wars literary movement, the Bloomsbury group. Like Virginia Woolf and Lytton Strachey and Clive Bell and the others, the Beats were close friends who helped and supported one another, mutual back-scratchers who corresponded voluminously when they were apart, who kept journals about one another, who promoted one another's work, and who used one another as characters in their books. Kerouac particularly made copious and impressionistic use of the others in book after book, and Ginsberg did so less directly in his poems. As the political commissar of the group, Ginsberg ceaselessly lobbied for the work of his friends, and managed to create an alternative support system of little magazines and sympathetic critics, in defiance of the established literary authorities.

There was of course little or no similarity in the writing of the three. In his use of landscape to evoke the life of the spirit, Kerouac harked back to Blake—"To see a world in a grain of sand, And a heaven in a wild flower." In his nostalgia and love of America he also harked back to Thomas Wolfe. Kerouac's theme in *On the Road* was how to assert possession of a birthright not through ownership but through mobility. The book was a pamphlet of lyrical instructions for criss-crossing the great American landscape, geographical and spiritual. For had not Walt Whitman said that "Americans should know the universe itself as a road, as many roads, as roads for traveling souls."

As for Allen, with his "Hebraic-Melvillian bardic strain," he had been able, through sheer self-belief and power of conviction, to expand his private agonies, the madness of his mother and the alienation of his friends, into the indictment of an entire society. In style he combined the dirgelike ethnic chant of the Hebrew psalms with the Whitmanesque long line, which was like a laundry line, in that you could hang anything you wanted on it, from dirty underwear to the effigies of your friends.

As for Burroughs, he was the Great Seceder, the artist as outlaw, in the line of Villon and Rimbaud, who had deliberately taken the literary game one step further by writing a nauseating book. His antipathy for all forms of control made him an uneasy leader of the movement, which he regarded at best as a flag of convenience. He felt no strong sense of membership under any literary banner, but having allies had its uses, for he would never have finished *Naked Lunch* without a little help from his friends.

They did have in common that their writing sprang from a reformist impulse at a time of cold-war hysteria and the smothering of the individual, which was essentially a restatement of Emerson's famous phrase, "Society everywhere is in conspiracy against the manhood of every one of its members." Their work stridently challenged the accepted rhetoric of the literary establishment. They created a community of the excluded against the like-minded, a band of unlike-minded. They took chances and lived out what they wrote and made themselves heard. Theirs was a literature of risk rather than a literature of tenure and awards.

Much of their growing fame came through the antagonism they provoked. Another of their bonds was that they were lumped together by their enemies. The day would soon come when J. Edgar Hoover, at the 1960 Republican Convention, would say that Communists, Beatniks, and eggheads were America's three menaces. And in 1958 came the attack from Norman Podhoretz, editor of *Commentary,* who complained for starters that Jack Kerouac in his jacket photograph was unshaven and his hair fell over his forehead. To the bald and clean-shaven Podhoretz, the lobes of whose mind had nineteenth-century European configurations, Kerouac was Struwelpeter, a disheveled ruffian of horrid excess. Podhoretz was against spontaneity, against enthusiasm, against energy. How could a man who in years to come would parrot the views of the Republican establishment grasp the authentic and exuberant American soul-searching of the Beats? If these young men had any sense, he seemed to be saying, they would be brown-nosing the powers that be just as he was instead of rattling bones in closets. So Podhoretz appointed himself spokesman of the rear guard, calling the Beats "the revolt of the spiritually underprivileged and the crippled of the soul—young men who can't think straight and so hate anyone who can." For good measure, he tied them in with the rise of juvenile crime. The complete buffoonery of his attack actually served to validate the Beats—by their enemies ye shall know them. As a result of such attacks, allies began to rally round. Rexroth, despite his personal squabbles with Ginsberg and Kerouac, predicted that the Beats would produce a literature considerably different from what was being produced by passing on the seven types of ambiguity to seminars of born idlers.

Returning to Paris in May 1958, Ginsberg and Corso found that there had been a small revolution, and that General Charles de Gaulle had come to power, on a platform of ending the Algerian war. Walking to the place de la Concorde with a friend, Allen saw the Champs-Élysées lined with hundreds of armed soldiers in battle dress, and squadrons of mounted police wearing silver helmets. It was almost noon, and Allen said, "At noon, two million Communists will swarm past the Madeleine and attack the Élysée Palace. What will you do?" The friend said he would dive into the Concorde fountain and stay underwater.

Back at the Beat Hotel, Burroughs was constantly being interrupted in his quest for a solitary life by young people wanting to meet him, for his underground reputation had spread, and he was now the resident wise man at 9 Git-le-Coeur. He explained to Gregory and Allen that he was working on a method, shown to him by Mack Thomas, for getting rid of unwanted callers. Being polite, he would invite them in, and then he would stare at them while repeating to himself, "I love you, I hate you, I love you, I hate you," and usually they became so uncomfortable they left. If that didn't work, he would visualize their spirit outside the door, and if the picture was strong enough the body soon followed.

One day near the Beat Hotel they ran into the poet Henri Michaux, an ancient and respected survivor of the Surrealist days. Very tall and very solemn, Michaux was a model of bourgeois respectability, but he had in common with Burroughs experiments with hallucinogenic drugs, for he had written some of his poems on mescaline, and had described his experiences with the drug in a book called *Miserable Miracle*. They started chatting, and Michaux promised to come and see them, but when he arrived at the Beat Hotel what did Gregory do but piss in the sink, and it was easy to see that Michaux was annoyed, because he thought Gregory was doing it to shock him. He was even more annoyed when they went for a walk, and while they were standing in a portal, a woman came up and started taking pictures. Michaux thought he had been set up to have his picture snapped with the brash Americans, but then the woman said, "Will you people please move aside so I can photograph this historic portal," and Michaux apologized for his unwarranted brusqueness.

It was easy to be suspicious of Allen and Gregory, however, for in Paris, perhaps in contrast to the decorum and formality of French life, they naturally took the unruly position, the "we-are-mischievous-boys" position. Thus, on June 15, 1958, they were invited to a party in honor of two of the great old Surrealists, Man Ray and Marcel Duchamp. Allen loved their Surrealist objects. Duchamp's birdcage filled with sugar cubes was, he thought, a riddle to free the mind. In any case, Allen got drunk and began to crawl on all fours in pursuit of Duchamp, feeling him up the pants leg and begging his blessing and calling him *cher maître*. Duchamp smiled and chuckled and kept saying, "I am only human." Allen asked Duchamp to kiss Burroughs, in a symbolic passing of the mantle from the great French Surrealist to his contemporary American successor, and Duchamp gamely went along with it, and pressed his thin lips to Burroughs' brow. Allen had a compulsion to meet all the writers and artists he admired, and at the top of the list was the novelist Louis-Ferdinand Céline, who was living in the lower-middle-class suburb of Meudon and was still practicing the profession of doctor as he had since his youth.

The author of *Journey to the End of the Night,* often mentioned as the greatest twentieth-century French novel, had narrowly missed prison or worse for his anti-Semitic views during the war, and had in fact fled with the Nazis in 1944, first to Germany, then to Denmark, where he spent some time in a Danish jail. Burroughs and Ginsberg thought that Céline's wartime record was despicable, but it did not cancel the fact that he was the greatest living French novelist, and that he had been a major influence on them, with his misanthropic vision, his ability to extract humor from the terrors of life, and his use of colloquial and ribald language. In spite of his wartime blunders, thought Burroughs, it would have been a gross miscarriage of aesthetics not to go see him.

They called on Michel Mohrt, an editor at Gallimard, Céline's publisher, for a letter of introduction, and again did not present themselves in a very good light, for Allen was high on cocaine, and disappeared into the bathroom every five minutes to take another snort. Mohrt was a good sport, however, and gave them a letter, and on a sunny day in July 1958, Burroughs and Ginsberg took a bus to Meudon, Corso having decided to stay in Paris to see a girl he was hoping to fuck.

Meudon was on the Seine, and Céline's house of reddish-brown stone was set back from the street and fenced off. When they rang the bell some fierce-looking dogs came out barking, followed by a tall frail man with a disorderly shock of gray hair, wrapped in scarves like an old concierge in spite of the summer heat. As Céline locked up the dogs, Allen asked, "Have they killed anybody?" Replying in English, which he spoke fluently, having made extended journeys to England and America, Céline said, "I just take them with me to the post office, to protect me from the Jews." He still received death threats and anonymous letters, he said, and had his hounds to guard him from fears of being hounded. He launched into classic Céline stories of everything going wrong—the neighbors harassed him, put out poisoned meat for his dogs, the druggist wouldn't fill his prescriptions. "*La vie est pleine de surprises désagréables,*" he said, which Allen and Burroughs thought was not a bad summing up.

"How's your clientele?" Allen asked. "Can you make a living?" Céline shook his head and said, "Oh no, most of the people who come to doctors are middle-aged women, and they only want to take their clothes off in front of a young man." Allen later saw that line in one of his books. Céline had reached the famous writer's plateau, where all he has to do is quote himself.

They sat in a little courtyard behind the house and listened to Céline embark on a rambling monologue, full of odd stops and starts and non sequiturs, like his prose style. He hated the Danes, they were an awful sniveling cowardly people. But when he had been told in Danish that he was going to be shot, it didn't have the same impact as in the mother tongue. It was much more shocking to be given bad news in one's own language. Céline liked to dwell on his prison experience. "One great brute," he said, "simply butted me in the stomach without a word."

Allen brought the conversation back to medicine and asked Céline whether he was a good doctor. "I don't know whether I'm good," Céline said, "but I'm reasonable." His next line was one that Burroughs recognized: "Sick people are less frightening than well ones," to which Burroughs replied, "And dead people are less frightening than live ones." Then they questioned him about the important writers of the day, but Céline dismissed every name they mentioned—Michaux, Beckett, Sartre, Jean Genet. "It is nothing," said Céline, "it is just another little fish in the literary pond." As they left, they handed him copies of *Howl* and *Junky,* which he quickly glanced at and set aside. It was clear that no other work but his own was worthy of serious attention.

At about that time, Allen went back to the States, and Burroughs started hanging out with Gregory Corso. They sat up for hours talking, and Gregory thought that it was almost like love. A warm and tension-free rapport had sprung up between them. Burroughs was back on heroin after a year on the wagon and one day when Gregory dropped by he had a batch and Gregory said, "Bill, can I try that," and Burroughs said, "Yeah, but it's poison, Gregory." Soon Gregory was hooked and joined Burroughs in the daily errands of finding and financing their habit. They became comrades-in-drugs. Gregory had the hotel's attic room, and one night Burroughs knocked on his door, and when Gregory opened it Burroughs looked at him and then said, "Sorry, sorry," and went back down, and Gregory wondered what the fuck it was all about; something had happened that he hadn't caught. Another time in Sinclair Beiles's room, Burroughs started telling Gregory that he was God, and that Gregory was there because of him. Gregory didn't know how to take it, it must be one of Bill's moods, but it was a heavy shot, which made him look at Bill a little askew. Was he full of shit, or did he really have some kind of power? Gregory decided that he did have powers, but they were human powers. When reminded of the incident many years later, Burroughs commented, "No one in his senses would want to be God, and certainly not me. I don't have the qualifications."

Gregory had heard about a rich French junky who was crippled with polio and sometimes hung around the Latin Quarter cafés, and who rode around in a chauffeured Bentley. One day he noticed a Bentley parked outside the Monaco Café, and peering inside, he saw a sharp-faced man in a wheelchair, and went up to him and said, "Would you like to meet a very wise man?"

The polio victim was Jacques Stern, member of a venerable and wealthy French Jewish family. He had spent the war years in the States and had graduated from Harvard. His money was tied up in various trusts, so that periods of flowing cash were followed by periods of bailiffs at the door. He had been to India with his friend Harry Phipps, where they sampled a cornucopia of drugs and amused themselves by conducting rickshaw races. When he tried heroin, he knew it was what he was looking for, it was a downer, like death, it was just what he wanted.

Jacques Stern represented the carriage-trade side of hard drugs, the wealthy young people who had no trouble obtaining it and whose money insulated them from the seedy aspects that Burroughs had come to know so well. Stern had a large apartment on the rue du Cirque, and boasted that he had spent half a million dollars decorating it. He had a long-limbed gorgeous American wife with thick red hair, named Dini. He had all the right baubles to which his money entitled him.

There were in Jacques Stern two opposing impulses playing tug of war inside his head. One was the need to be a masterful, successful hero. To convey that side of his personality he was always bragging. Before polio, he had been an outstanding athlete. His financial advice was sought out by the gnomes of Zurich. He was one of the three or four great lovers of the world. He was a bibliophile nonpareil, with one of the finest collections of Molière first editions. The other side of him was nihilistic and antilife, and it was this side that he satisfied with heroin. Combining both sides of his nature, Stern would give decorous dinners at Maxim's for a dozen friends, and afterward he would announce that he had been on drugs during the entire dinner, and he would launch into a lurid account of his slavery to heroin.

"Of course," Jacques Stern replied to Gregory, who took him out of his wheelchair and carried him (he must have weighed about eighty pounds) up the stairs of the Beat Hotel to Burroughs' room, dumping him on Burroughs' bed. Gregory later wondered whether he had done the right thing, for although Jacques Stern had flashes of brilliance, he was a total cuckoo. Burroughs, however, was impressed by his intelligence and the breadth of his knowledge, and they became fast friends. He sometimes felt that Stern was a more extreme version of himself, acting out instincts that he suppressed, in his megalomania and need for power over others. Burroughs was invited for dinner at the rue du Cirque, where the beautiful Dini took him aside to complain about how difficult Jacques was, his screaming, his tantrums. "He's a monster," she said. "Being in the same room with him is like being with death itself." He went scoring for dope with Jacques in the Bentley, and Jacques always paid. When he was in the chips, he was a great check-grabber. Sometimes Burroughs would call and be told, "*Monsieur est fatigué.*" He knew what that meant.

For a while, Burroughs was taken in by the picaresque accounts of his misadventures. With his lurid tales, he might have been a character in *Naked Lunch.* He was in constant danger, pursued by assassins. They had chased his Bentley, which he had crashed into a concrete island at 130 miles per hour, flipping over twice and turning right side up, with not a scratch on him or on the car. He would have to flee aboard his yacht, and would take Burroughs along (of course there was no yacht). Burroughs sent him to take the Dent cure, and Stern reported that he had come down with a severe sinus headache, the pain spreading to his spine and his entire body until two nurses had to hold him down and he bit a piece of wood right in two. Dent had to inject him with huge doses of heroin. Then he went into a catatonic state that lasted two days, and when he woke up he wrote a novel in a week. Burroughs later learned that the story of his stay with Dent was pure fantasy, but at the time he believed it. Impressed by the fragments of writing that Stern showed him, he wrote Allen Ginsberg that "Stern is I think the greatest writer of our time." Recently, Stern told him, he had fallen down a marble staircase and miraculously had suffered only a broken tooth. He certainly was a storm center, thought Burroughs . . . never a dull moment.

Then Stern announced that he and Dini had broken up, and she had thrown him out of the apartment. He wanted Burroughs to do a small favor for him. Burroughs should go over to the rue du Cirque, commiserate with Dini, find some pretext to go into the library, and slip a couple of his small Molière first editions into his pocket. As the recipient of so much of Jacques Stern's largesse, Burroughs found it hard to refuse.

"Dini, nice to see you," he said when she answered the door. "I hope this whole rift between you and Jacques can be solved." He was edging toward the library when she said, "Stop, I know what you're here for . . . you're here for the first editions. Well, instead of that you're going to leave." Muttering to himself, "All right, I did my best," he reported back to Jacques, who launched into a tirade: "You moron, you stupid dope, if you had any sense you could have managed it. You don't know how to do anything, you're totally useless." My heart wasn't in it, Burroughs thought. If it had been, I could have found a look-alike book on the *quais* and made a substitution, after creating a diversion.

That October of 1958, Stern asked Burroughs to accompany him to London to take the Dent cure again. He sent Burroughs over to the rue du Cirque to get $200 from his wife for travel expenses, which he did. Burroughs agreed to go to London, since Stern was footing the bill. After taking the cure, Stern rented a flat at 2 Mansfield Street, where they could continue to kick for a couple of weeks and hit Paris really clean. "You know," Burroughs wrote Gregory from London, "or rather I hope you don't get into a position to know, how it is after a kick. You can't do anything. Spent half an hour putting on cuff links."

Soon enough, however, Stern developed a craving for drugs and sent Burroughs out to make the buy. Burroughs picked up a stash of dope that was hidden under a telephone booth and brought it back to Mansfield Street. As soon as he got there, Stern gave vent to one of his irrational rages. "You conned my wife out of $200," he shouted. "You're nothing but a con man. Get out! Get out!" Burroughs could stand no more. Stern paid the bills but he took it out in abuse. As soon as Stern went out, Burroughs packed and left, after writing his host a note that said, "To call me a con man is one of the most grotesque pieces of miscasting since Tyrone Power played Jesse James." In the street he saw this headline on the newspaper boards: TYRONE POWER DEAD. It was yet another reminder of the magical universe, always weaving its hidden designs.

The situation with *Naked Lunch* was that Girodias had turned it down, but *Black Mountain Review* had published an excerpt. Thanks to Allen Ginsberg's efforts, another excerpt appeared in the spring of 1958 in the *Chicago Review,* a literary quarterly put out by the students at the University of Chicago, by which it was subsidized. Irving Rosenthal, a graduate student who had just been made editor, was excited by the Beats and the San Francisco poets and ran their work in the spring 1958 issue. Burroughs was delighted, and wrote Paul Bowles: "*Chicago Review* is completely sold on my work, publishing it in sections. One is already out—spring 1958—another will appear next issue. . . . Editor says he will publish all I send him." Burroughs rained material on Rosenthal, who wrote Allen Ginsberg: "Burroughs has been flooding me with mss., of which he's sparing me the obscene passages—I will have to clue him—he is the most uneven best writer I ever read, it's unbelievable." That was Irving Rosenthal, a small and contentious fellow, looking like the eighth dwarf in *Snow White*, the one called Quirky. But to Burroughs, Rosenthal was "the only editor who really understands what I am doing."

Rosenthal had in fact become so impressed with the importance of *Naked Lunch* that he published a nine-page section in the fall issue. Aside from its literary quality, Rosenthal felt that the book offered what he and many other homosexuals were looking for—a new image of homosexuality, a way out of the effeminate stereotype that had been imposed on them. Here was a man, assertive and unafraid, who took queerness out of the humiliating, faggoty, teacup-queen, limp-wrist typecasting. There was a liberating force in his writing. He had crossed a frontier for all of them.

When the autumn 1958 issue of the *Chicago Review* appeared that October, with the Burroughs text that included the words "shit," "ass," and "fuck," it aroused the wrath of *Chicago Daily News* columnist Jack Mabley. In an October twenty-fifth column entitled "Filthy Writing on the Midway," Mabley called the autumn issue "one of the foulest collections of printed filth I've seen publicly circulated." The obscene words were like "kids chalking a four-letter verb on the Oak Street underpass." The university "should take a long hard look at what is being circulated under its sponsorship."

Student editors of the review were supposed to have editorial autonomy, but Mabley's outrage put the university authorities on the defensive. Old grads were calling in to complain. Fund-raisers and public relations people said the review's excesses were undermining their efforts. If Rosenthal was allowed to go on unchecked, the endowment fund might be affected. The issue boiled down to fund-raising versus academic freedom. The five-man faculty review board of student publications met on November 3. The novelist and teacher Richard Stern, who was chairman of the board, asked Rosenthal for a list of the contributors to the winter issue, because "the dean wants to know." The issue was devoted to the work of three writers: William Burroughs, Jack Kerouac, and Edward Dahlberg.

Unfavorable winds were blowing, and Rosenthal went to see the dean of humanities, Napier Wilt, a strong supporter of the review, but Wilt told him, "You know, Irving, when it rains you put on a raincoat." The rain began to fall in November when it was decided at faculty meetings conducted by Chancellor Lawrence A. Kimpton that something had to be done to stop the review, because the winter issue promised to be even gamier than the others.

When Rosenthal went to the University of Chicago Press on November 17 to check the galley proofs of the winter issue, he was told by the shop supervisor that the copy had not been set in type. In effect, the issue had been suppressed, but when Rosenthal tried to drum up support, no one was interested. Not Philip Roth, then a young instructor, nor David Riesman, author of *The Lonely Crowd,* who was sympathetic but was leaving the university. Not Nelson Algren, the foremost Chicago novelist, whom one would have expected to champion freedom of expression, but who wrote a letter to a newspaper that said, "Now, in gaining influence so great that we can afford to support infantilism as a trade followed by professional infants, we score another first." Not Richard Stern, who turned against Rosenthal, saying he had used the magazine "as a showcase for one group of writers," and adding, "The faculty board *will pass* on the intellectual responsibility of student editors: those who print the work of cousins, those who print comic strips, and those who rob the till will be asked either to reform or resign." Rosenthal felt surrounded by Judases. He had not robbed the till or printed the work of cousins; in fact he had turned down the submissions of Richard Stern, considering them uneven.

Rosenthal and six members of the *Chicago Review* staff resigned in protest, and he and Paul Carroll, the poetry editor, started their own magazine, which would run the suppressed material in its first issue. When Jack Kerouac heard that they were looking for a title, he sent a telegram suggesting *Big Table.* It derived from a note he had left to himself on his writing desk: "Get a bigger table."

Discouraged by the *Chicago Review*'s demise, Burroughs wrote Paul Bowles in January 1959: "The *Chicago Review* folded out from under me. . . . Also I was denounced in *The Nation* as an international homo and all-around sex fiend. . . . Reminds me of old-time junky talking about the uptown citizens coming down to the Village, he is trying to hustle for the price of an H cap: 'Jesus, Bill, sex orgies they want yet.' "

The first issue of *Big Table* that came out in March included ten episodes from *Naked Lunch,* Kerouac's "Old Angel Midnight," and three poems by Gregory Corso. The issue's subtitle was "The Complete Contents of the Suppressed Winter 1959 *Chicago Review*." The postmaster general at the time, Arthur Summerfield, was known as a hardliner on pornography. He was the one who had shown President Eisenhower one of the juicier passages from *Lady Chatterley,* with the dirty words underlined. "Terrible, we can't have any of that," Ike was quoted as saying. In March, several hundred copies of *Big Table* were held up by the Chicago post office, which didn't deter Rosenthal and Carroll, who had the entire printing of 10,000 copies trucked to New York and San Francisco. In fact, the post office impounding made the magazine nationally known, and the issue sold out.

The A.C.L.U. took the post office to court, and at a trial in federal court in Chicago on June 30, 1960, Judge Julius J. Hoffman, who would later preside at the Chicago Seven conspiracy trial, ruled that the magazine was not obscene, and that the post office decision that it was not mailable should be set aside. Concerning the Burroughs episodes, Judge Hoffman wrote that "the dominant theme or effect is that of shocking the contemporary society, in order perhaps to better point out its flaws and weaknesses, but that clinical appeal is not akin to lustful thoughts." On the issue as a whole, the judge allowed that although the magazine contained "an overwhelming galaxy of four-letter, Anglo-Saxon words or other expressions usually consigned to the category of obscene parlance, it need not appeal to a salacious interest in sex. The use of obscenities in a work is insufficient to classify it as obscene. In this instance the use of shit and fuck violates a cultural and social taboo, to be sure, but not the law." Two years after its suppression by one of the leading citadels of liberal thought, the right of free expression was restored thanks to a federal judge under a Republican administration, and new writing captured a beachhead in the Second City. Thanks to the stir, Burroughs found a following, and *Naked Lunch* became a desirable literary property. *Big Table* continued to publish, five issues in all, and all were mailed. It was a kamikaze magazine, in that it self-destructed when its mission was accomplished.

While the *Chicago Review* and *Big Table* skirmishes were being fought out, Burroughs in Paris was going through strange graveyard days, where frightful fiends did close behind him tread, in the words of Coleridge. Once again the magical universe had opened up before him, yawning and abysmal, and he went through what was perhaps the strangest year of his life, 1959, the scariest and yet the most rewarding, unrepeatable and unendurable, and all because of a chance encounter in the street with the

Tangier painter and restaurateur Brion Gysin, with whom he had previously had no rapport at all.

Gysin, as it developed, became a close associate, friend, and catalyst, in the dictionary sense of speeding up certain processes in Burroughs' mind. He became a pivotal figure in Burroughs' life and work, through the implantation of two or three ideas. Perhaps that was his true vocation, and he was essentially that recurring archetypal figure, the *consigliere*. One can see him down the ages, whispering in the doge's ear, drafting designs for the king's gardens, official astrologer to the czar—conjuring up ideas and prophecies, always presented with perfect pitch for the attentive ear.

In his own art, Gysin was a one-man band, the fellow one sees on street corners with cymbals on top of his head, beating the drum with his foot, as he alternately plays the harmonica and the trumpet. He was a painter, he was a writer, he was a concrete poet, he was a composer and singer. What was he not? Single-handedly, he had made inroads into nearly every art. His versatility was in a sense his demise, for he was unable to commit himself to any one discipline, needing always an escape hatch in case the particular ship he was piloting sprang a leak. Thus, to those whose job it is to measure the work of artists, he seemed to be scattering his gifts. Critics like to slot you, and Gysin was unslottable. He did not function well in the modern cultural world of galleries and publishers, and would have been far happier at court, with a royal patron.

Aside from talent, which he had to spare, what kept Gysin going was a king-size ego, an unusual capacity for self-absorption. What he said about his infancy could serve as the maxim for his entire life: "The world has just recently been invented and it revolves around Me . . . Everything belongs to Me, everything everywhere." He was born on January 19, 1916, in Taplow, Buckinghamshire. His father was a Swiss from Basel raised in England, and Brion inherited the Alpine look, a ruddy complexion (capillaries later bursting in his cheeks), "well planted" hair (as the Swiss say), a long nose made for breathing thin air, and narrow blue eyes as bright as aquamarines. In 1903, Brion's father went to Canada and bought a ranch on the Manitoba prairie, near the town of Roblin. There he later met a girl who was working as secretary for the official historian of Canada. She was one of thirteen children, and when he asked her what her name was, she said, "Just call me Tillie the Toiler." They were married in 1915, but soon left England because of the war. Brion's father joined the 8th Canadians, an infantry regiment known as the Little Black Devils. He was killed in the battle of the Somme, in September

1916. Brion was not yet nine months old. The early loss of his father in war gave him an inability to commit himself to any national purpose. What after all was the true nationality of this Swiss-Canadian hybrid? Was it the language he spoke? He spoke four. Was it the country he lived in? He lived in so many. Brion was a man without predetermined allegiances. What he would become he would choose to become.

After his father's death, he and his mother returned to Canada, where he grew up near Edmonton. He remembered at the age of seven going by sleigh to a winter wedding in a cabin. A shotgun leaned against a wooden chest, on top of which a Hudson Bay blanket was folded. Two wartime buddies had built the cabin and lived in it, and now one of them was getting married. They were all outside in the snow, stained yellow by horse piss, when they heard the shot—the unmarried buddy had blown off the top of his head with the shotgun.

At fourteen, Brion was sent to Downside, a fine old Catholic school in England, run by the Benedictines in a monastery that went back to the Middle Ages. Uninterested in the opposite sex, he started masturbating while looking at the illustrations of Greek statues in the *Petit Dictionnaire Classique.*

Instead of going on to university, he went to Paris, where at the age of nineteen he attached himself to the Surrealist group. Several of his pen-and-ink drawings were hung in the Surrealist exhibit of 1935. But at the last minute, the quarrelsome Surrealist leader André Breton removed the drawings and expelled Brion from the movement. After all, what was the fun of leading a movement if you didn't expel anyone? Breton was famous for his excommunications. He had expelled the poet Tristan Tzara, after Tzara had pulled cut-up words out of a hat at a Surrealist rally and made a poem out of them. But to Brion, knocked off his perch at age nineteen, the expulsion had the significance of a curse, so that all of his later failures seemed to go back to that initial incident—the curse was still at work.

The fuss with Breton had to do not with the quality of Brion's drawings but with the whim of a man in power. It caused Brion to develop a conspiracy theory of his life in the arts. The reception of his work would not be based on merit but on other reasons. Certain interests were working with him or against him. The world was divided into allies and enemies. One result of this cabalistic view was to absolve him of responsibility. If his paintings did not sell, it wasn't because they were derivative but because the art world, controlled by Jews in New York and by cultural bureaucrats in Paris, was out to get him. If his novel *The Process* was ignored by reviewers, it was not because of its overblown style but because the ideas in it were so dangerous that it was being deliberately suppressed. On the other side of the ledger, only when the fix was in did anything positive occur. When he won a Fulbright right after the war, a gay professor who was one of the judges told him, "We gave it to you on the strength of your photograph."

After Paris, he went to Athens, where he got involved with a Greek woman who had a son by him, tall and fair like Brion, whereas she was small and dark. Brion did not recognize or even see his son, who killed himself while still in his teens. He was convinced that the mother of his son had given him syphilis, which in those days took a year to cure. It was another grudge to chalk up against women, whom he had disliked from birth, starting with his mother, who had him circumcised when he was two, against his will, he said.

Brion was the Great Misogynist, a calling he reinforced in Burroughs, who despite his air of impenetrability was quite suggestible, as when he thought for a while that Jacques Stern was a great writer. Burroughs saw his homosexuality as a hindrance, and sometimes talked about switching to women. In fact one night, drunk at a party in Paris, he took a woman home and spent the night with her. But Brion never let up on his sermon that women were no good. Woman was made from Adam's rib, she was a troublesome creature that had once been a part of you. There was a conspiracy of cunts, all out to get you, they were dangerous to meddle with, they gave you diseases. Their interests were not your interests, the main thing being that they didn't have to get it up. That was what it was all about. In sex with a woman, you got a little plus and a little minus plugging into each other, back and forth, to no good purpose.

Brion had his "misogyny rap," a sample of which went like this: "Look at the States, a world run entirely by women. They do a lot more hunting since the Pill—look at the ones who prey on homosexuals, old lionesses with their teeth a bit loose in their jaws, they go out of their way to break up homosexual couples, it's their main hunting-ground, they spot the one that's easiest to devour first. Of course the reason I'm a flop is that I don't have a really potent built-in widow as a wife working for my success morning noon and night. Just exactly what Gala did for Dali all those years. While he was producing, she was on the phone setting the prices and arranging dinner parties. Darling, we're going out with so-and-so tonight and you'd better say so-and-so." Such was the rap, which Brion could turn on like a faucet.

Having no desire to follow in his father's footsteps as cannon fodder,

Brion left for New York via Lisbon in 1940, thanks to a transit visa provided by the American consul. There he met John La Touche, lyricist of *Cabin in the Sky* and *The Golden Apple*, who took him on a tour of Harlem, where Brion graduated from Greek statues to black men. The peculiar form that his self-dislike took was the conviction that the white race were albino freaks. His own oatmealy freckled skin he called "bad packaging."

He worked as a stagehand and assistant costume designer on Broadway, but since he was not a citizen he couldn't join the union, so he found a job as a welder in a New Jersey shipyard. In 1943 he was drafted and sent to Japanese language school, where he learned the rudiments of the calligraphic techniques that would become an important element in his painting. In the army he met the great-grandson of the original Uncle Tom, the Reverend Josiah Henson, whose biography he wrote. On the strength of that, he was awarded a Fulbright in 1949 to study the slave trade in Bordeaux.

Bordeaux he soon found boring, and he headed for Paris, where he ran into Paul and Jane Bowles, whom he had met in New York. Paul remembers him shooting flaming bamboo arrows out his hotel window, which terrified Jane, who was sure they would all be arrested. A friend just back from Tibet had brought the arrows, with cotton tips soaked in alcohol. Brion was at loose ends, and Paul suggested he visit Morocco. He went for a week, and stayed twenty-three years. It was the *coup de foudre* (love at first sight), as the French say. In Morocco, Brion found his culture of choice, and immersed himself in it, thanks to his painter friend Hamri, who showed him all the special details of Moroccan life— how to wash himself, how to fold a blanket, how to prepare a *sebsi* (kif pipe). Thanks to Hamri, he had an entrée into Moroccan circles where he would not normally have been accepted. In Fez, the father of one of Hamri's friends told him, "You are the first Christian to have entered my house in a thousand years, except for slaves." Brion, who always knew the right thing to say, replied, "Are we all not the slaves of Allah?"

Brion had gone native with a vengeance, thought Paul Bowles. He dressed like a Moroccan, he ate like a Moroccan, he lived with Moroccans. Like Pierre Loti, he was in search of the picturesque. Paul thought the whole process was false. Since he was not Moroccan and had nothing to do with Moroccans, to try to be like them was absurd. Paul's attitude was that of an outsider, a tourist who had taken root but was still a tourist. He didn't think of himself as Moroccan, but as a New Yorker who happened to be living in Tangier. What, he wondered, was the urge that prompted people to disguise themselves? Perhaps Brion was suffering from identity diffusion, having already had four nationalities—English, then Swiss, then Canadian, then American. Having no idea who he was, he had decided to be Moroccan.

Of course, thought Paul, he had a natural inclination toward Moroccan life, since he was always intent on making everything strange and exotic. He was a self-described mythomaniac, who would embroider on a story with a basis of truth, and what was amazing was that he always remembered what he had told you. Also, he was a bad drunk, and had once gone after Hamri with a candelabra after closing hours, when he was running his restaurant, the 1001 Nights. Paul's Moroccan friend Mrabit thought Brion was a monster, because Brion had come around drunk one night and started saying Moroccans were no good, all they knew how to do was wash their asses, and the king was a whore, and Mrabit loved the king. Another time, Mrabit caught Brion sneaking a pill into his glass of mint tea, and was sure that Brion was trying to poison him, and he never forgave Brion for that. Jane didn't like Brion either; she said he was sadistic and an alarmist, who wanted to upset everyone and make everyone unhappy.

What Paul did not see was that by going native, Brion learned things unavailable to an outsider, and among these was an initiation into Moroccan magic. Hamri was a great believer in and student of magic, and a great client of magicians. Brion saw that magic was a routine part of daily life, that every day in every village in Morocco, potions were being brewed and spells were being cast. He was in the thick of *"la magique étude que nul l'élude"* ("the magical study that no one escapes"), in the words of Rimbaud. In Hamri's naïve renderings of Moroccan life there was magic—a witch on a terrace calling the full moon down into a basin of water, forming decipherable images. There were connections in this magical universe, quite apart from the flim-flam of crystal balls.

There was no doubt in Brion's mind that much of what happened in Morocco was the result of magic. He had direct evidence of it when he was operating the 1001 Nights. A ventilator shaft led out of the kitchen into the calle Garibaldi, and one day Brion decided to check whether it had been oiled. "Give me a ladder," he told Hamri, "I want to take a look." Inside the ventilator he found a small packet. Enveloping the packet were seven shards of mirror, seven spotted pebbles, and seven large seeds of some kind, all stuck together with chewing gum and pubic hair and menstrual blood. Inside the packet there was a message in Arabic that Brion could not read, and two little objects carved out of a piece of lead sheeting. One of them was the head of a bull, as big as a fingernail, and the other was a recognizable silhouette of Brion. The Moroccans working in the kitchen, most of them relatives of Hamri's, screeched and ran out when they saw the packet. Brion showed the message to a teacher of Arabic. The writing went across the page from right to left and across the page again, at a right angle, so that it formed a grid. The teacher said it was addressed to the Djinn of smoke and what it said was this: May Massa Brahim depart from this house as the smoke departs from this chimney.

Three days later Brion quarreled with his backer, a wealthy woman named Mary Cook, who told him that she was taking over the restaurant and that his services were no longer required. To Brion, this was not the result of poor management and unpaid bills, but of the packet in the ventilator shaft. A spell had been cast, and he had been brought down by magic.

Through with the restaurant business, Brion wondered what to do next. He asked himself, "What do I have that's different?" The answer was, his year of Japanese calligraphic study. He imagined a grid that would hold Japanese calligraphy vertically and Arab calligraphy horizontally, filling the entire picture space. On the strength of his first picture, he was offered a show in London by Arthur Jeffers, a well-known homosexual dealer who later killed himself after being expelled from Venice, life being no longer worth living. Then Brion went to Paris, invited by Princess Ruspoli to stay on the Île Saint-Louis. That was the side of Brion that Burroughs would come to call "the princess circuit." He loved titles, which he liked to drop the way Hansel dropped pebbles, to help him find his way home.

It was while staying with the Ruspolis in the fall of 1958 that Brion ran into Burroughs in the place St. Michel. Burroughs asked, "Wanna score?" Brion had deliberately kept his distance from Burroughs in Tangier. He saw at once that Burroughs was going to live a Spanish life, since he had a Spanish boyfriend, whereas he was living a Moroccan life, and the two did not mix. In those days there were 20,000 Spaniards in Tangier, and they had a life of their own that Brion had no interest in. You couldn't have Moroccan friends and Spanish friends; it was like cats and dogs. He had no reason to bring someone as strange and foreign as Burroughs into his life, at a time when he was busy putting the restaurant together. But then in 1957 when Kerouac and Ginsberg came to Tangier, Paul Bowles told Brion, "These strange people are here and are promoting Burroughs as a great writer." Brion had no idea that he wrote. He thought of

Burroughs as a rather pathetic old junky. But Paul said, "I think you've misjudged Burroughs. If you ever got to know him you'd find him rather interesting."

Acting now to repair his previous mistake, Brion conversed charmingly with Burroughs, and told him he was looking for a place to stay, having outworn his welcome at the Ruspolis. Burroughs got him a room at the Beat Hotel, and they began to see each other daily. Brion was a hypnotic storyteller, and Burroughs found himself listening attentively to his tales of Moroccan life. Their minds converged on such matters as the evil nature of women and the importance of the magical universe. Brion conversing at his best was a stellar performance made up in equal parts of free association, baroque descriptions, bits and pieces of arcane information, puns, japes and drollery, snatches of French and Spanish phrases, and much imaginative embellishment. Listening to Brion talk was a little like watching a man covered with elaborate Japanese tattoos. You might wonder what the point of it all was, but it was hard to take your eyes away.

Burroughs was particularly taken with Brion's account of Hassan I Sabbah, a Persian figure of the eleventh century known as the Old Man of the Mountain, and a contemporary of Omar Khayyám. Hassan I Sabbah was a religious agitator who founded a sect called the Ismailis (today headed by the Aga Khan). For thirty-five years he lived in a mountaintop fortress called Alamout, at 10,000 feet, in a valley south of the Caspian, not far from present-day Teheran. He devised the maxim "Nothing is true, everything is permitted," and lived up to it, recruiting political assassins who were fed hashish for motivation.

Paul Bowles was sure that Brion's interest in Hassan I Sabbah stemmed from his fascination with power and intrigue and the idea that one man could manipulate hundreds of others through the use of drugs, just by staying in his castle on top of the mountain. It appealed strongly to his sense of the incongruous. But the story mesmerized Burroughs, for it fitted neatly into his own mythology, which was based on all the different forms of control, including drugs. "Nothing is true, everything is permitted" he adopted as his personal maxim, quoting it in letters to friends and in his work. At this point in his life, Burroughs fell under the spell of Brion Gysin.

Soon, in the shabby premises of the Beat Hotel, strange things began to happen. One day Burroughs bought a keychain in a magic shop called *La Table d'Émeraude*, with a small stainless-steel ball on the end, which he hung from a nail on the wall of his room. Brion came in and started staring at the ball rather fixedly, and suddenly recognized something he saw. Burroughs joined him, looking over his shoulder, and said, "Why yeah, it's your restaurant in Tangier, but where are those people coming from?" A group of Moroccans were coming down the staircase carrying a corpse, as in a Moslem funeral, and passed through the doors and went out. Since they had both seen exactly the same thing, it could not have been based on suggestion. This must be what the Elizabethans called scrying, Brion thought.

He next decided to experiment with mirror-gazing. He had in his room two high armoires with heavy plate-glass mirrors on the doors. He told Burroughs that he would gaze for twenty-four hours if he had help in being handed food and No-Doz pills and cigarettes and joints. The idea was that you could see your former incarnations and be in better touch with yourself. You had to keep staring without closing your eyes, paying no attention to the tears streaming down your cheeks.

Brion at first saw nineteenth-century scientists in their laboratories. Obviously something momentous was happening in their experiments. Then the scene shifted, and he saw much more ancient figures, like a horde coming off the Asian steppes, great chieftains wearing amazing headdresses, with deeply scarred and tattooed faces, fierce warriors, hundreds of them, perhaps from Siberia. Finally they disappeared completely, and Brion found himself looking into a space that was at the same time limiting and limitless—was it an enormous room, or was it a landscape? There was a layer of blue-gray cloud about waist-high, breathing, moving, pulsating, and that was the end—it was like looking at the void.

When Burroughs tried mirror-gazing, he saw his hands in the mirror with the fingers amputated, looking completely inhuman, black-pink and fibrous, with long white tendrils growing where the fingers should have been. As he was mirror-gazing, a young resident of the Beat Hotel named Jerry Gorsaline came into the room and said, "Jesus Christ, Bill, what's happened to your hands? They look all thick and pink." Burroughs wasn't sure what was going on, but the paranormal phenomena were flying thick and fast. He felt that he had crossed an important barrier, and that he was in a very dangerous place, but there was no going back. One thing he knew for sure—so-called death was not final, though a powerful lobby gave out bulletins to the contrary.

The word got around the Beat Hotel that some pretty weird things were going on in Brion's room. Another young American, Nick Smart, walked in one day and exclaimed, "Oh, shit!" Burroughs was looking into one of the mirrors, but reflected in the mirror was someone else's face. Nick Smart swore that the room smelled of sulphur.

Another of Kerouac's children who arrived at the Beat Hotel around that time was Bill Belli. Husky and wavy-haired, with the slightly sullen, knowing manner of the Italian hood he sometimes pretended to be, Belli was the son of a chef in a New Jersey country club and a Sicilian mother, who after reading *On the Road* had hitchhiked across America four times and was now traveling through Europe. He and his buddy Jerry Gorsaline, a freckle-faced redhead whose grandfather was the editor Maxwell Perkins, got rooms at the Beat Hotel and knocked on Burroughs' door. Burroughs invited them in and asked them what was happening in New York. "Ahhh," said Belli, "the only thing that's happening is juvenile delinquents."

They sat in on some of the sessions with Brion. One time he was wearing a *djellabah,* so that only his face was visible. He went into a trance as Bill Belli, Jerry Gorsaline, and Burroughs watched. The features of his face began to lose their distinctiveness. They began to melt and merge so that his face became blurred. He was standing against the window, and for an instant his face vanished, so that you could see the curtains behind it. Then it came partially back, like an out-of-focus image you're trying to adjust in your binoculars, then it flickered again, then it disappeared again. Bill Belli was sitting there staring at the curtain where Brion's face had been. Then suddenly his face was visible again and he fell to his knees, short of breath, exhausted. Bill Belli looked at Jerry and said, "Did you see what I saw?" and Jerry said, "Yeah," and they compared notes.

Bill Belli was a bit of a skeptic, and the next evening he went down alone to Brion's room and said, "Hey, Brion, I was impressed, but can you do it again? But this time don't get into a *djellabah* and don't look in the mirror, just sit right here in front of me." Brion sat on the bed and crossed his legs and started to go into a trance. The muscles on his face twitched and his face began to dissolve, like a person with brain damage, whose personality does not show on his face. The "Brionness" of the face was gone and in its place was a fleshy formless mass. But that was as far as he got and he said, "I can't do it tonight." He told Belli he had learned the face-vanishing technique from a nomadic tribe in the desert.

Jacques Stern sat in on some of the sessions and saw various changes wash over Burroughs' face. Once Burroughs turned into Paul Bowles, and another time he turned into Khrushchev, with a gold tooth in the front of his mouth. Once Stern felt Burroughs touch his arm across six feet of space. Once Burroughs saw a creature in the mirror wearing some sort of green uniform, its face full of black boiling fuzz; Brion and Jacques Stern also saw it.

Bill Belli had stumbled onto a scene the strangeness of which was hard to absorb. The year 1959 was when all the various ingredients that made up the Beat Hotel came to a boil. It was like a Marx Brothers movie directed by Madame Blavatsky. You had Sinclair Beiles, the South African poet, thin and wiry with a Peter Lorre look, smoking four cigarettes at a time and throwing his shoes into the Seine. He had a German girlfriend he used to chase on the roof with a sword, saying he would pay her back for what the Germans had done to the Jews. He had episodes of terror and paranoia. Seeing a van parked on a street, he would become convinced that it was loaded with electronic equipment intended to track him.

For comic relief you had Jacques Stern and Gregory Corso. Stern being carried up the stairs, cursing and fulminating and throwing money at people. Gregory, that charming little con-man hustler, putting out that the government was afraid of the Beats as a potential revolutionary force, and that they were already infiltrating the movement.

As for Burroughs and Gysin, they were so far out it was scary. They spoke of sinister forces at work, people on Venus, curtains of fire. An arch, clever look would come into Gysin's eyes that meant "I know something you don't." He saw hidden meanings in the time of day, and connections of cosmic proportions in random remarks, and Burroughs was sucked into it.

Brion was a charmer, a dazzler, with a great store of esoteric knowledge, but Belli didn't trust him the way he trusted Burroughs, whom he felt he'd known all his life. Burroughs had a deep, bedrock sanity, and a depth of feeling not worn on his shirtsleeve. One of the things about him that most intrigued Belli was his hang-up with women. At twenty-two, Belli was at the point where he resented women because he needed them. Disturbed by his sexual needs, he responded to Burroughs' misogyny. Belli's strong Sicilian mother had given him a lot of tough love. But Burroughs' mother had clearly resorted to more cunning and devious female techniques of control, and it had had a deeper effect on him. Mother love was smother love, cloying, playing upon guilt manipulation. Burroughs had a way of saying the word "cunt" that was much more eloquent than the written word: "What are you doing with that . . . cuuuunnnnttt . . . ," that lascivious and distasteful . . . thing.

Burroughs as literary outlaw. (*Bill Belli*)

William Burroughs, Sr., Burroughs' paternal grandfather and inventor of the adding machine. (*Burroughs Corporation*)

Laura Lee Burroughs, the writer's mother. (*Burroughs Archive*)

Mortimer Burroughs, the writer's father, with his two sons, Mort (left) and Bill. (*Burroughs Archive*)

Bill Burroughs at the Los Alamos Ranch School, age fifteen. (*Los Alamos County Historical Museum*)

A. J. Connell, director of the Ranch School, and his dog, Peggy. (*Los Alamos County Historical Museum*)

Edith Parker (above), who married Jack Kerouac, and Joan Vollmer (left), who became Burroughs' common-law wife, shared an apartment near Columbia University where the founders of the Beat Generation gathered. (*Photo of Edith Parker: Edith Dietz. Photo of Joan Vollmer: Ginsberg Deposit, Columbia University*)

Allen Ginsberg, Lucien Carr, and Burroughs in the Columbia days. (*Ginsberg Deposit, Columbia University*)

Herbert Huncke in East Texas, 1947. Huncke was one of the Times Square hustlers who introduced Burroughs to drugs. (*Ginsberg Deposit, Columbia University*)

Burroughs and Dave Tercerero, the pusher, in Mexico City in 1950. (*Burroughs Archive*)

Joan Vollmer shortly before her death in 1951. (*Ginsberg Deposit, Columbia University*)

Burroughs being questioned in the shooting of his wife,
Mexico City, 1951. (*Ginsberg Deposit, Columbia University*)

Kiki and Burroughs in Tangier in 1957. (*Ginsberg Deposit,
Columbia University*)

Kells Elvins, Burroughs'
boyhood friend, on a visit to
Tangier. (*Ginsberg Deposit,
Columbia University*)

Burroughs and Brion
Gysin outside the Beat
Hotel in Paris, 1960.
(*Burroughs Archive*)

Maurice Girodias, who first published *Naked Lunch*. (*Robert Doisneau*)

Bill Belli and
Burroughs,
Beat Hotel, 1959.
(*Burroughs Archive*)

Burroughs and Ian
Sommerville, Paris, 1959.
(*Burroughs Archive*)

The psychedelic summer of 1961, Tangier. Left to right: Mikey Portman,
Burroughs, Allen Ginsberg, Alan Ansen, Gregory Corso, Ian Sommerville.
Sitting in front: Paul Bowles. (*Ginsberg Deposit, Columbia University*)

Billy Burroughs with his
grandfather, Mortimer
Burroughs, 1953.
(*Burroughs Archive*)

Laura Lee Burroughs
in Palm Beach. (*Coca-
Cola Co., Inc.*)

Burroughs and sixteen-year-old Billy in Tangier in 1963. (*Burroughs Archive*)

"Dilly Boy" John Brady with Burroughs in London, 1972. (*Burroughs Archive*)

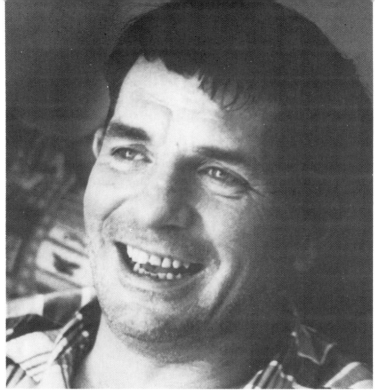

Jack Kerouac, shortly before his death in 1969. (*Ginsberg Deposit, Columbia University*)

Brion Gysin, several years before his death in 1986. (*Burroughs Archive*)

John Giorno photographed by Burroughs, Hotel Chelsea, New York, August 31, 1965. (*William S. Burroughs*)

Terry Southern with Burroughs. (*Bill Yoscary*)

Allen Ginsberg, Peggy Mellon Hitchcock with Timothy Leary, and Lawrence Ferlinghetti. (*Burroughs Archive*)

James Grauerholz, Burroughs' secretary since 1973, before the grave of Raymond Radiguet in Paris. (*Philip Heying*)

Allen Ginsberg, Gregory Corso, Burroughs, and Anne Waldman at Naropa Institute, Boulder, Colorado. (*Burroughs Archive*)

Billy and his father, not long after Billy's liver transplant in 1976. (*Burroughs Archive*)

Burroughs at seventy, in 1984, wearing the rosette of the Institute of Arts and Letters. (*Maarten Corbyn*)

To Burroughs, women were dangerous and inimical, an "I'll-get-you-if-you-aren't-careful" force. And yet, when Belli asked him about Joan, the wife he had shot, he picked up that Burroughs had genuinely loved her and had got it on with her. Belli began to wonder whether Burroughs was a closet heterosexual. Perhaps he lusted after women, but was stuck at some sort of arrested adolescent stage, so that he was so goddamned bashful and frightened, so vulnerable and so exposed, that he had to protect himself. One day when they were sitting in a café, Belli saw him staring at something and he turned around and it was a gal wearing a tight sweater. "Did ya see the treasure chest on that, Billy?" he said. "Bill, are you putting me on or do you like women?" Belli asked. "No, man, no," Burroughs said, getting flustered. Belli thought to himself, I wouldn't be surprised if he fantasized about chicks when he was in bed with a guy. Another time they went to a creepy after-hours place where an old broad was dancing with a gigolo. It looked kinky, and Belli said, "Come on, Bill, let's go." At this point a woman arrived in a long mink coat and it turned out she was a stripper. "You don't want to miss the cabaret, do you, Billy?" Burroughs asked. Belli thought, I'm a cunt-hound and I want to get out of here, and he's queer and he wants to watch this gal strip? So they put some music on the jukebox and the gal did her thing, and Burroughs gave her his undivided attention—he was eating it up.

It seemed to Belli that the level of Burroughs' sexuality was about age sixteen, at the stage when there's an incredible mystery surrounding sex, an incredible excitement and fear. Hot summer days, a hard-on at twilight in the damp grass, the smell of the river-bottom, all the stuff of masturbatory fantasies. Belli could see that a lot of Burroughs' sexual energy went into fantasy, and that his sexual life was more a fantasy thing than a physical sharing, more like masturbating in the company of someone else, private and removed. He was divided between a puritan obsession with dirty sex and his own true romantic nature, as expressed in pining over Allen. He had to defend himself against his own capacity for going completely overboard.

While Burroughs was exploring the magical universe, on the other side of the pond the Beats had become a full-fledged literary movement. Perhaps all bohemian movements begin as a protest against the triumph of the market economy, in the course of which they learn to market their own antibourgeois notoriety. In a healthy society, the impulse to clean out the cobwebs is bound to gain support. Allen Ginsberg saw the poet as a force for social change, Shelley's "unacknowledged legislators." Jack Kerouac was trying to ingest the entire experience of America. Gregory Corso was the poet as anarchist. Burroughs, who was not a part of the hoopla, maintained his stance of loner. In their discontent with American values, with cold-war suspicions, with loving the bomb, with a society shaped by corporate power and moral smugness, they had come up with something more vital. They had restored a sense of adventure to American culture. In their rejection of the boring, the conventional, and the academic, in their adoption of a venturesome lifestyle, they gave everyone the green light to plumb their own experience.

The Beats mastered showmanship; they were attention-getting pranksters, full of hijinks. In subway ads for the *Evergreen Review*, there was Allen Ginsberg in an Uncle Sam top hat, saying, "Join the Underground." Grove Press, which published *Evergreen*, was becoming an iconoclastic force in American publishing. In San Francisco, City Lights was going great guns with its Pocket Poets series. Everyone had been waiting for the shift, for the end of the lull in American poetry, and it had come with *Howl*—the shift from academic credentials to personal brilliance, from a search for values to a search for experience. There was actually now a Beat bandwagon that people were trying to climb up on, for Beat had become synonymous with rebellious.

The Beats, Allen Ginsberg wrote Burroughs in February 1959, had entered the whole social-psychic fabric of America, capitalizing on the thaw from the McCarthy era. Everyone was touched by their individuality and nonconformism and eccentricity. The media mills were grinding, and every day telegrams arrived asking Allen to appear on TV shows. Jack's agent said he could make $500 a night in public appearances. Bob Hope did a skit on the Three Bleats—Talent Ginsberg, Gregorius Corset, and Peter Lovekiss. At Columbia, 1,400 attended a Beat poetry reading and many more were kept out by the police. It was a triumph and a vindication for Allen, who had been scorned by his teachers and who was now invited to the temple to chastise the philistines. "We broke Columbia's back in one night," he wrote Burroughs.

Lord Byron called fame "the thirst of youth," and Allen was thirsty, even though he knew he might be drinking hemlock. "There's no end in sight to fame," he wrote Burroughs, "and I really see what you mean about the hideousness of all that. I'm such a myth in the Village, every time I go in a bar people rush up and talk to some idealized image they have of me . . . I hardly exist and talk as simple Allen any more." Simple Allen was evaporating in the glare of Allen the-poet-as-public-figure.

• • •

In April 1959, Burroughs went to Tangier for a vacation, wanting a change of scene, and landed with both feet in the middle of a big mess. Six months before, he had written Paul Lund, half-jocularly suggesting that they smuggle some Moroccan weed into France, concealed in the camel saddles sold in bazaars to tourists. Now it happened that a pal of Lund's, Captain Stevens, master of the *Amphitrite,* stopped off in the Canary Islands on his way to the West Indies and was arrested for punching a Spanish cop. The boat was impounded in Gibraltar pending litigation, and Captain Stevens, having nothing better to do, came back to Tangier and bought half a kilo of opium from Old Black Joe, the same fellow who had sold the sick-making hash to Jack Kerouac. Arrested for possession of drugs (the carefree tolerant days were over), Stevens implicated Paul Lund and "an American with glasses." The police searched Lund's place and found Burroughs' "camel saddles" letter. Threatened with deportation to England, where he was facing Pen Indef as a habitual criminal, Paul Lund fingered Burroughs as the mastermind of an opium-smuggling scheme. The Moroccan police concluded that Burroughs was the Paris connection for the opium that Captain Stevens had purchased. The police investigation of Lund was going on just as Burroughs arrived on his holiday. One day when he dropped in on Lund the police were there questioning him. Miraculously, they ignored Burroughs, not even asking him for his passport. At the time, he had five grams of hashish in his pocket. If they had searched him, he would have been arrested on the spot and seen the inside of the Tangier jail, known to locals as *la casa.*

Given the untimely presence of the police, Lund had to admit that he had handed over to them Burroughs' letter. Burroughs was furious. What a professional rat Lund was! Anything to salvage the old skin, what? He had really fucked up his vacation. The situation in Tangier was not conducive to relaxation. "I blame myself for knowing you in the first place," Burroughs said. But then Lund said, "You know, Bill, there comes a time when you're broken. . . . They broke me." Burroughs understood only too well, and all his annoyance evaporated. His only hope was that the Moroccan police, having his Paris address, would be too inefficient to pass his dossier on to their French colleagues.

When Burroughs got back to Paris, a copy of *Big Table #1* was waiting, courtesy of Allen Ginsberg. But his delight turned sour when in May he heard that the magazine had been declared obscene by the U.S. Post Office. This, he knew, would make publication of *Naked Lunch* in the

United States impossible. Because of the controversy, however, *Naked Lunch* was discussed, and it came to the ears of Maurice Girodias, who had rejected it the previous year, that the book was being suppressed. Publishing suppressed books was his specialty, and he got in touch with Burroughs through Sinclair Beiles, who was doing editorial work for Olympia, and who had also written a d.b. Or rather, he had rewritten the Chinese classic, *Psi Men and His Many Wives,* giving it to Girodias as *House of Joy,* by Wu Wu Meng. Beiles was the sort who frightens little children, thought Maurice, but he was not without charm or intelligence.

Girodias invited Burroughs to dinner at the Grande Séverine, with Art Buchwald and the French novelist Antoine Blondin, who was drunk as usual. He was a beer drinker, and he had to piss all the time, and to facilitate matters he closed his fly with a safety pin. Burroughs spoke very little French and Blondin spoke no English, but Girodias saw an eye exchange go on between them that expressed complete mutual understanding. As for Girodias, he found Burroughs impossible to grasp, being a completely unprecedented type, a man who looked so intensely respectable and puritanical, and who wrote such obscene prose. He was difficult to talk to because he was so silent and ghostly. Girodias thought of him as a *passe-muraille,* someone who walks through walls. He looked frail and terminal, as though it was a superhuman effort to go on living and carrying suitcases from hotel to hotel. Once, seeing him in the street with a big suitcase, Girodias picked it up because he was slightly stronger and healthier, but Burroughs got very offended and grabbed it back.

Now, aside from publishing, Girodias had a secret passion, which was the tango. All his life, he had wanted to be an accomplished tango dancer, and this was one of the reasons he had gone into the nightclub business, so that he could have a Latin band in the same building as his office. Every day he would take an hour or two off and rehearse tango steps with his teacher, Judy Smith, as the Brazilian band played for them alone. One evening in May he was in the middle of a dip that required his full concentration when he was distracted by a figure coming slowly down the stairs and onto the dance floor. Recovering his balance and his aplomb, he saw that it was Burroughs, who told him that there had been a police raid that morning at the Beat Hotel, and they had come straight to his room and arrested him, having found a gram of hash. It was the fallout from the Paul Lund business. They had driven up in their black Citroëns, tires screeching, although they could easily have walked, since police headquarters was directly across the river, but it was much more impressive to see them being disgorged from their old-fashioned *traction avants,* just like the Jean Gabin gangster movies. Burroughs had spent a horrible junk-sick day while they typed their forms and took his picture. He had been detained at the Préfecture for twelve hours, in the vast Kafkaesque labyrinth of French bureaucracy, and had then been released on his own recognizance. What was he going to do now? Girodias put him in touch with his English-speaking lawyer, Maître Bumsell.

By this time, Girodias had decided that he might be making a mistake in not publishing Burroughs, and wrote him on June 6: "Dear Mr. Burroughs, What about letting me have another look at *Naked Lunch*?" From then on, things happened very fast. Girodias decided to publish, and a contract was drawn up, giving Burroughs an $800 advance, and giving Maurice one-third of the English-language rights. Allen wrote from New York, warning Burroughs to "make sure he doesn't own half of you, as if you were a prizefighter." Girodias invited Burroughs to his restaurant and said: "This is a complicated business full of angles. I know them— you don't. Let me handle it. You will have to trust me." Okay, Burroughs decided, for better or for worse, in sickness or on the nod. He knew that under his timid and confused manner, Maurice was very smart—he also might get lucky with the book. Having seen Kerouac fuck around for five years trying to get *On the Road* published, he figured this was the best deal around. Girodias explained that if the book was sold in America he had a method for avoiding U.S. taxes by transferring royalties to Switzerland, where they would be funneled through his agent, Odette Hummel. Burroughs agreed to this, too, a decision he would come to regret.

In July 1959, Sinclair Beiles, acting as Girodias's go-between, told Burroughs that he had exactly ten days to prepare the manuscript for the printer. The deadline pressure helped to weld the book into one organic whole, with Beiles and Brion Gysin helping with the editing, as section after section was carried by Beiles from the Beat Hotel to the Olympia offices a few blocks away. The sections were sent to the printer in random order, but when the galleys came back the order seemed to work, and they were kept that way, except for a couple of changes. Burroughs corrected the proofs and designed the jacket, and by the end of July the book was rolling off the presses for a run of 10,000 copies, twice the usual Olympia printing.

Quite quickly, there was a small flurry of acquisition. Limes Verlag offered $400 for German rights. Mondadori took it for Italy, but Burroughs was told they were buying it to keep it off the market. Barney Rosset of Grove Press bought the American rights for $3,000. In France,

Gallimard took it, in a translation by Girodias's brother, Eric Kahane, but the book appeared with a *barre noire* (black stripe), meaning that under prevailing laws, it could not be placed in bookstore windows (*interdiction de mise en devanture*). Burroughs made fun of Girodias's crafty publishing arrangements in this mock description of the German sale to Allen Ginsberg: "Contract signed processing through Switzerland where it is registered in the name of a Turkish widow resident of Hong Kong branch office in Amsterdam. Girodias is such a devious fellow who you never know to whom you are a speak." In truth, however, he was gratified, after all these years, to be getting some measure of recognition. The publication of one book gave him the assurance that other books by him could get published, too. In his own hidden way, he had the competitive streak of his entrepreneurial forebears, and measured himself against other writers, as in this inscription in the copy of *Naked Lunch* he sent Paul Bowles: "To Paul Bowles, *****, from William S. Burroughs ****."

Burroughs also had some money in his pocket from the advance, which was not entirely beneficial, for he spent it on drugs. He was back to sitting in his room and staring at his big toe that summer. The poet Harold Norse, recently arrived in Paris, had heard about the strange addict writer who had produced a great book and one day he went to the Beat Hotel and knocked on his door. His room was austere, a bed, two chairs, a table, black-marker drawings of amoeba-like shapes on the walls. Conversation was difficult. He must be on junk, Norse thought.

"I just came here," Norse said.

Silence.

"From where?"

"Italy. I've been living in Italy."

Silence.

"Italy?" A faraway, sepulchral voice, slightly disdainful.

"Yeah."

Silence.

"Don't . . . like . . . Italy."

"Oh, I like the people, the sun."

Silence.

"Hate . . . the . . . sun."

"Uh, haha, well . . . *Paris* is great."

Silence.

"Never . . . go . . . out."

Behind the laconic manner, Norse sensed a forceful personality, but it was a bit like talking to a lizard. Burroughs must be the most haunted writer since Edgar Allan Poe, thought Norse. Despite this unpromising beginning, he started hanging around the Beat Hotel and made friends with the group of writers there. He also hung around the Mistral bookstore, which was run by a tall, thin, sandy-haired, bearded American named George Whitman, who claimed to be a descendant of Walt. His sprawling and rickety two-story building was a combination salon, reading room, and youth hostel. He had beds upstairs for people passing through. Norse noticed the attractive though scrawny English kid Whitman had working for him that summer, and asked him out to dinner. His name was Ian Sommerville and he was attending Cambridge. In spite of his Yorkshire accent and his rapid mumbling speech, Norse could tell that he was bright. He was from Darlington, in the north of England, where his father was a clerk for the railroad, and he had made it into Cambridge on the strength of his mathematical brilliance. He looked like a bird, with sharp features and reddish-blond hair that stood up as though electricity was running out of it.

Norse knew that Burroughs was trying to kick with the apomorphine that Dr. Dent had given him on the 1958 trip to London with Jacques Stern, but he needed someone in attendance. Brion Gysin wanted nothing to do with it, fearful of the psychic changes Burroughs would go through. "Bill," Norse said, "there's a nice-looking English kid working at George Whitman's." "I've never been able to pick anyone up there," Burroughs said. "This kid likes older guys," Norse said.

Burroughs went over to the Mistral and saw Ian standing on a ladder reaching for a book, which slipped out of his hands and landed on Burroughs' shoulder. When Ian excused himself, he provided Burroughs with an opening gambit. Burroughs told Brion Gysin that Ian looked like just the sort of person he could depend upon to be his nurse and run errands and administer the apomorphine, and, as young and inexperienced as he was, still to have a bit of severity.

On August 24, Harold Norse knocked on the door of Room 15, which was opened by someone tall and skinny and stripped to the waist. In the dim light, Norse thought it was Burroughs. "You're not the first," said Ian Sommerville. "I'm just a replica. Bill's trying to kick. You can't see him. He's sick as a dog."

Norse wondered whether Ian could handle it. This innocent young hick from the sticks of England had been catapulted into a wrenching experience with this weird genius with multiple personalities. Ian had adopted Burroughs' laconic manner and slightly nasal voice, like a clone.

"Well, I hope Bill pulls through," Norse said.

"I can't tell you what it's been like, man, it's been fuckin' unbelievable," Ian said, friendlier now, as if trying to make up for his initial abruptness. His hand moved nervously to his head, sweeping back his long straight hair. "I never want to go through this again, man. Hallucinations, convulsions, freakouts, the edge of insanity. I had to hang on to *my* sanity by my fingernails, and they're bitten down to the moons. But it's worth it, man, Bill's getting better."

He was coming down from a codeine habit, and it took him a week. A week of tea and milk toast, of sneezing fits and flu symptoms, of feeling a desperate need for something you don't have, of a feeling of deadness, of visions and psychic occurrences, of blue music and Uranian people in robes, while Ian doled out the apomorphine and the diminishing doses of codeine, until the craving disappeared.

Burroughs did get better, and Ian Sommerville became his lover, and their attachment would last in various forms for seventeen years, until Ian's death in 1976. It was the first emotional commitment Burroughs had risked since Allen Ginsberg. Burroughs deferred to Ian as an authority in the sciences, and Ian deferred to him as a writer of great talent. They spoke as equals. "Ian was William's little Einstein, explaining what the stars were up to," said a friend. Ian was at the other end of the spectrum from the Spanish boys Burroughs had kept for convenience and sex. Where they had been placid and uncomplicated and frankly and reassuringly materialistic, he was nervous and high-strung and moody. He had two sides, one campy and giggly, the other reserved and scientific and fastidious. Everything had to be arranged just so, from the furniture in a room to the way he lined up his pencils on his desk. He had a shy side, which came out prickly, and an uptight English side, where he played the crusty governess, and a donnish side, where he would patiently explain to you the theory of free-floating equations.

For the first time in his life, Burroughs had a lasting love affair, even though it eventually lapsed into a fitful friendship. There was not with Ian the built-in failure factor that there had been with Gene Allerton, because he was basically straight, and with Allen Ginsberg and his need for autonomy. At forty-five, Burroughs was more than twice Ian's age, and initially there was a feeling of respect on the part of the untried younger man for the worldly and accomplished older man. Ian's world was limited to Darlington and Cambridge, and Burroughs opened the door onto exotic vistas, with the possibility of travel and membership in the counterculture tribe.

For the time being, however, although Ian wanted to remain in Paris,

Burroughs urged him to return to his studies at Corpus Christi College in Cambridge and his activities as secretary of the Cantab Heretics Society, a group of iconoclasts who invited like-minded notables to speak and then tried to pick apart their arguments. Back in Cambridge that October, Ian reported that a medical checkup had revealed white pus cells in his urine. The doctor who examined him said it was VD, but another doctor said nonsense, it was kidney disease. In any case, "The antibiotic pills cured all and had the effect of lessening the depth of my habitual melancholy. As much as one can live in symbiosis with other people one can live in symbiosis with one's past and future, so who is to tell what were the important events in Paris?"

One important event for Burroughs was that his drug case was going through the wheels of the French judicial system. On September 25, he appeared before the *juge d'instruction,* or examining magistrate, whose function it was to draw up the indictment and make a recommendation to the court. Maître Bumsell explained to Burroughs that the *juge d'instruction* was very important, and that if you made a bad impression on him your goose might be cooked. Maître Bumsell had managed to get a *juge d'instruction* whose wife had been an addict and who might be expected to show some understanding.

The *juge d'instruction* had a copy of the "camel saddles" letter to Paul Lund and asked Burroughs what it meant. When Burroughs waffled, the *juge d'instruction* said in effect, "Look, I don't want to make a big deal out of this, but don't treat me like a fool." So Burroughs leveled with him, admitting that the letter referred to hashish but had never been put into practice.

In October, Burroughs went on trial before three judges. Maître Bumsell had coached him: If a judge addresses you, stand up, and give very clear, precise, brief answers. If a judge laughs about something, don't you ever laugh—that's one of the worst mistakes you can make. . . . Oh, you think this court is a joke, do you? In fact, all that Burroughs had to say was *Oui, monsieur le juge,* or *Non, monsieur le juge.* Maître Bumsell did most of the talking, his defense being that Burroughs was a man of letters who had unfortunately fallen in with dubious companions, as had so many men of letters in the past. It happened that Burroughs' preface to *Naked Lunch,* on drug use, had just been published in the *Nouvelle Revue Française,* an illustrious literary magazine. Maître Bumsell read portions of it to the court, establishing Burroughs' bona fides as a man of letters. When the judges gave him a suspended sentence and fined him eighty dollars, a huge sigh of relief rose from his lungs. He was lucky to be in what was perhaps the only country in the world where a literary reputation was a mitigating factor in a criminal case. In the United States it would have worked against you. He compared himself to his young friend Mack Thomas, who had recently been sentenced in Texas to twenty years for heroin possession (of which he served five). He had heard from Mack that he had been busted at the height of an antinarcotics crusade under Governor Price Daniels. The feeling in Texas, where Burroughs had once grown marijuana, was rabid—dope fiends were worse than murderers. The stripper Candy Barr got fifteen years for having a joint in her bra. Mack Thomas went through a nightmare, upon which he based his 1965 book, *Total Beast*. When the police questioned him, they handcuffed him around a tree and hooked the electrodes to his balls and to the alternator of their car—if you weren't talkative, that made you think twice. In prison, if you died in the summer, your autopsy report said "sunstroke," and if you died in the winter it said "pneumonia." Burroughs knew he was a lucky man to be out of Texas and out of the United States at that time.

He was now recognized as a writer, not only by publishers in various countries but by the French judicial system. Further recognition arrived on October 1, in the form of David Snell and Loomis Dean, a reporter-photographer team from *Life*, which was preparing a story on the Beats. They spent a couple of days with Burroughs, wining and dining him and handing out Cuban cigars "from Mr. Luce's private stock," and he found them vastly entertaining. They let him know right away that they had read *Naked Lunch*. The first thing Snell said was, "Have an Old Gold, Mr. Burroughs," a reference to a scene in the book where William Lee is being questioned by a tough cop and a nice cop: "O'Brien gives you an Old Gold—just like a cop to smoke Old Golds somehow." It seemed to Burroughs that Snell and Dean were themselves doing a nice-cop, tough-cop routine. Their techniques of ingratiation were to pour on the flattery, telling Burroughs that *Naked Lunch* was the greatest American novel since *Moby Dick,* and to tell stories that seemed connected to the material in the book, so that they began to seem practically like two of his own characters, the guys who have inside information about everything.

Excerpts from Snell file to *Life:* "We're packeting herewith negatives, contacts and prints on five rolls taken yesterday by Loomis Dean, showing the novelist William Burroughs in his Paris haunts. . . . Roll two shows Burroughs autographing copies of his book in a Left Bank bookstore near his hotel. . . . In rest of roll he has afternoon coffee in the bistro of the

Beat Hotel. . . . Roll one shows Burroughs alone in his second-floor room in the Beat Hotel. Room is lighted by a single forty-watt bulb, maximum allowed by management. Burroughs pays 13,000 francs per month for this single room where he sleeps and writes. Roll three shows Burroughs in the bistro of the Beat Hotel, where he has a morning coffee with his publisher, Maurice Girodias. Then we see Burroughs upstairs in the room of one of his few friends, Swiss-born U.S. artist Brion Gysin. . . . In roll four we see Burroughs wearing a pair of magnifying spectacles to see depth and detail in the Gysin paintings. In roll five, more shots of the afternoon coffee session.

"Note: Burroughs, while currently off the habit-forming narcotics, does freely use marijuana. Fortunately or unfortunately, however, we do not see him smoking marijuana in any of the Dean pictures. He was fresh out. All the smoke you see curling about his nostrils is tobacco. 'When I speak of drug addiction,' says Burroughs, 'I do not refer to kif, marijuana or any preparation of hashish, mescaline, sacred mushrooms or any other drugs of the hallucinogen group. There is no evidence that the use of any hallucinogen results in physical dependence. The action of these drugs is physiologically opposite to the action of junk.' "

Burroughs was forthcoming with Snell and Dean, even though he was ambivalent about the loss of his privacy. When he had told Bill Belli that he aspired to anonymity, he had meant it, and not long after the *Life* visit he sent this biographical note to Allen Ginsberg:

"I have no past life at all, being a notorious plant or 'intrusion.'

"Harvard 1936 A.B. Nobody saw him there but he had the papers on them.

"Functioned once as an exterminator in Chicago and learned some basic principles of *force majeure*.

"Achieved a state of inanimate matter in Tangier with chemical assistance.

"And never hope of ground that is yours."

Appearing in November 1959, the article in *Life* by Paul O'Neill ridiculed the Beats. "The bulk of Beat writers," it said, "are undisciplined and slovenly amateurs who have deluded themselves into believing their lugubrious absurdities are art simply because they have rejected the form, style, and attitudes of previous generations and have seized upon obscenity as an expression of 'total personality.' " The treatment of Burroughs, however, was slightly more respectful, reflecting no doubt a sympathetic tone in the material filed by Snell: "For sheer horror, no member of the Beat generation has achieved effects to compare with

William S. Burroughs. . . . The *Naked Lunch* could be described as an effort to communicate the degradation of addiction in epic terms."

One result of the article was an angry letter from his mother. Friends were calling: "Did you see the article in *Life* about your son?" She and Mort were getting the ripple effect. Burroughs had brought various forms of torment upon his parents, but this was the worst, to have him publicly branded as a Beatnik drug addict, and author of a scandalous novel. His father had recently suffered a heart attack and the article certainly didn't help his condition any. She hoped he would stay in Tangier, or wherever he was, and never return to the United States, under pain of forfeiting his monthly allowance.

"I counted to ten before answering your letter," Burroughs replied, "and I hope you have done the same, since nothing could be more unworthy than a quarrel between us at this point. . . . Yes, I have read the article in *Life* and after all . . . a bit silly perhaps . . . but it is a mass medium . . . and sensation factors must be played up at the expense often of fact. . . . In order to earn my reputation I may have to start drinking my tea from a skull since this is the only vice remaining to me . . . four pots a day and heavy sugar . . . did nurse make tea all the time? It's an English practice that seems to come natural to me. . . . I hope I am not ludicrously miscast as the wickedest man alive, a title vacated by the late Aleister Crowley—who by the way could have had his pick of Palm Beach invitations in a much more straitlaced era despite publicity a great deal more extreme. . . . And remember the others who have held the title before . . . Byron, Baudelaire, people are very glad to claim kinship now. But really, anyone in the public eye, that is anyone who enjoys any measure of success in his field is open to sensational publicity. . . . If I visit a waterfront bar in Tangier half a block from my house, I am rubbing shoulder with the riff-raff of the world. . . . You can do that in any naborhood bar USA and not least in Palm Beach. A rundown on some of the good burghers of Palm Beach would quite eclipse the Beatniks. Personally I would prefer to avoid publicity, but it is the only way to sell books. A writer who keeps his name out of the papers doesn't publish and doesn't make money if he does manage to publish. As regards my return to the family hearth, perhaps we had best shelve any decision for the present. Please keep me informed as to Dad's condition and give him my heart-felt wish for his recovery."

Although the tone of his letter was restrained and humorously courteous, privately Burroughs was furious. So his mother had thrown off her shopkeeper guise and revealed her hideous rank in Matriarch Inc., he thought. "I Queen Bee Laura of Worth Avenue—stay out of my territory, punk." So now she had forbidden him on pain of financial excommunication ever to set foot in Palm Beach, making him officially and at last a remittance man. She had shown her true colors.

Eventually Laura Burroughs simmered down, although she continued to refer to *Naked Lunch* as "that wretched book." In the meantime, in the fall of 1959, Burroughs was continuing his psychic experiments with Brion Gysin. There was an old woman on the corner who ran a newspaper kiosk, and one day, as Burroughs was buying a paper, a dog jumped up at him and he shoved it off. "*Pourquoi vous frappez la petite bête?*" the woman asked. ("Why are you beating the little beast?") Burroughs said the dog had jumped up on his coat. "*Quand même,*" the woman said. ("That's no excuse.") Feeling considerable ill will on the woman's part, Burroughs put a curse on her. Three days later, she was filling a Primus stove and it blew up in her face and put her in the hospital. The most casual curse was the most effective, thought Burroughs; he had hardly been conscious of doing it.

One day, in fact the same October day that Dean and Snell took Burroughs to lunch, while cutting a mount for a drawing, Brion Gysin sliced through a pile of newspapers with his Stanley blade, and made a mosaic out of the strips of newspapers, because it looked visually interesting. Then when he read it he thought it was hilarious. When Burroughs got back from lunch, Brion said, "By the way, look at this." Brion thought it was just an amusing accident, in the line of the old Surrealist games. But for Burroughs, who was looking for ways to escape from antiquated concepts of the novel, from the nineteenth-century structure of moving characters around within a plot, Gysin's cut-up newspapers switched on the electric light bulb over the cartoon character's head.

To Burroughs, the cut-up introduced an element of randomness and an element of time. Instead of writing being like a still life, writing with the use of cut-ups was like walking around the block. It made explicit a simple sensory process that was going on all the time anyway—which is that when you're reading a newspaper, say, you're reading one column but you see the other columns as well, and the bus you're on and the person sitting next to you. There was a juxtaposition of what you were doing and what was happening around you. What the cut-up method did was to incorporate that juxtaposition. Marcel Duchamp had done it years before by placing four unconnected texts in four divisions of a square. Von Neumann had introduced the cut-up principle of random action in his *Theory of Games and Economic Behavior.*

Burroughs now began to devote himself entirely to cut-ups, putting in eight-hour days. Gysin got him a couple of correspondence baskets and file cabinets and he spent his days cutting into strips pages from his favorite writers and his own writing, randomly rearranging the strips while looking away, and typing up the result. He even cut up his letters to friends, so that a December 7 letter to Paul Bowles went like this: "Smashed and tumbled the Thirsty off once more . . . sums of dwellings and darkness across the somewhere in that masonry of shattered fragments Castle Host set . . . Good-bye to their desert the riot-blown tombs, disemboweled houses marking the site . . . Black hinterland garden with a meaning of dust." This text, Burroughs explained, was a cut-up arrangement of a passage by Lawrence Durrell.

Paul couldn't see the cut-up method as an idiom for narration. Basically, it was an idiom to alienate the reader, which didn't make sense. It was even harder to read than Gertrude Stein. You could read it, you could force yourself to go from word to word, but you came out at the other end no happier and no wiser. And it wasn't any fun. It was clear to Paul that Burroughs was under the influence of Brion Gysin, who, having allied himself with Burroughs, had a stake in his reputation. Brion now felt possessive about Burroughs, thinking that he'd put him on the right track with the cut-ups. He had a strong vested interest in the cut-ups. Brion said that writing was fifty years behind painting, which to Paul made no sense at all; it was like saying that an orange had a better form than an apple. You looked at a painting in the same way that you looked at any object, but writing still had to be read on a printed page, left to right, line by line, word by word, and if the words had no meaning the reader was lost. Why not use the Cyrillic alphabet? That would be the ultimate cut-up.

For Burroughs, however, cut-up was the great breakthrough he had been seeking. So what if people couldn't read it? They would get used to it. Any advance in the arts was at first misunderstood. When people first saw Cézannes they attacked the canvases with umbrellas . . . but they got used to it. As he got deeper into cut-ups, he came to believe that his accidental combinations of words were prophetic subliminal announcements, coming to him from a collective, extratemporal consciousness. In other words, through the cut-ups he had become a medium for the disclosure of events about to happen. This was another breakthrough, since the guiding principle of fiction was "once upon a time." But Burroughs' cut-up principle was "once in future time." For instance, when he wrote a cut-up text called "Afternoon Ticker Tape," he had the line

"Come on, Tom, it's your turn now." A few days later, in the *St. Louis Post-Dispatch,* he saw this headline: TOM CREEK OVERFLOWS ITS BANKS. "I tell you, boss, you write it and it happens," Burroughs thought.

It was during this time, when Gysin and Burroughs were spending their days shredding and recombining texts, that an invitation came from Girodias for dinner at the Grande Séverine. Barney Rosset of Grove Press was in town, and told Maurice that he should call his restaurant Chez Lolita. John Calder, the English publisher who was fighting censorship laws in his country, was there; when he saw the Grande Séverine, he thought, my God, what is this consortium of restaurants, each run by a different girlfriend, all scratching each other's eyes out the whole time. Lo and behold, who should turn up but the Great Recluse himself, Samuel Beckett, who sat across the table from Burroughs. The two masters of postmodernism sat stolidly facing each other, motionless and silent amid the deafening racket of a bossa nova band, surrounded by scantily clad *danseuses*, as Marpessa Dawn sang the songs from her movie *Orfeo Negro*.

Finally, Beckett leaned forward and said, "What can you tell me, Mr. Burroughs, about this cut-up method of yours?"

"Well, Mr. Beckett," Burroughs said, "what I do is I take a page of my writing and a page of the *Herald Tribune*, I cut them up and then I put them back together, and I gradually decipher new texts. Then I might take a page of your writing, and line it up with what I already have, and do the same thing all over again."

Suddenly indignant, Beckett asked, "You're using other writers' words?"

"Words don't have brands on them the way cattle do," Burroughs said. "Ever heard of a word rustler?"

"You can't do that!" Beckett said. "You can't take my writing and mix it up with the newspapers."

"Well, I've done it," Burroughs said.

"That's not writing," Beckett snorted, "it's plumbing."

They continued their discussion, fueled by drink, until they went home. The propriety of using other writers' words in cut-ups was left unresolved.

By this time, Burroughs and Gysin were planning a book of cut-ups, and brought in two other collaborators: Sinclair Beiles, who was enthusiastic, and Gregory Corso, who was lukewarm. What Gregory liked was working with Burroughs, the exquisite conversations and the laughter, and making language magical by mixing up a Shakespeare sonnet and an Eisenhower speech. What he didn't like were Gysin's theories about rubbing out the word and destroying poetry. What, he told Gysin, you're not even a writer, and you're coming into the writing game and saying you want to destroy it, that's bullshit, you're only going to add to it. What Gysin was writing was totally mechanical. All that fucking cut-up shit, Corso told him, after a while it's going to be redundant.

Gregory didn't like Brion in any case, because Gregory had told Burroughs that his greatest fear was forgetting to lock his door at night, since having had a premonition of death—a man in a black suit with a face half black and half white had appeared to him. And what did Brion do but knock on his door late one night with a stocking on his face, and scare the shit out of him. But Burroughs, that was another matter, cutting the texts, putting the bowl out, then mixing the texts in the bowl, a line from Rimbaud—okay, Bill said, we'll use it. Bill actually thought that by mixing up medical articles they would locate a cure for cancer. Well, maybe they would. To Gregory, Burroughs was the most brilliant man on the planet, the top of all heads.

Beiles found two backers, Jean Fanchette, a little man from Mauritius who published a magazine called *Two Cities* that was written partly in French and partly in English, and Gait Frogé, a blond Breton woman who ran the English bookshop on the rue de Seine, another gathering place for writers, where young people came in, read for an hour or two, and left. Gysin chose the title when Beiles came around one day, in his usual manic state of urgency, and said, "You've got to get this going, there are only minutes to go."

Minutes to Go was published in March 1960 in a limited edition, and was kicked off with a memorable party at the English bookshop. Maurice Girodias provided the vodka, and poured out his heart to Gait Frogé. He was in love with his six-foot blues singer, Mae Mercer, and was covered with bruises from their combative encounters. Maurice was in a dark mood, distressed by the overhead on his restaurants, and said, "I don't know what I'm doing." Gregory Corso arrived with his girlfriend Sally November, and Gait Frogé asked, "Do you have one for every other month as well?" She had covered all the books on her shelves with black paper to reduce pilferage. All four authors were there, signing away.

Minutes to Go included a postscript by Gregory Corso expressing his ambivalence about the project: "I join this venture unwillingly *and* willingly," he said. "Unwillingly because the poetry I have written was from the soul and not from the dictionary; willingly because if it can be destroyed by the cut-up method, then it is poetry I care not for, and so should be cut up. . . . Unwillingly because my poetry is a natural cut-up, and need not be created by a pair of scissors. Willingly, because I . . . agreed to join . . . this venture."

The curious thing about *Minutes to Go* is that far from being a homogenized shredding operation where all the contributions sound alike, cloned by scissors, the individual voices come through with plenty of resonance.

Really throwing himself into it, Sinclair Beiles came closest to total incomprehension in his cut-ups of newspaper articles, as in, "This was followed by point to modern revolvers from three pheasants roasted to a turn-Czechoslovakia which have been cap with puree turned from the gangs of cold accomplishments."

Brion Gysin betrayed his thirties Surrealist origins in that what he really wanted was to push a program, to come out with a manifesto, as André Breton used to do. His efforts were didactic and mechanical, as in a page of permutations on the phrase "Rub the Word Right Out," which becomes "Word Right Rub the Out," etc.

Gregory Corso couldn't quite let go of the narrative anchor. His contributions made too much sense to qualify as authentic cut-ups, and did not entirely escape banality, as in

> Bomb decade
> Mother decade
> Good-bye values decade
> Dulles wanted to be Mr. Decade
> Marx Freud Einstein decade . . .

Burroughs came closest to the spirit of the enterprise in composing cut-ups that didn't quite make sense in the usual way, but had a skewed logic of their own, as in this cut-up from a *Saturday Evening Post* article called "New Clues to Cancer Cure":

> The beautiful disease and
> the government falls
> along the weed rooms
> flesh among the weed government . . .

> The girls eat morning
> dying people to a white bone monkey
> in the winter sun
> touching tree of the house.

It was April 1960 in Paris, with chestnuts in blossom, and holiday tables under the trees, and Burroughs was hearing voices. One of the voices was an American tycoon giving him orders: "Goddamn it, Burroughs, you better get back to America before I kick your ass." One afternoon at the hotel there was a message to call a certain number—it was the Narcotics Bureau office in the American Embassy, and they would like to see him.

Burroughs went over and introduced himself to a square-faced man with a tan—he must have just come back from a vacation on the Riviera. "Now, Mr. Burroughs," the narc said, "you have been convicted of a narcotics offense in a French court, which entitles us to confiscate your passport, but we don't want to do that. I suggest that you go back to America, because the French government is making moves to deport you. And keep yourself pretty clean between now and then, and keep your room clean."

Burroughs asked Maître Bumsell to look into French government efforts, and it turned out to be a complete bluff—there was no move to deport him at all. But this talk about keeping his room clean—that meant to Burroughs that they were going to plant something, and that he had better leave Paris. Once again, he had burned down the place he was living in. Oh, well, it was time to go. People were paying too much attention to him here. And had not the great Céline said, "The only thing that matters is to keep people from paying attention to you." England was the place, where he could join Ian Sommerville and start afresh.

· FOURTEEN ·

NAKED LUNCH

1959–1966

Although the Olympia Press edition of *Naked Lunch* appeared in July 1959, the American edition brought out by Grove Press was delayed for more than three years, due to a comedy of errors rarely equaled in the annals of publishing.

Behind Grove Press stood the inimitable Barney Rosset, son of a wealthy Jewish banker from Chicago and an Irish Catholic mother, whose immigrant father still spoke Gaelic and had done all right as a sewer contractor in Michigan. The product of a volatile genetic mix, Barney was one of those "why" children, always wanting to know the reason for everything: Why is the sky blue, why are some people poor and other people rich? Barney was rich, but he wasn't the polo-playing, coupon-clipping type. He was the rebellious type, who instinctively took the view opposed to conventional wisdom. He was the type that, when choosing sides for a sandlot game, you would pick for your team, not because he was that great a player, but just so you wouldn't have him yelling at you the entire time.

In high school, Barney co-edited a newspaper called *Anti-Everything*. At Swarthmore, he made censorship his hobbyhorse, and wrote his freshman essay on Henry Miller's *Tropic of Cancer,* as an example of an acclaimed book by an important American writer that was banned. With his inherited wealth and anticensorship views, Barney was in a position to make a mark in the growing counterculture movement fueled by the Beats, which he did by founding Grove Press in 1951. He started off in a stately manner, however, with a new edition of Henry James's *The Golden Bowl.*

It was in 1957, when he was thirty-four, that he took the leap that would make him the American equivalent of Maurice Girodias. Like Maurice, he was willing to take on the mighty apparatus of government in order to defeat censorship. His first effort was *Lady Chatterley's Lover,* which had been published by Knopf in an expurgated edition. Barney reasoned that with an accepted author like D. H. Lawrence, and a book that had first been published as far back as 1928, he might have a chance. With the help of Mark Schorer, head of the English Department at Berkeley and biographer of Sinclair Lewis, he fought the post office ban and won, the Supreme Court declining to review. It was a Pyrrhic victory—the book was out of copyright and thus was immediately pirated—and it was an expensive victory, with all the appeals, but to Barney it was worth it to have the satisfaction of seeing the full text of a great book in print for the first time.

His next goal was to publish *Tropic of Cancer,* but Henry Miller, now living in Big Sur and getting along in years, was an old warhorse out to pasture—he wanted no more conflict. When Barney went to see him, Miller painted an alarmist picture of vigilante groups sent out by the American Legion to burn his house down. It wasn't just the climate of the times, which were bad enough, thought Barney, it was that Miller had become completely paranoid. Thanks to the intercession of Maurice Girodias, however, who had considerable influence with Miller, Barney eventually signed up *Tropic of Cancer,* which he planned to publish in 1961.

In the meantime, he saw in *Naked Lunch* another scandalous and proscribed book which Grove Press could lead into battle, and in November 1959 he agreed to pay Girodias a $3,000 advance and a 17.5 percent royalty on all copies after the first 10,000, which would be split one third–two thirds between Girodias and Burroughs. As they wrangled over terms, Barney could not resist needling Maurice over his outside interests. "When I hear you talk about new kitchens, new doors, orchestras, violinists, I grow paler," he said.

Barney, however, had given Girodias a strong incentive to accept in offering to omit from the contract the warranty clause, which meant that the author would not be held responsible in case of a legal test in the United States. Anticipating legal problems, Barney asked the respected critic John Ciardi to write an introduction to *Naked Lunch,* but Ciardi gave the standard author's regret—he would like to do it, "especially since the P.O. bastards will be hard after it as I have no doubt," but he was nailed to deadlines.

Drumming up support for *Naked Lunch,* Barney sent it to Henry Miller, who gave it a mixed review, in January 1961: "I've tried now for the third time to read it, but I can't stick it. The truth is, it bores me. The Marquis de Sade bores me too, perhaps in a different way, or for different reasons.

There's no question in my mind, however, as to the author's abilities. There's a ferocity in his writing which is equaled, in my opinion, only by Céline. No writer I know of has made more daring use of the language. I wish I might read him on some other subject than sex and drugs—read him on St. Thomas Aquinas, for example, or on eschatology. Or better yet . . . a disquisition on the Grand Inquisitor."

At this time, Girodias was devoutly hoping for early U.S. publication of *Naked Lunch.* He was counting on strong U.S. sales to rescue him from pending bankruptcy. Every day lost put him deeper in the hole. But Barney's strategy was to publish *Tropic of Cancer* first, since Henry Miller had a formidable group of admirers behind him. He would delay the publication of *Naked Lunch* until the legal cases sure to arise over the Miller book were settled, for if they lost on *Tropic* they would sure as hell lose on *Lunch.* This to Maurice was the most painful of ironies, for he had convinced Miller to allow U.S. publication and now he was being punished for it.

The more Maurice fretted, the more Barney rubbed it in about the Grande Séverine, writing him on February 28 that "it really is not very realistic to live in the hope that *Naked Lunch* will make up for all of the other type lunches you have been serving . . . perhaps what is cruel irony is that so much money sunk into food has brought you to have a desperate dependence on one little *Naked Lunch.*"

Maurice didn't think it was funny. While Barney was laughing, Olympia Press was sinking. The royalties from *Naked Lunch,* which should have been in his pocket, were still in the distant future. Frantic and exasperated, he wrote Barney on March 31, 1961: "Publish the damned book, for God's sake."

But the book Barney published that April was *Tropic of Cancer.* Even though the Doubleday and Brentano bookstores refused to carry it, it jumped on the bestseller list. But with success came a legal battle of a magnitude that Barney could not have imagined, which threatened to place Grove Press on the same precarious footing as Olympia Press in Paris.

For to get the bookstores to carry *Tropic,* Barney had been obliged to guarantee to take up the legal defense of any wholesaler or retailer who was arrested for selling the book. These were criminal arrests, and if Barney had not promised to pay the legal expenses of arrested booksellers, the book would not have been distributed. It was a necessary investment, but it was also a dangerous one, leaving him open to having to pay for trials all over the country. Every day, more bad news arrived, until, by July, there had been fifty arrests, with trials scheduled in fourteen cities. Never was there a book in the history of publishing in the United States that gave rise to as many trials and lawsuits as *Tropic of Cancer*. They were coming from all directions, from Philadelphia and Cincinnati, from Los Angeles and Cleveland, from Boston and Dallas, from Miami and Chicago—even Honolulu got into the act. The estimates of legal costs took logarithmic leaps, draining the coffers of Grove Press. Charles Rembar, in charge of the defense, had to prepare a kit to send to other lawyers in the various venues.

It was a disastrous situation, so that when Girodias kept harping on *Naked Lunch*, it seemed to Barney that Maurice's problem was like the blow of a feather compared to the heavy artillery being fired at Grove. Barney had 10,000 copies of *Naked Lunch* printed and bound, but they would have to sit in the warehouse until the *Tropic of Cancer* smoke cleared. His patience wearing thin, Barney wrote Maurice: "If you think we or anybody else could do the same for *Naked Lunch* right now, you are crazy. We couldn't even get any decent number of testimonials for *Naked Lunch*, and we have tried very hard. Do you think we enjoy sitting around with 10,000 books costing more than $1.00 each to manufacture? Come on now—stop this insane badgering. We all have to sit this out together."

Adding to the confusion was an incident that October of 1961 that made Barney even more cautious about bringing out *Naked Lunch*. LeRoi Jones and Diane Di Prima were arrested by two postal inspectors for sending obscenity through the mails, specifically the Burroughs text "Roosevelt After Inauguration," contained in issue number 9 of their magazine *Floating Bear*. The text was a parody or routine in which Cabinet offices are given to pimps, thieves, hookers, and hustlers, which was not that wide of the mark, in a metaphorical sense, given the peculiarities of some members of the first Roosevelt Cabinet. In Burroughs' routine, when the Supreme Court invalidated New Deal legislation, the members of that august body were forced to submit to intercourse with a purple-assed baboon. In fact, they were forced to submit to a court-packing scheme which they fought off as ferociously as they would have the advances of a baboon, so that this too was plausible on the level of Rabelaisian metaphor. Burroughs concluded by having F.D.R. institute a series of contests—Most Unsavory Act contest, Cheapest Trick contest, Turn in Your Best Friend Week, and so on—which again was not so distant from the wheeling and dealing and double-dealing and secret compacts of the Roosevelt administration.

Although a grand jury refused to return indictments in the *Floating Bear* case, the seizure of *Floating Bear* reinforced Barney's decision to postpone publication of *Naked Lunch*. Maurice could bear it no longer, and tried to negotiate a separate deal with Dial Press, who would buy Grove's 10,000 ready copies and publish at once. Feeling that he had been stabbed in the back, Barney wrote Maurice on December 6, "Calm down those greedy eyes for a moment. There isn't any more money coming out of that book just now and you are going to have legal fees to pay if you don't stop selling something you don't own. . . . We will start in on you if this sabotage of yours keeps up. . . . Please, Maurice, don't precipitate a battle. We have so many going now that one more may not be as rough on us as it would be on you."

In contrast to Girodias's panic, Burroughs was sanguine about the delay, writing Barney on December 12: "I am sorry to see the difficulties between you and Girodias taking such an acrimonious turn—my own position remains clear and unchanged: I agree with you that it is not practical to publish *Naked Lunch* at this time in America."

Maurice, however, was sure that it was not he but Barney who had gone crazy. Barney kidded him about the folly of the Grande Séverine, but this was folly tenfold, to put *Naked Lunch* on a back burner. When Maurice wrote to say that he did not understand why Barney was spending thousands of dollars on lawsuits, Barney replied, "I'll tell you why—if you don't, you go to jail."

At the start of 1962, Barney was still bogged down in lawsuits. Two New York City booksellers had been called before a grand jury. There were trials on in Los Angeles and Chicago. "Only a suicidal maniac would plunge in with *Naked Lunch* at this moment," Barney wrote Girodias in January. "At least that is the opinion of everyone whom I have talked to, including Burroughs. We are not sitting on 10,000 books to spite you, believe me."

The situation improved when Barney won in Chicago, with a little help from his friends. The judge trying the case was an old friend of his father's, and the judge's son contacted Barney in the middle of the trial and told him, "My dad says that if you changed your argument in such and such a way he might see it in a different light." In addition, Richard Ellmann, the biographer of Joyce, was a splendid witness, who remembered chapter and verse of *Tropic,* which an aggressive district attorney would not allow him to consult. Nor did it hurt that Barney brought to the trial his Swarthmore essay, so that when the district attorney said he was only in it for the money, he said, "I happen to have with me an essay I wrote in college," which he proceeded to read. It was an ugly situation in the Chicago area, with police harassing booksellers, and Grove sued ten police chiefs for denying the booksellers their First Amendment rights.

After the judge ruled that *Tropic of Cancer* was not obscene, he received death threats. It took time, of course, for the various cases to go through appeals, and it was finally a Florida case that was reviewed by the Supreme Court, which ruled that Henry Miller's book was constitutionally protected, and that freed it all over the country. But by that time, there had been other events favorable to the publication of *Naked Lunch*.

In London, the ruddy-faced Scottish publisher John Calder had taken up the anticensorship cudgel. England was more proper than the United States or France—you couldn't print the word "fuck" in a book without finding yourself in court. The criterion was whether a book tended to "corrupt and deprave," which was given a broad application by judges and juries.

In 1962, Calder saw a way to advance the cause of new writing. Each year in his hometown of Edinburgh, during three weeks in August and September, there was a huge festival of the arts, with 800 events—opera, theater, twenty-five symphony orchestras: a great overspilling cornucopia of the arts. Calder was no wild-eyed Beatnik, but a well-connected member of the landed gentry, who rented his estate for grouse shoots. He talked the festival director, Lord Harwood, into letting him organize a conference of writers who would be invited from all over the world to discuss pregnant topics. Lord Harwood assented, saying, "Try to organize it so it pays its way."

Calder took the biggest auditorium at Edinburgh University, McEwan Hall, an architectural oddity that was shaped like a gargantuan beer barrel and seated 3,000. He installed his seventy writers, with microphones and translators in three languages. The American delegation consisted of Mary McCarthy, Henry Miller, Norman Mailer, and the still relatively unknown William S. Burroughs, whose book remained unpublished except by Olympia Press. It was quite an effective quartet, if Calder said so himself, even though no one had heard of Burroughs.

The writers' conference lasted five days, from August 20 to 25, and it turned into one of those "the-lines-are-drawn-and-which-side-are-you-on" running battles between "ancients" and "moderns," with various sideshows concerning regional and national issues. Calder was gratified to see a paying audience of about 2,500 attending the sessions, at which a chairman and a panel of six addressed themselves to the topic of the day, as a wandering microphone went round the hall encouraging others to speak up.

The first day started off tamely under British control. The topic was "How does the novel form stand today?" which, chairman Malcolm Muggeridge declared, he was highly unsuited to comment upon, since he practically never read novels. It was left to the diminutive and snowy-haired Angus Wilson to make the proper triumphalist statement showing how the English novel shored up English values. Was not the English novel a defense of English roots, on the assumption that there was something wrong with the rootless? Was not the revolution in language, as seen by Mr. Joyce and Mr. Beckett, a dead end? For Angus Wilson, the novelist who pointed the way was Ivy Compton-Burnett, who had kept the old moral/social values and stayed within the bounds of tradition.

Next came a voice from a former colony, in the person of Mary McCarthy, who allowed that the national novel, like the nation-state, was dying. This was a patently absurd remark, since each year there arrived at the already groaning United Nations table new nation-states, whose flags and names, such as Bangladesh and Sri Lanka, the other members had to learn, and who would soon produce a literature of the Third World.

But no matter, logic is not a requirement at writers' conferences, and Mary McCarthy pursued her theory of the stateless novel, saying that among recent books she had liked were "the work of Nabokov . . . which I personally have gone overboard for, and I would also cite Mr. Burroughs, who is here now. . . . The *Naked Lunch* is laid everywhere and is sort of speeded up like jet travel and it has that somewhat supersonic quality. It also has some of the qualities of Action Painting. It is a kind of action novel. And you could not possibly consider this as a description of American life." Whereas, Miss McCarthy added, when she read Compton-Burnett's novels, she had the impression she was always reading the same one.

Thus, whatever the merit of Mary McCarthy's theory of the stateless novel, she had managed, on the very first day of the conference, to put Burroughs on the map.

The second day, Tuesday, August 21, was devoted to Scottish writers and consisted mainly of a border skirmish between two of the above, Hugh MacDiarmid, the Grand Old Man of Scottish letters, who was one of those porridges that only Scotland can produce, being at the same time a Scottish Nationalist and a Communist, and who showed up wearing his kilt; and Alexander Trocchi, representing *les jeunes,* and author of a scandalous novel, *Cain's Book.* Speaking out of an angry parochialism, and a hatred of England for having imposed its language on the Scots, MacDiarmid said that since the death of Burns, there were only three or four Scottish writers who weren't writing "stuff for singers." It was deplorable that he had to use English to be read.

Trocchi did not disagree, considering the atmosphere in Scotland to be "turgid, petty, provincial, the stale porridge, Bible-class nonsense." But he also delivered himself of a personal attack on the seventy-year-old MacDiarmid, who was, he said, "an old fossil. . . . His old-fashioned hatred of the novel is just too crummy to be commented upon. . . . I don't want to be too hard or superior, but I think frankly that of what is interesting in the last twenty years of Scottish writing, I have written it all."

MacDiarmid countered with the charge that "Mr. Trocchi seems to imagine that the burning questions in the world today are lesbianism, homosexuality, and matters of that kind."

Sarcastically, Trocchi agreed that "I am only interested in lesbianism and sodomy," adding, "Isn't it high time we transcended nationalistic borders?"

"I want no uniformity," said MacDiarmid.

"I want no uniformity either," responded Trocchi, "not even a kilt."

The chairman for the day, David Daiches, had to silence the two adversaries, but sympathy for the Scottish situation was expressed by writers of other overshadowed nations, such as the Yugoslavs, and soon you had the Serbs insulting the Croats—they were just exactly like the younger and older Scots. And then some fellow got up and said, "I will read in my native language," which turned out to be an untranslatable Indian dialect, but he was extended every courtesy. It was amazing how far the fragmentation could go. It was a great day, thought Calder; it made headlines in the British papers, who increased their daily coverage.

The next day, Wednesday, August 22, was on "The Writer and Commitment." Simon Raven gave a sedate British view by saying that he was an old-fashioned novelist who wrote to make a living and pay for his expensive tastes. He was committed to trying to tell a good story in an intelligent and amusing way.

There was more to it than that, said Norman Mailer, for the West was Faustian in that "one always enters into a contract with something outside oneself. It can be anything from an ideal to a drug to a passion to a political party to an alienation from society." Thus the Western writer was, perforce, committed.

Trocchi claimed "the commitment of exile. I would claim that for myself as well as for Burroughs, as well for certain of the Beatnik writers in America." At a press conference later, Trocchi described himself as a "cosmonaut of inner space."

Burroughs liked the phrase, and he liked Trocchi, who was a fellow addict. In fact they were staying with Trocchi's doctor, who filled his heroin prescriptions. Since publishing *Cain's Book,* Alex was stuck with a large writing block. He'd rather do anything than write, and he'd stung every publisher in London. He was supposed to be working on something called "The Long Book," and Calder gave him translation jobs to keep him going. Then he got into stamps and rare books. It was demeaning to go from writer to book dealer, but he just would not write anymore. His family situation was a disaster. His wife, Lynn, died of an overdose, and one of his two sons died of cancer of the spine at age seventeen. Alex eventually had one cancerous lung removed and died in 1983 of pneumonia. He was always in trouble—once for possession of heroin, and another time when some people left some stolen jewelry in his apartment and he was charged with "guilty knowledge," which was the next thing to receiving. Burroughs and Calder testified at his trial and he was exonerated. Even after he stopped writing, Burroughs continued to think, "Alex has the courage to be a writer."

Burroughs was enjoying the conference, enjoying even the glares he was getting from the British "Dames" like Victoria Sackville-West and Rebecca West, as if he was the devil personified. No doubt, the conference was breaking up into cliques, but he was not alone. At a large party where everyone was drinking sherry, he found himself face to face with Henry Miller, who said, "So you're Burroughs." Burroughs did not feel up to saying, "Yes, *Maître,*" and to say, "And so you're Miller" didn't seem quite right, so he said, as a younger writer whose work had also been ruled obscene, "A longtime admirer," and they smiled. The next time they met at a party, Miller looked at him quizzically and said, "So you're Burroughs." Burroughs thought he must be over the hill. The only thing he'd said at the conference was that he had visited the Royal Academy to look at the Scottish painters.

At the censorship panel, Burroughs made a dispassionate and well-reasoned statement that helped to dispel the wild and woolly Beatnik image that he was by now associated with. "Censorship, of course," he said, "is the presumed right of governmental agencies to decide what words and images the citizen is permitted to see. That is precisely thought control. What is considered harmful would of course depend on the government exercising the censorship. In the Middle Ages when the Church controlled censoring agencies the emphasis was on heretical doctrine. In Communist countries, the censorship is said to be most close in the area of politics. In English-speaking countries the weight of censorship falls on sexual words and images as dangerous. . . . The excuse usually given for censorship is the necessity of protecting children. . . . But I can't think how they would be harmed by reading the work of Rabelais, Plutonius, Henry Miller, and my own work for that matter. And it is rather unlikely that they would read these works even if they were available to them, being in many cases virtually illiterate. . . . If censorship were removed, perhaps books would be judged more on literary merit, and a dull, poorly written book on a sexual subject would find few readers. Fewer people would be stimulated by the sight of a four-letter word on the printed page. The anxiety and prurience of which censorship is the overt political expression has so far prevented any serious scientific investigation of sexual phenomena."

Bored with defending the obvious civil liberties position, Mailer played devil's advocate, taking the part of the censor. "I have heard Mr. Miller and Mr. Burroughs," he said, "with great pleasure and great concern and yet I must ask myself, finally, is their work useful or desirable for the vitality of my nation?" Because the argument for censorship was not that such works corrupted the young but that they weakened the young, making them too civilized and sophisticated and insufficiently warlike. There was also the danger that the absence of censorship would bring about a totalitarian reaction, a clean-the-temple repressive movement. So it was an impasse, Mailer said, and perhaps the fate of the Western world depended on not having writers like Miller and Burroughs.

Mary McCarthy said it was clear why the Church had suppressed heretical books and the Communists political books, but why had capitalism chosen to suppress sexual books? Was it really that sex weakened people for war? What was Burroughs' explanation for the hostility of bourgeois capitalism toward sex? Was it the need to hold together the monogamous marriage?

"I think it is partly that," Burroughs said. "I think it is a very complicated phenomenon. But in general I would say that it involved channeling the sexual instinct into production and purchase of consumer goods."

"You mean the use that advertising makes of sex?" Mary McCarthy asked.

"That is what advertising is about," Burroughs said.

Mailer repeated that "a nation that has too much sexual sophistication is not a warlike nation. . . . The people who are controlling the country never talk about it this way, but once in a while may decide that it is very bad to have sexual freedom because it is going to make America weak vis-à-vis Russia."

"I don't see how this explains the extreme puritanism of America in periods of almost total disarmament," Mary McCarthy said.

"I can counter that with the various repressive laws that Stalin had passed all through the late thirties," Mailer said, "and you can draw a connection between that and his desire to build Russia into a warlike nation. When people are effectively repressed they tend to be more warlike. The proof of it is that it is considered sacrilege for a boxer even to have a woman when he is training."

Then the Great Banned One, Henry Miller, whom everyone thought had been asleep, finally spoke up: "What we are all trying for is to get as much freedom, as much liberty of expression, not only in writing, not on paper, not in talk, but in action, and the whole world today is in my mind strangled. We have no freedom of action, really, we are all talking nonsense. What we all would like to do when we see a good interesting woman is sleep with her, we should not make any bones about that. There is nothing wrong with lust or with obscenity, we all have impure desires. We should have the pure and impure, they exist together. Good and evil belong together, you can't separate them. Let's stop talking about censorship, let's do it, think it, talk it."

Concluding, Mailer said that "one had to enter this terrible borderland of sex, sadism, obscenity, horror, and anything else because somehow the conscience of Western man has become altogether muddy in refusing to enter it, and because the Nazis were so horrible, must we for the rest of our lives refuse to look at these phenomena? We have got to get into it, that is why I salute Mr. Burroughs' work, because he has gone further into it than any other Western writer today."

In tandem with the talk of sadism and horror at the conference, there was violence in the streets of Edinburgh, with youth gangs roaming the city and attacking visitors. That evening, Mailer was at a party when another writer came up the stairs, whining and complaining that he had just been beaten up in the street. There was something so piteous about the fellow that Mailer was reminded of the joke where someone keeps complaining to God about how badly he's being treated and says, "Why are you so unfair?" and God replies, "Because you bug me." And Mailer, too, was bugged listening to his fellow writer's lament, and he said, "Oh, they beat you up, did they, oh, isn't that horrible, well, here my fella, have some more," and proceeded to give the man a shove, and he fell down the stairs, got up, gave one frightened look over his shoulder at this madman at the top, and took off. Mailer thought of that incident as perhaps the worst single thing he had ever done—a gratuitous act of violence against someone he didn't even know who had just been victimized—but in his mind it was tied in with Burroughs and the day's proceedings and the need to explore the dark and irrational side of life. All in all, Edinburgh was the most frightening literary conference he had ever attended.

Friday, August 24, was the windup, on the future of the novel, when the rear guard mustered its troops to discredit the new writing. In an oblique attack on Burroughs and Trocchi, H. Raynor Heppenstall (who sounded like the author of books on English antique furniture) deplored "the junky sex novel, which is very much the American novel of the present, but about which one is already beginning to feel that it belongs in the past."

"I am going to have to be the one who is going to have to defend the American novel against being the junky sex novel," Mary McCarthy said. "I gathered from the tone that there was a sort of hysterical chauvinism at work." But what of Faulkner and Saul Bellow? Would she have to go on explaining that each American novelist was not the junky sex novelist?

Trocchi, whose writer's block did not extend to speaking, said: "I feel that I personally am being attacked when there is all this mention of drugs and sex. Drugs and sex do come into my books. . . . No doubt I shall go on writing, stumbling across tundras of unmeaning, planting words like bloody flags in my wake. Loose ends, things unrelated, shifts, night journeys, cities arrived at and left, meetings, desertions, betrayals, all manner of unions, triumphs, defeats. . . ."

Weighing in for the rear guard, Steven Spender said: "I would like to point out that everything that Mr. Trocchi has said had been said in 1905. That is that the fragmentation of values in the modern world should be reflected by fragmentation in modern writing. It led to a complete dead end and in fact I think that the history of modern literature since 1914–1920 or so is the attempt to recover from this point of view."

After some more sparring on junkies and sex as appropriate subject matter for the novel, it was Burroughs' turn to explain himself. "In writing I am acting as a mapmaker," he said, "an explorer of psychic areas. . . . And I see no point in exploring areas that have already been thoroughly surveyed." To do so required new techniques, and Burroughs explained that in the two novels he had written after *Naked Lunch*, *Nova Express* and *The Ticket That Exploded,* he had used an extension of the cut-up method, which he called the fold-in method:

"A page of text, my own or someone else's, is folded down the middle of and placed on another page. The composite text is then read across, half one text and half the other. . . . I edit, delete, and rearrange as in any other method of composition. . . . It need not be in any sense Dadaist. . . . After all, what does any writer do but choose and rearrange the material at his disposal. . . . I have made and used fold-ins from Shakespeare, Rimbaud, newspapers, magazines, conversations, letters, and so forth. So the novels that I have written in this method are in fact composites of many writers. I would like to emphasize that the cut-ups and the fold-ins are techniques and, like any technique, may be useful to some writers and not to others."

There were some in the audience who thought their leg was being pulled, that this talk of splicing texts was an elaborate joke, and from the floor, an Indian writer rose and asked, "Are you being serious?" "Yes, of course," Burroughs replied.

On this last day, there were thirty scheduled speakers, each of whom was allotted seven minutes, and Norman Mailer and Angus Wilson were the two moderators who were supposed to hold the speakers to their time limit. When the Italian writer Niccolò Tucci went on and on, for instance, Wilson rapped his gavel and finally leaned forward and said, "Mr. Tucci, you've written your letter, now mail it!" Tucci gave him the *malocchio* and gathered up his papers and stormed off the rostrum.

But in the case of Burroughs, Mailer made an exception, saying: "Out of respect for what I consider your vast talent and because you have not taken much trouble to speak before, we are going to break the rule in your case . . . and we are going to give you an extra five minutes." Burroughs was obviously the hit of the day, thought Mailer, even though he himself did not respond at all to this theorizing about cut-ups. The attempt to convey to the reader a sense of randomness and of the outside world interfering was to him as much of an abstraction as pure thought. The reality of good writing, he thought, was to shape experience to such a degree that the reader had no sense at all of the process of shaping. To give the reader the process of recording was as false as recording an experience in any other form.

After reading *Naked Lunch*, Mailer thought that Burroughs would go on and create some kind of demonic vision of existence that would make Céline look like a travel writer. But instead he had involved himself in cut-ups, which seemed to Mailer like a retreat. He seemed to want to epitomize the avant-garde, which Mailer found hard to take seriously because they didn't work hard enough for their ideas, being indifferent not only to the media but the very notion that people might be influenced by what they were up to. In that sense, Mailer was completely literal; he didn't think you had the right to influence people if you were not serious about your ideas. Although novelistically, he could conceive of someone with serious ideas who had no interest in influencing people . . . there was a vague claim in that direction at the end of Tolstoy's "Kreutzer Sonata." So whatever Mailer's personal misgivings were, he felt Burroughs deserved more time to express his views.

Given the extra time, Burroughs said that "the conferring writers have been accused by the press of not paying sufficient attention to the question of human survival. In *Nova Express*, and the reference as you probably know is to an exploding planet or star, and *The Ticket That Exploded*, I emphasize our concern with survival, with Nova conspiracies, Nova criminals, and Nova police. I feel that a new mythology is now possible in the space age and that we can again have heroes and villains, with respect toward the planet, and in closing I would say that the future of writing is in space and not in time."

This was too much even for Mailer, who interjected: "I have the vastest respect for you as a writer, and I think we are completely opposed to one another in every single one of our ideas. I think the future of writing is in time precisely and never in space, and one of us is going to be right." Mailer at that time was obsessively working on what he thought would be his big novel, which was about time, about a character who was born four times, but he could never figure out how to do it and had to give it up. But at the conference, he still thought he had this huge contribution to make about time, and when Burroughs started talking about space, Mailer thought, "Hey, we're completely at odds."

At this point there was a roundtable discussion, which strayed from its subject, the future of the novel, to focus on Burroughs. "We have here on this platform a number of distinguished writers," Colin MacInnes said, "of whom one can say that if one is a novelist, the other certainly cannot be. For example, if Mr. Lawrence Durrell, who in my view most surely is, then can Mr. Burroughs be with his passionate speculation bordering on the insanity barrier? If a writer like this is a novelist then clearly the word is practically meaningless."

"It seems to me," Stephen Spender said, "that what Mr. Burroughs was making was an analogy between science and writing. He was suggesting that a novelist, by putting out page one and page one hundred and facing them in page ten, was doing something similar to the rocket maker, and I was wondering whether this analogy really works. It sounds to me like a rather medieval form of magic rather than modern science . . ."

"The analogy that I was making," Burroughs responded, "was between the flashback method in film and the method I was using. Not anything so vague as an analogy with rocket makers."

Seeing that the conference was caught up with the novelty of Burroughs' idea, Mailer said, "Mr. Burroughs, there is a specific and I think rather intense bit of curiosity on several sides about the technique you called, I am not being facetious now, I really don't remember, it was 'fold-in,' or 'fold-out' . . . Seriously, what was the name you gave it?"

"Fold-in," Burroughs said.

"May I tell you," Mailer went on, "that I just have a *déjà vu* about this. At any rate, there are some people, including a newspaper man, who are most interested in this notion of the fold-in."

"I see," said Burroughs, "that this has been completely misunderstood, it really is not as arbitrary as it sounds, and I really can't properly illustrate it without a typewriter and pages of text to show it in actual operation, because it is a technique and like all techniques something to experiment with, something to do rather than something to talk about."

A question came from the floor: "Mixing up Shakespeare sonnets as has been done in a literary magazine—would you consider that a serious experiment? It doesn't seem to me a technique at all, it is simply a mix-up."

"I would consider it an interesting experiment," Burroughs said. "It would depend entirely on the result. I do think our mind sometimes does similar things. . . . Of thinking on the borderline of things, only here the methods are much more artificial."

The conference ended that afternoon, and it was clear that Burroughs had run away with it. He had come into it unknown, and emerged a luminary. Far from being a wild man in the Beatnik media image, he was serious and quiet and conservatively dressed, like a Harvard professor. The day after his comments about space, *The Scotsman* headline said WRITERS' CONFERENCE GOES INTO ORBIT. His description of the fold-in technique was reported in detail in *The Times* of London. The true proof of celebrity is to be spoofed, which he was in *Books & Bookmen*, in an article purportedly written in Beatnik style: "When some Dutch scribe said he was a homo, Bill responded by keeping his plastic mac on the whole time, as though he didn't wanna be violated or something. I don't suppose the Dutch guy cared; there were plenty of other queens on that trip anyway."

Burroughs' curious position as a writer whose notoriety preceded the publication of his book in the United States was caught in a *New York Times* column by Raymond Walters, Jr.: "At Edinburgh, when Norman Mailer joined Mary McCarthy in proclaiming William Burroughs the writer of this century who'd most deeply affected the literary cognoscenti, the hall was drenched in puzzled silence. No one present, it seemed, had ever heard of Burroughs.

"It would have been almost—though not quite—the same in this country. . . . He's long been living in such places as Paris and Mexico and now occupies a position roughly comparable to that of Henry Miller before the war. His fellow countrymen know him only as the author of *Naked Lunch* and other Paris-published works whose spicy content raises the gorge of the customs officials and other keepers of American morals." The implication was that *Naked Lunch*, like *Tropic of Cancer*, having found backers in the literary community, would eventually find its way into America's bookstores.

This was in any case the way Barney Rosset saw matters, for after Edinburgh, he decided to print more copies of *Naked Lunch* than the 10,000 in the warehouse, making the most of his author's notoriety. In October, however, there was an initial hurdle when both the printer and the binder (two different outfits) refused to handle the book. Russell Halliday, owner of Halliday Lithograph of West Hanover, Massachusetts, which had done *Lady Chatterley*, wrote Barney: "I am returning this order as I will not allow my name to be associated with this type of literature for reproduction in my plant. . . . Any book that we cannot be proud of here, one that we cannot give to friends and take into our homes is the title we would not be interested in producing."

This had happened to Barney once before, when a printer in Buffalo had refused to run off an issue of the *Evergreen Review* with a poem by Julian Beck of the Living Theater, the last line of which was "Fuck the United States." The printer had said, "We don't mind it if you say 'Fuck the Soviet Union,' but not 'Fuck the United States,' " and Barney had to find another printer, which he also did this time, Book Press in Brattleboro, Vermont.

The book was in the stores by November 20, 1962, and sold briskly—almost 8,000 copies in less than a month. But in January 1963 Grove Press came to another hurdle. Detectives in Boston arrested Theodore Mavrikos, owner of a bookstore at 545 Washington Street, a couple of blocks from the "combat zone" of bars and strip joints, for selling an obscene book—*Naked Lunch*. The arrest came at a time when there was a public clamor to clean up the zone, and Mavrikos had already been arrested nine times for selling obscene material.

After the *Tropic of Cancer* experience, which had almost ruined Grove Press, Barney Rosset did not intend to pay the legal costs of booksellers who were arrested for selling *Naked Lunch*. But there was only one case, in Boston, a state renowned for its institutions of higher learning and for banning books. In 1930, the Massachusetts Supreme Court had held that Theodore Dreiser's *An American Tragedy* was "lewd and obscene." In the 1940s, it suppressed Lillian Smith's novel about an interracial love affair, *Strange Fruit*. Since there was only the Boston case, Barney Rosset asked Edward de Grazia, a lawyer who specialized in First Amendment cases and whom Barney had on retainer, to defend it. De Grazia, a slightly, scholarly looking man who actually reads the books he has to defend, and who considered *Naked Lunch* an important book and perhaps a great book, arranged with the Massachusetts attorney general's office that instead of proceeding with a criminal trial against a single bookseller, the book itself should be put on trial for obscenity. In addition, he waived a jury trial.

In the meantime, Barney Rosset had nominated *Naked Lunch* for the 1963 Prix Formentor, a sort of avant-garde Nobel Prize supported by a group of seven publishers, which had in the past gone to "difficult" writers such as Jorge Luis Borges and Samuel Beckett. Having been thrown out of the Balearic island of Formentor by the puritanical Franco regime, the deliberations were held in May 1963 in a castle in Salzburg. Mary McCarthy, who was on the jury, got up to speak in favor of Burroughs, and after speaking for about five minutes, she broke down, inexplicably, and began to cry, and could not go on, and had to sit down. To Barney Rosset it was as embarrassing as it was dramatic . . . she simply could not continue speaking, and no one knew why. The chairman went on with other matters, and eventually Miss McCarthy rose as if nothing had happened, and in her usual composed and authoritative manner finished her remarks on behalf of Burroughs. No one understood what had happened, and no one had the rudeness to inquire, but it was an extraordinary moment, as well as an ill omen, it turned out, for Burroughs did not win the prize, which might have proved useful in the upcoming trial. (It was awarded to the French novelist Nathalie Sarraute.)

The Boston trial was set for January 1965. As it happened, Burroughs was visiting the United States at the time, and Ed de Grazia wondered whether he should call him as a witness. Barney thought it was a good idea, as it hadn't been done before, in the previous trial over Henry Miller and D. H. Lawrence. Why not call the author? What better spokesman could there be for his book?

Ed de Grazia had met Burroughs at a Grove Press party, and thought he would make a good impression on the stand. They had talked about Jean Genet, the convict-writer, and Burroughs said that the difference between them was that Genet was fond of prison while he was not. Later when he met Genet, de Grazia asked him about that, and Genet said yes, it might be so, for in prison he felt attractive to the other convicts and even to the guards, but in any case how would Burroughs know about jail since he had always had enough money to get himself sprung?

In this case, thought de Grazia, it was not Burroughs who was on trial but his book, and de Grazia was hoping to validate the doctrine that material with literary value could not be held obscene, no matter how much sex and bad language it contained. He was concerned that there might be a line of "when-did-you-stop-beating-your-wife" questioning if Burroughs took the stand, in connection with the shooting of his wife, and decided not to use him as a witness. In any event, he had plenty of other impressive witnesses.

The trial opened on January 12, 1965, with Massachusetts Superior Court Judge Eugene A. Hudson presiding. The prosecutor was William I. Cowin from the attorney general's office. Norman N. Holland, an English professor at M.I.T. who was due to testify on behalf of the book, found himself in the men's room with Cowin, who unburdened himself of what he really thought of the trial, which was that "I'm prosecuting this case because various old ladies are getting on the attorney general's back and insist that he do something about this book or that book. I wish I was devoting my time to something more important, and so does the A. G., but we have to bow to public opinion" . . . which didn't make Cowin any less determined to win the case.

The first witness was John Ciardi, poetry editor of the *Saturday Review* and translator of Dante's *Divine Comedy*, which, as he explained, also had its obscene passages and four-letter words—when Dante dipped the sins in excrement, he called it shit. In the *Inferno*, there was a parody of a military grafter who signaled his commander by making a trumpet of his ass and breaking wind in imitation of a military trumpet, which was not unlike the "talking asshole" passage in *Naked Lunch*. There was also a passage in which two sinners frozen in ice up to their necks ate the head of a third, which was similar to a cannibalistic passage in *Naked Lunch*.

Prosecutor Cowin asked Ciardi why the book contained so many references to baboons. "Burroughs finds himself in a nightmare world," Ciardi explained, "a kind of Hieronymus Bosch world of unreality and topsy-turviness; and inevitably some of those purple rumps of baboons flash through it. It's part of the pictograph of his particular madness."

Ciardi, while not an unconditional admirer of the book, said that it was "a substantial work by an author of some talent and of serious commitment. I do not think *Naked Lunch* is a great work of art. It is, however, memorable, serious, and important."

There followed a number of witnesses from the academic community who brought out that Burroughs was ultimately a moral writer, whose scenes of perversity were meant to revolt rather than titillate the reader. *Naked Lunch* was a highly literary work, with allusions to Anglo-Saxon battle poetry, Shakespeare, eighteenth-century mock-heroic, and the "Ancient Mariner," all of them distorted or altered in some way. "The total effect," said Gabrielle Bernhard Jackson, who taught English at Wellesley, "is of a literary tradition which has lost force and vitality, which presents a series of unacceptable verbal actions, or verbal actions acceptable only as parody, just as the contemporary society which relies on this tradition presents a series of unacceptable real actions."

Then Norman N. Holland, who had chatted with prosecutor Cowin in the men's room, testified that *Naked Lunch* was "a religious novel about original sin. . . . If Saint Augustine were writing today he might well write something like *Naked Lunch*."

"What was that again, please?" asked Judge Hudson, a prim and blinkered Irish Catholic who was convinced from the start to the finish of the trial that the book was revolting, and who among many outrageous remarks had now heard it mentioned in the same breath with one of the great theologians of the holy and apostolic Church. Holland imagined that Judge Hudson might have asked at that point, with his Irish brogue, "Do you mean to say, Professor, that the blessed saint would write something like *this book*?"—holding it up like a dead mackerel between thumb and forefinger.

Then Norman Mailer took the stand, and said he had read *Naked Lunch* three times and had liked it better each time. "The man has extraordinary talent," he said. "Perhaps he is the most talented writer in America, [and] as a professional writer I don't like to go about bestowing credit on any other writers."

Mailer saw "a deep work, a calculated work, a planned work . . . the artistry was more deliberate and more profound than I thought before. There is a structure to the book, you see, which is doubtless imperfect. I think one reason we can't call it a great book like *Remembrance of Things Past* or *Ulysses* is the imperfection of this structure. There is no doubt as to the man's talent; while it was, perhaps, excited and inflamed by drug addiction, it was also hurt. This man might have been one of the greatest geniuses of the English language if he had never been an addict."

"I don't want you to feel hurt that I haven't read any of your books,"

Judge Hudson interjected, ". . . but in any one of those books did your style involve sex in the naked sense?"

". . . Nothing that would be comparable to this," Mailer replied, "because I write in a far chaster tradition."

Mailer was followed by Allen Ginsberg, who was wearing a shirt and tie and collar for the occasion, but his shirt collar was twisted. Judge Hudson, grimacing slightly, observed him as he took the stand, and said, "Straighten your collar." Allen explained that the book's theme was not only drug addiction, but addiction on a larger scale, addiction to power, addiction to material goods, addiction to controlling others. Ed de Grazia, who by now did not consider his changes were worth a hill of Boston baked beans with Judge Hudson on the bench, thought Allen's presentation was bound to help in the appellate review.

Prosecutor Cowin argued that the book met the three recognized tests of hard-core pornography—lack of social value, appeal to prurient interests, and patent offensiveness. On March 23, 1965, Judge Hudson ruled that *Naked Lunch* was obscene. He had failed to appreciate the book's merit, thought Ed de Grazia, and had decided that the book was obscene by the standards of his own mind rather than by the standard of Justice William J. Brennan's opinion in the *Tropic of Cancer* case.

Ed de Grazia appealed, and argued his case before the Massachusetts Supreme Court on October 8, 1965. But the court delayed its decision on *Naked Lunch* pending the outcome of three other obscenity cases being reviewed by the U.S. Supreme Court, which would test and further define the so-called Brennan doctrine. The doctrine had already been tested in the *Tropic of Cancer* case, when in June 1964, five out of the nine justices voted to reverse a Florida decision that the book was obscene. Formulated by Justice William J. Brennan, the doctrine stated that a work declared obscene was excluded from constitutional protection only if it was held to be "utterly without redeeming social importance. The portrayal of sex in art, literature, and scientific works is not in itself sufficient reason to deny material the constitutional protection of freedom of speech and press." Following the *Tropic* case, the doctrine had to be spelled out, since the Court did not want to be put in the position of having to rule over and over again what was or was not too filthy for the American public. As Chief Justice Earl Warren put it, "I'm sure the Court doesn't want to be a final censor in reading all the prurient literature in the country to determine whether it has any social value."

Thus, on March 21, 1966, decisions were handed down on the three other obscenity cases under review. Ralph Ginzburg, who had been sentenced to five years in prison for using the mails to sell his magazine *Eros*, saw his conviction upheld, because his "stock in trade [was] the sordid business of pandering—the business of purveying textual or graphic matter openly advertised to appeal to the erotic interest of their customers."

Edward Mishkin, who had been sentenced to three years in prison for publishing pornographic books with such titles as *Screaming Flesh* and *Cult of the Spankers*, also saw his conviction upheld, although Justice Black's dissenting opinion said that the Supreme Court had no business acting as a "national board of censors over speech and press."

In the third case, however, *The Memoirs of Fanny Hill* was ruled not to be obscene in an opinion by Justice Brennan which clearly defined three tests for obscenity:

1. The dominant theme of the material taken as a whole appeals to a prurient interest in sex.

2. The material is patently offensive because it affronts contemporary community standards relating to the description or representation of sexual matters.

3. The material is utterly without redeeming social value.

All three elements had to be present for a work to be declared obscene.

With these firm guidelines, knowing where the High Court stood, the Massachusetts Supreme Court ruled on July 7, 1966, that *Naked Lunch* was not obscene, in the first application of the new tests to a contemporary work of literature. By a vote of five to two, the Massachusetts court ruled that although the book met the first two tests it could not be said to be "utterly without redeeming social value," and was thus not obscene. Dissenting Justice Paul C. Reardon said that he had found the book to be "a revolting miasma of unrelieved perversion and disease, graphically described. . . . It is, in truth, literary sewage." But his was the minority view.

The ruling on *Naked Lunch* in effect marked the end of literary censorship in the United States. Americans were finally allowed to read what they wanted to read.

It was fitting that the final battle between First Amendment rights and America's puritan heritage should have been fought in the city which made "banned in Boston" part of the national culture. No book like *Naked Lunch* had been cleared before—a book that made *Tropic of Cancer* seem sedate. Since nothing that would come after it would come close in bad language and objectionable scenes, it would set the standard for what was not obscene. Thus, *Naked Lunch* was the last work of literature to be censored by the post office, the Customs Service, and by a state government. And, as we all know, today's dirty book becomes tomorrow's college textbook. The *Naked Lunch* decision also left the door ajar for hard-core pornography, which squeezed into the opening, and this raises the question of whether the right to be sexually aroused is guaranteed by the First Amendment . . . but that's another matter.

All during the period of the book's publication and the trial in Boston, Burroughs had a more immediate problem, which was that he was finding it impossible to collect his share of the American royalties from Maurice Girodias. The arrangement was that Grove sent the royalties to Girodias's agent in Switzerland, Odette Hummel. In October 1963, for example, Barney Rosset cabled $9,500 to Odette Hummel, representing the royalties on 9,405 copies of *Naked Lunch* sold between January and June 1963. At that time, Burroughs, who was supposed to be getting his share of the American royalties, was in Tangier, so broke he could not pay his rent or repair his typewriter. He was in fact truly destitute, for he had told his parents he no longer needed the $200-a-month allowance they had been sending him since his graduation from Harvard, now that he had his royalties. For the first time in his life he was financially independent, or would have been had not Girodias siphoned off his royalties to settle his mounting debts.

Burroughs mentioned his predicament to Paul Bowles, who was also published by Grove, and who wrote his editor Richard Seaver (the one-time editor of *Merlin* in Paris, who had gone to Grove in 1959), "Too bad what happened to Bill Burroughs: your whole advance to him for *Naked Lunch* lost by Girodias, and no hope of ever recovering any of it, obviously."

Seaver had not realized there was a problem, and at once wrote Burroughs to ask what could be done to make sure he got his royalties. Burroughs replied that as far as collecting from Maurice, "It is a question of find a lawyer and get in line and the line is long and the till is empty. The plain fact is he spent the money to cover what he evidently considered more pressing debts and I was barely able to squeeze out of him enough to get myself back to Tangier.

"Despite my understandable annoyance with Maurice," Burroughs went on, "I still sympathize with his position, which could hardly be worse. More and more trouble with the French authorities, suspended sentences piling up, a twenty-year publishing ban, inevitable debacle of that unfortunate restaurant venture, owing money to his staff, social security to the government, fines, lawsuits, the lot."

Girodias was going under, and was frantically trying to bail himself out with every dollar that came in. In February 1964, Burroughs arrived in Paris to confront him and was greeted with the words, "I have a terrible confession to make." It was utterly hopeless. As Burroughs wrote Alan Ansen on February 27, "Some people are self-destructive and want to lose money, it's a thing I read about in the *Reader's Digest*. What a stupid bastard he is—and you know, I found out most of the money he spends on cunt and doesn't even get that he is a John." Feeling guilty about his treatment of Burroughs, Girodias wrote Barney on March 19 that "he is actually starving in Tangier and, as I am in a similar position in Paris, I simply cannot send him anything."

Thus, Grove Press began to send Burroughs his two-thirds share of the American royalties direct, and by 1967 he had received a total of $39,008.52 for *Naked Lunch*. But there continued to be some activity in Switzerland, with Odette Hummel selling foreign rights to Burroughs' books without his knowledge.

As Speaker of the House "Uncle Joe" Cannon used to say, the same sun that brings out the lilies bring out the snakes. This adage could well be applied to the critical reaction to *Naked Lunch*—Burroughs had his share of both. Mary McCarthy praised the book in *Encounter* and in the first issue of the *New York Review of Books*, and wondered whether Burroughs felt "more and more like the groom in a shotgun wedding, seeing my name yoked with his as it were indissolubly." There were other admiring reviews in *Newsweek*, which called the book "indeed a masterpiece," in the *Herald Tribune*, where Richard Kluger called Burroughs "a writer of rare power," and in the Sunday *New York Times*, where Herbert Gold called the book "a booty brought back from a nightmare."

There was also a chorus of disgust, about which Burroughs was understandably thin-skinned, since this was the first time he had been reviewed. He came to think of book reviewers as people who come onto a battlefield after the battle is over to finish off the wounded. The review that really drew his ire was the one in *Time*, because it was an inaccurate personal attack.

"He is not only an ex-junky," said *Time*, "but an ex-con and a killer. In Mexico, having acquired a wife, he shot her between the eyes playing William Tell with a revolver. . . . He has even been in the army but not for long; he reacted to being drafted by cutting off a finger joint, and was discharged with the notation 'not to be recalled or reclassified.' " Burroughs had cut off his finger joint under entirely different circumstances, and the review brought him to the boiling point. He sued for libel in

London, where he was then living, and won. But the damages he collected, which the court deemed to be just compensation for the damage to his reputation, amounted to five pounds.

In form, *Naked Lunch* was startling, bearing as much resemblance to the conventional novel as a videotape to the Bayeux tapestry, or a strobe light to a candle. Instead of characters, with backgrounds, families, personalities, and activities, characters that the reader might come to care about, Burroughs shuffled a series of bit players from his central-casting office: the Gimp, the Vigilante, the Paregoric Kid, the Shoe Store Kid, the Rube, Pantopon Rose, Clem Snide the Private Asshole. To which he added a few noncharacter actors, such as A.J., Dr. Benway, and Clem and Jody. These exist usually to perform a single function, as the drone exists to fertilize the queen. Clem and Jody are Russian agents masquerading as good ol' boys, whose function it is to cast the United States in an unpopular light. A.J., an agent of chaos, exists to play disgusting practical jokes—he puts piranhas in a socialist's swimming pool, and adds a drug mixture to the punch at a Fourth of July celebration in the U.S. Embassy. Dr. Benway is the stock figure of the outrageous doctor, going back to Molière.

Nor is there any "story" or plot in the usual sense, for the book jumps from place to place and scene to scene in a dizzying manner, according to the original random arrangement made by the printer. There is no psychological analysis of the characters' emotion, since there are no characters and practically no emotions except fear and loathing. Instead, Burroughs delivers a series of rapid-fire sketches or routines, in which he dredges up, from his experience as an addict and wanderer, a vision of the post-Bomb society. After the Bomb, there was rubble and the smell of death, and dust over everything, and subterranean creatures surfacing—and that is the scene he describes.

I am not a recording instrument . . . I do not presume to impose "story," "plot," "continuity" . . . Insofar as I succeed in direct recording of certain areas of psychic process I may have limited function . . . I am not an entertainer.

Burroughs' intention was to adopt the oldest fiction format in the world, the picaresque novel: a series of events, horrific and humorous, that occur on a trip, as in Petronius's *Satyricon*. The author's narrator and alter ego, William Lee, is an antihero, like Jack Wilton in *The Unfortunate Traveler*.

Burroughs' antihero is operating from the angle of vision of the drug addict. The fragmentation of the text is like the discontinuity of the addict's life between fixes. Junk means relief, from the whole life process, "from caring about the atom bomb and the cancer rent." But junk also means stagnation and fear of the police. As the book opens, the narrator, Bill Lee, is a hunted man. The addict society is divided among hustlers, marks, and cops. Junk permeates every moment, and the book is full of references to "the junk-sick dawn" and "the old junky walk." Junk is also connected to the magical universe, it is "surrounded by magic and taboos, curses and amulets." Junk is an international subculture, there is a "world network of junkies, tuned in on a cord of rancid jissom, tying up in furnished rooms, shivering in the junk-sick morning." In the attraction/revulsion duality of junk, there is a strong element of self-loathing, both autobiographical and visionary.

For Burroughs sees addiction as a general condition not limited to drugs. Politics, religion, the family, love, are all forms of addiction. In the post-Bomb society, all the mainstays of the social order have lost their meaning, and bankrupt nation-states are run by "control addicts."

The theory of addiction came into my head when the junk went into my arm. It was a metaphor for society. You start bending the word addiction out of shape and you see what it means. You can see withdrawal symptoms in the face of someone like Nixon, when the power ain't there no more. Addiction means somethin' that you've gotta have or you're sick. Power and junk are symmetrical and quantitative: How much? If you're a C.I.A. man you don't want to be the cop on the beat.

Thus the power addicts entrench themselves in self-perpetuating hierarchies using sophisticated control methods. Bureaucracy is their instrument: "Democracy is cancerous, and bureaus are its cancer." Corruption is another instrument: "As one judge said to another: 'Be just, and if you can't be just, be arbitrary.' " Political systems generate what Burroughs calls "a virus power," which manifests itself in such out-of-control phenomena as the proliferation of nuclear weapons and the pollution of the environment.

It's actually a common theme of twentieth-century literature to view the men in charge as grotesque, as in the work of Céline, Nathanael West, or Sinclair Lewis. Burroughs, however, isn't interested in satire but in the actual description of what he sees as a functioning system based on control and addiction. He reminds us that in the twentieth century the lunatics have taken over the asylum—we have seen the rise of the pathological leader, such as Hitler, Stalin, de Gaulle, Richard Nixon, and Lyndon Johnson (with plenty of more recent minor examples, from Idi Amin to Ferdinand Marcos and Papa Doc). Things have gotten too much out of control for there to be any point to reform. To concern oneself with politics, says Burroughs, is to make the mistake of the bull in the ring, which is to charge the cloth. In exactly the same way that the bull-fighter conditions the bull to follow the cloth, politics teaches the masses to follow images and illusions. We're in a state of emergency, says Burroughs, and the only thing to do is go back to the drawing board.

The book may have come from the feeling that the whole human organism and its way of propagating itself is repellent and inefficient. A living being is an artifact, like the flintlock. Well, what's wrong with the flintlock? Just about everything. It's unworkable in a driving rain, it has a low rate of fire-power, you have to keep cleaning out the touch-hole. Whereas in the modern assault rifle, the bullets have no casings, hence no cartridges to eject. This may be getting close to the final development of small arms, but the human artifact is back there with the flintlock. They will produce themselves into the sea, as Joselito says. [This prophecy of devolution is uttered by one of the characters in *Naked Lunch*.] *There are possibilities of more efficient organisms. If you don't use it you lose it.*

What gives the book credibility is that Burroughs is writing out of his own experience. He's been there. The situation of the society is his situation. Every page is strewn with autobiographical clues, which the uninformed reader would not recognize. The use of the English slang word "grassed" (for squealed) is a reminder of his friendship with the gangster Paul Lund in Tangier. A line from a World War II song, "Eager beaver wooing him (her) much too fast," is a glimpse of the first war years when Burroughs tried in vain to serve his country as an officer. The line "would stand still for Joe Gould's Seagull Act" evokes the Greenwich Village of the forties where Burroughs lived. Old Ike is Old Dave, his Mexico City connection, with whom he took speedballs (morphine and cocaine).

K.E. is Kells Elvins, with whom Burroughs went to Sweden: "Sweden . . . brings you all the way down. . . . I said, 'K.E., let's get right back on that ferry.' " "Overdose of H. His old lady shaking him and holding hot coffee under his nose" is a scene that took place between Burroughs and Joan in Yonkers, in the forties. The death of Joan, the tragedy that freed him to be a writer, is obliquely described. In Mexico, Joan disappears with a pimp trombone player. Then they are smoking tea, "and her flesh crystallizes" (in death), and the narrator leaps up screaming, "I got the fear!" and runs out of the house. "A year later in Tangier I heard she was dead."

The description of the political party of Interzone was based on the nationalist Moroccan party, the Istiqlal, which Burroughs came to know while living in Tangier, with its anticolonialist rhetoric and jingoistic anti-foreigner appeals. The Istiqlal platform, translated into day-to-day life, meant a Tangier shoeshine boy snarling, "We will push you into the sea."

In Burroughs' version, the one worthwhile party is the Factualists, who are against the misuse of control techniques: "We oppose, as we oppose atomic war, the use of such knowledge to control, coerce, debase, exploit, or annihilate the individuality of another living creature." The other parties, the Liquefactionists, the Divisionists, and the Senders, all want to rule the world through parasitic possession. The Liquefactionists want to eliminate everyone but themselves. The Divisionists, who are all latent or overt homosexuals, want to flood the world with replicas of themselves and create a one-sex society. The Senders, who want to control everyone through telepathy, are not even human, but examples of a virus. Under the control of these parties, "the broken image of Man moves in minute by minute and cell by cell. . . . Poverty, hatred, war, police-criminals, bureaucracy, all symptoms of the Human Virus."

Each party is infiltrated by agents of the others. In fact, the agent emerges as the key figure in the postnuclear society, which is riddled with people who are not acting on their own, but for some outside interest, and have thus given up their autonomy. *Jesus was the first agent: I am nothing compared with He who sent me. A C.I.A. agent is nothing compared with Langley, Virginia. Agents do what they are assigned to do by whoever they represent. There's an element of deceit, since they don't represent themselves as agents, and deceit has become an addiction in itself. The agent is hostile. William Lee the narrator is himself an agent, representing Hassan I Sabbah, the master of the assassins.* (Nothing is true, everything is permitted.)

The world after the Bomb, ruled by men addicted to power, is in a sorry state. How can the leaders, as they manufacture weapons that could end human life on the planet, expect any kind of order or restraint? How can they ask for a barrier to obscenity when the government supports the greatest obscenity of all, a nuclear arsenal? Thus, what we get in *Naked Lunch*, as analogy to the inventory of nuclear weapons, is an inventory of sexual fantasies and perversions that are meant to revolt. If they show anything about the author, it is his puritan disgust with the flesh. The nuclear age means "anything goes," on all levels, including the sexual, which becomes as monstrous as a pile of irradiated, ash-covered corpses.

"A coprophage calls for a plate, shits on it and eats the shit, exclaiming 'Mmmmmmm, that's my rich substance.' "

"A beastly young hooligan has gouged out the eye of his confrere and fucks him in the brain."

"I am fucking this citizen . . . he comes to a climax and turns himself into some kinda awful crab . . ."

Burroughs is writing in the tradition of seventeenth-century Puritan ideology, in which the sins of the flesh take you straight to hell. He is at once horrified by and attracted to the untamed part of the human personality. Acting out his most extreme impulses in writing was a way of suppressing them in real life.

He also longs for the innocent pastoral prenuclear American landscape in nostalgic passages that summon up his St. Louis boyhood: "Through the bars of East St. Louis lies the dead frontier, riverboat days." "Frogs croak in vacant lots where corn grows and boys catch little green garter snakes under broken limestone stelae." Behind the hanging scenes and the gang-bangs and the images of discharge and defecation is an authentic American wistfulness for the way things used to be: *What I want for dinner is a bass fished in Lake Huron in 1920.*

But post-Bomb America is old and dirty and evil—always cops and always trouble. "The U.S. drag closes around us like no other drag in the world." Again, Burroughs was writing from life, from his brushes with the law in New York, Texas, and Louisiana, and from his hatred of government regulation while a farmer in East Texas.

It's no fun to have such a sour vision of life, to see humanity as degraded and malign, to be on the lookout for the monstrous and disgusting to the exclusion of almost everything else. It's bound to affect you, so that you retreat into fatalism (*son cosas de la vida*) or hopelessness (many of Burroughs' characters are suffering from incurable afflictions, such as Irreducible Neural Damage). And yet Burroughs is able finally to shuck off all the pessimism and come up with a moral in the Emersonian vein, the moral of the autonomous man, who is not an agent or a creature of control systems: He is an individual, he is his own authority.

There's something heroic in Burroughs' ability to tramp through the swamps without sinking: the swamp of addiction, the swamp of homosexuality, the swamp of pessimism. In a sense, he writes his way out, for his material is not composed in the ordinary way, but dredged up from dreams and *majoun* hallucinations—it is an articulation of his own panic. Small wonder he repeatedly invokes Coleridge, another drug-assisted writer. When Burroughs writes something scary, you can be sure that it has scared him first.

A light sleeper, Burroughs was in the habit of waking after a dream and jotting it down. In this manner entire passages were transcribed from dreams. The end of *Naked Lunch* came in a nightmare he had while attending Dr. Dent's nursing home. He was walking through a rubbish heap after an atomic blast. Five Arabs were coming toward him: "He carries an open can of gasoline. . . . Throw the gasoline on them and light it." "I woke up with the taste of metal in my mouth back from the dead."

As much as Burroughs protests that he's just a recording device, he secretly knows he's more than that. There's a visionary side to *Naked Lunch*, perhaps only a logical result of the chaotic world he's describing, where the worst-case scenario comes true. Repeatedly, for instance, he mentions LSD, which no one then had heard of, years before Timothy Leary gave a generation its nonmarching orders.

In another passage, he predicts the coming of a viral venereal disease that originates in Africa, as AIDS is believed to have done. It starts in Addis Ababa and spreads from New Orleans to Capetown. The disease shows a predilection for blacks, but whites are not immune. There is no treatment. "Males who resign themselves up for passive intercourse to infected partners . . . may also nourish a little stranger." This may have seemed fantastic when it was published in 1959, but in 1988 it's just an echo of the six o'clock news.

Still another episode that seemed revoltingly farfetched was that of orgasm by hanging. But this, too, has become a social phenomenon chronicled in articles in *The New York Times* and *Vanity Fair*, in a book entitled *Autoerotic Fatalities*, and on *The Oprah Winfrey Show*. It seems that there are between 500 and 1,000 such asphyxiations a year, in which thrill-seeking young men tie a noose around their necks and cut off the blood supply to the brain via the carotid arteries, to heighten the pleasure of masturbation. A little slip, a false move, and they're twisting in the wind. The product of Burroughs' fantasy in 1959 has become a documented practice a quarter century later.

In fact, all of *Naked Lunch*, which seemed to the reviewers a sick and outlandish dream, can today be read as a literal account of what has come to pass at the end of the twentieth century. There is in *Naked Lunch* an oracular element, as Burroughs describes certain things about to happen. It is not, however, the work of a wild-eyed and turbaned seer who reads palms and tea leaves; it is a book written by a Harvard-educated, enormously well-read man who has absorbed all of Western literature. *Naked Lunch* fits quite properly in the same American literary tradition as *Moby Dick*, of the quest without fulfillment; of the one that got away, whether a fish or a civilization.

There are many literary allusions in the text, but as Burroughs' friend Alan Ansen pointed out, "Where in Pound and Eliot they achieve the mournful dignity of old columns, in Burroughs they often lie around like discarded Coca Cola caps." Rather than pile up references as the scaffolding for a new poem, which is what Eliot does in *The Waste Land*, rather than repeat passages in classical Greek or Chinese that are incomprehensible to the general reader, as Pound does in the *Cantos*, Burroughs' allusions are often throwaway lines, so that you hardly notice them, as when someone says he's going to "cowboy [kill] the white whale."

In one scene at least, however, there is a sustained allusion, taken from Joseph Conrad's *Under Western Eyes*. The scene is called "The Examination," in which Carl Petersen, whose sense of identity has been destroyed by the modern state, is summoned to the Ministry of Mental Hygiene to be questioned by Dr. Benway. It is based on the scene in Conrad's book in which Razumov, a student in St. Petersburg, who has turned in his fellow student Haldin for committing a political assassination, is called in for questioning by Councillor Mikulin.

Under Western Eyes: "[Mikulin's] mild gaze rested on him, not curious, not inquisitive, certainly not suspicious—almost without expression. In its passionless persistence there was something resembling sympathy."

Naked Lunch: "For the first time the doctor's eyes flickered across Carl's face, eyes without any emotion Carl had ever experienced in himself or seen in another—at once cold and intense, predatory and impersonal."

Razumov rebels under questioning, saying: "I protest against this comedy of persecution. The whole affair is becoming too comical altogether for my taste. A comedy of errors, phantoms, and suspicions. . . . Really, I must claim the right to be done once for all with that man. And in order to accomplish this I shall take the liberty . . . to retire—simply to retire."

Carl also wants to remove himself, saying: "It's just that the whole thing is unreal . . . I'm going now. I don't care. You can't force me to stay."

Razumov: "He walked to the door, thinking, 'Now he must show his hand. He must ring and have me arrested before I am out of the building, or he must let me go. And either way' . . ."

Carl: "He was walking across the room toward the door. He had been walking a long time. A creeping numbness dragged his legs. The door seemed to recede."

Razumov: "Razumov at the door turned his head. 'To retire,' he repeated.

" 'Where to?' asked Councillor Mikulin softly."

Carl: " 'Where can you go, Carl?' The doctor's voice reached him from a great distance. 'Out . . . Away . . . Through the door . . .

" 'The Green Door, Carl?' "

In both scenes, the police figure knows there is no place to hide. Razumov will be recruited by the czarist police to go to Geneva and spy on the Russian émigré colony. A betrayal sets off a chain reaction, and you can never get out from under, as Burroughs knew from having been set up by Paul Lund. Carl Petersen, the post-Kafka, post-Orwell, post-Bomb Razumov, doesn't even know what he's charged with, but he too will become an agent.

Look in the sky—dropping down like paratroopers over Burroughs' prostrate form are platoons of doctoral candidates, their chutes billowing against the blue, loaded down with backpacks full of dissertations—*sauve qui peut*! Actually, their interest validates *Naked Lunch* as an important work, one that survived the initial scandal to become a classic in its own time. There is a richness in the text that lends itself to multiple interpretations. Take for instance the "talking asshole" routine, which on the obvious level takes the form of an overelaborate scatological joke. "Did I ever tell you about the man who taught his asshole to talk?" Dr. Benway asks. "His whole abdomen would move up and down you dig farting out the words."

Over the years serious critics have read all sorts of things into this passage. Clearly, it seems to be an attempt to overcome that great error of Western thinking, the mind-body duality, which Burroughs sees as a control method based on fraudulent, either-or differentiation. (You think as much with your big toe as with your mind, Korzybski used to say.) Confounding the orifice of language with the orifice of evacuation is one way of overcoming the duality.

Or is it a conflict between the oral and the anal, between mouth and anus, with one organ victorious in its struggle with the ego? Is it a defense against Burroughs' psychic masochism?

Or does it have to do with the relation between language and matter? Language in the wrong hands is another control method, as Burroughs knew firsthand from the career of his uncle, Ivy Lee. If anus and mouth become a single orifice, language loses its privileged position, it sinks to the same level as the shit that gets flushed down the toilet. There is a warning in the "talking asshole" routine about the power of language, which is not to be trusted. "Documents are forgeries by nature," Burroughs says. The connection between the name and the object is arbitrary, and Burroughs is trying to liberate the reader from the snares of "in the beginning was The Word."

Or is it an allegory, with the "talking asshole" representing the body politic, and the triumph of bureaucracy, and the bureaucrats shoveling their gobbledygook shit?

One critic, Robin Lydenberg, finds that the "talking asshole" routine connects Burroughs to a tradition of "man-as-beast" imagery that goes back to Cervantes. In one passage in *Don Quixote*, two aldermen try to coax a lost donkey out of hiding by imitating its braying. The two aldermen making asses of themselves seem like precursors of the talking asshole. Later, when Sancho Panza asks for a raise, his master tells him, "An ass you are and an ass you must be, and an ass you will end when the course of your life is run." The lesson is that man becomes a beast when he seeks material rewards. Burroughs is on the same track. Like Don Quixote, he seeks to transcend the earthly realm, not heavenward but by looking for ways to leave this accursed planet spaceward.

All these latter-day assessments, all these critical responses, all these ingenious theories, are a source of amusement to the author, to whom they had not occurred. Inspired by the Pétomane, the French vaudeville performer who could fart the "Marseillaise," he merely wanted to write a routine about a man who taught his asshole to talk. He did not see the implication of what he wrote. Perhaps that is the mark of the major writer, one whose work is rich with implication, and who therefore attracts repeated critical scrutiny.

Of course some critics thought the experimentation went too far. *Naked Lunch* was too fragmented, too episodic, too arcane. As he went along, Burroughs burned his bridges. It was as bad as *Finnegans Wake*. The irony was that Burroughs never imagined he was writing an experimental work. He was writing as simply and straightforwardly as he could, just setting it down as it came to him. He was, however, trying to avoid manipulating the reader with plot twists and heart tugs. Yes, he shocks the reader with some outrageous scenes, but nothing in the book, he likes to point out, is as absurd as what one reads in the daily newspaper.

He was quite open about his intention in *Naked Lunch*, which was not to entertain but to instruct. When the *Titanic* is sinking, the only sensible thing to do is point the way to the lifeboats. As Anthony Burgess noted, "Burroughs' strength lies in his uninhibited prose, his ability to attack the nerves, but this prose is, in *Naked Lunch*, in the service of a didactic aim, not an artistic one." And yet here is another either/or: Why cannot a book be both didactic and artistic, as much of Swift was, as Dante and Milton were? Surely the two have been often reconciled in Western literature.

Naked Lunch continues to be read, more than a quarter century after its publication. It has never been out of print. Indeed, it remains something of a cult book among the young, and is often stolen from the shelves of college libraries. It has also become a tasty meal for doctoral candidates and critics, who recognize it as one of the important works of post–World War II American literature. As Tony Tanner put it in *City of Words*, "William Burroughs, too often seen as a peripheral figure mongering in his own obscene nightmares and eccentric experiments, in a profound way is an important writer, concerning himself precisely with many of those themes and problems which are central to American fiction."

FIFTEEN

BURROUGHS
MEETS LEARY

1960–1961

In April 1960, following his drug bust in Paris, Burroughs left for London, settling into a room in the Empress Hotel, at 25 Lillie Road. He occasionally saw Ian Sommerville, who was in his last year at Cambridge, and he lectured to the Heretics Club on the cut-ups. He lived quietly, writing his next novel, *The Soft Machine*, a cut-up work based on material left over from *Naked Lunch*. This material was his "Word Hoard," a mass of notes and routines that he would continue to recycle into two additional novels, *The Ticket That Exploded* and *Nova Express*. Mired in work, Burroughs did little socializing. For relaxation, he would spend a quiet afternoon in the cemetery near the hotel. You couldn't find a more pleasant place to sit in all of London.

With the publication of *Naked Lunch* in Paris and his growing fame as the mystery man of the literary underground, Burroughs had changed, as if he had become a character in his own book. Like his narrator, William Lee, he now thought of himself as an agent surrounded by hostile forces and menacing viruses. Writing was the all-important activity that would protect him—he had to get down on paper the instructions for survival on the planet.

He sent a typescript of cut-ups by himself and Brion Gysin to Dave L. Haselwood, who ran a small press in San Francisco, explaining that his writing was "only a transcription of voices along the streets and quarters where I pass. Abstract literature. Not Personal Opinions. Do these plots really exist? How in the fuck should I know? Just a writer is all. Just an artisan. Not running for office. Just writing what I see and hear in my imagination. Pure abstract literature."

Burroughs now dated his letters "present time," and told Haselwood that he wanted *Exterminator!* (as the collection was called) published "in response to present need." When Haselwood asked for biographical data, he responded: "I have no past life. Talk to my medium."

His medium was Brion Gysin, who was not so detached from worldly concerns, for he wrote Haselwood to complain that his name was not mentioned in the ad for the book, whereas he was the inventor of the cut-up technique. "There is no literary bucking for place here," Gysin said. "Times are just hard enough as it is without any misunderstanding."

Like *Minutes to Go, Exterminator!* was a book of cut-ups, with Gysin still trying to RUB OUT THE WORDS/OUT THE WORDS RUB, and playing with other permutations such as CAN MOTHER BE WRONG, and JUNK IS NO GOOD BABY. Whereas Burroughs prepared his mixture as before, of newspapers and literary texts, coming up with pithy phrases such as, "Is this shit necessary language of life?"

As the flap copy explained, "Burroughs in this his latest work has thrown away all traces of a polite regard for the sacred cows of narrative fiction. . . . Magazine and newspaper articles, headlines and catch-phrases of the day are cut up, scrambled and thrown at the reader, or rather, sprayed at him in the same way a machine gun sprays its target."

Concerned about "claim-jumping" on the cut-up method, Burroughs urged speedy publication. Not only were there no claim-jumpers, there were practically no readers, so that when he asked for royalties, as he was "short of the ready," there were no royalties, because the book, in an edition of about 1,000 copies, had not sold. Having just made a futile trip to Paris to collect some money from Girodias, Burroughs was understandably vexed, and took it out on David Haselwood, to whom he wrote: "You seem to be running a mighty loose ship. This is the 5th letter I have sent you and now I hear that you do not intend to publish Exterminator II. I consider your behavior sloppy, dishonest, and downright stupid. Is that clear enough or should I make it even clearer?" Recovering his equanimity, Burroughs accepted the failure of *Exterminator!* since there was always a time lag in the acceptance of new concepts.

When Paul Bowles received a copy of *Exterminator!* from Jack Kerouac's friend John Montgomery, he wrote: "I'm not really convinced of the importance of Burroughs' new kick . . . because I don't believe that abstract literature can help writing much. . . . What does it mean, really, save the expression of unsatisfied desire on the part of the mind to be autonomous?"

That March of 1960, traveling in Marrakesh, Paul found *Naked Lunch* on sale at the bookstore in the Hotel Mamounia. Two tourists were looking at it, and one said, "It's rather expensive. I don't know as I want to pay a pound for it." "Oh, is it a pound, I didn't realize," said the other. "Anyway, I've got the *Tropic of Capricorn* book. That's quite enough."

Still in Paris at the Beat Hotel, Brion Gysin wrote Burroughs that May: "We had the police in again the other day and they gave me a bad moment because they would not believe that it was my passport because I looked too young." In August Ian Sommerville arrived in Paris on his summer holiday and he and Brion did some mirror gazing and saw "lots of powerfully hatted ladies of about 1910."

In London that October, the tranquillity of Burroughs' life was shattered when one day there was a knock on the door of his hotel room and he opened it to find a young man of unusual beauty. Seventeen-year-old Mikey Portman, who had the pouty lips and mischievous eyes of the Caravaggio Bacchus, the kind of face in which youthful self-indulgence is already tinged with decay, was the first of a new breed—the Burroughs worshiper. He had read *Naked Lunch*, had been knocked out by it, and was determined to sit at the author's feet.

But as Burroughs would learn, having Mikey at your feet was not unlike having Missouri chiggers nipping at your ankles. Mikey was selfish, greedy, weak, and undisciplined. Already at seventeen, he had every major vice—homosexuality, drug addiction, and alcoholism. He also had, which made things worse, the funds to gratify his vices, for his family owned large chunks of London real estate. Whenever he ran out of money all he had to do was sign a check. His father had died when he was fifteen, and his bubble-headed mother was wrapped up in her Greek lover. The only stabilizing factor in his life was his godfather, Lord Goodman, who was head of the Arts Council and private lawyer to Harold Wilson. Portly and avuncular, he looked like Alfred Hitchcock. He was a liberal, who refused to serve South African sherry in his home. As the Portman family solicitor, he put Mikey on an allowance and did his best to curb his excesses. Privately, Lord Goodman referred to Mikey as "a poor, shattered thing."

Mikey was one of those young men on whom you could smell trouble. You could almost see a sign around his neck that said HANDLE AT YOUR OWN RISK. Although still in his teens, he already had a reputation for general irresponsibility, such as smoking in bed, or borrowing clothes and not returning them. Michael Wishart, an English painter and man-about-town who invited Mikey to his house in the south of France, wrote in his memoirs, *High Diver*, that when Mikey was around, the gramophone records became ashtrays and the sheets became tourniquets. His house became a rallying ground for the *tout Marseille, quartier Arabe*. Mikey took Wishart's Citroën and crashed it into a ravine, escaping unhurt. "He has nine lives, that boy," his doctor often said. But he was not equipped for terra firma. Wishart concluded, "He is far more beautiful, capricious and unpredictable than any of the monkeys and marmosets I have entertained and been obliged to dispose of in despair."

Burroughs at first was not amused by Mikey's craven attempt at ingratiation. Mikey wanted to take a room in the Empress Hotel at once so he could be near his idol, but Burroughs blocked his move, and he flounced out in a huff. Burroughs had been reading newspaper articles about the Soviet Party Congress, some of whose members had described KGB chief Beria as "crude and rampant," and "an enemy of the Soviet people." He wrote Brion Gysin that Mikey was "crude and rampant." In somewhat the same way as Beria, he could be viewed as an enemy of those he wished to befriend. But Mikey kept coming back, wearing Burroughs down so that finally he felt flattered to have this young hanger-on, whose beauty, he found, produced an aphrodisiac effect.

Of course, it was always touch and go, because Mikey could be infuriating, and although his family was rich, he was always broke and borrowing money and not paying his share. Burroughs tried to get him to stop using heroin, but that was hopeless. And when he was on junk he was a blank. Mikey was a definite liability, but whenever Burroughs said he'd had enough, he would come bouncing back, as in this letter in which he explains that he has split up completely with a friend who had a bad influence on him: "I gather by your letter that this may be exactly the way you feel about me. I am sorry if I have hindered you by my incompetence and sloth but please believe me when I say that, as far as I consciously am, am wholeheartedly for you and what you stand for, and if you think my presence is a hindrance, I will understand with no bad feelings." In the face of Mikey's mea culpas, Burroughs always relented.

On January 5, 1961, Burroughs received a letter from a Harvard professor named Timothy Leary, director of the Center for Research in Personality, Department of Social Relations, Harvard University. Under the auspices of Harvard, Dr. Leary was studying the effects of consciousness-expanding drugs. He wanted to know whether Burroughs, as a leading expert on the subject, would like to try some of his magic mushrooms. "There exists a group of people," Leary wrote, "who are interested in the potentialities of such new substances as mescaline and psilocybin. The latter is the synthesis of the Mexican mushroom. Under the right circumstances with the right people these drugs give not only a memorable high but leave the vision and mind uncluttered—in an enduring way. We—and I refer here to mainly Allen [Ginsberg] and me, with counsel from Aldous Huxley, Alan Watts, etc.—are concerned about the politics of the stuff. . . . I know you see the issue. Medicine has already preempted LSD, marijuana is the football for two other powerful groups—Bohemia and the narcotics agents. Mescaline and psilocybin are still up for grabs and it is our hope to keep them ungrabbed, uncontrolled, available. We are working along these two lines: We are turning on as many well-known opinion-making people as we can. When the issue comes up for legislation we hope to have a strong team to fight the noncontrol game. . . . I've got approval for a seminar next semester in which graduate students regularly take mescaline and psilocybin. . . . So specifically, would you be interested in trying the mushrooms? Perhaps you have already had a go at them. . . . In either case we'd be pleased to have your reaction both to the drug and our vedic aspirations" (Veda being the sacred literature of Hinduism).

This letter from Leary to Burroughs could be said to mark the beginning of the sixties "movement." It shows Leary, at the birth of his "psychedelic revolution," seeking an alliance with those fifties renegades, the Beats. At the same time it shows how, with Leary as their mediator, Burroughs and Ginsberg made the transition from the fifties to the sixties, keeping up with the changing style of the counterculture, while Kerouac remained frozen in time, an icon of the fifties. Neal Cassady made the transition, too, from the Beats to the hippies, via Ken Kesey's Merry Pranksters, for whom he became the driver. It was like the circle closing on the first forays into the world of drugs, with Huncke in the forties, and growing pot in Texas, and bringing it to New York to sell in mason jars, with Neal at the wheel. In the sixties, Neal was again at the wheel, driving the Merry Pranksters bus around as they celebrated acid.

On the run from the anthill, the Beats had been the *coureurs de bois* of the counterculture, blazing trails through the underbrush. They represented the affirmation of existence at a time when America seemed to be suffering from a collective nervous breakdown, the fruit of World War II, which had shaken up the society like nothing else since the Civil War. Mailer in 1957 wrote about the White Negro, the new man, who feels the danger that a black man feels from a hostile society, and who says, why not encourage the psychopath in oneself, as society is doing?

Briefly a Beat movement flourished, whipped up by the media after the success of *On the Road*, but its energy soon flagged. Self-parody was a sure sign of decline, as when Ted Joans advertised himself in the *Village Voice* as a Beatnik for hire at parties. And yet there would have been no *Village Voice* without the energy of the Beats.

So, with the closing of the Eisenhower years, a new set of boat-rockers arrived on the scene. The mutation from Beat to hippie meant a switch from grass to acid, from literature to music, from a small group of writers and artists and jazz musicians to a mass youth movement, from an antipolitical stance to a coalition of antiwar, civil rights, and environmental movements, a great nest into which flew birds of every feather, from yippies to radical nuns and priests.

The Beat mission of expanding consciousness mutated into ecological and antiwar consciousness. The questioning of authority, the drugs, the experimental lifestyle, the leaning toward Eastern philosophy, all were a carryover from the Beats. But in the sixties, concerts began to drown out poetry readings. The sixties people were on an audio trip and didn't need much more poetry than John Lennon's lyrics and Bob Dylan's lyrics, Dylan who had started out writing long Surrealist poems that he sent to *City Lights*, and whose early songs reflected his reading of *Howl* and *On the Road*.

At the heart of this transition, of this generational upheaval, was Dr. Leary, proclaiming that he had the answer in LSD, which would enlighten and free its users. There was a time in the sixties when people wore a blue-and-orange button that said "Leary is God." Of course he had to compete for the title with John Lennon, Bob Dylan, Jim Morrison, and several other contenders.

In 1960, however, Dr. Leary was not yet God, he was a Harvard professor who had not yet stumbled on LSD but who had, through some moment of aberration on the part of the university authorities, been empowered to administer hallucinogenic drugs to graduate students and prominent people in various fields. Although it's not generally known, Harvard had pioneered LSD experiments before Leary, in the mid-fifties, when ads appeared in the *Harvard Crimson* asking for volunteers at twenty-five dollars a day. The undergraduates who responded were taken to Boston's Psychopathic Hospital and given doses of LSD. It was part of a research program into death and dying. But when several of the volunteers freaked out, the LSD testing was discontinued. Later, Harvard gave Leary the go-ahead, in which were planted the seeds of the sixties counterculture. As the Beats got started by being expelled from Columbia, it was when Leary was fired from Harvard in 1963 and went out on his own that he became a leader of the young, "upleveling," as he would put it, failure into success.

At the time that he wrote Burroughs, Leary was a boyish, aggressively clean-cut and tweedy forty-year-old, having been born in 1920 in Springfield, Massachusetts, of a Catholic mother and an army dentist father, who fixed Eisenhower's teeth, among others. An army brat raised mostly by his mother, Leary went to Holy Cross in 1938 but rebelled against the Jesuits, and then got into West Point, where he made it through Beast Barracks before falling from grace. Drunk on the troop train returning to West Point after the Army-Navy game, he missed reveille the following morning. When questioned by the company commander, he would not admit that he was the one who had brought the booze on the train, and he was ordered to report before an Honor Committee made up of other cadets.

When the Honor Committee asked him to resign from the Corps of Cadets, he refused as a matter of pride. His punishment was the Silent Treatment. No cadet was allowed to sit next to him in the mess hall, and he had to request food by writing on a pad. He was a nonperson, completely ignored. In August 1941 he went before a court-martial, which acquitted him, so the Honor Committee decided to demerit him out. Demerits poured down for the flimsiest of reasons, for untrimmed hairs in his nostrils, for a shaving cut cited as "careless injury to government property." Leary agreed to resign from the Point in exchange for vindication by the Honor Committee. He had fought the system to a draw, and would continue to fight it, for the West Point experience had turned him into a subversive, who had decided that "nothing good for America can come from those gray Gothic piles."

There was indeed a pattern of expulsion from military and academic institutions, from West Point, from the University of Alabama in 1942, where he had sneaked into a girls' dormitory, and later from Harvard. But he also obtained his academic credentials at Berkeley, with a doctorate in philosophy, which eventually led to his Harvard appointment.

Leary's adoption of psychedelic drugs came almost by accident. Vacationing in Mexico in the summer of 1960, he took some magic mushrooms in Cuernavaca, obtained from the witch doctor of a nearby village. He went into trances, had visions, and experienced what amounted to a religious conversion. He had seen the face of God, and would never be the same.

Back at Harvard that fall, Leary decided to devote himself to the study of mind expansion through the use of hallucinogenic drugs. He moved to a big house in Newton, five miles from Cambridge. He discovered that the Swiss chemical company Sandoz had isolated psilocybin, the active ingredient of the mushroom. On Harvard stationery, he dictated a letter asking for a supply for research purposes. The pink pills arrived labeled: NOT TO BE SOLD: FOR RESEARCH INVESTIGATION.

Then Leary learned that the Grand Old Man of psychedelic experimentation, Aldous Huxley, who had written two books on mescaline, *The Doors of Perception* and *Heaven and Hell*, was right there in Cambridge, as a visiting professor at M.I.T. It seemed providential. Tall, gray, stooped, and nearly blind, the sixty-six-year-old Huxley reminded Leary's wife Susan of Gandalf the Grey Wizard in Tolkien's *Fellowship of the Ring*.

That October and November Leary and Huxley met to design a research program. They took psilocybin together. Huxley saw it in religious terms, calling it a gratuitous grace. Leary wanted to spread the word of mind expansion, which he saw as a tool for "cracking the psychotic crust" that covered America. The Tree of Knowledge, he thought, had been the first controlled substance, which Adam and Eve had been expelled from paradise for using. The Bible had enforced food and drug prohibitions. The idea was to distribute psilocybin, selectively, and to prevent the government and other meddlers from regulating it.

Leary's ambition was to turn on the entire country, the clergy, the bureaucrats, the politicians, the lawyers, the military, to pop his pills down the nation's throat. But he had to start slowly, and this is where Allen Ginsberg came in—Allen had his ear so close to the ground it was full of grasshoppers, and he heard about Leary's work and asked to visit. Allen came up that December and took some pills, and began recommending people that Leary could contact, for Allen had all sorts of connections—his address book was the *Who's Who* of the counterculture.

Allen of course recommended his friends. Jack Kerouac took the mushrooms, but he was a juicer, who had never liked drugs. His reaction to the claims of instant enlightenment was, "Walking on water wasn't done in a day." Neal Cassady was more receptive, calling psilocybin "the Rolls-Royce of dope." Leary wanted well-known people from the artistic community, whom Allen rounded up—Dizzy Gillespie, Willem de Kooning, Robert Lowell.

"You've got to write a big, enthusiastic letter to Burroughs," Allen said, "and get him interested in taking psilocybin. He knows more about drugs than anyone alive." Responding to Leary's January 5 letter, Burroughs replied on January 20: "I can only say that I think what you are doing is vitally important. Yes, I would be very much interested in trying the mushrooms and writing up the trip as I have done with mescaline. . . . I think the wider use of these drugs would lead to better conditions at all levels. Perhaps whole areas of neurosis could be mapped and eradicated in mass therapy."

Leary sent him the mushrooms in February, reporting that Arthur Koestler had come to stay for three days. His reaction to the mushrooms had been amazingly mixed. The author of *Darkness at Noon* called drugs an obscene short-cut, insisting that he preferred whiskey and good wine, and yet after taking the mushrooms he admitted that they put you in touch with God. He asked Leary for a supply to take back to London so he could turn on his friends. Charles Olson, the two-meter-tall Black Mountain poet, had turned on with Koestler, but Leary found that great writers sparring interfered with the trip. And yet Olson, who had always been down on drugs, was now saying, "Give them all mushrooms."

Leary was already moving into his second phase, which was a group therapy project in a state prison in Concord, Massachusetts, where a hip black prison psychiatrist named Madison Presnell was receptive to his ideas. They would give mushrooms to the convicts every two weeks and hold discussions afterwards. Leary was pretty sure they could turn on some of the guards as well. He also planned a reaching-out program for ex-cons in the area, in which a few would be hired as community liaison to help other ex-cons in trouble, giving them whatever they needed— lawyers, schooling, cash, or mushrooms.

Leary was in a unique position. By using the name and authority of Harvard, he had obtained an unlimited supply of psilocybin, of which he was the sole dispenser, without any faculty supervision. He was happily infiltrating the society with a substance he knew little about, except that it gave you trances and opened the doors of perception. He attributed to it miraculous, behavior-modifying properties, seeing it as a way to change such a normally unregenerate segment of society as the prison population.

Riding the crest of his Utopian wave, he had arranged a symposium at the annual meeting of the American Psychological Association, which was being held that September of 1961 in New York, on "Drugs and the Empirical Expansion of Consciousness," and he wanted Burroughs to be a member of the panel. "We need your moral support," he wrote on February 14. "I know you will understand the tightrope we walk. . . . [the meeting] could be the equivalent of the Armory Show for modern art. Once the snowball starts rolling it's amazing and really shocking to see how everyone, including the most implausible everyone, starts jumping on. I see it this way, that I'm just an academic second-baseman playing in a ball game that you started, and I'd feel a lot better to have you around when we start playing the crucial series."

Burroughs agreed to attend, even though he tried the psilocybin in Paris that March of 1961 and found it awful. It made him nauseated and irritable, and the visions he had were not pleasant—he saw green boys with purple fungoid gills.

In April 1961, he went to Tangier to spend the rest of the spring and summer, staying at the Hotel Muniria. He was sorry to see that the Spanish were all gone, which meant no more boys. It was a changed and sadder place, and all the trees in the Gran Socco had been cut down. Coming through the sidewalk in their place were bearded, sandaled, long-haired creatures of the late Beatnik or early hippie species, the female members with blackened eyes and whitened lips, who had included Tangier on their Occident-to-Orient itinerary. There were so many of them that the town looked like Greenwich Village. Burroughs deplored the presence of these untidy young people, who were in a sense his constituents, who read his books, and whose lifestyle he had helped to spawn.

He tried a hallucinogenic powder called Prestonin (actually dimethyltryptamine, known as "the businessman's buzz," because the high only lasted half an hour), made with ether, which gave him nightmarish visions: "Trips to the ovens like white hot bees through your flesh. But I was only in the ovens for thirty seconds and pretty good for a goy they said, and showed me around a very small planet." Burroughs decided to offer some to Paul Bowles, who was still around, and who was friendly, "but shifty like you know the color he was born," as he wrote to Allen Ginsberg. He went to Paul's apartment and said, "How do you want to take it, inject it or sniff it?" No injections, thank you, thought Paul. He didn't want to get hepatitis from a dirty needle. "All right, I'll sniff it." From a dirty gray bottle, Burroughs took out a substance that looked to Paul like the powder that was ground up out of fried worms to make mescal in Mexico. He made a little paper cone and took a sniff, and then Paul took a sniff, and there was a terrific explosion inside his head. He felt as though his head was a garage, and one of the walls of the garage had blown out, and he had a vision of the side of his head burst open, as in a comic strip. Then he thought he was thousands of miles from anywhere, far far away by himself, like a baby bird melting on a bough. In the meantime, Burroughs had gone into the kitchen to shoot up some more, and came back and asked, "Well, how is it?" A terrified Paul replied,

"I don't know," and Burroughs said, "You're probably gettin' bum kicks." Well, thought Paul, nobody could call it fun. Burroughs didn't like it much either, and was increasingly sure that hallucinogenic drugs were not for him. Going to the ovens reminded him of the ergot outbreaks in medieval France from rotten bread, known as St. Anthony's fire. It was about as unpleasant an effect as you could have with a drug.

The day after he tried Prestonin a cool mist came in from the sea and covered the waterfront. In his hotel room, Burroughs started experimenting with photo montages, which would eventually fill many scrapbooks. He spread some snapshots out on the bed with a gray silk dressing gown he had bought in Gilbraltar and several other objects, and rephotographed the ensemble. It was a sort of photographic cut-up of random objects.

As it turned out, that summer of 1961 in Tangier was a gathering of the tribe. Allen Ginsberg, Alan Ansen, and Gregory Corso turned up, and Burroughs was joined by Ian Sommerville and Mikey Portman. The only counterculture statesman absent from the conclave was Jack Kerouac, who was stuck in the states with a paternity suit.

His wife, Joan Haverty, had given birth to a daughter, Jan, in 1952, and Jack was sure he was not the father, having been told by doctors that he was not fertile as the result of his mumps. As he wrote Neal Cassady that April of 1961: "One night when I went to visit her to try to tell her *On the Road* had been rejected by Giroux 'because the sales manager Ed Hodge wouldn't like it,' she was in bed with a Puerto Rican dishwasher called Rosario. . . . I never knew his second name. . . . I'm certain the girl is not my seed, and I'm going to have the court order the blood test when the time comes. This bitch is trying to take my own mother's life away. You remember as well as I do my mother worked in the shoe factory for years while I wrote most of my books. Now she's retired, on $84 a month Social Security and I take care of the rest. . . . But now this bitch with a shitass tight-faced Jew lawyer is closing in on me for what's left after taxes. . . . There you have the salacious picture of a typical American marriage whore." Jack's conviction that the child was not his should be balanced against Jan Kerouac's striking resemblance to her father. But whoever the father was, how sad and ironic that the man who had eulogized the road was still tied to his mother's apron strings!

That summer of 1961 in Tangier became known as "the psychedelic summer" because they all sampled Leary's pills. Leary-induced chemical euphoria was in the air, but there were many undercurrents as well, having to do with the changing identities of the principal players and with the muddying of waters caused by the presence of new players.

Allen had not seen Burroughs since his departure from the Beat Hotel in 1958, and was still a little worried that Bill's obsession for him remained. In their correspondence, when Allen mentioned that he and Peter Orlovsky had gotten hot and horny with a couple of girls, Bill spitefully replied that Allen would always regret making it with women, that they had teeth in their vaginas, and so on. And then, when Allen, trying to show Bill that no relationship was idyllic, told him that sometimes he had to nag Peter for sex, Bill responded rather superciliously that he had never had that problem with his Spanish boys.

They had both changed. Allen now saw himself as one of the venerables elected by youth to lead them. He had a position, his manuscripts were in demand, even the proofs were sold to a collector, which he found rather ghastly, like selling fingernail clippings. Allen noticed that after the publication of *Naked Lunch* Bill seemed to go through an amazing transformation, seemed to gather strength, seemed to go beyond Allen in ordering his mind and emotions, expanding into a more solid artist role, so that pretty soon, instead of being a suitor, he became a teacher, more and more identified with his writing. His human fallibility and vulnerability dropped off, and he seemed to take on a kind of armor, so that Allen began to feel that he had lost something in the bargain. Bill was no longer dependent on him—or rather, the sexual role had been transposed into the role of editor and agent, a role that Allen gladly took on to compensate for not being able to satisfy him physically. It was another way of showing devotion. Underlying all these feelings was the conviction that they would join up again, which was realized in 1961 when Allen raised some money to go abroad with Peter Orlovsky.

He went first to Paris, where in the Beat Hotel he met Brion Gysin for the first time, writing Burroughs that he considered Brion "unhealthily superstitious." Brion had a big, red, garishly florid face, which frightened Allen. He was coming on with this galloping paranoia, as if everything was a plot and everyone was an agent, seeing conspiracies and correspondences everywhere. Allen was repelled by his hashish-induced performance. He wasn't really able to relax with Brion until years later, when he was giving a reading in Vancouver and looked up Brion's mother, Stella. When he told Brion, the paranoia dissolved. Allen realized that the origin of Brion's anxiety was a feeling of shame about his background. His mother was a farm girl who did not fit in with "the princess circuit." Allen had been through so many twists and turns with his own mother that anyone else's mother was all right with him. He understood that Brion wanted people to think he was self-generated, whereas he had a mom like everyone else.

His other reason for disliking Brion at first was that Brion had so much influence over Bill, and he was a little jealous. Somehow Brion had conned Bill, who had always been a practical and common-sense person, into playing arcane magical games. And it seemed to Allen that he had lost the authority that Brion had gained, and that Brion was making fun of him and undermining whatever authority he had left, so of course he was wary of Brion, although he was careful not to bad-mouth him. He did, however, feel that with the cut-ups Brion had led Bill right down the garden path. Allen liked linear narrative, and thought Bill's prose was enough of a cut-up as it was. The mind already cut material up. Then when Bill started saying that he was doing cut-ups to get messages from other worlds, well, to put it politely, Allen thought that was balls.

When Allen arrived in Tangier that May with Peter Orlovsky, he found a different Bill, aloof and guarded, who seemed no longer to value the old ties of friendship. Allen wondered what it was: Was it the influence of Brion Gysin, who with the cut-up method was pushing him into dehumanization, cutting up people the way he cut up texts? Perhaps the cut-ups were a useful passage, to see where he was going, but working in that mode seemed to be making him humanly unreachable. Or was it, Allen wondered, that Bill was still trying to work out the frustration of their old relationship, that he was now questioning habitual patterns, and asking himself why he had been so long obsessed with someone who was not receptive?

In any case, Allen was startled when at their first meeting Burroughs asked, "Who are you an agent for?" Allen knew he didn't mean a government agent; he meant that one's personality was a composite of all the influences and viruses that had already been contracted, of the imprints that had already been laid on. Burroughs told Allen that he had been imprinted by Lionel Trilling at Columbia. He said he saw Trilling in his face. Allen protested that it wasn't so, but in hindsight, he recognized that the statement had some validity. There was a certain part of his consciousness that had tried to please authority figures, which was a once-removed way of pleasing his father. But Bill was using his insights in a menacing manner, which made Allen go through a period of doubting his own identity and the value of his work.

And then Bill was always flanked by his two attendants or puerile bodyguards, Ian Sommerville and Mikey Portman, whom Allen found difficult, possessive, and malevolent. They were living together in an arrangement that Allen never understood, although it was clear that Bill had a crush on Mikey, who was encouraging his worst tendencies. Mikey had the new-wave indifference to anything classical, as well as an adolescent cattiness. He had a way of patronizing Peter when they went out to supper, which made Peter frightened and angry. Peter was made to feel unwanted, and Allen was caught in the middle. Bill, who thought Peter was dumb, encouraged the baiting. On one occasion, Allen was invited to dinner without Peter, who got upset at being so pointedly excluded, and decided to take off on his own. Allen wanted to stay in Tangier, and felt that Peter should have stuck it out. They argued to the point that Allen said Peter was a firing squad, with the usual orders: ready, aim, fire . . . followed by the coup de grace. But Peter felt rejected, and they parted temporarily that August, amid a good deal of grief, with Peter predicting they would not see each other again "for years."

Ian confided to Allen that he didn't like Mikey either, who was slavishly copying Bill. When Bill drank mint tea, Mikey drank mint tea. When Bill wore a trench coat, Mikey wore a trench coat. He even imitated the way Bill walked, with brisk, short steps. Mikey had a taste for black cock, Ian told Allen, and would probably end up with a knife between the ribs. Well, at least he had an adventurous soul, thought Allen, who recited to himself these lines of Auden's:

> Sing then the witty angels,
> Who come only to the beasts,
> Of heirs apparent who prefer
> Low dives to formal feasts.

In spite of these problems with the crew, Allen and the others made the most of their stay. On June 4, Allen, Peter, and Gregory Corso sat on woven mats under a fig tree and drank green mint tea. Later, they smoked pot in alabaster pipes and gazed at the ocean, which seemed to Allen a vast animal back, a blue wall of living jewels and fire. They seemed to be conversing on the hide of the sea.

On July 9, on the roof of the Armor Hotel overlooking the beach, Allen's typewriter clicked as the windowpanes rattled with the roar of a levanter. He thought of his mother, Naomi, in the madhouse, the mother to whom in sex with a woman he was afraid to return. Peter was sick in bed, and Gregory was curled up in his room with a cut finger. Allen knocked off at two that afternoon and stopped by Bill's room. He was lying in bed with his clothes on, and Mikey Portman was at his desk, faithful as a hound dog. Bill said he had been high on *majoun*, entering a very exquisite place. He had seen the ghost of Truman Capote, with the skin rotting and hanging from his body like Spanish moss. Allen thought of Peter, who was leaving for Istanbul in August, and wept at all the years they had spent together. With his departure, Allen's sense of assurance and unity would be gone.

In mid-July, Alan Ansen arrived from Athens, which he reported "was no cock-sucker's dream," but when you could get it it was cheap, "from seventy cents to a dollar a crack." He had not seen Burroughs since 1957, but had much admired *Naked Lunch*, although he felt that some of the obscenity was unnecessary. There were "too many fucks in a little room. And of course if you're trying to show sex as something nice, obscenity is a very two-edged tool. . . . What description wants to do is suggest. . . . boy is a sexier word than cock." As for the cut-ups, Ansen said that "when you smash a mirror because you don't like what it reflects, the fragments continue to wink the old message. Only an obsessed writer can make cut-ups fascinating, but the fascination is not that of total victory."

It seemed to Ansen that Gregory Corso was the life of the Tangier party, part Groucho and part Harpo, saying things that no one would think to say. When they went to see Paul Bowles, Gregory asked, "Why are you so polite?" "Well, maybe I am too polite," Paul admitted. But there came a day when Gregory rose up in wrath. He didn't like Mikey Portman either, whom he called "replica Bill Burroughs." So Mikey drank this thick sugary mint tea—to show what? He was a bore, really. One morning Mikey came by to give Gregory some *majoun* he had made. Now Mikey could seldom do anything right, and he had used kif mixed with tobacco to make the *majoun*, which makes it inedible. When Gregory ate it, he immediately got sick and started retching, and became convinced that he was the victim of a cabal masterminded by Burroughs, who had complete control over those two wretched kids, Ian and Mikey, the light and the dark. Doubled over in pain in his hotel room, Gregory kept repeating, "Omygod, I been poisoned, he coulda killed me." Then he decided: "I'm goin' after the motherfuckers!"

He ran over to Burroughs' hotel, finding him with Alan Ansen, and called him "Willie the Weasel." Burroughs had no idea what he was incensed about. "You're not any big guru," Gregory said. "All you care about is getting your cock up those boys' asses." Burroughs had heard enough and said, "Get out of here, you little wop."

"And ya didn't kill me with your air rifle, did ya," Gregory said, "the way ya said ya would."

Interceding, Ansen said, "The trouble with you, Gregory, is that you can never be a leader of men the way William can."

But Gregory, for the moment anyway, no longer trusted Burroughs. Even though he did not think he would ever encounter a "more genius or dignified type," he had lost faith in him. He had bad taste in his Gysin trick and in accepting Mikey the replica, who was a dolt to begin with—every word he uttered was "Bill says this" and "Bill says that"—the poor mother! What a sorry mess. And to think that once he had offered to aid Bill in everything, and they had been close, and now there was no more closeness. So what? Without Burroughs, the world was a less sinister hang-up.

Paul Bowles often had the whole crew over at his apartment, while viewing them through his "what-fools-these-mortals-be" lenses. Allen Ginsberg had a good mind, in spite of always trying to *épater* one, while Peter Orlovsky didn't seem to have any mind at all. Allen talked a great deal about getting all the Beats together, and somehow connecting the Beat movement to the Communist Party, an idea to which Gregory Corso responded with enthusiasm, while Burroughs didn't react at all. Ian Sommerville, Paul thought, was so high-strung he could explode at any moment. But he knew all about electronics, and was brilliant at repairing tape recorders. He would talk mathematics when he got high, and no one knew what he was talking about. As for Mikey Portman, he didn't know north from south. His father had left him a heavy platinum cigarette case, which he forgot at the Café de Paris, to the delight of some waiter or street Arab, no doubt. And one evening there was a party on the ground floor of Paul's building, and Mikey arrived at seven thirty, and it must have been one thirty in the morning when Mikey came pounding on his door, asking to borrow 25,000 francs—he had forgotten he had a taxi waiting the whole time. Paul thought that he should have had in his passport "Profession: Lost Soul."

Now that Burroughs had been published, he was not so deferential toward Paul, and did not hesitate to disagree with him. When Burroughs went into his "we-must-leave-the-planet" routine, Paul said, "We must never allow anyone to leave this planet, and I am perfectly content to stay here with shit inside me." "Well, Paul," Burroughs said, "that's your point of view, don't expect me to share it." They were philosophical opposites. Burroughs was a visionary and Paul was an eighteenth-century *encyclopédiste*. It annoyed Burroughs that Paul would not admit that he was interested in magic. As a matter of New England principle, he had to ignore such things, saying, "I have never had a psychic experience."

"Nonsense, Paul," Burroughs said, "everyone has psychic experiences, it's part of life."

It seemed to Burroughs that during the entire summer there were too many psychic forces jumping around, too many tensions and undercurrents, from which he protected himself by donning his Reichian character armor. Mikey Portman's West Indian friend summed it all up when he said, "Mikey, it is terrible what is going on here, spirits fighting . . . all the time spirits fighting."

In early August, Leary arrived, hoping to fold the Beat legacy into the psychedelic movement. Allen was the bridge, the Marco Polo of the counterculture, the cultural carrier and transmitter, the electrician who connected the wires. Leary was convinced that his cultural role was more important than his poetry, and that in the final analysis they were all pawns on Allen's big chessboard.

Leary took a cab from the airport to the Hotel Armor, where Allen had reserved a room at two dollars a night. It was his first time in Morocco, a culture built on drugs, with the whole country basking in the soft mellow haze of hashish and pot. The Royal Fair was in town and the king's picture was draped around every lamppost. You could hear the distant music of pipes and drums and see the gleam of fair-ground lanterns. There were tightrope walkers and jugglers on the Avenida de España.

After dinner, he and Allen went to Burroughs' hotel. In his dark cave of a room, with hundreds of photographs pasted together, and three deliberately untuned radios blaring noise and static, Leary was introduced to a tall, stooped, courtly man, flanked by two handsome English boys. "Well," said Allen, "everyone's been waiting for you to arrive with the legendary mushrooms of intercontinental fame. Montezuma's medicine. O fabled poets."

The session began in the dim-lit, crowded, smoky room in the Villa Muniria (dubbed by Gregory Villa Delirium), with the unmade bed and the paper-littered desk. Burroughs lay back on his bed, and the rest of them went out into the garden overlooking the harbor, where they could see lights twinkling in the rigging of ships. Alan Ansen was laughing and shaking his head. "This can't be true," he said, as the psilocybin spread through his cells. "So beautiful! Heaven! But where is the devil's price? Anything this great must have a terrible flaw in it. It can't be this good. Will we ever come down?"

Allen was affected differently, being depressed over Peter's departure and the situation with Bill and the boys, which was still a bit like a cold war. He told Leary that Burroughs was antilove. Allen was clinging to his identity as a poet and as Peter's lover, but Peter was gone, and Bill had told him that poetry was finished, because the world was moving on to a new consciousness that might eliminate words and ideas. Allen's pride was hurt, since part of his security depended on his identity as a poet. And now that the mushrooms took effect, he was filled with anxiety upon realizing that he had no separate self, but was the same as everyone else.

They went back in to find Burroughs and waited outside his door, and after a while it slowly creaked open, and there he stood, almost collapsed against the wall. He rubbed his haggard, damp face with his left hand and stared blankly ahead, like someone who has seen a ghost. "Bill, how are you doing?" Leary asked.

"I would like to sound a word of warning," Leary recalled Burroughs as saying. "I'm not feeling too well. I was struck by juxtaposition of purple fire mushroomed from the pain banks. Urgent warning. I think I'll stay here in shriveling envelopes of larval flesh. I'm going to take some apomorphine. One of the nastiest cases ever processed by this department. You fellows go down to the fair and see film and brain waves tuning in on soulless insect people."

Clearly, the mushrooms were not for him. He had not liked them the first time, and the second time even less. Alan Ansen pointed out that he had taken a very large dose, fifteen pills to Ansen's five. But Burroughs said that didn't make any difference. He had taken smaller doses, it just wasn't quite as disagreeable.

The others, however, were impressed. As Ian Sommerville wrote Brion Gysin: "Leary arrived and laid us all low with mushrooms to the extent that even Gregory had nothing but good to say and was as friendly as hell and universal love reared its ugly head then things got back to normal."

Allen, his pride wounded by Bill's statement that poetry was finished, went to his room the next day and told him he wanted to see him alone. But the ever-present Mikey was there, hovering around the door as they were talking inside. When Bill told Mikey that he and Allen were going out to lunch, Mikey said, "Guess I'll come along." There was no getting rid of him. When Mikey went to the men's room during lunch, Bill, sensing Allen's annoyance, said, "He is too dependent on me, that's the problem." So that Allen began to see things less as a conspiracy of Bill and Mikey against him. Bill did want everyone included, though the basis of inclusion was that they had to alter their minds, in the sense that Allen's mind told him that he was a poet and Peter's lover, both of which Burroughs thought were pointless. Just as he seemed to think sex was pointless. When Allen told him that sex was a part of the reaffirmation and support of identity, he admitted that sex might be a way to merge souls on an egoless basis, and that he only put it down when it was corrupted, as when it was part of the power-ego grab in America and other so-called civilized nations.

Then things came to a head when Mikey's friend Mark Groetchen arrived. A fat and loutish boy who worshiped Mikey in the same way that Mikey worshiped Burroughs, Mark was an obvious scapegoat, drawing to his pathetic person all the tensions and cruelties in the psychic atmosphere.

As Burroughs recalled the incident in a conversation with Alan Ansen many years later: "There was an occasion at Paul's when Mark Groetchen took *majoun* and flipped out with the horrors. 'I have a feeling of heat,' he said, and Paul said 'Oh, my God, it's hot in here, isn't it?' and Allen looked askance and said, 'What in hell is Paul doing?' He was making it worse. And Leary was trying to talk to Mark and get him out of the horrors he was experiencing."

"Yes," said Ansen, "there's a very unpleasant side to Paul, and that was a very good example of it."

"Well, you know," Burroughs said, "he gave Cyril Connolly *majoun*, and Bob Rauschenberg, who hates him to this day, saying that he gave him this stuff and he didn't know what was happening or what was in it, and he was in a state of fear, and far from reassuring him, Paul was making things worse . . . saying, 'Yes, it sometimes has these terrible effects on people . . . there have been a number of suicides.' Just building it up. Paul enjoys seeing the discomfort of others."

"That isn't a very attractive trait, is it?" Ansen asked. "Of course, his father was a dentist, a *profession oblige*, wouldn't you say?"

"I don't imagine he was a particularly painless dentist," Burroughs said. "He was one of those 'a-little-pain-won't-hurt-you' kinds of dentists."

"Ahmed Yacoubi [Paul's Moroccan painter friend] was the one who had the *majoun*," Ansen said. "It had some opium in it."

"I talked to Yacoubi," Burroughs said, "and he admitted to me that he and Paul did this quite deliberately, giving *majoun* to people who often had not even smoked pot before, and enjoying their discomfort. See, the danger of *majoun* is that it takes an hour or an hour and a half to hit, and people think it's had no effect and take some more. And the first thing they know, they feel terrible."

Allen Ginsberg, however, describing the incident in a letter to Peter

Orlovsky a few days after it happened, saw it rather differently: "Bill and Mikey were too high to notice—I took care of Mark, who was suffering isolation, and realized they were too fucked up to notice and care for him. I brought Mark out of it, and Bill said he was in error. I think it was nastiness on Mikey's part."

When Leary left, Allen was convinced that he would start a beautiful consciousness alteration of the whole world. He was sold on the mushrooms, and on Leary's claim that they cut off the ego part of the brain in the cortex, leaving an "open brain" without any loss of the idea of self. Leary never imagined there could be any academic opposition to his drug experiments. He had grandiose plans to turn on people high up in government. In this the first year of the Kennedy presidency, a new age seemed to be dawning. Kennedy's first term had begun inauspiciously, with the Bay of Pigs disaster, but no matter, Kennedy was a symbol of youth and change and a thaw in the ice age of the fifties. He had created the Peace Corps, and Freedom Riders were demonstrating in Alabama. A twenty-year-old Minnesotan who had changed his name from Robert Zimmerman to Bob Dylan was singing in Greenwich Village coffeehouses. Just as Kerouac, Ginsberg, and Burroughs had provided the counterculture with its primers, just as Leary was offering his "psychedelic revolution" package, Dylan would give the counterculture its anthems, "Blowin' in the Wind," and "The Times They Are A-Changin'." Leary saw a good omen in the appointment of some of his Harvard colleagues, such as the historian Arthur Schlesinger, Jr., as presidential advisers. Overflowing with optimism, he told Allen, "We'll turn on Schlesinger, and then we'll turn on Kennedy." Paul Bowles took Leary with a grain of salt, and had a vision of him as a bishop blessing 5,000 people in a cathedral. He always loved everything, and never had a disparaging word to say, and never showed any *angst* at all, which made Paul a bit suspicious. Maybe his mind was blown, as though he'd had a lobotomy. Burroughs, however, found Leary aware, confident, and well-intentioned, and accepted his invitation to come to Cambridge and take part in experiments in white noise and sensory deprivation. Although Burroughs had confirmed his aversion to psilocybin, Leary said there were other drugs he could try, such as peyote.

With Leary's departure, the psychedelic summer ended and the little band split up. Gregory left for London, where he was knocked out by pub names such as Queen's Head and Artichoke. Alan Ansen and Allen Ginsberg went to Greece, the latter feeling guilty at not having stuck by Peter. In Athens he ran into the critic Leslie Fiedler, who expounded another depressing theory, that criticism was now more important than poetry. Allen was still worrying about the problem that Burroughs had posed, that of cutting off one's identity. He did not find an answer until he met the Buddhists in Tibet, who told him that if you see something horrible, don't cling to it, and if you see something beautiful, don't cling to it.

Burroughs and his two disciples returned to the Empress Hotel in London. Burroughs was fed up with Mikey Portman, who, as he put it, "Was always overdrawing his account." Mikey took the Dent cure, establishing a pattern for years to come, of drinking himself into a stupor, going on junk, and taking the cure. What could you do with a beautiful boy who had so little sense that he drank a quart of vodka a day on top of heroin? When Mikey said he was going to Paris while Bill was in Cambridge with Leary, Burroughs warned Brion Gysin: "For God's sake no open bank with Mikey. I pass along urgent warning: Watch that little fucker. Give him the conducted tour routine and see he misses anything important."

Gregory came to say good-bye to Bill before he flew off to Cambridge and found that the scene was Tangier all over again. There he was in his smoky hotel room with Ian and Mikey playing the courtiers. How could Burroughs be a good man, Gregory wondered, when he left in his wake basket cases like Sinclair Beiles and Mikey Portman? What was he but a dead zombie junky out to fuck all human beings, in spite of his surefire style of writing?

Burroughs flew to Boston on August 23, all expenses paid by Leary's Harvard outfit. Leary's big, rambling house in Newton was a sort of Ivy League commune. He lived there with his son, daughter, and girlfriend, and all sorts of people came and went, Harvard people, people taking mushrooms, and distinguished hangers-on such as Gerald Heard and Alan Watts, two Englishmen who had gravitated westward to America, while their minds were turned eastward toward Vedanta and Buddhism. Heard, who was said to be a living example of the Wellsian supermind, had come to California in 1937 and espoused Eastern philosophy, yoga, and vegetarianism. He was a close friend and adviser of Aldous Huxley, to whom he fed ideas for his book *Eyeless in Gaza*. Alan Watts had arrived in 1938 and was considered responsible, along with Allen Ginsberg and the poet Gary Snyder, for the Buddhist influence on Beat writing, through his various books and articles selling mysticism without tears. A prodigious drinker and self-proclaimed adulterer, Watts was a happy mixture of hedonist and Buddhist, the very prototype of the rascal-guru. Both

Heard and Watts were scheduled to join Leary and Burroughs on the panel at the American Psychological Association.

Burroughs went to work on his paper, on the difference between narcotic and psychedelic drugs, but his first impressions of the Leary operation were decidedly negative. He was upset by the waste and conspicuous consumption at the Leary household. Enough food to feed a regiment was left out to spoil all over a vast kitchen by Leary's overfed and undisciplined children. In the other rooms typewriters, cameras, TV sets, record players, and toys of every description were stacked to the ceiling. It was a real nightmare of surfeit, indicative to Burroughs of the unhealthy state of American society.

He had been hoping that Leary would have other drugs besides mushrooms, but such was not the case. He refused to take any more psilocybin, writing Paul Bowles: "Nothing will ever get another psilocybin pill down this throat. I am of course not expressing my feelings on the subject to Leary lest he cut off the $."

In early September they went to New York for the panel at the Statler Hotel. Leary felt that he was making history. Here, before the cream of the psychological establishment, he was leading the first scientific panel on mind-expanding drugs. They had him in a room seating 200, and he went to the manager of the Statler and said, "Listen, we need a bigger room, we've got some big names here." But it was too late, and he played to an SRO audience—there were people standing in the hallway. Fortified by two joints, Burroughs gave an effective presentation, going through the different classes of drugs, and warning against lumping them together—stimulants like cocaine and Benzedrine, narcotics like heroin, sleeping drugs like barbiturates, and psychedelics, which were supposed to give you heightened awareness.

Back in Newton, Burroughs was hoping to take part in serious scientific experiments—he wanted to talk about computers and brain localization and biofeedback—but all Leary was interested in was turning people on. "The scene here is really frantic," he wrote Brion Gysin. "Leary has gone berserk. He is giving mushrooms to hat-check girls, cabdrivers, waiters, in fact anybody who will stand still for it."

Leary could see that Burroughs was cross, that the program was a joke to him. It was clear that Burroughs saw him as a buffoon, the head coach of the mind expansion set, giving his players locker-room pep talks about inner freedom. Burroughs had not come to Harvard to join psychedelic encounter sessions or to listen to blatherings about love and cosmic unity. He wanted to talk about neurological implants and brain wave generators.

The rub was, as he made it all too clear, that he didn't like psychedelic drugs. All he could talk about was the wonder of apomorphine. He was not using heroin then—God knows where he could have gotten it—but he was using a lot of gin and tonic. In any case, he seemed to Leary to be growing increasingly disgruntled and paranoid.

Leary tried to get him involved in the program in Concord. They visited the prison, and Burroughs talked to the inmates, but it seemed to him that the program was built on illusion. The convicts would say whatever Leary wanted them to say; all they were after was a chance of getting out. Leary gave them mushrooms, and told them the game they were playing was the wrong game, that there were better games than the cops-and-robbers game. With the help of mushrooms, they were supposed to see their motivations and become rehabilitated. As part of the experiment, some of the inmates were released into Leary's custody, and then one of them held up a store, which sent everyone back to the drawing board.

Burroughs lasted about a month in Newton, and then quietly jumped ship, leaving behind what he called "Leary and his pestiferous project." He wrote Allen Ginsberg that the project was "completely ill-intentioned," and that the money came from Henry Luce and other dubious quarters. (Henry Luce was reported to have said after taking LSD that he had talked to God on the golf course.) "They had utterly no interest in any scientific work," Burroughs said, "no equipment other than a faulty tape recorder. I was supposed to sell the Beatniks on mushrooms. When I flatly refused to push the mushrooms but volunteered instead to work on flicker [biofeedback] and other nonchemical methods, the money and return ticket they had promised were immediately withdrawn. I received not one cent from Leary beyond the fare to Boston. And I hope never to set eyes on that horse's ass again. A real wrong number." This was a paranoid reaction, and the low point of a friendship which has survived to this day.

Leary also wrote Allen, giving his side of the story: "From the moment Bill hit the USA he started putting mushrooms down. A crazy situation developed. We were facing a rising storm of opposition here and Bill was saying dreadful things about the mushrooms within our group. This left his research work in an ambiguous state. . . . I admire Burroughs' game. Tremendously. But only one can play. He declined to join our game—which is developing into a religious, do-good cult, etc. About ten Harvard people are ready to junk everything to work on the project. Start a new social institution. Bill left for New York and reports filtered back that he was attacking us. Too bad. I learned a lot from Bill. I only wish he had learned something from us. Too bad. Big decision coming up. Harvard pressure. They offer protection, prestige, money—if we play the research game.''

Thus, the initial attempt at fusion between the Beats and psychedelics (soon to be hippies) was a fiasco. This was but an episode, however, for over the years the two movements merged on many levels, and Burroughs got over his pique and came to admire Leary for his feisty, "let's-make-it-happen'' quality, his ebullience, his optimism. Leary felt he had a mission to turn people on, and that he would become the High Priest of a Great Awakening, and in a sense he did.

For that November of 1961, only two months after Burroughs' departure, he found something better than mushrooms. What he found had been discovered by accident in 1938 by Albert Hofmann, who was director of research for the Swiss chemical company Sandoz. At that time, Hofmann was studying the properties of the rye fungus ergot, in the course of looking for a substance that would stimulate blood circulation (or so he said: the rumor was that he was looking for an abortifacient). He was the first to synthesize the active ingredient in ergot, which had driven an entire village mad in the Middle Ages—lysergic acid diethylamide. He called it LSD-25, for it was the twenty-fifth of the ergot derivatives he had concocted. He tried it on mice, but nothing much happened, and the project was shelved. Five years later, in 1943, he made a new batch, and accidentally absorbed a small dose through his fingertips. He went into such a giddy condition that he had to stop work, and started home on his bicycle—this was the first acid trip—this scholarly, bespectacled Swiss chemist, cycling home from his laboratory in Basel to his home in the country, with clips on his trousers, trying not to weave in the road, under the influence of the most powerful mind-changing substance known to man. He was, he later said, in a "not unpleasant intoxicated condition, characterized by an extremely stimulated imagination.'' LSD would have such large social implications that Hofmann later told Leary that he wished he had never heard of it. He called it his "problem child.''

The turning point for Leary came when an enigmatic Englishman named Michael Hollingshead landed on his doorstep with 10,000 doses of LSD he had obtained from Sandoz to study its effects on the web-spinning of spiders. Instead, human webs would be spun, some splendidly intricate, some darkly chaotic. Leary tried it, and gave it to his friends Maynard and Flo Ferguson—the genie was out of the bottle.

Leary saw himself as a psychic pioneer who would lead society down unexplored paths for its betterment. He had a "single answer" kind of mind, and saw LSD as the way to spiritual awakening, and to artistic and political freedom. Intuitively, he placed himself at the center of that strange phenomenon known as "the spirit of the sixties."

In 1962 and 1963 he conducted LSD experiments in Mexico, with strains of acid he called "Morning Glory" and "Heavenly Blue." It was while in Mexico in May 1963 that he learned he had been fired from Harvard. It was, thought Leary, the Semmelweis effect—the Austrian doctor Semmelweis had been banished from the Viennese medical establishment for insisting that doctors wash their hands to prevent the spread of infection. Leary was in a lot of trouble. Newspaper headlines said DRUG SCANDAL AT HARVARD, and he was investigated by the Massachusetts Narcotics Bureau. Ah, well, he thought, he was in an honored tradition—Emerson had been banned from Harvard in 1838 for giving a lecture urging his audience to drop out of organized Christianity and find God within.

Burroughs' rather ungenerous reaction to Leary's troubles was recorded in a letter to Allen Ginsberg: "I see Leary has been thrown out of Harvard for distributing his noxious wares too freely, and some undergraduate decides he is God and takes off through traffic in Harvard Square." But by this time, the ripple effect was at work. A network of people had sprouted up, forming a loose-knit, many-stranded psychedelic movement. In San Francisco, Ken Kesey and his Merry Pranksters celebrated the benefits of acid. In Los Angeles, the psychiatrist Oscar Janiger turned on the stars—Cary Grant, James Coburn, Jack Nicholson. Leary moved to the Hitchcock estate in Millbrook, New York, where he set up the Castalia Foundation, after the fellowship of mystic scientists in *The Glass Bead Game* by Hermann Hesse, a writer whose "psychic quest" books like *Siddhartha* had an audience in the millions.

As the movement gained momentum, Leary was pushed step by step into political opposition. In 1965, he was arrested in Laredo for possession of marijuana. Singled out for special attention at the border crossing, a pinch of weed was found in his daughter's bra. The full weight of government might came bearing down on him, and he was given a twenty-year maximum sentence, later overturned by the Supreme Court. The sentencing judge called him "an insidious menace" and a "pleasure-seeking, irresponsible Madison Avenue advocate of the free use of drugs."

Leary was placed in the same outlaw position that the Beats had earlier found themselves in. They, too, had been expelled by the system. They, too, had been hounded and arrested. They were like himself in an old tradition of civil disobedience among writers and thinkers that went back to Thoreau. Emerson, Leary recalled, came to see Thoreau, who was in jail for not paying taxes. "David, what are you doing in jail?" he asked. "What are you doing not in jail?" Thoreau replied. Burroughs and the others were in that line, Leary thought. Burroughs had been arrested a number of times, and had never given an inch. All he wanted was the freedom to live his life as he saw fit, without government interference. Leary could relate to that. Obviously, the state hated drugs because drugs gave people power over themselves, and were a tremendous tool for individual search and Socratic inquiry.

After his bust, Leary bent his purpose to creating an alternative American society. He became the cheerleader for change: Turn on, tune in, drop out. "Turning on" meant an absolute faith in the beneficial properties of acid. Allen Ginsberg proposed in the *East Village Other* in January 1967 "that everybody who hears my voice try the chemical LSD at least once, every man, woman, and child in good health over the age of fourteen." Urging teenagers to drop acid seems in retrospect irresponsible, but such was the euphoria of the times that these and many other things were said ingenuously.

"Dropping out" meant that Leary wanted nothing to do with leftist activists who were clamoring for "student power," whom he called "young men with menopausal minds." He did not want the psychedelic movement to become contaminated by the mirror image of a political system. Passive resistance was his response to Vietnam. "The only way to stop the war," he said, "is for 100 high school kids to quit school tomorrow. Don't picket, don't get involved in it at all."

Leary's League for Spiritual Discovery gathered leading counterculture figures like Ginsberg, Gary Snyder, and Alan Watts, who thought up strategies for dropping out. They had a program of sorts, which amounted to a critique of conventional society while remaining in the good old American "how-to" tradition, for it was basically aimed at how to be a successful dropout, how to breathe, how to meditate, how to drop acid and not have a bad trip.

Basic to the program was a heavy reliance on drugs, an automatic form of rebellion, since drugs were illegal. King Leary with his acid rap, in white pajamas at a league meeting, was something to see, as he went on about "the latticework of cellular wisdom," "the chemical bibles of the nervous system," "tumbling down the capillary networks," and "the protein memory banks, waiting with a million card files." The league was a sort of religion, trying to legalize acid, which Leary called a sacrament that should be taken in a state of grace. Paraphrasing the Gospels, he said, "I am here to lead the broken-hearted." He prescribed LSD for seven-year-olds, "because children are less entrapped in their minds," while warning that "for every ecstasy there is terror and paranoia."

Leary and his cohorts established a sort of counterculture code of conduct. There was the idea that everyone can be good at everything, that everyone can be an artist, that desire is more important than apprenticeship. There was the willingness to take any kind of job in order to have more leisure to do the thing that mattered. There was the tendency toward communal living, so that people could pool their incomes, buy land, and live the way they wanted to. There was a contempt for urban life, Gary Snyder preaching the nauseous city—New York should be leveled and made into a buffalo pasture. There was the politics of farce, Ken Kesey and the Merry Pranksters mixing LSD in Kool-Aid, black students on a college campus campaigning for the right to black vanilla ice cream.

The head trip was passing through the national mind, rippling over the continent, affecting those who said they hated it, firing up everyone's imagination. In fact, the movement ran away from Leary, who was unable to keep it out of politics. The hippies dropped out, lit up their pipes, swallowed their acid tabs, and pelted the cops with daffodils at love-ins. And then what? They moved from rejection group to militant vanguard, from passive to active resistance. They marched and got arrested and burned their draft cards. A broad alliance formed, among the hippies, the New Left, the civil rights militants, the Vietnam draft resisters, and multiple fringe groups from the Diggers to the Yippies. There was a moving, shifting, meandering spectrum of dissent, which could be labeled the "hippie-pacifist-activist-visionary-orgiastic-anarchist-Buddhist-psychedelic-acid-rock underground."

The middle class blamed Leary for subverting its children, although Leary by this time was a general who had to catch up with his troops. He was, however, seen as the creator of the movement, a position he was not averse to accepting. All these young people in open rebellion against society were his flock. "After all," he said, "I am a religious leader and I must behave like one."

In 1967, the *Time* Man of the Year was "anyone under twenty-five." It was the time of the ashram, of Allen Ginsberg testifying before a Senate committee on LSD, of 10,000 hippies in Haight-Ashbury. Life was like a tape on Fast Forward, spinning on an acid spool, with events crystallized in catchwords: "flower power," "black is beautiful," "sit-ins," "generation gap," "do your own thing." Sitting out the sixties in Europe, and saved from the silly season by his own peculiar fastidiousness, Burroughs reflected that "95 percent of these people have no idea at all of what their 'own thing' is."

And yet he was one of their gurus, enshrined on the cover of the "Sergeant Pepper" album as one of the sixty-two faces gathered around the Beatles, along with Edgar Allan Poe, Oscar Wilde, H. G. Wells, Marx, Jung, W. C. Fields, and Lawrence of Arabia.

The death of the hippie was announced in a funeral notice in the *Village Voice* in November 1967. According to the devil theory of hippiedom, it was all the media's fault, but what about that segment of the movement that courted the media? On the David Susskind show, Abbie Hoffman opened a box and let out a duck labeled "hippie." The duck ran all over the aisle honking and flapping its wings and finally threw up. Susskind didn't want to run the footage. "But you said it was okay," Abbie said. "Yes, Abbie," Susskind said, "but the duck freaked out. You let him get out of control."

That's what was happening to the movement: it was out of control. It was now making headlines through drug-related acts of deviltry—the Manson murders, which showed just how bad things could get when the love beads were broken, when a mix of ex-cons and misfits infiltrated the innocent but doomed hippie movement and contaminated it; the Altamont riot, resulting in the death of a bystander, was a classic example of deluded optimism, when the Rolling Stones gave the Hell's Angels the security detail. The breakup of the Beatles was emblematic of a more widespread disintegration. Among the great public events of the counterculture, you could take your pick in terms of the horrible and the wonderful. You could toss a coin and come up Kent State or Woodstock. Woodstock was Leary's communion breakfast, with its estimated 100,000 acid trips among half a million participants, and its absence of violence.

It was also in a sense a grand finale, both for the movement, which was wrecked by the discrepancy between its noble aims and its bad behavior, and for Leary, who was still in the grip of the Justice Department. For when the Supreme Court ruled in his favor on the Laredo bust, the feds refiled on a technicality, charging him with the transportation of marijuana, and in 1970 he was sentenced to two consecutive ten-year terms for possession of less than an ounce of grass. Sprung from his California jail by the Weathermen, he ended up in Algiers, as the misfit ally of Eldridge Cleaver and the Black Panthers. Then, after many picaresque adventures, he went to Switzerland, and was eventually captured in Afghanistan in 1973. He once computed that during his years on the

lam, he served time in forty different jails on four continents. Such was
the price of leading the hippie troops—you became the most visible target.
Leary was released in 1976, somewhat discredited on the basis of rumors
that he had given information to the FBI.

But he had had his moment of triumph, continuing what Ginsberg and
Burroughs and Kerouac had begun. There was, Leary would be the first
to admit, some validity in saying that the hippies were second-generation
Beats.

SIXTEEN

BURROUGHS
AT LARGE

1962–1965

Following his discouraging stay with Leary, Burroughs was glad to get back to Europe in December 1961, after spending a couple of months in a basement apartment in Brooklyn working on *Nova Express*, for which Barney Rosset had given him an advance. He hated the New York cocktail party circuit, where people, instead of looking at you, looked at the door to see who was about to arrive. He hated the jockeying for position, what Freud once referred to as "the banal hankering after priority," the inflated reputations, the shooting stars, the writers who spent 20 percent of their time on their work and 80 percent on their image. He hated the people who claimed to admire your book when it was clear they hadn't read it. He was far happier in his old Paris haunts, at the Beat Hotel with Brion Gysin and Ian Sommerville, working on cut-ups and tapes. The newest twist was to record street sounds and mix them up and combine them with a cut-up text.

Brion Gysin reported that he had a long cut-up poem appearing in England where it was sure to make quite a fuss—the most violent fuss, my dear. He was going to be talking on Europe 1, the most powerful French radio chain. The French, of course, were dying inside their fossil language and needed to be shaken up a bit. All this did not produce *de quoi vivre* (wherewithal), however, for Brion had been too busy writing to get out there and kiss asses as they had to be kissed. "There's nothing I like better than kissing a nice fat ass," he wrote Paul Bowles, with only partial irony.

With Ian Sommerville, Brion had been working on a device which he hoped had commercial potential. It was a cylinder with slits that revolved on a phonograph turntable and produced, lit from the inside, alpha waves corresponding to thirteen flashes per second, which hit the optic nerve in such a way that they induced visions. Brion called it the Dream Machine, and it was shown that December at an exhibit called "L'Objet" at the Musée des Arts Décoratifs.

Looking around for a patron, he heard that Helena Rubinstein, who was then in Paris, had started a foundation to help struggling artists. Brion called her secretary, Patrick O'Higgins, a charming carrot-haired former Guardsman, who, it turned out, had been at Brion's old school, Downside. Brion took a Dream Machine to show Madame (as she was known), and she said, "Does it have to be black?" He made her a big white one, a meter in diameter, which she placed in the round window of her spectacular apartment on the quai de Béthune. O'Higgins was fascinated by it, and placed inside it a mummified Egyptian cat, 2,000 years old, swathed in bandages. The effect was interesting, but when Madame saw it she shrieked. "Patrick! My best cat!"

To give the Dream Machine some exposure, O'Higgins announced: "Madame, all the ladies from Seventh Avenue are here for the collections and we're going to give a little breakfast for them." On the appointed morning, the Dream Machine was spinning, and the ladies took their places in the grand salon and shoveled down their scrambled eggs, knowing they had a long day of fashion watching ahead of them. Madame made her entrance, wearing a little Yves St. Laurent hat that looked like a relic from the Boer War. O'Higgins was pushing her in the right direction with one finger on her shoulder, and someone was heard to say, "I think Patrick O'Higgins is the greatest toymaker in the world."

It became apparent as she came closer that Madame had two black eyes. O'Higgins told Brion in a stage whisper, "Madame's money has hurt her." In the bathroom, Madame had two safe deposit boxes fitted into the wall across from the toilet. She was in the habit, in the midst of her morning ablutions, of unlocking the boxes and playing with her cash and jewelry. "Greedy old girl," Patrick told Brion, "she pulled out the bottom drawer, and the other one slipped and hit her in the eyes."

O'Higgins kept plugging the Dream Machine, which was again in evidence at a fashion show Madame gave on her roof garden. Brion was happily ensconced at the heart of the princess circuit. Madame was herself a princess, having married a Georgian prince named Gourielli. When plump Princess Mdivani arrived, her monocle screwed in one puffy eye, it was "How are you this morning, princess," "Very well, thank you, princess," "You're looking beautiful, princess," "And you're looking very slim, princess."

Designed by a Mexican faggot, the dresses, Brion noted, were intended to trip women up. The cruelest clothes I've ever seen, he thought. Harry Winston was doing the jewels. Spotting a flash of green on a model's hand, Princess Mdivani called her over and took the girl's hand in one of her bearlike paws, and scrutinized the ring through her monocle. She then turned to Harry Winston, who was sitting next to her, and said with princess-like disdain, "Mr. Winston, in India the elephants wear better emeralds."

Madame next placed the Dream Machine in the window of her shop in the Faubourg St. Honoré. But she didn't buy it, she still had it on loan. Brion was so exasperated that one day he walked into the shop, picked it up out of the window, and walked off with it, and that was the end of Madame's sponsorship of the Dream Machine. Later, he took one to Venice to show Peggy Guggenheim, but Alfred Barr of the Museum of Modern Art was there, and said, "The kinetic thing is over, what it is now is pop." Brion was privy to the secret power, but could never get a piece of it. All these people who knew him and liked him, and yet always the taste of failure in his mouth.

Burroughs was completely supportive of Brion. He thought the Dream Machine was terrific, and had strange visions peering at it. It was time, however, to move back to London and resume his life as head of household with his two acolytes, Ian and Mikey. By February 1962, he was back at the Empress Hotel, much satisfied with his move. With a good English breakfast under his belt—porridge, bacon and eggs, toast and tea—he felt like a new man and got twice as much done. He was abstaining from drugs and sex.

He was shocked to learn on February 5, 1962, in a letter from Kells Elvins' mother, that his old friend had died in New York of a heart attack. He was only forty-seven years old, and had once had great vitality and élan. But Burroughs remembered Kells telling him that he had felt "the dying feeling" on a trip to Corfu. He had been in the street, walking up a hill, when sweat started pouring out of him and he had to sit down.

Burroughs later learned that Kells had been in New York with his wife Mimi, who was promoting Danish fashions. They were staying at the Biltmore Hotel, and Kells had died in bed. Mimi had him buried in Texas. At that time she was broke, and she was glad to get the $150 the magazine *Dude/Gent* paid for one of his stories.

As a writer, Kells hadn't accomplished much. When he was visiting his son, Peter, in Brighton, Massachusetts, he talked about what a committed writer he was, but Peter, who watched him fill his glass with vodka all day long, saw that his real commitment was to booze. Kells was convinced that his health had been ruined in the marines, so why bother? He had let himself get fat and out of condition, and was always going on about his lousy ticker.

Burroughs remembered a friendship that went back to childhood and had lasted all their adult lives. Perhaps each was looking at the other as someone he wished to be. Burroughs admired Kells' social ease and success with women. Boy, he sure had a way with women. Why, he could get right into *any* woman, and always had three or four beauties on a string. Also, it was thanks to Kells that he had started writing again, when they had collaborated on that routine about the sinking ship. If it hadn't been for that, he would have given up writing completely. Burroughs remembered that in his garden on Price Road, he and Kells had seen a blacksnake shaking its tail in dead leaves, pretending to be a rattlesnake, an image he had used in *Junky*. Kells had once written a song called "When Your Time Comes to Go," with the line "I'm gonna go on boozin' till my time comes to go."

In Burroughs' own life, the old points of argument with Mikey had disappeared, although there were some difficulties between Ian and Mikey. But Ian was one head he couldn't walk on. He wasn't tractable like Mikey, he was stubborn and high-strung, and retreated into a sullen remoteness when displeased. Mikey, however, seemed to have no identity of his own, and his faculty for imitating others was such that Burroughs began to see him as a body waiting to be possessed, perhaps by inhospitable forces. Once, when Mikey had a cold sore on his lip, Burroughs refused to see him, because a cold sore was a point of entry for those forces. Another time, Burroughs accompanied Mikey to Lord Goodman's to discuss what could be done about his heroin habit. Lady Frankau, a psychiatrist who treated junkies, was there. She was ardently opposed to the Dent apomorphine treatment, and urged that Mikey be admitted to a sanitarium. When they got back to Burroughs' basement flat in Bayswater, he saw something silvery slip off Mikey's shoulder, like silver light. He could see it quite clearly. It hit him right in the chest. He stood up to get a glass of water and passed out. A couple of minutes later he came around. Burroughs felt that he was the target of a curse which had come via Mikey from Lady Frankau. She and Dr. Dent at the time were struggling over Mikey. She was in agreement with the U.S. Department of Narcotics, which did not want the apomorphine treatment to spread. Just about that time, in 1961, Dr. Dent died, but his treatment continued to be administered by his assistants.

Back in London in August 1962 after the Edinburgh conference, he met through Brion Gysin a languid, lanky filmmaker named Anthony Balch, who had made several low-budget horror films such as *Horror Hospital*. He had an office in Wardour Street, the center of the marginal film business, and earned his bread by buying the rights to European soft-core porn films for distribution in the United Kingdom. It turned out that Balch was a Burroughs fan, and wanted to experiment with filming some of his cut-up texts. The film's working title was *Towers Open Fire*, and in January 1963 they shot a scene with Anthony's antiquated windup World War II 35mm camera in the board room of the British Film Institute, in which Burroughs, as the chairman of the board, rose and said, "Gentlemen, this was to be expected—after all, he's been a medium all his life."

More and more, Burroughs was operating under the conviction, constantly reinforced by Brion Gysin, that his writing placed him in danger, that he was surrounded by enemies who were out to do him in. He had a kind of "it's-them-or-us" siege mentality. When *Dead Fingers Talk*, an amalgam of Burroughs texts, was brought out by John Calder at the start of 1963, there were predictably hostile reviews, and Gysin wrote Burroughs, "Do you take your dish of tea with lemon or with venom, my dear?"

Burroughs now saw himself as one of his characters, inspector J. Lee of the Nova Police. He began to wonder whether Mikey was an agent sent to perturb his existence. Mikey had a sister named Suna who was fed up with his addiction and who, in March 1963, informed their mother that he was a junky. Suna portrayed Burroughs as an evil influence who had no interest in Mikey's recovery and would be of no assistance in helping him find a cure. Mrs. Portman's Greek boyfriend recommended cutting off Mikey's allowance. Burroughs, when apprised of the situation, was irate. He had done everything he could to get Mikey off heroin, but that was something no one could do for you. As for the boyfriend, he was just an opportunist, exploiting Mikey's mother for all he could get. Seeking advice, Mrs. Portman went to Lord Goodman, who told her that Burroughs had a positive influence on her son. Cleared of all charges, Burroughs was introduced to Mikey's mother, who was cordial in that uppity British way.

Burroughs wanted to spend the summer of 1963 in Tangier, but was concerned that it was infested with Beatniks and hippies. Paul Bowles reported that "the only way to live in Morocco now is to remember constantly that the world outside is still more repulsive." Burroughs agreed, arriving in June with Ian, Mikey, and Brion Gysin. He took a house on the Marshan, the plateau overlooking the sea, at 4 calle Larache. Alan Ansen arrived, and there was a new crop of Americans on hand—Irving Rosenthal, who had edited *Naked Lunch* for Grove; the New York writer Alfred Chester; the tall, bearded, rabbinical writer-photographer Ira Cohen; and that diminutive veteran of the Beat Hotel, Harold Norse.

Harold thought of himself as "dark-horse Norse," ignored and unpublished. He harbored bitter thoughts about his colleagues, whom he thought had more success than he did, while deserving it less. Irving Rosenthal he considered a monstrous shit, aberrated and power-struck, a diseased faggot clear through. He didn't trust Brion, whom he called SOBrion—he had to be the prima donna, and for all his charm, there was a spurious side. These days he talked only to Burroughs, who talked only to God, with contempt for all else. When the Russians announced that they were sending a woman into space, Harold was amused to see Brion's and Bill's reaction—they thought it was an ominous threat to carry the matriarchy, the cunt, the Bitch Goddess, into space. What new turn, Harold wondered, would this lead to in Bill's work? Lesbian colonels attacking fish boys on Mars?

Allen Ginsberg was in India, and one day Burroughs said to Norse: "Allen's always talking about attaining an egoless state through Indian meditation. Hell, I can do that anytime." "What do you mean?" Norse asked. "Well, man, like your personality disappears and you're not in your body. Look—watch." Burroughs stood up and his eyes went dead. His face was blank. Norse felt as if he was looking at an Egyptian mummy. He called, "Bill, Bill," but there was no reply. Finally, Bill looked at him and said, "See what I mean?" Norse told him the story of the two magicians, each trying to scare the other. The first one went through a series of elaborately frightening tricks, and then it was the other one's turn, and the other one said, "Boo!"

As for the other leading Beats, Jack Kerouac had moved to Northport, Long Island, in December 1962 with his mother. The house and garden were surrounded by a six-foot-high Alaskan cedar fence so that nobody could see him reading in the sun, or walking among his tomato plants, or Mémère feeding the birds. Mémère protected him from the outside world and "pain-in-the-ass visitors." She smilingly approved of his retreat from all-embracing acceptance into blinkered redneck suspicion. Of the white civil rights activists, Kerouac said that they "would hire Negroes to wash their toilet bowls," and the Jews had "flung the Negro at America so that we'd forget anti-Semitism." When friends showed up, Mémère repeated her favorite joke: "I sure had a hard time when I made Jack, and he's still giving me a hard time." Publicly, she bemoaned his drinking, but privately, she encouraged it by matching him drink for drink, and kept a bottle of Southern Comfort under her bed. Jack wrote drunken letters to friends excoriating women forever. Some dopey Jap Vassar cunt, he complained, had psychoanalyzed him by using the material in *Subterraneans*. It was a real square Vassar shot, with some idiot conclusions. So the heroine was based on a "living woman." What did they want him to do, screw cadavers? Jack had a horrible vision of the too-muchness of the world—of his mind essence completely blasted by music, people, books, papers, movies, games, sex, talk, business, taxes, cars, asses, gases, etc. He wanted to return to the simplicity of former times.

As for Gregory Corso, he was now a heroin addict, in thrall to the white muse. He had married Sally November (a onetime girlfriend of Bob Dylan's) and had a daughter, but had lost both, as well, he was sure, as the talent that burned within him. All these years the muse and the companionship of his fellow poets had carried him, but now he would be deathly ill without the white muse. He had been a poet, writing with chastising arrogance, his name and fame were spread far and wide, and it had felt good to be recognized. But suddenly it no longer felt good, he became immensely shy, his life was split in two. The boy with six sets of parents who had gone to jail surfaced from his subconscious and made him feel his fame was not deserved. The poet and the boy fluctuated back and forth. Unlike those who took drugs for kicks, he wanted to get off, he had never enjoyed the blood running down his arms.

And yet there were some good moments. At a Larry Rivers party in early 1963 in New York, he had overheard an elderly lady asking her husband, "Is that Gregory Corso?" and the husband admonished her for being so embarrassingly fanlike, and led her away down the elevator, and Gregory raced down the steps and met them outside and put his arms around the woman and said, "I am Gregorio and how are you and lo spring is coming." When he said good-bye he could see that she and her husband were glowing, that he had made them happy and was admired by them, and it made him feel wonderful all over because he knew that he was through with that creepy time when he and Allen and the others were seen as spider-eyed conspirators when in truth they were the best people in the world.

In Palm Beach, Billy Burroughs was growing up with his grandparents, whom he loved. Except that sometimes he secretly thought, "If they were dead, my father would have to take care of me." Palm Beach, where the police were so polite, and the lawns were so cropped and green, and the members of the Coral Beach Club suffered from terminal complacency, and strollers on Worth Avenue wore pastel clothes. At Cobblestone Gardens, on Worth Avenue, Laura and Mote sold Victorian chairs with taloned paws, porcelain dogs, music boxes, green pine cones from Maine, and large red strawberries made out of soap.

At the end of the day, after dusting the artificial flowers, they drove home to their two-bedroom, one-story house at 202 Sanford Avenue, a street lined with royal palms at the north end of town. The house was a bit run down; the sliding windows didn't slide, their aluminum frames being corroded by the salt air. Laura played records on a Victrola in a wooden box. One of her favorites was "Que Serà, Serà." The song seemed to Billy to reflect a fatalistic strain in her character. She did not wish to face things, and one of her sayings was "Some things are better left unsaid." It seemed to Billy that Mote loved Laura so much that he had allowed her to submerge his identity. Mote told Billy that he must never look over his shoulder while driving, because if you did your hand might turn the wheel without your realizing it—a certain European king had been killed that way. Billy later reflected that this was his grandfather's worldview, expressed in Mote language.

Sometimes Billy asked himself: What do I really remember? He didn't even know what his mother looked like, never having seen a photograph. In Mexico there was a tiled circular staircase, always cool, and a friend downstairs who kept a rabbit that hopped across the courtyard and bit him on the toe, after which his mother bought him a pair of shoes.

His father was a vague and distant figure, who came to visit from time to time. Once he took Billy to Stouffer's and told him a story about two little monsters who cut off a cat's head with garden shears. It was refreshing to Billy to hear something that wasn't a hundred percent wholesome. Even though Billy rarely saw his father, they kept in touch. Surprising items arrived in the mail—a collection of beautiful Amazonian butterflies in little glass cases; an edition of Rimbaud's poems with the English translation on the facing page. Everything he received from his father Billy kept in a locked green tin box in the bottom drawer of his bureau. Also locked away, as yet unexamined, was Billy's dilemma: How would he be able to love the man who had, as he knew from his grandmother, killed his mother and abandoned him? How would he be able to emulate and respect this man?

Every weekday Billy rode his English bicycle to a Palm Beach private school, where he attended classes with Kelloggs and Dodges and Posts.

He wrote his father that he had won the trophy for being the outstanding boy in the fifth grade. He had made the Safety Patrol, the football team, the scholastic honor roll and the citizenship honor roll. "I'm afraid there is an awful lot about me in this letter," he wrote. Under his signature there was a heart with an arrow through it. In the seventh grade, he informed his father he had written an essay on the value of turning in homework. He grew into his teens, an overweight boy with a high forehead, large apprehensive eyes, and brown hair that fell across his brow. Once he grabbed a potato chip from a buffet table set up for a school function and was reprimanded by the principal, who called him "chubby."

In 1960, at age thirteen, Mote reported, Billy was quite a big boy, "plump as a partridge," but he was lazy and his marks were not very good, though he had a good vocabulary and wrote well—but he tended to inject an irreverent sense of humor that was not appreciated by his teachers. He was being tutored four and a half hours a week in Latin and three hours a week in French. He had six book reports to write, including one on Henry James's *Turn of the Screw*, which seemed to Mote beyond the comprehension of a thirteen-year-old in its extremely difficult and involved sentences.

As he grew older, Billy was less interested in schoolwork than he was in fun and games. He sneaked into the north tower of the Biltmore Hotel, a vantage point for peeping at the naked ladies in the solarium, and came upon a baby owl. Forgetting the naked ladies, he wrapped the little white creature in his shirt and exited bare-chested through the elegant lobby, restoring it to health and freedom. With a friend, he heisted one of the big bronze lions off the steps of the public library and somehow hauled it—it felt like it weighed a ton—down the Via Mizner to the back door of one of the richest persons in town. Three days later it was back on its perch in front of the library. He broke a front tooth showing off to some girls that he could drink champagne from the bottle. Just call me Zorba the Schmuck. His grandmother took him to the dentist to have a good tooth put in and told him, "Try to keep your mouth closed whenever possible."

In 1962, when he was fifteen, Laura and Mote gave him a motorbike for his birthday. One summer evening he was drinking Roma port cooking wine with Bobby Furey and Al Morton (names changed), who broke the empty bottle and held a jagged spar against his forearm: "Think I'm chicken?" "Oh, haw haw yes," roared the other two. Pearls of blood formed on his arm like red sweat. Billy took him to the emergency room on his motorbike.

Billy's best friend, Lawrence Reeves, had an air rifle with which he shot woodpeckers, on the pretext of keeping them out of his father's mango trees. When Billy saw their stove-in backs and the deeper red on the red feathers he felt real fear.

Mote's sons had grown up with guns, and he gave his grandson a .22 rifle. One day in the fall of 1962, Larry and Billy were in Billy's room after school. Larry was sitting on the bed and Billy sat across from him on a chair, aiming his .22 at him, sighting through the scope. In the circle he saw Larry's face, a little quizzical, a little scornful, the cross hairs intersecting right between and a little above his eyebrows. His finger twitched, there was a concussion in the air, and he saw a red dot the size of a thumbtack on Larry's neck, an inch to the right of his Adam's apple. He had been certain the gun was empty. At the same time he was surprised that it had fired so low. The sound of his friend's voice screaming, "He shot me!" rang in his ears. Then there was the pandemonium of ambulance-calling and hand-wringing, and the arrival of Larry's parents, and the look and passing blow Larry's father gave Billy. The doctor said that if the bullet had struck half an inch in any other direction Larry would have been killed. The next day the police came with a stenographer who had a little machine on a tripod and took Billy's statement. They also took the bullet. He and Larry never spoke again. Billy wondered to what extent he was destined to duplicate the acts of his father. "Cursed" would be a better word. Was there something inside him that made him act out, in compulsive repetition, what had gone on before? Was he but an echo of his father's voice?

After the shooting, Billy was depressed. His schoolwork was increasingly erratic. Laura and Mote thought he needed a change. Billy said he wanted to be with his father. Burroughs agreed to take him. It was arranged that Billy would join him in Tangier in July 1963, when he had turned sixteen. There was an American school in Tangier (the headmaster was Omar Pound, son of Ezra) that he could attend in the fall. And so it was that Billy said good-bye to his grandparents and flew to New York, where he connected with a flight to Lisbon. In the Lisbon airport, on the other side of the customs barrier, an odd-looking man, wearing a suit and a hat in the summer heat, waved at him. He looked like an English bank clerk. When he approached, greeting him with awkward gestures and a smile that seemed forced, Billy noticed that his fingers were stained a dark nicotine yellow. Almost at once, to relieve the tension, he lit a cigarette from a pack of Players.

For Burroughs, bringing Billy to Tangier was an overdue attempt to connect with his estranged son. He was loaded with guilt because of Joan's death, and because he had so long avoided his responsibility as a father. He would now make it up to Billy by taking care of him. But raising a son in Tangier had about as much chance of success as growing orchids in the Moroccan desert. Billy was being brought into a homosexual household consisting of Burroughs and his two lovers, one of whom was barely older than he was; a household in which drugs were regularly and freely used. Through his father, Billy would meet the members of Tangier's expatriate homosexual set. It was a bizarre and dislocating setting for a suggestible sixteen-year-old. In assuming the responsibility for his son, Burroughs was inadvertently contributing to the delinquency of a minor.

They arrived at the house on calle Larache after dark. Billy was exhausted, and everything was disorganized. His father had not given any thought to where Billy would sleep, and blankets were hastily thrown over a couch. The lights weren't working. Burroughs lit candles until Ian arrived and hit a power pole with a broomstick. Mikey at once started one-upping him saying, "You needn't *insist* you're fresh from America." The next morning, Billy was awakened by Ian, who sat on his bed and talked to him and gently took his hand and tried to draw it to his groin. He hadn't been there twenty-four hours and they were already putting the make on him. What next?

After breakfast, Burroughs said, "Ian, take Billy down to the Gran Socco and help him pick out a pipe." That evening he had his pipe and smoked his first kif, pleased to be included in his father's entourage rather than treated like a child.

It was a job adapting to his father's way of life. In a sense he had more freedom in Palm Beach, where he could be out of the house with friends his own age. Here he had to hang around while his father banged away on his typewriter or sat in his orgone box in the upstairs hall, or smoked kif. When they went to bars, he had to fight off the advances of the simpering Tangier queens:

"We all knew you were coming and wondered what you looked like."

"I know I'm old, but I really haven't lost my figure, dear."

"Well, baby! I mean if you ever want your nuts blowed!"

Burroughs took Billy to the American School to introduce him to the headmaster, but he was surly and uncooperative—he didn't open his mouth. When school started in September, he attended for three days and quit. Burroughs asked him what the matter was, and Billy said he didn't want to go to school—it was too much trouble. He had brought his guitar with him, and said he wanted to learn to play flamenco. Burroughs, whose life and work were devoted to the cultivation of unfettered personal freedom, was unable to tell his son that he *must* go to school. He was in no position, either by temperament or logic, to be a disciplinarian.

One night, when Burroughs lay in bed, listening to Billy play the guitar in the next room, he was filled with an overwhelming sadness. "Where are you, Billy, where are you?" he asked himself, and there was no reply. He knew they were not connecting. Their conversations were strained and hollow. The right thing was said at the wrong time, and the wrong thing at the right time. It was all so stilted and difficult. What could you do when someone was operating out of a deliberate flaunting mechanism? Every suggestion Burroughs made was resisted. It was Billy's way of making his old man pay. He told Billy, "I don't want you to leave the kif and the dope right out on the goddamned living room table where anyone can walk in and see it. What if it gets back to the consulate?" But every goddamned time he'd find it out there and put it away himself and find it out there again the next day.

What struck Burroughs the most was that when he was sixteen years old the idea of going to Tangier would have been the most romantic thing he could imagine . . . smoking hashish in the native quarter . . . drinking mint tea in an Arab café . . . to an imaginative sixteen-year-old schoolboy that was Nirvana. But Billy never seemed to give a shit. He had no enthusiasm whatever. He never wanted to go anywhere. It did not impress him that he was in contact with a new reality. Where was his sense of wonder? At sixteen Burroughs would have been transported, but it did not make any more difference to Billy than if he was in Toledo, Ohio. Too bad, thought Burroughs, because no matter how badly you wanted to get back at somebody, it wasn't worth doing at the cost of total apathy— you had to have something of your own.

Father and son soon came to realize that the arrangement was not going to work out. Billy made Burroughs uncomfortable, hanging around like a living reproach. Billy began to miss Palm Beach and his grandparents, old and square as they were, screening his friends, telling him this boy's parents had each been divorced twice, and that such-and-such a girl seemed to be quite loose. With all its drawbacks, Palm Beach seemed like an improvement over the weird and aimless Tangier life and his father's homosexual clique. He realized that his father was making as much of an effort as he was capable of. He was trying to make the house more of a home, and had fashioned a ten-foot-long mahogany table from some wood he had bought. He was having Billy tutored in math by Ian, and was doing some English tutoring himself. But Billy knew that wasn't enough, and he had to think about graduating from high school. Finally it was Ian, who had become protective of Billy after his initial pass, who told him, "You don't want to live in a household of fags."

Billy told his father that he wanted to go back to Palm Beach and get his high school diploma, and to put a brighter face on his departure, added, "I'm sure this [Tangier] is where I'll wind up." The day came in January 1964 when Burroughs took him to the airport and said good-bye. His last words were "Billy, for God's sakes don't try to take anything out with you back to the States." Billy swore up and down he was clean. He must have looked awfully nervous at the customs line in New York because he was singled out right away, and it didn't take them long to find the *majoun*. He was lucky; the customs supervisor let him go, saying, "You're much too young to spend the night in jail." But from then on, the Burroughs name was on their books.

Burroughs went into a depression after his son's departure, mulling over what had gone wrong. When Billy was a baby, he thought, I was absolutely devoted to him. I carried him around and fed him more than Joan did. But then I lost him. There was just such a gap, he wasn't the same person. We didn't connect. It was a total failure. He was here six months, and we never got to know each other at all. From the beginning to the end, Billy had been inaccessible and emotionally dead.

Burroughs blamed himself for his inability to communicate. He knew that he was suffering from a deep emotional blockage that made him unable to really level with Billy and explain to him the true circumstances of Joan's death. The opportunity for catharsis, where father and son might have wept and hugged and shared their grief, had come and gone. It was that frustrating family trait, the inability to express emotion. It also made him unable to show anger with Billy. There was never an overt quarrel. In the Burroughs family, to make a scene was unthinkable. He had never heard his mother or father raise their voices to each other. It was good in one way, but bad in another, for making a scene cleared the air, and in Billy's case it would have broken the logjam.

It may have been because of Billy that the trouble with the neighbors started. Billy had made the mistake of going up on the roof, where unveiled women did the wash and gossiped. For a Nazarene to see them without their veils was a major infraction of the Koran, and retribution was swift—mud was flung at their front door.

Or it may have been Ian, who was then going through a very difficult paranoid period. Ian had "hot brains," as one of his Moroccan friends put it. He was being deliberately promiscuous with Arabs, as a way of freeing himself from what he felt was the hold that Burroughs had over him. He was trying to get away from that "merging-of-souls" side that Burroughs had pushed on Allen. Ira Cohen, the writer-photographer, recalls standing with Ian in front of the Hotel Muniria, located at the bottom of a hill. Ian had his back to the top of the hill, where Burroughs suddenly appeared. Ira saw him but didn't show it. Suddenly, as Ira was talking to him, Ian began walking backward up the hill as if pulled by a magnet, and kept walking without turning around until he was level with Burroughs. It was spooky. There seemed to be some occult takeover of personality at work.

Actually, at that time, Burroughs was trying to demonstrate an absence of possessiveness. He told Ian he did not require fidelity, and did not object to his liaisons with Arabs. But Ian was in a bad state. He started seeing a deaf-mute, who forced him into degrading situations with other Arabs. He even began to speak a little Arabic, which was not helpful, because he began to understand what they were saying about him. Ian was no empire-builder; if anything, he felt inferior to the Arabs.

Ian's abandoned behavior with local young Arab men may have earned the disdain and hostility of the neighbors. Burroughs and company were the only foreigners on calle Larache, and they made the mistake of not employing Moslems. If you employed a Moslem or two, they told the others, I work for these people and they are all right. Burroughs began to feel under siege. Every time he stepped out the door, he was showered with insults. People pounded on the door at six in the morning, shouting Arabic imprecations, and he was not sure why. What exactly had they done? Children threw rocks at the house, and on one occasion they broke the skylight. One evening, Burroughs heard a low wailing in the street, a sort of "*ul-ul-ul-ul-al-aiiiii*" and stepped out on the balcony, and there was a group of fifty veiled and white-robed women gathered in front of the house, chanting away. He thought of Orpheus, torn to pieces by madwomen, and stuck out his arm, spreading the fingers of his hand. With that one gesture, the women scattered. They obviously know, he thought, that I am not a friend of women.

Burroughs badly wanted to move to another part of town, but he was broke. It infuriated him that Girodias owed him $5,000—his royalties were not yet coming directly from Grove in New York—and in January 1964 he made a special trip to Paris to collect, only to be met by Maurice's "I-am-helpless" shrug with hands widespread to illustrate the utter void of his financial situation. "So put me in jail," Maurice said, holding out his hands for the cuffs. "I don't want to put you in jail," Burroughs said. "I want what you owe me for Chrissakes." But it was hopeless.

Stopping off in London on the way back to Tangier for a television interview, he had another nasty surprise. The customs official at Heathrow checked his name against a list, crossed out the "three months" on his visa, and stamped "permitted to land on condition does not stay longer than two weeks." "Why have you come to England Mr. Burroughs?" he inquired. Deadpan, he replied, "For the food and the climate." He was indignant at being treated like an undesirable character. Having a two-week visa looked bad on his passport. It was the Lenny Bruce treatment. He vowed not to return to England unless he was treated like any other visitor.

For lack of money, he was forced to remain at calle Larache, but despite the harrassment, he was able to work. He was still producing cut-ups, and wrote the New York poet Ted Berrigan that "to me the most interesting aspect of the cut-ups is that it introduces the unexpected into writing, that is you never know what will happen next and many of my best characters have cut in from the cut-ups. Also lines of straight narrative arise from cut-ups." He was contributing an "Uncle William" column to *My Own Mag*, a creation of the London counterculture figure Jeff Nuttall. This satire on the standard corny advice column had its moments, as in:

"Dear Uncle William, I am dating a transvestite and wonder whether I should go 'all the way.' Sincerely yours, Prince Philip."

"Dear Phil, Watch out for the 'I've got the rag on lemme pull you off' routine. Uncle William."

"Dear Uncle William, I hear the bugle calling me to the service of the flesh. Should I go? Yours Truly, Tommy Atkins, homosap."

"Not much choice, Tommy. Uncle William."

"One has to think of writing as any other job," Burroughs wrote his mother. "You work at it all day and every day if you want to make a living." His mother reported that Billy was having problems with schoolwork, and wondered whether he should see a therapist. Burroughs was against it, having had unrewarding experiences in that direction. Responding like a true alumnus of the Los Alamos school, with its emphasis on physical fitness, he recommended that Billy take boxing and jujitsu, which would build up his confidence. Burroughs himself had been made to take boxing at Los Alamos and had loathed it.

When Burroughs told Paul Bowles about his neighbor trouble, Paul just shrugged and kept his thoughts to himself. The trouble with Burroughs was that he never seemed to realize that he was living in Morocco. He wouldn't have anything to do with Moroccans, which was not quite the right attitude. His problems probably started with some tiny thing. Some kids may have annoyed him, and he may have slapped one, whereas one had to go out of one's way to be friendly. But Paul couldn't tell him that, because he didn't want to be playing the role of the old Morocco hand. He did not think A could save B from trouble. Nor did he think A should try. But A always did, or nearly always. He felt that people only learned when their ignorance made them suffer.

Look at Alfred Chester, who seemed to Paul totally unsuited to life in Morocco. Brooklyn-born, Chester had studied to become a rabbi, but a fever had deprived him of all facial and body hair, and you couldn't be a hairless rabbi. His mother made him wear a toupée. Paul noticed that when he went to the bathroom he would stay there for half an hour, and when he emerged there would be a strange odor of collodion in the air. Paul thought he was shooting up, but all he was doing was regluing his reddish wig.

Once he invited Paul and Jane to lunch and when they got there he was lying on the floor as though unconscious, completely bald. "I want to read you a letter," he said. "I've just written my father and I want to see if you think it's all right." Paul read the letter and said, "Well, he shouldn't be too upset by it. After all, if that's the way you feel." "I know," said Chester, "but there's a great problem. I don't know where to send it." "Isn't he with your mother, and if not, wouldn't she be able to give you his address?" "He died eight years ago," Chester said. Paul thought at first he must be joking, but he wasn't, he was absolutely serious.

Chester was an interesting writer, Paul thought; he had a story in the *O. Henry Prize Stories*, and another in *Best American Short Stories*, and he contributed a monthly review column to *Book Week*, but to call him bizarre was an understatement. One summer he rented a house on the beach at Arsilah, a pretty coastal town twenty miles south of Tangier, and he filled one entire room with several tons of oranges, which of course rotted. He took in two runaway dogs who bit several small children, and he had to pay bribes and fines. Since it was a very hot summer, he fixed a pulley on the roof, and paid some urchins to bring seawater up in buckets, so that he had a perfect roof pool for himself and his dogs. Of course the water leaked through into the entire house and wrecked everything.

Chester fell under the spell of a Moroccan named Driss. Like Brion Gysin, he was dying to know all about magic. But as soon as he began to practice it, he became convinced that it was being practiced against him. He started hearing voices, and went to see Paul to demand that he stop broadcasting. No matter what Paul said, Chester replied, "I know, I know, you don't know watcher doing, do you?" Because of the magic, ordinary objects took on an ominous significance. Paul had a sweet potato hanging in his hall and Chester told him to get rid of it, saying, "It's evil, it grows too fast." Paul said he wanted to see how long the vine would get. The next time Chester came he gave an awful cry and shouted, "It has the evil eye!" and lurched forward and fell on the floor.

At that time, the entrepreneurial writer-photographer Ira Cohen was soliciting contributions from Tangier writers for a magazine he wanted to put out called *Gnaoua*, after a spiritual brotherhood of Moroccan trance dancers. He had heard their incredible music, and it was precisely that kind of energy he wanted in his magazine. Through his duties as editor, Ira was caught in a little drama where egos clashed and behavior spilled over into the irrational. Apparently, Irving Rosenthal, one of the contributors to *Gnaoua*, was annoyed because he always had to visit Paul and Paul never came to visit him. To express his pique, he changed a line in his story, which originally said, "Some of the campiest queens I know have cocks drier than the mouth of an Arab caught between Taroudant and Tafraout with plenty of teeth and no water," substituting "Paul Bowles" for "an Arab."

Ira Cohen did not know what to do. If he cut the line, Irving would withdraw his story and the magazine was already in proof. But Paul had also contributed a story, which Ira wanted to lose even less. When Ira showed the proofs to Paul, he zeroed in like an eagle on that line of Irving's, before looking at his own story. Paul asked Ira what he was going to do, and Ira said, "Maybe I should just print a different copy of the magazine for each of the contributors."

Then Burroughs, having gotten wind of the incident, and being a contributor himself, came by Ira's house that March. Ira knew he was not there just to see the proofs; he wanted to know what all the fuss was about, and Ira told him. "Well," said Burroughs, "I guess controversy is a good thing."

Now it happened that when Burroughs dropped by, Alfred Chester was visiting Ira. When Ira unbolted the front door and said, "Hello, Bill," Chester jumped up and ran upstairs. He had written a negative review of *Naked Lunch* in *Commentary*, and knew that he had done it in a glib reviewer way, and that he couldn't stand behind what he'd written, and he was too embarrassed to face Burroughs (who, incidentally, had not seen the review).

Alfred Chester took the quarrel between Paul Bowles and Irving Rosenthal as a matter of crucial importance. A few days later he burst into Ira Cohen's house as though he was on fire and said: "I've got it all worked out. You know that thing of Irving's . . . I've made an appointment to see Jane and I'm going to tell her that for $5,000 I will get you to drop that line."

"Listen," Ira Cohen said, "you're out of your mind."

"Don't worry," Chester said, "you'll get half the money."

"You should give Irving half the money," Ira Cohen said.

"Fuck Irving," Chester said. "You want to give Irving anything you give it to him out of your share. You're in this up to your neck and you're in it with me."

"You're totally crazy," Ira Cohen said.

Then Chester said, "Give me that letter."

He was referring to a note that Paul Bowles had sent Ira. Paul prided himself on never showing any emotion, but Alfred Chester had so infuriated him that he had thrown a dish on the floor and broken it. It was after losing his temper that Paul wrote Ira in a jocular vein: "Alfred Chester is being impossible and I've arranged to have him knocked off."

Ira had unfortunately told Alfred Chester about the letter, which he now demanded, to help him in his scheme to collect $5,000—he would tell Jane that he had received a death threat from Paul and that he was going to send a copy to the State Department in Washington.

"Don't do it," Ira said, but then another visitor arrived, and Ira told his girlfriend Rosalyn, "Look, Alfred is totally out of his mind, just keep him busy while I deal with this other thing." A few minutes later, Chester raced out the door, screaming, "I've got it ha ha ha." It turned out that Rosalyn, instead of calming him, had given him the letter and urged him to ask for $10,000 instead of $5,000.

Alfred Chester went to see Jane Bowles, who, as he explained his scheme, kept saying, "But Alfred, I love you." "Don't talk to me about love," he said, "I want the $10,000 and I want it in unmarked bills."

Getting nowhere, Chester went to see the American consul and said, "Paul Bowles is trying to assassinate me through Moroccans." The next thing Paul knew he was summoned before the consul, a man named Schultz, who said: "You must understand that I don't take this seriously, but I'm obliged to ask you about it, because an American citizen says that you threatened to kill him. He has requested the protection of the marines." Schultz accepted Paul's explanation but shook his head and said, "In my entire consular career, this is the only place I've ever been posted where I understand *nothing* of what is going on."

Even in Tangier, where there was a high degree of tolerance for eccentric behavior, there were limits, which Alfred Chester exceeded, and soon after the "death threat" incident, the Moroccan authorities deported him. He moved to Jerusalem where he committed suicide. He was in a sense, Paul reflected, one of the casualties of Tangier, a city which tended to intensify whatever tendencies one had.

That May of 1964, Burroughs' first substantial payment from Grove Press arrived, which allowed him to move into a penthouse in the heart of Tangier, at 16 rue Delacroix, in the Loteria building. Proud of being financially independent at last, he wrote his mother that he had $2,000 in the bank at Gibraltar and was planning to see a good lawyer so that he could set up a trust fund that would provide Billy with a comfortable income for life. His mother replied with a mild dig about the obscenity in his books: "Someday I wish you would write a book that we can read and dedicate it to Billy—he would like that."

Paul came to visit Burroughs in his splendid penthouse, which had a distinctly nautical look, with porthole windows and leather chairs, and a huge balcony like the deck of a ship. All around the living room there were shelves, and each one was piled with large folios filled with newspaper clippings and photographs and bits of pasted-up prose. "I'll show you how I work," Burroughs said, and Paul followed him around the room as he dipped from notebook to notebook. "Let's see," he said, "*New York Times*, April 16, 1917, yeah, uh-uh, tornado in Illinois." Then he picked up another and said, "*Herald Tribune*, March 5, 1934, tornado in Oklahoma." "See," he explained to Paul, "I get them all put together, I collate them." Paul did not tell him what he thought of the cut-up system, but was amused by Burroughs' ultimate defense of it: "It works in the hand of a master."

Burroughs continued to have trouble with the locals in his new neighborhood. One time, as he was coming home from a rather festive evening, an Arab shoeshine boy began to shout insults at him. Enough was enough. Burroughs slammed an elbow in his face and chased him into a vacant lot where the cornered Arab picked up a rock and threw it, hitting him in the knee, which was cut and bruised.

That summer there was another infestation of hippies. Jane Bowles was right, thought Burroughs, when she said they were a menace to her way of life. She was afraid that the resident foreign colony would suffer as a result of the attention they attracted. There were periodic crackdowns and arrests. One man, arrested for photographing Arab boys in pornographic poses, was sentenced to five years and served five months.

The Istiqlal, the Nationalist party, which was antiforeign and antiqueer, was putting on pressure to rid Morocco of these degenerate foreigners.

In October, Burroughs wrote Brion Gysin that he was disgusted with Tangier "like I turn sick with the sight of crabs. The whole town solid cunt territory and everyone knocks himself or herself out to show you how worthless they can be. . . . All this happened since about the time of the Kennedy assassination. . . . I must get out before I open up with laser guns on the wretched idiot inhabitants. These people are going to fight Israel? What you see here is the Arabs at their worst. . . . There is not even material here for a riot. No guts left in this miserable town."

Burroughs decided to leave for New York, since Brion Gysin was going to be there marketing his Dream Machine. He claimed to have signed a contract with a toy manufacturer who was going to produce them en masse, and was ready to pick the money tree. Skeptical as usual, Paul Bowles said of the Dream Machine, "It promises a new kick to the juvenile delinquents."

Burroughs arrived in New York on December 8, aboard the *Independence*, gratified that he had been invited to the captain's cocktail party as a famous author. Upon landing, however, he got the "right-this-way" treatment. He was detained at customs for three hours while two narcotics agents named Ahearn and Cohen went through seven suitcases filled with books and papers. It was, Burroughs was certain, the fallout from Billy's *majoun* bust at the airport in January. "What, more books?" they complained. "More folders?" Where was the kilo of hashish? They read his diaries and saw something about feeling sick, and asked, "Does this refer to narcotic withdrawal?" Such was the police mind, Burroughs reflected, as limited as a beagle's. They found nothing to confiscate, and when they released him, they said, "We treated you like a gentleman." But they told Brion Gysin, who was waiting outside: "Are you a friend of that man in there? He sure writes some filthy stuff."

Burroughs had a "return-to-St.-Louis" assignment for *Playboy*, and took the train from New York on December 22. The long train ride put him in mind of former trips with the family: *The Green Hat* in his mother's lap, a delicate gray cone forming on the tip of his father's cigar. He was on the lookout for all signs of offensive change. Where were the old brass spittoons? Where was the smell of worn leather? In other words, who put the sand in the spinach? Gazing out the window, he saw acres of rusting car bodies, streams crusted with sewage, American flags over empty fields, crooked crosses in winter stubble—Church of Christ. A knock on the door: Half an hour out of St. Louis, sir.

The nudes were still there across from the station. Burroughs remembered hitting a parked car one night long ago, and being thrown out of his car, and rolling across the pavement, and standing up and feeling for broken bones right under those monumental bronze nudes by Carl Milles, depicting the meeting of the Missouri and Mississippi river waters.

At the Chase Plaza Hotel, he bounced on the bed and tested the hot water taps, like a good European. The next day he took a walk in Forest Park and thought of the times he had gone there with his Welsh nurse, who always said, "Don't ask questions and don't pass remarks." The first part of that injunction he had been forced to disregard for professional reasons, while for years he had remained uncertain as to what exactly constituted the second part, finally settling for "You spilled gravy down your tie."

He looked for anything that might remind him of 1920—a store sign, a lamppost, sunlight on a vacant lot. Down Pershing Avenue to 4664, its solid red brick façade unchanged. "Do you mind if I take pictures? I used to live here, you know." Where, he wondered, was Rives Matthews, his next-door neighbor? His mother had been to dancing school with Tommy Eliot, whose socks wouldn't stay up. That evening, he had dinner with Miggy and Mort, still an engineer with Emerson Electric. They lived at 6617 Pershing—hmm, 4664 and 6617 added up to twenty. It seemed emblematic of the permanence and sameness of Mort's life.

The next day, he drove around with Mort and took pictures. Clayton and the suburbs were built up beyond recognition. At the John Burroughs School, he looked for the locker-room door where he had stood one afternoon, watching the sky turn black and green. In the center of town, there was the old courthouse. The Arch, still under construction, had an ominous look, as though it might one day be the only landmark to survive an atomic blast. Cobblestone streets along the levee, a remnant of riverboat days. The *River Queen* and the *Admiral*, just like they used to be, floating down the Mississippi on a quiet afternoon. MacArthur bridge—just there a truck will crash through the guardrail and fall seventy-five feet, Burroughs imagined, killing the driver. He could see the dotted line in the *Post-Dispatch* picture. Rejected by *Playboy*, "Return to St. Louis" was published by the *Paris Review*.

Back in New York with the New Year, 1965, Burroughs checked into the Chelsea Hotel, which was very much to his liking. It had suites with large fireplaces that reminded him of Sherlock Holmes's Baker Street days, and Stanley Bard, the proprietor, was a patron of the arts known on occasion to accept paintings in lieu of rent. Arthur C. Clarke, the science fiction writer, had a suite on the top floor, and invited Burroughs to look through his pride and joy, a $3,000 Questar telescope. He claimed that he could read a newspaper over someone's shoulder in Union Square, nine blocks away. He showed Burroughs a man and a women eating dinner in their apartment across the street, and you could see exactly what it was they were eating and lip-read their dinner conversation. Clarke struck Burroughs as being like one of his own science fiction characters. He had a way of sliding around the margin of your vision like some semivisible intergalactic mentor. They talked about life on other planets, and Burroughs said that whatever could be written about must exist. In any case, they didn't all have to breathe oxygen. Clarke showed him a cartoon—a creature staggering out of a spacecraft and gasping "Ammonia!" Also on hand was the composer George Kleinsinger, who kept a menagerie of exotic animals in his room. He was worried about his python's loss of appetite. He tried canned quail, mice, and white rats. Once the python had to be rescued from a white rat that was biting it. "Oh, you lazy serpent," Kleinsinger said.

Herbert Huncke, who all these years had been in New York, living by his wits and off his friends, scoring when he could, stealing when he must, in and out of jail, heard that Burroughs was in town, and was offended that he did not get in touch. That was Bill, thought Huncke, he really didn't give a damn about old friends. But then Bill called and they arranged to meet. On January 19, 1965, however, Bill canceled their appointment because his father had just died. From his tone of voice, Huncke assumed that Bill was taking it in stride.

Burroughs went to Palm Beach for the funeral. His mother seemed to be taking it well. She and Mote had given up Cobblestone Gardens and had been living the senior-citizen Palm Beach life. Billy was not there, he was away at boarding school, and for some reason could not get back in time, but his brother, Mort, was there. Mortimer Burroughs had died of heart failure a few months short of his eightieth birthday. He had always been an enigma to his son. Mortimer's own father, the inventor, had had no time for his children, and had been unable to express his affection, and perhaps this was the root of his father's reticence. The list was long of subjects he wouldn't discuss—sex; Uncle Horace the black sheep; Mrs. White, the woman Burroughs' inventor grandfather had married shortly before his death. Burroughs knew that she had come to the house once to ask for money and Mortimer had refused to see her. Why? Too late to ask. As he thought of his father, his own identity faded out into a gray impalpable world. It seemed amazing that so close a tie as father and son could have existed between two men who had known each other hardly at all. He wished it could have been otherwise. He would have liked to have told his father that he was grateful for all the years of financial support. Over and out from Cobblestone Gardens.

Back in New York, Burroughs found a loft through Finkelstein the Loft King, also known as the Artist's Friend, at 210 Centre Street. On the ground floor there was a machine shop called Atomic Machinery Exchange, a name that fitted right into his scheme of things. The loft's sparsely furnished austerity suited him. There was a bed, a table, a few chairs, and a refrigerator in the corner. An interviewer who came to see him shortly after he moved in reported that instead of finding a warped genius like the Marquis de Sade, he had found a gentleman of the old school, a courteous scholarly person with the serenity of a Chinese sage, who quietly brewed tea, having sworn off drugs. His thoughts were on saving mankind from nuclear destruction, which would occur, he said, "just as soon as the U.S. and Russia sign a mutual nonaggression pact. When you read about that, run for the South Pole. The bombs will start dropping on China before the ink is dry."

Wanting Ian Sommerville to join him, Burroughs sent him $450 in traveler's checks. But Ian did not seem eager to leave London. He wrote that with a visitor's visa he would not be able to work. Did Burroughs really need him there? Burroughs did not insist, and later reflected that the year in New York had been the crucial turning point in their relationship. If he had come to America then things might have been very different. Or would they? The Egyptian hieroglyph for "question" was reeds and water.

In the meantime, Brion Gysin was trying to market the Dream Machine and found a young literary agent named Peter Matson, who was working in his uncle Harold's literary agency, to help him. Matson ended up as the agent for both Brion and Burroughs, but the Dream Machine project came to nothing. Brion had thought it might work as a psychedelic toy, an emblem of the sixties, but the businessmen were scared off by reports that flicker machines caused epileptic seizures. No one wanted to risk lawsuits. Brion began to think of New York as a city of darkness, a nest of Jews and matriarchy, where hostile forces worked against him.

Burroughs, on the other hand, was a hit, taken up by the downtown crowd. On April 23, 1965, he gave a reading in the Bowery loft of Wyn Chamberlain, an action painter who served a useful social function as a connector of people and giver of parties. In the vapor-lamp dusk, a line of derelicts waited for admittance to the Bowery Mission, while across the street, at 222 Bowery, a former Y.M.C.A., the glitterati assembled to meet a man whose reputation had been enhanced by his absence from the New York scene. The sculptress Marisol was there, with a green bow tie in her hair, and the poets Ron Padgett and Ted Berrigan and Frank O'Hara, and the photographers Diane Arbus and Richard Avedon, and the painters Larry Rivers and Larry Poons and Barnett Newman and Andy Warhol. It was a quorum of the downtown art scene, a charged, electric, high-energy event, recognized as such by *The New York Times*, who sent a reporter to cover it. Mack Thomas, Burroughs' friend from the Beat Hotel days, recently sprung from a Texas jail, read from his boyhood memoir *Gumbo* and sang Methodist hymns with his East Texas drawl. Then Burroughs read, striking the *Times* reporter, Harry Gilroy, as a latter-day Will Rogers, cracking dry jokes. As he read, he ripped down a white sheet backdrop to reveal a giant rubber tarantula on the wall, illustrating his text. Someone described Burroughs as a "hot spot"— that is, a figure that others converged around.

He gave another reading at a tiny, 129-seat theater on East Fourth Street, produced by the American Theater for Poets at two dollars a ticket. The word had spread among the young Village people that Burroughs was in town, and they wanted to take a look at the mystery man of the underground, whom they knew only through his work. They sat there in tight, buzzing intimacy, the lank-haired chicks in boots and leather, the guys with long hair and shades, carrying copies of *Nova Express*, passports to the hip scene.

Burroughs appeared through yards of furled red curtains, in complete antithesis to the sartorial informality and East Village chic of his constituents. He removed his topcoat and felt hat, placed them carefully on top of a white chair, positioned his polished leather briefcase on the table in front of him, and eased his thin frame, encased in a three-piece suit, into a high-backed leather chair. Part of the effectiveness of his reading had to do with the contrast between his proper and conservative appearance and the improper and far-out content of his material. It had the incongruous effect of a classic Surrealist juxtaposition—the umbrella on the operating table, or a Mother Superior naked from the waist down. The response to the Burroughs blend of extravagant humor, read with a slightly nasal, slightly raspy midwestern twang by a man who looked as though he should have been addressing a convention of morticians, was unrestrained laughter. It was as though he was up there doing pratfalls instead of merely reading.

Burroughs then played a tape that was a collage of four themes—a plane crash over Jones Beach, an official dispatch from the American forces in Vietnam, the last words of Dutch Schultz, and a cops-and-robbers caper. "I do all the voices," he explained. It was the audience's first exposure to cut-ups, but they sat still for it. After about an hour, Burroughs got up, and without acknowledging the applause, gathered his belongings and vanished behind the red curtains, leaving some in the audience wondering whether they had really seen him or whether it had all been done with mirrors.

Burroughs was lionized. People wanted to press the flesh and get his autograph. Conrad Rooks, a young man who had come into a family fortune, wanted him to act in his avant-garde film with Jean-Louis Barrault and Ravi Shankar, whom Tim Leary called "the Liberace of India." He did a period gangster sequence with black 1930 Cadillacs in which he and Rooks (who was starring as well as directing) mowed each other down with tommy guns firing blanks. Then Rooks fired his cameraman, Robert Frank, and hired some character he met in a bar who didn't know his ass from a light meter and who underexposed the film, and they had to shoot the sequence over.

There was a kind of New York hostess in the sixties who collected the poets and artists of the counterculture. The reigning member of this species was probably Panna Grady, the daughter of a Hungarian aristocrat, Tibor de Cholnoky, and an American heiress named Louise Marie St. John. Panna grew up on a country estate in Greenwich, Connecticut, came out as a debutante, and went to Wellesley. Then she transferred to Berkeley, where she was exposed to the San Francisco poetry renaissance, and met Allen Ginsberg. To the world of privilege and formality she preferred the world of the Beats, who were so unconstrained and outspoken and who revealed themselves with a candor that dispelled secretiveness, deception, and tactics.

In the sixties, Panna married a poet named Grady, who looked like an Irish bartender, moved to New York, and bought a spectacular apartment in the Dakota, where she threw memorable parties that brought the downtown people uptown. She had formed the idea of having a salon, after the eighteenth-century French tradition of Madame de Rambouillet, which would give her entrée to the art scene as a patroness and hostess. She loved art, which was pure and refreshed the heart. She gave and gave and all she asked in return was the company of artists. According to Brion Gysin, the Mick Jagger line, "You think you're the Queen of the Underground, don't send me dead flowers in the mail," was about her.

When she met Burroughs, the mystery man of the underground, she was mesmerized and felt something akin to love. She loved his humor, his serious clowning, the way he stretched things until one had to laugh, his tight-lipped chortle, his endurance and lack of greed, his haunting and tranquil old-soul's eyes, his decency and good manners, and his infallible insight into others. When she was with him, she knew that she was being seen attentively by an undistorting intelligence. He took her into account without passing judgment, without misunderstandings, quarrels, competition, domination, or crowding. She even liked his remote side, the side that left people alone and things unsaid. He never told you his troubles. And she liked his gentleman's hat that seemed to top off the ghosts of his respectability.

In the spring of 1965 she gave a party in his honor that had all the elements of a cultural event. It was an incredible mingling of every New York scene, the Beats, the flower children, the famous and trying-to-be, the Warhol people, the eminent English novelist, the cliques and the claques, and the hostess's uptown friends, peering down their noses at the fringed jackets, bandannas, beads, and long flowing skirts. So many crashed that Panna Grady had to tell the doorman not to let anyone else in. It was then that LeRoi Jones arrived and got into a tussle with a doorman, resulting in a broken arm—accounts differed as to whose. Another footnote to literary history was that Norman Mailer went up to Anthony Burgess and said, "Burgess, your last book was shit." Burgess thought that, considering the amount of buggery in Mailer's novels, he was being paid a compliment.

By the Edwardian mantelpiece in the music room stood the guest of honor, greeting well-wishers with uneffusive cordiality. Herbert Huncke complimented him on his new suit, and Burroughs said: "I'm going to leave very soon, I don't like parties. But Panna invited me and I felt I should put in an appearance." In the crowded main room there was a commotion. Word-of-mouth had it that an avant-garde poet had urinated in Mailer's jacket pocket.

Panna Grady, who was by then a widow, entertained thoughts of marrying Burroughs. Just as some people want to marry into noble or royal families, she wanted to marry into Bohemia, at an appropriate level— and Burroughs was right up there. After all, he had been married before. She began to look for occasions to lure him, arranging dinners and parties as pretext. One evening, she invited him with Marshall McLuhan, Robert Lowell, and John Wain. Carried away with the ambience of the evening and the excellent wine, Burroughs in appreciation said something about going to live in Chile with Panna, but she knew he wasn't serious. It was at this same dinner that Burroughs confronted John Wain for writing a vicious review of *Naked Lunch*. The cornered reviewer muttered, "The principal character has no interest in scenery." "What do you mean?" Burroughs indignantly replied. "I am a connoisseur of scenery."

Panna Grady continued to imagine a life together with Burroughs, where she could advance his career and become the Madame de Rambouillet of the counterculture, but Burroughs was evasive. Whenever togetherness was discussed, he pleaded "tired blood." Herbert Huncke exploited her fondness for Burroughs by selling her information. He would tell her the latest Burroughs story, and she would slip him fifty or a hundred dollars, depending on the quality of the information. She became known as such a soft touch when it came to Burroughs that she was called "Pan of Gravy." Burroughs himself never took a penny from Panna, and his privately held conviction was that there is no more miserable specimen than a homosexual who marries a woman for her money.

It was through Panna Grady that Burroughs met John Giorno, a young poet who would become a close friend and collaborator. In his own development, Giorno was a living artifact of the counterculture of the sixties. He came from an upper-middle-class family in Roslyn, Long Island, and after graduating from Columbia in 1958, he followed in the footsteps of his stockbroker father. He did the Wall Street trip for about four years and then met Andy Warhol and became his lover. Warhol was a foot fetishist who liked to lick Giorno's toes and feet, which Giorno thought was pretty dismal. Warhol wasn't famous yet, but was toying with the idea of making a movie. "Why don't people make great movies when there are so many great things?" he said with his customary profundity. He bought a Bolex and started to film Giorno sleeping. He would set the lights and camera up and Giorno would go to sleep, usually drunk, and he would shoot for an hour or two. It took months to get what he wanted, a six-hour movie of Giorno asleep, a concept that made twisting and turning and snoring avant-garde.

Thanks to his inert performance (a part, he could rightly say, in which there was absolutely no acting), Giorno was launched in the downtown New York scene. At the Panna Grady party for Burroughs, he met Brion Gysin, who thought he looked in profile like Piero della Francesca's portrait of the one-eyed duke of Montefeltro. They became lovers and took about fourteen acid trips together in the Chelsea Hotel. When Brion was awakened by the chatter of maids in the hall, he covered their mouths with dollar bills, telling them it was "hush money." The acid trips were completely sexual, and opened Giorno's heart, so that he felt a deep emotional involvement. Brion was the first person who had ever given him a worldview, combining elements of esoteric knowledge, magic, and a beguilingly paranoid view of history. Giorno was hooked, totally enchanted—every day was a learning process. He was the adept and Brion was the teacher, and his teaching was transmitted like an arrow, from the heart to the heart.

Thinking he was in love with Brion, Giorno gave up his apartment on Ninth Street between Avenues C and D and followed him to Tangier in 1965. It was a magical time, a time of enchanting conversations and daily visits with Paul and Jane Bowles, who lived in Brion's building. There was a theory that Jane had not had a stroke, but had been poisoned by her Moroccan friend Cherifa. One day in the fall of 1965 Paul stormed into Brion's apartment and said, "Do you know what just happened? The parrot died." Apparently, Jane had given the parrot some of her food and the parrot literally fell off its perch, legs up. Paul and Brion stood there facing each other and went through their poison routine: "Don't you notice how pale Jane is getting?" "Whiter than white." It was so convincing that Giorno found himself believing that Jane had been poisoned by a jealous Moroccan woman. He realized later that the poison theory was ludicrous, but at the time he was completely under Brion's influence. It took him years to discern that you couldn't take Brion with a grain of salt, you needed the entire shaker.

Brion took Giorno to Fez, where they dropped acid before visiting the tomb of the Merinides kings. There was a big hole in the ground, and the soil was still fresh, and Brion said, "It's been looted." All the looters had left were the bones. Giorno gathered up some tiny bones and broken bits of tile and pottery and wrapped them in his handkerchief. He saw himself as a saint, although occasionally he would float down and be a king. But he thought, "Being a king is not nearly so good as being a saint." Brion got nervous because they were on the edge of a cliff and it was pitch black and a pack of howling dogs was coming closer. They stumbled down a path in the cliff, which was pockmarked with caves where bandits lived. Giorno was the Merinid king entering the royal city of Fez, past the dyers, knee deep in their vats, their bodies stained with the colors of their dyes, past the silk merchants, arms extended, offering bolts of embroidered cloth, past the silversmiths embossing the metal with their points and hammers, past the desert and mountain people, sandaled and turbaned.

That was the sort of endless magical thing that happened with Brion. Giorno thought it was wonderful, but after a while he saw that Brion was dissatisfied, which was his great fault. Nothing was ever good enough. Brion complained that Giorno was sponging off him, that he never talked about anything but money, and that he had arrived with thirty-two pieces of luggage, as if he was planning to stay forever. Also, it seemed to Giorno that any ongoing homosexual relationship was extremely difficult, and it was particularly so with Brion, who preferred Arab men. Giorno felt neglected. He had come to Tangier for a six-month trial, and it hadn't worked out, so he left. In later years, when he thought of his affair with Brion, he thought of homosexual sex in general, and how the fag world had pioneered drugs and sex so that sex could be prolonged for hours, which led to multiple contacts and eventually to AIDS. As a Buddhist, Giorno had a theory that in the use of those sex drugs they had transgressed certain other realms, whose attendants had become angry, with a lethal anger from the spirit world.

When Giorno returned to New York in 1966 he became the lover of Robert Rauschenberg, and after that the lover of Jasper Johns, in 1969. But at a time when the counterculture was exploding and the shrapnel was flying, Jasper Johns was interested only in painting. He wanted to live a domestic married life where you saw no one and talked only about food. He refused to take any drugs, and he was a scold. It was like the horrible 1950s. He wasn't interested in Woodstock and he wasn't interested in the Vietnam demonstrations, and when he and Giorno discussed the student protest at Berkeley, he said, "I disapprove of it because it's nothing but the transference of power." "But Jasper, that precludes everything from changing," Giorno said, and went his own way.

His itinerary took him in an increasingly political direction. In 1969 he thought up Dial-A-Poem, which was launched at the Museum of Modern Art. There were twelve lines with twelve poets and when you dialed you randomly got one of the twelve, reading a two-and-one-half minute poem. It was so popular that the museum kept it going for six months—they were getting 20,000 calls a day. Giorno made it political—he put on Bobby Seale of the Black Panthers and Yippie leader Abbie Hoffman, and the Beat writer Diane Di Prima, describing how to make a Molotov cocktail. A poem on how to make a bomb was read on the day a real bomb exploded in the IBM building, and the New York newspapers ran stories that you could call David Rockefeller's museum and find out how to build a bomb. The trustees panicked, and the program was discontinued. Giorno had presented a total of thirty poets, who had received a total of 800,000 calls. He often thought, imagine if he had patented Dial-A-Poem and collected royalties from the telephone company. As it was, they made millions copying his idea. They started a dial-a-something department, with everything from recipes to horoscopes.

Giorno's next endeavor was as columnist for *Culture Hero*, a magazine edited by the conceptual artist Les Levine, which ran for five issues in 1969 and 1970. It was a distillation of the downtown scene, a mix of interviews and "heard-on-the-Rialto" type gossip. Giorno wrote a column called Vitamin G, in which he managed to offend almost everyone of note in the art world. His idea was that true art history, consisting of the talk exchanged among artists, was not being recorded. The way careers were being engineered, the reality of the artists' lives, were kept in the dark. So Giorno revealed very personal items about the artists. When something true about someone appeared in print, he felt, an invaluable moment was created. So Giorno told what they liked to do in bed, and listed the cock sizes of his best-known lovers: Gysin, Burroughs, Warhol, Johns, and Rauschenberg. He ran items such as this: "Andy Warhol said to Jasper Johns, 'Can I play with your cock as a work of art?' Jasper should let Andy do it. Andy is light-fingered, as opposed to heavy-handed." Les Levine told him, "You say things about people that even their worst enemies wouldn't say."

Giorno's attempt to cut through the cant and pretense and preening self-importance of the New York art world brought him ostracism from his peers. He was identified as the enemy for reporting indiscretions. Feedback from the cock-size column included the following from Brion Gysin: "Vitamin Giorno poison pills came in the mail. Since you last measured my cock with your big mouth, cortisone has shrunk it still further. [Gysin was being treated with cortisone after a motorcycle accident]. Anything you like to print about my nipples or my anal sphincter now would not surprise me. You may yet be the Pepys of the pariah set. If you cannot be the first, be the last, the very last."

Burned in the art world, Giorno turned to political protest with Abbie Hoffman. They taped radio programs that they sent to Radio Hanoi, which broadcast them to the American soldiers in South Vietnam. The programs were a mix of country-western, rock 'n' roll, news, and antiwar messages. They made a total of thirteen tapes, each three hours long. When the first tapes were broadcast in the spring of 1971, Vice President Spiro Agnew dubbed Giorno and Hoffman the Hanoi Hannahs, would-be Tokyo Roses, and called for their arrest on charges of treason. Wow! thought Giorno, no one had been arrested for treason since Aaron Burr, and here he was in direct line. His lawyer assured him that under the Logan Act, which specified that treason could be committed only in a war declared by Congress, he would not be charged.

And yet he had an uneasy feeling that he was under surveillance. One day in October 1971, a package arrived, and when he opened it, two detectives who just happened to be there arrested him for possession of marijuana. He was jailed in the Tombs, where he slept on the floor in a cell with two spade junkies who had been there a month. The occupant of the adjacent cell had shoved a clothes-hanger wire up his arm and bled to death. One thing sure to radicalize any human being, Giorno reflected, was to spend twenty-four hours in an American prison. The next day Wyn Chamberlain raised his bail and Giorno was sprung. He left for India, where he stayed six months and became a Buddhist.

In 1965, the year Burroughs spent in New York, Giorno knew him mainly through Brion Gysin. Burroughs and Gysin were collaborating on a book called *The Third Mind*, and Giorno often had dinner with them after a day's work. Burroughs also saw quite a lot of the painter David Budd, whom he had known in the Beat Hotel days. It was Budd who gave him a book called *The Desperate Years*, in which there was a passage quoting the strange stream-of-consciousness last words of the dying gangster Dutch Schultz. Fascinated by the text, which seemed to him a natural cut-up, Burroughs wrote a routine inspired by it. Panna Grady, still pursuing Burroughs and eager to be helpful, rented a theater where he could read his new work. She also arranged a meeting with Andy Warhol, who arrived at Burroughs' loft carrying several bags. "What is that?" Burroughs asked, as they prepared to go out to dinner. "Recording equipment," said Warhol. "Leave it there," Burroughs said. He and Warhol did not hit it off. They went to a Chinese restaurant, where an uncouth friend of Warhol's, as he finished his food, pushed his plates over onto another table where some Chinese people were eating. One thing Burroughs had no patience with was rude behavior, and he got up in the middle of dinner and walked out, with Panna Grady following.

Missing from the scene during Burroughs' first months in New York was Allen Ginsberg, who was traveling in Europe and was that May deported from Czechoslovakia. One fine spring evening, Allen was strolling in the streets of Prague with a young couple when a man came up to him, shouted "*Bouzerant!*" (fairy), and knocked him down. Allen ran down the street, but the man knocked him down again, and suddenly five policemen were standing over him with lifted clubs. Uh-oh, Allen thought, now I'm going to get it, and started humming the mantra "Hari Om" to the pavement. But instead of hitting him, they took him to the police station. The man who had approached him was obviously a provocateur. After he was released, he noticed that one of his notebooks was missing. The next day, plainclothesmen found him in a restaurant and asked him to come to the station and get his notebook back. When he signed a paper identifying it as his, their faces went blank and they said, "And now we must inform you that we are turning your notebook over to the public prosecutor for closer examination, as a rapid survey of the contents indicates illegal writings." Allen wondered what he might have written that might qualify as illegal writing. Maybe it was the line "I lie in bed with teenage boys afraid of the red police." A few days later he was detained again and told, "Due to many complaints about your presence in Prague from parents and educators who disapprove of your sexual theories, we are shortening your visa and you will leave Czechoslovakia today." Detectives took him to his hotel, watched him pack, and put him on a plane to London.

When Allen got back to New York he told Burroughs about his adventures. Burroughs reflected that Czechoslovakia was not that different from New York, where there seemed to be rampant drug hysteria. You could get arrested just for talking about drugs. He began to feel uncomfortable, particularly after Huncke reported that a narcotics agent had approached him, asking him to set up Burroughs and Ginsberg. Allen went straight to Mayor John Lindsay and complained that distinguished writers were the victims of a police conspiracy. Also, the political scene was oppressive, with the "Why not bomb Peking now?" sort of thing. Burroughs wrote Ian Sommerville on July 28: "I have missed you a great deal. Life in America is really a bore. Nothing here really, I just stay in my loft and work." He decided in August that the New York climate was uncongenial and that he had better head back to Europe. He had a lease on the Centre Street loft, but a young painter friend, David Prentice, promised to look after it in his absence and find a sublet.

Just before he left, who should show up but Paul and Jane Bowles on one of their rare visits to the United States. They had been in Florida visiting Jane's mother and stepfather, and reported that it was a terrible place, giving the impression of predigested existence. Everything was softened up and decayed, including the people. It was a land of sprinklers, lawns, and fancy trees. When a car went by it had a boat trailing after it.

It was all too obvious to Burroughs that Jane was not well. Her speech was halting and she dragged her feet, and the two of them were infuriatingly indecisive. It took them half an hour of soul-searching to get out of their room in the Chelsea and reach the bar for a drink. Paul saw himself at the center of an ordered universe, Burroughs reflected, and never blamed himself for anything. When Jane had her stroke he agreed to shock therapy, which should never be given if there was any suspicion of organic brain damage. But Paul had said, "You pay doctors to tell you what to do and you have to do it then, don't you?'' Paul was a genius at keeping his actual motivations concealed from everyone else, and Burroughs was convinced that one of his motivations, on a conscious level, was the ruination of Jane. But all this he kept to himself as he watched them that evening, Paul impassive and solicitous, and Jane clearly brain-damaged, a blurred and impoverished travesty of her true self.

At Gatwick airport in early September 1965, Burroughs again had trouble at customs. They wanted to limit his stay to one month instead of the usual three. He went to Lord Goodman, who personally took his passport to the Home Secretary to have it amended, and who told him, "Of course, dear boy, come as often as you like and stay as long as you please.'' London was gray, and Burroughs was busy taping street sounds and doctoring the tapes and playing them back on location. Hearing from David Prentice that Huncke was interested in renting his loft with a painter friend, Burroughs wrote: "There are no more undesirable tenants than Huncke or anyone he plans to live with and for your own protection and mine lock him out and bar the door. If he gets a foothold you will have the law in bugging everyone. He is not only a junky but a thief, strong both against the deed, in the words of the immortal bard. The raven himself is harsh who croaks the fatal entrance of Huncke under my battlement.''

Forced to leave England at the end of three months because of his visa, Burroughs spent the holiday season in Tangier, taking an apartment on the calle Goya. On Christmas day, Brion Gysin dropped by with his Moroccan friend Targuisti and a load of wood for his fireplace. "Heard the Christmas news?'' Brion asked. "Jay Haselwood just dropped dead at the Parade.'' The owner of the Parade Bar, the genial Kentuckian, the Tangier fixture everyone liked, had died of a heart attack.

Burroughs went to the funeral on December 30 at St. Andrew's Church. It was quite a turnout, the *tout-Tanger*, with all the cooks and waiters who had worked for him over the years, and the old biddies that Jay used to have lunch with, and the patrons of the Parade, from the *beau monde* to the naughty boys, and the shameless moochers who were always cadging drinks. "This man was loved by people in all walks of life,'' said the minister. Apparently, Burroughs was told at the funeral, Haselwood had come out of the bathroom with sweat streaming down his face, lain down on the floor in front of the bar, and died. One of the shameless moochers had taken advantage of the confusion to steal some money out of someone's purse, the very same one who at the funeral came up to him and said: "Oh, Bill, it's so nice to see you. Could you lend me 1,000 francs?''

As they followed the coffin to the grave, Burroughs reflected that it was the end of an era. Gone with Jay Haselwood was the old Tangier, with its colorful characters and live-and-let-live attitude. Now it was like every other place—the government had both feet in your business.

That evening, Burroughs went to Paul Bowles's for dinner. Paul had missed the funeral. He was looking after Jane, whose anxiety and depression had been aggravated by the news of Haselwood's death. She was under a lot of medication and drinking too much, a dangerous combination. Burroughs arrived immaculately dressed, all in black with a tightly furled umbrella. As he peeled off his gloves, he said, "Well, Paul, you missed a very enjoyable funeral." Paul wondered how he should take the remark. Was it said seriously, in the sense that some funerals were better than others, or was it black humor, or was it "we were happy to see the end of that one"? One never knew with Bill.

By the end of 1965, Burroughs had finished what he called his "mythology for the space age," a trilogy of books made up mainly of overflow material from *Naked Lunch*, with quite a lot of cut-up material thrown in. *The Soft Machine* was published by Olympia in 1961 and by Grove in 1966. *The Ticket That Exploded* was brought out in 1962 by Olympia and in 1967 by Grove, which also published *Nova Express* in 1964, Olympia having by then gone out of business.

All three books were concerned with the struggle between controllers and those who want to throw off control. The virus power is still entrenched. The consumer is an addict. The old mythologies have broken down and we are dealing here with a space-age war between the Nova Police and the Nova Mob. The Nova Mob is a band of aliens from outer space who control human beings by assuming the form of a parasitic virus. They are fought by the Nova Police, the good guys, who disappear once their task is done, unlike other police forces.

All of this draws heavily from Burroughs' reading in science fiction, but is filtered through his various preoccupations, such as the Mayan civilization, scientology, and a Reichian view of sex, as well as through his addiction and past experiences in Tangier and South America. The result is a fantasy world peopled with cartoon figures rather than characters, and dreamlike episodes rather than a plot, but lacking the compression and urgency of *Naked Lunch*. After all, this was material left over from *Naked Lunch*, and it has a bit of that warmed-over flavor. Like any sequel, it doesn't have the shock value the original had. The first man to jump off the Empire State Building in a parachute makes the six o'clock news. The second man walks away unnoticed, and can't even get himself arrested. Other problems were the numerous patches of cut-up writing, breaking the compact of intelligibility with the reader, and obsessively repetitive homoerotic passages.

Allen Ginsberg asked Burroughs: "Well, how can you expect anybody to read through all of this if you don't make big, categorical distinctions? . . . It's like reading one large series of prose-poems that have no end."

"No, no, no," Burroughs said, "it's quite comprehensible and as accessible as any book you pick up at the airport. People are demanding less and less in the way of plot and structure, I find. So I don't think there's any difficulty in understanding." In fact, all three books demand a degree of concentration hard to sustain. *The Soft Machine*, which consists of seventeen routines, opens with autobiographical reminiscences of junky days, as a way of grounding the narrative in memory: Burroughs rolling drunks on the subway with Phil White (the Sailor). Scenes of small-time pushing. Then the scene shifts to Morocco: "Got up and fixed in the sick dawn flutes of Ramadan." Hearing of Bill Garver's death in Mexico: "The consul would give me no information other than place of burial in the American cemetery. . . . He gave me an alarm clock ran for a year after his death." Kiki's death in Madrid: "This frantic Cuban fruit finds Kiki with a *novia* and stabs him with a kitchen knife in the heart." The Demerol cure in the Jewish hospital in Tangier.

There follows a passage in which it is made abundantly clear that sex is dirty: "Made it three times slow fuck on knees in the stink sewage looking at the black water." Sex is also a way to occupy and take over someone's body.

Then we have "The Trak Reservation" (*trak* means "thank you" in Danish), a satire on capitalist-consumer societies, and the introduction of Bradley-Martin, inventor of the double-cross and leader of the Nova Mob, who says, "Don't care myself if the whole fucking shithouse goes up in chunks—I've sat out Novas before—I was born in a Nova."

In "The Mayan Caper," Burroughs shows how the Mayan priest-rulers controlled the masses through the calendar, and describes "the transfer operation," a way of moving into someone else's body during an orgasm-by-hanging scene.

The book ends with its best passage, Burroughs' version of the creation myth, called "Cross the Wounded Galaxies." This is not the biblical Genesis, with its reassuring deity creating order out of chaos, but creation as it actually must have felt to the first upright beings, a thing of total fear, life *as* disorder. Millions of years of evolution are compressed in a few pages of powerful images: "Torn we crawled out of the mud. Faces and bodies covered with purple sex-flesh. . . . When we came out of the mud we had names." Man discovers language, "the talking sickness." Man discovers the need of others: "And the other did not want to touch me because of the white-worm thing inside but no one could refuse if I wanted and ate the fear-softness in other men." Man discovers war: "Once we caught one of the hairy men with our vine nets and tied him over a slow fire and left him there until he died." Man discovers methods of survival: "Sitting naked at the bottom of a well, the cool mud of evening touched our rectums. We share a piece of armadillo gristle, eating it out of each other's mouths. Above us a dry husk of insect bodies along the stone well wall and thistles over the well mouth against green evening sky." The situation is one of permanent horror, but there is always the possibility of escape to another planet: "Migrants of ape in gasoline crack of history, explosive bio-advance out of space to neon." "Cross the Wounded Galaxies" is so strong that it gives the impression of having been written by a man in a trance, who saw beyond what the rest of us see.

Like *The Soft Machine*, *The Ticket That Exploded* opens with an autobiographical sequence, a reminiscence of Burroughs' trip to South America with Eugene Allerton, but Allerton has now become an enemy, underlining the futility of love: "Basically he was completely hard and self-seeking and thought entirely in terms of position and advantage—an effective but severely limited intelligence. . . . But then who am I to be critical few things in my own past I'd just as soon forget." This is followed by a parody of love done through popular song titles: "Who's Sorry Now . . . Do I Love You . . . You Were Meant for Me."

The nature of the Nova conspiracy is finally described: "Always create as many insoluble conflicts as possible and always aggravate existing conflicts. . . . This is done by dumping on the same planet life forms with incompatible conditions of existence. . . ." One of these incompatible forms, being, of course, the opposite sex.

Burroughs postulates "Operation Other Half," which imprisons human life in conflict and duality, and counters it with "Operation Rewrite," in which binary thinking is dismantled. Such is the power of writing, he says, that it can change the conditions of our lives. He rejects the conventional solution: "Why don't I work for your uncle's company? Work for a company and what do they give you? . . . Member of the country club . . . house and garden . . . a wife . . . heart attack at fifty-five . . . no thanks."

And yet Burroughs has gone to the other extreme and become someone who sees nothing but the menace of life, an apocalyptic chronicler, a soured Utopian. The book ends with nostalgia for a lost childhood: "Stale dreams Billy . . . boy I was who never would be now . . . I lost him long ago.''

In *Nova Express*, the most didactic of the three books, Burroughs has a tendency to lecture the reader: "Who monopolized Immortality? Who monopolized Cosmic Consciousness? Who monopolized Love Sex and Dreams? Who monopolized Life Time and Fortune? Who took from you what is yours?" In other words, the battle between the Nova Mob and the Nova Police is analogous to the battle men should be waging to regain their freedom from control groups. "The purpose of my writing is to expose and arrest Nova Criminals. . . . To retake their Universe of Fear, Death, and Monopoly." Women as a controlling force are again excoriated: "You cunts constitute a disposal problem in the worst form there is and raise the nastiest whine ever heard anywhere: 'Do you love me? Do you love me? Do you love me?' Why don't you go back to Venus and fertilize a forest?"

The cut-up passages are more frequent here, sometimes as a parody of newswriting, with its claim to objectivity and "just the facts, ma'am." "Attorney-General for Fear announced yesterday the discovery that cries of nepotism might 'form a new mineral damaging to the President.' " "Police juice and the law are no cure for widespread public petting in chow lines, the Soviet Union said yesterday." Another purpose of the cut-ups is to show that nobody owns the language, and there are many references to the words of other authors, among them e. e. cummings and T. S. Eliot.

As usual the reviews were a mixed bag. Reviewers who were themselves writers of talent tended to appreciate Burroughs more than literary critics.

Nor were people at Grove Press too happy at the direction his work was taking. After *Naked Lunch*, sales slumped badly because the trilogy was inaccessible to the general reader, and appealed only to unconditional Burroughs fans. Dick Seaver, his editor, tried to tell him as gently as possible that it was madness to perpetuate the cup-up method, that it was hurting his sales and his reputation, that his writing was too good to get stuck in an arbitrary groove. But Burroughs could theorize for hours on the validity of cut-ups, how they went back to the Surrealist tradition, and how he was convinced that there were many important connections he could not make in the linear method of writing, which he could only find in juxtaposition and happenstance. "Sure, it's interesting," Seaver said, "but don't think of it as a life's work." "Anyone can use scissors," Burroughs replied, "but some can use them better than others. . . . It takes a master."

Seaver could not help thinking that that kind of narrow and obsessive focus was related to drugs. It was like Alex Trocchi, doing nothing for years but carving tiny wooden sculptures. Making cut-ups was just another aspect of the drugged state of mind. Also, he had this mountain of material that he didn't know what to do with, so he cut it up and recycled it. And yet the feeling at Grove was that they would continue to publish what he wrote, for he was one of their flagships. It would be a mistake to turn him down. All they could do was try and steer him away from the cut-up method.

· SEVENTEEN ·

THE LONDON YEARS

1966–1973

When Burroughs returned to London in January 1966, there was a murder on the train from Gatwick airport, which he saw as an ominous sign. He settled into the Hotel Rushmore, at 11 Trebovir Road, Earl's Court. He was reading Truman Capote's *In Cold Blood*, and wondered how it could be a bestseller. My God, what a bore it was, with its dull victims, their church suppers and 4-H clubs, and even duller killers. It must be that someone pressed a button somewhere and people bought any tripe at all. He was glad to see a full page of disfavor in *The Observer*, which said that Capote had deliberately let the killers hang, refusing to pull strings and release psychiatric testimony, in order to sell his crappy book.

In Burroughs' absence, Ian Sommerville, now twenty-six, had taken up with a younger man from his hometown of Darlington, Alan Watson, whose parents were pastry cooks. Alan was small and blond and swishy, and liked to camp it up. He worked in the canteen at Scotland Yard, where, if bought enough pints, he would dance on the tables. When he walked down Jermyn Street, where they were building the Cavendish Hotel, he sashayed past the construction crews in the scaffolding with one hand on his hip, blowing kisses with his other hand, and laughing at their gibes.

Burroughs considered himself the victim of a classic case of alienation of affection. It was entirely his fault for not having taken Ian to New York. He had relinquished and then tried to reclaim, and had no grounds to reclaim. While he was away, Ian had found someone he was attracted to, and it was futile for Burroughs to protest, or show his jealousy. He was in the humiliating position of having to put up with Watson, and hoping it would blow over. Sexual desire was so fleeting. There was a time, in Tangier, when Ian had wanted him but he wasn't interested. And now that Burroughs wanted Ian, Ian didn't respond. It happened very seldom that both wanted it—it just didn't coincide. Sexually, Burroughs reflected, he had always got it wrong.

Ian was riding high, having met the Beatles, who set him up in a recording studio. Paul McCartney wanted to launch a "Spoken Word" label, which would release a monthly record, like an avant-garde monthly magazine, with bits of poetry, interviews, and experimental music. Ringo Starr had an empty flat on Montague Square, a nouveau-riche sort of place with purple silk wallpaper, where Ian kept the expensive Beatle-bought equipment. Ian operated the studio like a crusty governess, with little supervision from the Beatles, who had their own problems.

Burroughs was at first glad that Ian had something to do, and a chance to make money. He marveled at the studio, which had equipment to rival the BBC's. He went by a few times and met Paul, who played the acetate of the *Rubber Soul* album for him. Burroughs just sat there nodding and not saying anything, and McCartney thought he hadn't liked it. What was bothering Burroughs was not the music, but that he had begun to see the recording studio as a conspiracy to alienate Ian from him even further.

Now, whenever he asked Ian to record something for him, Ian did it grudgingly and reluctantly. And Miss Alan Watson was always swishing around the studio, spraying perfume and fixing her hair, and fleeing with her bird-brain to cunt headquarters. He had to face the fact: Ian was married to a cunt. In May, when Ian and Alan went to Paris for a holiday, he told himself that he had never been so glad to see two people walk out of his life. He would refuse to see Ian again as long as he had a wife sticking to him like a barnacle. The trouble with Ian was that he had a snobbish, celebrity-loving side that Alan Watson brought out. Miss Watson was an exaggerated version of Ian's worst traits, the flighty side, easily impressed by names.

In July, Burroughs moved into a flat in Anthony Balch's building, at 8 Duke Street, a good location, near Piccadilly Circus on one side and Pall Mall on the other. Ian and Alan were broke, the largesse of the Beatles having come to an end, and in August asked if they could move in. Alan would do the cooking. Burroughs, out of weakness, agreed, initiating living conditions that were sure to make him miserable.

He had no sympathy with his own behavior. He knew perfectly well that he would find it difficult to live in close quarters on a day-to-day basis with Miss Watson while holding back his hostility. He was disgusted with himself. He felt that he was rolling around in his weakness like a dog rolling in manure. He had completely lost the upper hand. Brion Gysin told him, "Well, if you're going to let someone walk all over you . . ." Which was exactly what he was doing. He should have said, "If it's Alan you want, take him and get out of here." But he was too devoted to Ian to do that. Brion had always told him that the barking of dogs had a meaning, and on a short trip to Tangier he listened to the dogs and heard them bark "Boss, Bosses, Boss Bill"—the dogs were reminding him that he had lost the boss position.

Not that it was all bad. Alan was cordial and flexible, and cooked some excellent meals. But he played Maria Callas records from morning to night. "There goes that graveyard howl again," Burroughs said. Alan could tell when Burroughs was annoyed; he would make a nervous gesture through his hair and purse his mouth disdainfully. Then he would lock himself up in his room.

Nor did it seem to Alan that Ian and Burroughs got along all that well. They were like an old married couple, either bickering or silent. Ian was high-strung, overreacting to little things. When Burroughs knocked over a teacup, Ian said, "Oh, really, William, that's too much." Ian complained that Burroughs was a creature of habit. He had to have his first drink at six, and then he was drunk by eight. Ian did not think that was the way for an important writer to live, and told Alan, "I am not going to waste the rest of my young life on that old drunk." And yet when Burroughs went on the wagon, Ian stayed away. It was as though he was put out at having lost his major reason for complaint.

One sunny September day, Alan Watson went to Hampton Court and took some cassettes along. As he sat on a bench sunning himself, he played one of the cassettes and was horrified to hear his own voice being mimicked by Burroughs, saying things he often said. It was so spooky that he took the cassette off the machine and flung it into the canal. Burroughs had put a curse on Alan Watson, hoping it would make him leave. Later, when he thought about it, Burroughs told himself that no curse originating in lust and anger could ever work. The only curses that worked were those that were done with real detachment. What he had done to Miss Watson was rotten weeds . . . utterly indefensible.

In September 1966, Burroughs' attention was distracted from the Ian-Alan situation when he got the news that Billy had vanished. On his return from Tangier in 1964, Billy had struck his Palm Beach friends as completely changed. His closest female friend, Berteina Barnum, found him hurt and bitter and withdrawn. He was hurt, she surmised, because in Tangier he had realized that his father was unable to take care of him.

While this had remained untested, there was still hope. But now that he had actually gone and tried it, the illusion was lost. Billy became so difficult that his grandparents sent him to boarding school in the fall of 1964.

About the only place that would have him was the Green Valley School, in central Florida, outside Orange City, "Home of Pure Water." Occupying an old monastery, the school was run by the Reverend George Von Hilsheimer, a tall, clean-cut, energetic fellow with what the army calls "command presence." Hilsheimer was a licensed Baptist minister with a doctorate in philosophy from the Humanistic Psychology Institute in San Francisco. A disciple of A. S. Neill's Summerhill, he founded Green Valley as one of those noble educational experiments of the sixties, a school that kids would regard as a great experience rather than a prison sentence. He told the students not to call him "Sir," so they called him "George the Bear" and "Revvy Baby." In his office there was a framed statement called "Winners and Losers":

> A winner always has a program.
> A loser always has an excuse.
>
> A winner says let me do it for you.
> A loser says that's not my job.

And so on.

There was a gap between aspiration and reality, however, and Green Valley soon came to be known as a school of last resort for messed-up kids—dopers, hippies, and out-and-out crazies. When Billy arrived there in the fall of 1964 he struck the Reverend Von Hilsheimer as a mature-looking seventeen-year-old—you wouldn't card him at a bar. In turn, Billy found Von Hilsheimer larger than life and compassionate. Billy was popular with girls, and one day Von Hilsheimer told him, "Goddamn it, Burroughs, I started this school so I could get laid, not you." His general attitude to students having affairs was: "If I know about it, it becomes my business, so be discreet. As far as I'm concerned, privacy is the basis of all morality."

It did not take Billy long to realize that some of the Green Valley students were seriously disturbed. Around Easter of 1965, an eighteen-year-old boy named Nigel, recently released from a mental hospital, broke into the gun locker, removed a 9mm pistol, wrapped himself up in a sleeping bag, put the pistol in his mouth, and blew his brains out. Assigned to clean Nigel's room the next morning, Billy saw a piece of skull with hairs attached to it that was stuck to the wall, and the splattered crater the bullet had made next to it.

Billy had this on his conscience: The night in January 1965 when Laura called to tell him that Mote was dead, her husband, his father's father, he did not go at once to the school superintendent and say he needed a car, right away. It would have taken him four hours to be at her side. Crippled by inertia, he hadn't bothered.

With Mote dead, Laura at seventy-seven was short of money. She didn't see how she was going to pay for Billy's tuition. But this time Burroughs was able to help, and his grateful mother wrote: "I never had to worry about money before, and now all I want is to get Billy educated. Mote always managed the family finances and I suppose he tried to keep me from worrying. . . . Mote and I always talked things over—and it is hard to plan alone."

Billy started his second year at Green Valley in the fall of 1965, and it was not long afterward that he started taking drugs. One day the school's business manager came to see the headmaster, Ron Nowicki, and said, "We have an unusually large bill from the pharmacy this month." They asked for an itemized bill, which listed numerous purchases of a drug containing paregoric. It turned out that Billy's roommate had been to see a doctor for an ear infection and had obtained a prescription for a painkiller. Every week Billy and his roommate duplicated the prescription, going to the pharmacy in Orange City, charging the medicine to the school, cooking it up in their room, and shooting the paregoric. They were signing a staff member's name to the scrips, but Nowicki obtained their descriptions from the pharmacist and had their room searched. The syringes were found in the tone arm of their record player.

Billy was not dismissed from the school. Von Hilsheimer believed in giving kids a second chance and did not want to lose any tuition-paying students. That summer of 1966, having graduated from Green Valley, and hanging around Palm Beach, with his grandmother increasingly lost in a world of her own, he started taking speed. In mid-September, he told Laura he was going on a camping trip, and vanished. On September 19, Burroughs' brother, Mort, wrote him that Laura was in a panic. She would not eat or sleep or leave the house, she just sat by the phone waiting. This was a new low in irresponsibility. Obviously, Billy could no longer live with his grandmother. At the same time, he was nineteen and not ready for the world. He should go to his father in London, who should get him started in life. Not being wanted was a large part of his present trouble.

Billy had hitchhiked to New York, where he showed a real propensity for trouble, managing to get himself busted twice in two weeks. The first time, at the end of September, he was taking speed with friends in a hotel when detectives crashed in, waving guns, and made him stand against the wall with his hands up. He was taken to the Brooklyn House of Detention, where he killed time in his cell, as the guards did their rounds, yelling "On the Gate," meaning that the inmates had to stand at the front of their cells. He called Allen Ginsberg, who posted bail. The bondsman brought him two hot dogs and a glass of milk. When he went by Allen's to say thanks, Allen said, "For God's sake, be careful." Billy paid no attention, and went out looking for more speed. At his first court hearing, Allen provided a lawyer, and he was released on grounds of illegal search and seizure.

Then, on October 8, 1966, he was arrested with six others in a Bleecker Street pad where police found opium, marijuana, barbiturates, and guns. It was pure bad luck, thought Billy. Too embarrassed to call Allen again, he was taken to the Tombs, where a cellmate told him: "When the cart comes, grab the meat out of a couple of sandwiches and stick it in yours. They don't watch so good." Allen found out where he was and again bailed him out, asking, "Why don't you have the sense to stay out of places like that?" and again he was released for illegal search and seizure. He wrote his father asking for $300 to pay the lawyer, adding: "These fiascos are part of an education for me. Because of many things in the past, I've had to see just a bit of despair, and to experience a lot of mental fuckup. All this, not in any attempt to be like you, but rather to become able to understand my father. In Tangier, I was too afraid and had to leave." And yet it seemed that Billy was copying his father's drug-taking and criminality, but without his father's core of discipline and sense of survival. Perhaps it was a role-model situation: If your father was Pete Rose you were likely to take up baseball, and if your father was William Burroughs you were likely to take up drugs.

Allen Ginsberg didn't know what to make of Billy. He had Joan's dome forehead and Bill's gray eyes and grayish complexion and very fine brown hair—there was no trace of Whitey that he could see. (For there were those who said that Joan's gangster lover Whitey was Billy's real father.) He was intelligent but vague, and usually in need of a bath. He had called Allen to be rescued, and then he had disappeared, and then he had called to be rescued again, and then he had disappeared again. Allen tracked him down to a grungy place on Avenue B, and urged him to leave town before he got arrested a third time.

Burroughs agreed with his brother that Billy should join him in London, and plans were made to that effect. He had no idea what he would do with Billy, or how he would fit into the already complicated *ménage* with Ian and Alan Watson. Matters had improved in that department, however. His silly jealousy had evaporated, and he found himself actually liking Alan, who was tidy and willing and who fixed his breakfast each morning, and made elaborate dinners such as wild duck *à l'orange*. If Billy arrived, he would try to find another flat for Ian and Alan in the building.

But each time Billy was set to fly to London something came up. One time he said he was sick from Benzedrine withdrawal. The next time he had a really bad tooth. Then, in mid-November, he was arrested in West Palm Beach as he was leaving Henry's drugstore, where he had tried to fill a forged scrip for Desoxyn, which was prescribed as an antidepressant. The police found some pills under the front seat of his car. As Billy put it, "When you want speed, you're ready to walk ten miles and pose for skin pix."

Mort wrote Burroughs that their poor mother was at her wit's end. It was going to be a pretty messy thing for a lone old lady to handle. If they didn't get Billy away from her it was going to kill her. She had aged years in the last few months. Billy had been arraigned and was out on bail and his trial was set for August 1967. Mort was afraid Billy would be in another jam before August, and then things would be twice as bad. "I think the issue is clear," Mort said. "Either take care of him or write him off— without help he will never make it."

What was wrong with his son, Burroughs wondered? My God, three busts in a few months was too much. "I am convinced," he wrote his mother, "it is the difficulty of young men today, arising from the fact that he does not have anything to do or any goals which have meaning for him. I am ready to give any amount of time and effort to find something for him to do."

In fact, however, Burroughs was equivocating. He did not want to go to Palm Beach. He would do almost anything to avoid it, writing his mother on November 25 a classic example of mealy-mouthed reasoning: "I feel that for me to come to Palm Beach at this point would be unwise for several reasons. First of course is the question of expenses. Air fare plus living, it means a thousand dollars more or less . . . that much less money to provide for Billy. For that amount Billy could be treated for a week in a nursing home with the best care. . . . What concerns me is that (because of my past record) I am not a suitable guardian for Billy. In short my presence in Palm Beach might do more harm than good to

Billy's case. Whereas if I am not there questions are less likely to arise. Does Mort know about the situation? If he could come down for a few days that would be much more to the point."

The last time Mort had "come down for a few days" was when Burroughs had shot his wife and he had gone to Mexico to retrieve Billy. Mort now made it clear that he was through pulling his brother's chestnuts out of the fire. "Not that I doubt my own ability to make a good impression on any unprejudiced person," Burroughs continued. "However, the narcotics department is completely prejudiced. They say once an addict always an addict and they discount the possibility of cure. . . . I will almost certainly have trouble with them if I return. They told me when I came in last time I was subject to fine and imprisonment for not registering with the department when I left the U.S."

His son was bereft, facing criminal charges and a jail sentence in a state that treated drug users harshly, needing a father's presence and assistance, and here was Burroughs hemming and hawing and ducking his responsibility. He did not give the real reason for his reluctance, which was that he had a habit. If he went to Palm Beach, where what he needed was not obtainable, he would go through withdrawal. But as repeated pleas arrived from his mother and his brother, he had to bite the bullet. Billy was depressed, his mother was unable to cope, and Mort was unwilling to be a surrogate father. Burroughs finally decided to go to Palm Beach over Christmas 1966 and do what he could.

He arrived in the midst of a situation that was far from merry. Billy's prospects were as bad as could be. There were three felony counts, and he could not leave the country without posting some outrageous bond. His case was coming up before one of the most severe judges in Florida, Russell MacIntosh, who automatically handed down the maximum sentence to everyone who appeared before him. His mother was hallucinating and calling the police, saying she heard voices. She was driving him round the bend with her continual fretting and loss of memory. He had to explain some points to her fifty times. Friends of the family had faded into thin air. There were no servants and no car. The house was in a state of unbelievable disorder and, Burroughs was sure, quite literally haunted. On New Year's Day 1967 his mother fell and broke her wrist. Burroughs called Dr. Murphy, the family doctor, who was in trouble for having prescribed Benzedrine to Billy, and he wouldn't give Laura an injection, so Burroughs had to take her to the hospital.

Burroughs wasn't feeling that great himself, having arrived with the tail end of a tincture of opium habit plus various other disabilities—pain and tension in the back of the neck, swelling in the glands at the side of the neck with a high fever, and swelling in the groin. Which did not improve his mood, nor did Billy's incredible carelessness, for Burroughs found empty paregoric bottles and syringes all over the house.

"You're no help at all," he exploded. "And Mother is calling me Mort, and asking me to move things that aren't there, and calling me by any name that comes to mind. And I can't get a decent night's sleep in that back room, and when I do, it's all nightmares. All this on top of those stupid cops is frustrating."

Billy, however, found his father a pleasure to have around. He'd been there. He understood. He gave Billy the gospel according to Burroughs: Dress well, be punctual, speak when spoken to. Be attentive and not impatient. If a small mind with power began to feel inferior, there would be all hell to pay. Above all, there was no such thing as a nice cop. The cop mentality was, "If you're not guilty, how come you're bleeding?"

Burroughs went to see the lawyer his mother had found, and saw himself through the lawyer's eyes: this seedy, shifty, addict father . . . No wonder the son . . . He heard the lawyer say, quite distinctly, "Lousy father." The lawyer, however, thought there might be a way to get the charges dropped. He knew someone in the district attorney's office who was willing to make a deal. The deal was that they would place Billy on probation if he agreed to take the cure at the federal hospital in Lexington, Kentucky. Judge MacIntosh went along, imposing four years' probation, with every restriction in the book. But it was certainly better than standing trial, particularly since Billy, though off speed, was still taking paregoric, morphine, and Dilaudid.

In early February, 1967, Burroughs took Billy to Lexington. They flew together as far as Atlanta, but Billy, who was afraid of planes, was in a panic, despite a large dose of tranquilizers, and rented a car the rest of the way. Billy told himself that he had to get over this fixation about flying, but there was nothing down there but air, man, and what if the pilot didn't get laid last night and decides to take the whole shitload with him. As he waited in his hotel room for Billy to arrive, Burroughs was overcome with sadness. Tears streamed from his eyes. He saw Billy's future spread out before him, like a canvas covered with meaningless scratches, and he knew that it would end in tragedy, and that he was powerless to change it. He dried his eyes, thinking, "Crying is nothing to be ashamed of." The next day, when he and Billy presented themselves at the hospital, the admittance clerk looked at father and son and asked, "Which one of you is checking in here?" He knew an old junky when he saw one.

By mid-March, Burroughs was back in London, relieved to have escaped from all the family horrors. He was even glad to see Alan Watson. He started a new novel, *The Wild Boys*, but the flat was too crowded to work, and in May he left for Marrakesh, where he stayed with a friend from Memphis, Bill Willis, who was decorating a house for John Paul Getty, Jr. The only trouble was that Getty's checks kept bouncing. Marrakesh he found confining. The social circuit was too small. You kept seeing the same people over and over. The poverty and the begging were more obtrusive. The heat was oppressive. You had to close the shutters in the morning to keep the cool air in. When Willis sent the servant girl out to buy potatoes at one-thirty in the afternoon, she refused to go. What kind of respect did they expect from their servants, when they dragged in every boy off the streets? The only thing he liked about Marrakesh was Mr. Verygood, who came to the door each day with his hashish cookies. After a month, he moved to Tangier, writing through from 10:00 A.M. to dinnertime in his room in the Atlas Hotel, copiously supplied with *majoun*, and making notes while he ate dinner. From London there were occasional communications from Ian, a postcard that said "gloom doom spoon moon love Ian," and a note reporting "that the city makes its own weather is confirmed. Clouds hang heavy and low over London. We carry on."

Returning to London in July, Burroughs was greeted with another crisis, but one that mercifully did not require his presence in Palm Beach. His mother, it was clear, was losing her mind. She had appeared to be the stronger of his parents, while actually her degree of reliance on Mote had been complete, and without his steadying hand she was distressed and alone. Billy was back at Green Valley, and she constantly worried over whether he was complying with the conditions of his probation. Her Palm Beach fair-weather friends had deserted her. Ellis, the black gardener, would come in for tea out of kindness and sit there with a little white cup in his huge hand, finding her alone on the pink couch, white as whalebone, thin as a blade, one-breasted from cancer, talking about ghosts.

When Ellis left she drank cocktails and hallucinated, seeing drunken gauchos playing cards in her living room. She saw men coming out of the television set and sitting on her bed. She didn't understand how the men got in and out, disappearing so quickly. She called the police, asking them to chase the little people out, and blaming her neighbors for sending them around. Several times a day, she called Mort and Miggy in St. Louis. Dr. Murphy said it was hardening of the arteries.

The house was up for sale, but Bob Bissett, the real estate man, called Mort to say he couldn't possibly sell it as long as she was in it, because when he was showing clients around they were very definitely put off by her remarks about the little people in the corner playing bingo. The only solution, Mort and Miggy wrote Burroughs, was to move her to St. Louis and put her in a nursing home. But Mort didn't have the guts to do it unless she was willing, and one day she thought it was a good idea and the next day she changed her mind. You had to plan ahead to get into these places, however, and Mort put her name on the waiting list. The cost was rather high, but no worse than living alone, and her condition was bound to improve in a place where she could talk to real people instead of imaginary ones for a change.

In the fall of 1967, Mort and Miggy moved her to a St. Louis nursing home at twenty-five dollars a day. Mort wrote Burroughs that he would pay for it but wanted Burroughs to handle Billy's financial needs, for Billy had begun to call him from Green Valley to beg for money. Billy was back at Green Valley as a teacher's assistant—that school for kooks where maybe you could get some schooling if you were enterprising enough to hunt up a teacher and ask for it. Mort couldn't help him—he didn't even like the kid.

Finally the house was sold, and Laura was barely able to sign the deed. Mort had to guide her hand. When the check arrived she couldn't sign it and Mort had to forge her name on it to cash it. Laura's mind was deteriorating rapidly, and she rarely recognized Mort when he came to visit. The whole thing was a nightmare, and as usual, Mort had to handle it while his brother was off living the good life in London.

Not long after Laura Burroughs had entered the nursing home, Billy was sent to Alaska, where Green Valley ran a fishing camp in keeping with the Reverend Von Hilsheimer's "strenuous life" approach to education. On his way to Halibut Cove, as the place was called, Billy stopped off in St. Louis to see his grandmother. The nursing home was on a dirt road behind a Piggly Wiggly Supermarket. Old eyes in rocking chairs on the porch watched him approach. "She may not know you," the nurse said. Laura was in a pink robe, strapped to a chair. "She removes her clothing," the nurse explained. Billy found her purse and took the money out of it. He needed it more than she did. It was a long way to Alaska. The nurse came in and said, "Your time is up." "No, lady, not mine," Billy said. He started to cry, and Laura looked up from the chair where she was strapped and asked, "Billy, what's wrong, lamb?"

Billy returned from Alaska to the Green Valley School at the start of 1968 and promptly fell for a bright and vivacious seventeen-year-old girl named Karen Perry, the daughter of an entomologist who worked for the government in Savannah. Karen hooked him like he'd never been hooked before. At first, she was timid in bed, but then, oh God! The Reverend Von Hilsheimer remembers Karen as the distillation of the Jewish-American princess. She was gorgeous, but did she have a mouth on her, and did she have a temper.

The last week of July, Billy wrote his father: "I'm twenty-one years old now and in order to lead the fullest possible life before the bomb comes and grinds against me, I'm getting married. How'd you like to bounce a diarrhetic runny-nosed grandson on your knee?" Cut to close-up of Burroughs, shaking his head and grimacing. "I have found a fine complex exciting evil cunt whom I'm ready to devote a portion of my life to. . . . She is Karen, she is five foot two, enormously brown-eyed, sexual, and I love her for the thrust and parry, ying yang, cosmic ping-pong of the whole thing."

The idea was that they would get married in Savannah and live there, but Billy had to convince his probation officer, William J. Cain, to let him leave Florida. Cain called Karen in and told her: "This here paper is Bill's probation order. This is Bill's Bible. This little piece of paper is all that stands between Bill and the penitentiary."

Billy and Karen were married in August 1968 in the Perrys' backyard by a justice of the peace with a wart on his nose. The rabbi wouldn't officiate because Billy wasn't Jewish. Billy thought his in-laws must be saying, "What is our *gefilte* daughter doing with this *goyische* writer," but in spite of everything they were friendly and welcoming—Al Perry, kind though mildly skeptical, and his tiny wife, Libby, who clapped her hands when she was impatient. Billy had wanted a red cummerbund with his rented tux, but that was too flamboyant for the Perrys. He shook hands with people he didn't know, who said, "It was lovely, it really was." As he left with Karen he thought they were throwing the rice in his face and on his neck just a bit harder than necessary. His father did not attend but wondered from London how his son was going to support a family when he couldn't support himself.

They rented a two-bedroom house behind a Japanese restaurant in Savannah Beach, which was known for its strip bars and nightclubs. Billy was writing and Karen was a cocktail waitress, first at the Angle, then at Kitten's Korner, then at the Black Lace, a strip joint. Billy came by and drank free beer in the lounge. He had started drinking in Alaska and alcohol had become a very good friend. He struck up conversations with customers. He talked to a man who was so far right he'd been blackballed by the John Birch Society. Once a guerrilla in the Philippines, he'd brought back a recipe for Jap Suey.

The Black Lace was a raunchy place. One of the strippers had an act where she took a maraschino cherry from a customer's drink, put it up her snatch, and shot it out at the audience like a tiny red cannonball. At first, the ass-grabbing drunks provoked Karen to tears—"Hey baby, watcher got under there?" But she wised up fast, and soon developed the authority of a cop.

As for Billy, he was full of plans. He was going to attend the state college. He was going down on the docks to get a job on one of the shrimp boats. He bought a book called *Bargain Paradises of the World*, and was thinking of going to Australia when he was off probation. For Billy the thought was the deed. Whenever he did accomplish something, it invariably went wrong. He bought an old Mustang and drove it to Denver, where he got a tattoo at Frenchie's Tattoo Parlor, from Frenchie himself, a huge fat man wearing only overalls. It was a snake curled around a rose, but the rose got infected, turning into a huge scab, which he had to soak hourly in Listerine. Then he traded the Mustang for $200 and a shotgun, and the new owner took off with the car after paying fifty dollars. Billy sawed off the shotgun, making it unusable, and traded it in a bar for a six-pack. . . . From a car to a six-pack. He was glad that Karen put up with him, loony as he was, even though, with his drinking having passed the gusto stage, his sex life had begun to droop. At this time, he wrote in his diary, "I begin to fit into my role as a traveling exercise in other people's patience."

While Billy was falling in love and getting married, Burroughs was in London, where he heard from Allen that February of 1968 that Neal Cassady had died, a few days short of his forty-second birthday. Allen had seen it coming. Too much booze and drugs. A few months before, he and Neal had driven down from Bellingham, Washington, to San Francisco, and spent the night together in a motel on Van Ness. Neal's skin had been cold, sweaty, and corpselike—the chemical cast of amphetamines. It was the first time Allen had ever gotten out of bed with Neal voluntarily, and in despair he walked the streets, pondering the deathly fate that had overtaken the miracle of his youthful romance. In February, Neal had gone to the Mexican town of San Miguel de Allende. On February 3, passing the door of a wedding party, he was invited in. The next morning he was found collapsed by the railroad tracks outside town, and he died later that day in the hospital.

Burroughs lamented the loss of another member of the core group, and remembered their days together in East Texas. At that time, however, he was consumed by a new passion—Scientology. The teaching of L. Ron Hubbard attracted him as a fresh area of psychic investigation, which also might help him where psychoanalysis had failed. Hubbard's basic premise was that words heard in an unconscious or semiconscious state—a state induced by infantile trauma, anesthesia, or drunkenness—were recorded by the subject. These recorded words he called "engrams," which loaded you down with emotionally crippling although suppressed memories. For instance, words heard during an operation would, when repeated, cause pain and anxiety. The system of therapy was for the subject to be "audited" on an E-meter—a machine like a lie detector that measured galvanic skin response, when psychic stress created changes in the electrical resistance of the skin. The needle moved when there was a "reading," which indicated anxiety in response to a question. When you came to a painful incident, you kept running it (repeating the question) until you got a floating needle, showing that the subject was no longer disturbed by the incident. In other words, you repeated the material until it lost its emotional charge and became neutral.

Still suffering from a childhood trauma that he had never been able to unravel, Burroughs thought Scientology auditing was of great benefit. It could do more in ten hours than psychoanalysis could do in ten years. After taking the beginner's course at the London headquarters, 37 Fitzroy Street, he took the "clear" course in mid-January 1968 at St. Hill, a fortress-like compound lacking only a moat and drawbridge, in East Grinstead, about fifty miles from London.

This was a two-month solo audit course, eight hours a day, five days a week—it was as grueling as a full-time job. At the end you were supposed to be "clear," that is, rid of your engrams.

The auditing sessions were so emotionally charged that at the first one, Burroughs blacked out. It started rather formally, with the male auditor facing the subject saying: "Pick up the cans, please. This is the session." As he held the two metal cans, the auditor asked questions and watched for movements of the needle.

"If you were talking to an army colonel, what would you talk about?"

"I couldn't talk to any army colonel I ever saw."

"Fine, thank you. All right. If you were talking to an army colonel about that, what would you say exactly?"

"I would tell him he is too stupid to find his own balls."

"Fine, thank you. And if you were talking to the President, what would you talk about?"

"Drug hysteria."

"Fine, thank you. And what would you say, exactly?"

"What are you trying to do, turn America into a nation of rats? Our pioneer ancestors would piss in their graves."

"And if you were talking to the Pope, what would you talk about?"
"Birth control."
"Fine, thank you. And what would you say exactly?"
"Sure as shit, they will multiply their assholes into the polluted seas."
"That's it, we'll take a break now," the auditor said, giving him an orange drink. He said that Scientology had the answers he was looking for. Step by step he could become an Operating Thetan (a higher degree of clear).

After the break, they began an exercise called Overts and Withholds. Burroughs talked about Kiki, his Tangier boy, and said that when Kiki went away, he felt dead. The auditor asked him to return to the incident and tell him everything, like what Kiki was wearing.

Burroughs got as far as "it was" when the room went dark and he lost consciousness. The last thing he felt was the hair on the back of his neck rising like a cat's. The needle was slamming around on the machine. When he came to, he heard the auditor say, "A Rock C slam" (a strong reaction).

As Burroughs continued the sessions, he saw that sometimes there were release points to readings that neither he nor the auditor understood. They were things buried in his unconscious that he didn't know he knew, but when they surfaced the auditor got a floating needle. When the auditor got a read on a question about hieroglyphs and asked what it meant, Burroughs said, "The emerald beginning and end of word," and the auditor got a floating needle. On another reading, the release point was the phrase "Why, it's just an old movie." Yet another release point was Scobie, the character in the Graham Greene novel *The Heart of the Matter*, with his rusty handcuffs on the wall.

As rewarding as the auditing process was, Burroughs was distressed by other aspects of Scientology. L. Ron Hubbard, whom no one ever saw, was idolized, particularly by the young female members, who came on at breakfast with thinly disguised sexual dreams about the Great Non-Presence, like young nuns dreaming about their bridegroom Jesus Christ. Burroughs was sharing a house with seven other Scientologists, and they would all pile into a car in the morning and drive like hell, because if you were late you would be put into a condition of Liability, which meant that you had to wear a gray armband and you were not allowed to wash or shave. You had to go around collecting signatures to be absolved of Liability. Also, the attitude toward non-Scientologists was militantly hostile. They were seen as the enemy, and were referred to by Hubbard in his taped lectures as WOGs, the old colonial acronym for Worthy Oriental Gentlemen.

What most disgusted Burroughs, however, were the Sec Checks, a sort of Orwellian thought police. You would be called in for a Sec Check and be asked the following questions on the E-meter: "Are you here for any other reason than what you say you are?" "Do you have any doubts about Scientology?" "Are you connected to a suppressive person [anyone in disagreement with Scientology]?" "Do you harbor any unkind thoughts about L. Ron Hubbard?" Burroughs got a reading on that one, and when the question was repeated, he weaseled out of it by saying, "Yes, I can't help resenting his perfection." You learned to say the right thing. But it was humiliating, like a return to kindergarten, and going to Sec Checks reminded him of a line in Céline: "All this time I felt my self-respect slipping away from me, and finally completely gone, as if officially removed."

Returning to Duke Street on weekends, he used postcard photographs of L. Ron Hubbard as targets for his air pistol, but while cocking the pistol the hammer snapped on his thumb and nearly broke it. Boy, ol' Ron was spittin' back the curse. Ian and Alan Watson were still in the flat, but Ian had found a job in computers and was in a much better frame of mind.

In June, as one of those under suspicion of harboring unkind thoughts about L. Ron Hubbard, Burroughs took the dreaded Joburg, a series of 104 questions about every conceivable form of criminal activity. Each question had to be cleared (floating needle), and it took three weeks and eighty hours of auditing, because there were too few auditors and too many applicants. Burroughs ran all the material flat until there wasn't a tick left.

Of course, on a question like "Did you ever fuck your mother?" you got a protest read, and then if you got a second read they would ask you what that meant, and you might say, "Well, I've had this fantasy." You worked through that, and if you still got a read, it started to look bad.

Burroughs was asked, "Have you ever concealed a body?"

"Of course not."

"There's a read here."

Burroughs saw himself hiding a body in an alley in some sort of ancient Egyptian setting. "I think it's Whole Track [all past lives]," he said.

The auditor rephrased the question: "In this life, have you ever concealed a body?"

"No."

"That is clear."

"Did you ever commit forgery?" the auditor asked. He said he had not. "There's a read," the auditor said. He suddenly remembered that he'd forged narcotics prescriptions. The machine knew things the mind had forgotten.

After taking the advanced clearing course in Edinburgh, Burroughs left Scientology, impressed by the auditing techniques but disgusted by the authoritarian organization and the stupidly fascistic utterances of L. Ron Hubbard. The aim of Scientology, complete freedom from past conditioning, was perverted to become a new form of conditioning. He had hoped to find a method of personal emancipation and had found instead another control system. Scientology roped you in and bound you. It was like a state, with its own courts and its own police, its own rewards and penalties, and its own ludicrous jargon.

Returning to his Duke Street flat in July 1968, Burroughs was pleased to find that Alan Watson had left for the south of France with some rich queen. What a relief it was to find him gone. You didn't know how someone dragged on you until he wasn't around. The trouble was that Ian had moved out, too, to a mean overpriced hovel in the heart of London's smogland, at 55 Red Lion Street, way on the wrong side of the British Museum. Burroughs wondered what he could do to get Ian back. It was the sexual attraction between Alan and Ian that made it difficult, like interfering in a boy-girl affair.

For Ian, Scientology was the last straw. Burroughs was on an auditing binge. He wanted to round up people in the street and chain them to E-meters. It was all he could talk about. He put a sign up in the Indica Book Shop, around the corner from Duke Street, which was run by Ian's friend Barry Miles, offering to do free audits. When he tried to audit Ian, Ian fled, telling Miles, "When Bill turns that Operating Thetan glare on me, I just know it's time to leave." It made his skin crawl to have Bill fixing him with this weird eyelock. He hated the whole Scientology movement; it was spurious and tacky, and Bill's intelligence was being wasted. Bill claimed he was just investigating it but in fact he was hooked. Since he couldn't audit Ian, he audited Harold Norse, who was spending a few months in London. Norse told him, "I'm lonely." Burroughs kept running it on the E-meter and discovered that loneliness was a cover, and his real problem was that his boyfriend didn't want to sleep with him.

Burroughs was cultivating people like John McMasters, who had originated many of the Scientology techniques but had broken with Hubbard. He was a compelling speaker who had traveled the world making thousands of converts to Scientology, and he described himself as "the happiest man alive." Once Burroughs and McMasters went out to dinner at a restaurant on Greek Street called La Cucaracha. They had quite a bit to drink, and Burroughs gave the waiter a pound to sing "La Cucaracha," which brought back fond memories of his days as an exterminator. When the song was over, McMasters leaned over close to Burroughs, as though intent on imparting a deep secret, and said, "Did I ever tell you that in my previous incarnation I was Rudolph Valentino?" Burroughs pursed his lips and said: "Really, John? Most interesting."

The auditing sessions were interrupted that August by an offer he couldn't refuse. *Esquire* wanted him to cover the Democratic convention in Chicago, along with Terry Southern and Jean Genet. A hard-hitting troika, thought Burroughs, delighted to get out of London.

The political situation in America was that after the Tet offensive in January and Eugene McCarthy's success in the early primaries on an antiwar platform, President Johnson had decided in March not to run. Robert Kennedy's bid ended in tragedy on June 5. The delegates at the Chicago convention would have to choose between McCarthy and Johnson's vice president, Hubert Horatio Humphrey.

Quite another story, however, was taking place outside the convention hall, in the streets of Chicago, which was like the site of a medieval engagement, like Agincourt or Poitiers, where two opposing armies gathered in formation on a designated field of battle. Ten thousand demonstrators, mostly young, represented a coalition of protest groups including Yippies, Black Panthers, and Students for a Democratic Society. They were outnumbered and outgunned by 16,000 Chicago police officers, 4,000 state police, and 4,000 National Guard troops in full battle dress, armed with machine guns, bazookas, and tanks.

When Burroughs landed at O'Hare on August 24, on his first visit to Chicago in twenty-six years, the customs official touched his cassette recorder and said, "The tools of your trade." He was staying at the Sheraton, there being no room at the Hilton, the center of the action, where Yippies had exploded a stink bomb in the lobby. At the hotel he met Jean Genet, dressed in old corduroys and an open-necked shirt, his pink and dimpled face reminding Burroughs of a bald, clean-shaven Santa. Genet told him that because he was a convicted criminal, he had been unable to obtain a visa, and had gone to Canada, where a group of Quebec separatists had smuggled him across the border. He had been walking past police lines, he said, and had seen blood-lust in the blue-helmeted cops' eyes. One cop had stared at him but Genet did not lower his eyes. He heard the cop's inner voice saying very distinctly, "There is the enemy."

Michigan Avenue was chaotic. Sandwiched between the police lines were hippies with flutes and finger cymbals, clergymen and other protesting elders (including Dr. Spock), girls with long earrings labeled "Eugene," and long-haired young men carrying placards that said "Welcome to Fort Daley" (in honor of Chicago's 200-pound, five-foot-eight mayor, Richard J. Daley), and "there can be no peace in the U.S. until there is peace in Vietnam." Cars in traffic honked the rhythm of "Hell No, We Won't Go."

The next day, August 25, Burroughs went to the airport to catch the arrival of Gene McCarthy. There he was, smiling broadly, and surrounded by his young, scrubbed supporters, who should all have been wearing name tags reading "righteous idealist," and who were shouting, "The GOP will cry in its beer, for here is a man who will change the scene . . . Geeeeene!"

That evening came the outbreak in hostilities, when the Yippies defied a mayoral decree that Lincoln Park had to be cleared by 11:00 P.M. Burroughs was there, having linked up with Allen Ginsberg and his sense-derangement crew, who were passing around honey spiked with acid. Campfires flickered, voices were raised in song in the summer night, hash pipes were aglow, and Ginsberg was leading his troops in mantras. The scene reminded Terry Southern, who was drinking tequila and taking an occasional hit of Panama Red with his fellow *Esquire* correspondents, of an updated Currier & Ives print.

At midnight, prowl cars entered the park, and a megaphone voice said: "All persons will leave this park at once! This is an order from the mayor of Chicago and from the Chicago police." Terry Southern saw someone step out and throw a brick at the windshield of a police car. The searchlights flashed on, and the cops burst out of the woods, riot sticks in hand, clubbing at random. The kids retaliated with rocks and bottles. Then came the tear gas, the sting of which no mantra could relieve. Kids rubbed Vaseline on their cheeks to keep it from burning their skins and tied wet handkerchiefs over their noses and mouths.

One cop came up to Allen Ginsberg, who sat there quietly in the lotus position and said, "Go in peace, brother," and the cop held back his arm, muttering something about "crazy hippies." It was later alleged by Terry Southern and Abbie Hoffman that the man who had thrown the brick was an F.B.I. provocateur.

Norman Mailer, also covering the convention and also in Lincoln Park that night, ran into Burroughs and Genet, who had "the determined miserable look of infantrymen trudging to the front. . . . Genet, large as Mickey Rooney, angelic in appearance, glanced at him with that hauteur it takes French intellectuals two decades to acquire. Burroughs merely nodded. Nothing surprised him favorably or unfavorably."

Actually, Burroughs was surprised. He could not believe that this was taking place in America. At the same time, he reflected, it was history as theater, which had existed from the Stone Age to the present. He had managed not to tangle with the cops by making himself *El Hombre Invisible*. But when he saw the kids being clubbed, he thought that there were no innocent bystanders. Jean Genet later told him that, pursued by the police, he had run into an apartment building and knocked on a door at random, saying, *"C'est monsieur Genet."* The occupant of the apartment, it turned out, was a graduate student who was writing a thesis on him.

Then, on August 28, there was a rally around the Grant Park bandshell. They were going to march, ten thousand strong, down Michigan Avenue to the Hilton. Burroughs had agreed to march in the second row with Allen Ginsberg and Jean Genet, in an impulsive display of participatory journalism, but was feeling uneasy about the whole enterprise. He was hoping he wouldn't have to march, not being ready for martyrdom, and fearing that his splendid record of never having had a cop lay a violent hand on him in all his brushes with the law might now be compromised. There was no way out, however, for the organizers were giving instructions: "Link arms . . . keep five feet between rows . . . keep your cool . . . you can obtain tear-gas rags from the medics." Down Michigan Avenue they started, with Burroughs calm and impassive under his gray fedora, all the while thinking, "I hope to God we stop." In the distance, a solid phalanx of police came into focus. It would be madness, thought Burroughs, to try to force their way through. Thankfully, the organizers did not want violence, and neither did the cops, and the marchers stopped and dispersed.

Although not a movement person, being ambivalent even about his affiliation with the Beats, Burroughs found Chicago a heady experience. He felt that the seeds that he and Allen and Jack had planted years ago were bearing magnificent fruit. These young people challenging the political establishment and battling the Chicago police were in a sense the spiritual offspring of *On the Road, Howl*, and *Naked Lunch*. He had really dug the Chicago scene, by comparison with stodgy old London. When you saw 10,000 people in front of Buckingham Palace screaming "Bugger the Queen," there would be hope for England. But that day would never come. Chicago made Burroughs realize that he could accomplish more in the United States than he could sitting on the godforsaken island like a nineteenth-century queen.

In New York, Burroughs and Genet checked into the Hotel Delmonico to write their stories. Genet had a row with *Esquire* editor Harold Hayes, objecting to the magazine's cover photograph, which showed the three correspondents standing over what was meant to be the body of a demonstrator. He refused to pose with this *faux mort* unless his fee was increased. Hayes called him a thief, and Genet said, "*Mais bien entendu, monsieur*" ("Well, of course"). Before sneaking back across the Canadian border, Genet got $3,800 out of *Esquire*, and told Burroughs that Chicago had been one of the great experiences of his life.

In town to tape the William F. Buckley program "Firing Line" was Jack Kerouac, who dropped in on Burroughs at the Delmonico with three buddies from his hometown of Lowell. One ran a bar, one ran a liquor store, and one was a boxer. Jack was drunk, and ordered more drinks from room service. His friends told Burroughs that he was always that way now—every morning when he woke up he drank a wineglass full of whiskey. He was throwing away his talent and his life but there was nothing they could do. Jack wanted Burroughs to accompany him to the studio, but Burroughs said, "No, Jack, don't go, you're not in any condition to go." In spite of his condition, Jack came off as far more genuine and witty than the supercilious Buckley. When Buckley tried to pin him down on Vietnam, Jack said the war was a conspiracy by North and South Vietnam to acquire American Jeeps. He also said that the hippies were a continuation of the Beats. "The hippies are good kids," he said. "They're better than the Beats."

In October, when Burroughs was back at Duke Street, his enthusiasm for the United States cooled down. His flat was quiet and conducive to work, and he did not think it was beneficial to maintain the state of excitability he had felt in Chicago. A period of calm was in order. Another factor was that he had met a young man in a bar who had moved in with him. John Culverwell was a "Dilly boy," as the Piccadilly Circus hustlers were called. He was very childlike and well-intentioned, a little like Mikey Portman without any of Mikey's sloppy habits. And to top it off, he could cook.

Burroughs was well aware of the dangers of domesticity. It was always a dubious decision to bring someone in, because then they were on your hands, and you could get yourself into nightmare situations. It was a very old story, and you could almost predict the stages it would go through. At first they were full of enthusiasm, they wanted to clean everything and cook seven-course meals. Then things began to slacken, and they didn't want to go near the kitchen or touch a broom. There was the same slackening process with sex. At first it was "You're the love of my life and it's so great," then three months later it wasn't so great anymore. It became more and more mechanical, and then it came to a complete halt. What could you do? *Son cosas de la vida.*

Still, it was a risk worth taking, because he needed someone, and Ian had broken away. He had a job and was living his own life, though Burroughs still saw him often. In any case, Culverwell seemed placid and eager to please, and Burroughs tried to teach him the secrets of keeping a place clean—for instance, every time you walk into a room you clean something up or straighten something. But Culverwell was naturally messy, and every time he entered a room he added to the mess. Burroughs saw after a few months that it wasn't working out, and tried to set him up on his own. He encouraged Culverwell to join the merchant marine, and he did make one trip. But then he was back on his doorstep. It was hopeless, because boys like Culverwell were used to the easy life, drinks and money just for putting out. When they could make five or six pounds a night whoring, they weren't going to do any other kind of work for less money. The bottom line was that they were bone lazy. Burroughs finally had to tell Culverwell, "So long, it's been good to know you."

In 1969, at the time of Culverwell's residence, Burroughs was working on *The Wild Boys* and *The Last Words of Dutch Schultz*. In his spare time, he played with his E-meter. When Ian called in March saying that a burst water main had caused traffic to be diverted in front of his building, making an unrelentingly deafening roar, Burroughs told him to run it through the E-meter. The next day Ian told him the traffic had been redirected. Burroughs had great faith in the powers of the E-meter. A thousand blacks with E-meters, he wrote Brion Gysin, could integrate the Bible Belt.

Brion reported that in Tangier, it was a very rainy spring. Children in ragged bands ran through the streets chanting *"Yalatif"*—"That's enough." His novel, *The Process*, had been published by Doubleday, who were, Brion wrote, passing on hate-filled reviews from the American heartland. Brion was convinced there was a conspiracy to muffle the book, writing that it was "a dead duck returned by the booksellers. It can be kept on ice for a few more days and must, then, go back to the pulper's before it rots in their storage space. This is because there has not been one single review anywhere. . . . Can they do it to me next time? If they can and will, there is not much use in doing what I am doing, is there?" That Brion could assert in the same letter that there were hate-filled reviews and not a single review was an example of his charming inconsistency.

Then, in April, coming back one night from the little restaurant at the caves of Hercules, on the back of a motorcycle driven by the young American writer John Hopkins, they sideswiped a truck, and two of

Brion's toes were lopped off. From the Spanish hospital, Brion wrote that Hopkins, a blond and handsome Princeton graduate with an independent income, was utterly indifferent to his plight. The idea of going to the law in Tangier was unthinkable. He had no useful allies or accomplices. The affluent expatriates on the mountain had abandoned him, singing, "Let's all be millionaires together, we don't want to know." Hopkins had once told him, "The nice thing about money is that you can shit on anybody and tell them to fuck off." Brion now felt that he was on the receiving end of that philosophy with his three-toed foot. Hopkins left for Amsterdam to see his Dutch girlfriend and asked Brion, in that flat, semiamused way he had, "What can I bring back, a Rembrandt, a diamond?" Hopkins hadn't just fucked up Brion's foot and his summer, he had fucked up his head with worry and anxiety.

Burroughs did not want to interrupt his work to visit Brion, but sent him 200 pounds in August. When Hopkins got back, he agreed to pay Brion $1,500 plus medical expenses. But Brion still felt that Hopkins had acted like a coldhearted bully. And yet, Brion thought, it was his own fault for not having made a clean break with him that night of the straw vote on the 1968 election, at the American Consulate, when he had voted for Wallace.

Nothing was going right for Brion. His manservant and lover, Salah, a tall, mustached, Ethiopian-looking Moroccan, was stealing money from him. When Brion entertained, Salah also stole from the purses of the women guests. Salah had two wives, who were always clamoring for money. Brion did not know what to do about it. The arrival in September 1969 of Jean Genet, mysterious and leprechaun-like, was a welcome relief. He came by every day to cheer Brion up. Brion asked the author-thief, "Do you think Salah finds it more fun to steal than to wheedle it out of me like all the others do?" Genet shrugged. He had his own problems, among them a serious Nembutal habit that kept him in drugged slumber sixteen hours out of twenty-four. In October, the cast came off Brion's foot. The doctor had done a good job with skin grafts, and he was able to walk without any trace of a limp. But the motorcycle accident was the start of a long period of physical decline.

October 22, 1969, was one of those gray London days, when the city seems ghostly and forlorn, like an attic full of mildewed trunks. Sitting at his desk, Burroughs felt terrible waves of depression pass through his body. He felt so low that he forgot to put the laundry out. The smell of stale flowers and hospitals filled the flat. Then a friend came by with the news that Jack Kerouac had died.

Jack had moved to St. Petersburg with Mémère and his third wife,

Stella. On October 20, Stella had heard him groaning in the bathroom. She found him on his knees, vomiting blood. He was taken to the hospital, where he died the next day, after twenty-six blood transfusions. It was the classic drunkard's death. The cirrhotic liver had rejected the blood that was supposed to flow through it. The backed-up blood broke through the weakest veins, the little veins in the esophagus. He had drowned in his own blood, at the age of forty-seven.

Burroughs wondered what had caused that kind of relentless drinking. Could it be his sick attachment to his mother, from whom he had never been able to free himself, or was it the penalty of success, when everyone wanted a piece of you? He preferred to remember Jack in the early days at Columbia, acting out a scene from Gide's *The Counterfeiters* in a bowler hat on Morningside Heights, trying to pick up girls in Times Square on VJ-Day, arm-wrestling with Lucien Carr in one of the booths in the West End.

It took a while for Burroughs to shake off the depression that came with Jack's death, which was compounded by the feeling that he was stagnating in London. He wasn't a part of the petty and incestuous literary scene. They were all on short rations, and it was "You write a preface to my book and I'll write a favorable review of yours." He occasionally went to Sonia Orwell's, where he once ran into Stephen Spender, his adversary at the Edinburgh Conference, looking very hangdog because it had recently come out that the C.I.A. was backing his magazine, *Encounter*. Burroughs had known it for years but everyone said he was paranoid.

He also went to the home of Panna Grady, who had moved to London with the poet Charles Olson and continued to entertain in lavish and dramatic fashion. Dramatic because at one of her parties two poets got into a fight, and at another the police arrived, and Panna asked one of her guests, the distinguished author of *Seven Types of Ambiguity*, William Empson, who was in a reasonably sober state, to go to the door and make the proper English noises.

When Olson died in 1970, at the age of sixty, she married Philip O'Connor, author of *Memoirs of a Public Baby*, and a reputed *enfant terrible*. He would introduce himself as "Panna Grady's terrible husband." Once, when he consulted Burroughs about a cure for alcoholism, he said, sizing him up, "You're bourgeois, aren't you?" and Burroughs replied, "Yes, I am bourgeois." For O'Connor, much of whose work was a critique of modern literature, Burroughs' remark was a key to the understanding of his writing. Much of avant-garde writing, he thought, was done by ideologically conservative authors, James Joyce and Beckett and Burroughs among them. What was Burroughs' position in the culture? He was a man in whom the tenderness had been warped, and so he attempted to convey meaning without humanity. Céline was a writer in a similar situation. It was human to hate humanity, but to ignore it was impossible. So that for O'Connor, Burroughs' work was a shell, at best a raincoat in bad weather.

And what was Burroughs' position as an artist? O'Connor asked himself. He was the antibourgeois provided by the bourgeoisie, ideologically bankrupt, writing out of emotional disappointment. What would his shocking novelties become but wrapping paper for yesterday's toys? His work left no lasting impression in the end. He was a blower of bubbles. In the end the reader said: There is no fun in the relish of destruction. In Burroughs there was an old-fashioned man, an authoritarian individualist, who tried to escape from his own narcissism through various out-of-the-body strategies. Burroughs might remain, but O'Connor doubted it, for as Gorky had said, "Some things are too disgusting to write about." But the truth was not disgusting, and shit was not food.

O'Connor's remarks were a distress signal, an SOS at the state of postmodern literature in general. Burroughs wrote as a postmodern artist, post-Marx, post-Freud, and post-Bomb, in an era when God was dead and literature was exhausted, when at any moment the planet might go off like a firecracker. What was the point of writing a coherent beginning-middle-end narrative, with its tripartite structure reminiscent of the Trinity, when history itself was incoherent, with its own tripartite progression from ancient to medieval to modern offering cold comfort in the nuclear age? Life no longer seemed grounded, the former certainties no longer served. The Word itself was suspect as a method of control, and Burroughs used cut-ups and fragmented episodes as a way to avoid manipulating the reader. The writing became very much like the nervous, distraught, uncertain quality of contemporary life, where "the center cannot hold, and mere anarchy is loosed upon the world." To call it "a raincoat in bad weather" was to wish for the good old days when the sun was always out.

Aside from the odd social occasion, Burroughs sometimes received admirers. He had a number of rock stars among his fans. David Bowie told him that his songs owed a lot to the cut-up method. Mick Jagger invited him to his wedding to Bianca. He would be flown to the south of France on a chartered plane with the other famous guests. But it wasn't his scene. He didn't want to be sitting on a hot terrace through an interminable wedding lunch, squeezed between the Begum and Marianne Faithfull. Mick was offended—it was lèse-majesté. He did go to Mick's farewell party outside London, but he hated it. He had never mastered the art of talking in the bedlam of a noisy party, and wondered how some people could do it day after day.

From time to time he traveled, mostly to Tangier. In the summer of 1970 he spent a couple of months in New York. His painter friend David Budd had some movie people interested in *The Last Words of Dutch Schultz*, and he went over to work on the script, but it came to nothing. Returning to London made him think: Wouldn't I rather be in New York where any hour of the day or night there's a place to eat . . . what the hell am I doing in London? Culverwell was gone and he had not found a replacement. Alan Watson cleaned his flat once but Burroughs decided that once was enough when he discovered that Alan was helping himself to his tincture of cannabis.

The news about his mother was not good. She had regressed to a childlike condition and was under sedation; at least she no longer took off her clothes and tore them into shreds. She would talk coherently for a moment and then drift off into nonsense. When Miggy came to visit, she would say, "Oh, this is the lady that does my laundry."

On October 20, 1970, a telegram arrived that said MOTHER DEAD. She was eighty-two. For a moment, he felt nothing at all, and then it came, like a kick in the stomach. Burroughs thought of her in the nursing home, her hair cut very short, clutching her pink robe, her bare feet blue-veined. No doubt about it, he had her physique, thin and long-boned, and the Lee forehead, high and straight up and down. She had a special ephemeral quality, and she was psychic. She had dreamed that Mort, his face covered with blood, had come to the door and said, "Mother, we've had an accident," and Mort had in fact been in an accident and suffered minor cuts. Once, long ago, she had said: "Suppose I was very sick? Would you come to see me? Look after me? Care for me? I'm counting on that . . ." He had promised that he would, but in the last years of her life, when she was in the nursing home, hallucinating and wandering around naked, he had never once gone to see her, even though he had been in the United States several times. All he did was send mawkish cards on Mother's Day. And now she was gone. Mistakes too monstrous for remorse.

His life in London was increasingly dreary. Nothing was happening. There were no surprises. He had no *amigo*. Ian was now a highly paid computer programmer, busy with his work. Mikey Portman was out of the picture with an alternate junk and alcohol habit. He had the record for apomorphine cures, averaging one every two months.

Then, in May 1971, there was a flurry of activity over a film version of *Naked Lunch*. Brion Gysin wrote a script and Anthony Balch wanted to direct. Mick Jagger was interested, but when he came to the Duke Street flat Burroughs could see it wasn't going to work. Mick did not want Balch as director. He didn't like him. He thought Balch was coming on to him sexually, and in any case he didn't have a reputation as a director in the industry. He wasn't bankable. Balch had formed Friendly Films for the *Naked Lunch* project, and Burroughs thought it was an education to see Mick's palace favorites go into action and sign him up for a different film part. It was just as well. Mick was inseparable from his groupies and his Nicaraguan bride.

In October 1971 Burroughs was offered a teaching appointment in Switzerland. Al de Grazia, a political scientist and the brother of Ed de Grazia, who had handled the *Naked Lunch* obscenity trial for Grove Press, had founded the University of the New World in the Alpine village of Haute-Nendaz. It was intended as an alternative to the over-structured American colleges, where young people could learn in an untrammeled spirit of inquiry, without regulations or deans' offices. Instead of classes, there were "studios" and "rapport groups." The students wore T-shirts that said, "No classes, no grades, no exams." They could have added, "No tuition," since very few of them were paid up.

Al de Grazia had hit on the novel scheme of printing his own currency, with bills called Cows, since they had a picture of a heifer on both sides. "On the first business day of any month," it was stated on the bills, "the University will pay to the bearer, in exchange for this coupon, its face value in Swiss francs. A 2% premium will be added. Not valid unless stamped with official University of the New World seal." There was, however, some resistance on the part of local shopkeepers to accepting Cows as legal tender.

Burroughs was looking forward to three months of light teaching in the clean mountain air. The brochure showed a lovely campus of Swiss chalets nestled in pine groves at 4,000 feet, with mountain peaks in the background. But when he took a taxi at the train station and asked for the University of the New World, he was taken to a broken-down shack in the middle of a field. No one seemed to be around. He walked to the village and found a hotel, where a room had been reserved in his name. At least he had a roof over his head. But where was everybody? He finally ran into a couple of students who clued him in.

The school had attracted the drifters and dropouts on the international hippie circuit, and the prim Swiss were up in arms over the open use of drugs in their little town. In addition, some black musicians from the "music studio" had begun dating local girls, a practice that was frowned on by the elders. Burroughs saw the University of the New World disintegrating before his eyes. He knew he would not be paid, and he hoped he would not get stuck with the bill at the Hotel Montcalm, where he had been put up. If he got his fare back to London it would be a miracle. What a mess! As for the clean mountain air, after London, it had incapacitated him with a racking cough. The nearest drugstore was fifteen miles away, but he managed to get a batch of codeine pills and took to his bed with a pile of science fiction novels.

When he felt better he gave a couple of lectures. But stupidity was rampant among the students. "Uhhh," one asked, "the heat in the radiators, where does it come from?" Another remarked that Tangier must be very hot because it was in Africa, while a third asserted that big planes were safer than small planes because they were bigger. My Gawd, thought Burroughs, this university is *pas sérieux*. He was practically the only teacher who had shown up. The instructor who was supposed to teach the film course had taken off with the only projector.

For once, Burroughs was genuinely glad to get back to London. Anything was better than this madness with the hippies and the Cows. And yet he continued to feel the need to move, and thought about Afghanistan and southern Morocco. He had a conversation with his imaginary godfather:

"My books aren't selling and soon I shall have no money. What shall I do?"

"I suppose you have thought of cutting expenses, going to live in Tangier perhaps and writing another novel perhaps in a more popular vein?"

"Well, that would be the logical thing to do."

"And how many times have I told you that when you are in difficulties the 'logical' thing to do is always wrong, since it is just this 'logic' that has put you in your present difficulties?"

Things happened more often because of the unexpected than because of logic. In April 1972, an invitation arrived from Terry Southern, who had established himself as a screenwriter with *Dr. Strangelove* and *Easy Rider*, to come to Hollywood. The deal was this: Chuck Barris, a producer who had made a fortune with a television program called "The Dating Game," was interested in making a movie of *Naked Lunch*. Why this clean-living, teetotaling, vegetarian "king of the game shows" was drawn to an avant-garde novel that had been banned for obscenity was not theirs to reason why.

Burroughs and Southern were met at the Los Angeles airport by a chauffeured Daimler and driven to their hotel on Sunset Boulevard. The next day, Barris invited them to his house in Bel-Air, but this time the car that came to get them was a Toyota. There had, it seemed, been a sharp decline in status. The car was a two-seater with a driver, so that Burroughs practically had to sit in Terry's lap. Moreover, when they were dropped off at the house, Barris was not there. "Not like old Chuck to do a thing like this," Terry said. "I hate to tell you," Burroughs replied, "but he don't like the script and we'd better get out of here before he refuses to pay the hotel bill." He'd obviously done this on purpose to put them in their place. Burroughs wondered what possible misconception could have led to such a fiasco, and how they were going to get back to their hotel. Luckily Terry had friends a block away, and they called a cab. Barris had left instructions at the hotel that he would pay for the rooms but not for room service. Reflecting on such recent events as the University of the New World and the Chuck Barris experience, it seemed to Burroughs that life was one humiliation after the other.

In New York his spirits picked up when he went to X-rated gay movies. He felt a small stirring of pride that he had played a role in the whittling down of censorship. Now these blue movies would put him out of business. Who was going to read *The Wild Boys* when they could see Jerry, Audrey, Johnny, Ali, and Jimmy do it all on the screen? It was a one-way street. Once you had seen the fuck films you could not go back to the semiclad. Sex was everything. Sex was time made solid enough to fuck.

That was another drawback to London. No blue movies. England now seemed to him a gloomy cold unlighted sinking ship that would disappear with a spectral cough. After the top men had split the take there wasn't enough left to pay a living wage.

Burroughs had been hoping that marriage would help Billy settle down, but trouble seemed to hound the boy. In 1970 he and Karen had returned to the Green Valley School as junior staff, a category that the Reverend Von Hilsheimer had thought up for former students who couldn't make it on the outside. Karen ran the kitchen and Billy did odd jobs, picking up supplies and driving students to the doctor. To Ron Nowicki, the headmaster, Billy's face already showed the ravages of drinking—it reminded him of a map of the Middle East. And the way he dressed! As though Helen Keller had picked out his wardrobe. Once, while driving from Orlando to Orange City, Billy had bent over to light a cigarette, taking both hands off the wheel, and driven into a culvert. The car flipped over and was totaled, but he was unhurt.

Now, in October 1972, Billy wrote his father: "Disaster. Wife leaving me. Or rather I'm informed that my absence is required. I desperately need about $250 to hustle my ass back out West and try to make a start. . . . I've got to go and I've got to go soon. . . . It's bad, Bill, it's very bad when a six-year investment in another person comes to bankruptcy." (In fact it was four years.)

Burroughs was unable to express any sympathy for his son's distress. His attitude was: We all have to take our lumps. I've taken mine, and you have to take yours. He seemed incapable of normal human compassion toward a son who he knew from past experience had a fragile sense of himself. "I never know what to say when someone tells me his wife is leaving him," he replied on October 30. "*Son cosas de la vida, hombre.*" He did, however, respond to Billy's "desperate need," enclosing a check for $500.

At about the time that Billy and Karen were breaking up, Burroughs met another "Dilly boy," a short, strong, black-haired young man named John Brady, the son of Irish farmers. He was a bad-tempered drinker, but Burroughs asked him to move in, because he was lonely. He was tired of eating dinner by himself every night. How many evenings had he sat alone at the Angus Steak House with his steak, his baked potato, his half-bottle of Beaujolais, and only the Italian waiter for company.

He knew it was a mistake, but sometimes mistakes had to be made. Boys like John Brady had no education, and you could tell yourself that you were going to help them, but very often you succeeded only in giving them a little glimpse of something beyond Piccadilly, beyond their way of life, and then they were left stranded. You could take them so far and no further, and they were better off not being taken at all, because it made them feel out of place, disoriented. Even so, John Brady was not stupid—he had the natural savoir-faire of the Irish.

John Brady did have one trait that Burroughs prized highly—he talked in his sleep, and the words that came out of his mouth were natural cut-ups, which Burroughs wrote down and collected in a scrapbook: "Balls, you get nothing . . . nothing." "What about her up in the sky?" "Where's it go, into her sleeping drawers?" "Prince's gold is only old cock . . . load of monkeys." And many more disjointed observations. So that in spite of the difficulties Brady created, Burroughs the writer got his pound of flesh.

In January 1973, he took John Brady to Morocco, where he had a magazine assignment. In a mountain village south of Tangier called Joujouka, reached over a twisting dirt road that reminded Burroughs of a Missouri country road in the 1920s, there lived a group of musicians known as the "Pipers of Pan." These men were a special caste who traced their lineage to pre-Christian times. Down the generations for more than two thousand years their music had been passed on from father to son, without written notation. Exempted from farm work by the Moroccan government, they did nothing but play from birth, learning the arduous breathing technique on the raita (Moroccan oboe) that allowed them to sustain notes for what seemed like interminable periods.

These master musicians of Joujouka were secretive, and seldom played outside their village, which was little known and hard to reach. They were more on the order of a religious brotherhood than a tourist attraction. Brion Gysin, in his quest for all things Moroccan, had discovered them through his painter friend Hamri. Brion had taken the Rolling Stones to hear them play, and Brian Jones had been so impressed that he returned with a sound engineer and recorded their music. But by the time the record was issued, Brian Jones was dead. What a cheapshit guy he had been, thought Gysin. He never paid his bills, and the musicians never got a penny. He had been as slippery as they come. When he brushed the bangs out of his forehead you saw two hard beady little eyes.

Once a year in Joujouka there occurred the feast of Bou Jeloud, the Goat God, and this was the event that Burroughs had come to cover. An added attraction was that the great jazz saxophonist Ornette Coleman would be there to study the master musicians' techniques and perhaps play along with them.

Arriving in the village of thatch-roofed houses with cactus-lined lanes, Burroughs was greeted by Hamri, who had appointed himself the master musicians' manager. Eyes and smile flashing, large head on short body, Hamri had prepared food for fifty people: "*Pinchitos* (meat on a skewer), chicken, fish, all what you like." It was chilly in the January air, and Burroughs donned a brown *djellabah*, which he thought made him look like a walking tent.

That evening, the thirty-odd musicians, all wearing white robes and brown wool turbans, began to play, raitas and drums standing next to one another in a single line in the village square. It was a continuous, sinuous rope of music, uncoiling at an ear-splitting volume, ancient and yet contemporary. When Ornette Coleman played, building up counter-harmonies, it seemed to Burroughs that he was listening to a 2,000-year-old rock 'n' roll band. When the two forms met, this music from Punic times and modern jazz, it created a new frontier of sound.

Suddenly, screaming women ran into the village green, and the musicians stepped up the tempo. The women were being pursued by Bou Jeloud, Pan the Goat God, Master of Skins and Master of Fear. Covered with black goatskins, his head hidden under a furry animal headdress, the athletic young villager playing Bou Jeloud jumped high in the air, chased the women, and flailed them with switches. They scattered, caught in the reality of the moment, feeling real fear. The Master of Skins was making them jump out of their skins.

They were acting out an ancient mating rite, as the women sang the song of Crazy Aisha, who lures the Goat God to the village to impregnate them, the song balancing the music of Bou Jeloud, marking the old balance of power between male and female forces. "We will give you cross-eyed Aisha," the women sang, "and we will give you humpbacked Zora," and Bou Jeloud was enticed by this promise of womanhood, for he was sexuality itself.

A bonfire was lit, and Burroughs saw Bou Jeloud throw himself into it and roll around in the hot coals, emerging with coals sticking to his bare feet. And through it all the music continued, this unbroken blast of pipes and drums, this anthem of a lost civilization. It was a shattering experience, and Burroughs could only agree with the little Moroccan drummer who kept repeating what were probably the only English words he knew: "Very good everything. Outasight."

Back in London, Burroughs continued with his psychic experiments. He was interested in out-of-the-body experiences, the idea that with the right techniques it was possible to leave one's body and then go back into it. Flying dreams, it was said, were a form of out-of-the-body experience. He took a course called Mind Dimensions to achieve deep relaxation in a waking state. In May, he attended a workshop given by a reputed healer, Major Bruce McManaway. A regular army officer, McManaway had discovered his healing powers during World War II, when his unit was cut off without medical kits and he found that he could relieve the pain of his wounded men by laying on hands. The navy later used him to locate German submarines in the North Atlantic. McManaway was a level-headed, feet-on-the-ground sort of person who just happened to have psychic powers. But when he said he had seen group concentration lift a grand piano, Burroughs said to himself, "I'm from the 'show-me state,' and I'd sure like to see it."

At the workshop they studied visualization techniques. Burroughs was given a name and an address and was asked to visualize the person's ailment. He saw swollen veins. It turned out that the person had varicose veins. Then they sat in a circle, about twenty of them, and Major Bruce said, "There is a pillar of light in the middle of the circle, and I want you all to go up through the pillar of light . . . and then you will come to a plateau and you will see men in white robes." Burroughs could feel himself climbing up the pillar of light, he could feel himself up there . . . but a couple of the others in the circle couldn't get back down. They were sitting there in a deep trance and Major Bruce had to coax them gently in.

That August of 1973 Burroughs heard from his son, who was in Savannah, reunited with Karen. Billy's book, *Speed*, an autobiographical account of his New York bust, was out, and Burroughs wrote him that he had found it "hypnotically readable." Billy had a small advance on a second book, but found it hard to get cranked up. "What I want to do," he said, "is write to change the way people feel in their hearts." He couldn't make a living writing, however, and needed to find some form of gainful employment. He asked his father to lend him $1,000 so he could take a six-week trucking school course in Atlanta. Ten trucking companies hired from the school, and he could make $15,000 a year driving heavy equipment long distance. This was no last-ditch thing, he emphasized, but something he'd been thinking about for years. But the move to Atlanta led to another breakup with Karen, this one final. In deep depression, Billy went to Boulder, Colorado, and drank himself out from under hangovers at the Coors plant, where the 3.2 beer flowed free. "How about the knowledge of what a God-awful mess you are," he wrote his father, "that knowledge sitting on your shoulders with the full weight of every fuckup you managed as far back as fractured memory serves? You're a long way from the ocean—but you know it's deep." He went to Santa Cruz and met a diminutive blond flower child named Georgette Larrouy, who was into astrology, acupuncture, the effects of colors on your psyche, the Rainbow Gathering of the Tribes. She was also addicted to helping castaways. Billy moved in with her and tried to write more and drink less. He was given a checkup at the welfare clinic, and the doctor put him down as a borderline psychopath; in other words, thought Billy, someone who doesn't learn from unpleasant experiences.

There wasn't much that Burroughs could do for Billy, except send him money from time to time. At the age of fifty-nine, he was himself at a point of crisis, certain that he had to leave England. Prices had doubled and the whole island was going downhill. Anywhere but here, he thought,

Ireland which had no tax on artists, or Costa Rica. He wanted to see some sun and water (other than rain), and do some fishing and walking, and cut wood.

"Is London Foundering?" was the name of a TV program. People were less pleasant and showed their worst side when a country started to decline. One woman on the program said, "I don't want to bring children up in this country." Burroughs fumed at what he was paying for his hole-in-the-wall apartment with a closet for a kitchen. And the rent was only the beginning, because you had to pay something called rates. And instead of central heating they had storage heaters that didn't work, and the only person allowed to fix them had to come from the Electricity Board. And when he finally came over he fiddled around and said, "We don't have the elements, this is an old heater." For six weeks that winter he froze, sometimes staying in bed all day under the covers, and he finally told the janitor, "Get this goddamn thing out of here," and started using a plug-in electric heater.

Burroughs began to feel that he was in enemy territory, and in a situation like that you had to defend yourself. There was a Soho espresso joint, the Moka Bar, at 29 Frith Street, where on several occasions a snarling counterman had treated him with outrageous and unprovoked discourtesy, and served him poisonous cheesecake that made him sick. He decided to retaliate by putting a curse on the place. On August 3, 1973, he took pictures and made recordings, in plain sight of the horrible old proprietor, his frizzy-haired wife, and his slack-jawed son. Then he strolled over to the Brewer Street Market and recorded a three-card monte game—now you see it, now you don't. He came back to the Moka Bar several days later to make new tapes over the first tapes and take more pictures. The idea was to place the Moka Bar out of time. You played back a tape that had taken place two days ago and you super-imposed it on what was happening now, which pulled them out of their time position. When the Moka Bar closed down on October 30 and was replaced by the Queen's Snack Bar, Burroughs was sure that his curse had worked.

Was London foundering? The answer was yes. Every day in London gave him a sense of utter hopelessness, in the smallest things, as when the man at Fortnum and Mason's slighted him: "Are you next, sir?" Then he pretended not to find what Burroughs was pointing at. "You mean this, sir . . . or this . . . or that?" It was a weary time. Every day just hanging on some hideous insult or humiliation. The change without thanks. "We don't sell it by the stalk, sir." Not being let into Rules because the friend he was with was wearing a leather jacket. And then, when they did let you in, you had to tip the guy that carved the meat. Guy Fawkes had the right idea—blow the whole shithouse sky-high.

More than London, however, his low spirits could be traced to John Brady, who was a mean drunk. All the other Dilly boys were scared of him. In the words of the old verse:

> After he'd had his tenth Scotch,
> A man to be careful of and watch.
> And when he was mixing gin and rum,
> A man to stay well away from.

Johnny started bringing strange Irish girls around to Duke Street. In the morning, Burroughs would be making his cup of tea when a girl with no top on would rush by on her way to the bathroom. Burroughs was horrified. Once, he had to post bail for one of Johnny's girls, who had been arrested for soliciting. In addition, Johnny started to steal. Every day Burroughs gave him five pounds and a bottle of whiskey, but it wasn't enough. He would say, "Johnny, I was going to give you five pounds out of my wallet, but I seem to be short five pounds." He didn't even bother to deny it—just looked insolent. When Burroughs pressed him, he said, "Well, put yourself in my shoes." "That's very difficult," Burroughs thought to himself.

Several times, Burroughs told him he would have to leave, which made him even sulkier and more hostile. Then one day he insolently, deliberately, threw ashes on the floor. "Pick up those ashes," Burroughs said, and Johnny went into the kitchen and came out, not with a dustpan but with a meat cleaver. Burroughs was sitting at his desk and Johnny slammed the meat cleaver down—*Thunk*—an inch away from his hand. Then, with a wild look in his eyes, he said, "Light my cigarette." Burroughs lit it with a steady hand and calmed him down until he was smiling. "How about a cup of coffee?" he asked Johnny. The danger was past. He told Anthony Balch what had happened, and Balch said: "You'd better get rid of that boy as quick as you can before he kills you. Don't you know he once threatened his mother with an axe?" Burroughs had seen it too many times: the deterioration of the impeccable boy.

Balch was a loyal friend, living in the same building, and picking Burroughs up for dinner each evening, and listening patiently as he went down his list of grievances. At the top of the list was Ian Sommerville, who had moved to Bath, where he had a good computer job. Burroughs wished he had tried to convince him to stay in London. But he had said nothing to hold him back. Then he would start in on what he didn't like about London—the pub life, the underground system, the VAT tax, where they had you constantly filling out forms, and you had to write down the cost of every cab ride . . . it was diabolical. He had no friends, he had no social life, he wasn't part of the literary scene, he never gave a reading, because all they offered you was a glass of sherry. All he did was work, eight days a week.

Burroughs needed money to escape from England, and the possibility arose that he might sell his archives. The idea came from Brion, who had kept a trunk filled with Burroughs material all these many years. They got Barry Miles of the Indica bookstore to help them catalogue it, and spent months going over it. They approached Andreas Brown of the Gotham Book Mart in New York, who said Columbia University, which already had the Allen Ginsberg deposit, was interested. But then Brion brought in another dealer, Richard Aaron, who said he had a buyer who would pay cash on delivery. They broke their written agreement with Andreas Brown, who was not pleased. Aaron's buyer was a mysterious financier in Liechtenstein, Roberto Altman, who had dreams of building a library and museum, and who believed the Burroughs archive would be a promising start for his collection.

In August 1973, with the archive indexed and catalogued, Burroughs took it to Vaduz, the capital of Liechtenstein, with Brion Gysin and Richard Aaron. Burroughs lived through what seemed to be one of the scenes in the thrillers he had written as a boy. In his vaulted and paneled office, the mysterious financier took possession of the archive. When he snapped his fingers, in came Igor, a feature of every Liechtenstein transaction, the holder of the cash. He counted it in their presence, flipping the bills with incredible speed and dexterity, and packed the banded sheaves into a briefcase. They spent the night in the financier's house, under the passive surveillance of Rembrandt portraits, and Burroughs thought that he should perhaps establish himself in Vaduz, close to his archives. But the billionaires who were packed into the tiny principality seemed to cry out with one voice: YOU CAN'T COME IN HERE. THERE SIMPLY ISN'T ROOM.

The next day they drove to Richard Aaron's bank in Switzerland in a blinding rain. When they stopped for a bite to eat, Burroughs never loosened his hold on the briefcase, to which he was shackled with imaginary handcuffs. In the banker's outer office, he saw a portly black man with tribal marks on his face, holding a briefcase just like his. He was led into a little private room, where, as he waited, he spotted on the banker's desk a card from the foreign minister of Ghana. Then the banker arrived, exuding good cheer, and when Burroughs asked about moving the money out if he needed it, the banker said, *"Il n'y a pas de problème."* After Richard Aaron's commission and Miles's fee, Burroughs and Brion split the rest and Burroughs was left with a little nest egg to hatch him out of England.

With the archive sold, the opportunity now existed for escape, thanks to Allen Ginsberg, who had a way of showing up whenever Burroughs needed a push in the right direction. Allen had seen Burroughs while passing through London, and had found him depressed and drinking too much, repeating himself, sodden and self-pitying and lacking the old brilliance. Working behind the scenes in New York, Allen had contacted Leo Hamalian, director of the creative writing program at City College, who told Edward Quinn, chairman of the English Department, that Burroughs was available for teaching. City College had just launched a three-month course taught by distinguished writers, which had been kicked off in 1973 by Anthony Burgess. In November 1973, Burroughs was invited to teach the 1974 course from February to May, for a fee of $7,000, and he accepted. Out of the blue had come this letter full of promise, at a time when he'd just about given up.

No matter how depressed he was, no matter how grim London seemed, no matter how friendless and alone he felt, there was one thing that Burroughs always managed to do, and that was write. To sit down at his desk and peck away at his typewriter in a drugged or trancelike state was more than a professional activity—it was a lifeline, an absolute necessity, a way of connecting with the world, a way of fleeing from the world into fantasy, and a way of reconstructing the world according to Burroughs.

Roughly half his characters and scenes came from dreams. A light sleeper, he kept a pen and notebook on a bedside table, writing them down as they occurred. If he didn't, by morning he forgot them. Sometimes they were precognitive dreams. In one, a landlady showed him a room with five beds and he protested that he did not want four roommates. Several weeks later he was shown a room with five beds. Other dreams, as recorded in his dream notes, had to do with people he knew:

"Paul and Jane came in and ordered some expensive dessert that looked like a house made of cake. I had just been in a boxing match where I felt I had lost on points."

"I was working in a glass factory. The key to my mailbox had broken.

Samuel Beckett had a key-making shop opposite the factory. But I went to another shop next door, not wishing to ask him to make the key. Then he was driving me home to Price Road in a bus driving very fast. We finally came to a sort of inn.''

"Terrible quarrel with Joan, who wouldn't let me alone to go to the toilet. I scream 'I hate you.' She is rubbing something on me like green fairy stone. 'Words,' she said." (Fairy Stone was a greasy pink cake people used to rub on for sunburn.) Burroughs' comment on his late wife's appearance was, "As Hoagy Carmichael sang, 'Talking is a woman, listening is a man.' "

Most of the dreams, however, were scenes that he could convert directly into his books, such as "A young boy was doused with gasoline and burned to death," or "A tall youth with red hair grins and dances, swinging a sort of bucket."

Another source of material was what Burroughs took from other writers. Bad writers borrow, the saying goes, good writers steal—that is, what they take they make their own. In the margins of passages he liked Burroughs would write GETS, which meant Good Enough to Steal, as in this sentence from "A Country Love Story," by Jean Stafford: "Sometimes she had to push away the dense sleep as if it were a door." That sentence or one very like it would turn up in one of his books.

During the London years, Burroughs produced four books. It did not embarrass him to hear them praised as landmarks marking the end of history they might otherwise deserve to go down in. At the same time, he had to compete with himself, with the albatross of *Naked Lunch*, for there were those who said, "Well, that was a great book, but nothing since has come close."

In 1970, Grove Press brought out *The Job*, a sort of "the-author-explains-himself" book in the form of a long interview with a French admirer, Daniel Odier. The title came from the ten-year-old son of his friends Sanche and Nancy de Gramont, Gabriel, who said, as he was leaving for school, "I have to go to my job." In the book, Burroughs tirelessly rode his various hobbyhorses.

On the prophetic nature of cut-ups: He had written about J. Paul Getty, "It's a bad thing to sue your own father." Three years later Getty's son sued him.

His struggle against control systems: The Mayans had the perfect control system through their calendar, which was a monopoly of the priestly caste, and which told the population what to do on a daily basis. In our society, Burroughs was combating the encroachment of the family and the nation. Children should be raised in communes, away from their parents. The nation was a bankrupt political form: "You draw a line around a piece of ground and say this is a nation. Then you have to have police, customs control, armies, and eventually trouble with the people on the other side of the line."

On his critics: Wright Morris had called *Naked Lunch* a "hemorrhage of the imagination." Burroughs wasn't sure that was a compliment, but in any case had no idea who Wright Morris was. In *Encounter*, George Steiner, expressing his repulsion for Burroughs' explicit sex scenes, said, "In the name of human privacy, enough!" In whose name, Burroughs wondered, was privacy being evoked? In the name of the C.I.A., which secretly subsidized *Encounter*? In the name of the F.B.I., which had bugged Martin Luther King's bedroom? The breakdown of privacy was officially sanctioned at the highest government levels.

On the Beat movement: "I don't associate with it at all, and never have, either with their objectives or their literary style. I have some close personal friends . . . but we're not doing at all the same thing, either in writing or in outlook." Burroughs owed a lot to his reputation as a Beat chieftain, but preferred to position himself as the Lone Gunman.

His misogyny, fueled by Brion Gysin, had not mellowed with the years: "In the words of one of the great misogynists, plain Mr. Jones in Joseph Conrad's *Victory*, 'Women are a perfect curse.' I think they were a basic mistake and the whole dualistic universe evolved from this error.

"American women are possibly one of the worst expressions of the female sex because they've been allowed to go further. . . . America is a matriarchal, white supremacist country. There seems to be a definite link between matriarchy and white supremacy."

All in all, it was a stimulating performance, by turns brilliant and cranky, mundane and apocalyptic. *The Job* to be done, of course, was the elimination of traditional thought patterns and the creation of some new way of living.

Also first published in 1970, *The Last Words of Dutch Schultz* was written in the form of a screenplay. In October 1935 in Newark's Palace Chop House, Arthur Flegenheimer, alias Dutch Schultz, then considered New York's leading gangster, was gunned down by three rival mobsters. He survived for two days, in a guarded hospital room, where a police stenographer at his bedside took down his stream-of-consciousness last words, a fevered rumination mixing the present and the past, which seemed to Burroughs a ready-made cut-up.

Burroughs reconstructed the spirit of the time, the gang wars, the double-crosses, the continuously threatened lives of the mob bosses. He used many of the strange phrases taken down by the stenographers, which were remarkably like his own cut-up compositions:

"Come on, open the soap duckets."

"The chimney sweeps take to the sword."

"A boy has never wept or dashed a thousand Kim."

"My gilt-edge stuff and those dirty rats have tuned in."

Publishers Weekly described the book as "a gruesome, hallucinatory exposition . . . an empirical brevity keeps the poetry of brutality from becoming unendurably tiresome."

Published by Grove in 1971, *The Wild Boys* was a turning point for Burroughs, in that it was based on new material, and in that it returned to straight narrative after the lengthy period of experimentation with cut-ups. The wild boys were homosexual warrior packs, originating in Marrakesh in 1969, who had spread all over the world, setting up their own tribal society, and speaking their own language. The first ones were born of woman and removed to communes after birth so that they never saw a woman's face or heard a woman's voice. When they grew up they devised a method of cloning, so that they became self-generating. They took drugs, they were violent, and they spent an immoderate amount of time having sex. It was Burroughs' Utopian vision of an alternative society, and, like all his writing, a search for a way to escape social conditioning, time, and his own body.

One of Burroughs' sources for *The Wild Boys* was a science-fiction work by Poul Anderson called *The Twilight World*. The way he adapted other writers' materials can be seen in the following example:

Twilight World: "The boy was small for his fourteen years, lean and ragged. Under ruffled brown hair his face was thin, straight-lined and delicately cut, but the huge blue eyes were vacant."

Wild Boys: "A dead leaf caught in Audrey's ruffled brown hair."

Twilight World: "The point of origin was named as St. Louis, Missouri, and the date was just prior to that recorded for the outbreak of the final war."

Wild Boys: "The old broken point of origin, St. Louis, Missouri."

The Wild Boys also saw the introduction of Audrey Carsons, a largely autobiographical character. Gone is the hard-boiled, cynical authorial voice of *Naked Lunch*, the narrator William Lee. He has been replaced by a self-conscious boy, a misfit, who is painfully aware of being unwholesome, and who will drag his unwholesomeness through most of Burroughs' next books.

On the theory that "what is rejected in the final typescript is often as good or better than what goes in," Burroughs took the leftover material from *Wild Boys* and turned it into another novel called *Port of Saints*, which might also be called *The Further Adventures of the Wild Boys*, or *Wild Boys Redux*. This time the wild boys have time-traveled back to 1845, and are acting as advisers to black guerrillas in the West Indies, who are fighting the combined colonial powers of England and Portugal. They triumph thanks to the invention of an advanced grenade. All the leftover boys are on hand, up to their old tricks—Karate Boys, Circus Boys, Elephant Boys, Shaman Boys, Music Boys, Green Boys, and Snake Boys. Sex has replaced drugs as the form of addiction. The Wild Boys will learn that "sex is power," that ejaculation is a magical phenomenon charged with multiple meanings. They will learn to conceive plans at the moment of orgasm, enhancing their chance of success.

Port of Saints jumps all over the place in what appears to be a series of randomly connected scenes. A man named Kelly goes to see the American consul to recover his dead brother's passport. Then we are in Los Alamos, "your old radioactive alma mater." Then Burroughs' room on Duke Street extends and opens at the sides and he is in Mexico. His lawyer, Bernabé Jurado, makes an appearance.

With the reappearance of Audrey Carsons, Burroughs introduces autobiographical reminiscing. He recalls Harbor Beach, where as a boy he spent the summers with his parents: "A cold clear day, wind from the lake. I had walked on to the railroad bridge to fish in the deep pool underneath it. Too cold to sit still, I gave up the idea of fishing and wound my line back onto a spool which I wrapped in oilcloth and shoved into my hip pocket."

Audrey Carsons "already possessed the writer's self-knowledge and self-disgust, and the God-guilt all writers feel in creation." Audrey dreamed of adventure. No one wanted him anywhere. What he hoped most of all was to escape from his tainted flesh through some heroic act.

A key scene from Burroughs' childhood, when the Los Alamos school director, Mr. Connell, came to see him in St. Louis, is reenacted and embroidered upon. His parents are out, and Jerry (another alter ego) is sitting in the living room with the director, feeling very ill at ease. The director suddenly says, "I'd like to see you stripped, Jerry." In what follows, Burroughs reproduces the actual incident of Connell's watching him strip, during which he experiences an embarrassing erection, but takes it further by having Connell remark, "Your little pecker is getting hard." To which Burroughs/Jerry replies, "Well, uh, I touch it sometimes . . ." The actual scene, which is more ambiguous since Connell contents himself with watching the boy strip, is changed in Burroughs' imagination into an overt seduction, when Connell, "with caressing fingers touches the crown of Jerry's cock. . . . As his fingers touch Jerry feels the wet dream in his tight nuts gasping head back he goes off."

Writing in *The New Yorker*, John Updike said that "*Port of Saints* is claptrap, but since it is murderous claptrap we feel we owe it some respect. We would like to dismiss this book but cannot, quite. A weird wit and integrity beyond corruption shine through its savage workings, and a genuine personal melancholy. The net effect Burroughs achieves is to convince us that he has seen and done things sad beyond description." The bard of the mundane had acknowledged the poet of extreme experience.

In 1973, *Exterminator!* was published by Viking, Burroughs having left Grove Press with his editor, Richard Seaver. A collection of short pieces, many of them previously published in magazines, *Exterminator!* was somewhat disingenuously presented as a novel.

In one of the pieces, "The Discipline of DE" (Do Easy), which had to do with the right technique for doing everything correctly, Burroughs' puritan WASP background came out of the closet. His thesis was that carelessness in small things would be repeated in large ones. In small daily occurrences lay the potential for disaster. Therefore, there was a correct technique for every activity: "Guide a dustpan lightly to the floor as if you were landing a plane." "Don't pull or tug at a zipper. Guide the little metal teeth smoothly along feeling the sinuous ripple of cloth and flexible metal." "Replacing the cap on a tube of toothpaste . . . let the very tips of your fingers protrude beyond the cap contacting the end of the tube, guiding the cap into place." "If you throw a match at a wastebasket and miss get right up and put that match in the wastebasket."

Had he continued in this vein, Burroughs could have made a reputation for himself in the self-improvement field. What he was saying, and felt deeply, was that spilling something or breaking something was not just a moment of clumsiness but a symptom of a larger disorder. "Who or what," Burroughs asked, "was this opponent that makes you spill drop and fumble slip and fall?" Groddeck had called it the IT, a built-in self-destructive mechanism. Hubbard called it the Reactive Mind. Burroughs had suffered its tragic consequence when the gun he had aimed at a glass had fired low. He now applied great care to every small task. DE, he believed, was helpful in all areas of life. What were illness and disability but questions of neglect? Wyatt Earp had been a practitioner of DE when he had said: "It's not the first shot that counts. It's the first shot that hits. Point is to draw aim and fire and deliver the slug an inch from the belt buckle."

Still sensitive about reviews, Burroughs nursed his resentment of the hired scribes who dismissed his work. One in particular he came to detest, because although he had an obvious aversion to his books, he repeatedly insisted on reviewing them, until it got to be like a vendetta. This was Anatole Broyard of *The New York Times*, who reviewed *Exterminator!* on August 23, 1973. Since Burroughs was "the grand guru of the fictive put-on," Broyard said, he would search his soul "for telltale signs of archaic preconceptions, uptightness, or heterosexual chauvinism. . . . every word in *Exterminator!* must be given the benefit of the doubt, lest I fall into the dread solecism of mistaking what Mr. Burroughs seems to be doing for what he is *really* up to. . . . Mr. Burroughs is such a portentous figure by now that it's one Establishment attacking another, a bit like two middle-aged businessmen wrestling on the floor of the Century Club."

Broyard found the book to be "a stale replay of *Dr. Strangelove*." It was too bad that Burroughs had not included from his last book the last words of Dutch Schultz, which "would have introduced an all-too-invidious comparison with his own deteriorating prose style." Referring to the final episode in *Exterminator!* which was called "Cold Lost Marbles," Broyard noted an air of sincerity in the last lines, adding, "I hope it consoles him for losing his marbles." Burroughs dearly wanted to shoot it out with Broyard at twenty paces with .45s, but a duel between an author and a reviewer was hopelessly one-sided, in that only the reviewer was armed. What, Burroughs wondered, if food critics were as devoid of consensual criteria as book critics? What if one Michelin inspector said of a restaurant, "Food superlative, service impeccable, kitchen spotless," while another Michelin inspector said of the same restaurant, "food abominable, service atrocious, kitchen filthy." He wondered whether there was any way a writer could settle a score with a reviewer.

· EIGHTEEN ·

NEW YORK

1974–1976

Burroughs returned to New York in February 1974, at about the time of his sixtieth birthday, to take up his teaching duties at City College. Except for visits, he had been living out of the country for more than twenty-four years. He was glad to be back in post-sixties America, a country which he felt owed something of its evolution to the writing and lifestyle of himself and his friends, particularly among the young people. One of these young people was about to enter his life, ostensibly as a secretary, but in fact, over the years, as much more. Being the secretary of an important writer sounds glamorous, but is often drudgery. Alan Ansen complained that when he worked for Auden, all he did was make travel arrangements. Alan Searle had to put up with Somerset Maugham's cross moods and remarks about his laziness and stupidity.

For James Grauerholz, a twenty-one-year-old from Coffeyville, Kansas, meeting Burroughs was the turning point of his life. It was also a turning point for Burroughs, who at last found someone willing to devote himself to managing his life, in much the same way that an impresario manages an opera singer. James became that impresario, that manager, that partner, as in partner of a law firm. His life became so intertwined with Burroughs' that he could say what Burroughs was about to say before he said it, as though there had been a role reversal between the ventriloquist and his dummy.

James came from two families of early Kansas settlers, the Paulks and the Grauerholzes. His mother, Selda, and his father, Alvin, were the first in their respective families to attend college, and met at the University of Kansas. Alvin became a lawyer and politician in Coffeyville, where James was born in 1952. His parents did not get along, and James grew up unhappy and alienated from his peers. He became so withdrawn that when he was ten his father sent him to the Menninger Clinic in Topeka for evaluation. After a five-day battery of tests, the diagnosis was that he was a gifted child, but disassociated, with suicidal tendencies. The following year, he was sent to the Spofford Home for emotionally disturbed children in Kansas City. There he saw that he was not alone. The other children were also "cases." He also realized that he was homosexual, which caused him no anguish beyond the anguish of frustration, although for the moment he concealed it.

Back in Coffeyville in 1967, he gravitated toward the offbeat and the antisocial. The counterculture was in full bloom, offering alternatives to conventional behavior. James read *Howl* and *On the Road* and *Naked Lunch*. He sniffed glue, ate nutmeg and morning glory seeds, and took LSD. He was a child of his time.

James arrived at the University of Kansas in Lawrence in the fall of 1969, the year of Woodstock. Two years before that had occurred the summer of love in Haight-Ashbury. Slowly, the style and substance of those events filtered into the heartland. James dropped acid about twenty times but did not join any of the revolutionary groups that were forming on campus. He felt disdain for the self-styled revolutionaries who read Régis Debray and the thoughts of Chairman Mao. He was majoring in Oriental philosophy, writing poetry, and playing guitar in a band.

James wrote Allen Ginsberg, who replied with a request for a photograph. James sent him one—short flaxen hair, long, narrow, high-browed face, blue eyes behind thick glasses, a thoughtful, almost valedictorian expression, a large mouth, and a sallow complexion. Allen wrote James to call him if he ever came to New York. James also wrote Burroughs in London, wanting to write an article about his early years. "Must say no to early years article," Burroughs replied. ". . . In any case writers don't really have biographies unless they are Hemingways whose work suffered from his determination to act out the least interesting aspects of his writing. Mostly my life has been solitary and uneventful except in an inner direction."

In May 1973, having dropped out of school, James drove from Kansas City straight to the Lower East Side of Manhattan, and took a room in a fleabag, the Valencia Hotel. As he walked down St. Mark's Place, an old bum called out, "Hey, you young Beatnik, got a quarter?" That was exactly James's fantasy, that he was a young Beatnik following in the footsteps of Ginsberg and Kerouac and Burroughs, and here it was confirmed as soon as he hit the city streets, which was worth a quarter. He went to see Allen, who was on his way to a radio interview at WBAI, and asked him to come along. "Here I am," thought James, "the cute new boy at Allen's side." But when Allen tried to get him into bed he resisted. Allen was giving him a meditation lesson and said, "It's more comfortable if you open the buttons of your jeans."

James went back to Lawrence, but in the fall of 1973 he moved to Kansas City and took a job running the machines that develop rolls of film. It was total drudgery, watching thousands upon thousands of pimply-faced high school graduates, coming by on belts through the bath and the dryer, in different sizes, eight by ten, five by seven, and wallet-sized. He worked until one in the morning, and to stay awake, he would wonder what was going on in the minds behind the faces. He had a room near the Club Royale, a country-western strip joint with a big flashing neon sign. As he lay in bed, listening to the drunk and raucous crowd pour out of the Royale, while the neon sign lit up his wall with a flickering pattern, he had the same train of thought night after night—that he must somehow get to New York. And yet he was frightened by his grandfather's stories that it was a place where people were killed for no reason. Where would he find a job? How would he get by? He began to sob, overcome by the fear of life, then suddenly he stopped, opened his eyes, looked at the ceiling, and said to himself, "Anything is better than this." That was the beginning of courage, the thought that "I'm going to New York, and the worst that can happen to me is that I'll die there."

His father staked him to $800, and cosigned a loan on a Volkswagen van, and James made his move in February 1974. He loaded his guitar and stereo and books in the van and drove to Pineapple Street in Brooklyn Heights, where a friend put him up. He called Allen, who said, "You're in luck, Burroughs just arrived in New York. He's here all spring, teaching at City College, and he needs a secretary, so here's his number . . . call him." A kid out of nowhere meeting his heroes, James thought.

Burroughs invited James to the loft he was subletting at 452 Broadway. James knocked on a big metal door, and there he stood, having just turned sixty—a bit stooped, the hair thinning and graying, and those searching gray-blue eyes, that uneffusively courteous manner—a system of defense, thought James, like someone parachuted behind enemy lines who must escape detection. They drank Dewar's and soda, and Burroughs talked about the class he had just started teaching. He was getting very little feedback from his students. They seemed to be in a state of total apathy. He wondered why some of them had signed up for the class, since they sat through it reading comic books. He felt that he was revealing secrets to an unreceptive audience, like a man giving away hundred-dollar bills that no one wanted. He would have liked to put all of them off the career of writing. "Be a plumber instead!" he felt like shouting, and keep your fucking king-size refrigerators full of Vienna sausage and Malvern spring water. Or be a proctologist; you won't have to worry that next year there'll be a shortage of assholes.

They went out to dinner to a place in Little Italy, with gold-specked mirrors and Formica tables, ordering more drinks and getting sloshed. A cold wind was blowing down Broadway as they walked back to the loft, and Burroughs said, "The wind that blew between the worlds it cut him like a knife," a line from Rudyard Kipling. In the loft, a drunken Burroughs reached out and put his hand on James and asked him to stay the night. Even though James was gay, he was completely lacking in experience, and he said very gently, "Mr. Burroughs, I just moved to New York two days ago, and I just met you, and I have no objection in principle to what you're talking about, but right now it's just too much, I'm on sensory overload . . . I can't do it."

A few days later James returned, and they got drunk together, and this time when Burroughs made a pass he was not rejected. James was not physically attracted to him, he had no predilection for older men, but he admired him deeply, and if that was what he wanted he would give it to him. It wasn't, "Hey, I've got a handle on this old geezer," it was more like an offering.

Burroughs asked James to move in with him and work as his secretary. James also had a part-time job at the Gotham Book Mart. It was a tribute to James's natural gift for diplomacy that he was able quite quickly to make the transition from lover to friend. The sex was awkward, and it seemed to James that Burroughs was deeply repressed and could only overcome his innate primness when drunk. He was uncomfortable with sex, and it was rarely satisfactory.

Burroughs and James were lovers for only a few weeks, for when James started working at the Gotham in March he met a twenty-year-old boy named Danny Bloom (name changed), with large brown eyes and long curly hair and a "lost waif" look. Bloom felt that James was using his connection with Burroughs as a bait to attract young men he was interested in, but he did admire Burroughs, and wanted to meet him, and came to lunch. Burroughs was barely polite, and gave off strong jealousy vibrations. "Don't bring him around again," he told James. But James started staying over with Bloom, and there was a difficult transitional phase, when Burroughs was sulking and slamming doors and having little outbursts. To Burroughs, it was Ian Sommerville and Alan Watson all over again— another case of alienation of affection. No sooner did he find an *amigo* than he was stolen away.

James had inherited from his lawyer-politician father a concept of service, and he saw that if he could get over this awkward time he could continue to serve Burroughs. Finally James confronted him, saying: "William, we can't go on being lovers and living together—we just can't. But if you'll just get over this, we can be great friends. I love you with all my heart and we can be a really powerful partnership."

And so it was that Burroughs realized that James was more valuable as a secretary than as a lover and that he must not be jealous of his attachments to young men his own age, and that on those terms the partnership could thrive. For Burroughs it was a sea change. He had left the Old World and the influence of Brion Gysin, who believed that success depended on appeasing the gods. He had arrived in the New World, and through the good offices of Allen Ginsberg, who was forever fine-tuning the lives of his friends, he had been put in touch with one of its young denizens, a Kansas boy whose great-grandfather had run the Cherokee Strip, and who, despite his adoption of the counterculture lifestyle, retained the old midwestern values. Someone was dropped into his life who was too young to have formed the notion that success and failure depended on favorable or unfavorable conspiracies; who believed in the marketplace rather than in magic; who did not think that being unintelligible was the necessary path to wisdom; and who, despite his admiration for Burroughs' dark vision, was basically positive and constructive. James believed in improvement, he had a "can-do" attitude. He carried with him his midwestern heritage of common sense and the value of hard work and a good reputation.

Although he did not yet know it, James was indispensable to Burroughs. For even though he was off hard drugs, Burroughs still had the junky mentality of sitting and staring at his big toe and never wanting anything; if you gave him a bottle of vodka and some grass and some frozen peas and a steak, he was happy, or at least in a state of approximate equilibrium. The one thing he did was write. So he badly needed someone to take care of the nuts and bolts of life. Someone to bring people around, for on his own Burroughs would rarely make the effort; someone to arrange his schedule, to get his career moving again; someone to be an energy source, someone to contribute enthusiasm.

All these things James could do, and did. When in school he had read the history of royal courts, he had not seen himself as the king but as the power behind the throne. And now he came to believe that he could form and shape and elevate this great person into a counterculture Louis XIV; and of course if Burroughs was Louis XIV, James would be Richelieu, standing behind the king and whispering in the king's ear. Burroughs was happy to let James do it, for it was beneficial to both of them. There was a curious dynamic at work when you delegated authority, a curious increase in power.

For James too it was a sea change, for he was with great suddenness thrust into the New York art scene of the seventies, with its odd acceptance rites and pecking order. He had to keep a rein on himself so as not to seem too much the wide-eyed country boy. A few days after his arrival he drove Allen Ginsberg to a show at the Whitney Museum—"Frank O'Hara, a Poet Among Painters." Allen was off mingling, and James was left to himself, the new kid in town, wearing a red flannel shirt and sneakers, thrown into the cultural pond. A fiftyish queen introduced himself as Herbert Machiz and asked, "Well, where have you been all my life?" "In Kansas," James straightforwardly replied, which had Machiz breathless with laughter—he thought it was a *bon mot.*

He had to work at not being goggle-eyed when he met famous people, as when Allen brought Yoko Ono over to meet Burroughs. One February morning he slogged through the snow with Michael Balog, the painter whose loft Burroughs was subletting, to visit Robert Rauschenberg, who had a place on Lafayette and Great Jones. The smell of breakfast was in the air, and Cy Twombley was there, and a big limo waited outside, ready to leave for Philadelphia for the opening of Twombley's retrospective. No one paid any attention to James, who felt like a Visigoth among the Romans. So he left, but then decided to go back and just hang out and soak up the scene. And when he returned, Rauschenberg said: "Is that what you do? You just come and go?" Feeling humiliated, and realizing that even though he had entrée into a world of fame and talent, acceptance was not automatic, James said, "No, I work for William Burroughs." He needed Burroughs to validate him.

His parents, in the meantime, didn't know what to think. What was he up to in New York, and who was this writer he was mixed up with? His father had a rich friend he wanted James to meet, but James wrote back: "I have much better friends than he, who though not as RICH are much more wealthy. . . . Don't write me any more letters designed (intentionally or unintentionally) to try and make me feel guilty or demand that I be more dependent."

Although he was not capable of being the traditional "good son" to his parents, James's filial feelings were transferred to Burroughs, now that the brief "lover" episode had passed. James genuinely wanted to be the "good son" to Burroughs, who was completely nonjudgmental and who approved of the one thing his parents so feared—his homosexuality.

When Billy turned up in March, James immediately understood that the father-son relationship was cursed, and that by comparison he was and always would be the "good son." Billy was a drain on his father, while James was a help. James got things done, while Billy frittered his life away. James was a provider, while Billy was a depleter, always asking for handouts.

James could see how awkward it was between father and son, how guarded their conversation was, how difficult it was for them to show affection. By any objective standard, he thought, Burroughs as a father was just an abject miserable failure. First of all he had killed the boy's mother, and then he had been unable to take charge of the boy. One part of James wanted to say, "This is utterly reprehensible," but another part of him said, "Well, this is just how it is—some relationships are doomed."

James also saw that Billy's manner of responding to his father was based on a misconception. Billy, wanting to be like his father so that his father would approve of him, tried to show him that he was a Beatnik, too. But the image he had of his father was inaccurate. Burroughs, for all his lapses, was a careful, tidy man, who believed in keeping his passport in his inside jacket pocket, and in not opening his mouth at the wrong time, whereas Billy was careless and garrulous, which did not please his father at all.

Brimming over with goodwill, James wanted to be best friends with Billy, even though he looked like a hobo. He went along when Billy was looking for some loft on the Bowerey where a girl he used to know lived, and they walked down Canal and up the Bowery in this fruitless search, while Billy raved about finding this girl, and he came across to James as manic and disconnected and impractical.

So James started seeing himself as the anti-Billy. Billy was trying to reach his father on a symbolic level by saying, "I can be just as irresponsible as you," which was a mistake, while James, by showing himself to be practical and responsible, was much closer to what Burroughs wanted.

Burroughs began to think of his return to New York as a rebirth. The more he saw of James, the more he thought of the old song: "He is the best there is, I can use him in my biz." The teaching gig had been a lesson in never again. You were giving out all this energy and nothing was coming back. His best student wasn't even enrolled but kept showing up at lectures. A frail-looking, small-boned, slightly pixieish twenty-six-year-old, Stewart Meyer had discovered his writer's vocation under the wheels of a truck, which had come within inches of squashing his head. When he got out of the hospital, he said to himself, "Fuck this shit, I'm going to be a writer." When he read Burroughs, he saw the product of a highly evolved criminal mind, autonomous and willing to be wrong. Here was someone who would do his own thinking no matter what the price. Here was a mind that came along every hundred years. Here was a conservative anarchist, who believed along with Emerson that the stronger the state the weaker the individual. When he heard that Burroughs was teaching, he went up there and introduced himself. He agreed with everything Burroughs said so eagerly that Burroughs got annoyed and muttered, "What do you think, I got some kind of answers or something?" Stewart Meyer called Burroughs "the doctor," and started the habit of taking pages to the doctor. Nobody could teach you to write, but proximity to a master sure as shit didn't hurt. Stewart Meyer became a member of a small band, somewhat akin to Sir Arthur Conan Doyle's Baker Street Irregulars, which might be called the Unconditional Burroughsians.

When the course was over in May, Burroughs had an offer to teach a semester at the University of Buffalo for $15,000, but he didn't think he could work with the head of the English Department, the critic Leslie Fiedler, whom he sized up as a bit of a martinet. In any case, thanks to James, he now had an alternative to teaching, which was readings. Why be pinned down in an awful place like Buffalo when you could be giving readings at $1,000 a crack in sunnier climes?

Burroughs had come to New York to test the waters and had found them temperate. Now that he had James and a burgeoning career in readings, he decided to stay. A quick trip to London was required to close down his Duke Street flat and get rid of Johnny Brady, who proved to be a bit of a headache. Every day he called Anthony Balch for money to keep him alive. He said he was an alcoholic and could not live without booze. Balch kept giving him small sums until the amount added up to 100 pounds. Then he gave him ten pounds to put an ad in *The Times* asking for a position with a suitable gentleman of means, but the ad never appeared. Then, when he came around to ask for two weeks' rent in advance for a room, Balch told him he would pay his fortnight's rent if he could produce a letter of employment. Alternatively, he would buy him an airplane ticket back to Ireland. Balch felt sorry for him, but some people you just couldn't help. Burroughs had also been sending Johnny money, but decided that enough was enough, and wrote him a stern letter, which said: "Hope you can get yourself organized and get a job. Keep in touch."

No more was heard from John Brady, though Burroughs did get a rather touching letter from his other Dilly boy, John Culverwell, who was in Stoke-on-Trent, Staffordshire: "Would you like to see me again, Bill? Mind you, I've changed, I'm more settled in my ways now—thank goodness. . . . Bill, I wish you would send me a ticket so I could come to you even if it was for just a few weeks. We could have a lovely time together, Bill, I know it. Wouldn't it be good, Bill, you and I together again? I learned a lot from the last time, Bill, I learned the true value of a real friend. I'm just keeping my fingers crossed now, Bill."

James did not start out with any specific strategy on the readings, although he knew in his heart that Burroughs must go over the heads of the critics and straight to the people. When the news got out that he was back in New York, this mythical figure that few had ever seen, invitations began to come in. In April, through John Giorno, he was asked to read at St. Mark's Church in the village, which had a well-attended poetry program. It happened that Brion Gysin was in New York at the time, and he clearly wanted to read with Burroughs, but Giorno did not invite him, so that the reading became a symbolic changing of the guard. Brion was excluded. He was part of the Old World setup that had come to an end. The New World setup was based on Burroughs' reaching out to his fans and finding new fans through the readings, under the benevolent guidance of John Giorno and James Grauerholz. Burroughs was deeply touched when after the first reading James told him, "I was so proud of you."

Burroughs was a natural performer, with a natural presence. He had, thought Giorno, the ability to project an inner power and grab the audience's heart. He also made the audience laugh, with the dry delivery of his outlandish routines. James quickly realized that he must take a show-biz approach. People expected a mysterious, rather awesome figure, and you didn't want to give them a toothless Dracula. Every detail of the performance had to be worked out, the sound and the lighting, the table at which to read, the way he dressed. It had to be professional and theatrical, a performance and not a lecture.

James found a lecture bureau, New Line Presentations, which took a 30 percent commission but guaranteed a minimum of $850. Many of the readings he arranged himself when colleges started asking for Burroughs. He was invited to conservative establishments like Notre Dame by the student union or someone in the English Department who liked his work. The Notre Dame faculty might frown on the event, but could not prevent it. Although he had never been overtly political, Burroughs came across as a living symbol of rebelliousness that many college students could identify with. He had maintained his visionary/anarchist position through all the cultural changes of the fifties, sixties, and seventies, and was now becoming, thanks to age and consistency, the Grand Old Man of the counterculture.

After the isolation of London, the readings energized and rejuvenated him. Once again, he walked with a spring in his step. He took great pains over his performances, rehearsing and timing them to the second, and he took pleasure in the audience response. Those great waves of appreciation were as invigorating and beneficial as a massage. He was carrying his words across the country, sometimes into the very citadels of his foes, and there was always a warm welcome and a cluster of admirers. As he wrote a friend, "I have become a traveling performer, giving readings all over the USA." Burroughs later estimated that between 1974 and 1984 he had done 150 readings, at an average fee of $500, for a total income of $75,000. It was ironic, because for years, Burroughs had said, "I don't see any point in people reading their work." And now people were coming up to him and saying they'd never really understood his work until they'd heard him read it.

James was both manager and bodyguard, dealing with hecklers and unreliable promoters. In Washington, D.C., a punk-rock singer known as DOG started screaming "Fuck William Burroughs" and had to be led away. When a promoter in San Francisco canceled a reading, owing James $750, James called him and was told that he couldn't get blood from a stone. "What makes you think you are made of stone?" James asked.

In Washington in 1975, Burroughs and Allen Ginsberg read at the Corcoran Gallery and stayed with a famous Washington hostess, Amy Huntington Block. She gave a dinner for forty in their honor, to which important government figures came, including Supreme Court justices and members of the Cabinet. It was a vindication of sorts for Burroughs the pariah, who had trouble just getting through customs in his own country, to be introduced to these men. "Mr. Burroughs, I would like to present Supreme Court Justice Potter Stewart." Well, he thought, if someone is presented to me, it means I'm the one. He looked around the table at the men from the State Department and the Pentagon, who had told him they had read his books, and thought, "My moles, all my moles."

Burroughs often read on programs with other writers. At New York University in 1981 he read with that other master of the macabre, Stephen King, and at Notre Dame in 1977 he read with Tennessee Williams. He often read with John Giorno as a warm-up act. In Grand Forks, North

Dakota, in 1977, he read with Eudora Welty, LeRoi Jones, Ring Lardner, Jr., and John Ashbery. After the reading, they all went to the hotel cocktail lounge, where a stage hypnotist called for volunteers from the audience. Ashbery, winner of many poetry prizes and a painfully reticent man, was in a congenial mood that night, chatting with James, and they both got up on the tiny stage with two other volunteers. The hypnotist told them they were the Beatles—Ashbery was John Lennon and James was Ringo. When he played the song "She Loves You," James started beating the air with imaginary drumsticks, as Ashbery pranced around, playing air guitar. Then the hypnotist told them they were strippers and gave them all women's names—Ashbery was "Bubbles." He put on some Minsky music and to James's surprise, the normally prim Ashbery started undressing. He took off his jacket and tie, he unbuttoned his shirt and took that off, as he smiled seductively and fluttered his eyelashes, and he would have taken it all off, thought James, had not the hypnotist stopped him.

After the strip, the hypnotist gave each volunteer a posthypnotic command—something to say and do when the show was over. James was told to bark like a dog when he heard the cue "Has anyone seen my dog Rover?" Just as the show was ending, Burroughs arrived in the cocktail lounge with Ring Lardner, Jr., author of M*A*S*H, and called James over to introduce him. At that moment the hypnotist said, "Has anyone seen my dog Rover?" and James shook Ring Lardner's hand and said, "Arf-arf." Lardner quickly departed.

The constant traveling placed a strain on James's relationship with Danny Bloom. When James was back in New York he and Danny fell to bickering. One night over dinner at Phoebe's on the Bowery, they started arguing about who was a better friend to Burroughs. "I've been a better friend to William than you, man, and don't you ever—ever, man—insult my integrity," Danny said. So saying, he swept the vodka tonic off the table and into a thousand splinters, and stalked off. The waitress came over to clean up the mess and said, "Violent, huh?"

It seemed that whatever they chose to talk about turned bitter. Once it was conceptual art. "You're full of shit," Danny said, "to have such dogmatic opinions about conceptual art which you know absolutely nothing about."

"Whaddya mean?" James said. "I can name ten conceptual artists right this minute."

"That's it, names, you're so hung up on names and celebrities, but what's their work about, huh?"

"It's about nothing, goddammit," James said.

Then Danny, who had a job waiting tables, would say, as if to cap the argument, "I *work* for a living," meaning that being Burroughs' secretary was not work.

By May of 1974, Burroughs had moved to a loft at 77 Franklin Street, up three steep flights of stairs. It was spacious but needed work, and one of the first jobs Burroughs had done was to ask his painter-carpenter friend David Prentice to build him an orgone box. Prentice made a luxury model, with rabbit fur draped over the iron lining, which Burroughs sat in contentedly almost every day. "Maybe I'm as crazy as Reich was," he said, "but I do think there is something here." He had tried a great many methods in his search for a clear starting point, but always with a grain of salt, among them psychoanalysis, Scientology, est, group meditation, Mind Dimension, General Semantics, acupuncture, the Alexander method, and out-of-the-body experience. In all cases, the words of his jujitsu master came back: "If your trick no work you better run." He had not found *the* answer but many answers. His current psychic interest was Carlos Castañeda and *The Teachings of Don Juan*. There *was*, he devoutly believed, a world of magical will and intention. Nothing happened unless someone willed it to happen. If someone fell down the stairs or ran his car into a tree, on some level he intended to do just that. If he was unable to contact the level of intention he said it was just an accident, from which there could be derived the definition of an "accident": an event over which one has no conscious control. In his own case, the death of his wife was to the best of his conscious knowledge an accident, but on some other level, which he still did not fully understand, it was intended.

From the attention he was getting, from the solicitations, from all the people who wanted a piece of him, including the practical jokers, it was clear that Burroughs had become a certified public figure, a celebrity, just by returning to his own country. He was ambivalent about the attention, for he felt that his celebrity, or notoriety, was based on an image that had nothing to do with him, an image arbitrarily assigned. But at the same time he was pleased and wrote Alan Ansen: "America holding up well, that is better than most other places. I shock the hairless cubs by saying America is now the freest country in the world."

America was holding up, and he was holding up, but across the pond, two of his close friends were in a bad way. Something was very wrong with Anthony Balch. None of the doctors he went to were able to diagnose the nature of his illness. But he knew he was sick, and the anxiety was such that he had a nervous breakdown. It would be some time before the doctors discovered that he had an inoperable cancer of the stomach.

Burroughs thought of him in better days, when at parties he did his little number: "I'm going to do the impossible" (and he juggled three oranges), "the immoral" (he swallowed two codeine pills), "and the illegal" (he burned a pound note). And now one had to add: the inoperable. Balch would die in 1980.

And then, in December 1974, Brion Gysin was operated on for a cancer of the colon at the Royal Free Hospital in Hempstead. He had known for some time that something was wrong, ever since the day in Tangier when he had gone to lunch at the home of those Old Mountain social climbers Sanche and Nancy de Gramont. After lunch, he was sitting on a couch covered in pale blue linen, having coffee, and when he got up, a round bloodstain the size of a saucer had soaked through the linen. But it was months before Brion could be persuaded to seek medical help, and by that time he had to have a colostomy. "Well, they got me, they really got me," Brion wrote Burroughs. "Every foolish word I ever said about my interest in pain has been paid out several thousand-fold."

In February 1975, upon hearing that he would have to undergo three more operations, Brion tried to kill himself. Tearing off his bandages, he was about to smash the window of his hospital room with a chair so he could jump out, when he caught a glimpse of himself in the mirror and decided that he needed towels to protect his face from the jagged glass. During that moment of delay a nurse who had befriended him came in and stopped him.

After the operation, Brion wrote Burroughs: "I am now but a Gruyère cheese, a man full of holes weighing about 120 pounds. . . . They took out my asshole and destroyed what sex impulses I had left after the cobalt bomb which destroyed all tissues to the cellular level. I had three operations in three weeks and there ain't much left of Brion. They tell me I'll get used to a sack of shit on my knees. I've decided to come back and finish my life's work. Like the old Chinese painter I intend to work on to the point where I can bow three times and disappear into my picture." There was however a bright side: The National Health would pay his bill, which ran into the thousands of pounds.

So vain of his appearance, Brion now had to face life with a bag attached to his middle. Who would ever want him sexually again, he wondered. He felt like a rotten old pumpkin. His toilette to keep fresh and dainty took up an hour or two a day. By mid-April of 1975 he was back in Paris, spinning down into the depths of depression and then struggling back up for air. His paranoia was still functioning, and he worried that people had dropped him since his operation. Why wasn't Burroughs keeping him abreast? Was it true that John Giorno was knocking him with the New York galleries? "Am I such a shit?" he asked Burroughs.

At the end of June, he had a show at the Germain Gallery. He was pleased at the turnout. At least two hundred people showed up for the *vernissage*. But all they talked about was where they were going for the summer, and the next day they went. No sales were rung up. "When we come back," they said.

Burroughs at the start of 1975 was also experiencing difficulties, although they were literary rather than medical. Perhaps as a result of his outside activities, his teaching job and his readings, his creativity had suffered; he felt depleted. To call it by its name he had a severe writer's block, resulting in a paralyzing depression. The act of writing had become almost unendurable. He dreamed that Venusian doctors were torturing him by burning his hands and breaking his fingers. And this just at the time when he was starting on a new novel called *Cities of the Red Night*.

The solution to Burroughs' block lay in a chance meeting with another Unconditional Burroughsian. Steven Lowe, lean and angular, with lively brown eyes, had recently arrived in New York from Miami, where his father ran a chain of funeral homes and was a member of the Association of Flying Morticians. He had grown up in a funereal atmosphere, where everything was dark and air-conditioned and sealed, and where, from time to time, a hurricane sent the caskets flying.

Steven Lowe had a job writing novels for a Mafia-controlled porn sweatshop. A goon with a cigar who could barely speak English would bring around some illustrations, and Steve would write the plot around them. This too was a result of the breakdown of censorship, that the Mafia, a bunch of Sicilian illiterates, had moved into the book business, competing with "legitimate" porno publishers like Girodias. The Mafia porn people had their own set of rules. You couldn't use the words "Christ" or "God" because the reader would be offended. You couldn't have depressing death scenes, but it was okay to torture women. You could have businessmen chasing cunt, but no drugs could be mentioned. Steve had signed a contract for a book a week at $600 per book, and he never left his loft. He was at it all day long, trying to come up with his 188 pages a week, and it was affecting his health. Then all of a sudden the company went into Chapter Eleven. Who had ever heard of a Mafia bankruptcy?

An ardent Burroughs fan, Steve Lowe knew many details of his life. He knew, for instance, that in 1965 Burroughs had lived in a loft at 210 Centre Street, where there was a sign that said Atomic Machinery. At this point in his life, when the porn outfit had collapsed, he was walking one day past 210 Centre Street when he recognized Burroughs on the opposite sidewalk. The coincidence was too good to pass up, and he went over and introduced himself. Burroughs invited him to Franklin Street, and in the course of their conversation, Steve mentioned his interest in pirates. It turned out that one of the principal themes of *Cities of the Red Night* was an eighteenth-century libertarian colony of gay pirates on the island of Madagascar. It was agreed that Steve would help Burroughs with the pirate research, and that they would be collaborators on the book, and soon Steve was digging up pirate material, and holding daily meetings with Burroughs, and writing great chunks of prose.

Steve Lowe fit right into the Burroughs inner circle, and he and his wife, Bonnie, often invited Burroughs and James to dinner. At one memorable dinner in 1975, the guest of honor was Christopher Isherwood, author of *I Am a Camera*, friend of W. H. Auden, now settled in Santa Monica. Small and dapper, well-mannered and reserved, Isherwood fell into the category of "high homosexual." He told Virginia Woolf stories, in itself a sign of invisible precedence, for there were not many left who could—how when she smoked she made extended sweeps with her cigarette as if holding the rest of the world at arm's length. Allen Ginsberg called to ask if he and Peter Orlovsky could come over, and Steve said there wasn't enough food, but Allen said they'd eaten. When they arrived, they sucked on the bones of two fresh chickens Steve had bought, with the heads and feet still on. As Isherwood was leaving, Allen fell to his knees and kissed his feet, saying, "Master, master." A look of profound distaste crossed Isherwood's face—his English sense of decorum had been offended.

Another dinner Burroughs went to at that time was given in his small apartment in the Dakota by Charles Henri Ford, who was the brother of the actress Ruth Ford and who had written a homosexual novel published by Girodias, called *The Young and the Evil*. Ford had moved to Katmandu, and was going on about an exhibit he had organized called the Katmandu Experience, which featured what looked to Burroughs like sculptures of the sort you might expect in an arts and crafts show in the World Trade Center. On top of that, no liquor was served, and the food was an inedible curry full of splintered chicken bones, which, had he been a dog, would have killed him. Never again. At yet another party he met Janet Flanner, lesbian author of *The New Yorker*'s "Letter from Paris," beak-nosed and white-haired, who was now retired, and deaf as a post, and who kept saying (rather flatteringly, he thought), "Speak up, young man, don't mutter."

His writer's block was momentarily forgotten in a blur of other activities. He had the readings coming up, four of them in Chicago with Allen Ginsberg. Who should turn up at one Chicago reading but his old friend from his exterminator days, Ray Masterson, who was now making stained glass and dealing in antique furniture. Running into the occasional pal of bygone days was a fringe benefit.

In spite of the readings, money was tight, and that April of 1975 Burroughs got the first grant of his life, at age sixty-one, a $4,000 New York State CAPS (Creative Artist Public Service) award. News of the grant provoked an outcry in the *SoHo Weekly News* by Susanna Cuyler, who wondered why the heir to the Burroughs millions was awarded a grant. Burroughs asked her on April 10 to "lay to rest for all time the myth of the Burroughs millions, which has plagued me for many years. One reviewer has even gone so far as to describe me as 'the world's richest ex-junky,' at a time when I had less than $1,000 in the bank. My grandfather, who invented the hydraulic device on which the adding machine is based, like many inventors received a very small share of the company stock; and my father sold the few shares in his possession in the 1920s. My last bequest from the Burroughs estate on the death of my mother in 1970 was the sum of $10,000."

To further supplement his income, Burroughs began writing a column for *Crawdaddy* magazine, which led him into occasional forays in the world of rock 'n' roll. He was an icon of sorts among these young musicians, who had adopted the drug culture of which he was the granddaddy. Several groups derived their name from his writing—"Steely Dan," "Soft Machine," "Naked Lunch."

Although the rock musicians adopted Burroughs as one of their own, he had absolutely no interest in their music and would go to considerable lengths to avoid listening to it. James, who had played guitar in several bands, encouraged meetings between Burroughs and rock musicians (one of whom told him, "You sit on your ass writing—I could be torn to pieces by me fans"), but when they came around, he had to be there to explain who they were and what they were about, like the cardinal whispering in the Pope's ear the name of the next supplicant—"Oh, yes, my dear friend the bishop of Khartoum"—and briefing Burroughs on the appropriate remark: "I understand you use sixty-cycle tones in your music."

In any case, they came around to pay homage, Frank Zappa, the Talking Heads, Chris Stein and Debbie Harry of Blondie, Patti Smith, Iggy Pop, David Bowie, and various members of the Rolling Stones. Burroughs tried to answer their sometimes inane questions, and was flattered by their interest, which kept him current in the rock and punk counterculture of the seventies. When the surly and bovine Lou Reed of the Velvet Underground came by, every word he said was obnoxious. "I'm surrounded by assholes," he asserted at one point. "Even these people with me are assholes." To which Stew Meyer replied, "There are some assholes who give assholes a bad name."

In May 1975, Burroughs had a change of scene when he was invited to lecture at the Naropa Institute in Boulder, Colorado. Naropa was an interesting graft of Tibetan Buddhism on the American counterculture. Its founder, a Buddhist monk named Chögyam Trungpa Rinpoche, was a product of the Tibetan diaspora of the fifties. From Scotland and Canada, Trungpa had moved to Vermont, where he set up a Tibetan Meditation Center. He saw himself as a healer, treating problems of spiritual health. He advocated "crazy wisdom," and "cutting through spiritual materialism." Having recruited the poet Anne Waldman, he moved to Boulder, founded Naropa, and became one of the more prosperous transplanted Buddhist gurus.

Within Naropa, Anne Waldman and Allen Ginsberg founded the Jack Kerouac School of Disembodied Poetics, which became a magnet and forum for counterculture alumni. The veterans of the Beat movement and the Black Mountain School and the San Francisco Renaissance and all the other anti-Establishment literary factions could gather there and lecture and teach and feel at ease. So that when Burroughs and James Grauerholz and Steven Lowe arrived in May of 1975, they found, already in attendance, Allen Ginsberg, who was suffering from a partial paralysis of the face, which made his smile look twisted; Gregory Corso, typecast as the all-licensed fool; the poet Philip Whalen, an ordained Zen monk, Buddha-like in his girth and smooth-headedness and serenity; the Buddhist poet Gary Snyder; and the poet Robert Bly, who one afternoon came by Burroughs' apartment, which had become the center for gatherings, and told the story of how a tribe of Australian aborigines had reacted to their first experience with a battery-operated radio. The first thing they heard was news from Sydney: "Two women were killed this morning and two others were badly burned in a fire that destroyed a roominghouse for the elderly." Disturbed by the plight of these distant people, the aborigines gathered food and blankets to take to the survivors. Only with difficulty were they convinced that there was nothing they could do to help. After that, gradually, they began to lose their ability to react to the human and social needs around their village. "So the medicine man breaks a leg," said Bly, "and they figure, oh well, it's just another broadcast from Sydney."

Burroughs found Naropa congenial, and the teaching was not arduous, but he wondered about Trungpa, the smiling Tibetan with the soft reedy voice and the Oxford accent, whom he called the "Whiskey Lama," after observing him imbibe heroic quantities of alcoholic beverages. On one occasion His Holiness got so drunk he fell down the stairs and suffered a severe concussion. He said it was his karma, which prompted Burroughs to think: O excellent foppery of the world! As if we were fools and drunkards by heavenly compulsion. Trungpa did not appear to be a model of ascetic behavior, with his drinking, his chain-smoking, and his habit of asking his female devotees to become his concubines. His English wife, Diana, was an equestrienne, an expert in dressage. He had a squad of guards, and a car and a driver, and seemed to run his operation along monarchical rather than democratic lines. Was Trungpa simply indoctrinating and fleecing the gullible children of the middle class? Burroughs thought that at the very least Naropa had the merit of bringing together like-minded people who could exchange ideas. He had little interest in Buddhism, and told James one evening after dinner that "in 3,000 years the Buddhists have not come up with the answer to this question: What is the real nature of the Word?"

Burroughs was a bit of a holdout when it came to Buddhism, to which many of his writer and poet friends were drawn. The attractive feature of Buddhism was that it had no gods, it was not a religion like Christianity or Islam or Judaism, there was no bearded authority figure threatening you with eternal damnation if you did not confess your sins, there was no powerful institutional church with its mosques and cathedrals and its army of priests. There was in Buddhism, with its teaching that existence was suffering, an existential postmodern dimension that appealed to the counterculture. Buddhism was flexible and formless enough, and had enough different branches, to appeal to men as different as Jack Kerouac, Allen Ginsberg, Gary Snyder, and John Giorno. Kerouac tirelessly quoted the Diamond Sutra's injunction to discard "all arbitrary conceptions" and also endorsed the doctrine of nonattachment. For Gary Snyder, who had studied Zen during his twelve-year residence in Japan, Buddhism tied into his mystical view of nature and his conviction that the healthy growth of society began with the healthy growth of the self. For Allen Ginsberg, who had become a Buddhist after a stay in India, Buddhism provided a model in the person of the *bodhisattva*, the perfected being who postpones entry into Nirvana until all others are similarly enlightened. For John Giorno, Buddhism was originally connected to the first acid trips he had taken in 1965, when he glimpsed another reality he could not quite reach, and which he came to understand better through strenuous meditation. Buddhism helped him to explore the nature of mind and the nature of emptiness.

At Naropa, thanks to Trungpa and Anne Waldman, Buddhism and the counterculture were in formal alliance. As for Trungpa, the stories about him were endless. One night he had gathered the student body in the converted basketball gym that served as an auditorium and told them to go home, cut their hair, and find normal jobs like bakers and printers. In a drinking bout with one of the long-haired students, he had drunk the student under the table and then cut his hair off at the neck with a hunting knife.

The most talked-about incident, however, occurred in November 1975 at the seminar Trungpa conducted in the Colorado Rockies, near Aspen, at the Snowmass ski resort. At a Halloween party, Trungpa stripped off his clothes and urged the other guests to do the same. One of the guests, the poet W. S. Merwin, slipped away with his Hawaiian girlfriend to escape what he considered an imposition. Trungpa ordered his guards to seize them in their room and bring them back. Merwin had locked his door, which the guards broke down. They subdued him forcibly when he tried to defend himself with a broken beer bottle. Then Trungpa had them forcibly stripped, explaining that he was teaching the stripping away of neuroses. Merwin described the scene as "Buddhist fascism." It gave a bad name to the gurus who were supposed to be bringing to the West the spiritual secrets of the Himalayas.

News of this unpleasant event soon spread among the faithful. Allen Ginsberg feared that the publicity would cause Naropa to lose a $4,000 grant from the National Endowment, and he was right—the grant was turned down. He saw the incident as a case of sexual rivalry between Merwin and Trungpa for the beautiful Hawaiian girl. It was, thought Allen, like a Burroughs routine: "You Oriental slick cunt, why are you hanging around with this honky?" But Trungpa explained to Allen that it had nothing to do with sex, that stripping was a traditional Buddhist practice that he had done with his teacher. In the Western context, the timing was appropriate, because it was Halloween, when you blow your top and get rid of constraints. The principle, said Trungpa, was that once Merwin had agreed to attend the seminar he should have conformed to its usages. He was like a man who signs up for cooking school and then goes on a hunger strike. It was the rational liberal mind refusing to take part in cleansing symbolic ceremonies.

"This Merwin story has been batted around so many times with so many different versions," Burroughs wrote a friend, "that it is getting to be the local *Rashomon*. One fact emerges: that the only person injured was one of the guards. . . . These things happen when people drink too much. . . . The whole Buddhist position, that anything wrong with anybody comes from his own psyche and not from the outside, is of course a handy thing for any mind controllers. As I told Allen you could say the same thing to a rat in a maze. . . . I am not much interested in Buddhism myself. The course I teach in the summer consists of three lectures on writing and literature."

Although Burroughs was not a joiner of religions, and kept his skepticism intact about Buddhism, he decided in November to spend two weeks in Barnet, Vermont, at a Trungpa-conducted retreat. The idea was complete isolation. You went into yourself and you saw what happened. James drove him up and accompanied him to his small wooden hut in a rickety tractor-drawn cart, and left him standing in front of the hut, dressed in khaki trousers and shirt, staring at the blade of grass in his fingers as though a bit embarrassed by what he was doing.

Trungpa said no typewriter—that would be like a carpenter taking along his tools. A carpenter could always carpenter, thought Burroughs, but a writer had to take it as it came—a glimpse once lost might never come again. That was the trouble with Buddhists, they didn't understand writers. Show me a good Buddhist novelist, he thought. When Aldous Huxley became a Buddhist he stopped writing novels and began to write tracts. He conceded the typewriter but not pen and paper, because he wanted to jot down his dream notes.

The first thing Burroughs did in his retreat hut was make a flyswatter out of an old whisk broom. The second thing he did was kill a brown spider that he found on the shelf above his bed. It might be a highly poisonous brown recluse, he thought, and he didn't want it on his face while he slept. In the woodshed he found a piece of cardboard on which the previous occupant had written, "How can I please myself when I have no self to please?" Sorry, young man, thought Burroughs, I think you are kidding yourself. As long as you talk to yourself, you have a self. The self is a pimping, blackmailing chauffeur who gets you from here to there on word lines.

Burroughs found that the time sped by, and he was never bored or lonely. He took long walks, and was joined at night by the characters in his dreams. In one dream, "Allen and I open restaurant. Citation from the Board on beef stew. Inspector: 'Well, I hope I can get you off with a fine but I dunno. Preliminary tests show definitive contamination. You're lucky I got here before the customers or you'd be up for manslaughter. Didn't eat any yourself, did you?'

" 'Well, oh no, I'm sort of a vegetarian.' "

" 'That stew would make a vegetarian out of anybody.' "

Was the stew a metaphor for writing? Burroughs had no idea. His only complaint when the two weeks were up was that there had been no shaving mirror, but he was able to shave daily by using a pan as a reflector. The retreat was a success. Although no more of a Buddhist than before, he had found the solitude appealing.

Back in New York in late November, Burroughs moved to an apartment in John Giorno's building, a converted Y.M.C.A. at 222 Bowery, which had been bought by the furniture store next door, whose owner rented space to artists. The small basketball gym had once been Mark Rothko's studio. Burroughs had a large but windowless concrete space that had been the locker room. In the bathroom stood two high white porcelain urinals. The light of day never reached his apartment, which became known as the Bunker, but he didn't mind, he liked the privacy and the quiet and the safety—there were three locked doors between himself and the street. On the mezzanine, Bunker-level landing, there was a design in the linoleum that showed the letters "XRM" in a four-foot circle, which stood for X-Ray Manufacturing, for after it had been a Y.M.C.A., but before it was rented by artists, the building had been used to make X-ray tubes and equipment. Burroughs had the Bunker painted white, floors and ceilings, and walls, which he hung with paintings by Brion Gysin, so it didn't look gloomy. An added advantage, he liked to say, were the heavy psychic traces of countless naked boys. But the best part of the deal was the rent: $250 a month.

Burroughs was content in the Bunker, where James joined him to live and work. At the start of 1976, things were going reasonably well. There was only one person he missed from the London days, and that was Ian Sommerville, to whom he wrote that he was "accepting reading and speaking engagements which have proven both rewarding and enjoyable; standing ovations, transportation and hotel paid for, even lovers. . . . For a five-minute reading on New Year's Day I spent three hours rehearsing." Ian was now living in Bath, working as a computer programmer for a manufacturer of pork pies. In his 1975 Christmas card, Ian had written: "Been working on computers again for last few months, blue suit and briefcase, that kind of thing. Keeping the wolves at the door plus body and soul firmly apart. Howzzaboutuuu?"

February 5, 1976, was Burroughs' sixty-second birthday, and he received the following wire from Ian: HAPPY BIRTHDAY. LOTS OF LOVE. LOTS OF PROMISE NO REALIZATION. This last phrase Burroughs took to refer to Ian's efforts to find a job in America. Later in the day another telegram arrived, this one from Anthony Balch, and it said: IAN SOMMERVILLE KILLED IN CAR ACCIDENT FEBRUARY 5. FUNERAL FEBRUARY 12, BATH. Ian, who was thirty-five, had recently learned to drive and had bought a little Morris, which was his pride and joy. Shortly after sending Burroughs the birthday telegram from the Bath post office, he had been hit by a car coming the other way that had signaled a right turn but made a left turn. A card was found on his body donating his kidneys for transplants, and later that year, when Billy had a transplant operation, Burroughs saw a certain symmetry between Ian donating his kidneys and Billy receiving a liver.

Shortly before his accident, Ian had called Brion Gysin in Paris, to tell him how proud he was of his new car—driving was the one worthwhile thing he had ever learned, he said. During their conversation, Brion passed on some news that made Ian extremely distraught. The latest issue of a magazine called *The Fanatic* had come out that day, with a scurrilous article about Ian.

It happened that the editor of *The Fanatic*, Bill Levy, a Baltimore-born counterculture figure who lived in Amsterdam, had a grudge against Ian. Bill Levy's Dutch girlfriend had recently stayed with Ian in Bath, and she seduced him. It was the first time he had slept with a woman. In retaliation, Levy wrote an article entitled "Electric Ian—A Tawdry Brief Life," in which he accused Ian of having a deformed penis and of being an "electric-razor queen who shaves his genitals."

"Burroughs writes only to get boys," Levy quoted Ian as telling the Dutch girl, to which she sensibly replied, "You were one of them."

"He spent his twenties as kept lover and literary policeman to William Burroughs," wrote Levy. ". . . His next employment was in the computer industry. (As the Grateful Dead sing, 'All that cannot sink or swim is just left there to float.') This characteristically disconnected period in his life was marked by a fascination with rough-trade. He would take home younger punks only to wake up in the morning to find his tape recorder stolen. . . . Lo and behold, at the age of thirty-four, after a lifetime of misogyny, he made love with a woman."

Ian was so upset by what Brion told him that when Brion heard about the accident, he thought it must be suicide. But then he thought, I am the living proof that those who go on about suicide don't get around to it. Ian was not an experienced driver, and his attention must have been on Bill Levy's attack rather than on the road.

As for Burroughs, in all his life he had rarely been more furious than he was about the article on Ian. It was meant to kill, he thought. Who in his right mind would want all his most horrible characteristics, words, actions, and deformities publicized? What if some creep published all the sloppy drunken things Burroughs had said ten years ago? He could not accept the rationale that held "Just get it all said, every disgusting thing you can think of and wallow around in it, why not? We're all a bunch of shits anyway." Burroughs was not motivated to disclose the worst traits of his friends; he wanted to see their best, not their worst. It was as if he should select his worst writing and present it as his magnum opus. It could become a contest to see who could write the most driveling stupid boring book. It was Burroughs' opinion that Bill Levy was responsible for Ian's death.

It was a terrible blow, coming on his birthday as it had. At night, before going to sleep, Burroughs saw Ian's sad accusing face. He had not been comfortable on earth. He had not been in his element. Many were the nights when Ian appeared in his dreams. Often they were back on the calle Larache, with the neighbor problem. Someone was pounding on the door and Burroughs told Ian, "Give him some money, send him away." What a horrible interlude that had been. Invariably Burroughs dreamed of Ian on his birthday, June 3—Ian asking him if he wanted to be cured. Ian recommending a sound textbook on economics. In this manner, Ian remained a vivid presence in Burroughs' life.

Now that Ian was gone, thank God he had James. But in the spring of 1976, having been with Burroughs two years, James took stock of his situation. He had not intended to spend his life as the secretary of a famous writer, and sometimes he felt that he had made the Faustian pact—that in exchange for being introduced to a world of fame, he had lost his soul. He had always told himself that he would have a destiny, but now that destiny was to be second fiddle. And he would argue with himself that he wasn't just second fiddle, that he was someone on his own. William was the famous one and got the applause, but without making the arrangements and organizing the readings and bringing in the income none of it would work. And yet, even knowing that, a sense of frustration was built into the job, for he felt that he was running out of time in terms of making a career for himself.

As for their life together, it had its ups and downs. Burroughs was easier to get along with than he must have been in England, when he was doing E-meters eight hours a day, and James tried to imagine being audited and having his personality ripped to shreds—he couldn't have stood that. Once Burroughs did scare him by standing over him in the middle of the night and telling him that he had to get ready at once to leave the planet. Respecting his judgment, James thought, "Well, maybe there's something to this, gosh, I'll have to leave my family and my friends." But then he realized that Burroughs was drunk.

In a letter to Brion Gysin, in which the emotions of the moment made him sound more desperate than he was, James deplored the drinking, which was getting worse. In spite of his success and his travels and his active life, Burroughs went through cycles of depression and application, of exhilaration and dejection, through which ran the continuous threads of alcoholism and flatly irrational behavior. He rarely ended the night without making himself drunk, and more often than not, dull and repetitive and obstinate as well. He would spend the afternoon reading and writing, and then at six he would start drinking. Often he got drunk on just those evenings when he should have stayed sober, that is, when someone he liked was coming to dinner. It was like a child's overexcitement at the anticipation of a party, followed by premature fatigue and slurred, bullheaded, one-sided conversation.

When he saw this man he loved and admired reduce himself nightly to a travesty, to a pitiable avuncular figure that his guests had to humor, James felt frustrated and broken-hearted and helpless. He was managing expenses, he was answering letters, he was working with agents and publishers, he was arranging speaking tours, he was giving Burroughs a thousand attentions and services, as well as his daily company, his own life force. But now he felt at his wit's end because it seemed to be getting out of control. He knew that he was only a twenty-three-year-old kid from Kansas and that Burroughs was a world-famous man of letters, but there was no point in going on as master of ceremonies for a juggler who dropped the pins.

But then, invariably, something happened to shake him out of his pessimism, and right about then Burroughs was invited to take part in a reading in Berlin, under the auspices of the Akademie der Künste, where he joined up with Allen Ginsberg and Susan Sontag, the well-known panelist, as well as with Fred Jordan of Grove Press and his English publisher, John Calder. Susan Sontag had had a mastectomy in 1975, and Allen questioned her tactlessly, as was his habit: "So did you have it completely cut off? . . . And how's your love life?" "Not so bad," Sontag said. "In fact better than before. I'm getting a lot of propositions." Burroughs was embarrassed. The conversation made him think of people who sleep with hunchbacks for good luck. But it turned out that Susan Sontag was eager to talk about her cancer.

Fred Jordan said Samuel Beckett was in Berlin to direct the German production of *End Game* and that he was going over to see him late that afternoon, and Sontag said she had always wanted to meet him, and they all ended up going. Jordan said they should bring their own liquor, as Beckett would offer none, and they brought a bottle of whiskey. Beckett had a sparsely furnished duplex overlooking the Tiergarten (the zoo), and received them cordially, the famous face, all in planes like a Juan Gris collage, emerging from a turtleneck. But Burroughs could see that he had no genuine interest in any of them. He had decided to make pleasant conversation for twenty minutes and that was it. It was as if they had entered a hiatus of indifference. Allen, shameless as always, asked Beckett, who had been Joyce's secretary, whether Joyce had ever composed any songs. Yes, said Beckett, Joyce had written some lyrics to music by Schubert. Sing it for us, Allen asked, and Beckett, to Fred Jordan's surprise, did, singing about three verses in a thin Irish tenor— too bad no one had a tape recorder, Fred Jordan thought, to capture this curious literary musicale. Burroughs reminded Beckett of their last meeting in Maurice Girodias's Grande Séverine, when they had argued about cut-ups. Trying to bring a little animation into the conversation, Burroughs said the Berlin zoo was one of the best, with nocturnal creatures in their natural habitat . . . they even had flying foxes. Beckett nodded, as if willing to take his word for it. He did say that he hated literary discussions. It was a great bore to be asked, "What is your connection to existentialism?"

Burroughs in the old Beat Hotel days had devised a method for getting rid of people who dropped in, by visualizing them outside his room. Beckett had an even better method: As the afternoon turned into evening and his apartment got dark, he neglected to turn on any lights, and pretty soon everybody left.

· NINETEEN ·

BILLY

1974–1981

Abandoned by his wife in Atlanta in 1974, Billy Burroughs adopted the life of a derelict, drank himself into a stupor, and bemoaned his fate. Somehow, he reflected, he had gotten hooked on Karen, who had exposed in him a streak of masochism, and who had cemented a vampire hold on him that would last for seven years. She had introduced him to her incredibly vulgar and kind parents, who played "The Songs of Camp Judea" on the stereo, and driven him to alcoholism, and been incredibly unfaithful, and then dumped him.

Self-pitying, but lucidly so, Billy wrote in his diary that he was "always good for at least a half a day of damp wormy doom and gloom. Man, when I get feeling properly sorry for myself, really into it, that's like one of my main 'poor me if only I'd' snivel-n-moan trips. I can easily do a whole night and most of a morning on that number. And it's *stupid*." Another source of "poor me" thinking was his mother's death, about which he regularly reminded his father, writing him in the spring of 1974: "My nagging trauma—Joan's death—nags insistently. I want it out. Cannot quite let go in meditation or exercise. . . . How to go about it? 6–7 sessions careful hypnosis?"

Billy hitched to Santa Cruz, which was known for its large hippie population, living on the taxpayers' money. But he was too depressed and apathetic even to apply for welfare. He slept under bridges on cardboard and found food in garbage cans. One day he found a piece of rope, which seemed to him an omen that he should hang himself. That night he was sitting on a curb with the rope in his pocket when a young woman with golden hair sat next to him and said, "You're coming home with me tonight." What the hell, Billy thought, I can always hang myself tomorrow. The one thing about rolling stones, they rolled when they were pushed, and he rolled to Georgette's apartment: Georgette Larrouy, vet's assistant of Basque descent, collector of strays, flower child, and faithful consultor of the I Ching.

The next day, Billy hit the streets because he felt scummy—his head hurt, his feet stank, and he didn't love Jesus. But Georgette went looking for him, and found him, and she was angry. Like the song goes, thought Billy, "First she hit me, then she bit me, then she threw me in the truck and said, 'You goin' wit' me.' " So he went, and for a while it was party time. But drinking made her sick—she was hypoglycemic. She finally told him not to bring booze if he was coming over. So he would sit by a stream and chug-a-lug to his heart's content before knocking on her door. Georgette was soon hip to that and put him into the Santa Cruz detox center on Christmas Eve 1975. Billy spent horrible hours staring at the Christmas tree. Just the tree tree tree.

When he got out he started drinking again. He had a job as a cook and was supplementing his income with pilferage on the one hand and General Assistance on the other. In exchange for the welfare, he promised to do sixty-two hours a month of public work. Georgette took him to see a doctor, who told him, "Well, my young friend, you have a liver the size of Baltimore." Not without a trace of pride, Billy checked back into detox—scared, this time.

The opportunity arose in the spring of 1976 to go to Boulder, where he could be a sort of assistant teacher at Naropa and do a few readings under the sponsorship of Allen Ginsberg. He wrote his father on March 8: "Long ago I promised myself something exceptional by the time I was thirty and I've certainly not found it, so it must have something to do with something as simple as my filing system."

By April, Billy and Georgette were in Boulder, a part of the Naropa community. Billy read from a work in progress at one of Allen's classes, and Allen wrote him a check for twenty-five dollars as a teaching fee. What a Jewish mother he was, thought Billy. He looked a lot better shaved, with all those little facial muscles moving. Billy gave a reading in a room at the Boulderado Hotel, where he went through the unavoidable experience of being heckled by Gregory Corso, doing his usual shit-stirrer number. "What kind of sentence is that?" "You ain't the writer your father is, Billy boy." "Is that a stanza?" And other interruptions.

Then, for good measure, Gregory told a Buddhist astrologer who was there with a pretty girl, "I'm going to fuck your girlfriend in the ass," adding, "You're Jewish so you won't mind." Then he smeared the avocado dip over his own face and shirt like an ointment. Naropa was supposed to be a haven of serenity where poetic sensibilities could find expression, but Gregory disrupted all that.

Billy tacked up little notes offering to help people with their writing efforts, but there were no takers, which was a bummer. Fortunately, Georgette had a job as a highway flag-waver. She came home covered with grime and bought a bag of powdered milk to take a bath in, saying it made your skin all silky. It was clear to Billy that she wanted to be touched, but he told her that the milk bath was decadent and made no move to touch her when she emerged from the bath. He thought of Karen—when he was too drunk to fuck her she showed up four hours late one night with a $100 tip. He would never be able to forget, he wrote in his diary, that he had driven the woman he loved to vengeful whoredom.

Billy was finally writing again, and he drank nothing stronger than Coca-Cola. His plan was to walk in the mountains so that he would be wiry by the time he was thirty, and then he would get rich and live in uncalled-for surroundings. James Grauerholz wrote from New York that he and Burroughs were arriving in July and that he would set up some father-and-son readings. "Two things bother me about reading with Bill," Billy replied. "One, I'm almost as shit scared of large numbers of people as I am of airplanes, and two, I really am nobody and as yet haven't done anything worthwhile. I'd feel like a sprig of parsley."

To this Burroughs senior replied, in his best paternal "we-writers-must-be-practical" tone: "Writing is a very depleting, exacting, dangerous and underpaid profession, and the most basic and vital advice that I can give to any young writer is: pay attention to your finances. In the words of Wilson Mizner: 'Don't turn down any money.' It seems now that in order to survive we must become performers as well, and peddle our wares like purveyors of snake oil. At the same time, readings can be fun, when seen as performance, and I am looking forward to our joint readings at Santa Cruz and Berkeley. How is your health? Take care of yourself—*hasta la vista.*"

"How is your health?" was a very good question, while taking care of himself was the last thing Billy Burroughs knew how to do. One night in May, he woke up with a lump in his throat, feeling nauseous. He felt his way to the bathroom in the dark and spat into the toilet. This is no ordinary regurgitation, he thought, it's grainy and thick. Flicking on the light, he saw that the toilet bowl was red. *I must have had tomatoes for dinner.* Georgette said it was blood and that he should go at once to the hospital. Billy didn't want to go. He was scared. Here he was getting along all right at last, it wasn't great but it was tolerable, and out of the blue came something like this, like something in a monster movie. "I'll be fine in the morning," he said.

Georgette drove him to the emergency room at Boulder Community

Hospital. The nurse on duty asked him to fill out a form as lights danced in front of his eyes. "What seems to be your problem?" she asked. By way of reply, Billy deposited a pint of blood on the white linoleum floor. The next thing he knew he was a mass of tubes, bottles, and bags. When a nasogastric tube was pushed down his throat, out of irrational fear he bit the doctor's hand. "You do that again, you sonofabitch," the doctor said, "I'll stitch you to the goddamn *floor!*" The bleeding was stopped by applying icepacks to the neck to freeze and constrict the hemorrhaging veins in his throat. His damaged liver was unable to receive the blood that flowed into it, so that the backed-up blood went into reverse and broke through in the first place where the veins were weak enough not to be able to withstand the extra pressure, which happened to be the esophageal varices, the little veins in the gullet. You could lose a lot of blood that way. It was the way Jack Kerouac had died.

When Burroughs arrived in July, he talked to the doctor who had treated his son, who told him that only three things could result in the kind of hemorrhage Billy had suffered—one was a perforated ulcer, one was cancer of the stomach, and the third was cirrhosis of the liver, which was Billy's problem. The doctor drew a diagram to show how the blood, unable to flow through the liver, backed up.

On August 21, there was a party in Allen Ginsberg's apartment, and at one point Billy came out of the bathroom and said to James Grauerholz, "Jim, you better look at this—something's wrong." James saw that the toilet bowl was filled with blood and showed it to Burroughs and Allen. They decided to take Billy back to the Boulder hospital. The doctor there, Dr. Ewing, told them this was a life-and-death situation that he did not feel competent to handle. As it happened, thirty miles away in Denver, at Colorado General Hospital, there existed the world's only surgical unit capable of performing liver transplants, and it was run by the man who had pioneered the operation, Thomas Earl Starzl.

Starzl came out of the small Iowa town of LeMars. His father was a local newspaperman and his uncle Frank Starzl became general manager of the Associated Press. Tom Starzl went to medical school at Northwestern, where he decided he didn't want to become the kind of house-calling G.P. he'd known back home. He wanted to be right up there on the frontier of medicine, and break new ground, becoming the medical equivalent of the astronaut with the right stuff.

He chose the infant discipline of organ transplants, and began at Northwestern to attempt kidney and liver transplants on dogs, developing new surgical techniques. These were operations where you couldn't go by the book, because there was no book. Starzl had some success, and one of his canine patients survived twelve years with a borrowed liver.

The results with dogs were encouraging enough for Starzl to advance to humans. Kidneys were fairly simple, for there was a backup system. If something went wrong with the donor kidney, you could put the patient on a dialysis machine. Starzl performed his first successful kidney transplant in 1962, on an identical twin, with the other twin as the donor. This was at Colorado General Hospital, where he had come to run the surgery department and start up a transplant unit.

Starzl came to think of surgeons who did only kidney transplants as technically minor league, and concentrated on the liver, where the problems were formidable. There was no backup with liver transplants. If the donor liver failed, the patient died. Techniques had to be developed for the preservation of the donor liver, which also had to be compatible in blood type and size, although Starzl had once transplanted the liver of a four-year-old child into an adult. But if you transplanted an adult liver in a child, when the abdomen was closed the oversized liver pressed down and squeezed off its own blood supply. Over the years, by finding the proper cold solution to inject in the donor liver and packing it in slushed ice, doctors were able to preserve it for twelve hours, which allowed donor livers to be shipped from city to city.

Once the donor liver was on hand, the operation could begin. Removal of the diseased liver was the most dangerous part. It had to be severed from the arteries, veins, bile ducts, and ligaments that held it in place, and then literally thousands of collateral blood vessels had to be tied off to keep the patient from bleeding to death. Many of these tiny blood vessels were hard to locate, as they were clustered in the layer of fat between the skin and the muscles of the abdominal wall. So that this was a process that could take a surgical team as long as ten hours, and during that time a single error could kill the patient. Another risk was the drainage of bile from the gall bladder, which was normally processed by the liver, so that the surgeon had to perform a secondary operation linking the gall bladder directly to the intestine. A liver transplant operation was a maze full of lethal traps, not the least of which was the danger of cardiac arrest from trauma.

Once the new liver was installed and tied up to all the arteries, veins, ducts, and ligaments, with the added obstacle of a frequent disparity in size, a whole set of postoperative problems arose, with the danger of the body rejecting the new liver. Most transplant patients, if left untreated, would have a rejection crisis, and would die of raging fevers, kinking of the hepatic arteries, septic hepatic gangrene, or a number of other more or less arcane medical malfunctions. The treatment was large doses of corticosteroids, which had hazardous side effects, including hypertension and feelings of depression and rage. The worst side effect, however, was that the corticosteroids, in lowering the body's ability to reject the new liver, lowered also its ability to combat outside infections, making the transplant patient a prey to all sorts of viral and bacterial invaders.

Being alone in his field made Dr. Starzl seem distant. He was extremely reticent to talk about himself or his work. At times he took on some of the "mad doctor" attributes of Burroughs' Dr. Benway, like life imitating a parody. Here he is one day in his office, on the phone to another doctor, sounding like a dealer in spare body parts: "Say, that kidney you sent me from Tampa was seventy-two hours old—it was as hard as a golf ball. You know, with the proliferation of transplant units, half these guys don't know what they're doing. That young girl I operated on last week—they sent me a Class Four liver instead of Class One—I couldn't even close her up."

Starzl's first attempt to replace a human liver took place at Colorado General on March 1, 1963. The child patient bled to death on the operating table. Between March and July of that year, three more attempts failed, the patients dying within twenty-three days of the operation. This dismal record led to a three-year moratorium. Liver transplants were still in "they-said-it-couldn't-be-done" country, beyond the realm of reality. In 1967, Starzl tried again. There were two more failures, and, finally, on July 23, he operated on a one-and-one-half-year-old girl who survived the transplant and lived for thirteen months.

The more liver transplant operations Starzl performed, the more the survival rate rose. From every failure, useful lessons could be learned. By the time in August 1976 that Billy Burroughs was admitted to Colorado General, Starzl had performed 111 such operations, and about thirty-five of the transplant patients had survived. At that time, Tom Starzl was fifty-three years old, a shade under six feet, lean and wiry and athletic in the tense, ever-alert manner of a shortstop. There was no gray in his straight brown hair, and his narrow face, tanned in the winter by skiing and in the summer by bicycle riding in the Rockies, looked boyish. But on closer inspection, you could see that it was lined with creases and furrows, as if each of the 111 operations had left its mark. The image of glowing and energetic good health had also to be balanced against a three-pack-a-day smoking habit. The overall impression he conveyed was that of a pressure cooker. So much was held in and kept compressed. If you lifted the lid, scalding steam would come hissing out.

In a way, Billy was in luck, like a man dying of thirst in the desert who happens upon a soft-drink stand. Practically next door, he had the superstar of surgeons, the only man in America who could perform a liver transplant. Colorado General was the state-of-the-art center for liver treatment. And in addition, the transplant ward was federally funded—by the National Institute of Health—in view of its path-breaking research, so that the care Billy received, which would eventually add up to about a quarter of a million dollars, would be billed to Uncle Sam. It would not cost him or his father one cent.

In other ways, however, he was not so lucky. When he was admitted to Colorado General and was given a preoperative physical examination, the nasogastric tube produced "coffee grounds," that is, gastric secretions mixed with old blood owing to the bleeding from the varices into the esophagus. An arteriogram, or X-ray of the liver vessels, was performed. This is done by inserting a catheter into the artery and then shooting a whitish dye into it to make it opaque, so it shows up on the X-ray. Retrograde flow was observed, that is, blood rejected by the liver and flowing backward through the portal vein, until it backed up in the esophagus. From May to August, there had been five hemorrhages.

Since the transplant unit did not have a donor liver on hand, it was decided to perform a porta-caval shunt, an operation to bypass the flow of portal venous blood to the liver and prevent backing up. But in doing that, the blood was no longer detoxified by the liver, it went directly from the portal vein, which carried blood from the bowels to the liver, to the vena cava, which went from the liver to the heart—that is, it was being pumped out of the heart and going right back into the heart, bypassing the liver and reducing the pressure on the venous system, so that his esophageal varices would not be constantly exploding. A surgeon at Colorado General Hospital told Burroughs: "The shunt is just buying a little time. There is a chance that sooner or later he will bleed to death."

The porta-caval shunt was performed on August 23. This is a fairly routine procedure, but after it was over, Billy's liver function deteriorated rapidly. He fell into a liver coma and did not regain consciousness. To keep him alive, he had to be hooked up to a life-support system. His lungs were medically paralyzed and he was placed on a breathing machine. Later it was discovered that his liver had died because it had become devascularized—no blood was reaching it. This was because the dye used to make the X-ray of his hepatic artery had expanded and weakened the artery wall until it split open, like a bulge in the inner tube of a bicycle tire. Thus, the medical team, in X-raying his hepatic artery, had destroyed it, killing his liver, a mishap that occasionally occurs in performing arteriograms. The venous blood was bypassing the liver due to the porta-caval shunt, and the arterial blood, which had been reaching the liver through the hepatic artery, was cut off as a result of the arteriogram. Starved of blood, Billy's liver died.

When Burroughs came to see his son, he found it hard to stay in the room. The presence of death was too overpowering. He lay there puffy and yellow, his face partly masked by the breathing machine. The only thing that might save him would be a liver transplant, but they had no donor. There was talk of "termination." The only heartening note was a visit from Trungpa, who told Burroughs, "To live or die, either one is good . . . I think he will live." His was an optimism that no one else was advancing. Trungpa was not a doctor, but he was a spiritual healer with considerable experience in life-and-death situations, and Burroughs clutched at the straw he offered.

Someone at Burroughs' side wanted to read a passage from the Tibetan Book of the Dead, an encouragement to the dying to continue on their peaceful route to the Great Beyond. "Dammit!" Burroughs exploded, thinking of L. Ron Hubbard's engram theory. "Don't read that thing to him, he's in a fucking coma and he might listen."

Billy Burroughs remained in a coma for six days. He later remembered the sensation of swimming in deep space. He had flipped off the side of a boat, in the same way that Lloyd Bridges used to do it in "Sea Hunt," except that he had flipped back thousands of miles. On the sixth day, Saturday, August 28, a doctor told Burroughs, "There is no chance of recovery from the coma and there is no donor." They might as well have told him flatly that Billy was dead. On the seventh day, Sunday, August 29, a twenty-five-year-old woman named Virginia Wojahn was admitted to Colorado General with a tumor on her carotid artery. She died that very day of a stroke, and it was decided to use her liver for Billy's transplant. She was young, the size was right, and she was the same blood type, A.

By seven-thirty that evening, Virginia Wojahn's liver had been "harvested," a two-hour process, and Burroughs and Karen, who had flown in from New York, were summoned to Colorado General as next-of-kin to sign releases. "A liver transplant is a very risky operation," Dr. Starzl advised them. "You're playing big poker. There's a 30 percent mortality rate on the table. But in this case, you really stand to gain something."

The papers were there to be signed, but Karen started reading the fine print. She wanted to know the name of the donor, and was told, "We're not allowed to give out that information." She looked some more and asked, "What's this?" "It's a permission to use an experimental drug," she was told. When she started hemming and hawing, Burroughs blurted out: "For God's sake, Karen, just shut up and sign it. They're waiting."

Dr. Starzl, who had recently operated on a three-year-old boy with a liver flown in from Los Angeles by commercial airliner, prepared to operate again on the night of August 29, 1976, and Virginia Wojahn's misfortune in having been admitted to the hospital and dying there became Billy Burroughs' last chance at life. Burroughs and Karen and James went up to the waiting room of the transplant unit, on the eighth floor. Doctors with beepers fixed to their pants pockets bustled in and out. Over a door, there was a plaque from a grateful patient: "Thanks—you really make miracles happen." A doctor, discussing a kidney transplant on the phone, said, "They all wear out eventually." On the walls were photographs of transplant babies, and one of Dr. Starzl pitching on the hospital baseball team. James snatched a few hours of sleep lying flat on the linoleum floor of the waiting-room lounge.

Starzl preferred patients under forty. The older they were, the harder it was for them to withstand the immuno-suppression medication. Patients with an advanced malignancy were hopeless and shouldn't even be given transplants since they only added to the mortality statistics. There might be a chance with this one, since he was only twenty-nine, and aside from his cinder of a liver, seemed fairly healthy. Truly, it took extraordinary dedication to destroy your liver while still in your twenties, for the liver was virtually indestructible, the body's largest and quintessential organ, performing so many duties—storing carbohydrates and fat, making changes in protein, secreting bile, eliminating toxic substances. The heart was only a pump, but the liver was an incredibly intricate piece of machinery. The heart was to the liver as a bagpipe was to a symphony orchestra.

Billy was wheeled into the operating room at around 9:00 P.M. From the nipples to the groin, his chest and abdomen were swabbed with tincture of iodine in alcohol. Dressed in his workclothes—a blue surgical suit, white face mask, and close-fitting white cap—Dr. Starzl reopened the incision used for the porta-caval shunt and extended it, which gave him very good exposure. He noticed that the porta-caval shunt was all right, but that the hepatic artery pulse was difficult to feel, which was not surprising, since the artery had been split open by the dye used in the arteriogram.

The next and critical stage was the removal of the diseased liver. It had to be isolated and lifted out of the patient's body in such a way that he did not bleed to death. In Billy's case, the problem was simplified, in the sense that his liver, already dead, was receiving no blood. But Starzl had to sever and ligate the major veins and arteries, using clamps to stop the flow of blood. He performed the secondary operation, connecting the bile duct to the intestine.

Removing Billy's liver, he noted that it weighed about three and a half pounds, and had a peculiar pink color with black spots, indicating a possible genetic abnormality. Later, when it was sectioned, it emitted large quantities of air bubbles. Then there was a careful inspection of bleeding points, and a great many small veins had to be located and tied up. Once this was done, Starzl inserted the young woman's liver in Billy's abdominal cavity and began the delicate task of joining up the new liver's veins and arteries with Billy's, a task complicated by abundant bleeding, in spite of the clamps and ligatures, because the liver produced most of the clotting factor in blood, and with Billy's liver failure, his blood did not clot.

Starzl lined up the portal vein of the donor with Billy's portal vein, cutting the donor vein to get the right fit, so that there would be a minimum of tension and twisting. After the tie-up, the portal venous blood was allowed to flow through the donor liver, which was achieved in the remarkably short time of two hours and five minutes after the start of the operation.

Then, looking through a loop at the magnified arteries, Starzl trimmed the donor liver's coeliac (abdominal) artery to a similar size as one of Billy's gastric arteries, which he chose as a replacement for his dissected and useless hepatic artery. At this point, one and a half hours later, the new liver was rearterialized and began to take on the glowing brown color of a normal liver.

At this stage of the operation, when the worst should have been over, a serious problem arose. The donor liver had been lacerated during its removal from Virginia Wojahn's body and was now bleeding profusely. To stop the bleeding took many hours of patient effort and a quantity of transfused blood that surprised Starzl himself—twenty-one quarts. But with the help of an infra-red, sapphire-headed coagulator, the bleeding was finally brought under control.

Then all that remained to be done was to close the abdomen with continuous layers of silk thread stitches, and make a stab incision above the belly button where the long latex limb of the T-tube, installed for the drainage of bile, could emerge from the body.

At around 11:00 A.M. on August 30, fourteen hours after it had begun, the operation was over. This was appropriately called "heroic surgery." It was heroic for the surgeon and his team of two assistants, who were able, through a combination of great technical skill and inspired improvisation, to keep the patient alive while a large and unwieldy organ was installed in his body, not unlike the installation of an automobile engine leaking gallons of oil. And it was heroic for the patient, who survived the trauma of a lifesaving though ghoulishly indefinite stay on the operating table.

When Billy came out of his coma and made blurred eye contact with the masked face of the operating surgeon hovering inquiringly over him, he came out angry, and his first words to Starzl were "Fuck off." He had in effect died and been brought back to life, a prospect that at first did not appear inviting. He later reflected that he would have been happy to go. In fact, he had "seen" his grandmother, who had said, "We've been waiting for you, dear." But, as he reconstructed it, the Holder of the Key told him that his didn't match, and that he wasn't getting out that easy. "Go back and get the key, the right one," he was told, "and while you're at it, straighten out the mess you made."

The average postoperative hospital stay for a liver transplant patient was three weeks, but Billy remained at Colorado General for more than four months, because of complications. He was not an easy patient. There was a school of thought that the personality profile was important in the selection of transplant patients, but in the case of Billy there had been no time for psychological evaluation. R. Y. Calne, the Cambridge surgeon who had, after Starzl, performed the most liver transplants, and who had edited a book on the subject, firmly held that some patients were unacceptable. "A positive psychological approach is essential," he wrote, "if recovery is to occur after the formidable trauma of a transplant operation." You had, after all, lost a part of yourself and been given an alien organ in exchange that your body was busily trying to reject. It was a distressing fact that you were alive only because someone else had died. A strong motivation was essential to withstand the physical and psychic complications. "A stable personality is a prerequisite," wrote Dr. Calne, "as those patients who lack the maturity and ability to cooperate with staff members in their treatments will become difficult to manage postoperatively. Family support is of the utmost importance." The side effects of steroid medication would result in angry outbursts, noncooperation with treatment, refusal to have blood tests, and suicide attempts. A large burden would be placed on the family in maintaining a patient's stability.

Now Billy Burroughs was a notoriously unstable personality, who had narrowly missed drinking himself to death by the age of twenty-nine. He did not have the maturity to cope with day-to-day life, much less with the trauma of a liver transplant. His family situation was the opposite of supportive, with a shadowy father who in the past had rarely been around. Billy was highly ambivalent about having been brought back to life. The steroids he was on, prednisone and Imuran, made him by turn depressed and enraged. In terms of personality profile, Billy was exactly the sort of person who should not have been given a transplant—and yet, in a life-and-death situation, such caveats went by the board.

Billy became the terror of the transplant ward, insulting the nurses, throwing his food tray on the floor, and shitting in bed instead of using the bedpan. Several times he was so belligerent he had to be straitjacketed. The nurses would hear a fracas in his room and say: "Oh, that's Billy throwing his food around. Well, this time he can just go hungry."

In his normal moments, Billy tried to come to terms with his condition, and with the woman's borrowed liver that had brought him back to life. At first he called it "an alien piece of meat." Then humor prevailed and he began calling it "Virginia," and saying: "Virginia and I have hit it off real good. We're growing very attached to each other. We're talking about getting married." He identified with the young woman donor, who was roughly the same age as his mother had been when he was born, and who had given him rebirth.

In his hospital bed, Billy rolled the I Ching, and it came out "splitting apart," which confirmed him in the belief of his fragmented identity. Billy had plenty of family support at first. His father elected to remain in Boulder and came daily to visit. Karen and Georgette were at his bedside, outwardly caring female presences with undercurrents of rivalry. Visitors arrived daily from the Naropa community.

Medically, Billy seemed to be doing quite well. Psychologically, one minute he was fine and the next minute he felt like Crazy Horse, and then the feeling went away. He felt well enough in the last week of September to do physical therapy, but was too weak to lift the little one-pound barbells, and didn't like getting worn out in front of the sympathetic lady. But physical therapy soon became impossible because of a lump on his right hip which grew to the size of a softball.

Billy had a clear understanding of his postoperative dilemma. He knew that the steroids were necessary because when alien tissues were placed in a body, they were treated by that body as an infection. All the antibodies rushed to the scene to attack the invader. To avoid this reaction, which would result in rejection and death, the steroids were administered to kill off the antibodies. But the steroids made the body less resistant to infections. If you so much as stuck your head out the window, you'd catch a cold. Billy was so full of steroids that he was placed on "reverse isolation." Anyone who came into his room had to wear a mask for fear of exhaling germs.

Now, as a result of his zero resistance, he had developed this painful lump and a fever. A couple of specialists were sent to investigate. They stood over him disagreeing as to whether it was arthritis or rheumatism. Then, late one night, Starzl was walking the ward and came in to take a look at Billy's softball. Suddenly his eyes lit up and he ran into the hall with his white coat flapping, shouting: "Get in here! Get in here! I've made a wonderful discovery! It's an abscess, get me a needle! I'm going to aspirate!"

Starzl returned with a needle that seemed to Billy the size of a bicycle pump, rolled Billy over, and *Jambo!* Then, in an apologetic voice, he said, "That's curious." But inspiration struck again, and an even bigger needle was brought in—it must be the emergency fire hose from the hall, thought Billy—and it was *Jambo!* again. This time Starzl managed to draw out a small amount of pus, and said with satisfaction: "There you are. You can operate tomorrow."

On October 3, Billy was on the operating table once again. To get at the abscess, they would have to open him up from the quarter-sized hole where the T-tube stuck out under his breast bone, down to his groin— or, as Billy put it in his chats with his new liver, "down to where your Mount of Venus would be, Virginia sweetheart." The anesthesiologist blew up three of his veins trying to get him to sleep, and was muttering in Spanish while the surgeons ribbed him: "Hey, Pancho, whassamatter? Hurry up, we're late for lunch."

When Billy awoke in his bed on the ward, a pint of pus had been drained from a massive abscess in the lower left pelvic pocket, and his fever had gone down. He looked down the length of his body and was horrified to see that they hadn't closed him up. He had a large, gaping, open wound three inches across and a foot long. He'd been gutted like a pig for a barbecue. When one of the nurses came to tend to his new excavation, she lost her cool and exclaimed, "Oh, my God!" And it took a lot to draw an exclamation from one of the transplant nurses, because Eight North, Government Experimental Transplant Ward, was like an ongoing *M*A*S*H* episode, with patients dying all the time, and a kind of war-zone attitude, with nurses wearing blue jeans and flipping coins to determine who was assigned to the room of a dying patient, and visitors sleeping on the couches, and patients like Billy being allowed to smoke (with no one asking what). And the doctors themselves affected a hardened attitude. They had seen it all, like pretty eight-year-old Gretchen rejecting her new liver and literally turning quince yellow and withering up and dying within days, and they weren't going to show any emotion. Billy had asked Dr. Thomas, one of the surgeons on the ward, "Will you admit to being driven by compassion?" "No," he replied, "I just like the work. If I was driven by compassion, I'd be a pediatrician. You don't have to be *driven* to be compassionate."

Billy's abdomen was left open because it had to be irrigated three times a day. One machine ran two liters of saline solution through his insides and another machine sucked it out with loud noises, like someone trying to get the last drops of an ice cream soda through a straw. It wasn't painful, because those slimy, bulgy things called guts didn't have effective pain sensors. There were no nerve endings on the intestines, which had not been designed for airing. But Billy had the unpleasant feeling of guts being handled, of the nurse lifting up his intestines to squirt water under them to the accompaniment of vacuuming noises. He didn't want to see it and he didn't want to hear it and he played Janis Joplin and Doc Watson on the tape recorder his father had brought him while they did the irrigation, thinking, just two more songs and they're through. After the irrigation, the hole had to be packed with nonstinging iodine-soaked gauze. Billy asked the nurse how deep the hole was, and she said deeper than she could reach without pushing the gauze in first. And she had long fingers for a little lady. Every day when they pulled out the old gauze caked with dry blood it felt like red-hot barbed wire coming out. Glenda, the tough nurse, not the one who'd said, "Oh, my God!" called his wound "the birdbath" and told him to stop feeling sorry for himself. Bravery, she said, was needed, not self-pity. But Billy's attitude following the abscess operation did not improve.

The steroids made him crazy and mean, and he tore to shreds the magazines the nurses gave him. When he wanted attention, he threw the ashtray across the room. He got so paranoid that he told Georgette that he was a guinea pig and that they had given him a monkey liver. "They've got a place in the basement where they do experiments on animals," he said. "They've got a two-headed dog down there." When Georgette replied that they were trying to save his life but he was no help, he accused her of being an agent for the hospital who had come to him in the name of love to pump him for information.

Once, in the middle of the night, he ripped the nose tube off and staggered down the hall, gaping guts and all, his life-support machinery trailing after him, looking like a walking junkyard, and saying, "I wanna take a goddamn walk," and had to be forcibly restrained and placed under sedation. And yet . . . there was a poster on the ward that said "Fury is a sign of life." Billy was definitely in a state of fury. The failure of a match to light on the first strike was enough to get him going. When he couldn't reach the call cord for the nurse was enough. He stopped shaving, and began to look like a youngish Howard Hughes, with the beard and the disheveled, bewildered air.

Life on the ward seemed to Billy just a series of humiliations designed to prove what a subhuman he was. One day Starzl came by with two visiting foreign colleagues, who observed him as they would have the elephant man. One of them asked, with a tone of faint disapproval, "How do they become so hirsute?" What he was really saying, thought Billy, was, "Do all your freaks get so hairy?" He felt like replying, "Yes, the entire ward is funded by a government program to grow beards on Indians." And then good old Starzl said, "Say, Billy, would you mind opening your pajama top so I can point out a few specific scars?" And Billy did, showing the scars that he hated, because he thought of himself as a monstrous, disfigured creature, and that he hated anyone else to see. And as he lay there, with his open wound, and his ugly, livid scars, Starzl lost himself in conversation with the visiting doctors on a completely unrelated matter, and they all swept out of the room without a word or a nod, leaving him gnashing his teeth and buttoning his pajama top, and feeling like a child's toy top. When he glanced at the nurse, before whom he had been humbled, he saw that she was looking at him with honest outrage. She knew how he felt, and he said, "Hirsute, my foot," making "foot" rhyme with "hirsute," which cracked her up.

By now, getting into November, Billy's liver functions were normal. He was being kept in the hospital only for the treatment of his abscess, which had to be aspirated again on November 28. There were fewer visitors now, and Karen and Georgette were gone. It had been like a soap opera at first, with both his wife and his girlfriend in attendance and Billy with tubes up his nose. At first it was all sweetness. There was a feeling of reverence that this miracle had taken place. But then Georgette began to feel that she couldn't compete because Karen was more beautiful. Then Karen had to go back to New York. Finally Georgette went back to Santa Cruz. The I Ching had not prepared her for nasogastric tubes and immunosuppressants and a paranoid madman who thought he had been given a monkey liver. "I don't feel you know how to give love," she told Billy, "because love to you means sadness and pain."

By this time, Billy was familiar with life on the ward, which he saw as a lottery. This man will live, the man next door will die, the child down the hall has a chance. And it looks like I'll learn to dance, he thought, but first I will have to pay the piper in a big way. With his intestines still out in the open and being flushed three times a day, a piece of his colon got infected, and a little hole, or fistula, formed, leaking feces. Two attempts were made to close the fistula, but each time it reopened. It was interesting to Billy how each remedy brought a side effect. The arteriogram had killed his hepatic artery. The steroids had weakened his immune system and caused his abscess. The cleansing of his abscess had brought on a colonic fistula.

But Billy could not be kept indefinitely on the ward, and on January 22, 1977, he was discharged. His liver function was normal, his abscess was gone, and his fistula was under control. He would live in Boulder where his father and the Naropa people would look after him, and come to the hospital three times a week as an outpatient. The hospital's social services department arranged for him to collect $179 a month in welfare.

When Billy was discharged, his friend John Steinbeck, Jr., the son of the writer, came to get him. After spending six years in Vietnam on a TV crew, Steinbeck had settled in Boulder. He had from the start felt a kinship with Billy, the kinship of being sons of famous writers, and the kinship of wretched excess. John, like Billy, had gone on epic drunks. John, like Billy, would burn out his liver, and would have to stop drinking, which his liver appreciated, returning to its normal size.

Steinbeck was sure that Billy already had several strikes against him at birth. Just as the fetus of a junky is born with a heroin habit, just as the fetus of an alcoholic is born with something called fetal alcohol syndrome, which can lead to growth retardation and brain damage, the fetus of an amphetamine addict will display abnormalities. Billy had tried to grow his fetal brain cells in a swirl of Benzedrine-eucalyptus amniotic fluid from his mother's habit during pregnancy of mainlining the soakings from nose inhalers. The first liver cell he ever owned had been put to indentured servitude even as it tried to mesoderm its way into mere helpfulness. So that Billy's bile-buster, thought Steinbeck, was a product not only of what he had done to it but of what his mother had done to it.

Billy was in a cranky mood, complaining about his doctors. He had a wound above his belly button that wouldn't close, a fistula where he was shitting out of the middle of his chest. It was like having an asshole in your chest, thought Steinbeck. And the scars! He looked like he'd been hit by an 80mm howitzer. Billy was in pain, and the doctors wouldn't give him any Percodan. "What is this aspirin bullshit," he asked Steinbeck, "and why the fuck shouldn't I drink?" The first thing he wanted was a six-pack. Steinbeck surmised that the main purpose of the new liver was to allow Billy Burroughs to enjoy a few more rounds of beer. What else did he have? He went on at some length about how repulsive he would be to women. "Who would want someone who smells like me," he asked, "who would want me but a stump freak?"

Steinbeck understood the way Billy felt. They'd brought him back, and he hadn't asked to be brought back. Billy walked around thinking, this hurts, that hurts, why should I mow the fuckin' lawn, let's just get out of this game. At the same time he had no patience with Billy's self-pitying streak. Steinbeck had seen people run through the jungle tripping on their own entrails, he wasn't impressed by wounds and the smell of shit, and when Billy started whining, John would say, "See ya later, stinkbag." And Billy would vanish, feeling hurt, but soon he'd be back, giving you one of his empathy-check glances, and telling you how he'd lost his Tibetan good-luck charm. He was loopy as hell, Steinbeck realized, but you couldn't say, "So what?" He was always making these weird connections, like saying, "Look, I picked up this piece of paper today that says Timex, and your watch is made by Timex." Steinbeck realized that it was theistic, it was about his Maker, who hadn't done that great a job, so that Billy had to keep trying to make some sense out of it. To him, the world was a pun, but it wasn't playful, it was desperate. And finally, friendship with Billy was exhausting, because he forced rejection. Whatever you gave him, he wanted more. Until you'd say, "I can't," and he'd say "Aha, I knew it." But Steinbeck never quite gave up on Billy, for they both fitted into the constellation of famous fathers and troubled sons.

A room was found for Billy at the Boulderado Hotel, and the Naropa community rallied around. Everyone was trying to help, to find him a typist, to give him a ride to Denver. Anne Waldman, the mother of Naropa, one of those purposeful Aries women, who ran the poetry school and who was living at the time with the writer Michael Brownstein, kept an eye on Billy and invited him over for dinner. She had seen his father change during the months of Billy's hospitalization, this tough old bird becoming weepy and remorseful, in complete contrast to Robert Bly's description of him as "just a green-skinned reptilian." And she saw that

Billy was troubled, with his scavenger, magpie quality, spending his days rummaging through trash cans for clothing and talismanic objects. Perhaps, she thought, it was a way for someone without heritage or heirlooms to grasp the fleeting world.

It seemed to Michael Brownstein that Billy had a grudge against the doctors who had saved his life and the system that had given him free medical care. He walked around with a level of pain that was incommunicable. They called it heroic surgery, but they should have called it ironic surgery. For the irony was to have to take drugs that would allow your body to accept your new liver but that also tampered with your immune system so that you became vulnerable to every other illness. Billy was like the character in the Edgar Allan Poe Story "The Pit and the Pendulum"—would the rats eat him or would the pendulum slice him to pieces?

Not that Billy helped his situation. He was walking around with a six-pack all the time, like an announcement that he was determined to burn out his second liver just as he had burned out the first. It was suicidal and he knew it. He endlessly complained about his digestive tract and yet he was hooked on Twinkies and French fries. He became insufferable because he exhausted your reserves of goodwill. When his father had to go back to New York, Billy called Brownstein to get his telephone number and then he called again to say, "Man, it's just, I dunno where it is and maybe if you came and talked to me I wouldn't lose it because it's lost, man, I wrote it down on some phone book and now I can't find it." "Come on, man," Brownstein said, "get it together, can't you write down a phone number and stick it in your pocket? This is ridiculous."

Billy could not take the slightest criticism, and thought Brownstein was being censorious, as if he was saying: "Why don't you just go away and stop trying? You'd be much missed for five minutes," or, "When are you going to stop trying to ride your father's coattails?" He sought out people who were warm and caring and nonjudgmental, like the Naropa student from British Columbia, Virginia Smith, who drove him around when he went rummaging, and marveled at what he picked up—a broken antler, a torn painting, a strange doll with big eyes, which Billy claimed moved and followed him around his room.

One night early in March 1977 she went to see him and he said, "I'm glad you're here because I've only got an hour left." She grabbed all his pills and his razor blades and his hunting knife and threw this little bag of self-destruction under the seat of her car and drove Billy to his father's apartment, and the two of them sat up with him all night, listening to his grievances—the pain, the confusion, the steroids, people weren't treating him right, the whole bit. They got him through the night, but Burroughs wondered what was next, and on March 10 he wrote Dr. Starzl that Billy was suicidal. Burroughs had told Billy that it was due to the prednisone, and he hoped that Dr. Starzl could reassure Billy that such was in fact the case.

On March 11, Billy was readmitted to Colorado General. He was in severe pain because the fistula kept slipping out of place and leaking mucus and feces. An operation was performed to close the fistula, but after five days it reopened. In the hospital, Billy again expressed suicidal thoughts, and the nurses kept him up all night talking. He was also hallucinating, saying that the doll he had found talked to him. Dr. Starzl referred him to Dr. Richard Warner, the young, genial, Kansas-born psychiatrist who worked with the transplant patients.

Dr. Warner saw Billy regularly over the next four years, and came to know him as well as anyone. He saw a young man who was panicky and upset, to whom this second chance at life was a burden. Billy saw only the dismal aspect of his situation, which was real enough. There had been an invasion of bodily integrity, and Billy was having major difficulties with the whole notion of the transplant and of his station in life. He felt that he was not completely male, since he was carrying around a woman's liver. There were frequent references to "Virginia," and Billy said that he was planning to move to the State of Virginia. Since Virginia was in him, he would also be in Virginia. He wore an earring with a picture of the Virgin Mary on it, as protection for Virginia.

Dr. Warner did not want to make too much of the process of feminization, which may have been Billy's little joke. It was like the natives of New Guinea making up stories for Margaret Mead. "Well, fellas, what'll we tell her today, that we bury our young after the full moon?" Billy's real worry was not being feminized but being disfigured. He said that the idea of disrobing in front of a woman was terrifying. "What are they gonna think when I take off my T-shirt?" he asked. He was worried about letting a woman get a look at his scarred stomach with the openings for the fistula and the T-tube. He said he had tried it once, and the woman had left the bed smack in the middle of everything, saying she couldn't stand it. Billy said he felt hideously ugly. He called it "the Frankenstein syndrome," the feeling of having been pieced together. He called himself "a pieced-together human slab." Why couldn't he have a straight scar like the others instead of this canyon with a bulge in it, he wondered?

A secondary theme that contributed to Billy's depression was his ambivalence about his father. He had never laid to rest the matter of his mother's death. So that at the same time that he would have willingly killed his father, he yearned to be loved by him, but that never materialized. He could not break through his father's remoteness. The one great disappointment of his life was that he had never been able to engage his father's full attention. There was always an entourage of hangers-on insulating him, whom Billy described as "the faggots around my father." The only one he held in any esteem was Allen Ginsberg, but the others were rivals for his father's attention. About James Grauerholz he had mixed feelings—James was useful, he could get things done. But when James was protective of Burroughs' interests and had to deny Billy something, he became infuriated. For Billy, people were often reduced to whether they facilitated or obstructed his access to his father.

Billy was unable to reconcile the image of his father's literary success with his total lack of success in dealing with him. Here was an accomplished man, highly regarded in the literary world, lionized, who knew nothing about how to conduct himself with his own son. His inability to connect made Billy lash out against him. He would say that some of his father's work was fraudulent, that the cut-up method was a pile of shit, a reflection on the man's inability to deal directly with his thoughts and feelings. What in the world was this man about? Billy could not grasp it to save his life. His father was impenetrable.

And yet Dr. Warner could see that beyond the transplant and the father-son dilemma, there was something actively self-defeating about Billy Burroughs. Why did he have to look so awful, unshaven and unwashed and wearing clothes out of trash bins? Why did he steal the magazines in the waiting room, so that Dr. Warner began to worry whether what was on his desk was safe? Why was he unable to handle the slightest responsibility? Dr. Warner assigned him to write a poem a day, but Billy didn't deliver, saying, "I can't write poems on demand, you need to be inspired to write poems." But that wasn't the point, whether they were good poems or not, Dr. Warner just wanted to see him engaged in something. At one point Billy talked about being a watchman in a dump. He could sit there and read and watch the world go by. That was about as high an aspiration as Dr. Warner could hold for Billy. When he started answering ads to work in day-care centers for children, Dr. Warner thought: "My God, I hope no one hires him. I certainly wouldn't want a child of mine entrusted to him." He didn't have to discourage him, though; the marketplace took care of that soon enough.

Billy was released on March 23, but was readmitted from May 24 to June 1 for reasons that were not strictly medical. He was suffering from anxiety, and Dr. Warner put him on Valium, and his mood improved. He also had to straighten out his financial arrangements with the social worker, Ursula Schaeffer. The transplant ward had become a second home, a place he could check into when the world got to be too much. Mrs. Schaeffer, a kindly widow, spent many hours trying to help Billy, but it was a strain. She recalled a typical scene when Billy had lost his food stamps.

"Don't come back here until you've got some food stamps," she said.

"But I don't know where the office is," he said.

"I'll show you where it is."

"I don't have any money to get there."

"I'll give you carfare."

He went out and got lost and came back, and she drove him there in her car. Billy Burroughs, she thought, would have tried the patience of a saint.

Back in Boulder, Billy did a couple of readings, where he showed up drunk. His fistula was leaking. His T-tube was leaking bile over his clothes and sheets. He thought of himself as a walking bile geyser. He was going off his bird waiting to be "finished." He thought a lot about women, and wondered whether he would ever spend the night with one again. He would be thirty in July—thirty going on seventy.

At Anne Waldman's Fourth of July party, Billy met the forty-three-year-old West Coast poet Jo-Anne Kyger. Jo-Anne represented the distaff side of the counterculture. The daughter of a naval officer, she had grown up as a navy brat, constantly on the move. She joined the mid-fifties San Francisco scene, ingesting deeply of that mixture of fun, pills, alcohol, and megalomania, when North Beach was host to many poets, some great and some who thought they were great. She married one of them, Gary Snyder, traveled with him to Japan, and studied Buddhism and Zen meditation. The following passage from one of her poems sums up the half-realized aspirations of so many of the "questers" in the movement, including Billy Burroughs:

> Nobody knows what they want. They
> can plan it out and get that beautiful con-
> struction. I mean
> mine is the most beautiful but I never get
> what I want. You
> can't put the rocks in your mouth on the
> seashore, rub them in your eyes.

At the party, Jo-Anne noticed Billy Burroughs trying to light a fire-cracker, but it wouldn't light, and he said, "Ahhh, it's not going to make it." She had heard stories about his odd behavior—how he had pushed a baby carriage with a dead pigeon in it through the lobby of the Boulderado Hotel. Jo-Anne's heart went out to him. Allen, the old match-maker, told her that Billy had no place to stay and asked if he could spend the night in her apartment in Varsity Manor. Fine, she said. She was ending her summer course, and was winding down physically and emotionally. She brought him sheets and sat on his bed and told him that he was tired and needed sleep. But when she touched his forehead he felt a definite spark in her fingertips. It had been so long since he had held a woman, and this lady was a beauty, tall, blond, long-legged, with a freckled body, a husky voice, a lovely smile, and clear blue eyes. He sensed that she wanted to be taken rather than play the seductress, but he was full of misgivings. She had, however, seen his scars and fistula and had not screamed and run for cover.

Billy rolled over to her, afraid he might be making a mistake but glad to see that he hadn't, and awed by the pleasure he felt. Her hips seemed to be a separate living part of her, existing only as a means of sending pleasure for her face to express, all pearly teeth and starry perspiration in the moonlight streaming through the window. They lay in bed and talked about Buddhism, and Billy asked, "So, what's a *bodhisattva*?" In the near dawn, curled under the sheet and facing away, and not seeming a day over sixteen, she said, "A *bodhisattva*'s a man who puts his joint out for his old lady when he doesn't really want to." Then Billy said he was hungry and would bring her back an orange. He left her sleeping, but did not come back, that day or the next. When he saw her again it was only for a moment in Allen's apartment, and she gave him a diagram of where she lived in Bolinas, north of San Francisco, with her phone number. When she was gone, Allen asked him with a touch of prurience, "How did it go the other night?" "Very nicely," Billy said. "We talked a long time. She's really a fine lady."

On August 30, Billy was readmitted to Colorado General for nearly a month, to have the infected piece of intestine removed. After three days of bowel preparation regime, the operation took place on September 2, and a piece of colon about one and a half inches long was dissected under the abdominal wall. The wound healed slowly, because Billy was still on steroids, and to speed up healing, a piece of pigskin was grafted onto his stomach to close the opening. Now Billy was part woman and part pig.

Discharged on September 26, he decided to go to Santa Cruz and retrieve Georgette. He looked a bit better now, with the fistula closed, and his night with Jo-Anne Kyger had awakened the hope that he could have a normal life with a woman again. Borrowing $100 from a Denver friend, he boarded the California Zephyr. Billy loved trains, and the morning hours brought him true pleasure—the flash of small-town highway stoplights, bums sleeping under newspapers on benches, cigar smoke in restrooms, and the whip of the wind between the cars combined with the gasp of steam hinges. Billy felt so good that he found himself in the bar car, having the first of many beers. At the hospital they had told him to avoid alcohol at all costs. But one thing about drinking was that once you started, you couldn't believe it was bad for you. So he continued during the many miles it took to get from Denver to Santa Cruz.

And now Billy was sitting on the couch in Georgette's Santa Cruz pad, and Georgette was kneeling, looking up at him with her hand on his knee, and saying, "Listen, Billy, I don't know how to tell you this, but I have some heavy news for you." Something cold and tearful formed deep inside Billy, not to be let out, and he asked, "What's his name?" "Felipe," Georgette said. "Thirteen cents," Billy said. "THIRTEEN GODDAMN CENTS the letter would have cost you!" "I thought a letter would have been too cold," Georgette said. "Letters aren't as cold as the highway, goddammit," Billy said.

Felipe arrived, a shy young Mexican, and suddenly Billy felt apologetic, and said he was sorry his timing was bad, and they got drunk together, and Billy tried to trade earrings but didn't succeed. The next day he got a ride north on a motorcycle, burned a hole in his ankle from the heat of the muffler, scored some heroin in San Francisco, and collapsed.

When Billy turned up at Jo-Anne Kyger's in a taxi from San Francisco, which she paid, she was glad to see him. She was touched by the mixture of lost soul and grandiose aspirations. Billy had told her he wanted to ride a white stallion like Trungpa's. She invited Billy to move in with her but soon realized she had made a mistake. All he did was sit around and drink and play Neil Young's "Southern Man" all day long. She told him not to drink in the house, and the woods were littered with blue and white Colt .45 cans with a bull's head on them. She was not prepared for his steroid-induced rages, which anything could set off. Once he was cooking a pork roast, and when one of Jo-Anne's friends asked if she could help, Billy blew up and yelled, "It's my pork!"

Jo-Anne realized that people who were ill devised strategies to get their own way, because they knew that you didn't want to upset them. It got worse and worse, with Billy losing his temper with everyone who came around. It was like living with an ongoing emergency, like a forest fire. One day she was sick to her stomach and threw up, and she realized that having Billy around was affecting her health. She had been too ambitious in thinking that she could handle it, and would have to find a way to get rid of him—she would tell him that Bolinas was too remote for his medical care, and that the rainy season was about to start.

One day, after he had been in Bolinas about two weeks, she took him to the Children's Hospital in San Francisco for a blood test, and waited for him in Gino and Carlo's at the bottom of Telegraph Hill, where she ran into Gregory Corso. "This is terrible," she told Gregory. "I don't know if this guy is trying to kill himself or what, I can't handle it." Soon Billy turned up, and Gregory asked, "What are you making this poor lady cry for?" Billy agreed to go back to Boulder, where Jo-Anne promised to join him in January for her semester of teaching.

When Billy returned to Boulder in mid-October 1977, having been rejected by two women, he was drunken and quarrelsome. Burroughs and James Grauerholz wondered what to do next. James threw the I Ching and came up with Number 39—"Obstruction, difficulty, and trouble." The second line he threw was "The king's minister meets with difficulty upon difficulty, but through no fault of his own." On the evening of October 15, they were having dinner in Burroughs' Varsity Manor apartment when Billy flew into a rage. He became so furious that his voice came out as a high-pitched hoarse whisper, like someone speaking out of a voice box. When he started throwing things, James dragged a screaming and kicking Billy out the door and down the hall to the fire escape. Billy went limp and said, "Don't throw me over, man." He thought James was going to dump him off the fourth-floor fire escape. James sat him down with a post between his knees, his legs dangling over the side, and they talked, and they were both upset. Billy knew that his father was thinking of taking him to Boulder Psychiatric Hospital. "You've got to cool out, settle down, man," James said. Billy began to whimper: "Don't institutionalize me. Please, man, don't ever do that. I've been in institutions all my life and I don't have much longer to live. Please, dear God, don't put me in another one." James hugged Billy and went back to the apartment, pouring himself a straight vodka. He threw it down and said, "Oh, shit!" Billy had watered the vodka.

The next day, October 16, they drove him to Boulder Psychiatric in Allen Ginsberg's old Volvo, telling him that commitment was voluntary and was only for three days. But on the third day Billy "escalated" by breaking a chair when he couldn't find his cigarettes, and they kept him in another two days against his will. Billy threw the I Ching and came up with the Number 18 hexagram, "Work on what has been spoiled by your father." When James came to see him, wearing his customary tennis shoes, a scowling Billy said, "I don't like people who wear sneakers and I don't like people who are sneakers."

When Billy was released from the Boulder hospital on October 20, Burroughs decided to take him to Colorado General. Before they left, Billy said, "I'm really broke." "Look, here's your passport and your October welfare check for $179," James said. "There's a bank eight blocks away over the Library Bridge where you can cash it." Billy went out and came back half an hour later saying he had lost the passport and the check.

"Look, Billy, what happened?" an exasperated Burroughs asked.

"I don't know," Billy said.

"Well, you left here with it."

"I know, but I don't have it."

"Did someone pick your pocket or what?"

"You mean to say you think I threw them away?" Billy asked.

"I think exactly that," his father said.

He took Billy back over the route, and went down to the river where it passed under the bridge, thinking that Billy had dumped check and passport in the drink, but he couldn't find anything, for the current was fairly strong. This, however, was the incident that convinced Burroughs that the situation was hopeless. Billy resented him so much that he would throw away his own money and passport in order to create a problem.

At Colorado General, Billy was admitted October 21 and 22. According to his medical record, "This thirty-year-old white male is admitted for evaluation following one month of heavy alcoholic intake." A year after the initial transplant, he was on his way to destroying his second liver. He was admitted again, from December 14 to 31, for further treatment of his alcoholic problems. Sent to Dr. Warner's psychiatric unit, he was evicted for refusing to cooperate, and was diagnosed as suffering from "chronic alcoholism" and "sociopathic personality disorder." For the rest of the holiday season, they kept him on the transplant ward. Thus, in the year 1977, Billy had been admitted to the transplant unit five times for the continuation of his treatment.

In January of 1978, in the second year of his transplanted life, Billy was given a room in one of Naropa's Buddhist residences, Yeshe House, but soon began to spend much of his time at the Boulderado Hotel, where Jo-Anne Kyger was staying. In the middle of winter, Jo-Anne noticed,

Billy had no coat, and she wondered who was going to support her to support him. She was teaching a class called Lineage to the Pacific, about American poets who had traveled to India and learned about Buddhism. She sponsored Billy to teach a course on American dialects, but soon realized that he was in no condition to teach. Occasionally she saw glimpses of this other, preoperation person, but too often he was in a steroid-fueled frenzy. Once he cooked a chicken, freezing the tidbits he liked, the giblets and heart and liver, but then he lost them, and went around weeping: "I worked so hard, and I gave of myself, and now look what's happened."

Jo-Anne had a poet friend named Bill Benton who was coming to Naropa to give a reading, and the very mention of Bill Benton made Billy hysterical, even though there was no romance. On the day of Bill Benton's arrival, Jo-Anne took him into the Boulderado's little bar for a hamburger. Suddenly Billy appeared, glowering, and put his cigarette out in the middle of Bill Benton's hamburger, and knocked the vase of daisies off the table. After that, Bill Benton was afraid to read—no telling what Billy would do. Jo-Anne was mightily vexed. She had invited Bill Benton, so that Billy's hostility was an insult to her. In addition, she had just met someone whom she envisaged as a possible boyfriend, and thought of her life as open, since she saw no future with Billy.

She went out drinking on the night of the aborted Bill Benton reading, and came back to her room around midnight, and there was Billy curled up in her bed. And she was so pissed off that after wrecking the reading he was lying there like a sleeping angel, and that she could see no way of disentangling herself from him, because he had the power of his temper and his transplant, that she went on a great Irish "bananas" trip.

"Okay, Billy," she said, "this is it," and she started throwing the contents of the room out the window, with a running commentary: "Here go my clothes, here goes the lamp, here goes the chair, here go my books." The room was on the third floor and the stuff fell into a little courtyard. Jo-Anne felt elated, because she had turned the tables on Billy; now she was the angry one while he was meek and subdued. When she had thrown out everything she could lift, she said, "Let's go downstairs now." They took a big plastic bag and climbed over a cement wall into the courtyard and hauled everything back up to the room, which was a complete wreck. The next morning the hotel management told her she would have to leave and pay $100 in damages.

"Did you throw your typewriter out?" Allen Ginsberg asked her the next day. That would have been the ultimate sign of madness for a poet. She said she hadn't, but that she had felt forced to make a violent statement, for otherwise Billy's violence would always exceed hers. Jo-Anne now realized that she had been suffering from a case of idiot compassion for someone she couldn't take care of. He hung out with the winos and the street people who had, like him, a burned-out understanding of life. "What is his father doing?" Jo-Anne wondered. She began to think of Burroughs as some kind of monster who had somehow caused Billy's self-destructive behavior. When she saw him, all she could think was, "What did you do to your poor son?" She felt an inhumaneness in the man.

And yet at no other time in his life had Burroughs made more of an effort to be a father to Billy. He had remained in Boulder most of the time since the transplant in order to look after him, and had regularly provided him with money. He felt love and compassion for Billy, but knew at the same time that Billy resented him so deeply that he was capable of self-destructive behavior in order to hurt him. Burroughs would try and talk to him, but there was always a block, as if what Billy really wanted to say was not accessible to him. And this inability to communicate was aggravated by the medical complications of the transplant and by his drinking, so that it had become a vicious circle. Was it Euripides, Burroughs wondered, who said that man causes himself more trouble than is ordained by the gods? Billy was about as self-destructive as a human being could be.

There was an added complication, which was that since the summer of 1977, with James Grauerholz spending much of the time in New York, Burroughs had a new *amigo*. Cabell Hardy, Naropa student and would-be writer, had moved in with him in the role of "impeccable boy." Lean and handsome in an angular way, Cabell had grown up in Richmond, Virginia, the son of a naval officer who called him "Stony," perhaps because he didn't talk until he was six years old. When Burroughs asked him why, Cabell said, "I couldn't be bothered." He became a junky and supported his habit by peddling his ass in drag in the streets of Richmond. One night he was on a corner as a car slowed down, raising his slit dress, when out jumped his father, who said he wanted nothing more to do with him. Busted for pushing, Cabell spent about eight months in jail, where he placed himself under the protection of a more powerful convict, who then owned him sexually. Burroughs reflected that being physically attractive had its drawbacks. He had always felt unattractive, and envied those whom everyone wanted. But imagine a really beautiful kid in the fucking jailhouse. He became a commodity, bought, sold and traded. Would he have wanted to be a beautiful boy? No way, José.

As always happened with the impeccable boy, there was some slippage.

Cabell Hardy started out by making himself useful, and cooking meals, but soon tired of the "housewife" role. He stayed out late with friends his own age, and brought his girlfriend back to the apartment, which was the one thing Burroughs could not abide, having already experienced it with John Brady. When Cabell was around, he became domineering, like the Servant transformed into the Master. He had a mean streak, which he took out on Billy. Burroughs, who hated quarrels, did very little to stop him. When Billy came around, Cabell Hardy acted like a bouncer. If he screamed at his father, if he made a scene, if he was given money and complained it wasn't enough, Cabell Hardy would take him by the arm and walk him out. "You're sponging off your dad," he said. But what Billy saw was that Cabell Hardy was living with his father and getting far more from him in terms of attention and affection than he was. If Billy wanted to sleep over, Cabell would find ways to humiliate him, telling him he smelled, and pulling the pillow from under his head, saying, "You don't deserve this."

It should also be said that much of the time Billy and Cabell got along fine. They kidded around, and traded hats, and took dope together. Cabell Hardy could understand Billy's problem, having been disowned by his own father. But his first loyalty was to Burroughs.

After the bust-up with Jo-Anne Kyger, Billy took a Valium overdose and had to have his stomach pumped out at the hospital. Ideally, thought Burroughs, he should have had a round-the-clock nurse. Once again, he was admitted to Colorado General from February 2 to March 5, 1978, for "social rehabilitation." He was diagnosed as alcohol-dependent, and a biopsy of his liver showed alcoholic hepatitis.

Alarmed by the diagnosis, Burroughs suggested to Dr. Starzl that if Billy was placed on a maintenance dose of morphine, he might stop drinking. On March 14, Dr. Starzl wrote Dr. Warner that "all things considered, I think it would be better to addict him to a nonhepatotoxic drug such as morphine rather than permit him to burn out his new liver. . . . I am in favor of the plan . . . providing Billy with a biweekly supply of morphine. And you know, this kind of controlled addiction works well in Britain and permits many street users to return to an active life." Billy, said Dr. Starzl, was "a deeply disturbed but very worthwhile young man."

Dr. Warner had misgivings about the hospital supporting a morphine addict. This was the first time such a thing had ever been tried. But he went along with it at Dr. Starzl's insistence, and began to notice that Billy did stop drinking, and that the morphine was less destructive than alcohol. The only problem was that Billy would lobby for increased doses, and Dr. Warner had to hold the line.

The morphine seemed to work, and Billy did not have to be admitted to Colorado General for the rest of 1978. In October, a young filmmaker named Howard Brookner, who was working on a Burroughs documentary, came to Boulder with James Grauerholz and shot some interesting conversations between Billy and his father that were not used in the finished film, interesting because they showed Billy being tentative and apologetic, while his father made pronouncements, always knew better, and set himself up as the voice of reason and expertise. In other words, the usual father-son scenario.

"Your room looks incredible," James said.

"It's like a carnival in here," Billy said. "Plants. I have to feed my spider."

"Where'd you catch him?" Burroughs asked.

"In the bathroom."

"That's where they hang out," Burroughs said.

Billy had stopped drinking, and said: "Last time I went into a cocktail bar in an airport I got my passport and everything else ripped off. Got into a dice game with a guy."

"Your passport?" Burroughs asked.

"Yeah, it was in my knapsack, and every time I would win playing dice he'd buy me another drink, and by the time I thought I was really lucky he'd ripped off everything I own."

"You should watch out for casual meetings with strangers in airports," Burroughs said.

"Well, that was the first time and the last."

Billy mentioned his fear of flying, and his father said: "Who gives a shit whether the plane crashes or not, I don't. Why worry about it? Driving is much more dangerous than flying."

"Those damn oak trees don't give an inch," Billy said.

"I never give it a thought while I'm on the plane," Burroughs said. "If it crashes, it crashes."

"I just get this awful feeling that there's nothing down there but air, and the stewardesses are all so, you know, veneered and confident, like everything's just fine-fine-fine, they scare me half to death."

The conversation turned to Billy's book, *Speed*. "*Speed* is bound to be made into a movie at some point," James said.

"At one point," Billy said, "there was a film crew that wanted to make a movie out of it but Pete [Peter Matson, the agent for Billy and his father] screwed it up. They wrote and said they'd give me $25,000 and 10 percent of the box office. Pete said, 'Until you've been in the business as long as I have you can't appreciate the shoddiness of this proposal.'

And that was $25,000. It still gives me lower-back pains."

"I've been hearing from Peter about film proposals," Burroughs said, "and he does not turn them out of hand at all. He says, will you please make this solid. Do you want an option or what do you want? He would never turn down $25,000. Definitely not. He would say, precisely what do you want, an opinion? But he would not just say no, I don't believe that at all."

"Well, I can show you the letter," Billy said. "It was the phrase 'incredible shoddiness' that stuck in my mind."

"The shoddiness may have been that they weren't about to put up any money. You can hear about $25,000, but you want to see it."

"Boy, do I," Billy said.

Commenting on his operation, he said that "for a long time I thought I'd died and gone to another planet where everyone was conspiring to do me good. You know that Dylan song, 'From the East down to the West I see my life come flashing'—went through all that kind of stuff, down through the childhood homes, had drinks of water from high school fountains."

"This is of course a classic experience that many people have who have come back from the dead," Burroughs said. "Complaining about being back. They want to stay there and some officious fuck says you've still got this to do."

"The classic thing again is that if you're really goin' out you're supposed to meet people that you know. But I complained about meeting people that I didn't know."

"And some of them don't have white robes on," Burroughs said.

"Chariots?" Billy said.

"They're all very reassuring—we're glad to see you, you're among friends."

From the afterlife, the conversation turned to Christianity. "Christianity institutionalized killing and torturing people," Burroughs said. "You would not have someone saying 'Kill a queer for Buddha' or 'Kill a Jew for Buddha.' Christianity has the worst record in the world for atrocities, from the Inquisition to the conquistadors to Hiroshima. It is one of the evilest goddamned things in the world."

"Well, man," Billy said, "that depends on what kind of concept you've got of Christianity. I mean, everybody sees Christianity as this wimpy kind of thing. Somehow, I don't feel like that's true. One thing I've been exercising is who gets a dime or a quarter. You know when I'm walkin' down the street, with all these spare changers. And it's gettin' to be fun, you know, if they got a dog, or they're a couple, or this guy's got a more honest attitude—one guy came up and said, 'Gimme a fuckin' quarter, I'm a wino.' He got his quarter real quick."

"That's an old, old technique," Burroughs said. "You shouldn't fall for it. This goes back forty years—'Listen, I'm not bullshittin' ya, I don't want a meal, I want a drink.' It's old."

"I know, but I can tell the difference. This guy had literally got himself up from some cardboard."

"Go to work, you should tell them," Burroughs said.

"I took one look at him," Billy said, "and I said, man, get all the wine you can get."

It was advice that Billy soon started following himself. Despite the morphine, he began to drink again in the final months of 1978. The situation was deteriorating at Yeshe House, an old boardinghouse with sixteen rooms, five bathrooms, and seven refrigerators. There were hours for meals, and hours for kitchen duty, and rules for keeping the rooms clean, but Billy violated all the standards of community living. His room was like a dumpster, full of the junk he scavenged in garbage cans. It was not merely untidy, it was chaotic. He presented himself as a social outcast, who was beyond conforming. He refused to do kitchen duty, left loose tobacco all over the dining room from his roll-your-own efforts, drank the milk of another boarder and denied it, and sat by himself at the cable-spool table in the rear patio downing forty-ounce bottles of Colt .45. At night he cruised the cupboards in the roach-infested kitchen. Boardinghouse warfare erupted, in the form of notes on the refrigerator door. Finally, Billy was asked to leave, on the grounds that Yeshe House was for Buddhists only.

The problem of where to go was solved when he developed another abscess and was admitted to Colorado General from December 15, 1978, to February 6, 1979. They told him they would have to open him up another two inches. At this rate, Billy thought, he would be back where he was two years ago, having his intestines irrigated three times a day. He'd been hoping to find a woman to share his borrowed time. The whole idea was to have a presentable torso. But now he would leave with scars as gruesome as those he came in with.

Billy was overcome by the complete hopelessness of his situation. He was in for surgery to repair the aftermath of surgery. It was a Catch-22 dilemma, with no end in sight. He began to think that his theme song should be "I don't wanna be me." And so they opened him up again, and again he had a large abdominal wound that would not heal. Each day, there was a painful procedure where the doctors collected blood from internal bleeding in a colostomy bag. One of the nurses came in while this was being done, and the doctor asked, "Did you come to watch this delicate procedure?" "Yeah, big delicate procedure," Billy said. "Ha, ha."

He developed a paranoid dislike of the doctors. He was under the impression that some of them felt he was taking up a bed unnecessarily. Why were they checking his pupils to see if they were dilated? Sometimes he couldn't tell who was with him and who was against him. When two nurses came in and one said to the other, "Can I talk to you for a second" and they both left the room, he suspected they were talking about him.

The one exception in Billy's eyes was the top man himself, Dr. Starzl, whom he had misjudged. Even though Starzl was stingy with pain medication and seemed indifferent to his patients' comfort, Billy felt that he really *cared* about his physical condition. One day Starzl came in to check his wound, found it filled with pus, and bawled out the nurse. Since Billy had to deal with the nurse every day, he didn't want her to feel offended, so he defended her, saying, "It was really clean this morning." "Well, it's filthy now," Starzl said.

Billy wondered what he would do when he was released from the hospital. He had no place to stay. His father and James were back in New York. He had no food stamp card. He would have to trudge to the different bureaus in the snow. Billy had had enough. He wanted to hang himself in the shower. But Ursula Schaeffer, the social worker for the transplant unit, found him a studio apartment a block from the hospital, and had him put on Aid to the Needy and Disabled, which meant $200 a month and food stamps.

Now, living in Denver, away from his friends and his father, the focus of Billy's life became the hospital. It was the source of all his misery, but also his true home, for he had no other. He was required to come in three times a week for his morphine, but in fact he came every day, to chat with Ursula Schaeffer or take a shower. She knew that he sold food stamps to buy wine; she could smell it on him. She also knew that he was alone a great deal, so she got him a television set, but it was stolen.

The hospital meant both comfort and humiliation. Once he came into Dr. Starzl's office when Starzl was unwrapping a gift from a grateful patient. "No!" he said. "Oh, my! Not another watch!" Turning to Nancy Barfield, his assistant, he asked, "Do you need a watch?" "No, I've got one," she said. Looking at Billy, so scruffy and obviously destitute, she added, "Besides, that's a man's watch." Starzl caught her look, snapped the box shut, and said: "Well, I have no use for this one. I think I'll just put them all away—it's a shame to see them go to waste."

Billy wondered whether he had been brought out of his coma to learn the real meaning of suffering, loneliness, and regret. He knew that he could not go on much longer. He had no one to turn to in any real way. He sat in his apartment, listening to the dripping of the kitchen faucet. There were no more hands to hold, no more beers to drink. Instead, he was always found wanting: "I talked with your landlady and we both wonder if you're able to take care of yourself." People moved away from him on the bus and stared at him in the street. Ever since the fluke of science had brought him back to life it had been downhill all the way. His inclination to write was flagging. All he did was poke around in garbage cans, which was fun/despair, finding porno mags and baby shoes, and make lists of dos and don'ts:

—Stop imitating your father.
—Go to hospital.
—Remember that clean persons attract clean persons.
—Solve yourself, Billy, you're too good to waste.

In late May 1979, Billy wrote his father to ask him for money to buy a car: "I need approx (brace yourself) $500 for a dependable vehicle. . . . I'm afraid I can hear your sigh of exasperation, but I wouldn't have asked if it wasn't imperative."

Burroughs replied on June 3: "Now suppose you have a $500 car. What next? Where are you going? What about your welfare check and your hospital checkups and your medication? What are you going to do about morphine habit and avoiding alcohol? . . . The question is not the $500 or paying me back. The question is just what do you want to do and where do you want to go? The days of moving around from one place to another are pretty much a thing of the past. And sooner or later you have to decide where you want to stay."

This sensible reply from his father provoked in Billy an excess of pure hate and rage, and for the first time he put down on paper his long-buried feelings:

"Father—I wouldn't *be* on goddamn welfare if I hadn't spent most of my life doped up, beginning with an attempt to understand you—Imfuckingpossible 'man'—what in God's name are you anyway with your wretchedly evil entourage of bullet, gun, and mayhem *freaks*? . . . I'm thirty-one years old and it's none of your goddamn bother where I'm going—did you answer a four-year-old child whose mother you had just murdered when he asked, 'Where are you going?'—And I have news for you, pal, two things, as far as you and I are concerned you have signed my death warrant. . . . And yes, it *is* a question of the $500, you don't impress me a bit with all this 'be careful' bullshit, you could care less, and *your fucking wallet is full of blood*. All my life I've tried to experience you as something approaching a human being—by God in heaven: You *blew* it—if you think a *car* is what's behind this and I know you do, you only prove my point—Last words—I've been fighting against *real* hunger at times when you and xyz sat happily chomping steaks, smoking pot, snorting cocaine and giggling among your evil selves not two *blocks* from where I lived on *one* potato a day for three weeks—and your idea of being helpful was to buy 'your son' (which title I formally disavow as of Sunday, June 7, 1979) a pair of fucking blue jeans—you got it now, buddy—thank your well-fed ego that the world doesn't know you as a person dying in Denver does—God's mercy on you and your blood-bought money—Your Cursed from Birth Offspring.

"P.S. From one who has intensely studied your work all his life let it be known that in this one's opinion, everything since *Naked Lunch* is tripe of the worst con-artist type—as far as art goes that's your only kind—Con."

Having released his cry of prednisone-fueled rage, Billy thought twice about sending it. Burroughs, having turned him down on the car, began sending him money with some regularity, $100 a month, half the allowance he had for so many years received from his parents. But he reasoned that if he sent Billy any more, he would hand it out to winos in the street.

Basic to Billy's state of mind was that he felt physically so rotten. Here it was nearly three years after the operation, and he was always in pain. Each morning he awoke with severe stomach pains. He was in a state of chronic fatigue. Just making it to the 7-Eleven wore him out. In medical terms, it was two steps forward and three steps back, and in 1979, he was admitted to Colorado General four times: once in December and January for his abscess, then from April 23 to 27, for chills and vomiting, which were diagnosed as the flu; then from June 21 to 26, for another operation on his leaking fistula; and finally from July 25 to August 3, for another operation on his most recent abscess. His abdomen was being opened and closed so often it might have been a manhole cover. Billy had hoped that he would get well, but finally realized that there was no getting well. He had survived only to suffer grotesque humiliations and indignities. As long as he was on steroids, he would keep getting infections, and they would keep opening him up. After all, he had been in a coma for six days, during which his liver had not filtered the impurities in his blood, and the bacteria had proliferated in his abdominal cavity, for which he continued to pay the price.

That November of 1979, Billy had been in Denver less than a year, but was already sick of the place, which had to do with the constant presence of the Rocky Mountains in the distance, constantly saying, "I'll be here long after your little mess is newly buffaloed prairie." He longed for the sleep of the conscience-free and the weary. But he picked up when he met a compassionate young woman who was not put off by his scars and who slept with him. It was the first time since Jo-Anne Kyger, and he cried, and shook, and trembled, and felt he was back on the planet.

The improvement in his romantic life prompted him into activity, and he wrote his father that December that he was "job-hunting steadily. Buses, buses, buses, mountains of dimes gobbled up by Ma Bell. Latest prospects: two shots at working with crazy kids. Got turned down at the hospital for 'insufficient background' for a janitor job. What did they consider background in the complex world of broom-pushing I don't know."

But then one night Billy had his new girlfriend over to dinner and forgot to turn off two burners on the stove. The next morning he was awakened by the sound of splintering wood. His door was being broken down by five firemen who charged into the kitchen and turned off the gas. Then they opened all the windows and turned on a fan to clear the air, and Billy nearly froze to death. He was evicted, which he felt was very unfair, because he always paid his rent on time, and had once stopped a knife fight in the hallway, at great risk of personal injury. Once again, the infinitely patient and tolerant Ursula Schaeffer came to his rescue and helped him find another small apartment.

In early 1980, Billy moved into his new place, a studio at 756 Colorado Boulevard, south of Hatcher's drugstore. Everything was going wrong. The plumbing was backed up, and the handyman wouldn't fix his curtain. Out of food stamps, he was reduced to eating cold ravioli out of the can, not having the strength to boil water. He had fallen asleep smoking and burned a hole in his mattress, which would come out of his damage deposit. He was too broke to buy paper and had to write on envelopes. In every letter to his father, there was the same refrain: "Ho, you thought you'd get by one letter without $$$$?" When he asked for money for stamps, he got back a sarcastic reply: "Here's the two dollars you so desperately need." When James called him self-pitying, Billy was thrown into a steroid-induced rage, writing back: "I've been 'goddamned' long enough without people I love slapping me in the face with a wet fish. . . . If you were in my position I wouldn't hit you with such a phrase."

What was it all about but Tinker to Evers to Chance? He had gone too far, beyond psychiatrists, social workers, beautiful women, drugs, mind control, delusions of grandeur, the birds of the field, and the passage of time. How ridiculous this survival game really was. As the James Brown song said, "Baby, it's getting a little cold outside. I wonder do you know what I'm talking about."

Billy began calling James Grauerholz collect late at night to say that he was going to commit suicide. "I'm a mess," he said, "women don't like me, I'm a failure, I'll just do it, it'll be easier for everybody. I've got it all worked out." James spoke to Dr. Warner, who said that Billy refused to be responsible for his actions and tended to attribute omnipotence to others, and then when they did not live up to his expectations he would blame his condition on them.

Burroughs thought of having him in the Bunker, but it would be a nightmare, he'd start hanging out with the Bowery bums, and Burroughs would have to go out and find him at three in the morning. There were sound reasons for keeping him in Denver where his medical connection was established—he got away with murder up there, they had infinite patience with his irresponsibility, he could check in anytime, use the hospital like a hotel.

Burroughs came to Boulder that summer of 1980 to teach and spend some time with his son, who moved up from Denver to Boulder but had a hard time finding a room because he was so disheveled, with a ragged beard and long disorderly hair. Billy was sick of hearing "I'm sorry we just rented the place, I'm really sorry," but did nothing to improve his appearance. He could, however, crash at his father's, for Cabell Hardy was no longer around, having outworn his welcome.

On August 29, after a Chinese dinner, they went back to Burroughs' place, but he turned in early because he had to catch a plane to New York the next day. Billy wouldn't see the old flub for another year, and wanted to tell him that he knew that many a time he'd been more than a pest, but he couldn't get it out. The next morning, before Billy had wiped the sleep from his eyes, he and Allen loaded up the trunk of the car and Burroughs was gone. Billy did not go to the airport because his father did not like good-bye scenes, he was embarrassed by displays of emotion. He was a rather unfortunate man to say the least, thought Billy. As it turned out, it was the last time that father and son would see each other.

That fall, there was a bombshell on the transplant ward. Dr. Starzl resigned to start a transplant unit at the University of Pittsburgh Health Center. Billy wrote Starzl: "I just read of your resignation. I can only say that I felt as if a lifelong friend just died. Could you possibly reconsider?"

But Starzl did leave, and Billy lost his protector. From October 2 to 23, he was admitted to Colorado General for the last time, for an operation to correct the occlusion of his bile duct. After Starzl's departure, Billy lost his status as mascot of the transplant ward. His morphine dose was drastically cut, and he was discouraged from coming to the hospital except when required.

Then, in November 1980, a friend from Billy's childhood reentered his life. Teina De Bakey (formerly Barnum), who had had a teenage crush on Billy when they were both at school in Palm Beach, had returned to Palm Beach after a failed marriage to the son of the heart transplant surgeon Michael E. De Bakey. On November 14, 1980, she wrote Burroughs:

"I am writing in an attempt to locate your son, Billy. You will not remember, but I met you once many years ago at your mother's house in Palm Beach—1964. You were there for your father's funeral. You ran outside to see the Goodyear Blimp. I have been told by previous classmates here that Billy is dead. I would appreciate your letting me know if this is so, and if not, if there is any way I could get in touch with him."

Burroughs sent Teina Billy's Denver address, and they began to correspond. Billy wrote her on December 17 that he was working on an account of his operation that would do for hospitals what *Jaws* had done for beaches. Being back in touch with Billy made Teina remember her fondness for him when he was sixteen. Partly out of a wish to reenact a childhood fantasy, partly from a need to return to more carefree times, she invited him to visit her in Palm Beach.

The invitation seemed providential to Billy. He would escape the awful Denver winter and the chilly post-Starzl atmosphere at the hospital. He would return to the scene of his childhood, the one place where he had been really happy, taken care of and loved by his grandparents. He could sit in the sun and work on his book, and, who knows, maybe a spark would be struck between himself and Teina. For Billy, a return to Palm Beach meant "Eureka! Sweet Bird of Youth."

Teina expected to see Billy as he hd been in the eighth grade, cute and lively and full of mischievous fun. When he got off the plane in late December, she saw a gaunt, long-haired, bearded, stooped, squalid-looking bum who looked more like Charles Manson than the boy she remembered. She knew at once that he shouldn't have come—he belonged on the Bowery in New York, not on Worth Avenue—but she felt responsible for him. She found a furnished apartment at 126 Peruvian Avenue, and paid the first month's rent, $600—it was the high season.

She took him to see a doctor, who drew her aside and said, "He doesn't belong here." She took him to the barber for a shave and a haircut and bought him some new clothes. Billy stayed three and a half weeks, and those three and a half weeks were hell. Teina was working in a real estate office and would check in on him two or three times a day. He spent most of his time sitting in his room, drinking and crying, and saying, "I'm going to die."

Teina was overcome by melancholy and hopelessness. She realized that there was no place for Billy. She had a brother called Skipper who was retarded from birth, and who had been placed in a home, where he was happy with kids like himself. But where could Billy have been happy? In a home for transplants? She understood something about transplants, having been married for seven years to the son of Dr. De Bakey, who didn't seem to understand the implications of what he was doing—to him, she thought, the heart was just a muscle. It was clear to Teina that the shock of the transplant and the steroids had made Billy emotionally disturbed. He couldn't handle being on his own. He couldn't even shop or cook a meal.

Out of compassion, and to prove to him that he wasn't repulsive, she slept with him. But then he became possessive. One time she dropped by with a friend, and Billy wrote her an angry note: "Because you decided to get drunk with that gorilla you dragged in, yourself stumbling over the heater. I told you I'd work on that book with the sincerest intentions and (God, what nerve!) you sat right down and practically spat in my eye: 'You don't want to work on the book.' Well, goddamn it, right then and there I started thinking: I can write you *straight* under the table. Then you proceed to drink my wine and tell me to be patient. And then you leave after that silly monster pipes up with 'Teina and I just came by to take your temper—I mean temperature.' "

Just as he had with Jo-Anne Kyger, Billy was burning down a situation where a caring woman wanted to help. He was making himself impossible to be around. When he mentioned going to see George Von Hilsheimer, the director of the Green Valley School, whom he liked and admired, she urged him to go and stay with Hilsheimer for a couple of months, and then come back to Palm Beach in the summer when the rents dropped.

At the end of January 1981 she put him on the bus to Orlando. The bus driver looked at this unshaven and glassy-eyed creature who seemed to be having trouble walking, and asked, "Are you sure he's going to be all right?" Barely able to get the words out, and knowing how false they sounded as soon as they were uttered, she said, "Yeah, he's going to be all right."

Billy was running out of people. His father didn't want him, the girl who had once loved him didn't want him, but Hilsheimer made a point of never turning away a former student. George Von Hilsheimer was living in a big house in De Land, where he practiced therapy, the Green Valley School having shut down. When Billy called, he said, "Come on over and stay awhile." He wanted to take a look at this creature who had someone else's liver in him. The very thought of it made him fume, for he hated the "gee whiz" doctors. They did all this fantastic hardware and then dumped the guy into the street. It was emblematic of what was wrong with the whole medical establishment. He would like to see one transplant who was living a decent life. The emphasis was on the miracle itself rather than on life after the miracle.

When Billy arrived, all of Hilsheimer's opinions of "heroic surgery" were confirmed, for he was obviously in trouble. First of all, he looked like a tramp. And then, when Hilsheimer offered him a glass of very good wine, he just swilled it down, without even bothering to appreciate the bouquet. Nonetheless, Hilsheimer sensed that Billy had no one to turn to, and that Billy thought of him as a father figure, and may have been seeking him out because he *was* cold and blunt and hard as nails. So he invited Billy to sleep on the living room couch.

The next day Billy took a walk around De Land and got lost. Hilsheimer went looking for him and found him passed out, leaning against a dumpster. Drops of blood were dripping from his face like perspiration. "Sometimes my pores open and I just bleed," Billy explained. The next night Billy came in drunk and broke a window and cut himself. Hilsheimer had no patience with drunks, having had an alcoholic mother. But Billy explained that he was drinking because he was off morphine.

A couple of days later, Hilsheimer was sitting around the kitchen table with some friends. Wanting to use Billy as an example for a point he was making, he said, "This creature in the next room . . ." Overhearing the remark, Billy was offended, and insisted on leaving at once. "Billy, come on," Hilsheimer said, "there's no need to leave now, it's raining, and there won't be a bus for hours, and you'll have to sit outside in the rain under an overhang." "I've got to go," Billy said. He would not stay a minute longer if that was what Hilsheimer thought of him.

Hilsheimer drove Billy to the bus station, and if truth be told, was relieved to be rid of him. Sometimes you got the feeling with a sick person that if you cared enough you could bring him around, but with Billy he didn't get that feeling. A couple of hours later, the police called, having picked up Billy, but Hilsheimer wouldn't take him back. "This man has had a liver transplant," he said, "and he's dying, and there's no way I have the capacity to help him. He should be hospitalized." Hilsheimer had read once that if you were at the bottom of a well and could see just a little patch of blue sky it would still be worth being alive, but he wondered. The police took Billy to the West Volusia County Hospital, where he was admitted on February 1, 1981.

He remained in the hospital for sixteen days, suffering from pneumonia, hepatitis, possible scabies, and lice. His clothes were so dirty the hospital wanted to burn them, but it upset Billy to lose the shirt he had bought in Alaska and other memorable articles, so they cleaned what they could. Frances Lewis, the West Volusia Hospital social worker, notified James Grauerholz and Teina De Bakey, who sent money. In addition, Teina sent a bouquet of jonquils, which noticeably improved Billy's morale.

When Billy was discharged, Frances Lewis found him a room at a big, rambling, run-down former resort hotel called the Landmark, and opened a bank account for him. Every day, the neighborhood Community Center brought him meals on wheels. One of the nurses, who had seen him reading the Bible, invited him to go to a Pentecostal church service two days after his discharge. She reported that he cussed through half the service and then got up and left.

Billy was now completely isolated and withdrawn. He had stopped taking morphine. He had stopped taking the steroids. He accepted, indeed welcomed, the inevitability of liver rejection and death. His body was not one that he wanted to be in. His mind was stringing disconnected thoughts that sometimes made him burst out laughing.

He remembered Morrison's Cafeteria in West Palm Beach, where his grandparents used to take him. There was an old man at the entrance with his eternal chant: "Myyammeee daily newspapuh—Ballooo Streek." Over and over in the warm twilight air—there was something timeless about it.

He remembered a conversation he'd had with Allen Ginsberg over the relative value of waxed and unwaxed dental floss, when thousands of people out there thought every comment Allen came up with was a cosmic utterance.

He wanted to bash a state trooper for a coal miner. He wanted to go to the Texas border with a bazooka and shoot down one of those helicopters that transfix wetbacks in a beacon of light.

On March 2 he walked to the bus station to pick up several boxes of new clothes that Teina De Bakey had sent him. The landlady scolded him for not taking a taxi. That evening, standing in front of the mirror over the sink, he shaved his head. No one would ever call him hirsute again. As he looked at himself, as bald as a Buddhist monk, he thought of driving a serrated carving knife through his face and going to the doctor and saying, "This is the only way I can convince you that the pain I feel is worse than this."

Billy tried to focus his thoughts: Vomiting at dawn. Unwarranted fear. Pouring perspiration at the approach of sleep. A terror of waking. A terror of retiring. Pain and exhaustion. Salting my food with tears. He knew what he wanted on his tombstone: "Raised his fist and lightning struck it."

Billy went walking in the night. Shivering with weariness, he stumbled into a ditch by the side of the road and lay down in it as if in a bed. With the first light of dawn, a passerby found him and took him to the hospital, where he died at 6:35 A.M. on March 3, 1981. The cause of death was "acute gastrointestinal hemorrhage associated with micronodular cirrhosis." Virginia had left him after giving him life for four and a half years. Billy was thirty-three years old. His remains were cremated in De Land and his ashes were scattered in the Rocky Mountains in Colorado, at the site of a Buddhist center.

His father thought it was remarkable that he had lived more than four years with a borrowed liver, drinking the way he did. Obviously, it was just a general collapse of the whole system. When he found Billy's angry unsent letter among his papers, he was puzzled. Why did Billy say that his wallet was full of blood, as if he were a merchant of death or an evil old tycoon whose money was tainted? As for that business about Billy eating potatoes when he was eating steak, it was a complete fabrication.

Burroughs petitioned the court to administer Billy's estate, which consisted mainly of unpublished manuscripts. But Karen Perry, from whom Billy was still not divorced, tried to block the petition, writing the court on April 20 that Buroughs was "father to the decedent in name only. . . . "

"I was Billy's father for thirty-three years," Burroughs responded, "and she his cohabiting wife for only six. I never 'rejected' or 'abandoned' him, although our relationship, and our lives, were troubled. I maintained contact with my son throughout his life. Karen's allegation that 'I never supported the decedent financially, psychologically, or emotionally' is absolutely untrue. . . . I have done all I could to assure that his needs were provided for. Since my return to New York in 1974, after living twenty-five years abroad, I have provided thousands of dollars for his financial support." The court granted Burroughs' petition.

It was impossible, James Grauerholz thought, not to observe Billy's ineradicable wish to punish his father, which coexisted with his heart's desire to love and admire and be close to him. Another child, even one orphaned at the age of four, might have healed his own soul by rejecting and denouncing his father at a much younger age. The tragedy was in the impasse that prevented father and son from fully opening up to each other. The same set of parents, Mote and Laura, *raised them both with the gospel of restraint*. Some things are unforgivable. The man who killed your mother cannot be forgiven, no matter if he is your father and no matter how much you want to forgive him. No one can say that William Burroughs killed his wife and got away scot-free. He was fortunate that a Mexican jail sentence was not added to the nightmare that he would live the rest of his days. If there was ever a man who had the right to sink into heroin addiction and alcoholism, and descend invisibly to the bottom of society, there to die, it was he. But he did not descend, he picked himself up. It was Billy who descended, and it was Billy who died.

· TWENTY ·

THE BUNKER

1976–1981

The years from 1976 to 1981 were overshadowed for Burroughs by his son's illness and death, but in the meantime his life went on, and he moved back and forth between Boulder and New York, and continued to write in the white and windowless environment of the Bunker, and gave readings and saw his friends.

On June 3, 1976, there was a great feast at the Bunker in honor of Allen Ginsberg's fiftieth birthday. James Grauerholz was distressed when amid all the fellow feeling and congratulations a quarrel erupted between Allen and John Giorno over the covers of poetry albums that John had begun to produce. It was pathetic, thought James, to see them both descend to the level of personal insult, with Allen screaming abuse and John uptight and hurt and defensively babbling, "Okay, James, Allen has just said that you and William hate the album covers . . ." "Yes," Allen interrupted, "and John just told me that you think I don't know anything about music and that I'm an embarrassment." Then after some more verbal sparring Allen lay back, absorbed in his thoughts, feeling good after having let out all his spleen, and feeling self-important because of his "Stop-anyone-who-disparages-the-Beat-movement-in-the-nineteen-seventies" attitude.

In the seventies the Beat movement was pretty much a memory, the granddaddy of the present punk scene, which had come out of the teenage garage bands of the late sixties, with their emphasis on adolescent nihilism and boredom. Iggy Pop and the Stooges and the New York Dolls were seen as the standard-bearers of the true garage-band sensibility, which evolved into punk rock. The punk scene flourished with the coming of age of the first generation raised on the concept of nuclear annihilation, the Soviets having announced in 1950 that they had the Bomb.

In distressing times, extravagant fringe groups emerged, such as the

Incroyables during the Reign of Terror, who wore foppish clothes and disorderly hair in a style called *cheveux à la victime*. In the same manner, the punk subculture stressed various forms of sartorial excess and eccentric hair styles. The idealism of the sixties had evaporated, and the protest movement had died with the end of the Vietnam War.

Punk had started as a movement of disaffected teenagers. So you were a fifteen-year-old in Topeka, Kansas, sitting at home in the dark, and the warm summer air was wafting through the screen doors, and the tornado warnings were out, and you were listening to the Talking Heads, and you knew that a very different life was within range. Then it spread to New York, and became "the downtown scene," with its performance artists, clothing designers, and filmmakers. The music headquarters was CBGB (Country, Bluegrass, and Blues), which was on the Bowery, right up the street from the Bunker. On St. Mark's Place there was a punk boutique called Manic Panic. In 1976, *Punk* magazine appeared, with its "why-bother-we're-all-doomed" sensibility, which was very Burroughsian. *Punk*'s special issue, "Mutant Monster Beach Party," was also Burroughsian.

There was, however, something essentially self-defeating about "punk," which prevented it from becoming a mass movement like the hippies. The punk "rude and ugly" style was a reaction against flower power, and a need to go beyond the excesses of the Beats and the hippies in both appearance and behavior. For a young person to "go punk" while living with his or her parents entailed heavy disapproval, so that the "punk scene" was necessarily limited to cities where extravagance was accepted. In addition, "punk" was aimless and leaderless, less a movement than a collection of hair styles. It was as if they were saying, "We have inherited the counterculture, but we don't know where to take it." So, in the arts, you had the artist/merchandisers, led by Andy Warhol, "the art world's answer to McDonald's," with his gift for total banality.

It was Warhol who backed the Velvet Underground, who took the romanticizing of drugs to a new level of silliness. "When I put a spike into my vein," went one of their songs, ". . . I feel like Jesus." "Waitin' for the Man," sang the moronic Lou Reed, "Twenty-six dollars in my hand . . . up to Lexington and 125th . . . Hey white boy chasin' our women around." Well, thought Burroughs when he heard that one, the one thing a drug addict would not do is chase black women. Like characters in a Burroughs novel, punk figures adopted pseudonyms, some of them taken from his novels, such as Johnny Vortex and the Inferential Kid, and sometimes not, such as Lydia Lunch and Pat Place and Rockets Redglare, who offered a dissenting opinion to the prevalent junk-punk scene with his observation that "the people who glamorize heroin are the true pornographers."

The whole scene was a travesty, and yet Burroughs was a sort of totemic figure for the punks because of his own history as a junky. Here was this recognized author of venerable years and conservative mien, and he was a junky, too, man. Burroughs seemed to validate the taking of hard drugs. It was like Daddy giving you permission.

Burroughs himself had been off junk for years, but was forever identified through his writing as an addict. Junk was nothing but trouble, as he was reminded in a letter from his London friend, the writer Alex Trocchi, who had been burned by another figure from his past, the older but no less irresponsible Mikey Portman. "You may have heard from the grapevine," wrote Alex, "that Mikey nearly got me crucified for supplying him with heroin. Since then my heart is a dried prune to all junky pleas." Alex Trocchi and Mikey Portman both died in 1983, Alex of pneumonia and Mikey of a heart attack at age thirty-nine.

Burroughs was by now an established figure in New York, so established that for the first time in his life he had tax problems. He was treated, he thought, with deference—an I.R.S. agent, Miss Rhoda Guskins, made a house call to help him sort out his records. Then, in May 1977, the *Village Voice* arranged a meeting with Tennessee Williams in the Élysée Hotel. Both writers had been born in St. Louis, and they had met in Tangier in 1960, introduced by Paul Bowles. Burroughs had once borrowed from Paul a copy of Ten's first collection of stories. Being on junk at the time, he dripped blood all over it while injecting himself, and Paul was annoyed. It should be quite a collector's item, Burroughs now told the bibulous and garrulous Tennessee. They discussed the line between fiction and autobiography, and Burroughs said, "When someone asks me to what extent my work is autobiographical, I say 'Every word is autobiographical and every word is fiction.'" They reminisced about fellow writers, and Burroughs recalled Graham Greene saying, "Of course Evelyn Waugh was a great friend of mine but we never talked about *writing*."

In 1977, the scent of movie deals was in the air. Elliott Gould wanted to buy *The Last Words of Dutch Schultz* and play the lead. That didn't work out, but something more solid came into view that March with the reappearance in Burroughs' life of the man he called "the wheelchair financier," Jacques Stern, the polio victim who was in one of his temporary periods of affluence. Through a Cayman Islands corporation he had formed, called Automatique, he proposed to pay $20,000 for a year's option on Burroughs' first book, *Junky*, to make it into a movie. He further proposed to hire Terry Southern as screenwriter and Dennis Hopper as director and star.

It seemed to James Grauerholz that with his $20,000, Jacques Stern would be buying himself a year's worth of delusions, for Terry Southern and Dennis Hopper had the two worst reputations in Hollywood. Terry's fondness for dope was legendary. He had a standing joke with Burroughs about a potion called Brompton's Mixture, which combined cocaine, morphine, alcohol, cherry syrup, and water. As for Dennis Hopper, after scoring in *Easy Rider*, he had gone off to the Andes to make *The Last Movie*, a production blanketed in cocaine. He had a habit so bad that the bridge of his nose was misshapen and discolored. He used to say that he could hear the telephone wires talking to him. He had just finished shooting *Apocalypse Now*, and reported that Marlon Brando had refused to act opposite him, so that in their scenes together each interchange was filmed with the other actor absent. Dennis *was* the frenetic character in *Apocalypse Now*, in cowboy hat and boots and faded jeans.

But apparently the money was real, and there was always the chance that the movie might get made, even though the presence of Southern and Hopper would make it unbankable as far as backers went, so James went along with the deal. One day in March, at the apartment of Jacques Stern's lawyer, Joe Bianco, a roly-poly prodigy who had made a fortune in commodities by the time he was twenty-three, Burroughs, Hopper, and Southern were each handed a check for $20,000 and went to a French restaurant to celebrate. "We'd better cash these fast," Burroughs said, " 'cause it's all we're likely to see."

Then there was a big party at the house Jacques Stern was renting on Gramercy Park, with caviar and champagne, and James got a glimpse of what it was like to have lots of money while being completely disorganized. There was no furniture to speak of in the living room with the exception of a grand piano, and the waiters looked like bit players in a Bela Lugosi movie. Jacques had two orderlies helping him in and out of his wheelchair; he constantly cussed them out. The party was one vast shooting gallery. Joe Bianco had never seen drugs done so openly.

Stern was rolling rapidly back and forth across the living room in short spurts, the only cripple James had ever seen who could pace in his wheelchair. Then one of the orderlies handed him a hospital syringe with about 60cc's of liquid cocaine in it, and he stuck it into his wrist and injected part of it, letting the syringe hang there like a leaf, and he started raving that he was going to get Samuel Beckett to play the part of Old Ike, and then he got on the phone with the needle still hanging from his wrist and started shouting, "Get me Paris—Samuel Beckett." And then he was talking into the phone as though he was connected with Beckett: "Hello, Beckett—this is Jacques Stern—you've read *Junky*, by William Burroughs . . . yes, right . . . I want you to play Old Ike in a movie we're shooting—what do you mean, you don't want to? Well, fuck you, you old fraud!" and resoundingly hung up. Jacques often called famous people, but Joe Bianco caught him once talking to a dial tone.

It was demented, but the money was real. For the next two months they worked on the script and held continuous meetings, and James could see thousands of dollars going up various noses. Dennis Hopper was particularly trying, with his irrelevant posturing. They would be working on a scene, and Hopper would suddenly jump up and say, "I'm from Dodge City, Kansas, man, and when I was a little kid I used to be, like, in my bedroom, man, and I'd look out the window, man, and there'd be a train goin' by, and a whistle, man, you know what I mean, man, a whistle, and that whistle was blowin', man, it was blowin'," and none of what he was saying had anything to do with the script, and the others would roll their eyes heavenward and wait for the stirring reminiscence to end.

Terry Southern in the meantime was ensconced in the Gramercy Park Hotel with a bevy of attractive lady typists, some of whom used only their index fingers, and was trying to impress Stern with the Hollywood technique of colored pages to show which rewrite he was on, but to James's sorrow, he was throwing in a lot of scenes that weren't in *Junky*. He had a cocktail party scene where businessmen were standing around saying things like "My company recycles used condoms," and "Yes, we're into bogus penicillin," which had nothing to do with the book. The opening scene was a red mushroom cloud, which was then seen to be blood going into a syringe that a junky was injecting into his arm.

"What can happen to your script is not to be believed," Burroughs wrote Brion Gysin on May 24. "It's like you came back from Istanbul and there was a Dali bent watch right in the middle of your picture. You write a part for James Coburn and you wind up with Liberace."

By that time, the expected West German financing had collapsed, leaving Jacques Stern with a budget of $1,930,522 that he could not meet. Stern's solution was to announce a different star daily—he had signed Jack Nicholson, he had signed David Bowie. Then he would call his collaborators and heap upon them torrents of abuse. He told James he was a meddler, conspiring to keep Burroughs out of the project and "split the posthumous take." "If I ever have the displeasure of seeing you again," he said, "I will make it unlikely that anyone shall see you again."

He called Burroughs and said, "I hired you as an actor, not a writer, so get out of that role. What have you produced? One trunk! That's where you get all your shit! Haven't done much since *Naked Lunch*, have you?" Burroughs just let him rave and then said, "Look, Jacques, I don't want to listen to any more of this," and hung up. Stewart Meyer, who was around the Bunker a lot, said that Jacques Stern had broadened his emotional range, because for the first time in his life he wanted to kill a cripple. Stern threw money your way, and he threw headaches your way. Once he called Stew at five in the morning because his wheelchair batteries were dead. "Why don't you call the elevator man?" Stew asked. "Because he's a C.I.A. agent," Stern said.

The flower of Stern's abuse was reserved for Dennis Hopper, whom he held responsible for losing the financing. When Dennis arrived forty-five minutes late at a meeting in a suite at the Hotel Carlyle, Jacques Stern refused to speak to him, and sent him snarling messages from an adjoining room through Joe Bianco, which Bianco toned down. Annoyed with Bianco, Dennis said, "Hey, you know, man, I got friends in Arizona, they carry guns, man," to which Bianco replied, "We're not in Arizona, Dennis, we're in New York, and the person with friends in New York is me." Jacques finally wheeled himself into the room, and Dennis said, "I'm sorry you feel that way, Jacques," to which he replied: "You're not sorry, you're through! Finished! Fired, you miserable ass! Now get out!" with his long bony finger quavering imperiously toward the door. Dennis stomped out, which Jacques couldn't do, but the next day, the two of them were happily snorting powder together.

Burroughs grew weary of Jacques' manic behavior—he claimed he had a four-picture deal, that the French minister of culture was his bosom pal, and that the French film board would finance all his projects. The truth, Burroughs wrote in the same letter to Brion, was that "the Baron de Stern is an incorrigible fuckup. He can be relied on to fuck up any project in which he is involved. After he fired everybody four times with a torrent of abuse, we went to a lawyer and gave Joe Bianco control of production."

Terry Southern in the meantime was getting his expenses paid at the Gramercy Park Hotel, with all the perks, and referred to Jacques Stern as "a grand guy . . . really a grand guy!" Behind Burroughs' back, he and Jacques wrote a script that Terry took to Hollywood to flog, as though it had Burroughs' endorsement, whereas Burroughs thought of it as blending "the worst features of Terry's sophomoric humor and Jacques' bad Italian surrealism."

James was furious. It was enough to make him blow his lunch over the railing. He didn't think Terry's slapstick haw-haw-didja-get-it humor had any business in this movie. Terry was afraid to admit that mooching off Jacques for pot and speed and coke wasn't the same thing as writing a script that played. He was showing indications of his true nature, thought James, but this fit of pique did not interfere with a warm friendship that has endured.

And then in March 1978 the option ran out and it was all over—the rushing around to these half-assed meetings, the white nights, the easy money, the dinners at One Fifth Avenue, and the telephone ravings. For a year, thought James, they had lived in the kingdom of illusion, each with a different agenda: He and William had genuinely wanted to make the movie. Dennis Hopper wanted to finance his cocaine habit. Terry Southern wanted to rehabilitate his reputation as a screenwriter by piggybacking on Burroughs. And Jacques Stern wanted to create havoc.

Stern remained in New York, except that now he was broke, and Burroughs had to bail him out on more than one occasion. Once he was summoned to a restaurant where Stern could not pay the bill. In 1979, he landed on Burroughs' doorstep at the Bunker after starting a fire in his hotel lobby. "We'll wheel you right out into the gutter where you belong," the manager said. He arrived with all his stuff in laundry bags, and was carried up the stairs by the cab driver, whom Stern started insulting, and who said, "Listen, don't get smart with me or I'll drop you." He gave Burroughs the name of a woman to call, but the woman said, "I cannot have this man here." Stern commandeered the Bunker, racing around in his wheelchair like a giant insect. After a couple of days, Burroughs couldn't stand it, decided "I'm going to walk out on this whole situation," and left for Naropa.

In spite of the *Junky* fiasco, and the fact that none of his books had been made into a film, Burroughs was infiltrating popular culture in odd and various ways. In Seattle, Washington, a women's fashion boutique called Nova Express opened. Clemson University in South Carolina asked him to write something for the fiftieth anniversary of the publication of *Look Homeward, Angel*, by Thomas Wolfe, an author with whom he had little in common. The University of Minnesota had a Burroughs Club, whose only purpose was to further the appreciation of his work. *Newsweek* wanted him for "My Turn." *Playgirl* wanted him for "His Turn." *Quest* wanted him to go to Guatemala. The gay magazines *Blueboy, The Advocate,* and *Gay Sunshine* wanted him for interviews. Patti Smith asked him to write lyrics for her songs, which he did, thinking, "Why not grab a piece of the punk action?" and which went like this:

My husband and I
The old school tie
Hyphenated names
Tired old games
It belongs in the bog
With the rest of the sog
Pull the chain on Buckingham
The drain calls you Ma'am.
BUGGER THE QUEEN.

"One has the feeling," Burroughs wrote Paul Bowles, "of being in the middle of something here, I don't know just what. Why, I was made an honorary citizen of Austin, Texas, by the mayor himself." Faithful to Tangier, Paul replied: "You apparently decided to experience the rigors of the decaying culture *sur place*. I can believe it would be instructive, but I can't conceive of its being enjoyable." Then Paul proceeded to describe how life in Tangier had deteriorated now that it was no longer an international zone. Jane had died in Málaga in 1973. The *muezzins* now had loudspeakers at the tops of the minarets, so that the calls for prayer awakened everyone within two miles. They used to last a minute or two, and now they lasted twenty-five minutes. You could no longer find imported food in the market. There was no running water in his apartment. He had to take care of the illnesses of his servants, Fatima's liver and Abdouahaid's appendix, and of the various scrapes of his bad-tempered friend Mrabet. Several score of workmen were banging away across the street, building a new lycée for students who would wreck it as soon as it was up. The German tourists shuffled through the streets in close-packed groups, as if expecting a savage attack. He couldn't keep warm in the winter, since the doors of his apartment reached only to within an inch of the floor, and the windows had been built off-kilter, and the wind blew in. He could not leave Tangier, having been arrested as a spy the last time he had traveled to another city, and having had to wait five hours in the office of the military commander of Tetouan. He was afraid to leave Morocco, as he had been told he would not be re-admitted. He couldn't even go to Gibraltar. It was like a form of house arrest.

If those were the pleasures of life in Tangier, thought Burroughs, Paul could have them. But that was Paul, he wasn't happy unless he had something to worry about. He wrote Paul that in New York, there were no gendarmes pounding on *his* door. As for Boulder, to which he had returned in March of 1978, it was "bland and innocuous, a middle-class town with no slums or minorities . . . beautiful blond boys everywhere on looks but strictly decorative rather than functional." To Alan Ansen, who had been expelled from Venice again, just as Burroughs had been forced to leave Mexico and other venues, he wrote: "If only we could create a composite country, codeine pills from France, the liquor mart from Boulder, police from New York, boys from remote underprivileged areas, and of course all the local culinary specialties. . . . isn't one important feature the unquestioned right to remain? One always pays for that."

One always paid, that was the rub, and Burroughs still found himself from time to time in a cash crunch. The one advantage of places like Tangier and Athens was that they were cheap. That May, the checks started bouncing all around him like crystal skulls in a Mayan ball court. The wolves were closing in. He was about to be stripped of his credit cards when he was rescued thanks to loans from friends, his Grove Press royalty statement, a payment for a reading, a German contract, and some money from Gallimard, his French publisher. In the words of the immortal bard, Burroughs reflected, "Let us repair and order well the state that like events may ne'er it ruinate."

That summer of 1978 he and James went to Los Angeles to visit the set of the movie *Heartbeat*, which was based on Carolyn Cassady's account of her triangular affair with Neal Cassady and Jack Kerouac. As they drove to their motel, the Tropicana, Burroughs observed: "The sky is thin as paper here. The whole place could go up in ten minutes. That's the charm in Los Angeles."

At the Universal Studio in Culver City, the set was a tract house in San Francisco with fifties furniture and kitchen and canned goods with fifties prices. The scene they were shooting had Jack, played by John Heard, coming home drunk with a black woman and trying to smuggle her past Carolyn to the attic room. The clowning, thought Burroughs, was uncannily realistic. At lunch with Nick Nolte, who was playing Neal, he asked if there was any psychic contact, and Nolte nodded, and Burroughs felt Neal sitting there in his cheap 1950s suit with the sleeves pulled up. That was what acting was all about, thought Burroughs, you had to open yourself up to possession by the character.

After lunch, he watched a scene where they learn that Allen Ginsberg's book of poems, *Howl*, has been seized by customs, and Neal says, "All it's going to do is make him famous, the poor bastard." Allen had not wanted his name used, because (for one thing) of a fictitious scene in a Thai restaurant where they had him shouting, "Waiter, there's a turd in my soup," so his character was called Ira Streiker. Nonetheless, as Burroughs watched the scene, the past hung in the air. There were multiple takes, and at one point, the director, John Byrum, broke his absorbed indifference to the visitors' presence by saying, "And you think you've had chaos in *your* life, Mr. Burroughs."

The visit to the set started Burroughs thinking that in Jack Kerouac there had been a lifelong incompatibility between his uneasy surface presentation of a nice, regular American who liked beer and Mom and TV and baseball, who worked as a brakeman and wanted to settle down with Carolyn Cassady, and the spy in his body, the writer whose status as a regular guy is belied by an obsessive need to write about it. Who had killed Neal Cassady, Burroughs asked himself? The character that Jack made of him in *On the Road*, Dean Moriarty, killed Neal Cassady. He had died of exposure. And who had killed Jack Kerouac? A spy in his body known as Jack Kerouac the writer.

At this point, James Grauerholz was going through another crisis and decided to spend some time in San Francisco by himself. He had now been with Burroughs four years, and periodically got upset by the frustrations built into the job. As long as he worked for Burroughs, he would not be able to pursue his own goal of a career in music. There were also periods of heavy drinking when James, himself no teetotaler, could not bear to be around him, and left notes such as this: "It breaks my heart to see you drink yourself into an insensible stupor. If you wish to die perhaps it were better you killed yourself outright. You said to me once, about Kerouac, 'If a man wants to drink himself to death, there's nothing you can do.' It hurts me very much either way. Do What Thou Wilt— and do you really want to present this sorry spectacle of a mumbling, incoherent, and repetitive old man?"

What to do? James didn't want to just leave, which would be disloyal. Burroughs depended on him in a hundred different ways. He would have to groom someone to take his place. Fed up with New York and its distraction factor, James thought of moving to Lawrence, Kansas, where he had gone to college and had friends. It would be like a return to innocence. He could continue to manage Burroughs' affairs from Lawrence until a replacement was found. The question was, would he be a nobody, living in Burroughs' reflected glory, or would he be somebody on his own? In the meantime, he would do one final thing to elevate Burroughs' name even further.

It happened that not long before the trip to Los Angeles, a Columbia professor named Sylvere Lotringer had approached John Giorno about organizing some sort of "homage to Burroughs," bringing together European and American academics for a series of seminars. Lotringer saw Burroughs as they did in France, where he was acclaimed as a philosopher of the future, the man who best understood postindustrial society.

Giorno discussed the idea with James, and they saw it more as a gathering of the counterculture tribe which would enshrine Burroughs as its leader. There would be seminars, but there would also be music and entertainment, and star attractions. It would be something to cap the decade, a memorable New York Event. James wanted to call it the Nova Convention, which Giorno at first didn't like because it reminded him of the car put out by Chevrolet, but he went along with it.

And so, over the next months, they organized the Nova Convention. On the Los Angeles trip, James obtained some seed money from Tom Forcade of the magazine *High Times*. In the Palace nightclub in Paris, Brion Gysin ran into Keith Richards of the Rolling Stones, who admired Burroughs and said he would like to be a part of it. Giorno, who was designing the poster, was happy to hear that, and headlined Keith's name, because he was a big draw.

Volunteers were recruited to help put the show on the road, among them a 115-pound bundle of sometimes irritating energy by the name of Victor Bockris, who looked like an adult foundling. English-born, Victor was the son of scientists, his father being a professor of physics and his mother a laboratory technician working on leukemia research. He moved to New York in 1973, attracted by the lifestyle of people who lived on the Lower East Side and didn't have jobs. With a friend named Andrew Wylie, Victor started an interview team. The idea was that they would be dapper and businesslike, and wear Brooks Brothers pinstripe suits, and carry rolled umbrellas and attaché cases, and that Bockris & Wylie would become as eminent in their field as Abercrombie & Fitch were in theirs.

In early 1974 they arranged to interview Burroughs, but when he first saw them he thought they were C.I.A. agents. Trying again, they invited him to dinner and did their nice cop/tough cop interview routine. Describing the shooting of his wife, Burroughs said, "Well, it was a shaky gun," to which Wylie replied, "Maybe you had a shaky hand." James deleted so much of what was in the drunken interview that it was unpublishable, and there were other problems with an interview that Mick Jagger would not release, so that in 1975 Bockris and Wylie came to an acrimonious parting of the ways. They had become known for their access to celebrities—calling up thirty-five of the famous and asking them, "Do you believe in love?" or "What does Nixon think about just before he goes to sleep?"

Bockris saw the Nova Convention as a means of further incorporating himself into the Burroughs entourage by running errands and being generally helpful. He was able in this way to make the transition from journalist to familiar, and soon Burroughs was fondly teasing him: "May I make a suggestion, Victor? I think it would be a very good idea if you would remove the phrase 'and stuff' from your vocabulary."

The Nova Convention took place on November 30, December 1, and December 2, 1978, with the principal performances being held on the last two days at the Entermedia Theater, on Second Avenue and Twelfth Street, which had in the fifties been the fabled Phoenix Theater. Attending were an odd mixture of academics, publishers, writers, artists, punk rockers, counterculture groupies, and an influx of bridge-and-tunnel kids drawn by Keith Richards, who made the event a sellout.

Acting as mistresses of ceremonies were two diminutive young ladies in top hats and tails, Julia Heyward and Laurie Anderson, who was soon to win fame as a performance artist. Brion Gysin, who had been flown in from Paris to perform one of his cut-up poems, was horrified at seeing "these two terrible cunts dressed up like men." Laurie Anderson was John Giorno's discovery. He recognized her raw talent and sense of purpose. She was, he said, a ruthless whippet, totally dedicated to the task at hand, and didn't drink or smoke pot. Someone told Giorno: "You know, Laurie Anderson's dimples? Well, William Burroughs is the other side of her dimples." All went well that evening, with performances from Anne Waldman, Ed Sanders, Allen Ginsberg, John Cage, and Merce Cunningham.

On Saturday afternoon, there was a panel moderated by the conceptual artist Les Levine, including Burroughs, Timothy Leary, and Robert Anton Wilson, during which Burroughs gave what amounted to the convention's keynote speech. "This is the Space Age," he said, "and we're here to go. However, the Space Program has to this day been restricted to a mediocre elite, who at great expense have gone to the moon in an aqualung. They aren't really looking for Space, they're looking for more time, like the lungfish and the walking catfish weren't looking for a new dimension—they were looking for more water. It is necessary to travel. It is not necessary—and becoming increasingly difficult—to live."

That was what he loved about Burroughs, thought Les Levine—he allowed for some level of mystery in human life, he accepted that not everything was known. It was amazing to Les how Burroughs could be on the one hand like a provocateur and on the other like your grandfather. He was a midwestern moralist with a few peculiar habits, conventionally dressed, not given to flash or flip, very prim and proper. He had a sometimes Archie Bunkerish view of the world, as when he had told Les that painters made too much money and were ripping off the public. It was paradoxical that this man who was associated with the Beats and their abandoned living was one of the most conservative persons he had ever met.

Les felt that the Nova Convention, this broad counterculture coalition of the old established avant-garde and the new punk scene, had crowned Burroughs king. In the heat of enthusiasm that afternoon, someone— was it the English publisher John Calder?—had jumped up and nominated him for the Nobel Prize. To the counterculture Burroughs was what John Kennedy was to the liberals. He embodied its values and summed it all up. When you said "Kennedy," as when you said "Burroughs," it was a magic word.

Saturday night the Entermedia Theater was packed, largely with young people waiting to see Keith Richards. There was a small hitch, however, which was that Keith Richards had canceled. He was having problems as the result of a heroin bust in Toronto, and his office convinced him that appearing on the same program with Burroughs was bad publicity.

But the show had to go on, and the composer Philip Glass, playing one of his repetitive pieces on the synthesizer, was thrown to the wolves. The disappointed kids who wanted Keith Richards shouted and booed. Then Brion Gysin went on amid cries of "Where's Keith?" and found himself hoping that the riot would not start until he had done his brief turn.

In a last-minute effort, James Grauerholz had recruited Frank Zappa to pinch-hit for Keith. He volunteered to read the "talking asshole" routine from *Naked Lunch*. But as Zappa was preparing to go on, Patti Smith had a fit of pique about following him. James did his best to make peace, saying, "Frank has come in at the last minute, and he's got to go on, and he's doing it for William, not to show you up." Patti Smith retreated to the privacy of her dressing room, and Zappa got a big hand, because that's what they wanted, a rock star.

Still, no one had explained Keith Richards' absence, and it was Patti Smith who gamely bit the bullet. She came out in a fur coat and a pair of genuine iguana-skin cowboy boots. When she announced that she was going to tell a story, a heckler shouted, "Tell it to the iguana." For Patti Smith, every performance was like a bullfight, the ultimate confrontation, as well as an act of lovemaking with the audience, which she sometimes achieved by masturbating on stage under a fur coat with a slit pocket. In 1976 she was doing something of the sort in Tampa when she fell off the stage and broke her neck. Soon she was back at CBGB's—Out of Traction, Back in Action. On this occasion, she did the heroic thing, telling her audience, "I know you guys came in to see Keith . . . well, Keith ain't here . . . he's in a plane right now between L.A. and Toronto . . . he asked me to tell you all that if anybody wants their money back they can come and get it right now . . . ," and she pulled some bills out of her pocket, but there were no takers. Although ill with bronchitis and running a fever, she hadn't stood them up. She couldn't sing, but she noodled around on the clarinet.

In the meantime, Burroughs was backstage waiting to read, and smoking joints with Terry Southern and Victor Bockris in his dressing room. Marcia Resnick, a photographer of the punk scene, dropped in and sat on Terry's lap. "She'd be much safer sitting in my lap," Burroughs said, and Bockris stood on a shelf across the small room to take a picture of the Great Misogynist with a cute punk chick in his lap. At that moment James walked in, and in his best Nurse Ratchett manner asked, "What is going on here?" Bockris fell and spilled his wine all over Burroughs. By that time, the audience had quieted down, and John Giorno read without too many interruptions, and Burroughs went out and read to a warm welcome.

Afterward, there was a party at Mickey Ruskin's, at One University Place, which featured a big aluminum washtub filled with "Guyana punch" (vodka and Kool-Aid), and Burroughs made some appropriately sardonic remarks about Jonestown, which was then in the news. Abbie Hoffman, who was wanted by the police, attended in disguise. Later in the evening, Tim Leary got pied by Aaron Kay, the professional pie-thrower, who had Mayor Koch and Andy Warhol to his credit. Burroughs told him that being pied by Kay was a sign that one had arrived. Leary took it well, saying, "Kay is wired to pie like a crow is to fly or a mole to dig."

James thought the Nova Convention had been a resounding success. The media coverage was extensive and appreciative, hailing the event as a high point in the Punk–New Wave movement, the attendance was standing room only, and Burroughs, after so many years of obscurity and exile, was recognized as the leading figure in the counterculture.

Perhaps the success of the Nova Convention was an example of the way the avant-garde had refined the modern consciousness, a bit like the monks preserving the classics in the Middle Ages. But now that the social freedoms pioneered by the counterculture were available to everyone, what was its purpose? Its leaders had gone from being outcasts whose works were banned to successful literary men who were wined and dined and decorated. The great maw of American society, with its capacity to ingest and tame its enemies, had absorbed the counterculture. As an example, Allen Ginsberg had been elected to the Institute of Arts and Letters, and in February 1979, he was awarded the Gold Medal for literary merit by the National Arts Club. Attending the award dinner, Burroughs was amused to see that the little old club ladies were shocked when he read "Cocksucker Blues." If they could have taken their medal back, he thought, they would have. But the very fact that Allen could read the poem in the dignified Gramercy Square headquarters of the club was proof that the literary outlaws were being mainstreamed and coopted. They had brought about changes in the culture, and the changed culture was now willing, nay, eager, to adopt them.

Burroughs, however, maintained his avant-garde credentials with books like *The Third Mind*, a defense and explanation of the cut-up method, written in collaboration with Brion Gysin, which Viking published in 1978. The idea for the title came from a book called *Think and Grow Rich*, which said that when you put two minds together there is always a third mind. It was also a reference to a line by T. S. Eliot, "Who is the third that walks beside you?" which referred to the hallucination of two Arctic explorers, who imagined that a third person was with them. While at Grove, Dick Seaver had for years kept the boards for collages and graphics in his office, and every time he looked at them it made him think of Burroughs' theory "that one plus one equals three." He didn't know how they could publish this huge oversize book that would cost thirty dollars. But then Seaver had moved to Viking, and started his own imprint, Seaver Books, with his wife, Jeannette, and decided to bring out *The Third Mind*, but with only a few illustrations.

In March 1979, James moved to Lawrence, telling Burroughs he needed a change of scene. It would not be a break. It would be a sabbatical, and he would continue to manage Burroughs' affairs. James felt trapped in his role. He had closed so many doors. He wanted once more to experience a broad range of possibilities. He had to get away from New York and the entourage and the bungled projects like the *Junky* film. He needed a sense of renewal.

Now Burroughs was alone in the Bunker, missing James, and still faced with the ongoing nightmare of Billy's transplant. The vacuum that James left was filled by several friends. John Giorno, who lived in the building, took on some of the duties of looking after him, often cooking dinner. He was a benign and unobtrusive presence that Burroughs appreciated. He was like a cat, thought Giorno, expecting the food to be there at a certain time. Then there was Victor Bockris, who moved in with his "come-see-the-bear-dance" routine. Victor brought around celebrities to meet Burroughs, acting as introducer, go-between, and master of ceremonies. John Giorno provided the bread, and Victor Bockris the circuses. He would call and say, "I'll be over at six with some corned beef and Bianca Jagger." It was in a sense a useful function to fulfill, for Burroughs was entertained, and Victor became to some extent the arranger of his social life. On the other hand, Burroughs was expected to perform at Victor's evenings, and to be ever more outrageous. Victor was of course motivated by fondness for Burroughs, as well as self-advancement. As Stew Meyer put it, Victor may have been an opportunist, but he was a helpful opportunist.

A disciple of Warhol's techniques in *From A to B and Back* and other books of unrelieved verbatim transcription, Bockris had a book project of conversations with Burroughs and whoever else happened to be around, often through his arrangement. Published by Seaver Books in 1981, it was called *With William Burroughs: Report from the Bunker*, and was a useful chronicle of that period of Burroughs' life.

On one occasion, Victor brought around Christopher Isherwood, and when they went into a Bowery bar to call Burroughs to be let in, the author of *Mr. Norris Changes Trains* said, "Oh, my dear, it's so Eugene O'Neill! I mean it's just so absolutely *The Iceman Cometh*."

Victor brought around the wildlife photographer Peter Beard, to whom Burroughs gave a fanciful explanation of his missing finger.

"How did you lose your finger?" Beard asked.

"Oh, er, an explosion," Burroughs said. "Nearly blew my whole hand off. . . . But I had a very good surgeon."

"Was that a gun explosion?" Bockris asked.

"No, it was, er, chemical—potassium chlorate and red phosphorus."

"What were you doing with it?" Beard asked.

"Chemicals," Burroughs said. "I was fourteen years old."

"Did you feel any pain?"

"Oh yes, I did. The doctor had to give me a morphine injection which he said was almost an adult dose. Yes indeed, I've been addicted ever since."

In fact Burroughs had remained unaddicted since arriving in New York in 1974, but with James gone, that situation, too, was about to change.

For in 1979, inexplicably, heroin suddenly became plentiful and inexpensive in the streets of New York. You could find it on every corner, at ten dollars a dose instead of thirty dollars. On Rivington Street, right across from the Bunker, there was a major dealer known as "Dr. Nova," after *Nova Express*.

Among the punk crowd, it was cool to be a junky. Many of the punk musicians were on heroin. And now that the Bunker had become a gathering place for all sorts of punk scene people, heroin made its appearance there. Offering heroin to Burroughs, the patriarch of junk, seemed a natural thing to do, like offering an apple to Johnny Appleseed. As noted in Stew Meyer's journal, it wasn't long after James's departure for Lawrence that Burroughs started chipping. On March 13, he noted that Burroughs was on a health food kick, smack and steak, shoot some smack and chew some steak. Burroughs was staring vacantly at the wall and saying: "Nothing comes out of the clear blue sky. You've got your memory track, everything you've seen and heard." On April 7, Stew noted that Burroughs was using heroin again for the first time in many years. Finding roaches in the kitchen, he snapped at them with a towel, saying, "Mother of God, kill them, they're an abomination."

Stew was glad to be in the daily company of "the doctor," as he called Burroughs, even if the occasion was caused by heroin. The truth was, the doctor was uncomfortable on this planet and junk relieved him. He wasn't basically atrocious enough to be well-adjusted, and he had a certain contempt for "the insect servants," as he so diplomatically referred to earthlings.

Dispirited over his son's inability to make a life for himself after his transplant operation, Burroughs was back on the junk time he had himself so eloquently described, when your whole day revolves around scoring and shooting up. When James came to visit in June, he saw at once what was going on—not only had he lost a lot of weight, but his junky friends would arrive and go into a room with him and close the door. Also, James noticed a serious outflow of cash in his Citibank account.

It saddened him to find this pathetic scene that was focused entirely on junk, with those awful dispiriting junky conversations: "It wasn't as strong as last time, man," or "This is kind of head stuff, man," or "Remember that stuff we had last week?" or "That other guy gives a better count, man." But after all, James thought, I'm not his nursemaid. When he did try to say something, Burroughs was very defensive, and James went back to Lawrence.

So life at the Bunker continued, with runners bringing glassine envelopes, and assorted visitors, some well known and some obscure, shooting up. One of the young regulars was badly beaten for stealing steaks to finance his habit, and another passed bad checks. Burroughs rarely went out, except that on September 14, Frank Zappa, who wanted to produce an off-Broadway musical based on *Naked Lunch*, took him to see *Best Little Whorehouse in Texas*. It was a soft audience, thought Burroughs; they laughed at everything.

On October 25, according to Stew Meyer's journal, someone brought around cocaine, and Burroughs said, "Put it away, we don't have to feed every vacant nostril in town." On November 30, Stew and Burroughs got high together and Stew presented the idea that Fagin in *Oliver Twist* was really a hero because he was keeping all these kids from starving to death. But Burroughs said his reasoning was too twisted, it was like trying to make a hero out of Iago.

On New Year's Eve, there was a party at John Giorno's, with hashish brownies, of which Burroughs and Stew took ample portions. They did some heroin to hold them while waiting for the brownies to hit. Other guests arrived, and Burroughs smoked joints and drank vodka. Stew was amazed at the amount of drugs and booze Burroughs could handle without apparent ill effect. After all, the man was almost sixty-six years old. Burroughs, however, held that there was no medical evidence that the use of opiates damaged the health or shortened life. De Quincey, an addict for forty years, had lived to be seventy-four. It was the failure of addicts to observe rules of hygiene that did them in.

During dinner, a visiting Swiss publisher, Carl Laszlo, started choking on a piece of steak and fell on the couch gasping. Burroughs thought they would have to improvise a tracheotomy with a kitchen knife à la Dr. Benway, and Anne Waldman started praying. Allen Ginsberg said, "Call an ambulance," but Burroughs thought, try to get an ambulance on New Year's Eve. Someone tried the Heimlich maneuver, squeezing the diaphragm to force the food up, but that didn't work, and Laszlo was gasping for breath and turning blue in the face. Then they tried the reverse Heimlich above the diaphragm, and the piece of steak loosened and went down. After a short rest downstairs in the Bunker, Laszlo returned, joking that "it is not nice to die at a party, it is nicer to die at home."

By this time, Burroughs had finished the novel he had been working on since 1974, *Cities of the Red Night*, and had sent a typescript to Brion Gysin to look at. Brion urged him to delete a couple of phrases that he felt would be construed as anti-Semitic, to which Burroughs replied: "As regards the Jew jokes . . . there is no basis to assume that opinions expressed by a writer's characters are the opinions of the writer. You have a Nazi character, he is going to talk like a Nazi. . . . Look at my other books—*Naked Lunch*: 'All a Jew wants to do is diddle a Christian girl.' *Nova Express*: 'Take your ovens with you and pay Hitler on the way out. Nearly got the place hot enough for you Jews, didn't he?' *Exterminator!*: 'And I want to say this to followers of the Jewish religion. We like nice Jews with Jew jokes so watch yourself Jewboy or we'll cut the rest of it off.' In *Cities*, Hitler Jugend boys sing 'And the dance that they do is enough to kill a Jew.' Well, what would one expect from Hitler Jugend boys?"

Burroughs told Brion that he had full confidence in his editor, Dick Seaver, who had paid a $25,000 advance. He was, second to Beckett, the most prestigious author that Seaver had brought to his new employer, Holt, Rinehart & Winston. Anyway, he wasn't writing for the Book-of-the-Month ladies and would lose his present readers if he tried. He was not trying to be a commercial writer, he was trying to be the best writer. He wasn't going to change a scene to sell books or get a review in *The New Yorker*. Concession was the thin edge of a very thick wedge. At the same time, he assured Brion, he wasn't an anti-Semite at all. "With Reagan and these born-again assholes putting in their two cents' worth," he wrote, "us minorities have to stick together." He recalled his embarrassment when someone had said about *The New Yorker*, "Smart bunch of kids run that mag. Went to school with 'em." It took him awhile to register that the person had said "yids," not "kids."

From Paris, Brion lamented his lack of success. He didn't have a dealer for his paintings. The art dealers told him he was too avant-garde. They were interested only in art objects they could sell over the phone. On the poetry scene, he wanted to see his songs published, but didn't know who to turn to. His problem was that he didn't work nearly hard enough at his various careers. Any one of them would be flourishing if he devoted full time to it but he didn't and things slipped away. He should work only at paintings, but went on writing instead.

In the Bunker, Burroughs was still on heroin, an old junky with translucent skin and collapsed veins. Allen Ginsberg tried to connect him with boys, but Burroughs said: "Why would a good-looking kid want to make it with me? I look like something out of Bergen-Belsen." He was back to staring at his big toe—the sluggishness, the lack of interest in anything but the next shot. Addiction was a horror and a bore. He thought of De Quincey's struggle to reduce his laudanum intake to one gram a day, which he called "weaning from laud." As De Quincey had long ago observed, opiates "defeat the steady habit of exertion." Except that in Burroughs' case that was not quite true, for he had started working on his next book, *Place of Dead Roads*, and found that he could work quite well on heroin. In fact, he worked better with it than without it.

Early in 1980, a young man named David Dalton asked Burroughs to contribute an article to a book he was editing to celebrate the twentieth anniversary of the Rolling Stones. Burroughs agreed, even though he didn't much like their music and thought Mick Jagger was arrogant. But when he got it down on paper, my God, it was dull—"Rock 'n' roll music is a sociological phenomenon of unprecedented scope and effect"—that sort of thing. Burroughs confided to Victor Bockris that the article didn't work, and Victor, who continued to bring people around, most recently David Bowie and Joe Strummer, the lead singer for the Clash, said he would arrange a dinner at the Bunker with Mick Jagger, so that Burroughs could chat with him, and that he would also ask Andy Warhol and the photographer Marcia Resnick.

March 9 was the evening of the great face-off between Jagger and Burroughs. Andy Warhol arrived first, soon followed by Marcia Resnick, who began setting up strobe lights, as though she was shooting a movie. Victor told her to stash her lights or she would wreck the evening. Mick arrived in a chauffeur-driven Lincoln sedan with his future bride, Jerry Hall, and another woman. They sat down at the conference table in the Bunker's large main room, as Mick fidgeted with suspicion. "What is the purpose of this dinner?" his eyes seemed to be saying. It soon became apparent that he knew nothing about David Dalton's project, so Burroughs brought up his name, to which Warhol responded, "Oh, he's one of my best friends." Glancing warily around, Mick asked why Marcia Resnick was taking pictures. "I'm documenting the event," she responded.

Informed about Dalton's book idea, Mick suggested that it could just as well be Andy's twentieth anniversary, since Andy must have been doing something for the last twenty years.

Bockris, trying to get the evening back on track, said, "I think it would be nice to have dinner regardless of this misunderstanding," to which everyone agreed.

"Bill's so great," Andy said, "I'm trying to find some young boys for him."

Burroughs then attempted to explain to Mick what he had in mind— his article would say that a book could sell hundreds of thousands of copies, while pop music immediately reached millions of people.

Mick, in his surly way, said that television and movies were more effective than rock 'n' roll.

Burroughs said that rock music, like the cultural revolution, was concerned with confrontation between the performer and the audience.

Mick said he thought that was passé.

"Aren't you actually paid to confront your audience?" Burroughs asked. "Isn't that what you're doing?"

Mick wasn't buying it, and asked, "What is this cultural revolution you're talking about?"

Gripping the arms of his chair, and speaking with slow deliberation as if to a backward child, Burroughs said: "Do you realize that thirty or forty years ago a four-letter word could not appear on a printed page? You're asking *what* cultural revolution? Holy shit, man, what'd you think we've been doing all these years."

"He's young enough that he doesn't think about it," Andy said. "A lot of people don't think about it."

"Pop music was one of the key things in the whole cultural revolution," Burroughs persisted. "Every time they got busted for drugs we got that much closer to decriminalization of pot all over the world because it was becoming a household word."

Looking supremely bored, Mick asked, "Is there a phone in this joint?"

When he returned from his call, Victor desperately tried to keep the conversation going, asking, "Well, Bill, when did you last see the Rolling Stones?"

"Mick's farewell in England at the Roundhouse," Burroughs said.

Perhaps recalling that Burroughs had declined to attend his wedding, Mick said rather pointedly that they had only met twice since and had spoken on neither occasion.

"I wouldn't say that, Mick," Burroughs said.

Then Victor said that Andy had recently been shot and that Burroughs had once shot someone, and Mick asked, "Who did you shoot?" and Burroughs said: "I haven't shot anyone right lately, Mick. Been on my good behavior."

Mick got up and said he had to go, and there were perfunctory handshakes and farewells. He had stayed all of fifteen minutes. Good riddance, thought Burroughs. He was convinced that Mick had bent over backward to be as obnoxious as possible, pretending to know nothing about the project, as if he was being tricked into something. It was the petulant paranoia of the superstar. In his dull-normal mind, he must have equated Burroughs with junk, and since Keith Richards had already had too much publicity in that department, he didn't want Burroughs writing about the Stones. So he had made very sure that he would sabotage the project, and in that he had succeeded. Well, that was one article he wouldn't have to write.

A disappointed Bockris turned on Marcia Resnick: "Marcia, you weren't supposed to be taking photographs during the conversation! How can people talk if someone is running around taking photographs the whole time?"

Burroughs in 1980 continued to find relief in heroin. That April, according to Stew Meyer's journal, he was high one night in the Bunker and going on about how fucked up the white race was. They were the only ones who had an army before they had an enemy, he said. The Indians weren't ready but the Anglos were. It was the old game of Castle Keep.

Addiction did not prevent him from giving readings, however, since in most cities he could score, and on April 9 he met James Grauerholz in Los Angeles. James was in one of those hexed periods where everything goes wrong. In Lawrence, he had broken his jaw in a fall from his bicycle, and it had to be wired shut for four weeks. At his father's place in Coffeyville, he had crushed the tip of his left index finger moving some limestone rocks. In Los Angeles, he reached into his shaving kit and nearly cut off the tip of his right index finger on a loose razor.

But all that was trivial compared to his father's collapse. Alvin Grauerholz—pillar of the community, vice-commander of the American Legion, onetime candidate for lieutenant governor of Kansas—suffered a complete nervous breakdown in February 1980 and was admitted to the psychiatric ward in the Veterans Hospital in Topeka, where he remained nine months. It developed that there had been some kind of misappropriation of funds in two estates that he was managing, and two charges of felony theft adding up to $30,000 were filed against him upon his release from the hospital.

The trial took place in Coffeyville in the summer of 1981. The attempted defense was insanity, which in Kansas is not a winning strategy. Al Grauerholz was convicted, his appeal was rejected, and at the sentencing in 1983 the district judge took a harsh view of his continued refusal to admit that the money had been deliberately stolen—Al insisted that he had borrowed it and intended to replace it. This broken man in his sixties was sentenced to two to six years in the state pen in Lansing. He served six weeks before a new lawyer obtained probation, and is now living in West Texas, still on probation, and sells encyclopedias for a living.

The father-son role was reversed. At the age of twenty-eight, James became his father's legal guardian, and had to show him the love and guidance one would show a child. He wrapped up his father's law business, liquidated his assets, and returned the $30,000 to the two estates. It was a harrowing time, and, as he put it, in spite of the ancient family conditioning, the bile turbines were on full throttle. He felt that he was being pulled apart like taffy, with his father in Topeka, Billy Burroughs in Denver, and Burroughs in New York, each with his critical problem, claiming his attention.

Caught up in his father's crisis, James was not monitoring Burroughs' heroin addiction as closely as he would have liked. As Stew Meyer put it, "We started taking it, and when the smoke cleared we were on the nod. James was away and the mice were playing. If he had been there none of this would have happened. We needed a stabilizing factor. We fucked up our cash flow. I was a partner in a printing business, and that came to an end, and so did my marriage, and the walls came tumbling down."

In what would be remembered as "the wild summer of 1980," things got completely out of hand. One night Stew Meyer and Burroughs were out with some Italian heroin dealers in a revved-up red Mustang. The driver was high and the tires were screeching, and Stew was thinking, "This is great, there are guns in the car and an ounce of heroin, and old Dominick is doing seventy miles per hour through the East Village, and I'm gonna read about it tomorrow in the *Daily News*, under the headline 'Author Arrested with Drug Dealers'!" So Stew said, "Take it easy, you'll upset Bill," but Bill was looking out the window and smiling contentedly, not upset at all.

It was far too dangerous for Burroughs himself to score in the battle zone of Alphabet City (avenues A, B, and C), so that Stew and other friends attended to that. Jim Prince, a boyish twenty-five-year-old would-be writer who had become a Bunker regular, was sent out on numerous missions. He was slightly built but gracefully feline in a preppy way. Prince would find a message on his answering machine in Burroughs' unmistakable twang: "Ahh, the electricity's out, I need three light bulbs," which meant three bags of heroin. Prince would bring over the smack and Burroughs would open the door before he knocked, saying, "I felt you coming from downstairs." His veins had receded through age and addiction, and he only had two good ones left, one in his hand and one in his foot, and since it was his right hand, Prince had to inject him. He didn't mind doing his hand, but every once in a while he would have to do his foot, which made him feel like Nurse Prince. After he'd had his injection Burroughs would come alive again, and be quite warm and affectionate, and then he would lapse into silence and just sit there and stare.

Alphabet City was a jungle, with literally dozens of competing drug crews working out of abandoned buildings. The best time to score, Jim learned, was between seven and eight in the morning, where there was a busy traffic of customers on their way to work. He would wait in line with Wall Street types in three-piece suits, sanitation workers with their garbage trucks parked outside, and mailmen wheeling their canvas bags, all scoring for heroin and cocaine. You got to know a crew, but then you'd hear that down the street the product was better, or they gave a better count (more for your money), and you tried that.

One evening Jim went down to score two bags, dressed as usual in a sports jacket, shirt, and tie. He walked through a hole in the wall into a room where five guys stood in a semicircle. One of them said, "That's him," and the next thing Jim knew, a half-Hispanic and half-Oriental dude dressed in white pants, white shirt, and white bandanna had wheeled around and given him a karate kick in the chest. Jim knew that it was all too easy to get killed in a case of mistaken identity, so he picked himself up and started running—he was in fair shape, because before taking heroin he had been running five to ten miles a day. He felt them close behind, he could sense the fingers trying to grab him, and he didn't stop running until he got to First Avenue, the demarcation line between the drug jungle and the rest of the city.

Another time, trying out a new crew, he gave his money to the "cake-taker" and was told to climb six floors to the roof of the building and walk across a plank to the next building. He found himself on a plank sixteen inches wide and ten feet long, crossing over a six-floor drop to concrete and broken glass, the plank trembling beneath his sneakers, and on the other side he was handed the machine-tucked and sealed glassine envelope of beige powder. He brought the envelope back to Burroughs, who took out the spoon where he cooked the powder, squirted in the water, shot up, and dabbed his hand with cotton. He saved the cottons, saying that if he was ever caught short, "at least I got a cotton shot."

On the Fourth of July, according to Stew Meyer's journal, at a party in the Bunker, Burroughs was stoned and made a rambling and discon-nected toast, sounding like one of his cut-ups: "I'd like to take this moment to thank George Washington for the utterly bestial strategy of attacking on God's birthday . . . if you can't win why play and if you can't be horrendous find another game . . . All right, gentlemen, line up neatly and commence firing . . . War was a gentleman's game in those days, not like now when it's just an excuse to depopulate areas for moneyed interests."

Then it was off to Santa Fe for the D. H. Lawrence festival, where he was one of the honored guests. At the panel Burroughs was on, the long-winded Leslie Fiedler held the floor, saying that Lawrence had no followers. Burroughs couldn't get a word in, and finally Allen Ginsberg interceded, saying that Burroughs had a point to make. Burroughs said that he had been very influenced by Lawrence's book on Mexico, *The Plumed Serpent*. His voice dripping with sarcasm, Fiedler said, "I always thought you have been more influenced by Edgar Rice Burroughs than by Lawrence." Well, thought Burroughs, Fiedler's novel, *Back to China*, had been described by a reviewer as "a mire of baloney."

Then in August, Burroughs left with John Giorno to attend an international poetry festival in Italy, which was being held on the sands of Castelporziano near Ostia, the ancient port of imperial Rome, and which turned out to be a reunion of the counterculture abroad, with Allen Ginsberg, Gregory Corso, Brion Gysin, Anne Waldman, and LeRoi Jones. Poets had arrived from all over the world, with Yevtushenko representing the Soviet Union, and were put up at a seaside hotel. The Italians had built a big wooden stage on the beach, with lighting towers, and an estimated 35,000 attended, sitting in the dunes facing the ocean. There was a carnival atmosphere, with vendors circulating through the crowd, and meat grilling over spits.

The audience, however, soon grew restive. When an eighty-year-old Sicilian poet went on at tiresome length, there were cries of *bastante* (enough). With the non-Italians, there was the added problem of translation. Yevtushenko wisely read in Italian, but when Brion Gysin took stage center and read his "British Bards Abroad—John Keats died in Rome, waiting for money from home," he was heckled. Burroughs kept it short, just two minutes, which, with translation, came to four minutes, and got a good hand. But by the time Giorno came on the audience had begun filling empty beer cans with sand and hurling them on stage like grenades, and he found himself ducking as well as reading. Then a Russian poet got up and said, "All flags are shit except for the flag of the Soviet Union," which prompted some right-wing disrupters to carry a caldron of soup onto the stage, as they shouted, *"Minestrone, non poesia."* Peter Orlovsky, who was known for his strength, single-handedly removed the caldron amid catcalls, thrown bottles, and fistfuls of sand whipping across the stage. A full-fledged riot was about to erupt when Allen Ginsberg leapt to his feet and with outstretched arms intoned a ceaseless *Ommmmmmmm*. The audience picked it up and calmed down, the multitude was pacified, and the evening was saved. The next day the festival wound up without incident, except that John Giorno suddenly felt the stage begin to tremble and ran to the edge and jumped off, twelve feet into the sand, as it collapsed in a pile of wood and broken glass. It was like a wild scene in a Fellini movie.

After the poetry festival, Burroughs went to St. Louis to film scenes of his childhood with the documentary filmmaker Howard Brookner. Visiting Pershing Avenue, he found an intact 1920s time pocket, with even the posts at Hortense Place that he used to jump from as a boy still the same. His brother, Mort, joked that now that he was wearing a pacemaker he had given up weight lifting. Filmed by Brookner, Mort said that he had never read his brother's books, finding them gratuitously offensive.

When Burroughs was back in the Bunker that September of 1980, the heroin problem had to be faced. For some time, a friend of Victor's named Ira Jaffe had been urging him to go on the methadone program. Jaffe, a counselor for the New York State Division of Substance Abuse Services, was convinced that methadone was a solution for Burroughs, because he could take his daily dose and lead a normal life, and not be trapped in the addict subculture, where you were on junk time, and everything was related to scoring and shooting up. Also, with the stuff off the street you never knew what you were getting. It wasn't healthy for a man of Burroughs' age, and too expensive for a man of his limited means. So every time he saw Burroughs, Ira Jaffe mentioned the methadone program, planting the seeds and waiting for them to grow, even though Burroughs insisted that he wasn't addicted, he was just chipping (shooting up occasionally).

Methadone was a synthetic morphine invented by the Germans during World War II, when their access to the Turkish opium fields was cut off. You could no more fight a war without morphine than without ammunition. So that in a sense the Third Reich rested on a solid methadone foundation, not to mention the fact that Goering and Goebbels were users. They called it Dolophine, after the Führer's first name. In the sixties, doctors Vincent P. Dole and Marie Nyswander began treating addicts with methadone, and put together a program that was adopted by the federal government. They found that addicts could be weaned from heroin and morphine by being put on a maintenance dosage of methadone.

Critics said all they were doing was replacing one form of addiction with another, which was true in a sense. But when addicts were offered a controlled, low-cost maintenance program, they were removed from the evils of the drug subculture. Under maintenance, they could go to their jobs and take care of their kids.

Jaffe kept lobbying for methadone, and at one point asked Burroughs to speak at a workshop at a Substance Abuse Conference at Grossinger's. In New York State, there were half a million addicts, but only 35,000 were on methadone. In the sixties, Burroughs had once said that going from heroin to methadone was like switching from whiskey to port wine, but now, at the workshop, he said that methadone was a viable form of treatment.

In mid-September, Burroughs wrote Brion Gysin: "My habit is becoming a bit of a problem and I may go on a very exclusive and discreet maintenance program. Whatever the cost it has been worth it to stop drinking. Drink has been for me a real curse and what a relief it is not to wake up not remembering how I got home or what I said last night. Of course ideally I should be able to put down both junk and alcohol."

The exclusive program that Ira Jaffe found for Burroughs was the methadone clinic operated by Dr. Harvey Karkus (what a name for a drug-abuse doctor, thought Burroughs) at 27 East Ninety-second Street. Dr. Karkus had an illustrious clientele that supposedly included a U.S. senator and a network anchorman. He catered to a whole stratum of attaché-case junkies. You could after all be an addict and a gentleman— De Quincey had contributed to Tory journals. The beauty of methadone maintenance was that it was cheap—twenty-eight dollars a week—and it wasn't time-consuming, for all he had to do was go to the clinic for his weekly dose. Also, it gave you a nice buzz, you could feel it in the back of the neck and the thighs, and it lasted about six hours. The only side effect was that it cut down your sex drive, which to Burroughs didn't matter that much anymore.

Thus came to an end the nearly two-year run of the "Bunker Follies," a comedy-drama with a resident headliner on daily display, a supporting cast of street junkies, cameos by famous players brought around by stage manager Victor Bockris, a "shooting gallery" set, and an enticing aura of illegality. Burroughs settled down once again to a quieter life of writing and occasional readings, having had his last fling with Lady H.

In October, he went to Lawrence for a reading that James had arranged, and got a standing ovation when he spoke out against Jerry Falwell and his "Moron Majority." He was taking every opportunity to castigate the born-agains. He found that he liked Lawrence, a small college town surrounded by hills and rivers almost exactly in the geographical center of the country. It was calm, it was quiet, it was cheap. You could live on $300 a month. He was staying in an apartment in a run-down, dead-end street by the railroad tracks, with weeds growing through cobblestones, and vacant lots, and houses that had an air of partial occupancy. There was no noise except train whistles. He adored the ghostly, deserted atmosphere, which prodded his imagination. He would write about the different species that inhabited these semivacant houses. Some were Odor Eaters, while others were Eye Eaters—that is, they ate images, a car accident for an appetizer, while excreting a slag heap of old photos. He would be quite content to settle down in Lawrence, he thought, and even looked at a house with oak floors and paneling, three bedrooms, and a big modern kitchen, on a third-of-an-acre lot with four big trees, for the reasonable price of $29,000.

"Yeah," he wrote Brion Gysin, "that place in Kansas could be a nice spot for old age, feeding your goldfish in the evening in the garden pool, bats and fireflies." Back in New York in November, he wondered what would happen now that Reagan and the Moron Majority were in. All ruinous disorders follow us disquietly to our graves, in the words of Shakespeare. The snippy old black queen at the methadone clinic said, "We'll just have to wait and see what happens."

The new year, 1981, found him in the best shape he had been in for some time. He was off heroin, he had some money in the bank, and *Cities of the Red Night* was about to be published. He wrote Alan Ansen on January 28 that he was living in "one of the most congenial locations I have ever inhabited. I call it the Bunker because there are no windows and the walls are three feet thick, and three doors between me and the street with an armed guard downstairs during the day. . . . I keep fantastically busy. In addition to writing I make about twenty reading appearances a year with miscellaneous talks and lectures to piece out the odds. Things like that I wouldn't do unless I needed the money, but I enjoy doing it and it is no doubt good for my character, like cooking."

As the reviews of *Cities* started coming in, however, he was irked by what seemed to be the betrayal of a former friend and ally, Anthony Burgess, who, writing in the *Saturday Review*, said that "Burroughs' cupboard of symbols is not well stocked and he becomes rather monotonous. . . . When we have pederastic thrusts on every page we soon begin to yawn. . . . Sexual strangulation is a recurrent, and soon boring, theme. . . . What Burroughs needs is a theology. Blake was a far greater fantasist and he demonstrated that no poet is big enough to create his own."

"That bastard Anthony Burgess, who has become a fucking Catholic, gave me a terrible review," he wrote Brion Gysin. "Maybe I'll get to review his next book: 'Mr. Burgess seems to be as inexhaustibly prolific as a warren of rabbits . . . but what has happened to the freshness and humor that made *A Clockwork Orange* such an exhilarating experience?' "

To balance Burgess, there was an excellent review from another prominent English writer, J. G. Ballard, who called him "the first mythographer of the mid-twentieth century, and the lineal successor to James Joyce, to whom he bears more than a passing resemblance—exile, publication in Paris, undeserved notoriety as a pornographer, and an absolute dedication to The Word. . . . His novels are the first definitive portrait of the inner landscape of our mid-century, using its unique language and manipulative techniques, its own fantasies and nightmares."

Cities of the Red Night was the first of a trilogy of novels written in straight narrative style, and linked by one central idea: The author, dissatisfied with the state of mankind, would rewrite history, inventing a society more to his liking. As Burroughs put it, "I parachute my characters behind enemy lines in time. Their mission is to correct retroactively certain fatal errors at crucial turning points in human history." It was a brave attempt to write himself out of the human condition, which he felt was intolerable.

The spark for *Cities* was a thriller by James Jones, set on the island of Spetsai (which Burroughs had visited in 1973), called *A Touch of Danger*. Burroughs liked the detective story form, which was adaptable to any quest, and he thought up a "Private Asshole" called Clem Snide, who was on a missing-person case. Then Steven Lowe came along with his research on gay pirates, and this became another strand in the book. For there had been, in the seventeenth century, a Captain Mission who had established a short-lived libertarian colony on the island of Madagascar. This was just what Burroughs was looking for, in his yearning to recapture "the right to live where you want, with companions of your choosing, under laws to which you agree." So the adventure of a band of homosexual pirates (in their ship *The Great White*, a reference to Melville) became a parallel plot to the story of Clem Snide.

A third theme was that of the cities themselves, imaginary cities located in the Gobi Desert 100,000 years ago, the names of which were magic words that Brion Gysin had once taught him, saying, "If you want to get to the bottom of something, you should repeat these words before going to sleep." The city of Waghdas is in the grip of a cholera epidemic, which turns out to be a virus that is sexual in origin, very much like the present AIDS epidemic, although Burroughs wrote the book before there was any talk of AIDS. In Tamaghis, a walled city of red adobe, there are nightly public hangings; Ba'dan, the oldest spaceport on planet earth, has been taken over by gunslingers; while the city of Yass-Waddah is a matriarchy run by a hereditary empress. The red night of the title is caused by a falling meteor, which lights up the sky and causes mutations in the inhabitants.

To indicate that he was now writing in a mainstream narrative tradition, Burroughs opened the book in the style of a Graham Greene novel. Farnsworth, the district health officer, is the typical Greene protagonist, the bad Catholic with a mission he doesn't really believe in. He was "a man so grudging in what he asked of life that every win was a loss," one of the rare instances of a psychological observation in a Burroughs novel, which are notable for their lack of character development. As Burroughs puts it, "They don't develop, they are just there. They are mythological characters, fairy story characters." So with a tip of the old fedora to Graham Greene, Burroughs appears to be signaling that he is at last writing a conventional novel, with characters and a plot.

But the Graham Greene opening is a *trompe l'oeil*, for soon the novel starts time-traveling, and we are back in 1702, with Noah Blake, the son of a Boston gunsmith, who has signed on with a pirate ship. This is one of the things that boys do in adventure books, they leave home and go to sea. It is as though Burroughs' view of human freedom had been fixed at an early age, by reading books like *Treasure Island* and *Two Years Before the Mast*.

Along with time travel, there are various instances of cloning and identity switching. The young man that Clem Snide is looking for, for instance, is found decapitated, but his missing head later turns up on the body of another character.

The book switches back and forth between the pirate community in 1702 and the contemporary detective story. The pirates establish an outpost in Panama, where they fight the Spanish colonial power and govern themselves under a set of articles: No man may be imprisoned for debt. No man may enslave another. No man may be subjected to torture. No man may interfere with the sexual practices of another. No man may be put to death except for violation of the articles. Clem Snide, in the meantime, hot on the trail, discovers that the missing-person case is part of a diabolical conspiracy to wipe out the planet with a virus. We are living in dangerous times.

Eventually, characters from past and present mingle in the mythical cities, which are at war. There is not only time traveling but space traveling, to such an extent that some of the characters get star-tanned. The book ends with the destruction of the cities of the red night. The only survivor is Audrey Carsons, the author's alter ego, who can write his way out.

The author's point of view, as stated repeatedly by Burroughs, is that of the Old Man of the Mountain, Hassan I Sabbah: Nothing is true, everything is permitted. Every taboo that is broken, every act of outrage that is committed, is a justifiable act of insurrection against a bankrupt system of morality. Whatever his characters are doing, Burroughs seems to be saying, the actual conditions on the planet, created by the villains and morons in power, are worse.

Is it possible to write one's way out? Can a book alter reality, or find the escape route? Burroughs ends on a melancholy note. All that he has been able to do is "blow a hole in time with a firecracker. Let others step through. Into what, bigger and better firecrackers? Better weapons lead to better and better weapons, until the earth is a grenade with the fuse burning.

"I remember a dream of my childhood. I am in a beautiful garden. As I reach out to touch the flowers they wither under my hands. A nightmare feeling of foreboding and desolation comes over me as a great mushroom-shaped cloud darkens the earth. A few may get through the gate in time. Like Spain, I am bound to the past."

And yet, despite its gloomy conclusion, *Cities of the Red Night* is certainly the most compelling and inventive of Burroughs' books since *Naked Lunch*. Reading it is not unlike playing a pinball machine, with the various characters being flicked hither and yon by the flippers, and bouncing off the brightly lit posts, and taking unexpected routes, and finally vanishing down the chute at the bottom on the machine, as on the glass screen above it the different settings light up in garish cartoon colors.

Dick Seaver, who published *Cities* for Holt, Rinehart & Winston in 1981, thought it was a major book, and spent a lot of time on it with Burroughs and with James Grauerholz, who did a major editing job. Seaver liked working with Burroughs, who never pulled rank or showed off his erudition. He could have enlarged his audience tenfold had he been willing to make concessions. Middle America was not going to put up with all this homosexual stuff and the hanging scenes. And yet, Seaver was sure that one day a whole generation of academics were going to have a field day with his books. Already one critical study had been published, *The Algebra of Need*, by Eric Mottram, and Jennie Skerl, a professor at Skidmore, was working on another one. *Cities* sold 20,000 copies in hard cover, which was very good for Burroughs, and fellow publishers, who were not habitually generous with their praise, wrote to say "Congratulations on having brought Burroughs back to life."

There had been a feeling in the publishing world that Burroughs was in hibernation, even though he kept producing books during his New York years; in fact, he produced so many that Mary McCarthy told Brion Gysin that he was "writing too much." In the seventies, there was a scattering of short works published by small presses—*Cobblestone Gardens* (Cherry Valley, 1976), which was drawn in part from the first draft of *Naked Lunch*, and in which he addressed his feelings about his parents in the cut-up style; *Ah Pook Is Here* (Calder, 1979), a Mayan caper in which the evil Mr. Hart discovers the lost books of the Mayans in his search for immortality and murders his fellow explorer to keep the secrets to himself; *Blade Runner: A Movie* (Blue Wind, 1979), a science-fiction screenplay exploring the coming medical care crisis, which showed Burroughs at his most Archie Bunkerish: "It's about plain middle-class middle-income Joe, the $15,000-a-year boy, sweating out two jobs, I.R.S. wringing the moonlit dollars out of him to keep the niggers and the spics on welfare and Medicare so they can keep their strength to mug his grandmother, rape his sister, and bugger his ten-year-old son"; *The Book of Breeething* (Blue Wind Press, 1980), a short text showing that there is no relation between a word and its meaning, and illustrated by Robert F. Gale.

Burroughs was asleep in the Bunker on March 3 when James received the call that Billy was dead. James waited until he was up and dressed and had taken his morning tea before breaking the news. It was not a surprise. Billy had been one of the walking dead for some time. Burroughs got up and went into his room and closed the door.

He hardly had time to grieve before leaving on a strenuous three-week publicity tour through Indiana, Minnesota, Wisconsin, and Missouri. Aside from book-signing events, he and John Giorno read in punk-rock clubs, where the audiences were small but enthusiastic.

That summer of 1981 Burroughs spent six weeks in Lawrence with James. He liked the town even more on his second visit, in contrast to the bustle and expense of New York, and began to think again of settling there. One day the temperature dropped ten degrees and the sky turned green-black like the sky in El Greco's *View of Toledo*. It was a Kansas twister. He listened for tornado warnings, ready to head for the basement with a sledgehammer and a crowbar, as the radio advised in case you were trapped, but the tornado did not touch his neighborhood; it struck Gaslight Village, a trailer camp on the outskirts of town, and took out the K mart at Thirty-first and Iowa. Hailstones the size of lemons fell on his porch.

In mid-August, he did a two-week teaching stint in Boulder, where he found His Holiness drinking on top of an ulcer. Then there was a two-week gig in Los Angeles and San Francisco with Laurie Anderson, whom Burroughs considered a remarkable performer, and who promised to become the only genuine pop star to have come out of the avant-garde.

When they got back to the Bunker in September there was a notice in their mailboxes that rents in the building would be doubled. Burroughs was paying $355, which would climb to $710. Giorno, according to his custom, which was to set problems aside for a time, put the letter away. But that afternoon, James came to tell him, "We've made a momentous decision . . . William and I have had a long talk about the rent increase and we've decided it's the will of the gods . . . and William is going to move out to Lawrence."

Giorno thought it was a mistake to make such a snap decision. Burroughs should have asked himself, "What is threatening me?" and found a way to deal with it. Giorno went on a rent strike, and the increase was declared illegal, and the rents were frozen. So for Burroughs it was premature to say that he was leaving New York because it was too expensive when he could have stayed for the same rent. The truth was, Giorno thought, that James wanted Burroughs in Lawrence. In New York, James was a small fish in a big pond, and he was happier out of the city, and he wanted Burroughs out of the city, too. John felt bereft. It had been a joy to have Burroughs there, and it was a disappointment to lose him. But at the same time he realized that Burroughs, approaching old age, was carrying the idea of the expatriate to Kansas. He would make it his own, as he had done with Tangier, Paris, London, and so many other places. He was moving back to his native Midwest and the virtues of small-town life. After living out of a suitcase he wanted to own a house and land. He was two years away from seventy, and in your seventies you slowed down. The Bunker in the last two years had been the scene of endless amounts of heroin and cocaine, so that going to Kansas was the correct move. James was the nanny and Stew Meyer and Victor Bockris and James Prince were the tempters, and, as in any morality play, the nanny had won out over the tempters.

Before leaving for Lawrence, Burroughs had one final performance to attend to. He had fans among the "Saturday Night Live" writers, one of whom convinced producer Dick Ebersol to let him read on the program. But in dress rehearsal, Ebersol found Burroughs "boring and dreadful," and ordered that his time slot be cut from six to three and a half minutes. The writers, however, conspired to let his performance stand as it was, and on November 7, he kicked off the show, sitting behind a desk, the lighting giving his face a sepulchral gauntness.

"The hospital lavatory has been locked for three hours solid," he read. "I think they are using it for an operating room.

"Nurse: "I can't find her pulse, doctor.'

"Dr. Benway: 'Cardiac arrest.' He looks around and picks up a toilet plunger, and advances on the patient. 'Make an incision, Dr. Limpf,' he says to his appalled assistant. 'I'm going to massage the heart.' "

Among writers, Burroughs had positioned himself as the Great Outsider, but on the night of November 7 he had reached the position where the actress Lauren Hutton could introduce him to an audience of 100 million viewers as America's greatest living writer.

· TWENTY-ONE ·

LAWRENCE

1981–1988

When Burroughs moved to Lawrence at the end of 1981, he felt sure he had done the right thing. The first house he rented was in the country, and that was fine, even though he did not drive, for James did the shopping, and he had his cat Ruski and the great outdoors for target practice, and was happier than he had been in New York. The one thing he missed was his old friends, and in May he wrote Brion Gysin, who was settled in Paris, urging him to come to Lawrence. "If you were here," he said, "James and I could get bookings for readings and talks. . . . After all, we've been doing it for eight years. Six or seven readings and you can realize few thou enough to look around. . . . We could set you up here for half the price of NYC. I know you think of Kansas as Nowheresville and think I am caught up in nostalgia. Really it is the other way around. The whole concept of place is dead and it's nostalgia to cling to it. Time was every creative person had to be in Paris, London, New York etc. That's all over and done with. Went out when the jets came in. . . . I am the cat that walks alone. And to me all Hiltons are alike. It simply isn't worth paying double to be in NYC. So I found a place that is cheap, comfortable, and where I can work. . . . All this prattle from John [Giorno] and Felicity [Mason, an old friend of Brion's] about me being an urban person. . . . Neither of them hit on the important fact about urban living: the continual stream of second attention awareness. Every license plate, street sign, passing strangers, are saying something to *you*."

Brion replied that he had told people he had come to Paris to die and now felt he had to live up to it. He was getting to be one of the old Parisians, sought after as a witness, like the people in Warren Beatty's movie *Reds*. "Financially," Brion added, "I am in ruins. Everyone I know sneers at me, saying, 'You always say that.' If I do, it's true. I'm spending the last of the Swiss money [from the sale of the Burroughs archive]. . . . What I am writing now will never sell. . . . I am short of breath and take some pills which make my hands shake. I am deeply depressed. Despite all this, I have the gall to be forming a group with young Ramuntcho Matta [the rock 'n' roll musician son of the Chilean Surrealist Matta] on guitar."

Burroughs could sympathize with Brion, for in 1982, despite the money saved by living in Lawrence, he, too, was broke. That summer he was so short of the ready that he had to hock his Colt .45 for $200. Then Peter Matson bailed him out with a $2,000 loan, and his editor Dick Seaver came through with a $5,000 advance on the Holt trade paperback edition of *Cities of the Red Night*, which was pure largesse on Seaver's part, as no advance was due. Later that year, Seaver advanced $12,500 on signature for *Place of Dead Roads*, with $12,500 more due on delivery. There was other money from a lithographic collaboration with Robert Rauschenberg and from retroactive Social Security benefits. Burroughs was able to make the down payment on a one-story house he had bought on Learnard Street for $36,000. His monthly mortgage payment was only $300. But there was never enough money, what with keeping himself and James and the office, and in the fall he hit the road again for readings.

Back in Lawrence in November 1982, Burroughs moved into his house, feeling like a true member of the midwestern tax-paying middle class with his front porch and his backyard and his almost-an-acre lot on a quiet tree-shaded street. He caught up on his correspondence, which consisted largely of the odd requests that people make of those they consider famous. There were quite a few letters beginning, "Please excuse me if I allow myself to make a claim on your precious time." A fifth grader from East Sandwich, Massachusetts, asked for a class report, "Do you believe in God?" J. Shannon, a graduate student at Concordia University in Montreal, whose assignment was to write one of the "Beats" and get an answer, said "I keep imagining you in a male whorehouse in Tangier or superciliously studying your sock somewhere." "No," Burroughs replied, "I do not live in a Tangier seraglio fanned with ostrich plumes by nude Arab youths. I live in a small house on a tree-lined street in Lawrence, Kansas, with my beloved cat Ruski. My hobbies are hunting, fishing, and pistol practice."

One fan addressed his letter to "the Master of all pus." Raymond Longley wrote from England, "You are truly God and I have been rewarded," to which Burroughs replied: "You got me wrong, Raymond, I am but a humble practitioner of the scrivener's trade. God? Not me. I don't have the qualifications. Old Sarge told me years ago: 'Don't be a volunteer, kid.' God is always trying to foist his lousy job onto someone else. You gotta be crazy to take it. Just a Tech Sergeant in the Shakespeare Squadron."

There were requests for interviews, some refused, some granted. One interviewer, Charles Platt, reported that "Burroughs turns out to be almost as difficult to talk to as I feared. He is polite and perfectly willing to tolerate my presence, but many of his remarks are dismissively brief, as if the questions bore him. He smokes a succession of Players Navy Cut cigarettes, moves his hands and arms in awkward nervous mannerisms, fidgets in his chair, and several times gets up, walks to and fro, then sits back down again while he continues talking. He's nearing seventy and the years show in the lines in his face, but he has a powerful assertive voice. Typically, he makes a brief categorical statement, then stops and regards me with his pale eyes as if waiting to see if I really intend to ask any more dumb questions."

Burroughs had come to Lawrence for peace and quiet, as opposed to the commotion and menaces of New York, but that February of 1983 he discovered that Lawrence had menaces of its own. A few blocks up the street was the campus of Haskell Junior College, which had a student body of Indians. People who lived near Haskell built high fences, and posted signs that said "No Trespassing or Police Will be Called," because when Uncle Milty's bar closed at eleven-thirty they wandered forth flown with beer and insolence, and if you left your door open some Indian would wander in and ask, "Where's the party?" and the next thing you knew he'd be looking through your refrigerator for beer. Everybody in the neighborhood had a drunken Indian story.

One cold night at around eleven-thirty, he was in bed when there was a knock on the door, and when Burroughs opened it a crack, this huge brawny Indian, who was obviously feeling no pain, shouldered his way in and asked, "Where's your daughter?" "I don't have a daughter," Burroughs said, "you must have the wrong address." "I'll just check it out," the huge Indian said, licking his lips and throwing wild glances around the room. Oh, Jesus, this is bad, Burroughs thought. If I have to, I'll go into the bedroom and get my gun, and I'll say, "Look, don't make me use this," and if he says, "I'm gonna take that gun away from you and shove it up your ass," I'll shoot him in the leg.

"Look, I don't have a daughter," Burroughs repeated. "Yes you do," the Indian drunkenly insisted. "No," Burroughs said, "my daughter and my wife died years ago. [In fact, his stepdaughter, Julie, was married and living in upstate New York, but Burroughs had not been in touch with her for years.] I'm just an old man alone with his cats." The Indian focused his eyes for a good look at this stooped, frail old man in pajamas with wisps of whitish hair over his ears and sagging pouches under the eyes and said, "Hey, you are old, dad, you're gettin' old all right." "Yes, yes," Burroughs said, playing the part of the ancient. "Yes, I'm just an old man alone in his house." Soon the Indian became so apologetic he was almost in tears. As he left he said, "Let's shake hands," and they did some sort of slap-me-five, hand-in-hand-out hippie handshake, and then the Indian was gone. His parting words were, "Remember we're out there and you're in here." The next day Burroughs had a deadbolt installed.

No sooner was the Indian incident forgotten than Burroughs was shaken by the death of his brother, Mort, at the age of seventy-three, and he flew to St. Louis in February with James for the funeral. He had seen very little of Mort over the years, and they disagreed on every subject, and Mort couldn't read his books, but Burroughs experienced an undeniable physical impact. There were about twelve people at the funeral, and they all recited the Lord's Prayer. He couldn't stay for the burial because he had a plane to catch, but he wrote Miggy about his belief in an afterlife. It did tend to cheer people up, he found, coming from such an improbable source. He refrained from adding that visits from the dead were not always an unmixed blessing, and that death did not necessarily mellow a shrewish nature.

Mort's death brought back the guilt that Burroughs felt about his family. My parents gave me a hell of a lot, he reminded himself, and I gave them fuck-all. There's no use pussy-footing around when you know you've been a miserable bastard. My mother always knew when I was on junk, but she never lectured me, except to say, "You look terrible, you look just like your uncle Horace, when he came into the room it was like somebody else had just left." At 202 Sanford Avenue, when Billy was arrested, drinking old-fashioneds with Mother each day at four. I walk out to the end of a sandy road by the sea to wait for four o'clock. One day Mother came in with a bag full of paregoric bottles just lying around for the narcs to find. I took the bag to Lake Worth and threw it in with a stone ballast. Outside the house waiting for a taxi to the airport. My mother's kind, unhappy face. The last time I ever saw her. Really a blessing, she's been ill for some time. Too late. One night in Price Road I went down to the icebox, wretchedly unhappy, no sex no work. Dad was there eating something, I could hear his inner voice pleading for love and I looked at him with cold hate and I saw him wither under my eyes and I muttered, "Hello" . . . Looking back now I feel an ache in my chest and I reach out DAD DAD DAD. Too late, always too late. Mistakes too monstrous . . . Anyone who has not made such mistakes, young lawyer never botched a case, young doctor never killed a patient, I trust them little in the commerce of the soul.

Another death that affected him at that time was that of Tennessee Williams. How pointless and undistinguished to have choked on a bottle cap, he thought; no doubt he was lying on his back with his head tilted back. He remembered Tennessee in Paris, saying he was "desperately ill." They had told him at the American Hospital in Paris that he had hepatitis and mononucleosis. "I have never heard of either of those disorders," he said. "Really, Ten," Burroughs said, "at age thirty, you've never heard of hepatitis? Or mono, the kissing disease?" In Rome, he complained that he spoke no Italian. Burroughs told him, "All you have to say is *Dove vai?*, where you headed, and *Quanto costa?*, how much." Ten was such a histrionic queen, always dying and writing "the jig is up" in his journal. But you had to admire his enthusiasm for the pleasures of the flesh. "Redheads have that wonderful skin full of pearly tints." It gave him something to live for. "Tommy would not turn over but one evening he smiled sheepishly and said, 'Mr. Williams, if you'd like you can bugger me tonight.' " On the *Queen Mary*, Ten and Truman went down the first-class corridors and picked up the gentlemen's shoes set out for shining, mixing them up and setting them doors from their proper places.

On April Fools' Day it rained like the biblical deluge, and his basement, where he had stored 150 boxes of papers and books, was flooded. But in Lawrence people helped one another, and half a dozen friends showed up for the rescue operation, with the result that only thirty-one boxes were soaked.

In May, Burroughs went to New York to be inducted into the American Academy and Institute of Arts and Letters. He had finally made it at the age of sixty-nine. Now he would be able to listen to Virgil Thomson snore. As Somerset Maugham had once pointed out, longevity was the most valuable attribute a writer could possess. He just hoped he wouldn't overdo it, like Maugham and Churchill, who had lived into their senile nineties. So come drunks and drug takers, come perverts unnerved, receive the laurel given, though late, on merit, to whom and wherever deserved. Parochial punks, trimmers, nice people, joiners, true blues, get the hell out of the way of the laurel. It is deathless and it is not for you.

What a *métier* was writing, Burroughs reflected. My attic room in St. Louis opens onto a New York loft, from which I step into a Tangier street. We writers are tidier, we fade out in firefly evenings, a prom and a distant train whistle, we live in a maid opening a boiled egg for a long-ago convalescent, we live in the snow on Ian's grave falling softly like the descent of their last end on all the living and the dead, we live in the green light at the end of Daisy's dock, in the last and greatest of human dreams. Beckett gave me the greatest compliment by saying, "Well, he's a writer." This means the real job of exploration. Someone who has been there and brought it back. You have to write in present time so that what you write actually happens. Not like Mishima writing about hara-kiri and then doing it. Anybody can write "and then he shot himself" and shoot himself. I'm talking about someone who writes "and then he was shot" and is himself shot by someone else.

> The intellect of man is forced to choose
> Perfection of the life, or of the work.
> And if it take the second must refuse
> A heavenly mansion, raging in the dark.

In the words of the immortal Yeats. No heavenly mansion for me. Hemingway chose his life. Maugham chose his life. I chose my work. What I would give now to go back and be a war correspondent in Vietnam. I was too busy writing. I missed my chance for real action and danger which I never had. Well, there is just so much of the real stuff the Muses can wring out of you and when they have got it all they leave you with NOTHING. Was it worth it? I don't know . . . So Gilmore, you want to be a great writer? All right, I will tell you why you never will be . . . The reason you can never be a great writer is because you're a check-dodger . . . Remember at the San Remo you invited some people to our table and stuck me with the check? Remember the bar where you kept ordering drinks and then walked out? You think you can get away with that shit? You pay or you get nothing. You can't dodge the Muse's check. The Muse don't like welshers. A writer becomes a writer by PAY-ING . . . I gave it all I had and there's nothing left. What happened to Paul Bowles? He wrote out of his own fear and then the fear left him. Now it's folklore at best, at worst fake folklore. Well, Paul, we expected more of you after *The Sheltering Sky* and *Let It Come Down*. A lot more. We didn't get it. What happened, Paul? Speak! Kerouac knew long before I did that the fictional version is the real one . . . "But Jack, I'M NOT

RICH!" "You are in my book." He decided I had a trust fund and that was that. Can I perhaps then take a liberty and implant the memory of Rainbow Jack's French-Canadian bean soup? Under a rainbow, by a mountain lake, a lumberjack is holding up a can of soup, on the label of which the same scene is repeated . . . A picture of a picture of a picture, like barber-shop mirrors. And now he has a park named after him.

In San Francisco, where he continued to operate the thriving City Lights bookstore, the poet Lawrence Ferlinghetti reflected that Burroughs joining the Academy was another nail in the counterculture's coffin. Where was the counterculture in the meretricious, money-grubbing age of Reagan, the age of insider trading and children turning in their parents for drug use? The counterculture was by a pool in L.A., sunning itself. It wasn't with the rock groups or with Bob Dylan, who hadn't rocked the boat in a long time. Allen Ginsberg had become the Establishment, he had a three-inch-thick volume of his collected poems about to be published by Harper & Row in hard cover. And he, too, was in the American Academy, hobnobbing with the Schlesingers and the Galbraiths. He was really at the top of the heap. It was the beatification of Allen Ginsberg. Allen was saying things these days like "the Beat generation was never political," and Ferlinghetti thought back to that day when he had gone to the first reading of "Howl" and been knocked out by it, and had sent Allen a telegram that said, "I greet you at the start of a great career." How could you read "Howl" without a political interpretation? When Allen came back from India he said that socialism had failed, and he made disparaging remarks about the Sandinistas in Nicaragua. Ferlinghetti could see that he and Allen had reached a parting of the ways politically. As for Burroughs, his worldview was post-Orwellian, it was based on international conspiracies, and he continued to be radical even though he wasn't overtly political.

But when the two principal surviving Beat writers joined the Academy, Ferlinghetti thought, it only served to prove Marcuse's view that the dominant culture in a capitalistic society has a tremendous capacity to absorb outsiders, to ingest its own dissident elements. *Naked Lunch*, once banned, was now on college curriculums. In other countries there was no free speech, while in America you could say anything you wanted but no one paid any attention. The radical artist went into the ring to slug it out with bourgeois society, and found that he was puching a tar baby, which unperturbed by his blows, stuck to him and enveloped him with its blandishments of success and fame. It was what Tom Wolfe and Joni Mitchell called the Boho Dance.

Ferlinghetti had published the poetry of Allen Ginsberg and Gregory Corso in his Pocket Book series, which had started in the fifties with Rexroth and a bunch of writers that no one else would publish, but as the years went by, fewer and fewer manuscripts came in that could qualify. Ferlinghetti kept looking for something that would carry forward the so-called movement, but nothing came in, and finally he decided to end the series, because you couldn't publish a movement that didn't exist anymore.

A friend of his, a tenured professor at the University of California at San Diego and a onetime colleague of Marcuse's, had been very active in the sixties in teach-ins and antiwar demonstrations, and in 1968 he was busted when he tapped a marine recruiter on campus with a rolled newspaper. Now, in the eighties, he was still a boat-rocker, and after reading something in the paper that infuriated him, he had spray-painted REAGAN MURDERER on the side of one of the campus buildings, on his way to class, and some students came up and took the can of paint away from him and called the campus police. It was a total reversal of the generational roles, with the yuppie students turning in the counterculture professor. The campus police came to his class and said, "You're under arrest, will you please come with us," and he told them, no, they would have to carry him off, so that his students could see democracy in action. In the story of his friend, thought Ferlinghetti, was summed up the life and death of the counterculture, from the end of World War II until the eighties, roughly a thirty-five-year life span, with a glorious decade in the sixties. But now the work no longer shocked or disturbed, and there were no new dissidents, with the possible exception of the Vietnam vets, victims of Agent Orange and the like, in whom there was a seething rage that might express itself through the written word, but aside from that, one could say of the counterculture: Rest in peace.

Burroughs and Ginsberg did not agree with Ferlinghetti that by joining the Institute they were being coopted by the Establishment. Ginsberg felt that he was infiltrating the Institute as a subversive and could work within it to change it, to bring in friends like the poets Robert Creeley and Gary Snyder, and to obtain grants for hard-up friends like Gregory Corso. Burroughs did not recognize the existence of an Establishment, and, as the great pariah of American literature, felt that any form of inclusion was an asset in helping him to compose the façade of respectability that he presented to the world. Thus, he was glad to belong to the Institute, and wore its purple-and-gold rosette in the buttonhole of his lapel on formal occasions. Norman Mailer, another boat-rocker, recalled that when he had been elected he had written the Academy a nasty letter asking whether Henry Miller was a member, but the reply came back that Henry Miller certainly was a member. He came to understand that the Establishment worked on the same principle as if you had eight people living in an apartment, who gathered all their clothing together and tossed it into one huge bureau, and then you photographed the bureau, as though by the act of photographing it you were bringing order to its contents—and that was the purpose the Establishment filled, just by everybody being there. Mailer was all for accepting awards and prizes, in fact he was guilty of saying that Sartre should not have refused the Nobel, but at the same time you had to be aware of the price—that once you joined the club some of the fire went out of you.

James Grauerholz thought that the process of cooption described by that guru of sixties radicals Herbert Marcuse was actually more of a two-way street. In the process of ingesting its rebellious avant-garde, society first got an upset stomach, and then took on aspects of what it had swallowed. It was ironic that there came a point in an artist's life when he seemed to be accepted, so much so that some of his old comrades accused him of selling out, while in fact he was barely accepted by the book-buying public, and could only survive by added exertions, still compensated at the avant-garde rates his publishers deemed adequate.

After a week in New York for his induction and visits with friends, Burroughs was glad to be back in Lawrence that June. James, however, was going through one of his self-doubt phases. He was by then living with a friend from New York, Ira Silverberg, a young man with a pronounced social gift (he later worked the door of the V.I.P. room in the Limelight nightclub and became head of the publicity department at Grove Press), who was taking classes at the university. On July 2, 1983, James wrote Danny Bloom, with whom he had remained friends: "I went through a period of panic over my life-commitment to William yesterday but then came to realize that an investment's an investment, and it were premature to bail out before the time were right. Bill is in good shape all in all, working and writing madly day and night." Having gotten that off his chest, James was ashamed at having described his relationship with Burroughs as an investment. What he meant was not investment but involvement, both psychic and emotional. Even though he sometimes felt trapped, he knew that the higher you climbed a hill, the more you could not give up and go back down. You didn't quit near the top. And in any case, Burroughs was family; he wasn't someone you could leave.

The biographer had expected flat prairie on the forty-mile drive from the Kansas City airport to Lawrence that summer of 1983, but instead there were rolling hills planted with corn and cows grazing in green pastures. The biographer thought of Burroughs as essentially a city-dweller, needing the seedy underside that cities produce to feel at ease, the Bowery in New York, the Beat Hotel in Paris, the Socco Chico in Tangier, and could not imagine him in a college town of 50,000, having assumed that Burroughs detested the neighborly, homespun, small-town aspects of midwestern life.

Of course, Lawrence did have a literary tradition of sorts. Frank Harris, the author of *My Life and Loves*, one of the great autobiographies in the Chaucerian vein of ribald frankness, had arrived there in 1873 at the age of eighteen and remained several years, making it the site of his first amorous escapades. The black poet Langston Hughes had grown up in Lawrence from 1909 to 1915, arriving when he was seven to live with his grandmother on Alabama Street, at the foot of the hill where the university stood, and leaving when he was thirteen. Frank Harris discovered sex in Lawrence, and Langston Hughes discovered segregation. Black schoolboys could not join the Boy Scouts or swim in the Y.M.C.A. pool or play on school teams, and the Patee Theater on Massachusetts Avenue had a sign that said "No colored admitted."

And now Burroughs had settled there, after a lifetime of roaming the cities of the world, and had bought a house and land. On the first of his many trips to tape Burroughs in his new home, the biographer wondered what kind of mess he had got himself into agreeing to write a book about a friend. The biographer knew that in his work he was capable of suspending all personal feelings and of approaching his subject with a clinical attitude. He would go where the material took him, without trimming or hedging or leniency. He knew in any case that Burroughs wanted an honest book. The truth coin would not tarnish in his hand. He viewed his past with detachment and bafflement, wondering what had possessed him on occasion to act the way that he had, but was disinclined to present a sanitized version, as if hoping that absolution might follow confession.

The biographer had known Burroughs since 1972, when he had met him in London through Brion Gysin. There had been an immediate current of sympathy, reinforced over the years. There was something self-invented about Burroughs that the biographer found appealing. He did not derive from any previously existing model. If you asked yourself who he was like, as a writer and as a man, you could not find any comparable person. His humor, his ideas (always provocative, however wrong-headed they might sometimes seem), the toe of his discourse, his way of presenting himself to the world, were entirely his own, entirely original. Burroughs was refreshing in an age of mass-produced personality types, bogus conviviality, buffoonery passing for wit, and conversation as flat as the sidewalk. One also sensed that his refusal to conform to a more acceptable social type, in the great American tradition of "go along to get along," had been maintained at the cost of much suffering and loneliness.

The biographer knew that Burroughs in his childhood had suffered a critical psychic wound. A child's innocence had been blunted and brutalized by an early experience. From that moment on, he had been convinced that others saw him as peculiar. Instead of trying to adapt to the norm, he adopted a "call-me-a-dog-and-I'll-bark" attitude. He would become what he was accused of being, with a vengeance, and turn his impediments into strengths.

The sympathy between the biographer and Burroughs was not based on any similarity, for the two could not have been more different. In fact, when the biographer had interviewed Irving Rosenthal, who was still operating his commune in the Mission District of San Francisco, Rosenthal had told him that he was the wrong person to write about Burroughs because he was not homosexual. The biographer replied that one did not have to be a dwarf to write a book about dwarves. On Rosenthal's premise, Shakespeare could not have written *Othello* or *Macbeth*, and Flaubert and Tolstoy could not have written *Madame Bovary* and *Anna Karenina*.

The biographer recalled something Norman Mailer had told him: "Burroughs may be gay, but he's a man. What I mean is that the fact that he's gay is incidental. He's very much a homosexual but when you meet him that's not what you think of him. You might think about him as a hermit, a mad prospector up in the mountains who'll shoot you if you come to his cabin at the wrong time. Or you can see him as a Vermont farmer who's been married to his wife for sixty years, and the day she dies someone says, 'I guess you're going to miss her a lot, Zeke,' and he says, 'No, never did get to like her much.' So that he's got all those qualities, and on top of it all he is very much a homosexual, but that's somehow not the axis. He also has that way that certain people in society act, very formal, which is a defense against indiscreet inquiry, when let's say they've been put in jail for twenty years and they come out, and you can never refer to it in their presence, you wouldn't dream of it."

Burroughs had known his sexual orientation by the time he was twelve. He also knew that he had no choice in the matter, any more than a heterosexual has a choice. Athletically inept, finding difficulty in making friends, rejected by his father from such male enclaves as the basement workshop, Burroughs fit the Kinsey Institute's definition of "gender non-conformity" in childhood as the single most important factor in future homosexuality. He was isolated from his father and his male peers, and his mother encouraged in subtle ways the feminine side of his nature. Starved for male affection, he started forming attachments to other boys in grade school, when he met Kells Elvins. It wasn't that he wanted to be that way, for it made life more difficult. But since that was the way he was, he accepted it.

Nor did the biographer share Burroughs' misogyny, which at the bottom was probably an attempt to smother his own contemptible femininity. Born in his hatred of the secret, covered-up part of himself that was maudlin and sentimental and womanly, misogyny was his form of self-loathing. One would never guess that this masculine, deeply reserved man was capable, in the act of love, of turning into a passive and senti-mental female. Burroughs really did believe that women were useless and parasitic creatures, a blight on the planet, and that man must learn to clone himself and become independent from them. Love was a con put down by the female sex. At the same time, he had been married, and had loved his wife and slept with her and had a child. He had a small number of female friends. So that he was in the same position as the anti-Semite who insists that "some of my best friends are Jews." He was antiwoman in the deepest sense, the biological sense, but in his day-to-day life he had cordial, friendly relations with women. And many women admired his writing, in spite of its occasional misogynistic outbursts.

The biographer admired Burroughs' writing, even though he knew no one was batting a thousand. Most writers' careers looked like CAT scans. For the biographer, the high points were *Junky*, *Naked Lunch*, and the trilogy, while the low points were the cut-up novels using the left-over material from *Naked Lunch*. The cut-up method was an interesting ex-periment, but it broke the standard author-reader contract, which was based on the writer's obligation to inspire belief in the story the reader was being told. Cut-ups could lead to stunning results, and introduced an element of randomness that made writing closer to life as it's lived, but were difficult to sustain for the length of a book without making the reader catatonic.

The biographer also admired Burroughs' *stance* as a writer. In a society where freedom of expression was protected by the Constitution, the other side of that protection was that nobody gave a damn what you wrote.

An American writer, free to turn out books that no one read, might actually envy a Soviet writer who was censored and imprisoned, for there was dignity and stature in being designated an enemy of the state. While in America, hundreds of college writing programs turned out graduates who produced novels and short stories that had about as much dignity and stature as paper napkins.

Burroughs had restored dignity to the profession of writer. As he put it, there were writers who were bullshitters, making passes with no bull there, and writers who were bullfighters, in the ring with a real sword and a real bull. Burroughs really believed that writing was *dangerous*. It was a magical activity in which one entered areas where harm could befall you. He depended heavily on dreams and drug-induced trancelike states to sustain his writer's vision, deliberately placing himself in an area bordering on the irrational. He had to cross the border and come back, while knowing that it is not always possible to come back. The reality of the danger conferred dignity and importance to the writing. The degree of his dedication, the absoluteness of his commitment to his work, placed it on a high level of seriousness. He wasn't just putting pen to paper, he was taking the same kind of risk that a soldier in combat takes or a pilot in a frail craft, trying to break a circumnavigation record. He was the writer as psychic explorer, who has been there and brought it back. Burroughs had the *courage* to be a writer, that is, to pursue his own vision, however disagreeable and obscure it might sometimes seem.

But here the biographer was in Lawrence, crossing the silty green crook of the Kansas River, and driving down the main drag of low brick and limestone buildings, Massachusetts Avenue. The biographer had previously written about men who were dead, whom he had never met. He knew what they looked like from photographs, and he knew their voices from recordings. It would be a blessing to work from life. The only disadvantage was that there would be no death scene, which would leave the book hanging in the air, without resolution. The biographer had an ugly thought which he immediately stifled—what if Burroughs were to die just as he was finishing up, wouldn't that be convenient? No, don't even think of it.

Turning left on Nineteenth, and right on Learnard, he arrived at a single-story white clapboard house with a front porch, on about an acre of land, with a garage and a vegetable garden. Burroughs worked on an electric typewriter at a desk in his bedroom, and there was a second bedroom, small bathroom, kitchen that opened onto a narrow screened back porch, and living room that was furnished with items from a garage sale—a five-dollar green imitation leather easy chair, a ten-dollar black-and-orange couch with a sunflower motif and frayed tassels, worn through at the arms, a three-dollar carpet, two bookcases, and a round wooden table, used for meals, in one corner, with a lamp on it and three chairs around it.

Burroughs at sixty-nine had lost most of his hair, and was noticeably stooped, but he looked fit and had not put on any weight. With his warily knowing look, which seemed to say "All supermarkets are alike," he might have been the dean of croupiers in a casino on the Nevada border.

Sitting at the round table after making tea, and lighting up a Players Navy Cut, he said, with a hard look of his gray-blue eyes, as if divining the biographer's thoughts: "Ted, there's one thing that bothers me. How are you going to deal with the problem of a biography about someone who's very much alive? You've always had subjects who were dead before. I'm not even sick. There won't be any death scene."

"William," the biographer said, "as a biographer I want resolution, but as a friend I want you alive." And those were words that he came to believe.

The front doorbell rang. It was George Kaull, come to take Burroughs shooting at the target range in the basement of the community building in downtown Lawrence. Kaull was a strong-looking, straight-backed, white-haired man in his seventies, with the kind of open midwestern face in which wrinkles have not completely worn away the traces of youth. A gun lover and an atheist, he was the Lawrence representative of the American Civil Liberties Union. George had a bumper sticker on his car that said, "When guns are outlawed, I'll be an outlaw."

"I gave my daughter a .22 for her graduation," he said. "That's all I could sell her on. I said just fire two shots and even if you don't kill him you'll mark him so he can't say he wasn't there."

Then it was off to the range, and Burroughs asked the biographer, "Do you want a cane?"

"Not yet," he said.

"I mean if you're attacked by dogs," Burroughs said. He was living with five cats, and had developed a hatred of dogs, against which he protected himself with canes, a sonar device called a Dog Chaser that emitted a high-pitched wail audible only to dogs, and cans of Mace. "I gave the Airedale at the corner a squirt last winter," he said, "and he stopped right enough. Last I saw of him he was wiping his face in the snow."

In a little cloth bag, he carried his German police pistol, his Colt .45, and his .38 Magnum. There was a stop at the Lawrence Pawn Shop and Shooters Supplies for ammunition and a copy of *Survive* magazine. As they drove to the community building, Burroughs spotted a dwarf walking in the street and said, "I'll lean out the window and ask, 'Who sawed off your legs?' " But of course he didn't. It was his way of making up routines as he went along.

In the community building, a high school basketball game was in progress. On the wall of the basement target range, rules were posted: You must have your headphones on at all times. Never place your finger inside the trigger guard while moving a gun. When you are finished shooting, remove the magazine immediately. Rack your gun.

"Good sound safety rules," Burroughs said as he put on his headphones. He stood with arms extended, holding the .38 with both hands, one eye shut, and the biographer noticed that his shoulders were exactly as wide as his hips. His upper body formed a narrow rectangle. The targets were placed and retrieved with a pulley system, and Burroughs' targets showed good close clusters.

Back at the house, over drinks, there was a serious discussion about guns, concerning velocity, penetration, caliber, and the misstatements of know-nothing writers. "He released the safety on his revolver," Burroughs said. "That's one you see all the time. Of course, there is no safety on a revolver."

"What about the movie that had a telescopic sight on a machine gun?" George Kaull asked. "That's like putting a telescopic sight on a garden hose."

Gun lovers, the biographer reflected, were like other obsessives, from lepidopterists to ichthyologists, and could discuss their favorite topics *ad nauseam*. They justified their fondness for playing with guns as the need for self-defense. "I go out and shoot a few rounds in my backyard," George said, "and it does my soul good, and it warns the would-be hoodlums and intruders. You've got to defend yourself."

Burroughs' other obsession, as the biographer realized that night when he tried to sleep in the second bedroom, was his cats. He had no scheduled feeding time for them, and all five seemed to eat at different hours, so that Burroughs was up several times during the night, keeping up a running commentary: "Here my little Calico beast, oh, she's such a sweetheart." "Yes, my little Ginger beast, I know you're hungry, oh, my, look at this collar, it's either too loose or too tight." And so on.

The biographer was astonished, for he had never seen Burroughs drop his emotional guard, and here he was talking to his cats in an unguarded, openly affectionate tone, a tone he found it impossible to adopt, except perhaps in one specific situation, with humans. The biographer wondered whether this was the last refuge of the misanthrope, on the order of Pascal saying late in life, "The more I see of humans, the better I like my dog." Or was it some form of atonement, a way of making up for the lapses of earlier days, when he had been unable to express his love for his parents, or his son, or his wife?

The biographer could not help thinking that Burroughs had once been a torturer of cats, an activity he had described in *Junky*, and now he was like the prize product of a behavior modification program, the perfect graduate of a Skinner school, the cat molester turned cat lover. When he was not feeding them or brushing them he was playing with them. "Such an affectionate little cat . . . When I stroke his feet he turns on his back and puts his paws up to my face."

When he had first moved to Lawrence at the end of 1981, Burroughs had lived in a stone house a few miles outside town, and inherited a pure Russian Blue, whose sleek gray coat had bluish overtones, and whom he called Ruski. When he moved into the house on Learnard Street with Ruski in 1982, a stray cat started hanging around, but Burroughs wouldn't let her into the house. He fed her but hoped she'd go away. When she dropped four brown-orange kittens, Burroughs gave them away. Then in the winter of 1982 they had a cold wave, and when the mercury dropped to twenty degrees, Burroughs let her in, haunted by the idea of finding a frozen corpse on his back porch. He called her Ginger, and soon Ruski and Ginger committed an indiscretion, and Ginger dropped four more kittens, two of which Burroughs kept, calling them Calico and Wimpy. Ginger went whimpering from room to room, looking for the other two under the couch and bed. Then one day James was downtown and heard a cat crying, and when he turned around a tiny black cat jumped into his arms, and he brought it to William, who called it Fletch.

Burroughs thought of cats as psychic familiars. Once wild, they had been recruited by the ancient Egyptians to kill the rats in their grain storage bins and were domesticated. They could, Burroughs felt sure, perform psychic reconnaissance missions, and they could put a receptive person in touch with the level of subverbal awareness in which they operated. Also, they could act as screens or representations of people in the past.

In this sense, each of his cats was someone from his past life. Ruski, for instance, was Kiki. Just as when he had seen Nick Nolte on the set of *Heartbeat* he had felt Neal Cassady right there, when he picked up

Ruski he could hear Kiki saying, "*Déjame*, William, *tu es loco*" ("Leave
me alone, you're crazy"). Once he slapped Ruski, as he had once slapped
Kiki, for jumping on him and waking him up. Sometimes Ruski moved
away from his hand as Kiki had, saying, "You shame me, William, I am
not a child." Ginger was like an old madam, sleepy and self-indulgent,
you could imagine her eating Turkish candy by the pound and sprinkling
the red velvet sofa with powdered sugar, like Pantapon Rose in the St.
Louis whorehouse on Westminster. In Wimpy, there was a lot of his poor
father, with his pathetic need for affection, and of Billy, with his dependent, helpless nature, while Calico was like Jane Bowles, his mother,
and his wife, Joan, ethereal and delicate. Fletch was a sort of mischievous
brat-cat desert boy, like a character in *The Wild Boys*, ill-tempered and
moody, prowling around the house, jumping on the table, going out,
looking around, not entirely tame.

　　As in many families, there was a problem cat, in this case Ruski, the
best loved, the first. When Fletch arrived, Ruski went from being friendly
and happy to being miserable and hostile. He pissed on Burroughs' bed,
and one day when Burroughs was packing for a reading, Ruski pissed on
his two-suiter. If Burroughs was in the living room with Fletch, as soon
as Ruski came up from the basement Fletch would start hissing. It became
a daily drama, with Ruski the marauder against all the other cats. Ginger's
neck was torn open, and who could it have been but Ruski? Burroughs
took Ginger to the vet, who kept her on antibiotics for two days and
billed him $117. The bills on those cats were something enormous! Rabies
shots, and vaccinations for feline leukemia. Then Ruski came in soaking
wet and caught pneumonia and was in there for three days, and that cost
$100 . . . Then when Calico had her first litter, that cost seventy-four
dollars for delivery. Burroughs spent more on the cats' health than on
his own.

　　It was with cats as it had been with people. Ruski represented the
deterioration of the impeccable cat. Burroughs finally turned Ruski over
to some friends who lived in the country. He was basically a country cat,
and away from the other cats he could work out his ill temper. Not long
after, Wimpy disappeared. Burroughs canvassed the neighborhood with
a photograph and put ads in the paper offering a fifty-dollar reward. For
weeks, he put out food where Wimpy had last been seen, a couple of
blocks up Learnard. If I could commit a miracle, he asked himself, what
miracle would I commit? To get my Wimpy back. He thought of the
Wordsworth poem, "Michael." An old farmer had a son, Michael. They
were building a wall together, but Michael ran away to London. Many

times the old farmer went out to the wall, *and never lifted a single stone*.
Now that was sublime, even though it was on the edge of the mawkish.

Well, he still had Fletch and the other two. He had to keep his ears
alert for Fletch sounds, and got up during the night to heat up his food,
while Fletch rubbed against his leg. Pieces of sleep, he thought, I keep
dreaming and waking up and dreaming, and suddenly I'm in Mexico D.F.,
I had to sign in on my bond every morning at seven, you could go back
inside if you were fifteen minutes late . . . Some of them signing with
thumbprints, or con-man signatures with a flourish . . . In jail, I pulled
myself together . . . *Necesita mucho calma y resignación*, the guard said.
Through the rains and sunlight of Colombia, and the eternal customs and
passport inspection through silence of the deep rain forest and birdcalls
of the Indian hunters to the end-of-the-road towns of Pucalpa and Macoa.
In a clay cubicle an Indian boy squatting naked on a mat, sunlight through
wooden grids in the window, brown animal eyes. No, it is not to me you
do this thing. And the mustached truck driver who threw a knife with
marvelous accuracy. We came to the land of the delta people who speak
in little birdcalls. And the nightingales sang in Berkeley Square . . . God,
what a dreary interlude . . . the hangovers, the dead-end hopelessness.
Looking for bodies on the downs, an old English custom. Gibbons, Connell called his boys, tailless apes. Well, gibbons are dangerous animals.
Best thing to do if you have a gibbon for a pet is give it to a zoo. God,
it was cold on those sleeping porches in the Big House. "Get down and
waddle like a duck." Where the balsam breezes blow . . . And a vast
mushroom cloud darkened the earth. Corner of Pershing and Walton,
mild jerk of leaves, a squirrel with an acorn in its teeth, the Veiled
Prophet, floats in the hot summer night, yellow glow of lights, pink cake
with cardboard round the edges, gray sky. Old Sarge with his hula dance—
I'd like to see some moa of Samoa. Jane Bowles got up a petition to save
the trees in the Gran Socco and Madame Porte refused to sign, saying,
"*Je n'ai pas d'opinion.*" When I got a dose I went to the drugstore and
bought penicillin and the *practicante* shot it into me on the spot . . . They
took pride in their work . . . One *practicante* threw the needle like a dart
then slipped the vial on . . . One would slap one buttock and inject the
other one to fool you . . . The winking green crosses of the Paris phar-
macies. Quail in the market, a piece of pork fat tied across their breast.
In the hotel next to the Pont-Royal when the maid came in she scattered
my breakfast all over the carpet. "*Vous prenez Le Monde, monsieur?*"
Les Halles on first solo trip in 1932 when I was eighteen. I asked the cab
driver into the café for a drink and he was talking about the Stavisky

riots—"*et tout d'un coup Brrrhhuuuuuppp*, a sound like ripping cloth—then you know it's serious." The Beat Hotel in 1959 was the best time—we all thought we were interplanetary agents involved in a deadly struggle—it seemed real enough at the time. There were casualties, quite a number. We were getting messages, making contacts, everything had meaning . . . Well, there isn't any transport out. There isn't any important assignment. It's every man for himself. So here I am in Lawrence, Kansas, like the honorary agent for a planet that went out light-years ago.

In the fall of 1983 Burroughs and Grauerholz left for Europe on a whirlwind tour—five countries in eight days: Finland, Sweden, Norway, Denmark, and Holland. In Amsterdam they shared the bill with Richard Brautigan, whom Burroughs met in the hotel bar, a tall overweight guy wearing a floppy hat, who was very drunk in that somnolent way of people who habitually drink a quart a day. His characteristic expression was a crinkling of the brows as if trying to decide whether something that had been said to him had an undercurrent of malice. He seemed sad and uncomprehending. When he excused himself to go to his room, Burroughs was startled to see him crawl away on all fours.

The readings took him away from his writing and his study of mutation, but they were a necessary chore because money was tight. He would be seventy the following February and there was no relief in sight. So now at the age of seventy, he thought, I have to read in nightclubs to eke out a living . . . Ah well . . . I feel that one should know how to come down in the world. Perhaps I will end up in a boxcar by the river living on collard greens, eggs from the neighbors, and catfish. It's the same old show with the life drained out of it.

Burroughs came to New York in October for the premiere at the New York Film Festival of the documentary that Howard Brookner had been putting together since 1978. It had started as a twenty-minute final project at New York University Film School, and later Brookner filmed in London, St. Louis, and the Bunker. As he sat in the box on the night of the premiere, with Burroughs sitting behind him, Brookner thought, what if he hates it and pushes me out of the box? But Burroughs congratulated him on a good job, and the film went into theatrical release in 1984 and was bought by the BBC.

Burroughs was again in New York for his seventieth birthday on February 5, 1984, the proverbial three-score and ten, and a seated dinner for 170 was given in his honor at the Limelight club, organized by Ira Silverberg and attended by such luminaries as the singer Sting, the writers Terry Southern and Kurt Vonnegut, and the poet Allen Ginsberg. Frank

Zappa sent two dozen long-stemmed roses. Burroughs enjoyed the festivities, but when he was back in his room in the small hours of the morning and lit a last cigarette before sleep, the echo chamber of his mind turned to the past.

What will life be like at seventy at seventy? In Tangier, packing for the boat, the whistle in the harbor, we have twenty minutes twenty minutes. *Chaque jour dans le Métro.* I can't find my ticket my ticket. John De Chadenedes turned to me and said, "I don't want my days changed." They did not fully understand the technique and in a very short time almost wrecked the planet the planet. How I loved the movies . . . *The Phantom of the Opera* . . . the scene where she comes up behind him while he's playing the organ and pulls his mask off . . . Feast your eyes. Before the movie there was a big rawboned fellow singing "Sailing On, Sailing On . . ." The full misery of the human condition hits me when I think of that long-ago singer. I remember the Texas farm, the windup Victrola, the records by Hoagy Carmichael, "Talking is a woman, listening is a man," Stan Kenton, and "Low Flame" by Dizzy Gillespie . . . Room 29 at the Empress Hotel overlooking the backyard, clothes on the line, leaves on the trees, it's Sunday, always gloomy in London, three shillings on the mantelpiece over the boarded-up fireplace, I am wondering when I can get more shillings for the gas meter, the pubs don't open till seven. All the old junkies, Dave Tercerero and his toothless mouth, Bill Garver, Huncke, Phil White, Mikey Portman, Alex Trocchi—he could find a vein in a mummy—Pat Cole in New Orleans, with me when I almost O.D.'d, took twenty dollars out of my watch pocket, figured I wouldn't need it. "You turned all blue so I thought you were dying and I took off." . . . Gregory, he's really great, such resilience, gets beat up in a police van and worked over by the cops and comes right back laughing . . . A man has to fit in somewhere but I violated every rule . . . Not a Catholic like Greene and Burgess, not a high Episcopalian pederast like Auden, not an atheist like Tennessee, not a Buddhist like Allen . . . What they have against me is that I have managed to hold myself together and remain self-contained . . . I dare. And I have no intention of stopping . . . All experience is an arc where through there gleams the untraveled world that recedes as I move . . . And at my back I always hear the Internal Revenue hurrying near. Old age is winter, the last test and the toughest. Nine-tenths of my activity is purposeless fidgeting around, lighting another cigarette, nine-tenths dead wood weighing you down. House odds. How do we live through the dreary years of dead wood? It was inconceivable that Homo Sap could last another thousand years in present form. People of such great stupidity and such barbarous manners.

Even though he was seventy, Burroughs saw during the days he spent in New York that young men were still willing to make themselves available, but he wasn't interested. What has happened, he wondered, to an activity that used to be an obsession, and suddenly . . . Not a joy that time can give but what it takes away. All the boys I admired and never had at Harvard and Los Alamos . . . A feeling of being skinned and exposed and you can't stand for anything to touch you. One wonders, is sex really pleasurable at all, it may be simply converted pain and fear and anxiety . . . That is really what I meant by a Dead Road. Too old to cut the mustard. I got the money honey you got the time? Well, yeah, but . . . All that sort of sexual interest has gone into my obsession with cats. Sometimes I feel I am an androgynous being that wants to give birth to a being half cat and half man. I wish it would happen. I want to break down the hybrid principle. Hybrids unlimited, cats with dogs, dogs with possums, God knows what. So many died in the saddle and don't want to admit it. Scott Fitzgerald died in the saddle with Sheila Graham, and Charlie Parker died fuckin' Helen Parker . . . Must be a great sensation. I still have my phantom fucks, they're so much better than the real ones, there's no comparison, baby. People don't like to talk about it, but I've done a lot of research. There's one woman who had visits from her husband after his death, and he fucked her better than he'd ever fucked her when he was alive. He also gave her some tips on the market, how about that? The best sex I ever had was with my phantoms. Unless you were very lucky with a real person, which few people are. Of innumerable orgasms with real people, I can only remember three, one was with Jack Anderson, one with Ian, and one with Jimmy Cookson at the Empress Hotel, and just at the crucial moment a knock on the door . . . telephone, sir. It was Kenneth Alsop's secretary to say he'd twisted his ankle and couldn't keep our appointment. Sex for me was always wanting to be someone else, to be the other person. That's the crucial factor in homosexual relationships, and you can't do it with a woman. When I was young I was so horny I'd get a hard-on if I saw two flies fucking. In my whorehouse days in St. Louis it was five dollars for half an hour. I did all kinds of things, came between her breasts. Today it seems as inviting as a hamper of dirty laundry.

In February 1984, the second novel in the trilogy, *Place of Dead Roads*, came out. The scene shifted to the American West at the turn of the century. Having written about two kinds of boyhood adventure heroes, the private detective and the pirate, Burroughs now focused on a third, the Western gunfighter. Partly, he was living out fantasies of danger and action, which arose from a sense of frustration that his life as a writer had been too sedentary and uneventful. Partly, he sought to reclaim models of masculine behavior for the gay community. As he had created gay pirates, he now created a gay gunslinger in the person of Kim Carsons. Why shouldn't gays have their masculine role models just as straights do, he seemed to be asking. It was yet another way of rewriting history to fit his own circumstances, by attempting to rehabilitate the limp-wrist image.

Kim Carsons was not your run-of-the-mill Western gunslinger. For one thing, he hated horses, "their hysteria, their stubborn malice, and their awful yellow teeth," much as the young Burroughs hated horses when he had to ride one at the Los Alamos Ranch School. For another, Kim had to be the first gunslinger in Westerns to carry in his pocket a volume of Rimbaud's poetry.

Kim's mother was into table-tapping, as Burroughs' mother was, and his father's name was Mortimer, the name of Burroughs' father. So that we should not be surprised to see the descriptions of Kim fit the author, or rather the author as he sees himself, as an alienated and unlikable person, who must escape a planet where there is no place for him. As Bat Masterson put it, "A man's got to fit in somewhere," and that was the trouble with Kim—he just did not fit.

"Kim is a slimy morbid youth of unwholesome proclivities with an insatiable appetite for the extreme and the sensational."

"He is everything a normal American boy is taught to detest."

"He was also given to the subversive practice of *thinking*. He was in fact incurably intelligent."

"Kim was the most unpopular boy in school, if not in the town of St. Louis."

"As a prisoner serving a life sentence can think only of escape, so Kim takes for granted that the only purpose of his life is space travel."

"Kim has never doubted the possibility of afterlife or the existence of gods. In fact he intends to become a god, to shoot his way to immortality, to invent his way, to write his way . . . Kim considers that immortality is the only goal worth striving for."

Place of Dead Roads is much more autobiographical than *Cities of the Red Night*, but it is a fantasized autobiography. In the course of rewriting history, Burroughs is rewriting himself as he would like to be—the fastest gun in the West. The despised homosexual wimp becomes a great shootist,

much like the "before" and "after" Charles Atlas photographs, in which the weakling who gets sand kicked in his face on the beach becomes a Hercules everyone is in awe of. Indulging two of his obsessions, the book is packed with gun lore and homosexual sex scenes.

It is also, in the tradition of the Western, an old-fashioned tale of "good guys" and "bad guys." The former are the Johnsons, modeled on the character in Jack Black's *You Can't Win*, that is to say all the people who mind their own business, honor their commitments, and provide help when needed. The bad guys are "the shits," that is to say the traditional authority figures, who never mind their own business, who are always right, who make laws against victimless crimes, and who persecute those who don't agree with them. As a Johnson, Kim goes after the types who shit in the water supply and put needles and blades in Halloween fruit and candy.

Grafted onto the Western genre are Burroughs' usual preoccupations with mutation and space travel. Man is like a fish about to exchange gills for lungs, but for some reason he is stalled and cannot quite make it. Burroughs wants to give him the final push, which he believes will come as the result of infection by a new virus. The antidote to the virus will help forge the new man, who will have thoughts and behavior patterns that are not imprinted or prerecorded. "Everything we have been taught," says Kim Carsons, "all the conventional feelings, do not apply."

Time is running out, for mankind and for the author. Seventy when *Place of Dead Roads* was published, Burroughs was having his own intimations of mortality. Death is everywhere present in the novel, not only in the gunfights but seeping through every page of the text. Burroughs is fascinated by last words, uttered when a man knows he is about to die. General Grant, "circuits in his brain flickering out like lightning in gray clouds," said this to his nurse: "It is raining, Anita Huffington." Billy the Kid stepped into a darkened room. Behind him, gun in hand, sat Pat Garrett. *"¿Quién es?"* ("Who is it?") Billy asked. The answer came from the barrel of Garrett's gun. It was death, in person. "What," the author asks by implication, "will be my last words?" Or anyone's?

The book ends as it began, with a shootout in the Boulder cemetery on September 17, 1899, between Kim Carsons and the gunman Mike Chase. Both men are killed, but not by each other. They have been killed by single rifle shots fired from a distance, one in the back and one in the chest.

Place of Dead Roads was reviewed in *The New York Times* by Anatole Broyard, who imagined Burroughs reading from it to the Institute of Arts and Letters he had just joined. What would they do as he detailed the book's indistinguishable acts of sodomy, its gloating over sadistic killings, its repeated evocations of excrement? Would they applaud, burst into tears, or sit there and nod? "There are so many nearly identical couplings and killings," he wrote, "that more than once I thought I'd lost my page and read the same passage over again.

"For a celebrated author to publish a novel as poor as *Place of Dead Roads*," Broyard went on, "requires a degree of collusion or encouragement on our part. He must have a certain confidence in our credulity, must assume that bad taste is a good bet, that age cannot wither nor custom stale the appeal of an established reputation. . . . There's a French proverb to the effect that we deserve what we inspire. What we ought to ask ourselves is whether we want to go on inspiring books like *Place of Dead Roads*."

There was a mild corrective in the more positive review by Perry Meisel in the Sunday *Times* book section on February 19. *Naked Lunch*, wrote Meisel, "prophesied the wider fate of the American sensibility well into the next two decades. . . . By the time the counterculture of the 1960s had succeeded the Beats, license had become the law, and Mr. Burroughs had become a principal avatar of the liberationist esthetic he helped create." In conclusion, however, Meisel saw Burroughs as emblematic of the decline of the postmodernist avant-garde.

Never refute or answer the critic, thought Burroughs. Do not let the critic teach you the cloth, as they say in bullfighting circles. Never charge the cloth even if the critic resorts to misquotation. Writing prejudicial reviews was an exercise in black magic. Reviewers were like the Assayer of Scribes under the ancient Egyptians, who was assigned to impose a uniformity of style. The reviewer could draw disagreeable associations by implying that the book was completely unimportant without saying exactly why.

Burroughs wanted to put a curse on all the Assayers of Scribes, but curses were tricky; they could bounce back and bounce back double. They had to be very casual, like Nixon saying about his opponents, "They should have problems." Jane Bowles was always talking about putting just a small curse on the Beatniks in Tangier, so they would go away. "I don't want to kill them," she said, "I just want to make them a little sick."

Burroughs could imagine the scene with the Assayer of Scribes: This afternoon he has delivered his latest review to the office . . . a perfect job of demolition and he knows it. The effect is disquieting, gathering to itself a legion of negation. A feeling that someone is at the door. He steps to the peephole, the hall is empty down to the elevator. He slides the deadbolt and opens the door. A small black dog slithers in without a sound, brushes against his leg as light as wind. When he tries to find the dog it is nowhere to be seen. He complains to the doorman—how could an unauthorized dog slink into the building?

Sometime later, Burroughs heard that Broyard had been shifted from his job as daily reviewer to a job as editor for the Sunday book section, where he would write an occasional column, but few reviews. "Well, I guess my curse hit," he said. "There must have been plenty out on him. It's amazing he lasted as long as he did."

As the single most important thing about Graham Greene was his viewpoint as a lapsed Catholic, the single most important thing about Burroughs was his belief in the magical universe. The same impulse that led him to put out curses was, as he saw it, the source of his writing: "All my writing comes from the psychic thing. You have satoris, you have enlightenments. I couldn't write a word without them. You sit down and a light turns on and you see a set or a character. In other words, writing a novel is like watching a film. I transcribe it. That's the way the writing of fiction is done. You've got to put yourself into a state where the projector is on, which is known as inspiration. Or, as Hemingway called it, juice."

That July, 1984, Burroughs left for Naropa to give a series of lectures with Allen Ginsberg and Norman Mailer. To Mailer, Burroughs looked older, he walked with a cane and a pronounced stoop, but he was still amazingly intact, and impressive in a crazy way. He was not someone you would mess with, because he had blind guts. It seemed to Mailer that Burroughs in his writing had destroyed his own future, because he had done so much to advance the threshold of shock, so that now, when you read the new stuff, as interesting as it was, the element of shock in it was routine. Like Burroughs, Mailer had assumed that sex was the last frontier. But with hindsight he saw that they had occupied the last frontier much too soon, and that now they had a bunch of suburban developments on that last frontier, making it very hard to write interestingly about sex. There was a superficial sophistication about it that didn't exist twenty-five years ago, but no great comprehension.

Ginsberg and Burroughs mixed it up in the unembarrassed way of old friends, with Allen saying, "I think Bill has abandoned the story line."

"I haven't abandoned the story line at all," Burroughs responded. "My last two books have had very definite, elaborate story lines."

"But you're coming to it late," Allen said. "Because now you're trying to write a bestseller."

"I am not trying to write a bestseller!" Burroughs said. "Allen, don't you realize that someone cannot just sit down and write a bestseller? Bestsellers are written up to the limit of a man's ability. The public may be stupid but they will immediately see the insincerity of a book that was written to be a bestseller."

"Bestsellers are like a successful assassination," Mailer said. "Only the badly conceived ones ever work. If you conceive a novel too well you're going to be out of fashion because the fashion must have been already hanging around long enough in one place for you to have conceived it that well . . . You can't 'write a bestseller' because that implies more control of the immediate literary universe than anyone has."

For Mailer, sharing the podium with Burroughs was an ordeal, it was like being on the same bill with W. C. Fields, because the kids loved Burroughs—every time he opened his mouth they fell on the floor laughing. He'd say something like "Well, it's goddamn chilly in the morning," and they would all whoop with laughter. It was because he was authentic, Mailer reflected. No one was authentic anymore, and here was this guy who was absolutely what he was, who hadn't been influenced by anyone. But their styles were so different that Mailer felt they irritated each other, even though they always treated each other with respect and courtesy. And Mailer kept thinking, let me out of here so I don't have to worry about what this phenomenon is going to say next.

The summer of 1984 was one of wrenching change for Burroughs, for he left his editor of many years, Dick Seaver, and his agent of many years, Peter Matson. That spring in New York he was approached by the enterprising thirty-seven-year-old agent Andrew Wylie. The Harvard-educated son of a Houghton Mifflin editor, Craig Wylie, Andrew had spent some years in the downtown/drug/counterculture New York scene before launching his agency. One of his clients was Allen Ginsberg, for whom he had arranged a six-book contract with Harper & Row. Wylie thought that the same kind of deal could work for Burroughs. He knew that Burroughs was broke, and a multivolume contract would give him some financial stability. He flew out to Lawrence for a three-day visit and went over Burroughs' inventory. It seemed to him that one high point of the deal would be Burroughs' early unpublished novel, *Queer*, which he had said he would never release—but now he relented. Another high point would be several volumes of correspondence. At any rate, Wylie ended up putting together a seven-book proposal, and on the basis of that, Burroughs dropped Matson. In the subsequent negotiations, considerable animosity developed between Wylie and Dick Seaver, so that it's probably better to present each of their accounts, *Rashomon*-style.

"I went to Holt to see Dick," Wylie recounted, "and I said, 'We're working on a seven-book proposal.' Dick said, 'I've worked with William for twenty-five years, and I know he doesn't want to publish *Queer*, and as for the two volumes of correspondence, in my experience collected letters don't sell—I was at Viking when we published Joyce's letters, and they didn't sell.' 'I will send you a proposal for seven books,' I told Dick. 'What we have in mind is a large commitment.' When he got the proposal, Dick said he was not interested in seven books, he reduced it to four books, which I said was too low. This became a big problem. It got quite heated when it came down to the wire. In any case, his offer was not the best, and we moved to Viking. The key to it was that Dick would not believe that William had changed his mind about not publishing *Queer*. It was the attitude of a publisher who has had long experience with a writer, an attitude not shared by a new publisher, who was perfectly ready to believe that Burroughs *would* publish *Queer*, and who agreed that the correspondence was some of his best work. Of course it was natural for Dick to be furious and of course my attitude was going to seem bad, but I was being asked to accomplish something for a writer and I had to accomplish it. Dick had a long and distinguished career in publishing and did wonders for Burroughs, and I understand why he was angry. Dick said, 'I've been asking Bill to publish *Queer* for twenty years,' and what was left unsaid was 'and now this young asshole comes in to sell it to me.' But the big thing for me was to learn that William was broke, and I asked myself, what can be done to remedy the situation? The solution was to draw on his written inventory to get a large advance for a multibook deal that would comprise *Queer*, *Western Lands*, *Interzone* (an early version of *Naked Lunch*), two volumes of correspondence and two volumes of nonfiction."

"I was having dinner with Peter Matson shortly after the publication of *Place of Dead Roads*," Seaver recalled, "and he said, 'I have to tell you that Bill and I are parting company.' And I said, 'That's too bad,' because I felt Peter was very capable, and did his best for him. But Andrew had gone out to Lawrence and done a hard sell on Bill and painted a glowing picture of how he could do ten times better. And Bill's vulnerable, quite frankly. So Andrew came to me and said, 'Look, I'm going to try and sell the collected works.' And I said, 'That poses a rather serious problem. (A) I think it's premature. And (B) a lot of these works are owned by various publishers, Grove, Seaver Books, Holt, small presses, and all you can do is hardcover editions because the paperbacks already exist in various forms, so I don't think that makes a lot of sense.' I said, 'Let's do a multibook contract on the mass of material that hasn't been published. Come up with what you think makes sense, talk to Bill, and we'll draw up a contract to get him some money right away.' The next thing I knew Andrew was taking this around town to five or six publishers, *my idea*, and seeing who he could pit one against the other, and I was furious. And I had a very strong conversation with him, and he said, 'We're closing, it's too late to do anything.' I wasn't even sure I wanted to go to this closing, I don't play games, life's too short. But the day before the closing, a Thursday, he called me. He was looking for $150,000 for a five-book contract, and clearly none of the other publishers had responded to his demands. I said, 'Look, I'm not happy with the way you've handled this, I think it's frankly atrocious, to the point that I don't even want to make an offer, but I go back twenty-five years with Bill, we really have been through thick and thin—I have carried the flag when people said it's going to land you in jail. And then people said you're going to sell 1,500 copies, you're going to lose thousands of dollars, which I did. If I'm pissed it's because I don't think a relationship like this should be summarily dismissed. This said, let me go put my numbers together and I'll call you tomorrow morning.' He said in his nasal voice, 'Well, remember, tomorrow is the closing,' which put me off again. But I came back and called him and we struck a deal, I think it was $140,000 or $150,000. At five minutes to twelve he called and said, 'I have another offer, you don't have to match it.' 'What do you mean, you have another offer?' I asked. 'We struck a deal.' 'I'm sorry,' he said, 'but that's what happened.' I said, 'Fuck you' and then I called Bill, who said, 'Look, I've put myself in the hands of this man and I can't go behind his back.' I said, 'I'm not asking you to go behind his back, I just think this is not the way to do it. I think you should talk to him and we should try to work it out.' Andrew called me back and said, 'We're not going to do anything—this is it.' All I could do was regret the end of a long relationship and reflect that Andrew was not one of my favorite people.''

In his role of adviser, James agreed that it was time to shake things up, and get rid of the Old Guard, who because of their long association kept invoking preferential ties of loyalty. As for Burroughs, he felt bad about leaving Seaver. It was an age-old, insoluble problem, and he hoped they would remain friends. He had thought about it a long time. Reluctant to leave, he had hoped right up to the end that it could be worked out.

He told Wylie to give Dick preference even if it meant less money, but one-third less was too much, and he realized that the time had come to move on.

Now that it was done, he looked for reasons to justify his decision: Dick, you're telling me to be loyal to you, he thought, you're telling me that because of me you've become a cynic, when the point is that you've been publishing my books for years and paying me very little money. Why shouldn't I take as much money as I can get? Loyalty is not a one-way street. It does not mean that the publisher can exploit you. You paid the minimum you could get away with. You want it on a business basis, you've got it on a business basis, now I'm trying to get the most I can get away with. It's like authors were tenant farmers or house niggers—he's getting fifty cents a day and he's very happy with it, he only works twelve hours. What the hell, I don't feel one twinge.

It wasn't true that he didn't feel one twinge, but to say it helped him overcome any nagging feelings of disloyalty, and made him convince himself that he had done the right thing.

The seven-book deal with Viking was announced in *The New York Times* on November 23. Gerald Howard, the Viking editor who had signed up the books, said that Burroughs "has had a sort of pop star persona over the last decade or so. He's much beloved by rock stars, for one thing, and by people on the leading edge of various cultural trends. But my belief is that Burroughs is, in fact, a literary figure on the order of Yeats or Ezra Pound, and that as time goes by he will be seen and accepted by the Establishment." Viking paid a total of $200,000, or about $28,000 per book, while the English deal with Pan was for 45,000 pounds, for a total package of about a quarter of a million dollars, spread over seven books and seven years. It was a financial turning point for Burroughs, who was able to pay off some debts and maintain a surer footing on the slippery slope of upward mobility.

By the time the seven-book deal was announced, Burroughs was visiting Arizona State University, having reached the level of eminence where his manuscripts and correspondence were collected by research libraries. The competition among universities for the papers of important authors was lively. There was more demand than there was supply, because the older universities like Harvard and Yale, and the universities with an aggressive acquisition program like Texas, had skimmed the cream. They had a lock on the Henry Jameses and the Emily Dickinsons and the T. S. Eliots, so that the younger universities had to shop around for the papers of living writers.

One such young institution, Arizona State University, in Tempe, barely a quarter of a century old, wanted to upgrade its library and go after something major. It was part of the rivalry with the University of Arizona in Tucson, like improving the football team. A dealer put A.S.U. in touch with a corporate and securities lawyer from Cleveland named Robert H. Jackson, who was also a collector of rare books and manuscripts, and who happened to own an important Burroughs archive, which was appraised at $200,000. Arizona State bought it for $100,000, with the other $100,000 as a gift and tax write-off.

The urge to acquire had superseded all caution. Arizona State was a very conservative place, with rock-ribbed Republican alumni who would have been horrified by Burroughs' books. As one librarian put it, in the understatement of the year, "Burroughs is a man who might offend local sensibilities." For Arizona State to collect the papers of William S. Burroughs was about as incongruous as the University of Tel Aviv collecting the papers of Ezra Pound. And yet the race to build up an important collection was uppermost, so that a sizable Burroughs archive ended up in the Sun Belt, on the campus at Tempe, among the tanned and pampered students whose fathers gave them sports cars and private planes as graduation presents. When Burroughs came to Tempe in November 1984 to read and pay a courtesy call, he was given a mixed reception. The attitude of the library seemed to be, "We're not fans, but we understand why we should collect him." At the reading, one student walked out, saying he could not understand "the drunk, mumbling old man," but at the end he got a standing ovation.

Over the Christmas holidays, the biographer returned to Lawrence for more taping. On the evening of his arrival, he found Burroughs in a cheerful mood, cooking a stew and conversing with his cats. Burroughs described his theory for running a small town: "What would you do with 15,000 people? There would be a triage, you would designate certain people to work out their destinies, and put the others in an accident pool, with so many deaths from this and so many deaths from that. You could expand that to take care of the whole planet, because there's only one in a million that's worth a shit. In a biological mutation, only a small fraction is going to make it, most of them will go down the drain. The human line is running out, just like the dinosaurs ran out, and we have to mutate."

On Christmas Day, 1984, Burroughs and James and the biographer were invited to dinner at the home of Pat and June Barelli, in Mission Hills, Kansas City. Pat Barelli was an ear-nose-and-throat man who had married James's aunt June. There were four generations of Grauerholzes, Paulks, and Barellis at the dinner, ranging in age from eleven months to James's ninety-four-year-old grandfather, John Paulk, who was there with his eighty-six-year-old wife, Viola—they had been married sixty-eight years. Grandpa had been raised in Oklahoma when it was Indian territory. Most of the time he seemed to be sleeping in his chair, but when a photograph of his son and three daughters was passed around he woke up and said, "Someone asked me, 'John, how many children have you got?' and I said, 'I've got one old man and three old ladies.' I can't tell a lie, can I?"

"Well," said Burroughs, "I'm seventy, I'm a member of the club." But Grandpa, reluctant to grant Burroughs membership, insisted on calling him "sonny." After the turkey with the oyster stuffing, after the rack of lamb, after the yams and the mushrooms and the peas and the cranberry sherbet and all the other dishes that were like a dream of well-prepared abundance, the biographer said good-bye to Grandpa, who gave him a firm handshake and said: "I want to live to be a hundred because very few people die at that age. Six years from now, ask Jamie if I'm still around." Grandpa was ninety-eight on May 5, 1988. But his wife, Viola Wolford Paulk, who had been a formative influence on James, passed away, in October 1985, at the age of eighty-nine.

In January 1985, the biographer went to Paris to see Brion Gysin, who was not well. It was during "the great cold," when the Métro stations, which normally shut down at 1:30 A.M., were kept open for the *clochards* (bums) to sleep in. Brion was wheezing and coughing, a low growl rising from his throat, but his emphysema did not stop him from smoking. "I don't sleep more than twenty minutes at a time," he said. From his fourth-floor apartment on the rue St. Martin, he looked out at the exposed yellow-and-blue intestines of the Beaubourg Museum, a model of the falsely new. He looked out the window, seldom going out, and drank bourbon, and smoked hashish, and received the willing listeners of his by now familiar tales, how he had been done out of his restaurant in Tangier, how the *marchesa* had taken a shine to him. His mood swung from a feeling of despondency, in which he went into his "I'm-a-flop-I'm-a-failure" routine, to one of grandiosity, in which he said, "I'm a star in Paris . . . a living legend."

Once the capital of the avant-garde, Paris was now a cultural backwater, where Brion could still function on the princess circuit ("My dear, Ann of Bavaria and I are competing for the favors of a beautiful boy") while warming his hands at the brazier of socialist culture. He called the Ministry of Culture about his promised decoration, and performed little verbal pirouettes for the minister, Jacques Lang, and worried that at the last reception he had forgotten to kiss Madame Lang's hand. He ingratiated himself with a purchasing committee for the Île-de-France Museum, all eight members of which arrived to look at his work but purchased nothing. He sold his Surrealist drawings to the Beaubourg, the ones that André Breton himself had removed from the walls at the exhibit of 1935. He lobbied for a studio from the city of Paris, or for a dinner invitation. He was so caught up in the politics of culture that there was little time left for producing the work. It was "I must call the Ministry today," and "Does Jacques Lang like me?" And yet there was a genuine gallantry in Brion, who despite his failing health and his doubts about his position in the arts, maintained an enthusiasm for life amid its disappointments. He grumbled and groaned, but he didn't want to miss anything.

In June 1985, the biographer was back in Lawrence, where he found Burroughs in one of his despondent, "it's-the-end-of-the-human-line" moods. "All the political and social chaos we seen now reflects a much deeper biological crisis," he said. "The life expectancy is way below what it should be. Most animals live four or five times the length of time it takes them to reach maturity. A cat is mature at two years and lives to fifteen years. Our counterfeit species is vaster than empires, and more slow. What would be the point in keeping most of them alive anyway? I would gladly get rid of a whole streetful of people to save one kaluga, the incomparable gliding lemur in the rain forest of Borneo. I'm not committed to the human species. I want to move into space. I can't tell you how utterly unhappy I am here. I can hardly stand it, my life is a torment, I just wonder how anyone can feel as awful as I do and live."

The biographer told him that in spite of his pessimism, he loved life, and Burroughs replied, "I love life, but not the one I have." Then, after an excellent fettuccine dinner cooked by James, he stood up and announced, "You're quite right, I do love life, and I love my cats, which is the same thing." A friend had given him a patented "wishing machine" that he was trying out, a small, plug-in appliance consisting of two copper plates, between which were placed a photograph or a nail paring of the person to be wished for. According to the friend, the wishing machine had been used by the Department of Agriculture in experiments to get rid of pests, with a 90 percent kill ratio for Japanese beetles and a 70 percent kill ratio for corn borers. Burroughs had used it successfully to get rid of a growth on Ginger's lower lip, sitting in front of the machine for hours and formulating his wish without words, in silence, and thinking of himself as a surfer of wishing, riding on the wish as a surfer rode the waves, until Ginger's growth disappeared. He now had a photograph of Brion between the plates, and was working on relieving his emphysema. He saw a great future for wishing machines, when millions of people would have them, and their wishes would be coordinated by a television announcer: "All you good people who wished for Mrs. Potter in Peoria, now listen here all you wishers, Mrs. Potter reports that her arthritis is much better." Of course you couldn't wish for something for yourself, that was just asking for trouble, but Burroughs thought there was no limit to it, and was planning to try it on someone with cancer or AIDS. It was sympathetic magic, the power of group concentration.

In July, there was a "Burroughs Week" at Naropa, and Burroughs and James returned to their old haunts, an apartment at the Varsity Manor in Boulder. At dinner the first night, Gregory Corso brought two bottles of Mumm's Cordon Rouge, complaining that it was Extra Dry and not Brut. Reminiscing, Allen said that Jack Kerouac used to call him "Jewboy." Allen took it for a while, but finally had enough, and said to Jack, "You eat shit out of your mother's cunt," which shut him up. Allen said that many of Burroughs' disputable opinions, such as his comments about women, were deliberately outrageous probes written as black humor, but once they were on the page in print he had to defend them as gospel. Burroughs nodded, and said he liked the kind of writer whose style you could recognize in a few words. He could recognize Jane Bowles in one sentence, he said, in the story about the man who ran an alligator farm, "but there was no security in the alligators." A recognizable style, however, was not necessarily good writing—look at Dryden, who had written the most breathtaking conceit in the English language when he commented on Lord Hasting's smallpox: "Each little pimple had a tear in it to wail the fault its rising did commit."

The next evening Burroughs had dinner at the home of Anne Waldman and her poet husband, Reed Bye. Burroughs was godfather to their four-year-old son, Ambrose. His approach to small children had not changed over the years; he still seemed to think that they liked to be scared, and so he came on as a sort of bogeyman, telling Ambrose, "I'm going to take you to the mountain." Ambrose, who in the past had run off in tears when faced with this threat of abduction, had now reached a stage of maturity where he refused to be intimidated by the elderly gentleman with his cane and three-piece suit, and replied, "And I'm going to kick you in the penis."

The next day there was a panel with Burroughs, Ginsberg, and Corso, which turned into an exercise in nostalgia as they went time-traveling back to the days of the Beat Hotel.

"Henri Michaux came to see us," Gregory recalled, "and what do we do, we piss in the sink, we don't go out and piss in the hall, all right, that's the lazy man's way. So he gets very bourgeois uptight, our friend the poet."

"I didn't piss in the sink," said Burroughs, always proper.

They were having problems with the microphone, and Burroughs, the old hand, told Gregory to stay six inches away from it. "The size of my dick," Gregory said. That was Gregory, turning every occasion into buffoonery. Several members of the Naropa faculty thought it was a poor example for the students.

But no one attempted to silence Gregory, who went on in the same vein: "Remember Guy Harloff, the Dutch painter who was fucking Kay Boyle's daughter? Everybody had to take a shit in those old French toilets where you had to squat, and he used to miss the hole, and you'd go in there and say, 'Oh my goodness, it's Guy Harloff again with his big ass.' "

Burroughs told about visiting Céline, who "looked like an old concierge, all covered with shawls."

"That's where I blew it," Gregory said. "I had to fuck that dumb cunt that day, Jules Dassin's daughter, and what am I gonna do, fuck her or go and see this bitter old man?"

Then Allen and Burroughs were recalling Kerouac's visit to Tangier in 1957. "He had an American reaction," Burroughs said. "He thought it was dirty and didn't like Arabs." "Did he have any Arab girls?" Allen asked. "Yes, I think so, but it wasn't very successful," Burroughs said. "Two old queens talking about fucking again," Gregory said, "there they go. Truth and finkery are very close—watch out."

You could say this for Gregory—his street-urchin style was still intact. He had avoided ingestion by the Establishment, and remained an outsider, unfit for polite society. In that sense, he was closer to the original spirit of the Beats than the two others, who now fitted better into the award-recipient, may-we-have-an-interview, poet-laureate mold.

In November 1985, Burroughs and James and Michael Emerton, his new *amigo*, left for Paris to see Brion, and Burroughs signed up for a reading in Amsterdam to defray the expenses of the trip. Brion's emphysema was so bad he had to take oxygen, but when James lit a cigarette he pleaded for a puff. He had been taken up by a hashish smuggler who called himself James Kennedy, but whose real name was Jim McCann. In the seventies, McCann had "played the green card." Under cover of helping the I.R.A., he had set up his dope-smuggling runs through Ireland. A Belfast boy known as "His Nibs," McCann spent some of the money he made on art. He gave Brion $4,000 a month, against a large, ten-panel work in progress called *Calligraffiti of Fire*, so that Brion could afford a male nurse.

Back in New York for a few days, Burroughs went strolling in the East Village and was quite happy to play his part as "Grand Old Man of the Counterculture." On the corner of Eighth Street, a cabdriver waved and shouted, "Hey, Burroughs," and he waved back. In the St. Mark's Bookshop, *Queer*, which had recently been published to favorable reviews, was in the window, and when he went in to sign a few copies, the manager said, "It's our biggest seller." When he went into a luncheonette for a sandwich, the waiter who took his order said, "Wow, you're a genius," and a man at the next table chimed in, "How does it feel to be a genius?" "Oh, I'm used to it," Burroughs said.

Queer was an important early work, written in the same reportorial style as *Junky*, detailing the author's obsession with Eugene Allerton while living in Mexico. Both books were about scoring, of one sort or another. In a new introduction, Burroughs asked himself why he had wanted to chronicle such painful and unpleasant memories. He decided that writing was a way of achieving immunity from the events described, as well as further similar events, like a vaccine. Writing was also his way of fighting back against the ugly spirit he felt possessed him, causing the death of his wife. In a cut-up he made in Paris years later were the words "Raw peeled winds of hate and mischance blew the shot." At first, he thought the words referred to blowing a shot of junk; then he realized that it was the shot that had killed Joan.

That night John Giorno made dinner for Burroughs, James, the biographer, and the painter Keith Haring, who said he had almost been tarred and feathered at his opening by disgruntled and envious East Village artists. Burroughs said he was having trouble with his eyes and would have to have a cataract operation. He could no longer go to target practice, he didn't see the target. He showed the biographer some recent letters from readers. "Mr. Burroughs," one asked, "does your obsession with weapons indicate a basic insecurity?" "It sure does," Burroughs said. "Like all people at this time, I'm terribly scared. What's a man without a weapon, faced by a deadly attack?" Another reader asked, "Do you consider yourself a religious man?" "My reply is," Burroughs said, "do you consider Einstein's field theory a religious statement?"

Then it was back to Lawrence and his beloved cats. Now that Ruski was in the country and Wimpy had vanished, he was down to three, Ginger, Calico, and Fletch. In a journal entry on March 13, 1986, he wrote: "I am in a panic. Fletch attacked me. I had gone to sit on the couch. He came over, got into my lap, and suddenly began to whine and attack me viciously. I slapped him with the medical thriller I was reading. He hissed and went down into the basement. Whatever possessed him permeates the house with a smell of menace and evil. Would anyone sitting on that couch at that moment have been attacked in the same manner? Don't know. I sense that he is sick physically and perhaps in some chronic pain. I stand in deadly fear of his anger. Of any anger? The fear is in my chest, gray-black like underexposed film."

On April 16, 1986, Burroughs saw in the paper that Jean Genet had died, and remembered their assignment for *Esquire* at the 1968 convention. Harold Hayes had called him a thief, and he had said, "But of course." Genet was a great person, an incredible person. He and Beckett were the two twentieth-century novelists who would definitely last. In the last ten years of his life, he didn't write, he was a barbiturate addict. There was the French language, he said, and there was myself, and I put one into the other, and it is done. He lived in small hotel rooms. He was used to jail cells and didn't want a big place. If someone recognized him he moved out the next day. He wanted to be anonymous. Genet said he was protected by his age, his white hair, and his money. All the old friends were dying. Burroughs could take as his own the words of Tennyson's Sir Bedivere: "And I the last go forth companionless."

A visit from Alan Ansen, a gay Falstaff, large and jolly in spite of his own health problems, cheered Burroughs up. Alan had a spot of uremia. His daily four giant martinis had caused him to fall off a barstool. Off the booze, he had a definite awareness of the closing of the shades, and felt that he was slipping into geriatric petulance. But he thought Burroughs looked great. With his longevity, he was on the way to becoming the George Burns of the counterculture.

Burroughs told him about a young friend named Dean Ripa, who caught rare snakes in Africa and sold them to zoos. "He arrived on my doorstep with eight very venomous snakes," Burroughs said. "A gaboon viper, one of the evilest-looking creatures I've ever seen. Four feet long and weighing thirty pounds. Instead of squiggling along like most snakes this thing walks on its ribs like a caterpillar, and the final thing is they growl like dogs. They have a head the size of a small shovel, huge fangs and a terrific amount of venom. Another was the green mamba, six feet long, with a neurotoxic venom."

"Sounds like 'The Adventure of the Speckled Band,' " Ansen said.

"They were all in the back of his car, and he's got a little heater in there, he has to keep them at a temperature of between seventy-five and eighty degrees. I couldn't have them in the house because of my cats, so we took them out to Fred Aldrich's where there's a gas heater, and he put the snakes through their paces. He has a special instrument like a concave cane, so if the cobra came at him he could push it away. 'If I give you the word, get out quick,' he said. He lost his best friend to a snakebite."

That evening over dinner, Burroughs told of a theory he had read about in the *National Enquirer*, advanced by Dr. John Seale of London, to the effect that AIDS was a man-made virus derived from the Visna virus that occurs in sheep, and that was being grown in Soviet laboratories to wipe out the people of the Free World. "Where did that virus come from," he asked, "from a Moscow laboratory, where else? It was developed by Soviet scientists as a biological weapon of war."

"This whole AIDS thing is a scenario right out of William's writing," James said. "The virus of sexual frenzy in *The Wild Boys*."

Ansen had in common with Burroughs that he, too, was a true original, whose opinions were not derivative. When the biographer asked him what Burroughs' motive had been in a certain incident, he replied, "We don't want to get into the situation of Goethe's biographer, who quoted Goethe as saying, 'I only fell in love five times in my entire life,' and then added a footnote saying, 'The master here in error was.' "

Later in April, Burroughs and James went to Germany and he gave readings in Berlin and Bremen to overflow crowds. They then spent four days in Paris with Brion, who knew he was going to die soon and was surrounded by a small circle of helpers. In his moments alone with Burroughs and James, Brion was open about his fear of death. He wept, and said he was terrified. A tumor in his side, which had not yet been diagnosed but was clearly cancerous, was causing him great pain. His emphysema was worse, and he was on oxygen at almost all times. He had, however, finished the pen-and-ink drawings for a short book by Burroughs called *The Cat Inside*, which was to be published in a deluxe edition of 250 copies.

They spent a few days in New York on the way back to Lawrence, and on May 2, at dinner at John Giorno's, Allen Ginsberg, who had seen galleys of the cat book, offered editing suggestions, saying that he should not describe someone as "a well-known Kansas sculptor," because "well-known" sounded like magazine prose. Nor did he like the phrase where

Burroughs described Ruski's disappearance and said he was depressed and in pain. What did he mean by "in pain"?

Distraught over Brion's decline, Burroughs exploded: "Don't you know what 'in pain' means? Don't you realize that I love my cats more than you love any of your fuckin' lovers? ANY OF YOUR FUCKIN' LOVERS?"

Allen did not rise to the bait, having found serenity through Buddhism. The talk turned to Brion, who had written John Giorno that he was thinking of suicide because he was in such pain from emphysema. Someone with Alzheimer's disease had just jumped off the top of the Beaubourg across the street, which had given him ideas. Burroughs said that he had never in his life contemplated suicide, which probably made him some sort of a freak. It would be far better to run amok—which, by the way, came from the Malay *amoq*, to engage furiously in battle—going out fighting and taking some of the bastards with you. But if you were talking about how you might do it, he wouldn't take pills, 'cause often they didn't work, or fall off a building, 'cause he was afraid of heights and you might land on a ledge. He'd blow his brains out with a shotgun the way Hemingway did.

In June, Allen Ginsberg, the spirit of youthful irreverence, reached the advanced age of sixty. He looked strong and fit, but complained about high blood pressure and kidney problems. In addition, Peter Orlovsky was acting up and had to be sent to various places for psychiatric help. As always, Allen was in the eye of the cyclone, managing the whirling circles of his life—his teaching job at Brooklyn College, the publication of the annotated edition of *Howl*, exhibits in New York and Texas of photographs he had taken over the years, and helping Peter and down-and-out friends like Harry Smith and Gregory Corso. Allen had become the curator and guardian of the Beat movement.

In July, Brion Gysin was diagnosed as having lung cancer, on top of his colostomy and his emphysema. His doctor did not give him long to live. John Giorno, who was traveling in Europe, went to Paris and saw him on July 3. Propped up on cushions, emaciated and ravaged, wheezing and coughing, Brion lay there like a half-demented diva, singing his last-act aria of self-pity, and still obsessed by his two phobias, women and Jews: "All the trouble in the world is caused by women and Jews . . . Moses, Christ, Marx, Freud, and Einstein." Burroughs wanted to be at Brion's side, but could not leave Lawrence before the beginning of August, because he could scarcely afford the ticket to Paris at full short-notice prices, and because there seemed to be a little more time. The biographer called

Brion on Wednesday, July 9, and told him to hang on until they got there in the first week of August. "That's too late," Brion said. "I'm going out on Saturday."

On Sunday morning, July 13, his male nurse arrived at the apartment on the rue St. Martin and found Brion dead in his bed, of a heart attack. He was seventy years old. Burroughs was grief-stricken, and guilt-ridden that he had not gotten there on time. Poor Brion. At least he had gotten his decoration and been made a *Chevalier* of the Order of Arts and Letters. He had worried that he had wasted his career. The publishers said he was a painter. The gallery owners said he was a writer. For Burroughs, Brion was the only man he had ever respected, a regal, impeccable presence without a trace of pretension, the only authentic heir to Hassan I Sabbah. Brion could never be a faker or a coward. As it turned out, his illustrations for the cat book had been their final collaboration.

Felicity Mason, another of Brion's closest friends, flew to Paris to make the funeral arrangements. She had known Brion since 1952, when, intrigued by his looks and manner, she had joined him at the café table where he was sitting in the *Djema el Fnaa* in Marrakesh. It turned out that they had been born a year apart in adjacent English villages, and that each had a sibling who had died. Brion decided that Felicity would be his new sister, and so she had remained for thirty-four years, weathering Brion's petulance and tantrums as the price to be paid for his brilliance and charisma. As for his sexual tastes, she saw nothing wrong with men liking men. She liked men herself, and had written about her busy sex life under the pen name Anne Cummings, and understood just what men saw in each other—good, hard cocks. While women were all soft and smelled like beauty salons.

Because of the Bastille Day fourteenth of July holiday, Felicity could not arrange for Brion's removal to the Père La Chaise cemetery until Thursday, July 17. On that day, it was bright and sunny, and street musicians were playing in front of the Beaubourg when the hearse pulled up at 135 rue St. Martin. A small band of the faithful followed the coffin from the apartment to the hearse, including the friends who had attended to his needs in the last days, and who recalled that even to the end, hooked to his oxygen tank, he had held court and cracked jokes, and Establishment ladies from the museums in whites and grays. Felicity laid two sprigs of white orchids on the coffin as a last farewell, and gave a luncheon for twelve in a little restaurant in the Beaubourg neighborhood that Brion had liked.

At the cemetery, there was a backup at the crematorium, so that Brion had to lie in cold storage on standby, which he would not have appreciated. Finally, on Tuesday, July 22, he was cremated, as the music of Jajouka he had loved so well was played. Kennedy/McCann, the dope smuggler/art collector, took custody of the ashes. Matilda, Duchess of Argyll, gave a postcremation reception. To the end, Brion had remained on the princess circuit.

It happened that Maurice Girodias, onetime head of the Olympia Press and now pursuing other interests, had recently moved to a penthouse apartment in the Ménilmontant section of Paris, with a direct and unobstructed view of Père La Chaise. Alerted by friends, he was on his terrace watching the crematorium, looking out over the endless rows of little white gravestones between clumps of leafy trees, where Oscar Wilde and so many other famous men were buried. The crematorium, a vaguely Oriental cupola with two short, round chimneys sticking up like animal snouts, was practically under Maurice's nose, and he saw it every day when he tended to his geranium boxes.

The crematorium had been built as a monument to free-thinkers after the French Revolution, a practical implement of the rationalist creed, an alternative to the Christian superstition of interment, announcing with each puff of smoke, "There is no life after death." It was a fitting end for Brion, who had believed only in himself, thought Maurice. It was also an egalitarian end, reducing men of high and low station to the same diminutive pile of ashes. And yet it seemed to Maurice that in this as in every other aspect of life there was an order of precedence, so that when a body was cremated, the puffs of black smoke were wispy and hesitant in the case of a nobody, and fuller and more abundant in the case of more prominent corpses. This impression lasted only for a moment, however, for the puffs of smoke were soon dispersed and carried away by the wind. When the puffs that had once been Brion went up, Maurice looked away.

In Lawrence, Burroughs was in a deep depression, where the smell of death clung to everything. Pale horse, pale rider, where are they now? Mikey Portman entwined with my brother, Mort, I had to laugh even to think of such a thing what are you in front of decent people? Stardust on each hurricane warnings out. Two adolescents both of us using the copper basin pubic hair dust of the dead before I met Kerouac in the peony-filled field. Who has provided for these needs? Two dollars extra. Interesting theory from the shopkeeper. Wanna get screwed, Skinny?

Michael Winkler of Lima, Ohio, age six, first case in medical history to recover from rabies. Garver got the job, is he dead, too? Oswald's mother reminding Johnson, "You would not be President except for my son's act." The alley behind MacPherson, where are you today, Pryne Hoxie? Kells and Kiki in front of the Café Central, where are you today? Kells in a dream, saying, "I was beaten in handcuffs." And Rex Weisenberger . . . "If you do, mother, I will cut the legs off the dining room table." And Dave Kammerer, rocks in his pockets, at the bottom of the Hudson. And Antony Balch burning the pound note.

Just an old man with his memories popping. On the way to the Greek restaurant on Moscow Street we passed our Paddington digs and I said, "Oh, there's where we used to live," and Ian snapped, "I don't want to be reminded of our life together."

We commit daily crimes against people by the fact of being alive. "What about your brother?" Brion asked at the Beat Hotel, and I burst into tears realizing the emptiness of Mort's life and my own, responsibility. And Billy with his room full of empty paregoric bottles, and Mother mixing cocktails at four in the afternoon. And Gene Angert in Menninger with his decorticated body. Oh yes, I was slight, but a slight build is an advantage in the long run. And Henry Beck, who helped me get married in Athens, died of Malta fever. Ilse would be in her eighties, she must be dead, though I heard she was living near Zurich. And when the Jew-boy asked, would you rather be a live coward or a dead hero, Masseck just looked at him. Ruski killed the birds, brought them in, and dropped them on the kitchen floor. At Los Alamos I threw a dead rabbit into the pigpen and they ate it, hair and all. Hogs will eat anything.

I look back on the things I've done, asking myself, "What in the hell did you do that for? What was in your mind, were you crazy or something? What possessed you to do such a stupid, destructive thing? Don't you realize that if you'd hit the glass you'd have endangered those people sitting on the couch?" My past is an evil river.

When I drove to New York from Harvard with Bill Gilmore and Richard Stern, it was night, and Stern was going seventy miles per hour through intersections. "Richard you are scaring me to death," I said, and he replied, "Are you worried about meeting death? Well, you won't meet him with me." "For sure I won't," I said. "If you don't slow down I'm going to get out of this car." He slowed down. The tide is coming in from Hiroshima, you dumb earth hicks. *Sauve qui peut.* Your death is always with you. You don't have to run around looking for it.

In the fall of 1986, Burroughs pulled himself out of his depression and resumed work on *Western Lands*, the last volume of his trilogy. He saw friends again, and attended the monthly meeting of the Lawrence Cat

Club in the fairgrounds building. He wanted to propose the construction of a no-kill cat shelter, but that was not on the agenda, and instead he had to sit through a demonstration on "showing your cat"—how to hold it and show it to the judge at cat shows. If your cat scratches the judge, that doesn't help.

In December, Burroughs finished *Western Lands*, and he and James came to New York for a festive week of dinners and parties. Many old friends came to a birthday party for James, including Allen Ginsberg, John Giorno, Barney Rosset, Stewart Meyer, and Howard Brookner. On Sunday, December 21, as Burroughs and James were in the Bunker packing for their return to Lawrence, Allen Ginsberg and Lucien Carr arrived, both bearded like the wise men of old.

Lucien was still in Washington with his news agency, which had gone through a change of ownership. The new president had called him in and told him, "You have an iron rice bowl," a Chinese expression meaning that he would not, like so many others, be fired. Allen recalled that when he had visited the English department of a Chinese university, half the faculty were ideologues appointed during the Cultural Revolution, who did not speak a word of English. When Allen was invited to a faculty meeting, the iron rice bowl contingent was not in attendance. Why bother, since they were tenured for life, whatever happened?

Lucien said he was on his way to the hospital to visit his eighty-eight-year-old mother, who had suffered her third stroke in a year. He poured himself some Old Overholt in a teacup, and Burroughs shuddered—he frowned on daytime drinking. "But William," James said, "you have advanced the hour of the sundowner farther that anyone I know." "Not this far," he said. "The sun is over the yardarm," Lucien said. Lucien and Allen left, saying good-bye to Burroughs, three old friends who went back forty years to the Columbia days, and whose lives were still intertwined.

In Lawrence, Burroughs finished *Western Lands*, which was due to be published in December 1987. Perhaps, he thought when it was done, it was his last book. There were times now when he felt he could no longer write. "I cannot express myself through writing anymore," he said. Writing was a part of his life that was over and done with. *Western Lands* was his finale, his sign-off, his last hurrah. He was leaving the stage and there would be no encores. He remembered what Jean Genet had said: "There was the French language and there was me and I put one into the other and now it's finished—*C'est fini*." For him, it was the same—*C'est fini*.

Or was it? In spite of what he said, there were days when he sat down at the typewriter and jotted down dream sequences or memories. It wasn't quite over as long as he had the recording urge.

November 5, 1986, journal entry: "I was a bit junk-sick. I had also smoked a joint, and suddenly this sex desire comes over me and I go into the bathroom and jack off standing up. A gentle touch and Ian is behind me, fucking me, just drop your pants, Bill, and let me fuck you. The feeling of merging and a click in my throat and I suddenly feel whole."

May 1987 dream notes: "Junk-sick in Tangier. I am going to show James 'the most horrible street in Tangier.' A ship a ship. Ian neglected me. In Morocco Jacques Stern was a drug clerk. I had an RX for chloral hydrate which he didn't want to cash. My time in Tangier with Billy was strained and hollow. Like the time he called long distance after an accident from the hospital. I could hear him but he couldn't hear me. I kept saying where are you, Billy, where are you? All my family and intimate relationships tend to be strained and off-key. Affection denied when needed or supplied when unwanted. Holding in my hand a limestone fragment I picked up at a Greek ruin in 1973 with John Brady—it was a testicle."

In lieu of writing, he turned to painting. Not only the gunshot paintings he had experimented with on wood panels, but works on paper reminiscent of the calligraphic paintings of Brion Gysin. He knew nothing about painting, but these were accomplished works, and he felt that Brion's hand was guiding him. What he was trying to do was put time into the painting, which he called the Big Bang technique. The pictures moved and changed, he found in them hidden faces and scenes. When he painted he felt a pleasant vertigo, a falling into the picture. So that he spent hours not only painting but looking at his paintings, and divining their hidden language. He gave his TV set to James, he no longer had any use for it: "I'd rather look at my paintings."

He did very few readings now, although in the summer he still went to Naropa to teach. He was there in July 1987 for a week, and found that the other guest lecturer was an old friend, the psychiatrist R. D. Laing, whom he had known in London in the seventies. Laing was then at the height of his fame, as the author of *Knots* and *The Divided Self*, and the head of a therapy center in which he encouraged his patients to accept and come to terms with their mental disorders. He told them to get inside their madness, to go through it and come out the other side.

As usual, Burroughs had an apartment at the Varsity Town House, where his friend from New York days, Steven Lowe, had joined him. One night they invited Allen Ginsberg and Laing to dinner, and Laing showed up with his attractive young girlfriend, Margaret. Laing seemed to have been drinking, and recounted a run-in he'd had with Allen's friend, Peter Orlovsky. "If I'd had my Glasgow pub buddies here," he said, "we wouldn't have put up with that shit."

Burroughs started talking about mandatory blood tests for AIDS, and how it was another form of government control, and as he spoke, Laing slumped down in his chair, as though returning to the fetal position. Suddenly he began shouting at Burroughs: "Talk to me! Talk to me!" "Oh, Ronnie," Margaret said, "quit winding people out."

Then Laing turned to Burroughs and said, "You're stupid." "What?" a startled Burroughs asked. "You're stupid," Laing replied. "I beg your pardon, Ronnie, I've been called many things in my life, but stupid wasn't one of them." "What do you mean by stupid?" Steve Lowe asked. "You're stupid," Laing said, "because you have all the information any one man can have, because you love your cats, and because you're innocent and naïve." "That's ridiculous," Steve said, "you're undermining the terms." Laing seemed not to hear, he was somewhere else, and he was saying, "The sky's too blue, the ocean is too wet, the snow is too white." God, thought Steve, mad Gregory was a blessing compared to this lunatic. Then Laing said, "I'm an agent, and we're still in telepathic control." What deterioration, thought Steve. Once a brilliant man, and now look at him. He had taught others to come out the other side, but where was he? Physician, heal thyself!

Margaret rose from the table, and a few minutes later said, "Ronnie, the taxi's here." Laing jumped up in Pavlovian reaction and Burroughs saw him to the door, saying, "Good to see you, Ronnie." That was Burroughs, thought Steve, unflappable and unfailingly courteous. It would have been so easy to trade insults with Ronnie, to say something wounding. People thought Burroughs was some kind of monster, whereas in fact he was a gentleman, in the best sense of the word.

In December 1987, Burroughs came to New York in his dual capacity as writer and painter. There was a publication party for *Western Lands* at the Gotham Book Mart and a signing at B. Dalton on Eighth Street and Sixth Avenue. And who should Burroughs find sitting in his chair at Dalton but Herbert Huncke, also in his seventies, one of the last survivors of the post–World War II Times Square scene. Huncke looked pretty good, considering it was miraculous that he was still alive, with all the drugs and booze he had ingested. At Dalton there were so many people on line for the signing that they ran out of books and had to cut the line, like a movie line: sold out. "If you live long enough," Burroughs said, "you become the Grand Old Man of letters."

Then there was a show of his paintings that opened on December 19 at the Tony Shafrazi gallery on Mercer Street. Shafrazi was an Iranian painter-turned-dealer who had made his reputation in the art world by defacing *Guernica*. He had walked into the Museum of Modern Art where Picasso's huge painting was hanging in the lobby and had written a message across it with a can of red spray paint. He had meant to say KILL ALL LIES but in the excitement of the moment it came out KILL LIES ALL. At the opening, there was a big crush, television cameras, celebrities, the downtown people, the art world, and Burroughs wearing a gray double-breasted suit. The gunshot paintings were upstairs (including the one that the Institute of Arts and Letters had turned down for its 1983 exhibit of new members' work), and the watercolors and drawings were downstairs. James, still the star-struck Coffeyville bumpkin, pointed to a bright orange gunshot painting and said: "Bianca Jagger put a reserve on that one. . . . There's a party afterward at the Canal Bar. A select group. Madonna's coming with Matt Dillon, and Chris [Stein] and Debbie [Harry] will be there." Burroughs' comment on the difference between painting and writing was "Painting is a hell of a lot easier than writing."

It was gratifying to be able to turn a senior citizen hobby (Irving Berlin at the age of 100 passing the time with his watercolors) to profit. In May 1988 Burroughs passed through New York on the way to Europe for gallery shows in Antwerp, Amsterdam, and London. "They're all pre-sold," he said. "It's the only way to go." He looked thin to the point of anorexia, an indication that James Grauerholz was not in strict attendance, for when Burroughs was left alone he forgot to eat. He had also rolled back the hour of his first drink, which had once been 6 P.M., to 3:30, threatening to turn the sundowner into a sunriser. The talk in the media about the legalization of drugs was like a vindication, for he had always said that if drugs were legal there would be no drug problem. "You do it gradually," he said, "like a prescription drug, with plenty of controls and safeguards. Just by having a standardized product, you'd be saving hundreds of lives." Perhaps he would see it in his lifetime. They could start with marijuana, which was no more addictive than nicotine.

Who killed Kim Carsons and Mike Chase? The answer was divulged in *Western Lands*. They were both killed by Joe the Dead, a hideously scarred character, blind in one eye, with a stump where his left hand should be, the victim of an exploding safe. Joe the Dead is described as a Natural Outlaw, dedicated to breaking the natural laws of the universe. A specialist in evolutionary biology, he intends to crack two biological laws: One, that hybrids are permitted only between closely related species. Two, that an evolutionary step requiring biological mutation must be irretrievable and irreversible.

Joe the Dead is a monstrous, inhuman character who has brought back strange knowledge from the grave. "His only lifeline is the love of animals. Cats see him as a friend."

From one book to the next, Burroughs had killed off one alter ego, Kim Carsons, and adopted the guise of another, Joe the Dead. For his purpose in *Western Lands* was to write his way out of death, to immortality. The Western Lands of the title have nothing to do with the American West. They are, according to the ancient Egyptians, the lands beyond death that a few can reach after a perilous journey, and after crossing the Duad, the river of excrement.

Western Lands is another quest book, but this time the quest is not space travel or mutation, but some form of life after death. "The road to Western Lands is unpredictable. Today's easy passage may be tomorrow's death trap. The obvious road is almost always a fool's road, and beware the Middle Roads, the roads of moderation, common sense, and careful planning."

As in the previous books, the sets and characters go through quick changes. In his quest for the Western Lands, Burroughs resurrects Kim Carsons and adds another character called Neferti. There are flashbacks to the Weimar Republic, the Russian front, and the fall of Berlin, like a series of false starts—these are not the way to the Western Lands. Kim moves to Tangier, and to Uruguay. Why, he wonders, did the Egyptians need to preserve the physical body in mummy form? It had to be because of women, who are parasites feeding on men's bodies. However, if the Western Lands could be reached by the contact of two males, the myth of duality would be exploded. Burroughs sees two roads to the Western Lands, through the love of danger and through homo-sex. But danger is a monopoly of the insensitive and noncreative, while homo-sex has been dealt a deadly blow by AIDS.

Western Lands is an account of a trip beyond death, a metaphor for the artist's longing for immortality. Written in an elegiac tone, it flashes back to scenes of Burroughs' childhood and early life: "The house on Pershing Avenue . . . Inside he stumbles on a heap of toys . . . One Christmas after another in layers . . . A crust of broken ornaments crunches underfoot like snow."

He imagines finally reaching the Grand Hôtel des Morts, where he sees Ian Sommerville, "vague and wispy and cool . . . a curious combination of a mathematician . . . and a cold, bitchy woman." He is in the Land of the Dead, where the silver coins that are the legal currency reflect the qualities the pilgrim has displayed during his lifetime. Cat coins are for cat lovers, kindness coins are for those who were helpful without consideration of payment. There are courage coins, integrity coins, and truth coins. Coins cannot be counterfeited or stolen, they tarnish and blacken in the wrong hands.

But have Burroughs and his characters reached the Western Lands? As Joe the Dead moves about the house making tea, smoking cigarettes, and reading trash, he feels a pain that he cannot locate in bodily terms. "It isn't exactly *his* pain, it's as if some creature inside him is suffering horribly, and he doesn't know exactly why, or what to do to alleviate the pain, which communicates itself to him as a paralyzing fatigue, an inability to do the simplest thing—like fill out the driver's license renewal form. . . . The thought of sitting down and doing it causes him the indirect pain that drains his strength, so that he can barely move."

As the book ends, they have been unable to cross the Duad. "I want to reach the Western Lands," writes Burroughs, now speaking in his own voice, but he is prevented from doing so by the river, down which flows "all the filth and horror, fear, hate, disease, and death of human history."

And then he asks himself the question that indicates the failure of the quest: "How long does it take a man to learn that he does not, cannot want what he 'wants'?" He has spent thirty years trying to write his way out of the human condition and must finally accept that it cannot be done. He has come to the end of words. The book ends with the phrase heard every night in English pubs: "Hurry up, please, it's time." The end is approaching, and the Duad is unpassable, but the writing itself will remain.

Acknowledgments
and Sources

I am very much indebted to William S. Burroughs for giving unsparingly of his time, almost on a day-by-day basis, over the four years that this book took to complete; to James Grauerholz, for his continuously diligent and enthusiastic cooperation, and for his editing help; to Robert H. Jackson, for allowing me to examine the crucial Burroughs archives in his possession; and to my editor, Robert Cowley, whose skill greatly improved the book.

I would like to thank the following for interviews and/or correspondence: Eugene Allerton, Alan Ansen, John Ashbery, Nancy Barfield, Mary Beach, Sinclair Beiles, William J. Belli, Joseph Bianco, Victor Bockris, Paul Bowles, Eileen Bresnahan, Howard Brookner, Chandler Brossard, Andreas Brown, Michael Brownstein, David Budd, Miggy Burroughs, John Calder, Hortense Calisher, Lucien Carr, Arthur Chase, Hal Chase, John Cherry, Judy Coffee, Ira Cohen, Gregory Corso, Malcolm Cowley, and Mark Coir and David Curry of the Burroughs Corporation; Beteina Barnum De Bakey, Edward de Grazia, Richard Dillon, Richard Elovich, Peter Elvins, Lawrence Ferlinghetti, Raymond Foye, and Dr. Richard A. R. Fraser of the New York Hospital–Cornell Medical Center; Allen Ginsberg, John Giorno, Maurice Girodias, Robert F. Giroux, Jeff Goldberg, Michael Barry Goodman, Brion Gysin, Cabell Hardy, Richard Hayes, Al and Helen Hinkle, John Hopkins, Herbert Huncke, Ira Jaffe, Fred Jordan, John Kingsland, Galway Kinnell, Seymour Krim, Jo-Anne Kyger, Timothy Leary, Les Levine, Fran Lewis, Kennet Love, Steven Lowe, Norman Mailer, Bernard Malamud, Felicity Mason, and Donald W. Meyer, superintendent of Bellefontaine Cemetery, St. Louis, Missouri; Stewart Meyer, Barry Miles, Robert Miller, John Montgomery, Bill Morgan, Edward Morgan, Gabriel Morgan, Gerald Nicosia, Harold Norse, Ron Nowicki, Panna Grady O'Connor, Philip O'Connor, June

Overgaard, Edith Kerouac Parker, Claude Peliu, David Prentice, Ann R. Prewitt, Bob Rosenthal, Irving Rosenthal, Barney Rosset, Ursula Schaeffer, Arthur Schlesinger, Jr., Richard Evans Schultes, Rogers Scudder, Richard Seaver, Sylvia Shorris, Eileen Simpson, Virginia Smith, Carl Solomon, Terry Southern, Dr. Thomas Earl Starzl, John Steinbeck, Jr., Richard Stern, Mack Thomas, Virgil Thomson, George Von Hilsheimer, Anne Waldman, Dr. Richard Warner, Alan Watson, Edwin J. Woods, Marianne Woolfe, and Andrew Wylie.

I would also like to thank the following institutions and their librarians for archival material: Carol O. Daniel, librarian of the John Burroughs School, St. Louis, Missouri; Linda Aldrich and Hedy M. Dunn of the Los Alamos Museum; the Manuscripts Room at Columbia University; Temple University; the Lilly Library in Bloomington, Indiana; the George Arents Research Library at Syracuse University; Washington University; the Northwestern University library; the Harry Ransom Humanities Research Center, University of Texas at Austin; the Frank Melville, Jr., Memorial Library, State University of New York at Stony Brook; the University of Delaware; the Special Collections Room, Arizona State University, Tempe, Arizona; and the University of Kansas, Lawrence, Kansas.

Notes

Abbreviated Titles of Sources Frequently Cited

BA:Burroughs archive, Lawrence, Kansas.
BI:Burroughs interviews with the author.
GD:Ginsberg deposit, Columbia University.
RJ:Burroughs archive, Robert H. Jackson collection,Cleveland, Ohio.
BJ:Billy Burroughs Journals.

Prologue

Induction of Burroughs and ceremonial proceedings: based on interviews with William S. Burroughs, James Grauerholz, Stewart Meyer, Malcolm Cowley, Bernard Malamud, Arthur Schlesinger, Jr., Hortense Calisher, Galway Kinnell, John Ashbery, and Allen Ginsberg. Transcript of Ralph Ellison speech and other material supplied by the library, American Academy and Institute of Arts and Letters.

Chapter 1: St. Louis

Burroughs family background and grandfather: BI, Archives of Burroughs Corporation, Detroit, Michigan.
Laura Burroughs: BI, Miggy Burroughs to author.
Ivy Lee: BI, and *Courtier to the Crowd*, by Ray Eldon Hiebert (Ames, Iowa, 1966).
St. Louis childhood and servants: BI.
John Burroughs School: BI, Ann Russ Prewitt to author.
Personal Magnetism essay: John Burroughs School library.
Class of 1931 fiftieth reunion: Ann Russ Prewitt to author, BA.

Chapter 2: Los Alamos

Founding of school: Los Alamos Museum archives.
A. J. Connell: BI, Rogers Scudder and Arthur Chase to author.
Burroughs at Los Alamos: BI, Burroughs School record, Los Alamos Museum, Rogers Scudder and Arthur Chase to author.

Chapter 3: Cambridge

Taylor school: BI, Ann Russ Prewitt to author.
Burroughs at Harvard: BI, Robert Miller and Richard Stern to author.
Kells Elvins: BI, Peter Elvins to author.
European tour: BI, Robert Miller to author.
Year in Vienna and marriage to Ilse Klapper: BI.

Chapter 4: New York

Visit to Huntsville and suicide of Toller: BI.
Burroughs and Korzybski: BI.
Burroughs and Jack Anderson: BI, BA.
Attempts to volunteer and ad agency career: BI.

Chapter 5: Chicago and New York

Discharge, Merritt Inc., and exterminator job: BI.
Lucien Carr: Carr to author, Kennet Love to author, GD.
David Kammerer: BI, Kennet Love to author, Chandler Brossard to author.
Allen Ginsberg: GD, Allen Ginsberg to author.
Ginsberg meets Burroughs: Carr and Ginsberg to author, GD.
Jack Kerouac: Ginsberg and Burroughs to author; *Memory Babe*, by Gerald Nicosia (New York, 1983).
Edie Parker and Jack Kerouac: Edie Kerouac Parker to author.
Joan Vollmer: Edie Kerouac Parker to author.
Joan Vollmer and John Kingsland: John Kingsland to author.
Hal Chase: Hal Chase to author.
Lucien Carr and Celine Young: GD.
Burroughs flying for Franco: Lucien Carr to author.
Funeral service for Jack: Edie Kerouac Parker to author.

Chapter 6: "And the Hippos Were Boiled in Their Tanks"

Carr-Kammerer dilemma: BI, GD.
Jack and Edie quarrel: Edie Kerouac Parker to author.
Jack and Lucien attempt to ship out: BI.
Allen and Lucien: GD.

Allen and Kammerer: Ginsberg to author.
Kammerer killing: BI, GD, Chandler Brossard to author, Ginsberg to author.
Celine Young to Kerouac: GD.
Lucien drops out: GD.
Hippos: BA.
Kerouac to Carl Solomon: GD.

Chapter 7: Junk

Jack and Edie: Edie Kerouac Parker to author.
Burroughs, Ginsberg, and Kerouac: BI, Ginsberg to author.
Allen suspended from Columbia: Ginsberg to author.
Joan Vollmer to Edie Parker: Edie Kerouac Parker.
The "libertine circle": BI, Ginsberg and Hal Chase to author.
Herbert Huncke: Huncke to author.
Burroughs meets Huncke: BI, BA.
Huncke and Kinsey: Huncke to author.
Burroughs moves in with Joan: BI, John Kingsland to author, Hal Chase to author.
Burroughs arrested: BI.
Bill Garver: BI, Huncke to author.
Phil White crime: BI, Huncke to author.
Burroughs in St. Louis: BI.
Burroughs moves to Texas: BI.
Huncke and Joan: Huncke to author.
Kingsland to Edie Parker: Edie Kerouac Parker.
Burroughs starts living with Joan: BI.

Chapter 8: Texas

Joan to Allen: GD.
Life in New Waverly: BI, Huncke to author.
Neal Cassady: GD.
Wilhelm Reich: BI; *Wilhelm Reich vs. the USA*, by Jerome Greenfield (New York, 1974).
Joan gives birth and Burroughs' parents visit: Huncke to author.
Allen and Neal visit: BI, Huncke and Ginsberg to author.
Return to New York: BI, Huncke to author.
Burroughs arrested in Beeville: BI.
Burroughs' farming experience: GD.
Kerouac and Lucien Carr in New York: GD.

Chapter 9: Louisiana

Burroughs in Algiers: BI.
Kerouac-Cassady trip to New York: Al Hinkle to author.

Helen Hinkle stays with Burroughs: Helen Hinkle to author.
Jack and Neal visit: BI, Al and Helen Hinkle to author.
Allen to Burroughs on Joan's sexual needs: GD.
Huncke staying with Allen: Ginsberg and Huncke to author.
Allen arrested: GD, Ginsberg and Huncke to author.
Allen meets Carl Solomon in hospital: Ginsberg and Carl Solomon to author.
Burroughs arrested: BI, BA.
Burroughs' views on farming and frontier heritage: GD.
Burroughs' view on wetback policy: GD.

Chapter 10: Mexico

Burroughs' initial fondness for Mexico: GD.
Joan to Ginsberg: GD.
Burroughs picking up a boy: *Junky.*
Bernabé Jurado and Old Dave: BI.
Fight with Joan: *Junky.*
Telepathic game: Carr to author.
Burroughs brings opium to Old Dave: *Junky.*
Pilgrimage with Old Dave: BI.
Burroughs and Kells Elvins: Marianne Woolfe to author.
New impression of Mexico: GD.
Scene with cat: *Junky.*
Burroughs drunk: BI and *Junky.*
Burroughs and homosexuality: GD.
Burroughs runs into Hal Chase: BI and Hal Chase to author.
The Bounty scene: BI, Eugene Allerton to author, Edwin Woods to author.
Burroughs and Allerton: BI, Allerton to author, *Queer.*
Joan to Ginsberg: GD.
Allerton and Burroughs in Latin America: BI, Allerton to author.
Ginsberg and Carr in Mexico: Ginsberg and Carr to author.
Hal Chase runs into Joan: Hal Chase to author.
Joan's death: BI, Allerton and Woods to author.
Ginsberg and Carr reaction: Ginsberg and Carr to author.
"I am forced to the appalling conclusion": *Queer.*
Burroughs and Mexican authorities: BI.
Burroughs and his brother: BI.
Ginsberg and *Junky*: Ginsberg to author.
Carl Solomon to Kerouac: GD.
Publication of *Junky*: Carl Solomon to author.
Burroughs to Kerouac and Ginsberg: GD.
Robert Giroux to Kerouac: Giroux to author.
Kerouac in Mexico: BI.
Bill Garver in Mexico: BI.
Allerton turns up, and Burroughs' departure: BI.

Chapter 11: Colombia

Billy in St. Louis: BJ.
Move to Palm Beach: BJ and Miggy Burroughs to author.
Burroughs in Latin America: BI and *Yage Letters*.
Meeting with Richard Evans Schultes: Dr. Schultes to author.
Quest for yage: BI and *Yage Letters*.
Ginsberg to Eisenhower: GD.
Gregory Corso: Corso to author, GD, University of Kansas.
Burroughs' sexual interest in Ginsberg: BI, Ginsberg to author.
Alan Ansen: Ansen to author.

Chapter 12: Tangier

Burroughs at forty, and the magical universe: BI.
Tangier: *Tangier—A Different Way*, by Lawdom Vaidon (David Woolman; The Scarecrow Press, Metuchen, New Jersey, 1977).
Tangier characters: BI.
Burroughs and Woolman and the two Arab boys: GD.
Paul Bowles: Bowles to author, and *Without Stopping*, by Paul Bowles (New York, 1972).
Burroughs to Ginsberg and Kerouac: GD.
Burroughs and Brion Gysin: GD.
Burroughs and Kiki: BI, GD.
Burroughs on junk: BI.
Ginsberg dream about Burroughs and visit to Cassadys: Ginsberg to author, GD.
Ginsberg to Kerouac: GD.
Burroughs runs into Carl Solomon: BI.
Burroughs and Ginsberg: GD.
Burroughs hooked again: BI.
Burroughs and Bowles: Bowles to author.
Ginsberg in San Francisco: Ginsberg to author; *Howl*, the annotated edition, edited by Barry Miles (New York, 1986).
Lawrence Ferlinghetti reaction to *Howl*: Ferlinghetti to author.
The Dent cure: BI.
Burroughs' visit to Venice: BI, Alan Ansen to author.
Burroughs back in Tangier: BI, Bowles to author.
Kerouac in Tangier: BI, *Memory Babe*.
Ginsberg and Orlovsky in Tangier: Ginsberg to author, BI, Ansen to author, Bowles to author.
Burroughs in Scandinavia: BI.
Kiki's death: BI.
Kerouac's success: GD, *Memory Babe*.
Burroughs leaves Tangier: GD, BI.

Chapter 13: Paris

Allen Ginsberg in Europe: Ginsberg to author.
Gregory Corso in Europe: Corso to author.
Corso and Mack Thomas: Mack Thomas to author.
Beat Hotel: BI, Ginsberg and Brion Gysin to author.
Girodias and Olympia Press: Girodias to author.
Ginsberg takes *Naked Lunch* to Girodias: Ginsberg and Girodias to author.
Burroughs sees Ginsberg again in Paris: Ginsberg to author.
Sinclair Beiles in Paris: Beiles to author.
Mason Hoffenberg in Paris: BI.
Mack Thomas on Burroughs: Mack Thomas to author.
"The first dreamy day of spring": GD.
John Huston party: Ginsberg and Corso to author.
Ginsberg and Corso in London: Ginsberg and Corso to author.
Beats and modernist tradition: Ginsberg to author.
Meeting Michaux: Corso and Ginsberg to author.
Meeting with Duchamp: Corso and Ginsberg to author.
Meeting with Céline: Burroughs and Ginsberg to author.
Corso and Burroughs: Corso to author.
Jacques Stern: Corso and Burroughs to author.
Chicago Review flap: Irving Rosenthal to author; *The Case History of Burroughs'
Naked Lunch*, by Michael Barry Goodman (New Jersey, 1981).
Brion Gysin: Gysin to author.
Paul Bowles on Gysin: Bowles to author.
Magic in the Beat Hotel: BI, Gysin to author, Bill Belli to author.
Belli on Burroughs: Belli to author.
Ginsberg to Burroughs, February 1959: GD.
Burroughs back in Tangier: BI.
Girodias invites Burroughs: Girodias to author.
Burroughs arrested: BI, Girodias to author.
Olympia publishes *Naked Lunch*: Girodias to author.
Harold Norse meets Burroughs: Norse to author.
Burroughs meets Ian Sommerville: BI, Norse to author.
Burroughs' drug case comes up: BI.
Life interviews Burroughs: BI.
Excerpt from Snell file: Time-Life archive.
Biographical note to Allen: GD.
Burroughs' letter to his mother: RJ.
Burroughs and the kiosk woman: BI.
Brion Gysin discovers cut-ups: BI, Gysin to author.
Burroughs meets Beckett: BI, John Calder and Barney Rosset to author.
Gregory Corso on Brion Gysin: Corso to author.
Sinclair Beiles and *Minutes to Go*: Beiles to author.
Burroughs leaves Paris: BI.

Chapter 14: *Naked Lunch*

Barney Rosset founds Grove Press: Barney Rosset to author.
Correspondence over *Naked Lunch*: George Arents Research Library, Syracuse University.
Tropic of Cancer case: Barney Rosset to author.
Calder and Edinburgh Festival: John Calder to author.
Events at Edinburgh Festival: transcript of proceedings, library of State University of New York at Stony Brook; BI, Norman Mailer to author.
Printer refuses to handle *Naked Lunch*: Barney Rosset to author.
Naked Lunch case: Rosset to author, BI, Syracuse (Grove Press papers), *The Case History of Burroughs'* Naked Lunch, and Edward de Grazia to author.
Naked Lunch trial: trial transcript, Grove Press.
Burroughs' troubles with Girodias: Syracuse collection.

Chapter 15: Burroughs Meets Leary

Burroughs in London: BI.
Correspondence with Haselwood: Bancroft Library, University of California, Berkeley.
Bowles to Montgomery: John Montgomery to author.
Mikey Portman meets Burroughs: BI; *High Diver*, by Michael Wishart (London, 1977).
Mikey Portman to Burroughs: RJ.
Leary to Burroughs: RJ.
Timothy Leary: Leary to author; *High Priest*, by Timothy Leary (New York, 1968); *Flashback*, by Timothy Leary (Los Angeles, 1983).
Allen Ginsberg to Leary: GD.
Leary to Burroughs: RJ.
Burroughs back in Tangier: BI, Bowles to author.
Kerouac and paternity suit: Kerouac correspondence, Humanities Research Center, Austin.
Ginsberg's views of Burroughs and Brion: Ginsberg to author.
Ginsberg and Mikey Portman: Ginsberg to author.
Alan Ansen on *Naked Lunch*: Ansen to Burroughs.
Mikey gives Gregory Corso bad *majoun*: Corso to author.
Bowles and the whole crew: Bowles to author.
Leary arrival: Leary to author.
Sommerville to Gysin: Jackson collection.
Incident with Groetchen: Burroughs and Ansen to author, GD.
Burroughs in Boston: BI, Jackson collection.
Leary becomes a counterculture leader: Leary to author, *High Priest*, *Flashback*.

Chapter 16: Burroughs at Large

Brion Gysin and the Dream Machine: Gysin to author, Patrick O'Higgins to author.

Death of Kells Elvins: BI.
Burroughs and Mikey: BI.
Harold Norse: Norse to author, Norse correspondence, Fales Collection, New York University.
Kerouac and Mémère: *Memory Babe*.
Corso in New York: Corso to author.
Billy Burroughs in Palm Beach: BJ.
Mote to Burroughs: RJ.
Billy shoots his friend: BJ.
Billy in Tangier: BJ, BI.
Trouble with the neighbors: BI.
My Own Mag: University of Kansas library, Lawrence, Kansas.
Alfred Chester in Tangier: Bowles to author, Ira Cohen to author.
Bowles visits Burroughs: Bowles to author.
Burroughs to Gysin: RJ.
Right-this-way treatment: BI.
Return to St. Louis: BI, BA.
Chelsea Hotel, father's death, life in New York: BI.
Burroughs' readings: BI.
Panna Grady and Burroughs: BI, Panna Grady O'Connor to author, Herbert Huncke to author.
Giorno and counterculture: BI, Giorno to author, Gysin to author.
Ginsberg in Czechoslovakia: GD.
Burroughs and the Bowleses: BI.
Jay Haselwood's death: BI, Bowles to author.
Seaver and the cut-up method: Seaver to author.

Chapter 17: The London Years

Burroughs and Alan Watson: BI, Alan Watson to author.
Billy at the Green Valley School: BJ, George Von Hilsheimer to author.
Laura Burroughs to Burroughs: RJ.
Billy in New York: BJ, Ginsberg to author.
Mort to Burroughs and Burroughs to Laura: RJ.
Burroughs in Miami, takes Billy to Lexington: BI.
Mother losing her mind, and move to nursing home: RJ.
Billy getting married: RJ.
Billy's married life: BJ.
Neal Cassady's death: GD.
Burroughs and Scientology: BI; Arizona State University, BA.
McMasters and Burroughs: Barry Miles to author.
1968 convention: BI, Ginsberg to author, Terry Southern to author.
Kerouac visit: BI.
Culverwell and Burroughs: BI.
Brion Gysin accident: Gysin to author, John Hopkins to author.

Kerouac's death: BI, *Memory Babe*.
Philip O'Connor on Burroughs: Philip O'Connor to author.
Death of mother: BI.
Visit to Hollywood: BI, Terry Southern to author.
Billy breaking up: RJ.
Burroughs and John Brady: BI.
Joujouka: BI, Brion Gysin to author.
Burroughs and McManaway: BI.
Billy leaves for Santa Cruz: BJ.
Burroughs' dislike of London and problems with John Brady: BI, Claude Pelieu
and Mary Beach to author.
Archive sale: BI, James Grauerholz to author.

Chapter 18: New York

James Grauerholz and family: Grauerholz to author.
Burroughs and James: BI, Grauerholz to author.
Billy and James: Grauerholz to author.
Burroughs and readings: Grauerholz to author.
Burroughs and Bloom: Grauerholz to author, Bloom to author.
Burroughs fan mail: BA.
Brion Gysin operation: Gysin to author.
Steven Lowe and Burroughs: Lowe to author.
Burroughs and rock musicians: BI, Grauerholz to author, Stewart Meyer to
author.
Burroughs and Naropa: BI; Ginsberg to author; *The Great Naropa Poetry Wars*,
by Tom Clark (Santa Barbara, 1980).
Burroughs' Vermont retreat: BI, Grauerholz to author.
Death of Ian Sommerville: BI, Gysin to author, issue of *The Fanatic* (courtesy
of Jeff Goldberg).
Burroughs and James: Grauerholz to author.
Visit to Beckett: BI, Ginsberg to author, Fred Jordan to author.

Chapter 19: Billy

Billy in Santa Cruz: BJ.
Gregory misbehaves: Richard Dillon to author.
Burroughs to Billy: BA.
Billy taken to hospital: BJ.
Thomas Earl Starzl: Starzl to author.
Billy's hepatic artery severed: Billy's medical record, supplied to author by Dr.
Starzl.

Billy's liver transplant: medical record.
Billy in hospital: BJ, medical record.
Billy discharged: BJ; John Steinbeck, Jr., to author.
Billy in Boulder: Anne Waldman, Michael Brownstein, and Virginia Smith to author.
Billy sees psychiatrist: Richard Warner to author.
Billy and Jo-Anne Kyger: Jo-Anne Kyger to author.
Billy in Santa Cruz: BJ.
Billy and Grauerholz: Grauerholz to author.
Billy loses passport: BI.
Cabell Hardy and Burroughs: BI, Cabell Hardy to author.
Starzl to Warner: Billy's medical record.
Howard Brookner out-takes: courtesy of Howard Brookner.
Billy in Denver: BJ, Starzl to author, Nancy Barfield to author, Ursula Schaeffer to author.
Angry letter to father: BA.
Billy suicidal: Grauerholz to author.
Billy in Boulder sees father: BJ, BI.
Billy to Starzl: Starzl to author.
Billy and Teina De Bakey: Teina De Bakey to author.
Billy and Von Hilsheimer: Von Hilsheimer to author.
Billy in West Volusia Hospital: Frances Lewis to Grauerholz, BA.
Billy's death: BJ, Frances Lewis to Grauerholz, BA.
Petition for estate: BA.

Chapter 20: The Bunker

Allen Ginsberg's fiftieth birthday: Grauerholz to author.
Trocchi to Burroughs: BA.
Burroughs to Tennessee Williams: *Village Voice*.
Movie version of *Junky*: BI, Grauerholz to author, Joe Bianco to author.
Burroughs to Bowles and Bowles to Burroughs: BA.
Burroughs to Ansen: Alan Ansen to author.
Visiting set of *Heartbeat*: BI.
Grauerholz and Burroughs: BA.
Nova Convention: John Giorno, James Grauerholz, Victor Bockris, Les Levine, Jeff Goldberg, and Brion Gysin to author.
Burroughs alone in Bunker: James Grauerholz, Victor Bockris, Stewart Meyer, and John Giorno to author.
Dinner with Mick Jagger: transcript in Burroughs archive.
Collapse of James Grauerholz's father: Grauerholz to author.
Scoring for Burroughs: Jim Prince to author.
Lawrence festival: Grauerholz to author.
Poetry festival in Italy: Ginsberg, Giorno, and Gysin to author, and BI.
Burroughs on methadone: Ira Jaffe to author.

Burroughs to Gysin on Kansas: BA.
Burroughs to Gysin on Burgess: BA.
Richard Seaver on *Cities of the Red Night*: Seaver to author.
Burroughs decides to go to Lawrence and appears on "Saturday Night Live": BI, Giorno and Grauerholz to author.

Chapter 21: Lawrence

Burroughs to Gysin: BA.
Gysin to Burroughs: BA.
Burroughs on the road: BI, Alan Ansen to author.
Fan mail: BA.
Scene with Indian: BI.
Death of brother: BI.
Death of Tennessee Williams: BI.
Induction into Institute: BI.
Ferlinghetti reaction: Ferlinghetti to author.
Burroughs, Ginsberg, and Grauerholz reaction: comments to author.
Burroughs and Grauerholz: Grauerholz to author.
Burroughs and cats: BI.
1983 tour, film premiere, and seventieth birthday: BI, Grauerholz to author.
Burroughs and Broyard: BI, BA.
Mailer and Burroughs at Naropa: Mailer to author.
Burroughs changes agent and editor: BI, Richard Seaver and Andrew Wylie to author.
Burroughs at Arizona State: BI, Grauerholz to author.
Burroughs Week at Naropa: author present.
Burroughs in New York and death of Genet: author present.
Alan Ansen visit: author present.
Death of Brion Gysin: Felicity Mason and Maurice Girodias to author.
Burroughs reflects on death: BI.
Burroughs in New York with Lucien Carr and Allen Ginsberg: author present.
Burroughs in December 1987: author present.

Index